S0-EHZ-642

Cyclopedia of World Authors II

Que-Z

CYCLOPEDIA of WORLD AUTHORS II

VOLUME FOUR—QUE-Z

Edited by

FRANK N. MAGILL

Salem Press
Pasadena, California Englewood Cliffs, New Jersey

∞ The paper used in these volumes conforms to the American National Standard for Permanence of Paper for Printed Library Materials, Z39.48-1984.

Library of Congress Cataloging-in-Publication Data

Cyclopedia of world authors II / edited by Frank N. Magill.

p. cm.

Includes bibliographical references.

ISBN 0-89356-512-1 (set)

1. Literature—Bio-bibliography. 2. Literature—Dictionaries. 3. Authors—Biography—Dictionaries. I. Magill, Frank Northen, 1907- . II. Title: Cyclopedia of world authors 2. III. Title: Cyclopedia of world authors two.

PN451.C93 1989

809—dc20

[B] 89-10659

CIP

ISBN 0-89356 512-1 (set)

ISBN 0-89356 516-4 (volume 4)

PRINTED IN THE UNITED STATES OF AMERICA

LIST OF AUTHORS IN VOLUME 4

LIST OF AUTHORS IN VOLUME 4

LIST OF AUTHORS IN VOLUME 4

Cyclopedia of World Authors II

Que-Z

JOSÉ MARIA EÇA DE QUEIRÓS

Born: Póvoa de Varzim, Portugal
Date: November 25, 1845

Died: Paris, France
Date: August 16, 1900

Principal Works

NOVELS: *O crime do Padre Amaro*, 1876, 1880 (*The Sin of Father Amaro*, 1962); *O Primo Basílio*, 1878 (*Cousin Bazílio*, 1953); *A relíquia*, 1887 (*The Relic*, 1925); *Os Maias*, 1888 (*The Maias*, 1965); *A ilustre casa de Ramires*, 1900 (*The Illustrious House of Ramires*, 1968); *A correspondência de Fradique Mendes*, 1900; *A cidade e as serras*, 1901 (*The City and the Mountain*, 1955); *A tragédia da rua das flores*, 1979, 1980.

SHORT FICTION: *O mandarim*, 1879 (*The Mandarin and Other Stories*, 1965); *Contos*, 1902.

NONFICTION: *Prosas bárbaras*, 1903; *Cartas de Inglaterra*, 1905 (*Letters from England*, 1970); *Ecos de Paris*, 1905.

José Maria Eça de Queirós (Queiróz, according to an older spelling) is generally regarded as Portugal's most important author of prose fiction. Eça, as he is known in Portuguese circles, was born an illegitimate child. His parents were later married, but he spent most of his childhood and adolescence separated from them. He completed secondary studies in Oporto and in 1865 received a law degree at the University of Coimbra, where he witnessed extensive polemics about the status of Portuguese literature and the ideas of positivism. After practicing law for a short period and directing a political journal, Eça traveled to Egypt to attend the opening ceremonies of the Suez Canal (1869), and then to the Holy Land, experiences which are reflected in his writings. Upon returning to Portugal, he became an intellectual activist. He was one of the principal organizers of a historic colloquium on modern thought in Lisbon, delivering an address entitled "Realism as a New Expression of Art" (1871). Here, the author argued for the moral and social roles of the artist, who should seek to better society by portraying it without traditional biases.

While publishing continually, Eça made a career of diplomacy; he served in Havana, Newcastle, and Bristol before settling in Paris in 1888. There he was married and found the tranquillity necessary to devote himself to his career in literature. He met Émile Zola, to whom he was compared by several contemporaries. Others have compared him to Stendhal and Benito Pérez Galdós. Eça spent the last days of his life in France. Many of his stories, travel diaries, and letters were published posthumously. Contemporary interest in his fiction was stimulated with the publication of *A tragédia da rua das flores* (tragedy on the street of flowers), a work of long fiction that Eça had left in manuscript form. In 1988, a major Portuguese critic challenged the assumptions that Eça had completed work on this novel and that he intended the work to be published.

The work of Eça de Queirós is customarily divided into three phases. In what may be termed the author's preparatory phase (1866-1875), he published journalistic articles and late Romantic stories. These initial years reveal an impetuous young writer in the process of developing a forceful style and a critical posture. In his realist phase (1875-1888), Eça superseded the sentimentalism of romance and instituted the realist novel in Portuguese letters. The author aimed at a social anatomy of contemporary problems, combating literarily the structures and values of society's fundamental institutions, the monarchy and the Church, as well as those of the bourgeoisie. He sought to create characters whose actions would be symbolic. Rather than exceptional individuals, Eça's literary figures tend to be social types, representing institutions or particular aspects of the historical environment. While *The Sin of Father Amaro* centers on a case of clerical impropriety, the narrow-mindedness of provincial life and the undue influence of local oligarchies are also exposed. The classic realist theme of adultery is treated in *Cousin Bazílio*, which is reminiscent of Gustave Flaubert's *Madame Bovary* (1857; English translation, 1886). The extramarital intrigue of a woman fond of popular Romantic literature is a springboard to investigate bourgeois marriages of convenience and the consequences of ignoring the education of women. While *The Relic* takes place mostly outside Portugal, the questions of religious hypocrisy the work raises were quite relevant to local nineteenth century reality. *The Maias* is Eça's most ambitious work. In this vast treatment of Lisbon's high society, the author applies his characteristic irony to politicians and their ignorance, financiers and their influence on government, the ostentatious behavior of the new rich, the shallowness of social climbers, and the futility of romantic imagination. In all these works, Eça focuses on customs, moral values, and exterior appearances, favoring a social psychology and adopting a consistently critical posture.

Eça's mature phase (1888-1900) reveals fictional worlds beyond orthodox realism and the iconoclasm associated with it. The fundamentally scientific approach of observation, documentation, and diagnostic commentary moves toward a more general humanitarianism with frequent spiritual overtones. The corrosive irony of earlier works becomes tempered, as the seemingly pessimistic outlook of the grand social portraits gives way to more constructive and hopeful attitudes. *The Illustrious House of Ramires*, built around the common novelistic structure of genealogy, frames a historical romance of picturesque medieval content, which is being written by the protagonist. While there are ambivalent and humorous elements, aristocratic personages, with their attempts to regenerate senses of heroism and achievement, are treated with evident sympathy. The work is by no means a simplistic appeal to patriotism, but it can be read as an effort to uphold integrity and to stimulate national pride and respect. *The City and the Mountain*, in turn, offers a kind of neopastoral optimism. Eça contrasts urban (especially Parisian) and rustic settings in an apology for the latter. Without the excesses of Romantic style or exaggerations of Romantic thought, the novel communicates an idealistic message: Happiness and fulfillment can best be achieved in bucolic surroundings, far from the distractions and corruption of urban civilization.

Eça was a prolific writer of stories, novels, letters, criticism, travel literature, and social commentary. As a consummate stylist, he is considered to have initiated modernity in Portugal and, along with Joaquim Maria Machado de Assis of Brazil, in the Portuguese language. While Eça's nonfictional writing is consistently insightful, it concerns a Portuguese public above all. The stories and novels he left achieved a more universal plane and have been translated into twelve languages; they clearly merit recognition in the canon of nineteenth century European fiction.

BIBLIOGRAPHICAL REFERENCES: There is an insightful essay on Eça by V. S. Pritchett in his critical collection *The Myth Makers: European and Latin American Writers*, 1979. For a book-length study in English of the author and the evolution of his work, see Alexander Coleman, *Eça de Queirós and European Realism*, 1980, which cites the major critical and stylistic studies in Portuguese, Spanish, and French. Among the items of periodical criticism in English, see the comparative study by James R. Stevens, "Eça and Flaubert," *Luso Brazilian Review*, III, no. 1 (1966), 47-62; and Peter Demetz, "Eça de Queiróz as a Literary Critic," *Comparative Literature*, XIX (1967), 289-307.

Charles A. Perrone

RACHEL DE QUEIROZ

Born: Fortaleza, Brazil
Date: December 19, 1910

PRINCIPAL WORKS

NOVELS: *O quinze*, 1930; *João Miguel*, 1932; *Caminho de pedras*, 1937; *As três Marias*, 1939 (*The Three Marias*, 1963); *Dôra Doralina*, 1975 (English translation, 1984).

PLAYS: *Lampião*, pb. 1953; *A beata Maria do Egito*, pb. 1958.

SHORT FICTION: *A donzela e a moura torta*, 1948; *O Brasileiro perplexo*, 1964; *O caçador de Tatu*, 1967.

NONFICTION: *Histórias e crônicas*, 1963.

Rachel de Queiroz is regarded as a significant voice of neoregionalism in Brazil and as a protofeminist writer. She was born in the capital city of the state of Ceará in Brazil's northeastern region, the setting of most of her fiction. After the great drought of 1915, her family moved to Rio de Janeiro and then to Belém do Pará. Returning to Fortaleza, she was graduated from a Catholic girls' school in 1925 and soon began work as a journalist. Throughout her career she has written *crônicas*, the Brazilian genre of commentary, social observation, or sketches of life and customs. At the age of twenty, Queiroz published her first novel, which received a national book award. Like many intellectuals of the day concerned with social issues, she had a brief association with the Communist Party (1931-1933) and faced imprisonment for expressing her ideas. In the late 1930's, Queiroz moved permanently to Rio de Janeiro, but she continued to make annual visits to the family ranch in the interior of Ceará. In recognition of her defense of the disadvantaged, she was chosen to represent her country at the 1966 United Nations Commission on Human Rights, after which she joined the Federal Council of Culture. In 1978, she became the first woman to be elected to the Brazilian Academy of Letters.

Queiroz is noted for her profound understanding of the language, landscape, and human drama of northeastern Brazil. The second generation of Brazilian modernism, which included such authors as Jorge Amado, was characterized by the nationally focused social novel of the 1930's. As a member of this generation, Queiroz sought to bring pressing issues to light in honest examinations of conditions in her land of birth. Themes of social conflict, poverty, and forced migration structure Queiroz's fiction. The physical and mental suffering caused by drought is examined in *O quinze* (fifteen, or 1915), which is based on firsthand acquaintance with the people and places of the backlands and cities affected by the drought. In the face of wretched situations, Queiroz avoids defeatism, preferring to portray the stoicism of the people. In *João Miguel* (John Michael), she turns to the social psychology of violence in the backlands. The novel is a study of a protagonist who is imprisoned for murder. *Caminho de pedras* (road of stones), more historically oriented, presents the persecution of political dissidents and organizers. Queiroz examines, in a provincial situation, stages of development, class structure, and relations of power. While less distinguished than her fiction, Queiroz's dramatic works also concern the problematic Northeast. Social banditry and heroic folk verse emerge in a play based on the life of a famous renegade, *Lampião*. *A beata Maria do Egito* (Saint Mary of Egypt) relates hagiological legend to parallel circumstances in Brazil.

Queiroz is also known for her treatment of women's issues, which are in varying degrees at issue in all of her fictional works. One of the prime figures of *O quinze* is a young woman who strives for an independent position in the midst of general crisis. The oppression of women is also taken up in the social portrait of *Caminho de pedras*. Such issues are at the fore of Queiroz's two works which have appeared in English. The protagonists of *The Three Marias* confront life in the fictional present through reminiscences about adolescent experiences in a convent school. The novel details their attempts to deal with current frustrations and to come to terms with their sexuality and their roles as citizens, mothers, and spouses. Queiroz addresses the inadequacies of the educational system, especially with regard to women, the inequalities of male-female relations, and the difficulties of emancipation. In *Dôra Doralina*, a retrospective narrative technique is again adopted. The heroines' trajectories are presented in three "books," or stages of life, as the relations of mother, daughter, and a male figure are examined. The women confront traditional values and interpersonal problems from different generational perspectives. Here one senses more positive imaging of self and greater potential for freedom and fulfillment.

Rachel de Queiroz occupies a dual position in the Brazilian canon. Besides having a significant role in the regionalist novel of the 1930's, she was the first to integrate gender issues into Brazilian fiction. She is thus an outstanding forerunner of contemporary writers who probe the social psychology of women's roles and dramatize their conflicts.

BIBLIOGRAPHICAL REFERENCES: There is a chapter on Queiroz in Fred Ellison, *Brazil's New Novel: Four Northeastern Masters*, 1954. For critical excerpts translated from the Portuguese, see David W. Foster and Virginia R. Foster, *Modern Latin American Literature*, Vol. 2, 1975. See also Benjamin Woodbridge, "The Art of Rachel de Queiroz," *Hispania*, XL (May, 1957), 144-148; and Joanna Courteau, "*A beata Maria do Egito*: Anatomy of Tyranny," *Chasqui*, XIII (May, 1984), 3-12.

Charles A. Perrone

RAYMOND QUENEAU

Born: Le Havre, France
Date: February 21, 1903

Died: Paris, France
Date: October 25, 1976

PRINCIPAL WORKS

NOVELS: *Le Chiendent*, 1933 (*The Bark Tree*, 1968); *Gueule de Pierre*, 1934; *Les Derniers Jours*, 1936; *Odile*, 1937; *Les Enfants du limon*, 1938; *Un Rude Hiver*, 1939 (*A Hard Winter*, 1948); *Les Temps mêlés: Gueule de Pierre II*, 1941; *Pierrot mon ami*, 1943 (*Pierrot*, 1950); *Loin de Rueil*, 1944 (*The Skin of Dreams*, 1948); *On est toujours trop bon avec les femmes*, 1947 (*We Always Treat Women Too Well*, 1981); *Saint-Glinglin*, 1948; *Journal intime*, 1950; *Le Dimanche de la vie*, 1951 (*The Sunday of Life*, 1976); *Zazie dans le métro*, 1959 (*Zazie in the Metro*, 1960); *Les Œuvres complètes de Sally Mara*, 1962; *Les Fleurs bleues*, 1965 (*The Blue Flowers*, 1967); *Le Vol d'Icare*, 1968 (*The Flight of Icarus*, 1973).

POETRY: *Chêne et chien*, 1937; *Les Ziaux*, 1943; *Foutaises*, 1944; *L'Instant fatal*, 1946; *Petite cosmogonie portative*, 1950; *Si tu t'imagines*, 1952; *Le Chien à la mandoline*, 1958; *Cent mille milliards de poèmes*, 1961 (*One Hundred Million Million Poems*, 1983); *Texticules*, 1961; *Courir les rues*, 1967; *Battre la campagne*, 1968; *Fendre les flots*, 1969; *Morale élémentaire*, 1975; *Pataphysical Poems*, 1985.

PLAY: *En passant*, pb. 1944.

NONFICTION: *Entretiens avec Georges Charbonnier*, 1962; *Bords: Mathématiciens, précurseurs, encyclopédistes*, 1963; *La Littérature potentielle*, 1973.

MISCELLANEOUS: *Exercices de style*, 1947 (*Exercises in Style*, 1958).

Raymond Queneau, novelist, poet, critic, editor, playwright, filmmaker, philosopher, mathematician, and painter, is regarded as one of the most audacious and ingenious French writers of the twentieth century, with a career spanning the period from Surrealism to the New Novel. Queneau was born in Le Havre at the beginning of the twentieth century. His mother was Josephine Mignot; his father, a businessman, was Auguste Queneau. After completing his studies at the *lycée* in Le Havre, Raymond Queneau went on to the University of Paris in 1920 and took his degree in philosophy in 1926. That same year he was called to military duty in Algeria and Morocco. A year later he returned to Paris; the next year, he married Janine Kahn, sister-in-law of André Breton, leader of the Surrealist movement. In 1934, they had a son, Jean-Marie, who became a painter. During the 1920's and 1930's, Queneau took jobs that allowed him a meager income: He worked in a bank, gave private lessons, sold paper tablecloths to inexpensive restaurants, translated books from English into French, and did some journalism, writing a column called "Connaissez-vous Paris?" (Do you know Paris?) for the daily *Intransigeant*, from 1936 to 1938. In 1938, he became a reader at the prestigious firm Gallimard, which had already published four of his first five books, all novels, and would produce most of his subsequent works.

Queneau's editorial career was briefly interrupted when he was drafted in August, 1939. Serving in small provincial towns, he was promoted to corporal just before being demobilized in July, 1940. Queneau then returned to Paris. Despite the hardships of the war, this period was one of intense literary production. In addition to his editorial duties at the Gallimard publishing house, where he became general secretary, he collaborated on clandestine publications and wrote a weekly column for *Front National* until 1945. He received his credentials as a professional journalist in the same year; however, he was to remain at Gallimard for the rest of his life.

The Surrealist movement had a significant influence on Queneau's writing, and he became involved in the movement in 1924-1925 and again from 1927 to 1929. Although he published a poem and two pieces of automatic writing in the *Révolution Surréaliste*, André Breton's journal, central to Queneau's interest in Surrealism was the way of life it represented: one of total revolt against the bourgeois values. Eventually quarreling with Breton over personal and not ideological concerns, according to Queneau, the latter left the group in 1929. His break with Surrealism, however, left Queneau somewhat unsettled. The crisis led him to reexamine his life through psychoanalytic therapy and to reevaluate his literary goals. Subsequently, Queneau abandoned Surrealist experimentation and began writing his own unique brand of fiction. His first novel, *The Bark Tree*, appeared in 1933. Although the work is considered one of his best because of its innovative narrative technique and meticulously planned arithmetical composition, it was not a commercial success. Queneau's reputation as a writer of originality and wit only began to be established with his autobiographical verse-narrative *Chêne et chien* (oak tree and dog) in 1937.

After the comic novel *Pierrot*, Queneau published *The Skin of Dreams*. Besides parodying the existential themes of freedom and absurdity, the work examines the mythmaking function of film as well as film's relation to wish fulfillment. Literature is the subject in Queneau's *Exercises in Style*. In this text, the author recounts an insignificant incident: A person boards a bus, gets his feet stepped on by another passenger, then sits down. This incident, however, is recounted in ninety-nine different styles, each one (like mathematical permutations) varying the arrangement of events, word choice, tone, and emphasis. Deflating the myth of literature, Queneau demonstrates that the writer can create literature out of the most banal, trivial subjects. *Exercises in Style* became one of Queneau's best-known works.

Zazie in the Metro became a best-seller when it was published in 1959. The novel's story of a young girl's two-day visit with her uncle and his wife in Paris becomes a quasi-epic battle with the forces of evil; the novel questions certain ordering factors in civilization and undermines outworn conventions of language and literature. In 1965, Queneau published what is perhaps his most complex and profound text, *The Blue Flowers*. In this novel, in which each character is the dream of the other, the author situates dreams in the context of the philosophical tradition of illusion and reality. In his dream, the dreamer is able to capture an essential part of his own identity. The variety of interpretations possible in this novel allow the reader to enjoy the novel on many different levels.

During his lifetime, Queneau, because of his distance from the mainstream of literary fashion and from literary movements, was given marginal attention by critics. His work, at times, was both greeted enthusiastically and underestimated. Although Queneau has been called everything from a literary lightweight (for his seemingly frivolous attitude toward literature and life) to a creative genius on the order of James Joyce (for his invention of new literary structures and for his linguistic virtuosity), many writers have found affinities with Queneau and have admitted his influence.

BIBLIOGRAPHICAL REFERENCES: Jacques Guicharnaud, *Raymond Queneau*, 1965, translated from the French by June Guicharnaud, is a pamphlet-length study that provides a general introduction to the author's works. In *The Flowers of Fiction: Time and Space in Raymond Queneau's "Les Fleurs bleues,"* 1982, Vivian Kogan attempts a poststructuralist reading that even with its limitations offers an original approach to the novel. W. D. Redfern, *Queneau: "Zazie dans le métro,"* 1980, is a critical guide to the novel that has much useful information for students, for whom it is written. Allen Thiker, *Raymond Queneau*, 1985, acquaints the reader with Queneau's major literary works and provides a useful bibliography. See also Germaine Brée and Margaret Guichot, "Fly in the Ointment," in *An Age of Fiction: The French Novel from Gide to Camus*, 1957; Mary Campbell-Sposito, "Ça c'est causer? Dialogue and Storytelling in Queneau's Novels," *French Forum*, XI (1986), 59-69; and Vivian Mercer, "Raymond Queneau: The Creator as Destroyer," in *The New Novel from Queneau to Pinget*, 1971.

Genevieve Slomski

WILHELM RAABE

Born: Eschershausen, Germany
Date: September 8, 1831

Died: Braunschweig, Germany
Date: November 15, 1910

Principal Works

NOVELS AND NOVELLAS: *Die Chronik der Sperlingsgasse*, 1856; *Die Leute aus dem Walde*, 1862; *Der Hunger Pastor*, 1863 (*The Hunger Pastor*, 1885); *Abu Telfan: Oder, Die Heimkehr vom Mondgebirge*, 1867 (*Abu Telfan: Or, The Return from the Mountains of the Moon*, 1881); *Der Schüdderrump*, 1870; *Der Dräumling*, 1872; *Horacker*, 1876 (English translation, 1983); *Alte Nester*, 1879; *Prinzessen Fisch*, 1883; *Villa Schönow*, 1884; *Pfisters Mühle*, 1884; *Unruhige Gäste*, 1885; *Im alten Eisen*, 1887; *Das Odfeld*, 1888; *Stopfkuchen: Eine See- und Mordgeschichte*, 1891 (*Tubby Schaumann: A Tale of Murder and the High Seas*, 1983); *Gutmanns Reisen*, 1892; *Die Akten des Vogelsangs*, 1896; *Hastenbeck*, 1899; *Altershausen*, 1911.

Wilhelm Raabe is a major representative of German realism, along with such writers as Gottfried Keller and Theodor Storm. Born in the small town of Eschershausen in the duchy of Braunschweig, Raabe was reared in Holzminden, where his grandfather, August Heinrich Raabe, a postmaster and local historian, had a great influence on him. His father worked for the judiciary and maintained a large personal library, from which Raabe read.

When his father was transferred to Stadtoldendorf in 1842, the lack of a *Gymnasium* meant that Raabe had to take private instruction. The experience developed in him a resistance to all formal schooling. In 1845, after the death of his father, Raabe's mother moved the family to Wolfenbüttel, where she had relatives. Raabe withdrew from school in 1849 and was sent to Magdeburg as an apprentice to a bookseller. His work gave him ample opportunity to read, but his attempt to pass the university entrance examination (*Abitur*) failed. In 1854 he attended the University of Berlin as a nonmatriculated student and began writing *Die Chronik der Sperlingsgasse* (the chronicle of Sparrow Alley), which was completed in 1855 and published the next year to some favorable reviews.

When Raabe returned to Wolfenbüttel in 1856, he had entered his career as a writer. During this time, he met editor Adolf Glaser, traveled some, and attended the theater. In 1862 he married Bertha Leiste, and he moved to Stuttgart, where he enjoyed the more stimulating cultural environment and was able to publish several novels in installments (*Roman-feuilleton*). Because of their belief in a united Germany under Prussia, Raabe and his wife felt somewhat alienated from his pro-Austria friends. Thus, in 1870, in spite of the war mobilization, Raabe moved his family to Braunschweig.

Raabe's time in Braunschweig, from 1870 to 1898, was extremely productive. He wrote some of his most important works during that period, including *Horacker*, *Pfisters Mühle* (Pfister's mill), *Das Odfeld* (Odin's field), and *Tubby Schaumann*. His income from writing was sufficient to support his family.

He completed *Die Akten des Vogelsangs* (documents of the birdsong) in 1895 and then wrote *Hastenbeck*, a historical novel. On his seventieth birthday he was honored by the city of Braunschweig and by the Universities of Tübingen and Göttingen. He died on November 15, 1910.

During his lifetime, Raabe was disappointed that his use of experimental style with multiple perspectives was not understood and that the satire inherent in his work was missed. He was praised for his humor, his themes showing traditional values, and his descriptions of everyday life. Yet critics often failed to notice his social criticism.

Tubby Schaumann, arguably Raabe's finest novel, is representative of his writing. Focused on the story of an outsider, Heinrich Schaumann, cruelly called "Tubby" (*Stopfkuchen* literally means "stuff cake") by his schoolmates, the novel shows a young man who, like Raabe, was a failure in school. Tubby, however, develops his talents and goes on to achieve his dream, ownership of a farm (which serves as his fortress). The narration is slow and rambling, but the characters and society are revealed one step at a time until the idealization of the rural town (and its postman) are shown to be an illusion. Criticism of society is embodied in Raabe's theme of the isolation of the individual and unjust accusations. His use of first-person narrative and reminiscences gave rise to the interrelated perspectives that are characteristic of his mature work.

Raabe's characters must find a way to survive in a world formed by the Industrial Revolution, a world where materialism seems to dominate humane action. Some cannot survive, such as Antonie in *Die Leute aus dem Walde* (people from the forest), but others, such as Schönow in *Villa Schönow* and Tubby in *Tubby Schaumann*, demonstrate human dignity and are able to live according to their own values of love, friendship, honesty, and genuine kindness. Raabe's reality is only superficially idyllic: Rustic environments may look pastoral, but they invariably hide human weakness, such as the meanness evidenced in *Tubby Schaumann* and the gossip and rumor of *Horacker*. Human suffering, rather than history, is viewed as the enduring, progressive force.

Raabe's position as a major nineteenth century novelist of the period of German realism (1850-1890) has not always been recognized. Furthermore, a lack of translations has made him less known, or perhaps even unknown, to the English-speaking public. In the 1950's and more recently, however, some critics have begun a reevaluation of his works, recognizing a more complex view of the world, which goes beyond a mere capturing of German regionalism. The modern reader, accustomed to the techniques of twentieth century narrative, will find Raabe's multiple perspective accessible and will especially respond to his themes of isolation and disillusionment.

BIBLIOGRAPHICAL REFERENCES: Horst S. Daemmrich, *Wilhelm Raabe*, 1981, is an extremely helpful orientation in English to Raabe's life and works. Jeffrey L. Sammons, *Wilhelm Raabe: The Fiction of the Alternative Community*, 1987, includes an extensive bibliography. See also the earlier, excellent insights into Raabe's major works by Barker Fairley, *Wilhelm Raabe: An Introduction to His Novels*, 1961; Roy Pascal, "Raabe," in *The German Novel: Studies*, 1956; and G. Wallis Field's short but helpful presentation as part of his chapter "Poetic Realists in Prose," in *The Nineteenth Century, 1830-1890*, 1975.

Susan L. Piepke

DAVID RABE

Born: Dubuque, Iowa
Date: March 10, 1940

Principal Works

PLAYS: *Sticks and Bones*, pr. 1969; *The Basic Training of Pavlo Hummel*, pr. 1971; *The Orphan*, pr. 1973; *Boom Boom Room*, pr. 1973 (best known as *In the Boom Boom Room*); *Burning*, pr. 1974; *Streamers*, pr. 1976; *Goose and Tom-Tom*, pr. 1982; *Hurlyburly*, pr. 1984; *The Rabbit and the Toyota Dealer*, pr. 1985.

SCREENPLAYS: *I'm Dancing As Fast As I Can*, 1982; *Streamers*, 1983.

David Rabe is one of America's most uncompromising dramatic commentators on the Vietnam War. The three major Rabe plays sometimes referred to as "the Vietnam trilogy" (*Sticks and Bones*, *The Basic Training of Pavlo Hummel*, and *Streamers*) are intense, compelling analyses of a society forever altered by a controversial war, of a generation that lost its innocence in battle.

David William Rabe was born in Dubuque, Iowa, on March 10, 1940, to William Rabe, a high-school teacher who later became a meat packer, and his wife, Ruth McCormick Rabe, a department store employee. Educated at two Catholic schools in Dubuque—Loras Academy and Loras College, where he earned his B.A. degree in 1962—Rabe went on to graduate school at Villanova University in Pennsylvania, where he began work on a degree in theater. Two years in the U.S. Army, which included eleven months in Vietnam, interrupted Rabe's graduate work; he resumed his study upon his return from Vietnam, completing his master's degree in 1968. The next year he married Elizabeth Pan. That marriage ended in divorce, and in 1979 Rabe married actress Jill Clayburgh.

Rabe's tour of duty in Vietnam proved to be a major turning point in the future playwright's life. Assigned to a hospital group, Rabe never actually experienced combat, although he witnessed the fighting at close range and observed the American troops both in and out of combat. It was the extreme youth and inexperience of these soldiers that made an impression on Rabe, who later described these "kids, just kids . . . standing around some bar like teenagers at a soda fountain, talking coolly about how many of their guys got killed in the last battle." His first two plays were the result of Rabe's frustrating return to society after Vietnam. Both were written while he was in graduate school but not produced until they came to the attention of the influential Joseph Papp, director of the New York Shakespeare Festival's Public Theatre.

The Basic Training of Pavlo Hummel, which opened on May 21, 1971, ran for 363 performances at the Newman Theatre in 1971 and 1972 and earned for Rabe an Obie Award and a Drama Desk Award. *Sticks and Bones* was even more critically successful than *The Basic Training of Pavlo Hummel*, winning for Rabe the 1972 Tony Award, the Outer Circle Award, and a special citation from the New York Drama Critics Circle. A *Variety* poll named Rabe the most promising playwright of 1972. The play was not, however, a popular success, and its Broadway run was supported in part by the New York Shakespeare Festival. Still drawing his themes from his experiences in Vietnam, Rabe based his next play on Aeschylus' Oresteia trilogy. *The Orphan*, an attempt to draw parallels between the Trojan War and twentieth century post-Vietnam violence, was unsuccessful, confusing both popular audiences and the critics. A departure from the Vietnam theme, *In the Boom Boom Room* was neither a critical nor a popular success, although it was nominated for a Tony Award during the 1973 season.

With *Streamers*, Rabe returned to the Vietnam War—and to critical acclaim. Opening at the Long Wharf Theatre in New Haven, Connecticut, the play moved to Lincoln Center's Newhouse Theatre and won for Rabe the New York Drama Critics Circle Award for the best American play of 1976. Eight years would pass before Rabe's next successful play, the controversial *Hurlyburly,* a dramatic exploration of the moral deterioration of modern America, was produced.

Although the most acclaimed of Rabe's plays dramatize the effect of war on the lives of average people, Rabe emphatically denies that he is an antiwar playwright. "I don't like to hear them called antiwar plays," he says in response to attempts to label his work. "All I'm trying to do is *define the event* for myself and for other people." His attempts to "define the event" are violent and sensational, marked by the lyrical seaminess and trenchant aggressiveness of their language and darkly powerful in their exploration of senseless violence in war and at home.

Perhaps the best known of David Rabe's plays is *The Basic Training of Pavlo Hummel*, the story of the making of a soldier. Pavlo Hummel is a teenage misfit who discovers in the Army and in Vietnam a niche, a place where he can function almost competently, though in a macabre sort of way. As a medic, he picks up the wounded and the dead from the battlefield. A nobody at home, Pavlo soon discovers that in the military the violence latent in his character is acceptable. Through his experiences he achieves a kind of brutal masculinity and maturity, but even that success proves inadequate to prevent his ignominious and senseless death. An argument with another soldier over a prostitute ends when the other man kills Pavlo with a grenade. Clearly the army is a dehumanizing institution, but in Rabe's theatrical world, civilian society is equally destructive to the soldier. Reaction to the news of Pavlo's death is minimal: Mickey, Pavlo's half brother, claims, "Vietnam don't even exist." Such was the civilian complacency and lack of involvement that Rabe found so disturbing upon his return from Vietnam.

David Rabe's gift to the American theater is a body of plays that are at once violent and lyrical, realistic and nightmarish, confrontational and symbolic. His is a powerful voice that is distinctive for its intense concern with post-Vietnam American society. As playwright Howard Richardson has remarked, "*Sticks and Bones* had more impact on those in a position to mold public opinion than any statement from President Nixon, and David Rabe can take as much credit for ending the war in Vietnam as any one individual." Yet Rabe's concerns go beyond the effects of a war to the all-too-human need to comprehend the meanings and causes of violence, to understand the chaos that is human life.

BIBLIOGRAPHICAL REFERENCES: "David Rabe," in *Dictionary of Literary Biography,* Vol. 7, 1978, is a good source of biographical information. For an in-depth discussion of Rabe's plays as symbols of the failure of language to overcome alienation, see Craig Werner, "Primal Screams and Nonsense Rhymes: David Rabe's Revolt," *Educational Theatre Journal*, December, 1978, 517-529. See also Bob Prochaska, "David Rabe," *Dramatics*, May/June, 1977, 18; Philip Beidler, *American Literature and the Experience of Vietnam*, 1982; Richard L. Homan, "American Playwrights in the 1970's: Rabe and Shepard," *Critical Quarterly,* XXIV (Spring, 1982), 73-82; Robert Brustein, "Painless Dentistry," *The New Republic*, August 6, 1984, 27-29; and James Reston, *Coming to Terms: American Plays and the Vietnam War,* 1985.

E. D. Huntley

RAJA RAO

Born: Hassan, Mysore State, South India
Date: November 5, 1908

PRINCIPAL WORKS

NOVELS: *Kanthapura*, 1938; *The Serpent and the Rope*, 1960; *The Cat and Shakespeare: A Tale of India*, 1965; *Comrade Kirillov*, 1976; *The Chessmaster and His Moves*, 1988.

SHORT FICTION: *The Cow of the Barricades and Other Stories*, 1947; *The Policeman and the Rose*, 1978.

Raja Rao, with Mulk Raj Anand and R. K. Narayan, is considered one of the most important twentieth century Indo-English novelists. The eldest in a Brahman family of nine children, he was born in Hassan, Mysore State, South India, on November 5, 1908 (although official records list his date of birth as November 21, 1909). Young Rao stayed with his grandfather, a Vedantist, while his father taught Kannada at Nizam's College in the neighboring state of Hyderabad. From his grandfather, Rao absorbed a spiritual foundation in Indian philosophy which is apparent in all of his work. In 1915, Rao joined his father in Hyderabad to attend school and then went to Aligarh Muslim University in North India in 1926. There, under the guidance of Eric Dickinson, a poet and visiting professor from the University of Oxford, Rao's literary sensibilities blossomed. In 1927, Rao enrolled in St. Nizam's College in Hyderabad, majoring in English and history, and was graduated with the B.A. in 1929.

In that same year, Rao's life changed dramatically. He won the Asiatic Scholarship of the Government of Hyderabad for study abroad and left India to study at the University of Montpellier in France. There, he met and married Camille Mouly, a French professor. She not only encouraged his writing but also supported him financially for several years. Between 1931 and 1933, Rao published three essays and a poem written in Kannada (his mother tongue) in *Jaya Karnataka*, an influential journal. His earliest short stories were published in such journals as *Cahiers du Sud* (Paris) and *Asia* (New York). During this time, he was also researching the influence of India on Irish literature, but he stopped in 1933 to devote himself fully to writing. At this time, Rao returned to India for the first of his many pilgrimages for spiritual and cultural nourishment. During the next ten years, he visited many different ashrams and religious teachers—for example, Pandit Taranth, Ramana Maharshi, Narayana Maharaj, and Mahatma Gandhi. In the 1930's and 1940's, Rao also was active in social and political causes there, such as the young Indian Socialist movement "Quit India," and worked with Indian cultural organizations. In 1938, Rao's first novel, *Kanthapura*, although written earlier, was published in London. Praised by E. M. Forster as the best novel ever written in English by an Indian, *Kanthapura* is an account of nonviolent Gandhian resistance in a South Indian village. In 1943, Rao's spiritual search appears to have been fulfilled when he met Sri Atmananda Guru of Trivandrum, and Rao returned to France in 1959 only after his guru's death. In the meantime, Rao's early short stories and others were collected and published in 1947 as *The Cow of the Barricades and Other Stories*.

In 1960, one year after his return to France and twenty-two years after *Kanthapura*, Rao's second novel appeared. His ambitious masterpiece, *The Serpent and the Rope*, explores the relationship of India and Europe through the marriage of a South Indian Brahman and his French wife. In 1965, its sequel, *The Cat and Shakespeare*, was published. Described as a metaphysical comedy by its author, this gentle allegory blends the naturalism of the short stories with the philosophical interests of *The Serpent and the Rope*. Though written earlier, Rao's minor work *Comrade Kirillov* was also first published in 1965 in French and then in English in 1976.

Rao has spent more than forty years in France and has traveled in most parts of the world. From 1965 until his retirement, he was Professor of Philosophy at the University of Texas at

Austin, teaching one semester a year. His first marriage having dissolved in 1939, Rao married American actress Katherine Jones in 1965; they would have a son, Christopher Rama. In 1978, a second collection of short stories, *The Policeman and the Rose*, was published. Rao's fifth novel, *The Chessmaster and His Moves*, appeared in 1988 and continued to explore Indian thought and its relationship to Western experience and challenges.

Although Rao never settled permanently in India, he is regarded as the most "Indian" of the Indo-English writers, as well as the most sophisticated and philosophically complex. Largely autobiographical, his works deal with the East-West encounter and the relationship between male and female. The central theme is the quest for the absolute, the ultimate reality of life, and Rao's major novels reflect his own spiritual search. *Kanthapura* explores the reawakening of the Indian spirit through the philosophy of action (*karma yoga*). *The Serpent and the Rope*, steeped in Vedantic philosophy of *Advaita* (nondualism), develops the path of knowledge (*gyana yoga*) as a means of self-realization. *The Cat and Shakespeare* is the first of Rao's novels in which a character not only seeks truth but also finds it and comes to live it through the path of love and devotion (*bhakti yoga*). Rao's works are likened in structure and style to Indian legendary history, especially the *puranas*. Inspired by William Butler Yeats, James Joyce, and others who created an Irish English, Rao skillfully adapts the English language to suit Indian sensibilities and his own narrative purposes in order to "convey in a language that is not one's own the spirit that is one's own," as he puts it.

Despite his small output and the long silences between works, Rao's challenging fiction has been well received. His short stories are universally acclaimed, and *The Serpent and the Rope* is perhaps the greatest metaphysical novel written in English. Rao was awarded the Indian Literary Academy Award in 1964 and was again recognized in 1988 with the Neustadt International Prize for Literature. Although criticized by some as too philosophical and digressive in style, Rao is internationally acknowledged as a significant modern novelist. He has created a truly Indian novel in English, saturated with epic vision, philosophical depth, and symbolic richness.

BIBLIOGRAPHICAL REFERENCES: An excellent starting place is the special issue of *World Literature Today*, LXII (Autumn, 1988), devoted to Raja Rao. This issue includes texts by Rao and essays on his work, a chronology, a selected bibliography, and illustrations. Two pioneering, full-length studies, M. K. Naik, *Raja Rao*, 1972, and C. D. Narasimhaiah, *Raja Rao: A Critical Study of His Work*, 1972, are among the most perceptive and significant assessments. Criticism is also available in Narsingh Srivastava, *The Mind and Art of Raja Rao*, 1980, and the eighteen essays anthologized and edited by K. K. Sharma, *Perspectives on Raja Rao*, 1980. K. R. Rao, *The Fiction of Raja Rao*, although published in 1980, does not include criticism of any of his works published after 1965. P. C. Bhattacharya, *Indo-Anglian Literature and the Works of Raja Rao*, 1983, presents Rao's fiction within an analysis of Indian authors writing in English. See also Richard R. Guzman, "The Saint and the Sage: The Fiction of Raja Rao," *The Virginia Quarterly Review*, LVI (Winter, 1980), 33-50; Janet P. Gemmil, "Dualities and Non-Duality in Raja Rao's 'The Serpent and the Rope,'" *World Literature Written in English*, XII (November, 1973), 247-259.

William S. Haney II

TERENCE RATTIGAN

Born: London, England
Date: June 10, 1911

Died: Bermuda
Date: November 30, 1977

PRINCIPAL WORKS

PLAYS: *French Without Tears*, pr. 1936; *Flare Path*, pr., pb. 1942; *While the Sun Shines*, pr. 1943; *Love in Idleness*, pr. 1944 (also known as *O Mistress Mine*); *The Winslow Boy*, pr., pb. 1946; *Playbill: The Browning Version and Harlequinade*, pr. 1948; *Adventure Story*, pr. 1949; *Who Is Sylvia?*, pr. 1950; *The Deep Blue Sea*, pr., pb. 1952; *The Sleeping Prince*, pr. 1953; *Separate Tables: Table by the Window and Table Number Seven*, pr. 1954 (best known as *Separate Tables*); *Variation on a Theme*, pr., pb. 1958; *Ross*, pr., pb. 1960; *Man and Boy*, pr. 1963; *A Bequest to the Nation*, pr., pb. 1970; *In Praise of Love: Before Dawn and After Lydia*, pb. 1973; *Cause Célèbre*, pr. 1977.

SCREENPLAYS: *French Without Tears*, 1939; *Uncensored*, 1942 (with Wolfgang Wilhelm and Rodney Ackland); *English Without Tears*, 1944 (with Anatole de Grunwald; also known as *Her Man Gilbey*); *Journey Together*, 1944; *The Way to the Stars*, 1945 (with de Grunwald; also known as *Johnny in the Clouds*); *While the Sun Shines*, 1946; *Brighton Rock*, 1947 (with Graham Greene; also known as *Young Scarface*); *Bond Street*, 1948 (with Ackland and de Grunwald); *The Browning Version*, 1951; *The Sound Barrier*, 1952 (also known as *Breaking the Sound Barrier*); *The Final Test*, 1953; *The Man Who Loved Redheads*, 1954; *The Deep Blue Sea*, 1955; *The Prince and the Showgirl*, 1957; *Variation on a Theme*, 1958; *The VIPs*, 1963; *The Yellow Rolls-Royce*, 1964; *A Bequest to the Nation*, 1973.

TELEPLAYS: *The Final Test*, 1951; *Adventure Story*, 1961; *Ninety Years On*, 1963 (with Nöel Coward); *Nelson: A Portrait in Miniature*, 1964; *Heart to Heart*, 1964; *All on Her Own*, 1968; *Nijinsky* (unproduced).

Born in Kensington, London, on June 10, 1911, to William Frank and Vera Houston Rattigan, Terence Mervyn Rattigan frequently mentioned the coronation of George V in that year, an event his mother was unable to attend because of her pregnancy. From a privileged background of diplomats on his father's side and barristers on his mother's side, he attended Harrow (where he wrote his first play, a short piece about Cesare Borgia) and Trinity College, Oxford (where he acted in a production of William Shakespeare's *Romeo and Juliet* with Edith Evans and Peggy Ashcroft, directed by John Gielgud). Unwilling to follow his father in diplomacy, Rattigan convinced his parents to finance him in a London residence and a playwriting career. His entire life was devoted to the theater: stage, film, and television.

He wrote plays from his own personal experiences, reflecting the rapidly changing times, beginning with the carefree, youthful experiences of schoolboys in *French Without Tears* in pre-World War II England. Later he wrote about English life during World War II, especially in an interesting trilogy composed of *Flare Path*, *While the Sun Shines*, and *Love in Idleness*; ultimately he became increasingly frank in his later plays, dealing with the personal failures of upper-middle-class, frequently public, figures.

One of two of England's most popular dramatists (Noël Coward being the other), Rattigan enjoyed success after success with plays such as *The Winslow Boy* and *The Browning Version* in the 1940's. It was in the latter drama that his dramatic technique matured in a change from the diffuseness of earlier plays to a tightly knit construction that focused on one principal character. Also, the farcical or romantic moods of the earlier plays took on a somber note, as the serious problems of middle-class characters living in the postwar era took form in his plays.

An entire family in *The Winslow Boy* (based on a sensationally popular trial) find themselves in virtual financial ruin in their attempt to vindicate their young son, Ronnie, who has been unfairly dismissed from school. In *The Browning Version*, a schoolmaster, having failed as a teacher and a husband, finds a remnant of dignity and life after twenty years of living with emotional repression that has caused his metamorphosis into a living corpse. The lonely and alienated characters Hester Collyer, the wife of a successful judge in *The Deep Blue Sea*, and Sybil Railton-Bell and Major Pollock in *Separate Tables* take on darker overtones, as they challenge the hypocrisy of prevailing attitudes.

The plays that emerged from the 1960's—*Man and Boy*, about a hardened financier and his son, and *A Bequest to the Nation*, dealing with Lord Nelson's emotional and insoluble problem caused by the conflict between his personal need for a mistress and the national admiration for a war hero's wife—continue Rattigan's themes in characters who enjoy public success. The Nelson story was so popular that it enjoyed successful performances on television, film, and stage. Other historical figures were dramatized in *Ross* and *Adventure Story*, the first about the political and personal life of the enigmatic T. E. Lawrence and the second about Alexander the Great.

When terminal illness struck actress Kay Kendall, wife of Rex Harrison, Rattigan used that experience as the source of *In Praise of Love*, one of the earliest plays about terminal illness. A few years later, his own bone cancer was diagnosed, and just before he died he was driven past a theater where *Cause Célèbre* (like *The Winslow Boy*, based on a sensational trial) was in rehearsal. In this manner, he bid his final farewell to the theater which he so loved and to which he had devoted his entire life.

As a popular playwright, Rattigan was frequently criticized for lacking ideas in his plays. Stung by the continuing criticism, he began a debate on the play of ideas in 1950 in *New Statesman*, a debate that drew letters during successive weeks from writers such as Sean O'Casey, Christopher Fry, and even George Bernard Shaw. Later that same decade, in 1956, when the London stage revolution began with the explosion of Jimmy Porter's anger at the Royal Court Theatre (in John Osborne's *Look Back in Anger*), Rattigan again came under fire from critics such as Kenneth Tynan who labeled him as a writer of the conventional, well-made play.

Yet some of the new dramatists, such as Harold Pinter, David Rudkin, and Tom Stoppard, found much to be admired in the characters Rattigan developed (*The Browning Version*, especially, has enjoyed successful revivals). Embodying the glamour of the film world in his writing for films such as *The Prince and the Showgirl*, *The VIPs*, and *The Yellow Rolls-Royce*, Rattigan is, at the other extreme, the stage chronicler of the very private, lonely, pained individuals who endure social disenfranchisement. Socially disenfranchised in a limited way by his own homosexuality and dogged by the "serious" critics, Rattigan's life paralleled the paradoxical successes and failures he dramatized in his dramas.

BIBLIOGRAPHICAL REFERENCES: Michael Darlow and Gillian Hodson, *Terence Rattigan: The Man and His Work*, 1979, a critical autobiography, traces the life and art of Rattigan from birth to death. One of the only critical studies of Rattigan's plays, Susan Rusinko, *Terence Rattigan*, 1983, categorizes Rattigan's plays by phases in his career. Included also are discussions of his film and television writing. One encyclopedic source of much detail is Holly Hill, *A Critical Analysis of the Plays of Terence Rattigan*, 1977 (dissertation). See also John Russell Taylor, "Terrence Rattigan," in *The Rise and Fall of the Well-Made Play*, 1967; Harold Hobson, "The Playwright Who Always Hid His Pain," *Sunday Times*, December 4, 1977; Martin Gottfried, "In Praise of Craftsmanship," *Stagebill*, November, 1974; and T. C. Worsley, "Rattigan and His Critics," *London Magazine*, September, 1964, 60-72.

Susan Rusinko

ISHMAEL REED

Born: Chattanooga, Tennessee
Date: February 22, 1938

PRINCIPAL WORKS

NOVELS: *The Free-Lance Pallbearers*, 1967; *Yellow Back Radio Broke-Down*, 1969; *Mumbo Jumbo*, 1972; *The Last Days of Louisiana Red*, 1974; *Flight to Canada*, 1976; *The Terrible Twos*, 1982; *Reckless Eyeballing*, 1986; *The Terrible Threes*, 1989.

POETRY: *Catechism of D Neoamerican Hoodoo Church*, 1970; *Conjure: Selected Poems, 1963-1970*, 1972; *Chattanooga*, 1973; *A Secretary to the Spirits*, 1977; *Cab Calloway Stands in for the Moon*, 1986; *New and Collected Poems*, 1988.

ESSAYS: *Shrovetide in Old New Orleans*, 1978; *God Made Alaska for the Indians*, 1982; *Writin' Is Fightin'*, 1988.

ANTHOLOGIES: *19 Necromancers from Now*, 1970; *Yardbird Lives!*, 1978; *Calafia: The California Poetry*, 1979.

Ishmael Reed is recognized as an important American satirist, an innovative poet, and a major part of the antirealist countertradition in black American fiction that includes authors such as Clarence Major, James Alan McPherson, Leon Forrest, Toni Morrison, and Alice Walker. Born in Chattanooga, Tennessee, on February 22, 1938, Reed moved to Buffalo, New York, when he was four years old. After he was graduated from Buffalo's East High School, Reed attended the University of Buffalo, but financial problems forced him to withdraw before graduation. He then married and moved into the notorious Talbert Mall Projects. The two years he spent there provided him with a painful but valuable experience of urban poverty.

In 1962, Reed moved to New York City. As well as being involved with the Civil Rights movement and the black power movement, he served as editor of *Advance* and helped to found the *East Village Other*, one of the first and most successful underground newspapers. He was an active member of the Umbra Workshop, a black writers' group. In 1967, Reed moved to California, began teaching at the University of California at Berkeley, and published his first novel, *The Free-Lance Pallbearers*, a parody of the African American literary tradition of first-person, confessional narratives and an unrestrained attack on the corruptive potential of power in American politics, received surprising critical attention and praise. It was soon followed by *Yellow Back Radio Broke-Down*, a fantastic parody of the popular western in which Reed satirizes America's repressive tendencies and argues for an aesthetic that gives priority to imagination, intelligence, and fantasy.

The 1970's were a prolific period for Reed. He published volumes of innovative poetry that presented a sensuous black aesthetic in a hip, jazz-inspired voice, and several poems were reprinted in college literature anthologies. In partnership with Al Young, Reed founded a series of publishing ventures designed to build a multicultural national literature by printing the work of minority authors. During the 1970's, Reed published three novels that strengthened his reputation as a satirist but went beyond the literary dismantling of America to propose a cultural alternative for nonwhite Americans. In *Mumbo Jumbo*, a complex mix of erudite scholarly paraphernalia and the formulas of detective fiction, and in *The Last Days of Louisiana Red*, another parody of detective fiction, Reed defined an African American aesthetic based on voodoo, Egyptian mythology, and improvisational musical forms. In *Flight to Canada*, set in the Civil War South, Reed concentrated on the question of authorial control, the idea that nonwhite Americans must create their own "stories." Reed's fictional reconstructions of the American West, the Harlem Renaissance, the American Civil War, and contemporary American politics, interwoven with ancient myths, non-European folk customs, and the formulas of popular culture, are liberating heresies meant to free readers from the limitations of the Judeo-Christian tradition.

The 1980's were a more difficult decade for Reed. Through essay collections such as *God Made Alaska for the Indians* and *Writin' Is Fightin'*, Reed has presented his political and aesthetic ideas directly. His poetry, particularly *New and Collected Poems*, has continued to receive favorable reviews; however, novels that he has published in the 1980's have been poorly received by most critics, and they have engendered accusations of sexism and anti-Semitism. *The Terrible Twos* and its sequel *The Terrible Threes* are heavy-handed satires of Reaganesque politics, but *Reckless Eyeballing* was more controversial. In it, Reed maintains that the American literary environment is dominated by New York women and Jews. Although Reed's ostensible target is a cultural establishment that creates and strengthens racial stereotypes, portions of the book seem to be direct and somewhat mean-spirited attacks on the success of Alice Walker's *The Color Purple* (1982).

Reed has created a substantial body of fiction that has established him as an important satirist and a leading proponent of a new black aesthetic. His innovative narrative technique, which combines the improvisational qualities of jazz with a documentary impulse to accumulate references and allusions, has stretched the limits of the American novel and dramatically broadened the scope of African American literature. It remains to be seen how his conflict with feminists and the literary establishment will affect his career.

BIBLIOGRAPHICAL REFERENCES: Reginald Martin, *Ishmael Reed and the New Black Aesthetic Critics*, 1986, is a comprehensive explication of Reed's aesthetic theories, but several articles provide overviews of his fiction. See James R. Lindroth, "From Krazy Kat to Hoodoo: Aesthetic Discourse in the Fiction of Ishmael Reed," *The Review of Contemporary Fiction*, IV (Summer, 1984), 227-233; Robert Murray Davis, "Scatting the Myths: Ishmael Reed," *Arizona Quarterly*, XXXIX (Winter, 1983) 406-420; Jerry H. Bryant, "Old Gods and New Demons: Ishmael Reed and His Fiction," *The Review of Contemporary Fiction*, IV (Summer, 1984), 195-202; Henry Louis Gates, Jr., "The 'Blackness of Blackness': A Critique of the Sign and the Signifying Monkey," *Critical Inquiry*, IX (June, 1983), 685-723; and Peter Nazareth, "Heading Them Off at the Pass: The Fiction of Ishmael Reed," *The Review of Contemporary Fiction*, IV (Summer, 1984), 208-226. See also Michel Fabre, "Postmodern Rhetoric in Ishmael Reed's *Yellow Back Radio Broke-Down*," in *The Afro-American Novel Since 1960: A Collection of Critical Essays*, 1982, edited by Peter Bruck and Wolfgang Karrer; "*The Last Days of Louisiana Red*," in Norman Harris, *Connecting Times: The Sixties in Afro-American Fiction*, 1988; "The Men" in Charles Richard Johnson, *Being and Race: Black Writing Since 1970*, 1988; John O'Brien, "Ishmael Reed" in *The New Fiction*, 1974, edited by Joe David Bellamy; Lizabeth Paravisini, "*Mumbo Jumbo* and the Uses of Parody," *Obsidian II*, I (Spring/Summer, 1986), 113-127; and Neil Schmitz, "Neo-HooDoo: The Experimental Fiction of Ishmael Reed," *Twentieth Century Literature*, XX (April, 1974), 126-140.

Carl Brucker

MARY RENAULT
Mary Challans

Born: London, England
Date: September 4, 1905

Died: Cape Town, South Africa
Date: December 13, 1983

Principal Works

NOVELS: *Purposes of Love*, 1939 (best known as *Promise of Love*); *Kind Are Her Answers*, 1940; *The Friendly Young Ladies*, 1944 (also known as *The Middle Mist*); *Return to Night*, 1946; *North Face*, 1948; *The Charioteer*, 1953; *The Last of the Wine*, 1956; *The King Must Die*, 1958; *The Bull from the Sea*, 1962; *The Mask of Apollo*, 1966; *Fire from Heaven*, 1969; *The Persian Boy*, 1972; *The Praise Singer*, 1978; *The Nature of Alexander*, 1980; *Funeral Games*, 1981; *The Alexander Trilogy*, 1984 (includes *Fire from Heaven*, *The Persian Boy*, and *Funeral Games*).

BIOGRAPHY: *The Nature of Alexander*, 1975.

CHILDREN'S LITERATURE: *The Lion in the Gateway: The Heroic Battles of the Greeks and Persians at Marathon, Salamis, and Thermopylae*, 1964.

Mary Renault is the pseudonym used by a British novelist who acquired popularity in the United States through her skillful and artistic reconstruction of Hellenic civilization and her biography of Alexander the Great. Born September 4, 1905, in London, England, where her father was a doctor, Mary Renault was the older of two daughters. Her earliest memory of London was of a Zeppelin raid during World War I, which she described in later life as a "splendid fireworks display." Renault attended Clifton High School, a boarding school near Bristol, from 1921 to 1925 and in 1927 was graduated with honors in English literature from St. Hugh's College, Oxford.

Although she had planned to teach after graduation, she realized that her main interest was writing. Convinced that successful writers must experience life in a personal way, Renault trained as a nurse at Radcliffe Infirmary, Oxford, from 1933 to 1937, during which time she wrote only a few Christmas skits. With the outbreak of World War II, she returned to Radcliffe, where she worked in the neurosurgical ward from 1938 to 1945. With the ending of the war she traveled extensively in France, Italy, Africa, Greece, and the Aegean Islands for three years. The enchantment she felt when viewing the ruins of classical Greece later served as a major source of inspiration for her Hellenic novels, and the allure of Africa resulted in her establishing a permanent residence in Dunbar, South Africa, in 1948.

Renault's literary career is best evaluated in two phases: The years 1939 to 1953 were her apprenticeship, and the period from 1956 to 1981, the time of her mature, historical fiction. Renault's apprenticeship saw six books published, all of which were a prelude to her Greek novels. Her first work, *Promise of Love*, drew upon her experience as a nurse and was so candidly written that many of her coworkers were uncomfortable with its content. Although the work received very favorable reviews, it was her fourth novel, *Return to Night*, that established her credibility as a novelist on both sides of the Atlantic. In denouncing apartheid and censorship laws in South Africa, *Return to Night* was awarded the prestigious Metro-Goldwyn-Mayer literary prize of $150,000. Renault's early work proved controversial in 1953, when her American publisher, William Morrow and Company, refused to publish *The Charioteer*, maintaining that American society was not ready for a work that described homosexual friendships as an ennobling experience. Six years after its appearance in Europe, Pantheon Books, a division of Random House, published the work and became Renault's permanent American publisher.

The six volumes published during her apprenticeship reflect, in part, the author's displeasure with the present and her veneration of the past. Increasingly she employed Hellenic situations as a medium for examining contemporary ones. This is reflected in her use of classical allusions and Platonic imagery to treat contemporary problems cast in a contemporary setting. Glory, honor, and the pursuit of excellence, all Greek ideals, were handled successfully in her early novels, but her treatment of homosexuality, another characteristic of antiquity, met with opposition. The difficulties she encountered with *The Charioteer* convinced Renault that if she was to progress as a novelist she must write about real Greeks in a Hellenic setting.

Historical fiction has its own critical canon which demands a creative use of sources, the interweaving of character and event, and a point of view that would be valid for the era in question. While Mary Renault successfully fulfilled all these mandates, she was more than simply a popular novelist. She was a sophisticated artist who believed that literature should instruct as well as please, and in her efforts to combine creativity with scholarship she willfully sacrificed vast, popular appeal. Unlike most popular fiction, Renault's novels manifest meticulous research and most contain maps, a selected bibliography, and author's notes on the use of primary sources. To make her books as authentic as possible, she never Latinized proper names, which tends to be troublesome for readers who are unfamiliar with Greek names. Renault's artistic skills are best reflected in her ability to transform the historical into the fictive. Her creative, but scholarly, use of written and archaeological sources resulted in a reconstruction of the ancient past with authentic flavor and color.

BIBLIOGRAPHICAL REFERENCES: Peter Wolfe, *Mary Renault*, 1969, is a critical analysis of Renault's works from 1939 to 1966 in which he argues persuasively that she deserves a higher standing among literary scholars than she has been accorded. Perhaps the best single work on Mary Renault is Bernard F. Dick, *The Hellenism of Mary Renault*, 1972. Dick's work contains valuable biographical information, background on Renault's attraction to Hellenism, and an enlightened discourse on historical fiction. Landon C. Burns, "Men Are Only Men: The Novels of Mary Renault," *Critique: Studies in Modern Fiction*, VI (Winter, 1963/1964), 102-121, studies character, theme, and the use of classical myth in *The Last of the Wine*, *The King Must Die*, and *The Bull from the Sea*. Bill Casey, "Nurse Novels," *Southwest Review*, XLIX (Autumn, 1964), 332-341, examines nurse novels since World War II. For an unfavorable review of Renault's work, see Kevin Herbert, "The Theseus Theme: Some Recent Versions," *Classical Journal*, LV (January, 1960), 175-185.

Wayne M. Bledsoe

KENNETH REXROTH

Born: South Bend, Indiana
Date: December 22, 1905

Died: Santa Barbara, California
Date: June 6, 1982

Principal Works

POETRY: *A Prolegomenon to a Theodicy*, 1932; *In What Hour*, 1940; *The Phoenix and the Tortoise*, 1944; *The Signature of All Things*, 1949; *The Dragon and the Unicorn*, 1952; *The Art of Worldly Wisdom*, 1953; *Thou Shalt Not Kill*, 1955; *A Bestiary*, 1955; *In Defense of the Earth*, 1956; *Natural Numbers*, 1963; *The Homestead Called Damascus*, 1963; *The Collected Shorter Poems*, 1966; *The Collected Longer Poems*, 1967; *The Heart's Garden, the Garden's Heart*, 1967; *The Spark in the Tinder of Knowing*, 1968; *Sky Sea Birds Trees Earth House Beast Flowers*, 1971; *New Poems*, 1974; *The Silver Swan*, 1976; *On Flower Wreath Hill*, 1976; *The Love Poems of Marichiko*, 1978; *The Morning Star*, 1979.

CRITICISM: *Bird in the Bush: Obvious Essays*, 1959; *Assays*, 1961; *Classics Revisited*, 1968; *The Alternative Society: Essays from the Other World*, 1970; *With Eye and Ear*, 1970; *American Poetry in the Twentieth Century*, 1971; *The Elastic Retort: Essays in Literature and Ideas*, 1973.

AUTOBIOGRAPHY: *An Autobiographical Novel*, 1966; *Excerpts from a Life*, 1981.

TRANSLATIONS: *One Hundred Poems from the French*, 1955; *One Hundred Poems from the Japanese*, 1955; *One Hundred Poems from the Chinese*, 1956; *Thirty Spanish Poems of Love and Exile*, 1956; *Poems from the Greek Anthology*, 1962; *Pierre Reverdy Selected Poems*, 1969; *The Orchid Boat: Women Poets of China*, 1972 (with Ling Chung); *The Burning Heart: Women Poets of Japan*, 1977 (with Atsumi Ikuko).

NONFICTION: *Communalism: From Its Origins to the Twentieth Century*, 1974.

One of America's great men of letters, Kenneth Rexroth was a polymathic genius, learned in literature, politics, music, languages, art, and religion. Rexroth was born December 22, 1905, in South Bend, Indiana, the son of Charles Rexroth and Delia Reed Rexroth. His mother, who passed on her strong feminist convictions to her son, died of complications of tuberculosis in 1916. Two years later, Charles Rexroth, whose pharmacy business had failed, died as a result of alcoholism. Kenneth was reared by his aunt on Chicago's South Side. He attended classes at the Chicago Art Institute and the University of Chicago. When he was only sixteen years old, he worked his way to the West Coast and back. Later, he shipped out to Europe, then, on his return, once again worked his way west and then to Mexico, before returning to Chicago.

Rexroth was married four times. His first wife, Andrée Dutcher, died in 1940, and in the same year he married Marie Cass. They were divorced in 1948. In 1949 Rexroth married Marthe Larsen, with whom he had two daughters, Mary in 1950 and Katherine in 1954, before the couple were divorced in 1961. In 1974 poet Carol Tinker became Rexroth's fourth wife.

Rexroth's activity between the world wars was largely political, though he did produce two long philosophical poems that were not published until later, *The Homestead Called Damascus* and *The Art of Worldly Wisdom*. One of his first published works was *In What Hour*, a book of poems that appeared in 1940, when Rexroth was almost thirty-five. *The Phoenix and the Tortoise* soon followed, and thereafter Rexroth published some fifty volumes of poetry, criticism, translations, and autobiography.

The Collected Shorter Poems, *The Collected Longer Poems*, *New Poems*, and *The Morning Star* contain all Rexroth's original verse. These books, individually and together, display the wide range of Rexroth's interests, from anarchism to Buddhism, from the environment to the Orient. Rexroth's early artistic enthusiasm for cubist painting, which he himself practiced, translates into the "objectivism" of his early poems, a style he shared with William Carlos

Williams and Louis Zukofsky. Thematically, *The Collected Shorter Poems* includes love poems such as "The Thin Edge of Your Pride," political poems such as "From the Paris Commune to the Kronstadt Rebellion," nature poems such as "A Lesson in Geography," social poems such as "Thou Shall Not Kill," travel poems such as "Vicenza," and translations, among other themes. Various poems are dedicated to different contemporaries, from the Dadaist poet Tristan Tzara to the Welsh bard Dylan Thomas. The net effect of reading these poems is a sense of both breadth and depth, range of subject and style combined with profundity and intensity of feeling.

Rexroth's translations are equally impressive. With his long-standing interest in Oriental culture, he was largely responsible for making Chinese and Japanese poetry available to a broad American audience. Of special note in this respect are *One Hundred Poems from the Japanese* and *One Hundred Poems from the Chinese*. Rexroth has also translated poetry from Greek, Latin, Spanish, and French, including the work of French cubist poet Pierre Reverdy. In return for his interest in their culture and literature, three books of Rexroth's poems have been rendered in Japanese by translators.

An Autobiographical Novel chronicles the first twenty-one years of Rexroth's life. Begun as a set of tapes made to inform his young daughters about their father's ancestors and early life and subsequently broadcast over the Pacifica Radio Network, the book was transcribed and edited by further dictation, to preserve its oral quality. In it Rexroth describes with factual detachment his early experiments in abstract painting, his adoption of the bohemian lifestyle, his political activisim, his spiritual odyssey, and his conservationism.

Rexroth's essays are pointed, trenchant, and individualistic. He brings his wealth of knowledge to bear in criticism that regularly shatters idols such as T. S. Eliot, undermines repressive authority such as that of the New Critics, reorganizes the traditional poetic canon to include forgotten poets such as Mina Loy, attacks the literary academy for superficiality and laziness, and generally enforces his vision that literature should be imaginative, international, innovative, and intelligent. From his position as outsider and given his extremely articulate—even arrogant—voice, Rexroth as a critic is able to speak the unspeakable and recognize the unrecognizable, leading often to insights that tend to explode prejudice, cut through cant, and refresh his readers' judgment, even when they do not agree with him.

In 1956 Rexroth gained special notoriety as the father of the San Francisco Poetry Renaissance, a flowering of creative activity in the Bay area that corresponded to the rise of the Beat movement in New York. In fact, it was Rexroth who acted as master of ceremonies for the famous Six Gallery reading, at which Allen Ginsberg first performed "Howl" (1956). That Rexroth subsequently rejected—and was in turn rejected by—some of the writers he initially supported is testimony to his integrity. As soon as he perceived that some of the new poets were encouraging a formulaic approach to literature, and so to life, he rejected them.

In the 1950's and 1960's, Rexroth won many prizes for his poetry and translations and taught sporadically in various universities. In 1967 a grant from the Rockefeller Foundation enabled him to travel around the world. Subsequently, his growing belief that the world is doomed to destruction by runaway technology started him on a new spiritual quest that led through Buddhism to Episcopalianism and finally to Roman Catholicism. The publication of *The Orchid Boat* and *The Burning Heart* in the 1970's fueled the growing interest in literature written by women; at about the same time Rexroth produced a radical social history, *Communalism*. Rexroth was baptized in the Catholic church in 1981, about a year before he died of heart disease in Santa Barbara, California. Though his reputation remains small, his literary output has seldom been equaled in scope, range, and quality.

BIBLIOGRAPHICAL REFERENCES: A collection of essays that is useful is *For Rexroth*, 1980, edited by Geoffrey Gardner. Morgan Gibson, a longtime friend, has published two brief books on Rexroth: *Kenneth Rexroth*, 1972, a basic introduction in the Twayne series, and *Revolutionary Rexroth: Poet of East-West Wisdom*, 1986. See also Lee Bartlett, *Kenneth Rexroth*, 1988. For a review of Rexroth's work by a contemporary poet, see William Carlos Williams, "Two New Books by Kenneth Rexroth," in *Poetry*, XC (June, 1957), 180-190.

James T. Jones

JEAN RHYS
Ella Gwendolen Rees Williams

Born: Roseau, Dominica Island, West Indies *Died:* Exeter, England
Date: August 24, 1894 *Date:* May 14, 1979

Principal Works

NOVELS: *Postures*, 1928 (also known as *Quartet*); *After Leaving Mr. Mackenzie*, 1930; *Voyage in the Dark*, 1934; *Good Morning, Midnight*, 1939; *Wide Sargasso Sea*, 1966.

SHORT FICTION: *The Left Bank: Sketches and Studies of Present-Day Bohemian Paris*, 1927; *Tigers Are Better-Looking*, 1968; *Sleep It Off, Lady*, 1976.

AUTOBIOGRAPHY: *Smile, Please: An Unfinished Autobiography*, 1979.

CORRESPONDENCE: *Jean Rhys: Letters, 1931-1966*, 1984.

In his introduction to Jean Rhys's *The Left Bank*, Ford Madox Ford captured the essence of all Rhys's work when he wrote that she had a "passion for stating the case of the underdog." Rhys was born Ella Gwendolen Rees Williams in Roseau, in the West Indies, on August 24, 1894. Rhys's mother, Minna Lockhart, was a white West Indian whose grandfather had been a Dominican slaveholder. Rhys's empathy for outcasts appears to have originated in her childhood. First, the young Rhys was aware of the tense relationship between blacks and whites in Dominica and of the disesteemed position that her great-grandfather had held. Her complicated feelings about her own relationships with blacks resulted in the creation of fictional relationships such as that between Anna and her black nurse, Francine, in *Voyage in the Dark*. Second, like Julie in *After Leaving Mr. Mackenzie*, Rhys believed that her mother preferred Rhys's younger sister. She remembered her father, a doctor, however, as acting caring toward her. Another event which had a tragic effect upon Rhys was her molestation as a young girl, an episode which she fictionalized in the short story "Good-bye Marcus, Good-bye Rose." Finally, even though her family was Anglican, Rhys was also influenced by Catholicism, as she was sent to a convent for schooling.

In 1907, Rhys left Dominica for England and eventually became a chorus girl. She stopped acting when she had her first love affair. Devastated when the relationship ended, Rhys found solace in keeping a diary, which later became the basis for *Voyage in the Dark*. In 1919, she married Jean Lenglet, a Dutch-French journalist, and they moved to Paris. In 1923, Rhys met writer and editor Ford Madox Ford, who created her pen name, Jean Rhys. Rhys's first published story, "Vienne," appeared in Ford's magazine, *The Transatlantic Review*, in December, 1924. Meanwhile, Rhys's husband was convicted of illegal entry into France, and during his imprisonment, Rhys became Ford's lover. When her affair with Ford ended, Rhys began the novel *Postures*, a fictionalized account of her relationship with Ford. This first novel, published in 1928, is viewed by many critics as Rhys's most unsuccessful work because she failed to achieve authorial objectivity. Rhys returned to England in 1927 and was divorced from Lenglet in 1932.

Rhys published *After Leaving Mr. Mackenzie* in 1930, *Voyage in the Dark* in 1934, and *Good Morning, Midnight* in 1939. She wrote little during World War II and did not publish again until March, 1966, when *Wide Sargasso Sea* appeared. In March, 1979, Rhys broke her hip, and on May 14, 1979, she died in the hospital in Exeter. She was survived by her daughter, Maryvonne Lenglet Moerman.

In her novels and short stories, Jean Rhys created detailed portraits of women who live marginal existences, outside conventional society. Embodying her work is a pessimistic view of a world in which the individual is isolated from others, trapped by fate, and possessed of little free will. At best, the individual can only hope to survive. Some critics explain this stark reality in Rhys's work by using feminist, Marxist, or psychoanalytical theories.

Although Rhys basically dealt with the same subject in all of her work, women who are alone, the intensity and vividness of her writing resulted in the creation of characters who are believable and themes which are enduring. One constant theme is rejection and loss. For the protagonists, love and happiness are remembered as brief and evanescent moments in childhood. As adults, the protagonists seek to regain love, but it is impossible. The women become victims of love and, consequently, experience disgrace. Connected to this theme are motifs of loneliness and isolation. Rhys's female protagonist often lacks a real home, lives alone in a single room, and drifts from one boardinghouse to another. This existence emphasizes the purposelessness of the heroine's life.

Furthermore, any meaning that the Rhys heroine can find for her existence is often based on her brief relationships with men. Ironically, these relationships allow the protagonist to break out of her isolation and momentarily experience some happiness; yet inevitably, when the men end the relationship, the woman is powerless so that she can do nothing but return to a room to be alone. Rhys also shows men to be emotional victims, unable to reveal themselves and form lasting relationships. Still, at the end of *Good Morning, Midnight*, Jean Rhys suggests that the human need for closeness with another person is so great that humiliation and failure in relationships will continue to be risked.

In her last and most critically acclaimed novel, *Wide Sargasso Sea*, Rhys explains how the madwoman in Charlotte Brontë's *Jane Eyre* (1847) became locked in the attic. Thus, for Rhys, the madwoman in the attic, like the outcast alone in a room, has a story to tell. The story reveals that labels, such as "mad," often hide and distort who people really are.

When Rhys's first five books were published, they were enjoyed by a small audience. Then, when Rhys did not publish anything in the 1940's, her books went out of print. In 1958, however, a radio broadcast of *Good Morning, Midnight* regenerated interest in her work, and by 1973, all Rhys's earlier novels had been reissued. Even with so much success, Rhys is still not appreciated by some critics. The main criticism against her work is that each book is the same story filled with unremitting pessimism and helpless women who contribute to their own victimization. Overall, appreciation for Rhys's work exists among a small but growing public and critical audience. What is often admired, besides her commitment to the "underdog," is her spare but forceful writing style, which coincides with the subject matter of her work; content and form are united and result in a powerful work of art.

BIBLIOGRAPHICAL REFERENCES: For a study of the relationship between Rhys's life and her writing, see Carole Angier, *Jean Rhys*, 1985. Nancy R. Harris, *Jean Rhys and the Novel as Women's Text*, 1988, investigates how Rhys uses male discourse and female discourse in *Voyage in the Dark* and *Wide Sargasso Sea* to give each novel prominent themes. Teresa F. O'Connor, *Jean Rhys: The West Indian Novels*, 1986, examines the linkage between *Voyage in the Dark* and *Wide Sargasso Sea* and the familial, cultural, and historical influences of Rhys's family and homeland in Dominica on her writing. David Plante, "Jean," in *Difficult Women: A Memoir of Three*, 1983, is a fascinating memoir of Plante's relationship with the then-elderly Jean Rhys. For other valuable readings of Rhys, see Arnold E. Davidson, *Jean Rhys*, 1985; Thomas F. Staley, *Jean Rhys: A Critical Study*, 1979; and Peter Wolfe, *Jean Rhys*, 1980. See also Elizabeth Abel, "Women and Schizophrenia: The Fiction of Jean Rhys," *Contemporary Literature*, XX (1979), 155-177; Frank Baldanza, "Jean Rhys on Insult and Injury," *Studies in the Literary Imagination*, II (1978), 55-65; Elgin W. Mellown, "Character and Themes in the Novels of Jean Rhys," *Contemporary Literature*, XIII (1972), 458-475; P. A. Packer, "The Four Early Novels of Jean Rhys," *Durham University Journal*, LXXI (1979), 252-265; Clara Thomas, "Mr. Rochester's First Marriage: *Wide Sargasso Sea* by Jean Rhys," *World Literature Written in English*, XVII (1978), 342-357; Helen Tiffin, "Mirror and Mask: Colonial Motifs in the Novels of Jean Rhys," *World Literature Written in English*, XVII (1978), 328-341; and Elizabeth Vreeland, "Jean Rhys," *The Paris Review*, XXI (1979), 218-237.

Michelle Van Tine

RONALD RIBMAN

Born: New York, New York
Date: May 28, 1932

Principal Works

PLAYS: *Harry, Noon and Night*, pr. 1965; *The Journey of the Fifth Horse*, pr. 1966; *The Ceremony of Innocence*, pr. 1967; *Passing Through from Exotic Places*, pr. 1969; *Fingernails Blue as Flowers*, pr. 1971; *A Break in the Skin*, pr. 1972; *The Poison Tree*, pr. 1973; *Cold Storage*, pr. 1977; *Buck*, pr., pb. 1983; *The Cannibal Masque*, pr. 1987; *A Serpent's Egg*, pr. 1987; *Sweet Table at the Richelieu*, pr. 1987.

TELEPLAYS: *The Final War of Olly Winter*, 1967; *Seize the Day*, 1987.

SCREENPLAY: *The Angel Levine*, 1970 (with William Gunn).

Ronald Burt Ribman's plays mirror the condition of twentieth century man by dealing with characters who are trapped by their societies, their circumstances, even by their own personalities and bodies into a severely restricted range of possibilities, a condition against which they rebel but from which they gain enlightenment. He was born in New York City on May 28, 1932, the son of Samuel M. Ribman, a lawyer, and Rosa (Lerner) Ribman. After attending New York grammar and high schools, Ribman went to Brooklyn College for a year before transferring to the University of Pittsburgh, where he obtained his bachelor of business administration degree in 1954. He served for the next two years in the U.S. Army, returning to the University of Pittsburgh in 1956, when he began graduate work in English literature. After receiving his master's degree in 1958, he continued his studies in English literature at Pittsburgh, obtaining his Ph.D. in 1962. He then taught English for a year at Otterbein College in Westerville, Ohio. In 1963, he left the Midwest and returned to New York, having decided to become a full-time writer.

The American Place Theater (APT) launched Ribman's career as a playwright. Along with the director Wynn Handman, Lanier wanted to develop new playwrights and to present literate and controversial plays that were not then being produced either on or off Broadway. Ribman's first play, *Harry, Noon and Night*, was produced under APT's Writers Development Program and given its guaranteed six-week run in 1965. As with several APT productions, *Harry, Noon and Night* was later presented Off-Broadway at the Pocket Theater, where it played for six performances. Ribman's black comedy centered on the descent of Harry, a homosexual artist, into the maelstrom of his own failures. Critics were strongly divided over the merits of the play. Some found its three scenes poorly unified, its situations brutally obscene, and its language gratuitously scatological. Others thought it was the best new play in New York that year, making a significant statement about the corruption that results when human beings try to dominate each other.

For his second play, Ribman transformed an Ivan Turgenev novella, *Dnevnik lishnego cheloveka* (1850; *The Diary of a Superfluous Man*, 1899), into a double portrait of human loneliness, but *The Journey of the Fifth Horse* was much more than an adaptation. Ribman took Turgenev's story of a nineteenth century landowner who dies friendless and added to it the character of a functionary in a publishing house who is forced to read the diary of the dead landowner. The reader, who masks his loneliness by sarcasm, is coarse, superficial, and self-righteous, whereas the landowner, who constantly anticipates rejection, is shy, melancholic, and self-doubting. In his play, Ribman reveals how similar these two men really are: They are both superfluous men, as useless to society as a fifth horse running tethered beside a carriage drawn by four horses. *The Journey of the Fifth Horse*, even though it had only a short run, was highly acclaimed by most New York critics, who also singled out Dustin Hoffman's portrait of the repressed clerk for special praise. Ribman's play received the Obie Award for the best Off-Broadway drama of the 1965-1966 season.

This early success led to a commission to write a teleplay for Columbia Broadcasting System (CBS) Playhouse, a series designed to generate original dramas for television. CBS gave Ribman freedom to choose his subject matter and theme. In *The Final War of Olly Winter*, the initial production of CBS Playhouse broadcast on January 29, 1967, Ribman chose the Vietnam War as his subject and pacifism as his theme. Olly Winter, a black master sergeant in the army, kills a guerrilla, who turns out to be a young girl, and reluctantly forms a friendship with another Vietnamese girl, with whom he eventually dies. Though some critics found the play conventional in sentiment and lacking in originality, most praised Ribman's mastery of this new medium and his compassionate portraits of his central characters. *The Final War of Olly Winter* was nominated for an Emmy award of the American Academy of Television Arts and Sciences. With his Obie Award and Emmy nomination, Ribman obtained financial support from the Rockefeller Foundation, and since a bright future in the theater seemed assured, he married Alice Rosen, a nurse, on August 27, 1967, a union that resulted in two children, a boy and a girl. The Rockefeller Grant gave Ribman the confidence to take greater risks in writing his third play, *The Ceremony of Innocence*, a historical drama set in medieval England and produced at the American Place Theater. Of all his plays, *The Ceremony of Innocence* most nearly approaches classical tragedy.

Passing Through from Exotic Places, Ribman's next offering, was presented by the Capricorn Company rather than APT. Composed of three short plays, it was neither a critical nor a popular success. During this time Ribman also wrote his first screenplay, *The Angel Levine*, with William Gunn. The film had an excellent cast (Zero Mostel, Harry Belafonte, Ida Kaminska, Milo O'Shea, Eli Wallach, and Anne Jackson) and a strong source (a story by Bernard Malamud), but its account of an impoverished Jewish tailor's encounter with a black angel left most audiences and critics skeptical and unmoved. In 1970, Ribman received a Guggenheim Fellowship, and in 1971, APT honored him by choosing his play *Fingernails Blue as Flowers* to be half of the double bill inaugurating APT's new theater in the basement of a skyscraper at 111 West 46th Street. Critics found Ribman's play much less interesting than Steve Tesich's *Lake of the Woods* (pr. 1971), the other half of the doublebill. After *A Break in the Skin*, a technological drama whose several versions never pleased its author or its audiences, Ribman's next play, *The Poison Tree*, achieved considerable success (it won for Ribman the Straw Hat Award for the best new play in 1973). Its triumph in provincial theaters led to its becoming Ribman's debut play on Broadway, where it opened early in 1976 at the Ambassador Theater. The image of the "poison tree" in the title represents the California prison that is the play's setting and that poisons both the prisoners and the guards who inhabit it. Using the obscene argot of the inmates, Ribman documents the brutalization of the prisoners, who are mostly black, by the guards, who are mostly white, but this theme does not exhaust the injustices that flow from this deeply corrupting situation. Ribman also uncovers other levels of inhumanity, for example, prisoners betraying prisoners. Like many of his other victim heroes, these prisoners in their claustrophobic environment are symbols of a more pervasive entrapment to which humankind subjects itself. Ribman's compassionate meditation on the penal system raised issues demanding public attention, but despite a very favorable critical reception, the play closed after a short run.

Following his Broadway *succès d'estime*, Ribman returned again to APT with *Cold Storage*, the play most critics see as his best. It won for Ribman the Elizabeth Hull-Kate Warriner Award of the Dramatists Guild. *Cold Storage* is essentially a therapeutic dialogue between two terminally ill cancer patients: Joseph Parmigian, an Armenian fruit dealer and an unstoppably loquacious explicator of the art of dying; and Richard Landau, an affluent Jewish art dealer and as reserved and taciturn as his companion is outspoken and garrulous. Landau does not at first enjoy Parmigian's playing a suicidal Hamlet at one moment and a jolly Falstaff the next. He also does not want to be told that he is dying, and he does not want Parmigian to know that his parents helped him escape the Nazi Holocaust at the expense of their own lives (this reason for his guilt-ridden taciturnity is uncovered in the second act).

Ribman uses these contrasting characters to explore such themes as death as escape, death as expiation of guilt, and death as the enhancer of life. Although *Cold Storage* had defects—a weak second act, a lack of dramatic action, and character running riot over theme—Ribman's celebration of life at the door of death was full of intelligent and witty writing as well as penetrating insights into some very human characters and the human condition. Parmigian goads not only Landau into assuming his responsibility for living life fully but the audience as well. After *Cold Storage*, Ribman disappeared from the New York theater scene for five years. Then, in 1983, APT produced his play *Buck*, a dark comedy that takes place in a cable television studio, a department store, and a bar. Like many of his other plays, it had a short run. During the 1980's, Ribman returned to teleplay writing: He based *Seize the Day* on Saul Bellow's novel of the same name. Ribman also continued writing plays for regional theater companies. For example, in 1987, *Sweet Table at the Richelieu* had its world premiere at the American Repertory Theatre in Cambridge, Massachusetts.

Although Ribman's oeuvre has been widely praised by critics and rewarded with several prestigious grants and awards, he has not achieved the public recognition and commercial success to which many feel his substantial literary gifts entitle him. For the most part, his plays have appeared Off-Broadway or in regional theaters and have had limited runs. There are several reasons for this: his originality and adventurousness in theme and setting, his highly literate writing, and his philosophical point of view. Critics have pointed out that there is no such thing as an easily categorizable Ribman play. He does not seem to work out of his personal life the way so many American playwrights do. He has written about homosexuals, a Russian landowner and clerk, a medieval king, black prisoners, and dying cancer patients. His plays have been set in modern Munich, nineteenth century St. Petersburg, and a contemporary tropical island, prison, and hospital roof. His writing is sensitive to the complex qualities of language, and he is able to adapt his English to suit the style and mood of his plays, be they absurdist, historical, comedic, or tragic. He has said that his plays are about words, and he accounts for their neglect by the general public because many theatergoers are overly visual—they go to see a production rather than to focus attention on what the playwright has to say. Ribman writes out of a deep humanity, based on powerful convictions and deep social insights.

BIBLIOGRAPHICAL REFERENCES: Robert Brustein has discussed Ribman's provenance as a playwright in *The Third Theatre*, 1969. Martin Gottfried has analyzed Ribman's role in the early history of the American Place Theater along with some of his early plays in *A Theater Divided: The Postwar American Stage*, 1967, and *Opening Nights: Theater Criticism of the Sixties*, 1969. Gerald Weales examines Ribman's early plays in his *The Jumping-Off Place: American Drama in the 1960's*, 1969. For a more acidulous discussion of some of Ribman's plays, see John Simon, *Uneasy Stages: A Chronicle of the New York Theater 1963-1973*, 1976. For excerpts from some of the more significant analyses and reviews of Ribman's plays, along with references to their sources, see *Contemporary Literary Criticism*, Vol. 7, 1977, edited by Phyllis Carmel Mendelson and Dedria Bryfonski. Aside from reviews of his plays and analyses of contemporary American playwrights, Ribman's work has not received extensive critical attention in scholarly journals. Occasionally, his plays are discussed to illustrate a theme; such is the case in Mary Otis Hivnor, "Adaptations and Adaptors," *The Kenyon Review*, XXX, no. 2 (1968), 265-273, where Ribman's adaptation of Turgenev in his *The Journey of the Fifth Horse* is treated.

Robert J. Paradowski

ELMER RICE
Elmer Leopold Reizenstein

Born: New York, New York
Date: September 28, 1892

Died: Southhampton, England
Date: May 8, 1967

Principal Works

PLAYS: *On Trial*, pr. 1914; *The Iron Cross*, pr. 1917 (with Frank Harris); *The Home of the Free*, pr., pb. 1917; *For the Defense*, pr. 1919; *Wake Up, Jonathan*, pr. 1921 (with Hatcher Hughes); *It Is the Law*, pr. 1922; *The Adding Machine*, pr., pb. 1923; *Close Harmony: Or, The Lady Next Door*, pr. 1924 (with Dorothy Parker); *Cock Robin*, pr. 1928 (with Philip Barry); *Street Scene*, pr., pb. 1929; *The Subway*, pr., pb. 1929; *See Naples and Die*, pr. 1929; *The Left Bank*, pr., pb. 1931; *Counsellor-at-Law*, pr., pb. 1931; *Black Sheep*, pr. 1932; *The House in Blind Alley*, pb. 1932; *We, the People*, pr., pb. 1933; *Judgment Day*, pr., pb. 1934; *Between Two Worlds*, pr. 1934; *Not for Children*, pr., pb. 1935; *American Landscape*, pr. 1938; *Two on an Island*, pr., pb. 1940; *Flight to the West*, pr. 1940; *A New Life*, pr. 1943; *Dream Girl*, pr. 1945; *The Grand Tour*, pr. 1951; *The Winner*, pr., pb. 1954; *Cue for Passion*, pr. 1958; *Love Among the Ruins*, pr., pb. 1963.

NONFICTION: *Minority Report: An Autobiography*, 1954; *The Living Theatre*, 1959.

NOVELS: *A Voyage to Purilia*, 1930; *Imperial City*, 1937; *The Show Must Go On*, 1949.

Elmer Rice, one of the major dramatists of the first half of the twentieth century, was instrumental in the emergence of American drama as an influential force in world theater. Born Elmer Leopold Reizenstein, he grew up in Manhattan, living with his parents Jacob and Fanny Lion Reizenstein. The family was poor, and Rice completed only two years of high school before quitting at age fourteen in order to work and contribute to the family's budget, being employed first as a claims clerk and then as a law clerk in his cousin's office. While working, he received a high school equivalency diploma, and in 1908 he entered New York Law School. His concern with social issues, which would be evident throughout his career, was developed early. His parents instilled in him the value of goodness and fairness, but his experience with law taught him that the world was otherwise. He observed that the law, rather than being used to uphold justice, often was manipulated to evade justice. In addition, his early reading of George Bernard Shaw and Henrik Ibsen imparted to him a respect for socialism and a guarded attitude toward capitalism. At the age of twenty-two, shortly after being admitted to the New York bar, he left his position at the law office determined to write plays. Eight months later, *On Trial* was playing in New York receiving the praise of critics. The play eventually earned more than $100,000 for him, enabling him to continue in the theater.

With *On Trial*, Rice began a professional life that would include the writing of more than thirty plays. In addition, Rice, starting with *Street Scene* and with the exception of *The Subway*, directed all of his plays, and after 1930 he also produced them. As a playwright, he is recognized for his experimentation and for his technical expertise. Even his first play demonstrates his interest in innovation. *On Trial* contains a rather conventional plot: An ill-treated woman goes on to a happy marriage only to be blackmailed by her early seducer into another sexual liaison. Incensed, her husband murders the man and is placed on trial. The play was a success not because of the plot but because of the structure. Opening with the trial scene, the play proceeds through a series of flashbacks, a technique previously unknown in theater that Rice had borrowed from film.

During this period he married Hazel Levy, had two children, and actively involved himself with social issues such as women's suffrage and child labor. Drama became his means to effect changes in the social system. He wrote about women's views of World War I in *The Iron Cross* and about child labor in *The House in Blind Alley*. When the difficulty of finding an outlet for these plays became apparent, he wrote more commercially acceptable plays, such as the two moderately successful mystery melodramas, *For the Defense* and *It Is the Law*, and the drama *Wake Up, Jonathan* written with Hatcher Hughes. Throughout his career, his plays can be divided into those that have a social message and those that fit the conventional Broadway mold.

After a two-year stint in Hollywood writing for film, Rice returned to New York and penned one of his most acclaimed plays, *The Adding Machine*. The play, innovative for its use of expressionism, illustrates the anti-individualistic effects of industrialization. Mr. Zero, a bookkeeper for twenty-five years, has worked methodically six days a week without a raise or any other acknowledgment from his boss. On the anniversary of his twenty-fifth year, he is fired; his replacement will be an adding machine. After receiving the news, he stabs his boss and then spends the evening with his wife and several other nondescript couples. As he expects, he is arrested, tried, and executed. To his amazement, he is transported to heaven where he encounters his fellow bookkeeper Daisy Devore who, secretly in love with him, had committed suicide. For the first time in his life, Zero has the opportunity to be happy, but he rejects it as immoral. Choosing to leave heaven, he is assigned to computing figures on a gigantic adding machine. Since souls are recycled, however, he is sent back to earth to another slavelike existence. The play received generally favorable reviews and has been revived and produced in New York, London, and Paris, and on innumerable college campuses throughout the United States.

After a few years in Paris, an experience later reflected in *The Left Bank*, Rice was again in New York City writing and then directing and producing what would become his most successful play, *Street Scene*. This play, for which he received the Pulitzer Prize, presents a slice of lower-middle-class life in New York. The many characters and numerous incidents are connected by the single stage setting, a tenement, and by the developing drama of the Maurrant family. Stifled by both life in the tenement and a cold, domineering husband, Anna Maurrant seeks happiness in a not-so-secret affair with a bill collector for a milk company. The climax of the play is reached when is Maurrant kills his wife and her lover and is soon captured. After a tearful meeting with her father, Rose Maurrant realizes that contentment can only lie within and that life in the tenement is not necessarily one of humiliation and brutality. While the play is a realistic depiction of the dehumanizing effect of tenement life and is a criticism of the capitalistic system that produces tenements, it affirms that fulfillment is within the reach of all.

During the 1930's, Rice continued his political activities, joining the American Civil Liberties Union, lecturing against censorship in the theater, and protesting the United States' involvement in World War II. Although his politics were socialistic, he never considered joining the Communist Party. His plays of the 1930's reflect his views. *We, the People* is a series of scenes illustrating the oppression of capitalism, while *Judgment Day* is against Fascism. *Between Two Worlds* is a presentation of the theories of capitalism and communism; both systems are found lacking. In 1938 he wrote, produced, and directed *American Landscape*, a play about the growing menace of Fascism on American soil. In *Flight to the West*, Rice, reversing his pacifist stance, argues the necessity of involvement in World War II. For years he believed that war was a tool of capitalistic expansion, but with World War II he concluded that war was the only way to stop Fascism and to protect democracy.

Reacting against hostile critics, Rice (for a period of four years in the 1930's) did not write any plays, but he nevertheless retained an involvement in the theater. He was director of the Federal Theater Project and in 1938 organized, along with other playwrights such as Maxwell Anderson and Robert Sherwood, the Playwrights' Producing Company whose aim was to encourage an uncensored environment for drama.

In the 1940's, he wrote what is considered his last success, *Dream Girl*, starring his second wife, Betty Field, whom he later divorced in 1955 in order to marry Barbara P. Marshall. This romantic comedy concerns a young woman's fantasies as she attempts to deal with a dull reality. His later plays, *The Grand Tour*, *The Winner*, *Cue for Passion*, and *Love Among the Ruins*, while containing memorable passages, are generally considered to be inferior to his earlier work from the early 1920's to the mid-1940's.

Rice was an accomplished playwright, writing more than thirty plays in a career that lasted fifty years. Partly because of his efforts, American drama gained in stature. He argued that theater should present serious ideas that challenge the political status quo. To that end, many of his plays had messages about the oppression of capitalism, the dehumanizing force of the machine age, the dangers of Fascism, and the importance of protecting democracy. He also fought the conventionality of typical Broadway plays, arguing for freedom of expression in form and content. Rice is a major American dramatist who did much to promote and advance the quality of American theater.

BIBLIOGRAPHICAL REFERENCES: For a playwright of Rice's stature, surprisingly little criticism has been devoted to his work. For a discussion of his plays in relation to his political ideas, see Robert Hogan, *The Independence of Elmer Rice*, 1970; Anthony F. R. Palmieri, *Elmer Rice: A Playwright's Vision of America*, 1980; and Jules Chametzky, "Elmer Rice, Liberation, and the Great Ethnic Question," in *From Hester Street to Hollywood: The Jewish-American Stage and Screen*, 1984, edited by Sarah Blacker Cohen. For an examination of his position in the theater, see Alan S. Downer, *Fifty Years of American Drama*, 1951; John Gassner, *Masters of Drama*, 1954; Malcolm Goldstein, *The Political Stage*, 1974; and Gerald Rabkin, "Elmer Rice and the Seriousness of Drama," in *Drama Commitment: Politics in the American Theatre of the Thirties*, 1964. Biographical information along with a study of his major plays is presented in Frank Durham, *Elmer Rice*, 1970.

Barbara Wiedemann

MORDECAI RICHLER

Born: Montreal, Canada
Date: January 27, 1931

PRINCIPAL WORKS

NOVELS: *The Acrobats*, 1954 (also known as *Wicked We Love*); *Son of a Smaller Hero*, 1955; *A Choice of Enemies*, 1957; *The Apprenticeship of Duddy Kravitz*, 1959; *The Incomparable Atuk*, 1963 (also known as *Stick Your Neck Out*); *Cocksure*, 1968; *St. Urbain's Horseman*, 1971; *Joshua Then and Now*, 1980.

SHORT FICTION: *The Street*, 1969.

ESSAYS: *Hunting Tigers Under Glass: Essays and Reports*, 1968; *Shovelling Trouble*, 1972; *Notes on an Endangered Species and Others*, 1974; *The Great Comic Book Heroes and Other Essays*, 1978; *Home Sweet Home*, 1984.

CHILDREN'S LITERATURE: *Jacob Two-Two Meets the Hooded Fang*, 1975.

TRAVEL SKETCH: *Images of Spain*, 1977 (with Peter Christopher).

ANTHOLOGY: *Canadian Writing Today*, 1970.

Mordecai Richler is a major Canadian novelist who treats contemporary mores with a mixture of amusement and censure. Born on January 27, 1931, Richler was one of two sons of Moses Isaac Richler and Lily (Rosenberg) Richler. He grew up in the area around St. Urbain's Street, a milieu he has frequently re-created in his novels and especially in his collection of stories, *The Street*. After loafing through Baron Byng High School (the Fletcher's Field of his fiction), he attended Sir George Williams College but withdrew in 1951. He spent most of the next twenty years abroad, at first living squalidly in Paris and then settling in London. Visits to Spain produced a fascination with that country which is manifest in several of his books.

His first novel, *The Acrobats*, is set in Valencia in April, 1951. This melodramatic novel, in places blatantly reminiscent of Ernest Hemingway's novels about Spain, incorporates several motifs that recur in Richler's work: alienated Jews, a sinister German, and a protagonist who feels trapped between the older generation, with its traditional values, and younger, iconoclastical rebels. Surprised at its success, Richler subsequently expressed a dislike for the book, though he continued to explore the themes he broached in it.

The Apprenticeship of Duddy Kravitz is Richler's best-known novel, and it was made into a successful film. After rendering life miserable for the teachers at Fletcher's Field High School, Duddy lands a hotel job at a summer resort area north of Montreal (as Richler did). A sympathetic chambermaid, Yvette, shows him an unspoiled lake which, following his grandfather's dictum that a man without land is nothing, Duddy vows to own, in spite of the anti-Semitism of the surrounding French Canadian farmers. Yet his despicable treatment of the innocent epileptic who is driving a truck for him so disgusts Yvette that she ceases to help him and reveals his dishonesty to his grandfather. Thus, when Duddy shows his family the lake he has finally acquired, his grandfather is not impressed and Duddy's triumph is diminished. Moral ambiguity is central to Duddy's character. On the one hand, he brazenly and ruthlessly exploits and betrays those who help him; on the other hand, he does rescue his brother from a dire predicament and gives compassionate help to a dying uncle. Similarly, Richler satirizes both Jews and Gentiles, often in amusing episodes.

Indeed, humor was to become increasingly prominent in Richler's work in the 1960's. Apparently inspired by the author's temporary return to and dealings with the Canadian media, *The Incomparable Atuk* uses the rise and spectacular fall of an Eskimo poet-turned-entrepreneur to satirize all kinds of current fads and phenomena. Richler especially mocks the kind of Canadian nationalism which expresses itself in strident anti-Americanism and the kinds of Jewishness which either proclaim the superiority of all things Jewish or ostentatiously pursue assimilation into the Gentile world. Satire and exaggeration are taken even further in *Cocksure*. Its protagonist is Mortimer Griffin, a Canadian blueblood who won the Victoria Cross during World War II. The novel contains several brilliant and hilarious episodes satirizing progressive education, the sadism of egocentric television interviewers, and the duplicity of documentary filmmakers. Praised by Anthony Burgess and other judicious critics, the novel was criticized by some for its hero, who embodies no positive alternatives to the evils he attacks.

Joshua Shapiro of *Joshua Then and Now* is another protagonist who bears a strong resemblance to his author: Born in 1931 in a Jewish area of Montreal, he learns more on the street than in Fletcher's Field High School. He makes his living as a journalist in England, has adventures in Spain in 1952, marries a Canadian Gentile (with whom he has several children), and, resettled in Montreal, strives to preserve his domestic stability. While struggling to keep their home functioning while his wife is in the hospital with a nervous breakdown, Joshua takes to breaking into the homes of his now-affluent former schoolmates and carrying out ingenious revenges. Since Richler was living in Montreal again while writing this novel in the 1970's, Canadian affairs are prominent, such as the panic among rich English-speaking Montrealers following the sensational victory of the separatist party in the Quebec provincial election of 1976.

Although Richler is a prolific writer of essays, scripts, and reviews, he seeks to make a lasting mark through his novels. The four he wrote in the 1950's, culminating with *The Apprenticeship of Duddy Kravitz*, depict a world in which acquisitiveness and expediency regularly succeed at the expense of affection and honesty. Nevertheless, their heroes maintain some integrity, flawed though it is in Duddy particularly. Later, in *The Incomparable Atuk* and *Cocksure*, even more destructive forces are at work, but their depressing implications are modified by Richler's comic inventiveness and satiric energy. *Joshua Then and Now* presents decent protagonists beset by contemporary decadence but emerging with confidence and hope renewed. Biting and wide-ranging in their satire, Richler's major novels escape total pessimism by virtue of his humor.

BIBLIOGRAPHICAL REFERENCES: George Woodcock, *Mordecai Richler*, 1970, perceptively covers Richler's writings up to *The Street*. *Mordecai Richler*, 1971, edited by David Sheps, is a useful collection of articles. Graeme Gibson, "Mordecai Richler," in *Eleven Canadian Novelists*, 1973, is a candid interview with the author. Mark Levine, *Mordecai Richler*, 1980, is a brief monograph. Arnold E. Davidson, *Mordecai Richler*, 1983, analyzes Richler's work up to *Joshua Then and Now*. Victor J. Ramraj, *Mordecai Richler*, 1983, thoughtfully evaluates Richler's strengths and weaknesses. *Perspectives on Mordecai Richler*, 1986, edited by Michael Darling, contains eight advanced essays on Richler's technique, include a computer-based study of his language in *The Apprenticeship of Duddy Kravitz*.

Christopher M. Armitage

RAINER MARIA RILKE

Born: Prague, Austria
Date: December 4, 1875

Died: Valmont, Switzerland
Date: December 29, 1926

Principal Works

POETRY: *Leben und Lieder*, 1894; *Das Buch der Bilder*, 1902, 1906; *Das Stundenbuch*, 1905 (*Poems from the Book of Hours*, 1941); *Neue Gedichte*, 1907-1908 (*New Poems*, 1964); *Requiem*, 1909 (*Requiem and Other Poems*, 1935); *Das Marienleben*, 1913 (*The Life of the Virgin Mary*, 1921); *Die Sonette an Orpheus*, 1923 (*Sonnets to Orpheus*, 1936); *Duineser Elegien*, 1923 (*Duinese Elegies*, 1930; better known as *Duino Elegies*).

SHORT FICTION: *Vom lieben Gott und Anderes*, 1900 (*Stories of God*, 1932).

MISCELLANEOUS: *Die Weise von Liebe und Tod des Cornets Christoph Rilke*, 1906 (*The Tale of the Love and Death of Cornet Christopher Rilke*, 1932).

BIOGRAPHY: *Auguste Rodin*, 1903 (English translation, 1919).

NOVEL: *Die Aufzeichnungen des Malte Laurids Brigge*, 1910 (*The Notebooks of Malte Laurids Brigge*, 1930; also known as *The Journal of My Other Self*).

PLAYS: *Nine Plays by Rainer Maria Rilke*, pb. 1979.

Rainer Maria Rilke is the most important and influential German poet of the twentieth century; along with the Anglo-Irish William Butler Yeats and the French Paul Valéry, he caused a transformation of lyric poetry, opening up new directions and potentialities. He was born (baptized René Karl Wilhelm Johann Josef Maria Rilke) on December 4, 1875, in Prague, then within the dominion of the Austro-Hungarian Empire, the second largest administrative unit in Europe. The Rilke family had long been established as fairly prosperous land agents near Prague and claimed descent from a long line of Carinthian nobility. Rilke's father had begun his adult life as a career military officer, but he was forced to resign his commission because of a chronic throat problem. Thereafter he worked as an Austrian railroad official, eventually transferring his dreams of military glory to his son, who would triumph where he had failed. Rilke's mother, a poet with aristocratic fantasies, had other ideas.

At the age of eleven, when Rilke had completed his early schooling, his parents' marriage dissolved. In that situation, Rilke had to be sent to boarding school; his father's will prevailing, he entered a rigorous military academy. He later reported that the Prussian discipline traumatized him; although some critics have doubted the severity of the training, Rilke certainly reacted against the bourgeois values of a society that supported such institutions and ideals. Chronic illnesses, probably psychosomatic, eventually forced his withdrawal. He was expected to take over his uncle's law practice in Prague, but he became increasingly disenchanted with law and attracted to poetry. With the publication of his first volume, *Leben und Lieder* (life and songs), in 1894, his vocation was set.

For the next several years he published regularly, though he would ultimately renounce as juvenile all this material, including his most popular work, *The Tale of the Love and Death of Cornet Christopher Rilke*, a rhythmical balladesque recounting of the experiences of a seventeenth century soldier, Rilke's ancestor. Yet his real breakthrough as a poet had already begun. It started with his discovery of Friedrich Nietzsche, who instilled a philosophy of struggle, and of the Danish novelist Jens Peter Jacobsen, who taught him to look at nature as a source of images corresponding to emotional states. He followed this with two trips to Russia, where he was overwhelmed with both the immense landscapes and the combination of piety and fatalistic resignation in the Russian soul. Contact with an artists' colony at Worpswede near Bremen fused these influences by helping him look for plastic equivalents for feelings, something akin to T. S. Eliot's theory of the objective correlative. Finally he went to Paris in 1902; he found the modern metropolis terrifying and spirit-robbing. The sculptor Auguste Rodin took him in, insulated him against the shock of the city, taught him more about the way sculpture could shape poetic images, and hired him as private secretary.

The employment lasted only eight months, but it moved Rilke to take an entirely fresh approach to lyric poetry. This revelation, however, was disclosed only gradually. The first traces appear in *Das Buch der Bilder* (book of images), to the second edition of which (1906) he added thirty-seven poems, including some of those for which he is best known. Even before this he published *Poems from the Book of Hours*, in which he adopts first the persona of a Russian monk meditating on the interrelationship of man, nature, and God, then that of the poverty-stricken street people of Paris. These poems introduce a unique pantheistic mysticism, a celebration of natural religion that absorbs familiar Christian images.

The transformation reached full flower in his *New Poems*, especially in the second volume (1908). These were different enough from anything he had done earlier that he distinguished them as "experiences"; the others were simply "feelings," immature approaches to the complex whole. He presents a version of his Parisian transformation in *The Notebooks of Malte Laurids Brigge*, in which the title character is a fictionalized counterpart of Rilke experiencing the isolation and depression of the sensitive soul in the modern cosmopolis. It begs comparison with James Joyce's parallel account in *A Portrait of the Artist as a Young Man* (1916), though it has never received the same public acclaim.

This frenzy of publication left Rilke exhausted. He sought solace in travel, first to North Africa, then to Spain, following which he occupied himself mostly in translations of French, Spanish, Italian, and English poets. Finally, while spending a season at Schloss Duino on the Adriatic, he felt new inspiration. He managed to finish two components of what would become *Duino Elegies*, but he became oppressed first with fears of and then with the fact of World War I. That oppression kept him from writing for ten full years, until 1922. When inspiration returned, it came with a vengeance: His writing became so compulsive that he was left physically debilitated afterward. Yet he was able to finish *Duino Elegies*—and to alter the course of not only German but also world poetry in the process.

This book consists of ten wide-ranging poems, loosely linked in a cycle, which explore Rilke's personal universe of spiritual struggle as a microcosm of the more general problem of human existence. The poems are obscure, dense, and laden with private symbolism, and unraveling them required the best efforts of a generation of scholars. One key, derived in part from his earlier poetry, has been found in Rilke's concept of nature, which he sees as the source of both poetic experience and human action. In his vision, however, both poet and humankind are profoundly alienated from nature; the attempts of both to reestablish the vital link repeatedly end in frustration. Humans are doomed to suffer defeat in their efforts to restore themselves to their source in nature; this makes tragedy the norm of human experience. Worse, in attempting to disclose this reality, the poet must work with words and images that reflect only dimly the truth of experience.

Finally eased of this terrible burden, Rilke turned to *Sonnets to Orpheus*, a Dionysian celebration that balances the Apollonian austerity of *Duino Elegies*. Rilke composed these fifty-five sonnets within a few weeks after finishing the earlier harrowing poems. The sonnets share the difficulty of style and obscurity of reference of *Duino Elegies*, but in all other respects they are a complete contrast. Their tone is ecstatic, celebratory, full of light, joyful rather than lamenting. The sonnets commemorate integration and reunion: Orpheus, the spirit of song, moves nature with his singing and harmonizes it with humankind. Imitating him, the poet becomes the means of spiritualizing nature and human experience in it. In balancing *Duino Elegies*, *Sonnets to Orpheus* demonstrates that Rilke's aesthetic and mysticism embrace both polarities. Where he would have gone from this point remains conjecture. He died in Switzerland, of a blood disorder, in 1926.

BIBLIOGRAPHICAL REFERENCES: The most authoritative and thorough biography of Rilke is Donald Prater, *A Ringing Glass: The Life of Rainer Maria Rilke*, 1986; it features a complete bibliography. E. M. Butler presents the approach and the judgment of the mid-twentieth century in *Rainer Maria Rilke*, 1941. A valuable attempt to assess Rilke's permanent position in literature appears in Timothy J. Casey, *Rainer Maria Rilke: A Centenary Essay*, 1976. Rilke's voluminous letters, in which he worked out his philosophical and theological positions, are represented in R. F. C. Hall, *Rilke: Selected Letters, 1902-1926*, 1946. The periodical *Modern Austrian Literature* collected several important essays in a special Rilke issue in 1982. A second useful compilation is *Rilke: The Alchemy of Alienation*, 1980, edited by Frank Baron, Ernst S. Dick, and Warren R. Maurer. Romano Guardini's analysis of the poetry in *Rilke's "Duino Elegies": An Interpretation*, 1961, remains illuminating.

James Livingston

TOMÁS RIVERA

Born: Crystal City, Texas *Died:* Riverside, California
Date: December 22, 1935 *Date:* May 16, 1984

PRINCIPAL WORK

NOVEL: . . . *y no se tragó la tierra* (1971; . . . *and the earth did not part*, 1971; better known as . . . *and the earth did not devour him*).

Rarely has a literary reputation been so securely based on one slim novel as Tomás Rivera's. Though he was also highly regarded as a college administrator and educator—becoming, in 1979, the first Chicano to be named a chancellor in the University of California system—and though he published a small collection of poems (*Always and Other Poems*) in 1972 and scattered poems, essays, and short stories afterward, it is on his striking episodic novel, . . . *and the earth did not devour him*, that his literary reputation rests.

Born on December 22, 1935, the son of migrant workers, Florencio Rivera and Josefa Hernández Rivera, Tomás Rivera himself did migrant work until 1957. He received his B.S. in education in 1958 and his Ph.D. in Romance languages and literature in 1969. His novel, . . . *and the earth did not devour him*, was first published in 1971, in an edition that printed both the original Spanish and its translation into English; it won the Quinto Sol National Chicano Literary Award. In 1978 he married Concepción Garza, and in 1979 he became chancellor of the University of California at Riverside.

Not a conventional novel, . . . *and the earth did not devour him* may appear to some at first reading to be a collection of loosely connected short stories and sketches. While the separate chapters are written and can be read as individual stories, contemporary critics of the text agree that the deeper structure of the work as a whole demands that it be read as a novel.

The book begins with a chapter entitled "The Lost Year," which introduces the theme of lost time that will continue through the novel. When the narrator describes a recurring dream in which the unnamed protagonist "would suddenly awaken and then realize that he was really asleep," the reader may be put in mind of the beginning of *À la recerche du temps perdu* (1913-1927; *Remembrance of Things Past*, 1922-1931, 1981), in which Marcel talks about waking up with the candle extinguished and not remembering whether he had slept. As the book goes on, the reader understands that the period he is describing as a year is actually several years, which have blended together into a single year. The fragmentation of the chapters that follow highlights less the memory loss of the protagonist than the slow regaining of memory he is experiencing.

The novel follows the effects of migrant living and working not only on the main character but also on the community of workers. Typically, the chapters alternate sections of tersely described action with equally terse dialogue between unnamed speakers—sometimes between the characters of the story being told and sometimes between two people who are discussing this story, which might be well known to both of them. At the end of "The Children Couldn't Wait," a story about a child being shot for taking a drink of water, two people talk about how the boss who shot him went crazy and lost all of his money. Similarly, both "The Little Burn Victims" and "The Night the Lights Went Out"—the first a story of children burned to death and the second a story of a jealous lover who electrocutes himself—end with the voices of people casually discussing these tragedies. Not only do the tragedies belong to the entire community, but they are accepted almost as everyday, if fascinating, occurrences.

Side by side with these apocalyptic stories are the stories that seem to center on the main protagonist himself—and though it is not certain that the young boy who appears in many of these stories is the same one, it is certain that the stories are presented as if they might be about the same person. Just as the tragedies belong not only to the people they happen to but also to the entire community, each story about the growth and disappointments of a young boy belong not only to the young boy himself but also to people like him. In "It's That It Hurts," the boy, having being expelled from school for fighting back when attacked by a couple of what the principal calls "our kids," and unable to imagine breaking the news to his parents, tries to convince himself that maybe he was not expelled. The irony is that his expulsion from school marks the beginning of his real education. Three stories, "A Silvery Night," "And the Earth Did Not Devour Him," and "First Communion," trace his growing mistrust of religion as he calls on the Devil to appear, curses God for letting his father and little brother both get sunstroke, and lies to a priest at confession. In each case, he expects some sort of retribution to occur, but instead what happens is the sudden recognition that the Devil will not appear and that the earth will not open up and swallow him.

His astonishment at learning that apocalypses need not occur leads up to the "The Portrait," in which a man who has been swindled by a person who promised to make a portrait of his dead son searches out the swindler and forces him to make the portrait from memory. For the first time in the book, forceful action taken by a Chicano against an exploiter produces a desirable result. In the penultimate chapter, "When We Arrive," migrant workers on a truck that has broken down discuss what they will do when they arrive, even after one of them says, "We never arrive." They never arrive at anything except waiting for the next job, the next arrival; still, in this constant waiting, a community is forged.

Before his death, Rivera was working on a second novel, *La casa grande*, sections of which had appeared in various journals, but no final product was released. Regardless, on the basis of his one short novel *. . . and the earth did not devour him*, which has become a standard text in North American Hispanic and Chicano literature classes, his literary reputation is secure. Partly because his novel was written in Spanish and was translated into English, many critics of Chicano literature view it as a text that liberated other Chicano writers to find their authentic voices. When the journal *Revista Chicano-Riqueña*, which Rivera helped to found, published a special double issue, *International Studies in Honor of Tomás Rivera*, after his death, many of the contributors recalled not only his presence as a writer but also his liberating generosity as an educator and friend.

BIBLIOGRAPHICAL REFERENCES: The double issue of *Revista Chicano-Riqueña*, *International Studies in Honor of Tomás Rivera*, edited by Julian Olivares, XIII, nos. 3/4, 1985, is the best source of information on Rivera and his work. This volume contains reminiscences of the man, a poem by Evangelina Vigil-Piñon written in his memory, close examinations of his work, and essays on Chicano and Hispanic literature. *Contemporary Chicano Fiction: A Critical Survey*, 1986, edited by Vernon E. Lattin, contains four essays that provide sharp critical insights into the relationship of the form and subject matter of Rivera's novel, and the appendix offers a good bibliography of works on Rivera. Similarly, *Modern Chicano Writers*, 1979, edited by Joseph Summers and Tomás Ybarro-Frausto, contains four essays on Rivera, under the heading "The Narrative: Focus on Tomás Rivera"; the reader who comes fresh wishes to place the novel within its twentieth century literary context might pay special attention to Summers' article "Interpreting Tomás Rivera." See also Vernon E. Lattin, "Novelistic Structure and Myth in *. . . y no se lo tragó la tierra*," *Bilingual Review/Revista Bilingüe*, IX (1982), 220-226; and "Tomás Rivera," an interview, in Juan Bruce-Novoa, *Chicano Authors: Inquiry by Interview*, 1980.

Thomas J. Cassidy

ALAIN ROBBE-GRILLET

Born: Brest, France
Date: August 18, 1922

Principal Works

NOVELS: *Les Gommes*, 1953 (*The Erasers*, 1964); *Le Voyeur*, 1955 (*The Voyeur*, 1955); *La Jalousie*, 1957 (*Jealousy*, 1959); *Dans le labyrinthe*, 1959 (*In the Labyrinth*, 1960); *La Maison de rendez-vous*, 1965 (English translation, 1966); *Projet pour une révolution à New York*, 1970 (*Project for a Revolution in New York*, 1972); *Topologie d'une cité fantôme*, 1976 (*Topology of a Phantom City*, 1977); *Souvenirs du triangle d'or*, 1978 (*Recollections of the Golden Triangle*, 1984); *Djinn*, 1981 (English translation, 1982).

SCREENPLAYS: *L'Année dernière à Marienbad*, 1961 (*Last Year at Marienbad*, 1962); *L'Immortelle*, 1963 (*The Immortal One*, 1971).

SHORT FICTION: *Instantanés*, 1962 (*Snapshots*, 1965).

LITERARY CRITICISM: *Pour un nouveau roman*, 1963 (*For a New Novel: Essays on Fiction*, 1965).

Alain Robbe-Grillet is the most articulate spokesman for and leading practitioner of the avant-garde movement in French fiction that has come to be known as the New Novel. He was born the son of Gaston and Yvonne Canu Robbe-Grillet. His father was an engineer, a profession that Robbe-Grillet later followed. The young Robbe-Grillet spent some time at a seaside locale much like the one he describes in perhaps his most famous novel, *The Voyeur*; the family soon moved to Paris, where Robbe-Grillet spent most of the remainder of his youth.

The German occupation of France in World War II was a nightmare for the entire nation, but it was especially traumatic for Robbe-Grillet, whose parents embraced extremely unpopular, conservative political views. Eventually, Robbe-Grillet was sent to work in German factories as a virtual slave laborer. Yet these traumatic years are reflected in no direct way in Robbe-Grillet's fiction; indeed, he vociferously objects to the use of fiction as a political tool.

Robbe-Grillet seems to have been largely unfazed by what could have been an embittering experience. Instead, he pursued his studies at the Institut National Agronomique, and in 1945 became *chargé de mission* at the Institut National des Statistics in Paris. From 1949 to 1951, Robbe-Grillet was an engineer with the Institut des Fruits et Agrumes Coloniaux, working in Morocco, French Guinea, Martinique, and Guadeloupe—the tropical locales of the latter three prefiguring the setting of his masterpiece, the novel *Jealousy*. Robbe-Grillet turned more and more toward literature in the early 1950's, finally publishing his first novel, *The Erasers*, in 1953.

Robbe-Grillet was an immediate sensation in a society that values its literature highly. *The Erasers* won for him the Fénelon Prize in 1954, and his next novel, *The Voyeur*, won for him the prestigious Prix des Critiques. Robbe-Grillet's influence on the direction of French literature was felt in another way, when he became literary adviser to the avant-garde publisher Éditions de Minuit in 1954. With the publication of *Jealousy* and *In the Labyrinth*, Robbe-Grillet clearly established himself as a leading figure—along with Nathalie Sarraute, Claude Simon, Michel Butor, and others—in the innovative New Novel movement. His position as unofficial chief spokesman for the movement was confirmed in 1963 with the publication of *For a New Novel*, a collection of criticism and reviews that Robbe-Grillet had published in newspapers and journals over the previous decade. At about this same time Robbe-Grillet's talents as a screenwriter became evident; he wrote the screenplay for *Last Year at Marienbad*, which won an Academy Award for Best Foreign Film.

Still, it is for his fiction that Robbe-Grillet is best known. One of the most interesting phenomena in post-World War II literature is the storm of debate that centered on Robbe-Grillet in the late 1950's and early 1960's. Few movements have sparked such controversy as the New Novel. In Robbe-Grillet's case the controversy was exacerbated by his undeniable fascination with sadomasochism, dramatized in such novels as *La Maison de rendez-vous* and especially *Project for a Revolution in New York*. Robbe-Grillet could not escape controversy even in marriage. His wife, Catherine Rstakian, is the rumored author of an underground pornographic novel.

No movement in literature can remain new forever, and the New Novel began to show its age in the late 1960's, especially as readers and young writers turned to Latin America and its "magic realism" for inspiration. Still, if Robbe-Grillet seemed to have begun reusing the same by-then-old strategies in his novels of the mid-1960's, his novels of the mid-1970's and later—*Topology of a Phantom City*, *Recollections of the Golden Triangle*, and *Djinn*—show him still striving to create new forms, still determined to ride point for the avant-garde.

Robbe-Grillet is best known for his formal innovations in such works as *Jealousy*, where, the percipient reader may eventually discover, the narrative point of view follows the gaze of a jealous husband as he spies on his wife and, intermittently, recollects or imagines suspicious scenes from his wife's past. As is almost always the case in a Robbe-Grillet fiction, determining not only what the character knows but also what the narrative eye can and cannot see is the fascinating and sometimes frustrating obligation of the reader.

Robbe-Grillet's fictions are interesting—or, depending upon one's view, outrageous—as much for what he does not do as for what he does. What he does not do, principally, is provide a theme. Repeatedly in his criticism Robbe-Grillet abjures "external" intent; psychological insights, philosophical argument, political rhetoric, even something as apparently basic as "meaning" are all, for Robbe-Grillet, worn-out conventions of dated fiction. Instead of holding a mirror up to reality, Robbe-Grillet's fictions are their own reality, more reflective of the rules of grammar and the tyranny of an often-neurotic narrative point of view than of any sense of "the real world" beyond fiction.

Judging the merits of a determinedly avant-garde writer is always difficult. Some, simply because what these writers create is new, tend to exaggerate their importance; others tend to undervalue their work because it does not fit some preconceived notion of what fiction should be. The real question is, after the shock of the new has subsided, what of value remains? Robbe-Grillet, for a furious two decades, was at the center of a critical and creative storm. The storm has now abated, and one can clearly see that Robbe-Grillet was indeed a brilliantly innovative writer who blazed a trail that few writers and fewer readers chose to follow.

BIBLIOGRAPHICAL REFERENCES: Bruce Morrissette, *The Novels of Robbe-Grillet*, 1975 (rev. ed.), is one of the earliest and still one of the most lucid analyses of Robbe-Grillet's art. John Sturrock, *The French New Novel: Claude Simon, Michel Butor, and Alain Robbe-Grillet*, 1969, analyzes Robbe-Grillet's fiction in the context of the New Novel as a whole. In *Narrative Consciousness: Structure and Perception in the Fiction of Kafka, Beckett, and Robbe-Grillet*, 1972, George H. Szanto discusses how Robbe-Grillet's perception of the operation of human consciousness is reflected in the narrative structures of his fictions. John Fletcher, *Alain Robbe-Grillet*, 1983, is a generally unsympathetic study which, nevertheless, is important for containing more personal information about the author than is found in most critical works. Dale W. Frazier, *Alain Robbe-Grillet: An Annotated Bibliography of Critical Studies, 1953-72,* 1973, is an indispensable reference tool. See also Vivian Mercier, "Alain Robbe-Grillet: Description and Narration," in *The New Novel from Queneau to Pinget*, 1971; Leon S. Roudiez, "Alain Robbe-Grillet," in *French Fiction Today: A New Direction*, 1972; Daniel P. Deneau, "Robbe-Grillet's 'Microtexts,'" *International French Review,* I (1974), 164-166; Hazel Barnes, "The Ins and Outs of Alain Robbe-Grillet," *Chicago Review,* XV, no. 3 (1962), 21-43; and James Lethcoe, "The Structure of Robbe-Grillet's *Labyrinth*," *French Review,* XXXVIII (1965), 499-507.

Dennis Vannatta

NED ROREM

Born: Richmond, Indiana
Date: October 23, 1923

Principal Works

AUTOBIOGRAPHY: *The Paris Diary of Ned Rorem*, 1966; *Music from Inside Out*, 1967; *The New York Diary of Ned Rorem*, 1967; *Music and People*, 1968; *Critical Affairs: A Composer's Journal*, 1970; *Pure Contraption*, 1973; *The Final Diary: 1961-1972*, 1974; *An Absolute Gift*, 1978; *Setting the Tone: Essays and a Diary*, 1983; *The Paris and New York Diaries of Ned Rorem: 1951-1961*, 1983; *Nantucket Diary of Ned Rorem: 1973-1985*, 1987.

Ned Rorem, who is best known as a musical composer and who describes himself as "a musican who happened to write, not an author who happened to compose," is the author of a series of diaries and collections of essays which, while they run a wide gamut of subjects, are primarily concerned with the narcissistic world of their author. He was born in Richmond, Indiana, on October 23, 1923, the son of medical economist Clarence Rufus Rorem and Gladys Miller Rorem. According to Rorem, his parents were financially lower-middle-class, culturally highbrow, liberal, and well-read left-of-center Quaker converts.

Although the elder Rorems were not especially musical, they arranged for Rorem to take piano lessons when he was seven. After the family moved to Chicago when Rorem was eight, his parents exposed him to music by taking him to concerts and recitals. Rorem, characteristically insisting that he was born an artist, denied that his choice of a musical career was influenced by his parents. Nevertheless, there was one event which did influence Rorem's choice of a career. When he was ten, his piano teacher introduced him to the music of Claude Debussy and Maurice Ravel; from that point onward, Rorem was determined to become a composer and to live in Paris.

At seventeen, Rorem began studies at Northwestern University's School of Music. In 1942, he received a scholarship to attend the Curtis Institute of Music in Philadelphia. From the Curtis Institute, Rorem went to The Juilliard School, where he received his bachelor's degree in 1946 and his master's degree in 1948. In 1948 he also won the George Gershwin Memorial Prize for Composition. In 1949, having accomplished his goal of becoming a composer, Rorem fulfilled his other goal by moving to Paris. For the next seven years he divided his time between Paris and Morocco.

Three years before his move to Paris, Rorem had begun keeping a diary, primarily "as a release from shyness, to investigate on paper what [he] could not say aloud." The diary soon became a catchall for Rorem's preoccupations outside musical composition, and in 1966 Rorem, never shy about self-revelation, published the first of what would become a series of diaries. *The Paris Diary of Ned Rorem* was followed by *The New York Diary of Ned Rorem*, *The Final Diary: 1961-1972*, and *The Nantucket Diary of Ned Rorem: 1973-1985*.

These diaries are, in Rorem's words, "random and bloody and self-indulgent." Entries are short, epigrammatic, outspoken, and, often, gossipy. The writing style is sometimes elegant, sometimes witty, and sometimes merely plainspoken. Since the diaries are primarily concerned with Ned Rorem, there is a continuity which is sustained from the earliest to the latest diary, with what some critics refer to as Rorem's "inflated egoism" providing both the tone and the plot. Later diaries, however, reveal a mellowing artist. In *The Nantucket Diary of Ned Rorem: 1973-1985*, Rorem is sadder, more meditative than dramatic, and more concerned with the transitory nature of art and the passions than with the preoccupations of a young artist living in Paris. The change in tone and mood probably reflects as much as anything Rorem's discovery that when a person reaches "a certain age, certain subjects become embarassingly dull and nobody's business." The earlier chronicles of roaring drunks and a completely uninhibited life-style, which were everybody's business, are replaced by perceptive and thought-provoking observations.

In addition to the diaries, Rorem has published a number of books which are essentially anthologies of his writings. The first of this series, *Music from Inside Out*, is a collection of lectures delivered at New York State University, Buffalo, while Rorem was Slee Professor of Composition. According to Rorem, the lectures deal with "how to answer other people's questions" about "the so-called concerns of creation."

The later books are less focused than *Music from Inside Out*. Like the diaries, they serve as catchalls and in general contain miscellaneous blends of essays, lectures, journal entries, critical reviews, and random diary entries not included in the diaries. For example, *Critical Affairs: A Composer's Journal* contains, among other things, a discussion of the poetry of music, a condemnation of rock music, tributes to a pair of fellow musicians, criticism of music critics, and a reflection on Rorem's Paris years from the vantage point of twenty years.

Ned Rorem's writing style in the essays does not differ dramatically from the style found in the diaries. His controversial opinionation, which characterizes much that may be found in the diaries, is somewhat mitigated in the essays by a genuine sensitivity to matters pertaining to the musical world. Even so, the constant personal references, the excessive name-dropping, and the often-interminable reiteration of the contents of various menus make extended readings more tedious than entertaining. Because of this self-absorption, some critics have downplayed the importance of Ned Rorem's published works. They suggest that, while his books do contain entries which are timely or timeless, Ned Rorem's preoccupation with Ned Rorem diminish their value to succeeding generations. They charge that as a "revealing profile of the artist," Rorem's works have "too much profile and so little art." Others, however, who are more concerned with the profile than with the art will find in these works a wealth of information about the artist and the man Ned Rorem.

BIBLIOGRAPHICAL REFERENCES: The best sources for a study of Ned Rorem are his own diaries and essays. The preface to *Setting the Tone: Essays and a Diary*, 1983, for example, provides insights into Rorem's reasons for and manner of keeping a diary. Valuable reviews of the diaries include Gavin Lambert, "Confessions of a Charmer," *The New York Times Book Review*, LXXI (July 10, 1986), 46; Robert Mazzocco, "To Tell You the Truth," *The New York Review of Books*, VII (September, 1966), 6-8; and C. K. Miller, review in *Library Journal*, XCI (May 1, 1966), 2326. See also David R. Slavitt's interview with Rorem, "Pose and Compose with Ned Rorem: It's Hard to Tell the Difference," *Philadelphia Magazine*, LXXIX (May, 1988), 89.

Chandice Johnson

RICHARD RORTY

Born: New York, New York
Date: October 4, 1931

PRINCIPAL WORKS

PHILOSOPHY: *Philosophy and the Mirror of Nature*, 1979; *The Consequences of Pragmatism*, 1982; *Contingency, Irony, and Solidarity*, 1989.

EDITED TEXTS: *The Linguistic Turn: Recent Essays in Philosophical Method*, 1967; *Philosophy in History: Essays on the Historiography of Philosophy*, 1984 (with J. B. Schneewind and Quentin Skinner).

Richard Rorty is one of the most controversial figures in the world of American philosophy in the late twentieth century. He was born October 4, 1931, in New York City, the son of James Hancock Rorty and Winifred Raushenbush Rorty. He took his B.A. and M.A. at the University of Chicago and his Ph.D. at Yale University. His teaching career has included positions at Yale, Wellesley, and Princeton universities and the University of Virginia. Rorty married Amelie Sarah Oskenberg in 1954, and they had one son before they were divorced in 1972. Mary R. Varney became Rorty's second wife in 1972; they have two children. Rorty was a Guggenheim Fellow in 1973-1974 and a MacArthur Fellow from 1981 to 1986.

From early in his career, Rorty has been interested in the history and methodology of philosophy. In his introduction to *The Linguistic Turn*, a book he also edited, Rorty focused on the metaphilosophical difficulties of linguistic philosophy. Two decades later, in *Philosophy in History*, which he coedited, Rorty divided the history of philosophy into four genres: accounts that treat a given philosopher, school, or period in context and without much reference to earlier or later developments; accounts that treat a given philosopher, school, or period in the light of subsequent "improvements" in philosophy; accounts that analyze the assumptions of a given philosopher, school, or period to discover their purposes; and accounts that treat philosophers of all schools and periods with reference to a few perennial philosophical problems.

Rorty's methodological and historical bent is evident in his two most important works, *The Consequences of Pragmatism* and *Philosophy and the Mirror of Nature*. The former work attempts to revive American pragmatism of the kind practiced by John Dewey and William James as a happy medium between analytic philosophy and continental philosophy. It is the latter work, however, that assured Rorty of a respected place among modern philosophers and made him the center of a decade-long debate.

Philosophy and the Mirror of Nature is an eminently readable book, especially for those who are not philosophers. This readability is most fitting, since Rorty argues in the book for a more practical, less professional approach to philosophy. He explains that all modern philosophy is based on a representational model for thought derived primarily from three philosophers: John Locke, René Descartes, and Immanuel Kant. Their emphasis on epistemology, Rorty claims, resulted from their successful attempt to free philosophy from the constraints of theology. In other words, he sees the Enlightenment as a response to cultural needs rather than to the nature of reality. Rorty identifies three philosophers—he calls them the three greatest philosophers of the twentieth century—who recognized and responded to the flaws in the philosophical "mirror" of the Enlightenment: Martin Heidegger, Ludwig Wittgenstein, and Dewey. Heidegger, Rorty says, created new categories for philosophy to replace the bankrupt terms of Cartesianism. Wittgenstein, in like manner, debunked the myth of the neutrality of science and scientific terminology. Dewey represents, for Rorty, the model of philosophy in the future, a model that will require that philosophy continue its search for knowledge without aggrandizing itself and with full awareness that it is satisfying its own self-interest in the process. The result will be a philosophy that is, to use Rorty's terms, "edifying" rather than "systematic."

Rorty's work has become a kind of self-fulfilling prophecy in the world of professional philosophy, creating a revolution in which members of all camps have taken every effort to maintain and fortify their positions, with the result of a quantum leap in the intensity and clarity of discussion. Rorty also became associated, by virtue of his historicist approach with the school of literary criticism called deconstruction, which held sway over academic literary circles from 1970 through the mid-1980's. His wide and deep influence has made Rorty one of the chief metaphilosophers of the twentieth century.

BIBLIOGRAPHICAL REFERENCES: Two contrasting examples of the many articles on Rorty's work to be found in philosophical journals are Dorothea Frede, "Beyond Realism and Anti-Realism: Rorty on Heidegger and Davidson," 1987, a critical account of Rorty's shortcomings in one limited area, and Frank G. Verges, "Rorty and the New Hermeneutics," 1987, a more appreciative explanation of the value of Rorty's contributions to philosophical method. For a review of *Philosophy and the Mirror of Nature*, see Quentin Skinner, *The New York Review of Books*, XXVIII (March 19, 1981), 46; *The Consequence of Pragmatism* is discussed by Jerome Miller, *America*, CXLVIII (February 19, 1983), 136. See also John E. Toews, review of *Philosophy in History*, *American Historical Review*, XCII (October, 1987), 902, and Leon H. Brody, review of *Contingency, Irony, and Solidarity*, *Library Journal*, CXIV (February 15, 1989), 161.

James T. Jones

ISAAC ROSENFELD

Born: Chicago, Illinois
Date: March 10, 1918

Died: Chicago, Illinois
Date: July 15, 1956

PRINCIPAL WORKS

ESSAYS: *An Age of Enormity: Life and Writing in the Forties and Fifties*, 1962.
SHORT FICTION: *Alpha and Omega*, 1966.
NOVEL: *Passage from Home*, 1946.

The title of Isaac Rosenfeld's only published novel, *Passage from Home*, is emblematic of his life and career. Rosenfeld was always in passage from a starting point which he ultimately rejected but for which he could find no meaningful substitute. Like Albert Camus, and like his friend and fellow Chicagoan Saul Bellow, Rosenfeld sought answers to questions about how to live in a world devoid of meaning.

Rosenfeld was born into a middle-class Jewish family in Chicago in 1918, and although he rejected Judaism, the experience of Jewish life remained a backdrop to his writings. His concerns mirror those of several other Jewish writers, particularly Sholom Aleichem and Franz Kafka. In 1941, Rosenfeld earned a master's degree in literature at the University of Chicago and then moved to New York to pursue a doctorate at New York University. He married his wife, Vasiliki, that same year and quickly became a part of the intellectual subculture of Greenwich Village. He began to publish and becamed an assistant editor of *The New Republic* while also contributing to other left-wing and Jewish publications such as *Commentary, The Nation, The Kenyon Review,* and *Partisan Review.* Many of the stories and essays he wrote for these periodicals are reprinted in the two posthumous collections, *Alpha and Omega* (short stories) and *An Age of Enormity* (nonfiction essays). In 1943 Rosenfeld left his position at *The New Republic* and took a job on a barge in New York Harbor. While he did not abandon the Greenwich Village society of which he was one of the leading lights, during this period Rosenfeld came close to embracing Wilhelm Reich's theories. Reich held that the ills of modern society are traceable to sexual repression.

In the early 1950's Rosenfeld moved to the Midwest again and taught at the University of Minnesota. He continued a pattern of disengagement by resigning that position and returning to Chicago, where he became an instructor of literature at the University of Chicago. By this time he had had two children but had divorced his wife. Rosenfeld finished another novel, "The Enemy," a Kafkaesque tale about a war commander who struggles to convince himself that what he is doing is just while at the same time trying to determine why he is doing it. This novel's failure to be accepted by a publisher apparently disillusioned Rosenfeld so greatly that he wrote little after 1951. He died alone of a heart attack in his furnished room near the university in 1956.

The concerns and technique of Rosenfeld's fiction can be seen in his autobiographical *Bildungsroman*, *Passage from Home*. The young protagonist, Bernard, is fascinated by two people who symbolize a rejection of the stale middle-class values by which he himself feels bound: his Aunt Minna, an acerbic woman who insists on living her own life free of convention, and Willy, a Gentile who had been married to Bernard's dead cousin Martha. Bernard contrives to unite the two free spirits. They begin to live together, and after a family quarrel Bernard moves in with them; he discovers that he is not well accepted in the relationship which he helped to create, and he returns home with a renewed sense of the values of the family life he had left behind. Unfortunately, Bernard's father does not respond well to the new sense of identity in his son, and at the end of the novel, Bernard realizes that his return home only makes him aware that he has no real home.

In his second, unpublished novel and in many of his short stories, Rosenfeld followed the lead of Kafka by creating characters who try to find homes in ideas rather than in places or with people. Perhaps the most compelling of these stories is "The Colony" (1945), which is about a newly empowered political leader in a Third World country. Although the leader has doubts about the effectiveness of the ideology which his predecessor espoused, he rather whimsically begins a revolt and is swiftly imprisoned. While in his jail cell, he thinks through the consequences of his thoughts and actions but comes to no definite conclusions. The story ends with the political situation and the mind of the protagonist still unresolved.

Rosenfeld's best writing appeared in the form of criticism and literary commentary, most of which was written for mass-circulation periodicals and was therefore limited to two or three pages. In these essays Rosenfeld surgically dissects the writing of authors who fail to unite "life" (description of human affairs) with "truth" (the underlying meanings behind human actions) or authors who fail to reveal the true human condition but take refuge behind a tough façade which masks sentimentality. Included in this category are such obvious targets as Irwin Shaw and Herman Wouk, but Rosenfeld also dismisses such giants as Ernest Hemingway and William Faulkner. Rosenfeld admired writers such as Kafka and André Gide, who avoided easy answers to modern dilemmas. He was also baffled by the figure of Mahatma Gandhi, whose successful political application of his belief in a transcendent reality confounded Rosenfeld's naturalism. While it could be said that, too often, Rosenfeld was unable to unite "life" and "truth" in his own fiction, the life he led was an inspiration to his contemporaries.

BIBLIOGRAPHICAL REFERENCES: Theodore Solotaroff provides an account of the facts of Rosenfeld's life as well as a critical appraisal of Rosenfeld's works in his article "Isaac Rosenfeld: The Human Use of Literature," *Commentary*, XXXIII (1962), 395-404, which also appears in a slightly different form as the introduction to Solotaroff's collection of Rosenfeld's essays, *The Age of Enormity*, and as "The Spirit of Isaac Rosenfeld" in Solotaroff's own collection of essays, *The Red Hot Vacuum*, 1970. Alfred Kazin, "Midtown and the Village," *Harper's Magazine*, CCXLII (1971), 82-89, gives an account of Rosenfeld's New York days in the early 1940's at *The New Republic*. The best overview of Rosenfeld's work is Mark Schechner, "Isaac Rosenfeld's World," *Partisan Review*, XLIII (1976), 524-543. See also David Ray, "Where Are the Little Magazines?" *The New Republic*, CXXXV (1956), 20; George Dennison, "Artist in His Skin," *Commentary*, XLII (1966), 102-104; Bonnie Lyons, "Isaac Rosenfeld's Fiction: A Reappraisal," *Studies in American Jewish Literature*, I (1975), 3-9; Myron R. Sharaf, "Rosenfeld and Reich," *Commentary*, XXXIV (1962), 352-353; John Berryman, "Of Isaac Rosenfeld," *Partisan Review*, XXIII (1956), 494; Ezra Greenspan, *The "Schlemiel" Comes to America*, 1983; and Morgan Blum, "For a Friend Who Died Alone," *The New Republic*, CXXXV (1956), 19.

James Baird

JOSEPH ROTH

Born: Brody, Austrian Galicia
Date: September 2, 1894

Died: Paris, France
Date: May 27, 1939

Principal Works

NOVELS: *Hotel Savoy*, 1924 (*Hotel Savoy*); *Die Rebellion*, 1924; *Die Flucht ohne Ende*, 1927 (*Flight Without End*); *Das Spinnennetz*, 1928 (*Spiders Web*); *Zipper und sein Vater*, 1928; *Rechts und Links*, 1929; *Hiob: Roman eines einfachen Mannes*, 1930 (*Job: The Story of a Simple Man*); *Radetzkymarsch*, 1932 (*The Radetzky March*); *Tarabas, ein Gast auf dieser Erde*, 1934 (*Tarabas, a Guest on Earth*); *Die Hundert Tage*, 1935 (*Ballad of the Hundert Days*); *Beichte eines Mörders, erzählt in einer Nacht*, 1936 (*The Confession of a Murderer, Told in One Night*); *Das falsche Gewicht: Die Geschichte eines Eichmeisters*, 1937; *Die Kapuzinergruft*, 1938; *Die Geschichte von der 1002 Nacht*, 1939; *Der stumme Prophet*, 1966 (*The Silent Prophet*); *Perlefter*, 1978.

SHORT FICTION: *April: Die Geschichte einer Liebe*, 1925; *Der blinde Spiegel*, 1925; *Ein kapitel Revolution*, 1929; *Stationschef Fallmerayer*, 1933; *Die Legende vom Heiligen Trinker*, 1939 (*The Legend of the Holy Drinker*); *Der Leviathan*, 1940; *Le Triomphe de la beauté*, 1934; *Le Buste de l'empereur.*

ESSAYS: *Reise durch Galizien*, 1924; *Im mittäglichen Frankreich*, 1925; *Der Rauch verbindet Städte*, 1926; *Bericht aus dem pariser Paradies*, 1926; *Die russische Grenze*, 1926; *Juden auf Wanderschaft*, 1927; *Artikel über Albanien*, 1927; *Das moskauer jüdische Theater*, 1928; *Leningrad*, 1928; *Briefe aus Deutschland*, 1929; *Panoptikum: Gestalten und Kulissen*, 1930; *Brief aus dem Harz*, 1930; *Bekenntnis zu Deutschland*, 1931; *Der Antichrist*, 1934 (*The Antichrist*); *Aus dem Tagebuch eines Schriftstellers*, 1937; *Über das "Dokumentarische,"* 1938; *Rede über den Alten Kaiser*, 1939.

CORRESPONDENCE: *Briefe, 1911-1939*, 1970.

OTHER NONFICTION: *Der neue Tag: Unbekannte politische Arbeiten, 1919 bis 1927, Wien, Berlin, Moskau*, 1970; *Berliner Saisonbericht: Reportagen und journlistische Arbeiten, 1920-1939*, 1984.

MISCELLANEOUS: *Werke in drei Bänden*, 1956; *Werke: Neue erweiterte Ausgabe in vier Bänden*, 1975-1976.

Joseph Roth was born Moses Joseph Roth on September 2, 1894, in Brody, in Austrian Galicia, which at that time was in the eastern part of the Austro-Hungarian empire and today is in the Ukraine. His parents were part of a large Orthodox Jewish community, not uncommon in that part of the old empire. His father, Nachum Roth, was an unsuccessful traveling businessman who died, the victim of a psychopathic disorder, in 1910. Joseph was reared by his mother, Maria (or Miriam) Roth, née Grübel, and his grandfather, Jechiel Grübel, a successful draper and orthodox Jew in Brody. As was customary, the boy attended the elementary school and the Royal-Imperial Crown Prince Rudolph Gymnasium in Brody, where German was the language of instruction. At home, the family spoke German, but Roth also learned Polish, Yiddish, and Ukrainian. After his graduation with honors in 1913, he attended the University of Lemberg (Lvov) for one semester and the University of Vienna from 1914 to 1916. He studied literature and began his career as a writer, publishing poetry, short stories, and essays in a Viennese newspaper. From 1916 until 1918, he served in the Austrian army.

For a number of years following World War I, Roth was concerned almost exclusively with political and social issues. Although he was essentially a conservative, at this time he embraced the socialist point of view—he even signed some of his newspaper articles "Red Joseph." He investigated the plight of the outsider, with special interest in the fate of the Eastern European Jews, the Ashkenazim. In 1924, he developed this same theme in a series of novels. Like most of his fictional work, these novels appeared serially in newspapers. *Hotel Savoy* appeared in the distinguished *Frankfurter Zeitung*, and *Die Rebellion* was serialized in the Berlin newspaper *Vorwärts* in 1924. Both novels treat the topic of social injustice that the outsiders and victims of the war encounter in Western European society. *Hotel Savoy* portrays a microcosm of a society suffering decay and corruption, while *Die Rebellion* illustrates the life of a crippled war veteran who loses his organ grinder's license and is thus another victim of capitalism.

From the mid-1920's to the late 1920's Roth traveled to Eastern Europe on assignment for a newspaper. He published his major essay *Juden auf Wanderschaft* (wandering Jews) in 1927. The essay portrays migrating Jews who were uprooted by the war from the small Jewish towns of the East, where they had celebrated their traditions and values, to be resettled in the major metropolitan centers of Berlin, Vienna, and Paris, where they were assimilated by western Jewry. The fate of the Eastern European Jew in postwar Western European society was articulated most poetically in *Job*. Through these journalistic and fictional writings preceding the time of the Holocaust, Roth served as an insightful and sensitive reporter on the terrible destiny awaiting the Jews of Europe.

The other major theme which preoccupied Roth for many years was the disintegration of the once-mighty Austro-Hungarian Empire. Although he had written on this topic throughout the 1920's, it was his best-known novel, *The Radetzky March*, that provided the most eloquent statement on this theme. Initially serialized in the *Frankfurter Zeitung* between April 17 and July 9, 1932, the novel traces the life of Austria and its Emperor Franz Joseph I from the Battle of Solferino in 1859, in which the French defeated the Austrians, until 1916, the year the emperor died. The fictional characters make up three generations of the von Trotta family. The grandfather, Lieutenant Joseph Trotta, the celebrated "hero of Solferino," risked his life to protect the young emperor in the Battle of Solferino. In recognition for this deed, the young lieutenant, whose forefathers were peasants, is elevated to the rank of nobility. His only son, Franz von Trotta, serves the empire as an exemplary civil servant, while his only grandson, Carl Joseph, has an undistinguished career in the military.

Shortly after Roth completed this major novel, another chapter began in his life. When Adolf Hitler became chancellor in 1933, Roth left Germany for a life of wandering and exile. He traveled in various Western European countries, but his last residence was Paris. He continued to be a prolific writer of fiction and essays, but because he was blacklisted as a Jew and vocal opponent of the Nazi regime in Germany, he lost the great majority of his readership. He lived in considerable poverty in a small hotel and frequented his favorite café, where he wrote and met with his many friends. He succumbed to alcohol in this period of exile and grief, his writings generally returning to the two major themes he had treated in his earlier works. He died on May 27, 1939. The inscription on his gravestone describes his work and defines his contribution to literature: "Écrivain autrichien—mort à Paris en exil."

Roth belongs to a generation of writers who were virtually forgotten because of the forced exile they experienced during the Nazi period in Germany from 1933 to 1945. That has changed largely through the efforts of his close friend, the writer Hermann Kesten, who has prepared several editions of his works. *The Radetzky March* has established him as one of the important Austrian writers, while many of his other novels and essays have confirmed him as a significant source on the plight of the Eastern European Jews. He is often cited by critics and readers for the elegance of his prose writings. Scholars have shown a continuing and increasing interest in his work and the readership, in both the English-speaking and the German-speaking world, has increased substantially over the years.

BIBLIOGRAPHICAL REFERENCES: David Bronsen's major biography, *Joseph Roth*, 1974, although written in German, serves as the basis for all that is known about the author, who was inclined to alter the facts of his own life. Bronsen interviewed 160 people in fifty cities and twelve countries to re-create the life and era. The Leo Baeck Institute in New York City, as trustee of Roth's literary estate, publishes the *Leo Baeck Institute Yearbook*, which often includes articles about Roth, including David Bronsen, "Austrian Versus Jew: The Torn Identity of Joseph Roth," XVIII (1973), 219-226; Sidney Rosenfeld, "The Chain of Generations: A Jewish Theme in Joseph Roth's Novels," XVIII (1973), 227-231; Otto W. Johnston, "Jewish Exile from Berlin to Paris: The Geographical Dialectics of Joseph Roth," XXXI (1986), 441-454; and Sidney Rosenfeld, "Joseph Roth and Austria: A Search for Identity," XXXI (1986), 455-464. Other significant articles are David Bronsen, "The Jew in Search of a Fatherland: The Relationship of Joseph Roth to the Hapsburg Monarchy," *The Germanic Review*, LIV (1979), 54-61; and David Dollenmayer, "History and Fiction: The Kaiser in Joseph Roth's *Radetzkymarsch*," *Modern Language Studies*, XVI, no. 3 (1986), 302-310. Major chapters on Joseph Roth in books are: "Joseph Roth: A Time out of Joint," in Cedric E. Williams, *The Broken Eagle: The Politics of Austrian Literature from Empire to Anschluss*, 1974; Barton W. Browning, "Joseph Roth's *Legende vom heiligen Trinker:* Essence and Elixer," in *Protest, Form, Tradition: Essays on German Exile Literature*, 1979, edited by Joseph P. Strelka; Philip Manger, "*The Radetzky March*: Joseph Roth and the Hapsburg Myth," in *The Viennese Enlightenment*, 1985, edited by Mark Francis; and Sidney Rosenfeld, "Joseph Roth," in *Major Figures of Modern Austrian Literature*, 1988, edited by Donald Daviau.

Thomas H. Falk

PHILIP ROTH

Born: Newark, New Jersey
Date: March 19, 1933

PRINCIPAL WORKS

NOVELS: *Letting Go*, 1962; *When She Was Good*, 1967; *Portnoy's Complaint*, 1969; *Our Gang*, 1971; *The Breast*, 1972, revised 1980; *The Great American Novel*, 1973; *My Life as a Man*, 1974; *The Professor of Desire*, 1977; *The Ghost Writer*, 1979; *Zuckerman Unbound*, 1981; *The Anatomy Lesson*, 1983; *Zuckerman Bound*, 1985; *The Counterlife*, 1987.

SHORT FICTION: *Goodbye, Columbus*, 1959.

NONFICTION: *Reading Myself and Others*, 1975; *The Facts: A Novelist's Autobiography*, 1988.

Along with Bernard Malamud and Saul Bellow, Philip Roth is the most prominent of the American Jewish novelists who emerged after World War II. Of all of his fictions with invented characters, only *When She Was Good* does not focus on a figure who is recognizably a second- or third-generation Jew struggling to come to terms with the attractions and repulsions of life in the United States. Roth was born in Newark, New Jersey, on March 19, 1933, and grew up in a lower-middle-class Jewish section of the city. His father was an insurance salesman and his mother a housewife. After one year at Newark College, Rutgers University, Roth transferred to Bucknell University, in rural Pennsylvania, where he edited the literary magazine and received a B.A. in English, magna cum laude, in 1954. After receiving an M.A. in English from the University of Chicago in 1955, he enlisted in the U.S. Army but, as a result of a back injury sustained in basic training, received a medical discharge. He returned to Chicago, where he spent a year as a Ph.D. candidate and an instructor in English. He later held teaching positions at the University of Iowa, Princeton University, the State University of New York at Stony Brook, and the University of Pennsylvania and maintained residences in both London and upstate New York. A champion of authors from Soviet Bloc nations, Roth in 1975 became editor of the Writers from the Other Europe series for Penguin Books.

Roth's first public literary acclaim came when "The Contest for Aaron Gold" was selected for inclusion in *The Best Short Stories of 1956*. In 1959, *Goodbye, Columbus*, a novella and five short stories about contemporary American Jews, won for Roth the National Book Award and the Houghton Mifflin Literary Fellowship, and its success lauched his national reputation. In the same year, he began a troubled marriage with Margaret Martinson Williams, a Gentile who furnished the model for fictional harpies in several of Roth's works. The two separated in 1963 and were divorced in 1966, two years before her death in an automobile accident. He subsequently began a long-term relationship with English actress Claire Bloom.

Roth's first novel, *Letting Go*, is a Jamesian study in individual freedom and moral choice. Five years later, in 1967, Roth published his second novel, *When She Was Good*, a severely naturalistic account of five generations of a compulsive Protestant family in a small Midwestern town. His next novel, *Portnoy's Complaint*, marked a radical departure in style and tone, however, and became the most controversial best-seller of 1969: The success of *Portnoy's Complaint* made Roth rich and infamous. Ribald, flamboyant, and deliberately outrageous, *Portnoy's Complaint* is the extended monologue that Alexander Portnoy, a responsible young city official with lascivious obsessions, delivers to his psychoanalyst. The book's notoriety drastically altered Roth's relationship to his reading public, a relationship that became a theme in his writing.

The unflattering portrait of Jewish assimilationists, hypocrites, and mediocrities in *Goodbye, Columbus* led to the denunciation of Roth from rabinnical pulpits as an enemy to his people. He was also attacked by influential critics for the paucity of his grounding in a genuinely Jewish tradition. The publication of *Portnoy's Complaint* led to further vilification, as it also contributed to his celebrity. Uncomfortable in the role of public figure and unrepentant of what he saw as his honest attempts to portray American Jewish life torn between traditional ethical restraint and the libidinous temptations of contemporary materialism, Roth insisted on expressing himself through his fictions. Increasingly, his novels concerned themselves with the burdens of fame, intellect, and Jewishness for recurring characters who seem an alter ego for Roth himself.

My Life as a Man, for example, is a reflexive fictional structure recounting the New Jersey childhood, rebellious adolescence, disastrous marriage, and literary ambitions of Nathan Zuckerman, who is himself a creation of American Jewish writer Peter Tarnopol. To the charge that his novels were only thinly disguised autobiography and that he was using fiction as a coy evasion of the facts, Roth responded with *The Facts: A Novelist's Autobiography*. Though it purports to recount his life directly, the book omits much and is framed, like Roth's most elaborate metafictions, with a critique by his own character Zuckerman. "Sheer Playfulness and Deadly Seriousness are my closest friends," declared Roth in a 1974 interview, and his novels may be grouped according to which mood prevails. It is when both styles contribute equally, primarily in the Zuckerman cycle, that Roth produces his most satisfying works.

In the 1961 essay "Writing American Fiction," later collected in *Reading Myself and Others*, Roth bemoans the imagination's inability to rival the grotesque reality of contemporary American experience—yet much of his fiction is energized by this desperate sense of its own inadequacy. A spirited, comic inventor and an incisive chronicler of life in the United States in the second half of the twentieth century, especially among Jews, academics, and writers, Roth has made a successful career out of the themes of family, ethnicity, and fiction itself, just as all three have become increasingly problematic in American culture.

BIBLIOGRAPHICAL REFERENCES: For a useful chronological survey of his career up to 1978, by someone without Roth's mischievousness or memory, see Bernard F. Rodgers, Jr., *Philip Roth*, 1978. Other book-length studies of Roth include Sanford Pinsker, *The Comedy That "Hoits": An Essay on the Fiction of Philip Roth*, 1975, which surveys Roth's work in terms of tensions between public and private and between laughter and pain; Hermione Lee, *Philip Roth*, 1982, an overview organized by theme; John N. McDaniel, *The Ficton of Philip Roth*, 1974, which studies the fiction through *My Life as a Man* via the categories of "victim-hero" and "activist-hero"; and Judith Paterson Jones and Guinevera A. Nance, *Philip Roth*, 1981, which analyzes Roth's first eleven books in terms of conflicts between the individual and society, men and women, adventure and security, myth and reality. *Philip Roth*, 1986, edited by Harold Bloom, collects fifteen essays ranging throughout Roth's canon. Roth also receives extended and prominent discussion in general studies of the American novel since World War II. The best of these include Frederick R. Karl, *American Fictions: 1940-1980*, 1983; Alfred Kazin, *Bright Book of Life*, 1973, Raymond Olderman, *Beyond the Waste Land*, 1972; and Tony Tanner, *City of Words*, 1971. See also studies of American Jewish literature, including Allen Guttmann, *The Jewish Writer in America: Assimilation and the Crisis of Identity*, 1971; and Irving Malin, *Jews and Americans*, 1965.

Steven G. Kellman

SALMAN RUSHDIE

Born: Bombay, India
Date: June 19, 1947

PRINCIPAL WORKS

NOVELS: *Grimus*, 1975; *Midnight's Children*, 1981; *Shame*, 1983; *The Satanic Verses*, 1988.
NONFICTION: *The Jaguar's Smile: A Nicaraguan Journey*, 1987.

Salman Rushdie may be the most famous (many would say infamous) novelist of the late 1980's, though unfortunately for the wrong reasons. Without his notoriety, however, he would still be a quality writer of some considerable promise, read, in the main, by the small number of intellectuals who are interested in the contemporary novel of high artistic intention. Rushdie was born to an affluent Muslim family and began his education in Bombay at the Cathedral School. His family had considerable admiration for Great Britain, and at the age of thirteen, he was sent to England to one of the finest boys' schools, Rugby School. He went on to the University of Cambridge, where he read history with some emphasis upon the history of Islamic religion and culture. After graduation, he returned to the East, joining his parents in the new state of Pakistan, but within a year, he was back in England, having run into difficulties (a warning of things to come) over his production of Edward Albee's play *The Zoo Story* (pr. 1959) because of a reference to "pork" in the text. In London, Rushdie tried to become a professional actor (1968-1970) but had to settle for work in advertising; through the 1970's, he worked at producing fiction on the side, but his first novel, *Grimus*, sold badly and was a critical failure. He married an Englishwoman, Clarissa Luard, in 1976, and had a son, but that marriage ended in the 1980's, and he then married the American writer Marianne Wiggins.

With the publication of *Midnight's Children* in 1981, Rushdie's literary fortunes changed. He won the most prestigious British literary award, the Booker Prize, and the novel sold extremely well for a work of such intellectual complication, not only in Great Britain but all over the world. He won the James Tait Black Memorial Prize in 1982, and he was made a Fellow of the Royal Society of Literature in 1983. His next book, *Shame*, was also received with critical enthusiasm and was also nominated for the Booker Prize. This time he did not win, and he astounded the company at the award ceremony by publicly protesting his loss—perhaps a sign that Rushdie does not lack confidence in his talents. It was not, however, until early in 1989 that Rushdie's work really came into the public eye. His novel *The Satanic Verses* appeared in England in the autumn of 1988, just in time to be nominated for the Booker Prize. Again, he missed the prize, although the work was reviewed with some favor, if not with the wide enthusiasm that he had received for *Midnight's Children*. From the beginning, however, there was some unrest in the large, immigrant Muslim community in England about references to their religion in the book, which exploded into worldwide controversy in early 1989: The spiritual ruler of Iran ordered the execution of Rushdie, putting a price for the killing at $2.6 million if accomplished by an Iranian and a more modest $1 million if by anyone else. Authors have often been at odds with the social, political, and religious world, sometimes dangerously so, but Rushdie's case is one of the most extreme examples of that discord. In response to the clamor and support for the Ayatollah Khomeini's demand for Rushdie's death from the more fundamentalist wing of the Muslim religious community (which is spread widely throughout the world), Rushdie was retired to a secret place in England, heavily protected by the police. Diplomatic relations between Iran and those countries which protested the attack on freedom of speech were very seriously disrupted and, in some cases, severed.

The Satanic Verses was burned by Muslims, shops selling the book were attacked, and the novel became a best-seller, usually sold from under the counter to avoid the possibility of spontaneous attack by Muslims enraged by Rushdie's handling of Muhammad in his text. Rushdie's use of artistic license endangered his life. Yet Rushdie is a very humorous writer who, on many occasions, in all of his work, takes generous liberties with the excesses of all forms of human authoritarianism. Another point is that he is not an easy writer; Rushdie demands considerable intelligence of his readers and a capacity to follow enormously complicated labyrinths of mischievous improvisation. The novel, as a literary form, has not always been confined to the realistic portrayal of character under the pressure of environment, for good or ill. There is a respectable wing of it which is less committed to reality and which can include fantasy of wide-ranging tonal implication; it can be digressive, unstructured, parodic, and it can be mockingly satiric, salacious, pornographic, and tasteless in a high-spirited way.

Midnight's Children is all these things, a collection of social, religious, political, and psychological comment, loosely hung together around the wild idea that at the midnight hour on the first day of Indian independence from Great Britain (August 14, 1947), one thousand and one children were born in India with unusual gifts which ranged from intense beauty for one, through the ability to change sex for another, and so on, to the hero of the tale, who can communicate with all of them in his head. Around that preposterous idea, Rushdie weaves the history of his family (beginning with his grandfather and grandmother and including all the wildly eccentric members of his family) and the history of Indian and Pakistani independence up to the 1970's. It is long, complicated, hilarious, and not loath to make comic and satiric mayhem about family, religion, and politics in ways which are consistently indiscreet and indiscriminating. The source of this style is possibly Laurence Sterne's great eighteenth century novel *The Life and Opinions of Tristram Shandy, Gent.* (1759-1767), but there are marks of technical excess in *Midnight's Children* which are reminiscent of Jonathan Swift's *A Tale of a Tub* (1704). Rushdie's *Shame* looks remarkably like an extension of *Midnight's Children* not only technically but also thematically. The characters are new but quite like those of *Midnight's Children* in many ways. *The Satanic Verses* is, again, more of the same: enormously entertaining, saucy, a virtuoso performance in the tradition of what has come to be known as "magic realism," in which telling a wild tale well is more important than credibility.

Rushdie will be remembered as the writer who in the supposedly enlightened twentieth century unmindfully unleashed the power of public reaction in ways which are alarming and disquieting. As a writer, he is something else again: a writer of enormous talent, overflowing imagination, and a fine comic-satiric eye for the hypocrisies, the stupidities, and the self-interest of humanity in general.

BIBLIOGRAPHICAL REFERENCES: As a result of the controversy surrounding Rushdie's *The Satanic Verses*, reviews and articles about Rushdie's work abound. Reviews of *The Satanic Verses* include Francis King, *The Spectator*, October 1, 1988, 31; Hermione Lee, *The Observer*, October 2, 1988, 46; William E. Smith, *Time*, February 27, 1989, 28; and the following: *The Times Literary Supplement*, September 30, 1988, 1067; *The New York Times Book Review*, XCIV (January 29, 1989), 3; and *The New York Review of Books*, XXXVI (March 2, 1989), 25. Articles about the controversy that has ensued since *The Satanic Verses* was published include Gerald Marzorati, "Fiction's Embattled Infidel," *The New York Times Magazine*, January 29, 1989, 24; Salman Rushdie, "The Book Burning," *The New York Review of Books*, XXXVI (March 2, 1989), 26; and John F. Baker, "To Kill for a Book?" *Publishers Weekly*, CCXXXV (March 3, 1989), 22. See also "Words for Salman Rushdie," *The New York Times Book Review*, XCIV (March 12, 1989), 1, with statements by twenty-eight distinguished writers in support of Rushdie. For further study of Rushdie's work, see Robert Towers, review of *Midnight's Children*, *The New York Review of Books*, September 24, 1981, 28, and on the same book, V. S. Pritchett, *The New Yorker*, LXIII (June 26, 1981), 26;

Bruce Allen, review of *Shame*, *The Christian Science Monitor*, December 5, 1983, 53, and also on *Shame*, D. J. Enright, *The New York Review of Books*, December 8, 1983, 26, and James Lasdun, *Encounter*, January, 1989, 69.

Charles Pullen

JOANNA RUSS

Born: New York, New York
Date: February 22, 1937

PRINCIPAL WORKS

SCIENCE FICTION: *Picnic on Paradise*, 1968; *And Chaos Died*, 1970; *The Female Man*, 1975; *We Who Are About To. . .*, 1977; *The Two of Them*, 1978; *On Strike Against God*, 1979.

LITERARY CRITICISM: "What Can a Heroine Do? Or, Why Women Can't Write," 1972; *How to Suppress Women's Writing*, 1983; *Magic Mommas, Trembling Sisters, Puritans, and Perverts: Feminist Essays*, 1985.

SHORT FICTION: "When It Changed," 1972; *Alyx*, 1976; *The Zanzibar Cat*, 1983; *Extra (Ordinary) People*, 1984; *The Hidden Side of the Moon*, 1987.

CHILDREN'S LITERATURE: *Kittatinny: A Tale of Magic*, 1978.

Joanna Russ has successfully used science fiction to develop feminist alternatives to myths of male heroism and dominance; her critical writing defends a strong feminist position. The daughter of two teachers, Evarett I. Russ and Bertha Zinner Russ, Russ was born on February 22, 1937, in the Bronx district of New York, where she spent her youth before going to college. In 1957, she received her B.A. in English literature from Cornell University. Three years later, Russ earned an M.F.A. in playwriting and dramatic literature from the Yale School of Drama. Married from 1963 to 1967, Russ has taught at various universities in the United States and, since 1977, has been a professor of English at the University of Washington in Seattle.

Before the publication of her first science-fiction novel, *Picnic on Paradise* (later collected in *Alyx*) in 1968, Russ wrote short fantasy pieces about a female Phoenician assassin struggling in a male-dominated world; now, Russ decided to abduct her heroine to the future, where Alyx once again combats machismo while trying to lead to safety a group of tourists stranded on a planet where no advanced technology can be used.

In her famous 1972 essay, "What Can a Heroine Do: Or, Why Women Can't Write," written after *And Chaos Died* (in which a male homosexual protagonist comes to terms with a race of telepaths), Russ defends science fiction as the only genre that allows a woman writer to avoid the anti-feminist requirements of "mainstream" literature: passive, submissive, and objectified females.

As a writer of science fiction and fantasy, Russ expands generic conventions by deliberately turning them on their heads. *The Female Man*, written in 1971 and finally published in 1975, promptly won for Russ the prestigious Nebula Award for the year's best science fiction and is perhaps Russ's most consequential work. Here, she employs the science-fiction commonplace of alternate universes to present four heroines who live in worlds where the status of men ranges from extinction to being the enemies in a merciless gender war. To survive in her world, which closely resembles Russ's America, the character of Joanna decides that she has to become the female man, whereas her assassin-counterpart Jael fights the men who have subjugated other men and turned them into sex dolls; Jael, however, indulges in sexual acts with her willing slave Davy—a satiric crux of the narrative, when the most male-oriented genre of them all, pornography, is claimed by a woman writer.

Russ's declared desire to present feminist alternatives has created female characters who go through rites of passages of which the style and form deliberately mimic traditional narratives. Thus, Irene of *Picnic on Paradise* resembles the earlier protagonist Alyx in *The Two of Them*, where the male helpmate is killed almost incidentally and where the relations between the female agent and a native girl are the sole emphasis.

On Strike Against God is a radical continuation of Russ's overall strategy, with a narrative focused on a lesbian love relationship; *Kittatinny: A Tale of Magic* is written to provide young girls with a positive female figure for the genre of fantasy. Russ's short fiction, which was collected and published in the 1980's, constitutes a body of feminist stories designed to replace, or at least complement, male-oriented texts.

As a feminist critic, Russ strongly fights the battle of the women's movement against a purely male-serving world. In her radical reclamation of all literary genres for women, Russ has not excluded pornography. She continues to praise the potential of science fiction as a medium through which women can gain an authentic voice of their own.

Critical reception of Russ's work has been generally encouraging, though with notable resistance to her marked feminist stance. Often, however, the wry humor and tongue-in-cheek satire of key scenes has not been understood, and her deliberate distortions (of Swiftian proportions) have been taken at face value, to the detriment of both text and reader. Occasionally, the schematic inversion of male mythology, whereby form and structure are maintained and only the gender of the protagonists exchanged, has led to charges of a mechanical approach to literature; this argument is counterbalanced by Russ's self-proclaimed drive to reverse radically cultural assumptions regarding "proper" sexual roles in the field of popular literature.

BIBLIOGRAPHICAL REFERENCES: Barbara Garland, "Joanna Russ," *Dictionary of Literary Biography*, Vol. 8, *Twentieth Century American Science Fiction Writers*, 1980, edited by David Cowart and Thomas L. Wymer, is the first substantial discussion of Russ. Paul Walker, "Joanna Russ," in *Speaking of Science Fiction*, 1978, and Charles Johnson, "A Dialogue: Samuel Delaney and Joanna Russ on Science Fiction," in *Callaloo*, VII (1984), 27-35, contain valuable interviews; Delaney also wrote "Orders of Chaos: The Science Fiction of Joanna Russ," published in *Woman Worldwalkers*, 1985, edited by Jane B. Weedman, which also contains Thelma J. Shinn's essay "Worlds of Words and Swords: Suzette Halden Elgin and Joanna Russ at Work." Robert Scholes and Eric S. Rabkin, in *Science Fiction: History, Science, Vision*, 1977, discuss *The Female Man*. E. Calkins and B. McGhan, *Teaching Tomorrow: A Handbook of Science Fiction for Teachers*, 1972, recommends Russ's early work for academic discussion. See also Gerald Jonas, "Review of *The Female Man*," *The New York Times Book Review*, May 4, 1975, 50; Brooks Landon, "Eve at the End of the World," in *Erotic Universe*, 1986, edited by Donald Palumbo; Natalie M. Rosinsky, "A Female Man," *Extrapolation*, XXIII (1982), 31-36; Samuel R. Delaney, introduction to *Alyx*, 1976; and *More Women of Wonder*, 1976, edited by Pamela Sargent. For brief biographical sketches, see Marilyn J. Holt, "Joanna Russ," in *Science Fiction Writers*, 1982, edited by E. F. Bleiler; *Contemporary Literary Criticism*, Vol. 15, 1980; and *Contemporary Authors, New Revision Series*, Vol. 11, 1983.

Reinhart Lutz

WITOLD RYBCZYNSKI

Born: Edinburgh, Scotland
Date: March 1, 1943

Principal Works

NONFICTION: *Paper Heroes: A Review of Appropriate Technology,* 1980; *Taming the Tiger: The Struggle to Control Technology,* 1983; *Home: A Short History of an Idea*, 1986; *The Most Beautiful House in the World*, 1989.

Witold Rybczynski was born in Edinburgh, Scotland, in 1943. The Rybczynskis, like many Polish families, were forced to flee to Scotland during World War II. After the war ended, they settled in Surrey, England, where Witold attended Jesuit schools. He subsequently emigrated to Canada, where he received bachelor of architecture and master of architecture degrees from McGill University in Montreal. This institution was later to receive him into its architectural faculty as professor of architecture. Rybczynski first attracted wide attention with the publication in 1980 of his first book: *Paper Heroes: A Review of Appropriate Technology.* Appropriate Technology (AT), of which Rybczynski is hailed as one of the founding fathers, is described by the architect as "part lay religion, part protest movement, and part economic theory." AT has as its aim the humanization of technology, which includes the adapting of methods of industrialization to the particular countries to be developed (this idea is especially valid for the Third World), a process which advocates the careful planning of industrial development with an eye toward the particular needs, abilities, and native, human, inventive resources of the particular developing country: AT in its practical guise. At its spiritual bottom, AT is concerned with redefining humankind's relationship to the machines it creates. AT seeks to foster an organic inter-reaction of man and machine; a relationship in which man is ever in control of the technology he creates, and in which work ceases to be a harrowing grind, but rather a fulfilling, creative task which emphasizes the creative being in man.

Rybczynski's next theoretical work, *Taming the Tiger,* which was published in 1983, is possessed of a much more philosophical bent than the previous *Paper Heroes*. In *Taming the Tiger,* Rybczynski discusses humankind's love/hate relationship with technology. Throughout the ages, Rybczynski notes, people have cautiously flirted with technological progress, moving further and further toward an ever more machine-oriented society, while gingerly protesting against said progress, afraid that the "monster" they have created may one day turn upon them. In his captivating historical overview of mechanical creativity, Rybczynski shows the reader how man is—and has always been—a technological being. He and his machines—from the earliest stone hammers up to the nuclear reactors of the twentieth century—are inextricably linked in the fabric of intellectual and social history. While it is obvious that man can never consider relinquishing his mastery over machine, the answer lies not in turning back the clock and renouncing technological progress (an absurd concept) but rather in educating people to understand technology as well as the technological impulse—educating people to make the right technological choices, so that they can remain in control of their increasingly sophisticated, "intelligent," and almost self-sufficient inventions.

Rybczynski's next book, *Home*, was all the more provocative a publication, in that it concerned itself with humankind's relationship to one of its most personal forms of expression: the dwelling place. In this book, Rybczynski showed forth his technical erudition as an architect, as well as his gift for provocative prose and sensitive description of a subject that is often approached/rather coldly. The ideas first broached in *Home*, the humanist, aesthetic choices to be made in the planning of a living space (and not merely a space to live in), are given further, more personal development in *The Most Beautiful House in the World*. This book, published in 1989, concerns the design and construction of Rybczynski's own house, the Boathouse, near Montreal.

The Most Beautiful House in the World is written with the same delicately philosophical, almost poetic style which characterizes *Taming the Tiger*. Rybczynski does more than simply describe the house he evolved for himself from his original plans of a workshed in which to build a sloop; he takes us on an odyssey through space and time in an evocative history of architecture, spanning medieval Europe, Hindu India, the America of Frank Lloyd Wright, and primeval Africa in an effort to emphasize the spiritual bases of man's initiative to design his dwellings, and the importance that the feeling, aesthetic eye should have for today's home-builders. Rybczynski describs the planning and building of one's own home in *The Most Beautiful House in the World* as a process requiring all the delicacy and feeling of the Zen tea ceremony or Japanese flower arrangement. This same delicacy characterizes all the author's literary endeavors. From each of the books mentioned above speaks the voice of a humanist, whose main concern is neither with the development of technology nor with the building of houses, but with the cultivation of the human soul.

BIBLIOGRAPHICAL REFERENCES: Reviews on Rybczynski's books are the main source of information on his work. For a review of *Taming the Tiger*, see Linda S. Robinson, *The New York Times Book Review*, LXXXVIII (November 6, 1983), 16. For reviews of *Home*, see Otto Friedrich, *Time*, CXXVIII (August 4, 1986), 64; John Lubaes, *The New Yorker*, LXII (September 1, 1986), 96; G. Woodcock, "*Home*," *Canadian Literature*, Summer/Fall, 1987, 253-259; and N. Z. Tausby, "*Home*," *University of Toronto Quarterly*, IX (Fall, 1988), 198-200. For a review of *The Most Beautiful House in the World*, see Genevieve Stuttaford, *Publishers Weekly*, CCXXXV (March 3, 1989), 95. See also P. Odell, "The Economics of the Oil Crisis," in *The Times Literary Supplement*, July 9, 1976, 859; Suzanne Slesin, "Modern Is Affordable (Witold Rybczynski on Contemporary Furniture)," *The New York Times Book Review*, XCI (August 3, 1986), 24; Pamela Young, "A Rebel in the Parlor (Architect Witold Rybczynski)," *Maclean's*, IC (August 18, 1986), 50; and Trudie Nelson, "Elements of Comfort," *Chatelaine*, LX (February, 1987), 72.

Charles Kraszewski

ERNESTO SÁBATO

Born: Rojas, Argentina
Date: June 24, 1911

PRINCIPAL WORKS

NOVELS: *El túnel*, 1948 (*The Outsider*, 1950; also known as *The Tunnel*); *Sobre héroes y tumbas*, 1961 (*On Heroes and Tombs*, 1981); *Abaddón, el exterminador*, 1974.

ESSAYS: *Uno y el universo*, 1945; *Hombres y engranajes: Reflecciones sobre el dinero, la razón y el derrumbe de nuestro tiempo*, 1951; *Heterodoxia*, 1953; *Tango: Discusión y clave*, 1963; *El escritor y sus fantasmas*, 1963; *Tres aproximaciones a la literatura de nuestro tiempo: Robbe-Grillet, Borges, Sartre*, 1968; *Itinerario*, 1969; *La convulsión política y social de nuestro tiempo*, 1969; *Mitomagia: Los temos del misterio*, 1969; *Ernesto Sábato: Claves políticas*, 1971; *La cultura en la encrucijada nacional*, 1973; *Diálogos*, 1976; *La robotización del hombre y otras páginas de ficción y reflexion*, 1981.

Ernesto Sábato emerged from the Argentine pampas to examine his nation's character and to explore the existential crisis of modern humanity. He was born on June 24, 1911, in Rojas, Argentina, where his Italian immigrant parents owned the local flour mill. One of the searing events in Sábato's life came in 1924, when his parents sent him to La Plata to attend secondary school. Torn from his community and large family, Sábato suffered a nervous collapse. He regained stability by immersing himself in the orderly world of mathematics and science. In 1929, he entered the Institute of Physics at the National University of La Plata, where he became involved with anarchist and Communist student groups. In 1934, he attended a student Communist congress in Brussels, Belgium, and once more fell into mental despondency. He fled to Paris, again finding peace by immersing himself in science. He returned to La Plata, completed his doctorate in 1937, and received a fellowship to study with French physicist Irène Joliot-Curie. After his time in France, he spent a year at the Massachusetts Institute of Technology. In 1940, he accepted professorships in theoretical physics at schools in La Plata and Buenos Aires.

Although science had provided him with needed mental stability, Sábato came to believe that humanity's desire to rest its physical, mental, and spiritual well-being on science and reason had led to disaster. Thus, he left science by using his teaching positions to finance his literary apprenticeship, served by writing regularly for *Sur* and *La Nación*. In 1945, dictator Juan Perón, offended by Sábato's writing, forced him to resign his professorships, freeing him to devote himself fully to literature. It was the first of several times that Sábato's staunch support of freedom of speech got him in trouble with Argentine caudillos. In 1945, Sábato published a book of essays, *Uno y el universo* (one and the universe), which earned for him national recognition. In 1948, with Albert Camus' help, he found a publisher for his first novel, *The Outsider*, which gained for Sábato international recognition. Two further volumes of essays followed, and in 1955, he became editor of *Mundo Argentino*, until his support of freedom of speech and press brought him into conflict with the military government of Pedro Aramburu. Sábato was forced to resign his position, a decision he made again in 1958, when, as Director of Cultural Relations in the Arturo Frondizi government, he became dissatisfied with government policy.

He had published further volumes of essays in the 1950's, but it was his second novel, *On Heroes and Tombs*, appearing in 1961, which assured his stature in Latin American letters. *On Heroes and Tombs* encompassed themes that concerned Sábato throughout his literary career. The novel begins in May, 1953, when seventeen-year-old Martín meets and falls in love with the mysterious Alejandra. In June, 1955, she kills her father, Fernando, and then commits suicide. To explain the events of those two years, Martín and other central characters journey through 150 years of Argentine history, come into contact with the major social classes and ethnic groups of Argentina, and confront the searing events of their own lives as they try to comprehend the tragedy of Fernando and Alejandra. Few writers have described the existential crisis of modern times more powerfully and clearly than does Sábato in *On Heroes and Tombs*.

More volumes of essays followed *On Heroes and Tombs*, and in 1974, Sábato published his third novel, *Abaddón, el exterminador* (Abaddón, the exterminator). A nervous condition restricted Sábato's further literary output, but he has retained his preeminent position in the Argentine literary world. His support of freedom continued to win for him respect. After the brutal military dictatorship that lasted from 1976 to 1983, President Raúl Alfonsín appointed Sábato to head the National Commission for the Disappearance of Persons. Sábato is in the forefront of the post-World War II Latin American writers. Recognition of his importance continues to grow in the United States and elsewhere.

BIBLIOGRAPHICAL REFERENCES: An excellent biography of Sábato is Harley Dean Oberhelman, *Ernesto Sábato*, 1970. Oberhelman brings together the man and his works in one of the best biographies in the Twayne series. See also Beverly Gibbs, "*El túnel*: Portrayal of Isolation," *Hispania*, XLVIII (1965), 429-436; John Fred Petersen, "Sábato's *El túnel*: More Freud than Sartre," *Hispania*, L (1967), 271-276; Richard Callan, "Sábato's Fiction: A Jungian Interpretation," *Bulletin of Hispanic Studies*, LI (1974), 48-59; and Luis González-del-Valle and Catherine Nickel, "Contemporary Poetics to the Rescue: The Enigmatic Narrator in Sábato's *El túnel*," *Rocky Mountain Review of Language and Literature*, XL (1986), 5-20.

William E. Pemberton

OLIVER SACKS

Born: London, England
Date: July 9, 1933

PRINCIPAL WORKS

SCIENCE: *Migraine: Evolution of a Common Disorder*, 1970 (revised as *Migraine: Understanding a Common Disorder*, 1985); *Awakenings*, 1973 (revised 1983, 1987); *A Leg to Stand On*, 1984; *The Man Who Mistook His Wife for a Hat and Other Clinical Tales*, 1985.

Hailed as "one of the great clinical writers of the 20th century," Oliver Sacks describes in his books the often-bizarre worlds of patients trapped by their neurological afflictions. He was born in London on July 9, 1933, the son of Samuel and Elsie (Landau) Sacks. Both of his parents were neurologists, and he took an early interest in medicine. He was graduated from Queen's College, Oxford, in 1958 and continued his medical studies at Middlesex Hospital in London until 1960. He completed his neurological residency at the University of California, Los Angeles. Since 1965, he has served as a professor of clinical neurology at the Albert Einstein College of Medicine in New York and as a consultant to Bronx State Hospital, as well as maintaining his own private neurology practice.

A talented clinician, Sacks has the literary gift of writing clearly and compassionately about a wide range of complex neurological disorders. In the tradition of his mentor, the great Russian neurologist A. R. Luria, Sacks is able to dramatize his patients' inner lives and, in his depictions of their bizarre and baffling symptoms, reflect on the mysteries of the human mind. Sacks is a frequent contributor to the *London Review of Books* and *The New York Review of Books*, where many of the chapters of his books first appeared as separate essays. Through the success of his books, he has been able to reach beyond his specialty to a broad general audience. Sacks's earliest book, *Migraine*, is a voluminous study of this strange and often excruciating neurological malady, which may beset a patient for an entire lifetime. Sacks, who suffers from migraines himself, has compiled a full account of the history and etiology of the disease, which is sometimes accompanied by visions of luminous wheels, auras, lights, or other psychovisual hallucinations. He describes the visionary experiences of some famous mystics, such as the medieval nun Hildegard von Bingen, in terms of their migraines. Sacks's revised edition of *Migraines* updates his original research and adds additional case histories and clinical material.

Awakenings presents case histories of twenty elderly New York patients with sleeping sickness who later developed symptoms of Parkinson's disease. Many of them had been hospitalized for decades in a nearly catatonic state until 1969, when the new drug L-dopa was administered to them. Sacks describes them as "dormant volcanoes" whose lives were suddenly transformed when they were "awakened" with L-dopa. *Awakenings* presents a detailed clinical account of these patients as they emerged from their isolation and tried to recover their lives. Sacks writes of the tremendous excitement at seeing these lives suddenly redeemed through these miraculous awakenings. Unfortunately, the recoveries experienced by Sacks's patients were often only temporary and were followed by such bizarre neurological reactions that their medication had to be curtailed. The text of *Awakenings* is divided into three sections: Introduction, Awakenings, and Perspectives. Sacks begins with a detailed discussion of Parkinsonism, discusses the individual case history of each patient, and offers some thoughts on the overall pattern of this disease and on what it reveals about the nature of memory, self, and identity. A revised edition provides a new introduction and an update on the progress of his twenty original patients.

Sacks's third book, *A Leg to Stand On*, is a remarkable personal account of the aftermath of a leg injury that he sustained while hiking in Norway. The damage to his left knee and muscle tissue was so great that he lost all neurological sensation in the entire limb. He describes in great detail the loss of proprioception or body sense of his limb, so that he had to struggle in physical therapy to repossess it and learn to use it again. Sacks offers many perceptive comments on what it is like to become a patient: the feeling of helplessness and dependence, the psychology of debilitation, and the importance of recovering one's inner harmony to promote healing and recovery. *The Man Who Mistook His Wife for a Hat and Other Clinical Tales* is perhaps the most conventional of Sacks's works, a collection of twenty-four fictionalized clinical accounts of patients with various bizarre neurological symptoms. Sacks recasts their illnesses in mythological or metaphorical terms, presenting in turn personalized accounts of neurological losses, excesses, transports, and impairment. His tales read like short stories, blending dialogue and character with abundant clinical details and background information to help make sense of these strange accounts of memory lapses, identity confusion, uncontrollable tics, visual agnosia, and prodigious musical memory. Sacks's patients become vividly alive in their potential despite their neurological afflictions.

Sacks has continued the tradition of the neurologist as writer that reaches back to the famous nineteenth century Philadelphia physician Silas Weir Mitchell, who wrote novels and magazine essays about his patients' disorders, and A. R. Luria, who spoke of how the classical and romantic tendencies in medicine needed to be combined in patient care. In his writing, Sacks has tried to recapture the inner lives of his patients in transforming the medical narrative into a new literary genre. His *Awakenings* served as the inspiration for a one-act play by Harold Pinter, *A Kind of Alaska* (pr. 1982), published in the trilogy *Other Places* (1983). In the play, Pinter dramatizes the plight of one of Sacks's patients. Sacks's tale "The Man Who Mistook His Wife for a Hat" has been set to music by a minimalist composer. In all of his books, Sacks has tried to convey the full human experience of neurological disorder.

BIBLIOGRAPHICAL REFERENCES: A good resource to start with is the body of interviews that have been conducted with Sacks. See Marek Kohn, *New Statesman*, CXII (November 28, 1986), 19-20; Holly Brubach, "Talking to . . . Oliver Sacks (A Neurologist on the Poetics of Medicine)," *Vogue*, CLXXVII (November, 1987), 230; and "When Nature Distorts Our Minds," *U.S. News & World Report*, CI (July 14, 1986), 57. Sacks's books have elicited many solid reviews; see Patricia O'Connor, review of *The Man Who Mistook His Wife for a Hat and Other Clinical Tales*, *The New York Times Book Review*, XCII (January 11, 1987), 34; Harold L. Klawans, review of *Awakenings*, *The Journal of the American Medical Association*, CCLX (July 8, 1988), 273; R. Liebmann-Smith, "More Clinical Tales," *The New Yorker*, CXIII (May 4, 1987), 30-31; and Daniel Goleman, "An Atmosphere of Eloquent Medicine," *The New York Times Book Review*, XCI (March 2, 1986), 3.

Andrew J. Angyal

EDWARD W. SAID

Born: Jerusalem, Palestine
Date: November 1, 1935

Principal Works

CRITICISM: *Joseph Conrad and the Fiction of Autobiography*, 1966; *Beginnings: Intention and Method*, 1975; *Literature and Society*, 1979 (editor); *The World, the Text, and the Critic*, 1983.

SOCIAL CRITICISM: *Orientalism*, 1978; *The Question of Palestine*, 1979; *Covering Islam*, 1981; *Blaming the Victims*, 1987 (editor; with Christopher Hutchens).

Edward Said has been the most articulate American critic of literary theory since the influx of European influence beginning in the 1960's, as well as its most politically sophisticated and experienced literary intellectual. Said was born in Jerusalem, Palestine, on November 1, 1935, to Wadie A. and Hilda (Musa) Said. He was educated at Princeton and Harvard universities. Although he has been a visiting professor at numerous major universities, he has remained at Columbia University since 1963, having been appointed as the Parr Professor of Comparative Literature in 1977.

There are three separate strands in Said's writing, which began to come together in the 1970's: scholarship on individual authors, such as Jonathan Swift, Gerard Manley Hopkins, and Joseph Conrad; the estimating and mapping of emerging critical theory, by reviewing it as well as incorporating it in his own original theoretical work; and political work, on behalf of the Palestinians. The moment of this conflation is the year spent as a Fellow at the Center for the Advanced Study in the Behavioral Sciences at Stanford University, 1975 to 1976. *Orientalism*, the product of this stay, is an exemplary combination of an original synthesis of the theoretical work of Antonio Gramsci, Michel Foucault, and, to a lesser extent, Jacques Derrida; a rigorous study of individual texts; and an insistent demonstration of how intellectual work leads to political consequences.

Orientalism argues that the West has dominated the East first of all through intellectual effort—the research and imaginative writing which always presupposes that the East is there, fated to be known by the West, its necessary interlocutor. Said followed with two more books, *The Question of Palestine*, a straightforward counterhistory from the point of view of the Palestinians, and *Covering Islam*, which critically exposes the racist assumptions behind the coverage of Islam and the Middle East. In 1987, Said published, together with Christopher Hutchens, *Blaming the Victims*, a series of essays which expose the popular misrepresentations of Palestinian history which have passed for the truth in the media.

Said is unusual in that he has not fixed himself in a specific theoretical position. Instead, he insists that the critic's job is to map the traveling of theory, not to follow or spread it. To be committed to a position but also outside positions is an idea which is present in one of his earliest publications, a translation of one of Erich Auerbach's last essays, in which Auerbach quotes Victor-Marie Hugo on the positive estrangement of all exiles and émigrés: "The man who finds his homeland sweet is still a tender beginner; he to whom every soil is as his native one is already strong; but he is perfect to whom the entire world is as a foreign land."

BIBLIOGRAPHICAL REFERENCES: For an important series of reviews of *Beginnings*, the book which established Said's influence on theory, see a special issue of *Diacritics*, VI (Fall, 1976); this issue also contains an interview with Said. For a review of *The World, the Text, and the Critic*, and *The Question of Palestine*, see Bruce Robbins, "Homelessness and Worldliness," *Diacritics*, Fall, 1983, 69-77. For a characteristic exchange between Said and the professional Orientalists, see Bernard Lewis, "The Question of Orientalism," *The New York Review of Books*, XXIX (June 24, 1982), 49-53, and Said's reply, also in *The New York*

Review of Books, XXIX (August 12, 1982), 44-46. For one of the most developed considerations of Said as a representative humanist intellectual, see Paul Bové, *Intellectuals in Power*, 1986.

W. A. Johnsen

J. D. SALINGER

Born: New York, New York
Date: January 1, 1919

PRINCIPAL WORKS

NOVEL: *The Catcher in the Rye*, 1951.

SHORT FICTION: *Nine Stories*, 1953; *Franny and Zooey*, 1961; *Raise High the Roof Beam, Carpenters, and Seymour: An Introduction*, 1963.

As famous for his flight from fame as for the one novel and thirteen short fictions that he produced before retreating into silence, Jerome David Salinger gave voice to the rejection of materialism and regimentation that attracted the generation growing up in the United States after World War II. He was born in New York City on New Year's Day, 1919, the son of a prosperous Jewish importer and his Scottish-Irish wife. From 1934 to 1936 he attended the Valley Forge Military Academy, a boarding school in Pennsylvania, which was to serve as the model for Pencey Prep in *The Catcher in the Rye*. After brief stints at Ursinus College and New York University, he studied short-story writing at Columbia University with Whit Burnett. His first commercial publication came in Burnett's own *Story* magazine. The following summer, 1941, *Collier's* became the first of several slick magazines, including *Cosmopolitan*, *Esquire*, *Mademoiselle*, and *The Saturday Evening Post*, to publish Salinger's short stories.

After the entry of the United States into World War II, Salinger volunteered for service and was sent to Europe, with the Army Signal Corps and then with the Counter Intelligence Corps. His marriage to a Frenchwoman, in 1945, lasted eight months. His marriage to Claire Douglas, in 1955, produced two children and lasted twelve years.

After his return to civilian life, Salinger began, in 1948, to publish in *The New Yorker* those studies in precociousness and poignancy that were to constitute the 1953 collection *Nine Stories* and that were to be widely anthologized and read. Several of them feature characters from the Glass family, a clan that was to populate his fiction of the 1960's. Yet it was his 1951 novel *The Catcher in the Rye* that made Salinger famous—and wealthy. The novel immediately attracted a wide, devoted, and enduring following, especially among those close to the age of its main character, a rebellious sixteen-year-old named Holden Caulfield. *The Catcher in the Rye* is Holden's first-person account of a long December weekend in New York following his expulsion from Pencey Prep. Holden's contempt for the "phoniness" of the adult establishment and his dream of becoming a "catcher in the rye," a sort of guardian for the pristine but vulnerable values of childhood, seemed to embody the nascent countercultural trends of the 1950's.

A celebrity now, Salinger was becomingly increasingly attracted to the doctrines of Oriental mysticism. His desire for a meditative retreat from worldly preoccupations was abetted by his decision to leave New York for the tiny, secluded New Hampshire town of Cornish on January 1, 1953. It was while he was living on his rustic estate, without a telephone, that Salinger's *Nine Stories* appeared and enjoyed a popular success extremely rare for a collection of short fiction. Salinger resisted the blandishments of publicity, and, when one of the local adolescents he befriended published an interview with him in her high-school newspaper, the author was offended. It was the last time that he allowed himself to be interviewed.

In 1961, Salinger published in one volume *Franny and Zooey*, the two novellas on which he had been working for almost seven years. Each focuses on a member of the extraordinary Glass family, whose gifted children—Seymour, Buddy, Boo Boo, Walter, Waker, Zooey, and Franny—have each been stars on a radio quiz show. *Franny* recounts a weekend that Franny Glass spends with her Ivy League boyfriend during which she berates him for his smug conventionalism and his preference for academe over art, reason over truth. *Zooey* extends

Salinger's religious preoccupations in its account of twenty-three-year-old Zooey's debt to the Buddhist teachings of his older brothers Buddy and Seymour.

Seymour: An Introduction, first published in *The New Yorker* in 1959 and, with *Raise High the Roof Beam, Carpenters*, in book form in 1963, is Buddy Glass's attempt to come to terms with the suicide of his beatific older brother Seymour. The latter novella is the story of Seymour's wedding day.

Meanwhile, as Salinger, in remote New Hampshire, withdrew more and more from worldly concerns, he was increasingly harried by intrusive journalists, inspired by the cult of this reclusive author. Salinger rebuffed each attempt to invade his privacy, and he even began to view the very act of publication as a betrayal of his art. His final appearance in print was in *The New Yorker* of June 19, 1965, with a twenty-thousand-word story entitled "Hapworth 16, 1924," a long letter written by Seymour Glass that brother Buddy finds forty years later. Salinger reportedly continues to write but steadfastly refuses to share any of his later work with his numerous and devoted readers. He took legal action to prevent unauthorized publication of some of his earlier stories, and he went to court to suppress a biography by Ian Hamilton. For more than a year, Hamilton was kept from publishing his study, and, when it finally appeared, in 1988, it was devoid of quotations from the private letters to which Salinger's lawyers had objected. Salinger received more publicity from this legal confrontation than if he had ignored the attempt to appropriate his life, though the Hamilton book is more of a study in biographical frustration than a satisfactory portrait of the elusive author.

Apart from *The Catcher in the Rye* and his published stories, Salinger's principal claim to fame is his principled contempt for fame. He is the Greta Garbo of American literature, the novelist who wants to be alone but whose dedicated readers remain jealous of his solitude. His last published fiction abandons the conventions of plot and characterization in the interests of theological speculation. It has interested most readers much less than the earlier work, which in its worldly details and its irreverent humor established Salinger's reputation and made possible his distaste for reputations and his reverent retreat from worldliness.

BIBLIOGRAPHICAL REFERENCES: The first volume-length biography of Salinger, Ian Hamilton, *In Search of J. D. Salinger*, 1988, was handicapped by legal barriers and the subject's extreme elusiveness. *Salinger: A Critical and Personal Portrait*, 1962, edited by Henry A. Grunwald, contains the attempts by investigative reporters from *Time* magazine to uncover Salinger's secrets, as well as other essays on the author's life and works. Warren French, *J. D. Salinger*, 1976, is an excellent overview of the author's career. For studies of Salinger's fiction, see *J. D. Salinger and the Critics*, 1962, edited by William F. Belcher and James E. Lee; *J. D. Salinger*, 1987, edited by Harold Bloom; Kenneth Hamilton, *J. D. Salinger: A Critical Essay*, 1967; James Lundquist, *J. D. Salinger*, 1979; and James E. Miller, Jr., *J. D. Salinger*, 1965. *"If You Really Want to Know": A Catcher in the Rye Casebook*, 1963, edited by Malcolm M. Marsden, and *Salinger's "Catcher in the Rye": Clamor vs. Criticism*, 1963, edited by Harold P. Simonson and E. P. Hager, both examine Salinger's novel from a variety of perspectives. Eberhard Alsen, *Salinger's Glass Stories as a Composite Novel*, 1983, establishes connections among the short fictions, with particular attention to Salinger's religious concerns.

Steven G. Kellman

SONIA SANCHEZ

Born: Birmingham, Alabama
Date: September 9, 1934

PRINCIPAL WORKS

POETRY: *Homecoming*, 1969; *We a BaddDDD People*, 1970; *Love Poems*, 1973; *A Blues Book for Blue Black Magical Women*, 1973; *I've Been a Woman: New and Selected Poems*, 1978; *homegirls & handgrenades*, 1984; *Under a Soprano Sky*, 1987.

PLAYS: *Sister Son/ji*, pb. 1969; *The Bronx Is Next*, pr. 1970; *Uh, Huh; But How Do It Free Us?*, pb. 1974; *Malcolm/Man Don't Live Here No Mo'*, pr. 1979; *I'm Black When I'm Singing, I'm Blue When I Ain't*, pr. 1982.

CHILDREN'S LITERATURE: *It's a New Day: Poems for Young Brothas and Sistuhs*, 1971; *The Adventures of Fat Head, Small Head, and Square Head*, 1973; *A Sound Investment and Other Stories*, 1979.

SOCIAL CRITICISM: *Ima Talken bout the Nation of Islam*, 1972; *Crisis in Culture—Two Speeches by Sonia Sanchez*, 1983.

Sonia Sanchez is one of the most influential and enduring writers to come to prominence during the Black Arts movement of the 1960's; her activism, editing, teaching, and performances over three decades establish her as one of the sustaining voices in nurturing what many critics regard as a second renaissance in black American letters and culture. Born in Birmingham, Alabama, on September 9, 1934, to Wilson and Lena (Jones) Driver as Wilsonia Driver, her mother died when Sanchez was a year old; consequently, she and her sister Pat spent their early years with various members of the Driver extended family. Shy as a child, perhaps because of prolonged childhood stuttering, Sanchez' earliest necessity for writing was an effort to avoid embarrassment. When Sanchez was nine years old, her father moved the family to Harlem, New York, where she came of age both enriched and provoked by the gaps between formal education and the verbal agility of black language in the street community.

In 1955, Sanchez received her undergraduate degree in political science from Hunter College in New York City, and, in the next year, she studied poetry with Louise Bogan at New York University. Following two more years of postgraduate study, Sanchez sought to use her writing and activist politics by working to create an integrationist social ideal through work for the Congress of Racial Equality, then a principal force in the Civil Rights movement. She contributed regularly to the leading black journals of the time—the *Liberator*, *Journal of Black Poetry*, *Negro Digest*, and *Black Dialogue*—and began her long teaching career in San Francisco. Involved with fellow activists such as Amiri Baraka, Ed Bullins, Huey Newton, Eldridge Cleaver, and Maulana Ron Karenga, Sanchez became an active proponent of black studies programs in college curricula. In the midst of turmoil on California campuses of the 1960's, Sanchez changed her political views on race relations from integrationist to black nationalist politics. As a result, she became subject to Federal Bureau of Investigation (FBI) scrutiny, most notably because of an introduction she had written to a book published by Assata Shakur, a member of the Black Liberation Army who had been convicted of the murder of a state trooper, sentenced to prison, and then had escaped. Such notoriety only strengthened Sanchez' resolve to change social attitudes, initiating her lifelong support of numerous grass-roots organizations.

During Sanchez' political transition in the mid-1960's, she developed a poetic militancy that echoed her nationalist stance in activism. Seeking a poetry accessible to the masses, textured by street culture and yet faithful to African American history and experience, she credited Malcolm X with inspiring her approach to language. Affirming the need for black-controlled publications, Sanchez, rather than seeking more lucrative major mainstream publishers, offered her first poetry collection *Homecoming* to Dudley Randall's Broadside Press, the most influential black publishing house of the 1960's and 1970's. In her early work, she used a style that drew heavily on the oral tradition of the African legacy and contemporary militant speech. Her poetic attack on "white America's" refusal to cope with personal and institutional racism was woven from a variety of techniques that included sharp, scornful images of violence and suffering and invective that was often laced with profanity. *Homecoming*, although consistently mapping personal references and acknowledging African American experience from slavery through Reconstruction to the northern migration of rural blacks in the South, relocated the source of black culture in the urban ghetto and emphasized themes of family life and personal responsibility as well as political resistance to acculturation in mainstream America. Perhaps as a result of her brief marriage to the black poet Etheridge Knight, who served time in prison on drug charges, Sanchez, while affirming the need for black males in positions of political leadership, refused to compromise her standards of equality even in matters of gender. Drawing some criticism from contemporary black male writers, Sanchez nevertheless identified with the needs of many single black women who were primary caretakers for their children, having now children of her own. Typical in Sanchez' work, personal experience became public concern, and she began regarding children as an important part of her audience, eventually writing three children's books, and the black cultural education of children as an important responsibility of black writers.

The poetry of Sanchez, including that in her second volume *We a BaddDDD People*, finds its best expression in her performance of it. While several recordings offer a reasonable approximation of her powerful voice, not even those duplicate her presence in her unique delivery at a poetry reading. Through more than five hundred readings at campuses and community centers around the country, her voice became nearly legendary for its use of traditional chants, lingering near-screams, playful but satirical intonations, and musical phrasing. After taking teaching positions in Pittsburgh and New York, Sanchez expanded her interest in performance to include dramatic writing. Her most acclaimed plays, *Sister Son/ji*, and *Uh, Huh; But How Do It Free Us?*, continued the development of her feminist politics by exposing the contradiction of a revolutionary movement for black power while the leaders of that movement, in too many cases, viewed black women as objects to be subjugated in the interest of black male pride. Refuting the notions that black women were most effective in submissive roles and that they ought to be "happy" about that status, Sanchez reaped a fair amount of vicious criticism from her fellow (male) writers. The resulting emotional stress in her personal life led to poetic experiments with haiku and tanka forms; these short, terse poems were to sustain her personally, to keep her poetics growing and to be published eventually as *Love Poems*.

In 1972, Sanchez began a three-year teaching post at Amherst College. That same year she joined the Nation of Islam, and, in 1973, she published *A Blues Book for Blue Black Magical Women*, in which she advocated the philosophy of Black Muslims and, through a long sequence of praise poems, offered a communal celebration of black women in the past, present, and future. Although she resigned from the Nation of Islam in 1975, her nationalist ethic and aesthetic continued in subsequent works. By the mid-1970's, Sanchez had moved to Philadelphia to accept what was to become a tenured position at Temple University. Her book *I've Been a Woman* offers a succinct overview of the various stages of her poetry: revolutionary, personal, Muslim, and feminist. By then, her stance against black male chauvinism with her unwavering nationalist politics, in hindsight, seemed ahead of its time, and she gained a new generation of readers, still moved by her performances as an earlier generation had been. In 1984, a new collection, though containing some revised earlier work, *homegirls & handgrenades*, which won for Sanchez the American Book Award in 1985, documented her continuing testimony to the ravages of alienation and the necessity for hope and activism. In this volume and in her 1987 collection *Under a Soprano Sky*, Sanchez includes themes of ecological survival, linking the well-being of blacks to the stability of the planet, and antinuclear activism.

Sanchez' place in American letters generally and African American literature specifically now seems beyond question. Early white reviewers dismissed her poetry as too political, too militant, and too obscene; and, after her rise to prominence in the late 1960's and her feminist criticism which provoked hostile rejection in the early 1970's, Sanchez' critics—both black and white—regard her as among the vanguard of black women writers, including novelists Alice Walker and Toni Morrison, who have expanded the province of American literature to reach people of color all over the world. Sanchez seems likely to remain one of the constant voices in American poetry and one of the crucial models in African American drama.

BIBLIOGRAPHICAL REFERENCES: Readers may usefully approach the study of Sanchez through these two pieces: Herbert Liebowitz, "Exploding Myths: An Interview with Sonia Sanchez," *Parnassus*, XII/XIII (1985), 357-368; and Sonia Sanchez, "Ruminations/Reflections," in *Black Women Writers (1950-1980): A Critical Evaluation*, 1984, edited by Mari Evans. Overviews of her poetry can be found in the same collection. A brief but essential introduction may be found in Kalamu ya Salaam, "Sonia Sanchez," *Dictionary of Literary Biography: Afro-American Poets Since 1955*, Vol. 61, 1985; a more thorough discussion is by Joyce Joyce, "The Development of Sonia Sanchez: A Continuing Journey," *Indian Journal of American Studies*, XIII (1983), 37-71. On Sanchez' drama, see Rosemary K. Curb, "Pre-Feminism in the Black Revolutionary Drama of Sonia Sanchez," *The Many Forms of Drama*, 1985, edited by Karelisa V. Hartigan; and Barbara Walker, "Sonia Sanchez Creates Poetry for the Stage," *Black Creation*, V (1973), 12-14. For further study, see discussions in Bernard W. Bell, *The Folk Roots of Contemporary Afro-American Poetry*, 1974; *The Second Black Renaissance: Essays in Black Literature*, 1980, edited by C. W. E. Bigsby; Dudley Randall, *Broadside Memories: Poets I Have Known*, 1975; and Eugene B. Redmond, *Drumvoices: The Mission of Afro-American Poetry, A Critical History*, 1976; Two early assessments are still accurate: see R. Roderick Palmer, "The Poetry of Three Revolutionists: Don L. Lee, Sonia Sanchez, and Nikki Giovanni," *CLA Journal*, XV (1971), 25-36; and Sebastian Clarke, "Sonia Sanchez and Her Work," *Black World*, XX (1971), 44-48, 96-98. See also Raymond Patterson, "What's Happening in Black Poetry?" *Poetry Review*, II (1985), 7-11.

Michael Loudon

MARI SANDOZ

Born: Sheridan County, Nebraska
Date: May 11, 1896

Died: New York, New York
Date: March 10, 1966

PRINCIPAL WORKS

BIOGRAPHY: *Old Jules*, 1935; *Crazy Horse: The Strange Men of the Oglalas*, 1942.

HISTORY: *Cheyenne Autumn*, 1953; *The Buffalo Hunters: The Story of the Hide Men*, 1954; *The Cattlemen of the Rio Grande Across the Far Marias*, 1958; *These Were the Sioux*, 1961; *Love Song to the Plains*, 1961; *The Beaver Men: Spearheads of Empire*, 1964; *The Battle of the Little Big Horn*, 1966.

NOVELS: *Slogum House*, 1937; *Capital City*, 1939; *The Tom Walker*, 1947; *Winter Thunder*, 1954; *Miss Morissa*, 1955; *The Horsecatcher*, 1957; *Son of the Gamblin' Man*, 1960; *The Story Catcher*, 1963.

MISCELLANEOUS: *Hostiles and Friendlies*, 1959; *Sandhills Sundays and Other Recollections*, 1970.

Mari Sandoz was a historian and novelist of the American West. She was born in Sheridan County, Nebraska, on May 11, 1896, the daughter of Jules Ami Sandoz and his wife, Mary Elizabeth Fehr. Her father, a Swiss immigrant who came to America in 1881 and homesteaded in western Nebraska in 1884, was a community builder and a champion of small farmers in their struggle with land-grabbing ranchers, but he was also a domestic tyrant whose heroic stature was diminished by a lifetime of legal quarrels and by savage acts of violence against his wife and children. As a child, Sandoz was required to perform brutal tasks which would have been dangerous for an adult. Once, for example, she was sent to bring in the cattle during a blizzard and suffered an attack of snow blindness that permanently blinded one eye; on another occasion her father, in a rage, broke a bone in her hand, which as a result was partially crippled for the rest of her life.

Sandoz received less than five years of sporadic education in country schools, but her determination to become a writer originated in childhood, and the environment of the Nebraska frontier, violent and dangerous as it was, provided a wealth of material that she was able to exploit throughout her career. Her father was a friend to the Sioux Indians who visited his ranch, some of them warriors who had only recently been at war with the United States Army, and Sandoz's early determination to do literary justice to them originated in these encounters.

Sandoz, in spite of her limited education, passed the rural teacher's examination in 1913 and conducted her first school in her father's barn. A year later, she married a young local rancher, Wray Macumber, but she was divorced from him in 1919. That year she went to Lincoln, Nebraska, to attend a business college, and during the next sixteen years she struggled to earn a living at a variety of jobs while getting an education and beginning to write. She attended the University of Nebraska when she could afford it but never took a degree; meanwhile she began to write short stories based upon her memories of western Nebraska. Before her father died in 1928, he asked her to write his biography, and though she had often thought of doing so his hold upon her and his contempt for writers and artists were so great that she hesitated to begin.

Old Jules, her first and probably her most important book, was first written as a novel and then rewritten several times as history. A thoroughly researched work, it is indispensable for an understanding of the development of the northern Great Plains, but the editors who rejected it considered it too dramatic to be entirely true, and they objected to her prose style. Her arguments with them were the first in her lifelong fight for a style which she believed was too tough for the taste of provincial Easterners.

Old Jules was her first achievement in the creation of the Trans-Missouri series, which she determined early in life to write. The books in this series—*The Beaver Men, Crazy Horse*, *Cheyenne Autumn*, *The Buffalo Hunters*, *The Cattlemen of the Rio Grande Across the Far Marias*, and *Old Jules*—recount the history of the region from earliest historical time to the twentieth century and, if she had lived longer, would have concluded with an account of the development of the petroleum industry on the plains.

Though she was devoted primarily to the writing of history, Sandoz produced novels throughout her career. Her early efforts, *Slogum House* and *Capital City*, were in part the products of her fear in the 1930's of the rise of Fascism in America, and the moral passion which motivated her is revealed in the allegorical methods she employed. Her later novels carry the weight of their social messages more successfully. The best of them are *Miss Morissa*, the story of a frontier woman doctor whose character resembles Sandoz's own, and *Son of the Gamblin' Man*, the story of the painter Robert Henri's father, whose passion to found a community in the West must have struck Sandoz as resembling that of her own father. In addition, two short novels on Indian themes, *The Horsecatcher* and *The Story Catcher*, are highly regarded.

Sandoz moved to New York in 1943 to be near research libraries and publishing houses. Except for research trips to the West and teaching at the University of Wisconsin in the summers from 1947 to 1955, she lived there for the rest of her life. In her last days she fought a heroic—and lonely—battle with cancer as she worked to complete her last book, *The Battle of the Little Big Horn*. She died in New York on March 10, 1966.

Sandoz wrote three books that will be read as long as the frontier experience remains a vivid possession of the American imagination: *Old Jules*, *Crazy Horse*, and *Cheyenne Autumn*. Jules Sandoz, who may seem a reprobate to the superficial reader, is actually a remarkably complex man—a romantic always dreaming of a freer life to the west and an idealized Europe to which he cannot return, yet a realist who struggles to create a community while brutalizing himself and those around him. His daughter's success in rendering the complexity of a man whom she simultaneously feared and admired makes this book both a masterpiece of Western history and one of a handful of the most important works of American biography. *Crazy Horse* and *Cheyenne Autumn* reveal a remarkable success in achieving empathy with the Plains Indian peoples, and the language Sandoz used seems to be exactly what the Indians would have used if they had told these stories themselves.

BIBLIOGRAPHICAL REFERENCES: One full-length biography of Mari Sandoz is Helen Winter Stauffer, *Mari Sandoz: Story Catcher of the Plains*, 1982. It includes a complete bibliography of writings by and about Sandoz before 1982. For futher study, see *Twentieth-Century Authors*, 1942, edited by Stanley Kunitz and Howard Haycraft; Bruce H. Nicoll, "Mari Sandoz, Nebraska Loner," *American West*, Spring, 1965, 32-36; Mamie Meredith, "Mari Sandoz," in *Roundup: A Nebraska Reader*, 1957, edited by Virginia Faulkner; Scott Greenwell, "The Literary Apprenticeship of Mari Sandoz," *Nebraska History*, LVII (Summer, 1976), 248-272; and Gail Baker, "Mari Sandoz," in *Notable American Women: The Modern Period*, 1980.

Robert L. Berner

WILLIAM SANSOM

Born: London, England
Date: January 18, 1912

Died: London, England
Date: April 20, 1976

PRINCIPAL WORKS

SHORT FICTION: *Fireman Flower and Other Stories*, 1944; *Three*, 1946; *Something Terrible, Something Lovely*, 1948; *South: Aspects and Images from Corsica, Italy, and Southern France*, 1948; *The Passionate North*, 1950; *A Touch of the Sun*, 1952; *Pleasures Strange and Simple*, 1953; *A Contest of Ladies*, 1956; *Among the Dahlias and Other Stories*, 1957; *Selected Short Stories, Chosen by the Author*, 1960; *The Stories of William Sansom*, 1963; *The Ulcerated Milkman*, 1966; *The Vertical Ladder and Other Stories*, 1969; *Hans Feet in Love*, 1971; *The Marmalade Bird*, 1973.

NOVELS: *The Body*, 1949; *The Face of Innocence*, 1951; *A Bed of Roses*, 1954; *The Loving Eye*, 1956; *The Cautious Heart*, 1958; *The Last Hours of Sandra Lee*, 1961 (also known as *The Wild Affair*); *Goodbye*, 1966; *A Young Wife's Tale*, 1974.

NONFICTION: *Jim Braidy: The Story of Britain's Firemen*, 1943, (with James Gordon and Stephen Spender); *The Icicle and The Sun*, 1958; *Blue Skies, Brown Studies*, 1961; *Away to It All*, 1964; *Marcel Proust and His World*, 1974.

EDITED TEXTS: *Choice: Some New Stories and Prose*, 1946; *The Tell-Tale Heart and Other Stories*, 1948 (by Edgar Allan Poe).

SONG LYRICS: *Lord Love Us*, 1954.

William Sansom wrote novels, essays, travel books, and children's books, but he is arguably one of the most important writers of short stories to emerge from England after World War II. He was born on January 18, 1912, in London, England, the son of Ernest Brooks and Mabel (Clark) Sansom. The product of a comfortable middle-class upbringing, Sansom attended Uppingham School. After he was graduated in 1940, Sansom studied for a short while in Europe, where he cultivated an interest in the arts. Without receiving a degree, Sansom returned to London after only a few months. Sansom worked in a bank for a short while before deciding to assist the fire department in the monumental task of putting out the fires caused by the Blitz of 1940-1941. His account of what he saw as an auxiliary fireman in a book entitled *Jim Braidy* marked the beginning of his literary career.

Sansom spent the next five years honing his skills as a short-story writer. In his first collection of short stories, *Fireman Flower and Other Stories*, Sansom once again attracted public attention through his vivid portrayal of the horrors of the bombing of London. The subjects and moods of these early stories focused on death and terror. Although Sansom was criticized for his wordy style, he was praised for the precision with which he analyzed character and motive.

Two more volumes of short stories came out in 1948. The stories collected in *South* center on the reactions of typical Englishmen to situations outside their normal realm of experience. The majority of the stories in *Something Terrible, Something Lovely* deal with characters who are thrust into horrible situations. The power of these stories is derived from the fact that they contain realistic descriptions of people and places.

Sansom's first novel, *The Body*, is also the most highly praised. *The Body* is a psychological portrayal of Henry Bishop, a suburban Londoner who suspects his wife of twenty years of infidelity. Even though some critics deplored the novel's "slick" style, most hailed *The Body* as a study in jealousy that had no contemporary peer. Sansom received more critical acclaim with the publication of his second novel, *The Face of Innocence*. This story of a handsome young woman who marries an old friend of the narrator emphasizes the humor and wit that were only hinted at in his first novel.

Between 1951 and 1954, many critics believed that the quality of Sansom's work declined.

In *A Touch of the Sun*, a collection of twelve short stories ranging from the macabre to the comic, Sansom once again exhibits his flair for observation as well as a tendency to manipulate two-dimensional characters. A novel, *A Bed of Roses*, also received only a lukewarm reception by the critics. The stories in *A Contest of Ladies* vividly convey a sense of place, but the characters, like the ones in *A Touch of the Sun*, fail to come to life.

In 1955, Sansom discovered the source of a second income when an American editor looked at some of Sansom's stories that were set in Naples. Sansom's talent for description was so evident in these stories that the editor suggested that Sansom write travel pieces for him. Within a few months, Sansom was writing travel pieces for major American magazines.

Sansom's literary reputation was greatly enhanced by the publication of *The Loving Eye* and *The Cautious Heart*. *The Loving Eye* is the satirical story of a middle-aged invalid, who becomes obsessed with a twenty-one-year-old girl that he observes outside his window with binoculars. In *The Cautious Heart*, Sansom once again employs humor to comment on the nature of love. This story of a nightclub pianist, his girlfriend, and her drunken escort is powered by the same sexual tensions and jealous acts that appeared in such successful works as *The Body* and *The Face of Innocence*.

By the 1960's, Sansom's reputation was so well established that each publication was eagerly awaited by the reading public. His last major work was a biography of Marcel Proust entitled *Marcel Proust and His World*. Sansom's compulsive observations and sensuous descriptions seem to have made him ideally suited to this undertaking. He died in London on April 20, 1976.

Sansom's best work reflects his keen ear for the idiom of post-World War II, lower-middle-class England and his sharp eye for detail. Equally adept at comedy, satire, and the macabre, Sansom was praised for his technically flawless prose—though critics deplored Sansom's habit of reducing human nature to a subject for social analysis. Even though he had been touted throughout his life as the logical successor to D. H. Lawrence, Sansom never really fulfilled the promise that was contained in his earliest stories and in his best novel, *The Body*. If Sansom is not classed as one of the world's greatest writers, perhaps the reason has less to do with skill or ability and more to do with his interest in the life of the average Englishman, not with the totality of human experience.

BIBLIOGRAPHICAL REFERENCES: "William Sansom" in *Contemporary Authors*, Vols. 5-8, 1969, edited by Barbara Harte and Carolyn Riley, provides an exhaustive bibliography of his major works as well as insights into themes that run through his major works. For further study, see "William Sansom" in *Contemporary Literary Criticism*, Vols. 2 and 6, 1976, edited by Carolyn Riley et al., which documents his strengths and weaknesses as a writer through reviews of several of his major works. See also Walter Allen, *The Modern Novel*, 1964; Kenneth Alsop, *The Angry Decade*, 1958; Herbert Barrows, "A Novel of Suspicion: *The Body*," *The New York Times Book Review*, LIV (August 7, 1949), 3; "Briefly Noted: *Goodbye*," *The New Yorker*, LXII (April 1, 1967), 148-149; "Fiendish Obsession: *The Body*," *The Atlantic Monthly*, September, 1949, 86; "The Innocent and the Guileless: *The Face of Innocence*," *The Atlantic Monthly*, September, 1951, 84; Edmund Fuller, "Window Watcher: *The Loving Eye*," *The New York Times Book Review*, LXII (February 10, 1957), 5; Alice S. Morris, "Characters Without Will: *A Contest of Ladies*," *The New York Times Book Review*, LXI (March 25, 1956), 4; Alice S. Morris, "Living Landscapes: *South: Aspects and Images from Corsica, Italy, and Southern France*," *The New York Times Book Review*, LV (September 10, 1950), 4; Alice S. Morris, "Pathways to Horror: *Something Terrible, Something Lovely*," *The New York Times Book Review*, LIX (October 10, 1954), 5; "Three's a Crowd: *The Cautious Heart*," *Time*, September 29, 1958, 100; and Eudora Welty, "Time and Place—and Suspense: The Short Stories of William Sansom," *The New York Times Book Review*, LXVIII (June 30, 1963), 5.

Alan Brown

FRANK SARGESON

Born: Hamilton, New Zealand
Date: March 23, 1903

Died: Auckland, New Zealand
Date: March 1, 1982

PRINCIPAL WORKS

CRITICISM: *Conversation in a Train and Other Critical Writing*, 1985.
EDITED TEXT: *Speaking for Ourselves: A Collection of New Zealand Stories*, 1945.
MEMOIRS: *Once Is Enough*, 1973; *More Than Enough*, 1975; *Never Enough!*, 1978.
NOVELS AND NOVELLAS: *When the Wind Blows*, 1945; *I Saw in My Dream*, 1949; *I for One*, 1954; *Memories of a Peon*, 1965; *The Hangover*, 1967; *Joy of the Worm*, 1969; *Man of England Now*, 1972 (includes *I for One* and *A Game of Hide and Seek*); *Sunset Village*, 1976.
PLAYS: *Wrestling with the Angel, Two Plays: "A Time for Sowing" and "The Cradle and the Egg,"* pb. 1964.
SHORT FICTION: *Conversation with My Uncle and Other Sketches*, 1936; *A Man and His Wife*, 1940; *That Summer and Other Stories*, 1946; *Collected Stories, 1935-1963*, 1965.

Frank Sargeson is the creator of a distinctly New Zealand tradition of fiction and, as well, is one of that tradition's finest writers. He was born in Hamilton, New Zealand, to middle-class parents with strong religious convictions. After attending Hamilton High School, he enrolled in 1920 at Auckland University College, where he prepared for a law career as a solicitor. He worked in a Hamilton law office before breaking with his puritanical family and moving to Auckland, where he was employed briefly as a solicitor. In 1927, he left for a tour of Europe, with the highlight of the trip being his extended stay in Bloomsbury, near the British Museum. His European travels convinced him that he was a displaced person abroad, and he returned to New Zealand in 1928 and began an abortive government career in Wellington. Unfitted temperamentally for the life that he had prepared to lead, he suffered a breakdown and visited his uncle's farm, a refuge for Sargeson since his childhood from his father's strict morality. He never returned to the conventional life and society that he subsequently satirized in his fiction. In 1931, he moved to a small cabin that his father owned at Takapuna, on Auckland's north shore.

During the 1930's, he wrote many articles and sketches, some of which began appearing in *Tomorrow* in the mid-1930's. In 1936, he published the autobiographical *Conversation with My Uncle and Other Sketches*, the first of many literary successes. His growing popularity and literary stature were such that in 1953, he was honored in *Landfall* on the occasion of his fiftieth birthday by sixteen other New Zealand writers. He was also the subject of critical essays in *The Puritan and the Waif* (1954); the title reflects the primary conflict in Sargeson's fiction. Drawing on his own position outside conventional society, he wrote short stories about outsiders, waifs, and social outcasts, all lonely people operating on the fringe of society and the brink of emotional collapse. Aware that they have somehow been hurt by a society that they perceive as destructive, they are inarticulate or unconscious of the cause or depth of their wounds. Through the use of a vernacular first-person narration, Sargeson suggests his characters' attitudes and responses to a situation; it is the character, not the situation or plot, that is his focus. His short story "Just Trespassing, Thanks" won for him the Katherine Mansfield Award in 1965.

His novels, which seem episodic, are also more concerned with character than plot. *Memories of a Peon*, a picaresque, comic novel, concerns the adventures of its nonconformist protagonist. The first part of *I Saw in My Dream*, *When the Wind Blows*, like James Joyce's *A Portrait of the Artist as a Young Man* (1916), concerns a young man's struggle to escape a sexually repressive past and discover his identity, but the frankly experimental novel also reflects Sargeson's movement from realism to psychological symbolism as well as a more fragmented narrative style. Sargeson returned to his study of the disturbed adolescent in *The*

Hangover, which also concerns the passage from youth to maturity.

Sargeson's world is a masculine one, and like Henry Lawson, his Australian counterpart, he celebrated "mateship," the loyal ties between men. In fact, though his male protagonists seem preoccupied with sex and actively struggle to free themselves from their inhibitions, Sargeson does not offer his readers portraits of healthy sexual relationships between men and women. Consequently, critics have seen homosexual overtones and subplots in many of his short stories and novels, though the homosexuality is muted and understated, clearly not Sargeson's focus. Though known primarily for his fiction, he ventured into other literary genres. When he turned his hand to drama in the late 1950's, he again had no tradition within which to work. *A Time for Sowing* and *The Cradle and the Egg* were tied to his fiction by content and experimental style. The story of a fallen missionary who was sexually involved with the Maori he came to serve, *A Time for Sowing* could easily have been a historical novel about an outsider struggling but failing, victim of his puritanical past.

Sargeson also wrote several memoirs in the 1970's, with titles that reflect his attitude toward life (for example, *Never Enough!*), and in 1985, he published a collection of essays concerning, in part, the literary form he had helped to develop. Sargeson was not only an innovative, experimental writer whose work evolved with New Zealand society but also the creator of the literary tradition in which he worked. His identification with New Zealand fiction is reflected in his editing of *Speaking for Ourselves*, and his work has influenced, in terms of its liberating effect, later writers. In fact, he was instrumental in assisting the development of Janet Frame, who has succeeded him as the foremost New Zealand writer of fiction. The literary history of New Zealand is inextricably related to Sargeson's literary career.

BIBLIOGRAPHICAL REFERENCES: A full-length study of Sargeson's life and work is H. Winston Rhodes, *Frank Sargeson*, 1969, which also contains a selected bibliography. An earlier, more comprehensive bibliography has been compiled by Bill Pearson and appended to *Collected Stories, 1935-1963*, 1964. A collection of essays, *The Puritan and the Waif: A Symposium of Critical Essays on the Work of Frank Sargeson*, 1954, edited by Helen Shaw, was published as a tribute to Sargeson on his fiftieth birthday. See also E. A. Horsman, "The Art of Frank Sargeson," *Landfall*, XIX (1965), 129-134; E. H. McCormick, *New Zealand Literature: A Survey*, 1959; Joan Stevens, *The New Zealand Novel, 1860-1960*, 1961; R. A. Copland, "The Goodly Roof: Some Comments on the Fiction of Frank Sargeson," *Landfall*, XXII (1968), 310-323; Howard McNaughton, "In Sargeson's World," *Landfall*, XXIV (1970), 39-43; J. B. Ower, "Wizard's Brew: Frank Sargeson's *Memories of a Peon*," *Landfall*, XXVI (1972), 308-321; W. H. New, "Enclosures: Frank Sargeson's *I Saw in My Dream*," *World Literature Written in English*, XIV (1975), 15-22; R. A. Copland, "Frank Sargeson: *Memories of a Peon*," in *Critical Essays on the New Zealand Novel*, 1976, edited by Cheryl Hankin; Murray S. Martin, "Speaking Through the Inarticulate: The Art of Frank Sargeson," *Journal of General Education*, XXXIII (1981), 123-134; and Jean-Pierre Durix, "An Interview with Frank Sargeson," *Commonwealth Essays and Studies*, III (1977/1978), 49-54.

Thomas L. Erskine

WILLIAM SAROYAN

Born: Fresno, California
Date: August 31, 1908

Died: Fresno, California
Date: May 18, 1981

PRINCIPAL WORKS

SHORT FICTION: *The Daring Young Man on the Flying Trapeze and Other Stories*, 1934; *Inhale and Exhale*, 1936; *Three Times Three*, 1936; *Little Children*, 1937; *Love, Here Is My Hat and Other Short Romances*, 1938; *The Trouble with Tigers*, 1938; *Peace, It's Wonderful*, 1939; *My Name Is Aram*, 1939; *Saroyan's Fables*, 1941; *Dear Baby*, 1944; *The Saroyan Special: Selected Stories*, 1948; *The Assyrian and Other Stories*, 1950; *The Whole Voyald and Other Stories*, 1956; *The Saroyan Reader*, 1958; *After Thirty Years: The Daring Young Man on the Flying Trapeze*, 1964; *Best Stories of William Saroyan*, 1964; *The Tooth and My Father*, 1974.

PLAYS: *The Hungerers: A Short Play*, pb. 1939; *My Heart's in the Highlands*, pr., pb. 1939; *The Time of Your Life*, pr., pb. 1939; *The Great American Goof*, pr. 1940; *Love's Old Sweet Song*, pr. 1940; *The Beautiful People*, pr. 1940; *Across the Board on Tomorrow Morning*, pr., pb. 1941; *Hello Out There*, pr. 1941; *Jim Dandy*, pr., pb. 1941; *Razzle Dazzle*, pb. 1942; *Talking to You*, pr., pb. 1942; *Get Away Old Man*, pr. 1943; *Sam Ego's House*, pr. 1947-1948; *A Decent Birth, a Happy Funeral*, pb. 1949; *Don't Go Away Mad*, pr., pb. 1949; *The Slaughter of the Innocents*, pb. 1952; *The Cave Dwellers*, pr. 1957; *Sam the Highest Jumper of Them All: Or, The London Comedy*, pr. 1960; *Settled Out of Court*, pr. 1960.

NOVELS: *The Human Comedy*, 1943; *The Adventures of Wesley Jackson*, 1946; *Rock Wagram*, 1951; *Tracy's Tiger*, 1951; *The Laughing Matter*, 1953 (also known as *The Secret Story*); *Mama I Love You*, 1956; *Papa You're Crazy*, 1957; *Boys and Girls Together*, 1963; *One Day in the Afternoon of the World*, 1964.

AUTOBIOGRAPHY: *The Twin Adventures: The Adventures of William Saroyan*, 1950; *The Bicycle Rider in Beverly Hills*, 1952; *Here Comes, There Goes, You Know Who*, 1961; *Not Dying*, 1963; *Short Drive, Sweet Chariot*, 1966; *Days of Life and Death and Escape to the Moon*, 1970; *Places Where I've Done Time*, 1972; *Sons Come and Go, Mothers Hang In Forever*, 1976; *Chance Meetings*, 1978; *Obituaries*, 1979; *Births*, 1983.

SCREENPLAYS: *The Good Job*, 1942; *The Human Comedy*, 1943.

MISCELLANEOUS: *My Name Is Saroyan*, 1983; *The New Saroyan Reader*, 1984.

During the 1930's and 1940's, William Saroyan was one of the best-known, most critically admired, and most popular American writers. His affirmation of humane values in the face of adversity, oppression, and human error was a source of comfort to the reading public, and his audacious stylistic experiments won for him the praise of critics. Later, Saroyan continued to write as much and as well as he had before, but the world changed—and with it critical reception and public taste. After Saroyan's death in 1981, however, audiences began to rediscover an author who was a unique blend of public figure, entertainer, and artist.

William Saroyan was born in Fresno, California, in 1908 to Armenian immigrants; he was the only one of his siblings to have been born in the United States. Saroyan was proud of his Armenian heritage and rarely allowed his readers to forget his ancestry for more than a few pages. Early in life he experienced two devastating losses: His father, a preacher and writer, died of appendicitis when Saroyan was three, and his mother, unable to care for her children while she worked, put them in an orphanage, where Saroyan lived for the next five years, effectively losing his mother as well.

Because of these experiences, Saroyan was determined not to be defeated by life, and he threw himself into his work with intense energy. He decided early to become a writer, and in 1934 he became a nationwide success with the story "The Daring Young Man on the Flying Trapeze." Its theme of the irrelevance of the artist in a brutal commercial society made the story socially significant, and the stream-of-consciousness technique fascinated critics, who saw in its writer an innovative talent.

Saroyan came from an oral literary tradition based on story-telling, a fact reflected in his next two successes. For a person who is accustomed to spoken art, playwriting seemed natural; Saroyan's play *The Time of Your Life*, set in a San Francisco bar and peopled with a collection of eccentrics, was the hit of the 1939 Broadway season and received the Pulitzer Prize, which Saroyan refused with characteristic quirkiness, stating that monied interests should not patronize art. The play's central character is a boozy philosopher named Joe who gently solves the problems of the people who inhabit the bar. After this early success, Broadway was unreceptive to Saroyan, and he did not have another work produced in New York until *The Cave Dwellers*, although he continued to write plays. Another success based on Saroyan's use of oral tradition was the collection of stories *My Name Is Aram*. The stories are about a boy maturing in an Armenian community in California. Many of them are based on incidents in Saroyan's life, particularly the continuing influence of a series of slightly mad uncles, who serve the boy as a sort of extended family.

In the 1940's, Saroyan became a favorite of Louis B. Mayer, head of the leading Hollywood film studio Metro-Goldwyn-Mayer. The result of this friendship was Saroyan's most successful work, *The Human Comedy*, which was first produced as a film starring Mickey Rooney and Van Johnson, the screenplay of which Saroyan converted into a best-selling novel. *The Human Comedy* draws on Saroyan's own life; the hero, Homer Macaulay, is a telegraph messenger boy, just as Saroyan had been in his youth. The novel concerns the coming-of-age of the boy and the learning experiences of his young brother Ulysses, as the family must finally face the tragic news that the oldest son, Marcus, has been killed in the war.

Saroyan was drafted in 1943 and assigned the job of writing training films. World War II was a turning point for his artistic career as well as his personal life. In 1943 he married socialite Carol Marcus; together they would have two children. Although the marriage ended in divorce, Saroyan once again married Marcus in 1951, with even more disastrous consequences and another divorce. The critics and the public turned against him after he published an idiosyncratic novel, *The Adventures of Wesley Jackson*, which, both critics and the public complained, had missed the point of what the Fascists had done to the world. After Auschwitz, Saroyan's wistful affirmation seemed a weak response.

During the last two decades of his life, Saroyan found some degree of emotional stability and shuttled between a Paris flat and two tract houses in Fresno, one of which was completely filled with memorabilia. For years before his death, it was fashionable to say that Saroyan was a sentimentalist who had lost touch with the realities of twentieth century life. Yet Saroyan's alleged sentimentality was a reaction to life's tragedy, not a retreat from it; Saroyan would not allow sweetness and hope to die no matter what the world did to him. That affirmation and that struggle are also evident in Saroyan's enormous literary output, which continued even after critics and most of the public had rejected him.

BIBLIOGRAPHICAL REFERENCES: Two biographies of the writer are helpful: *Saroyan*, 1984, by Barry Gifford and Lawrence Lee, who use an oral historical approach with excerpts from interviews with many who knew the writer, and *William Saroyan*, 1983, by Aram Saroyan, the writer's son. Aram Saroyan also describes his father's last weeks in *Last Rites*, 1982. The first full-length critical study of Saroyan is Howard H. Floan, *William Saroyan*, 1966, which has been followed by David Stephen Calonne, *William Saroyan: My Real Work Is Being*, 1983. Both these books contain bibliographies. *William Saroyan: The Writer and the Man Remembered*, 1983, edited by Leo Hamalian, is a collection of remembrances, tributes, and critical comments by various writers. David Kherdian, *A Bibliography of William Saroyan, 1934-1964*, 1965, provides a reasonably complete use of Saroyan's publications for the period indicated. See also Edwin B. Burgum, "The Lonesome Young Man on the Flying Trapeze," *The Virginia Quarterly Review*, XX (1944), 392-403; Frederic I. Carpenter, "The Time of Saroyan's Life," *Pacific Spectator*, I (1947) 88-96; John Dolman, Jr., "Jim Dandy: Pioneer,"

Quarterly Journal of Speech, XXX (1944), 71-75; and William J. Fisher, "Whatever Happened to Saroyan?" *College English*, XVI (1955), 336-340.

James Baird

NATHALIE SARRAUTE

Born: Ivanovo-Voznessensk, Russia
Date: July 18, 1900

Principal Works

NOVELS: *Portrait d'un inconnu*, 1948 (*Portrait of a Man Unknown*, 1958); *Martereau*, 1953 (English translation, 1959); *Le Planétarium*, 1959 (*The Planetarium*, 1960); *Les Fruits d'or*, 1963 (*The Golden Fruits*, 1964); *Entre la vie et la mort*, 1968 (*Between Life and Death*, 1969); *Vous les entendez?*, 1972 (*Do You Hear Them?*, 1973); *"Disent les imbéciles,"* 1976 (*"Fools Say,"* 1977).

SHORT FICTION: *Tropismes*, 1938, 1957 (*Tropisms*, 1963); *L'Usage de la parole*, 1980 (*The Uses of Speech*, 1980).

AUTOBIOGRAPHY: *Enfance*, 1984 (*Childhood*, 1984).

PLAYS: *Le Silence*, pb. 1964 (radio play; *The Silence*, 1981); *Le Mensonge*, pb. 1966 (radio play; *The Lie*, 1981); *C'est beau*, pb. 1973 (*It's Beautiful*, 1981); *Pour un oui ou pour un non*, pb. 1982.

ESSAYS: *L'Ère du soupçon*, 1956 (*The Age of Suspicion*, 1963).

Nathalie Sarraute has often been called the mother of the French New Novel. She was born in Russia on July 18, 1900, the daughter of Ilya Tcherniak, a chemist and owner of a dye factory, and Pauline Chatounowski. At the age of two, Sarraute's parents were divorced, and she spent much of her childhood moving back and forth between Russia, France, and Switzerland. Sarraute's mother eventually returned to Russia with her daughter, remarried, and published a number of novels and short stories under the male pseudonym Vichrowski. At the age of eight, Sarraute returned to Paris to live with her father in the hub of the Russian émigré community.

Sarraute studied English at the Sorbonne, history at the University of Oxford, and sociology at the Faculty of Letters, Berlin, before entering the University of Paris Law School in 1922. In 1925, she married Raymond Sarraute, a fellow law student. Sarraute was a member of the Paris bar for twelve years, during which time she became the mother of three daughters and began her writing career.

Her first work, *Tropisms*, demonstrates the theoretical and innovative approach to writing that sets Sarraute in the forefront of contemporary artists. The term "tropism" comes from the field of biochemistry and describes a preverbal, instinctive, psychic movement, as primitive and tiny as that of a plant's response to light and water. Beneath any overt human act or word, these authentic responses prefigure the superficial, socially acceptable behavior people learn to enact. The notion of "tropisms" leads Sarraute to create worlds in which the ego and identity play little importance. In many of her works, characters are indistinguishable from one another in the normal sense (their ages and occupations are not known). Instead, Sarraute focuses on their shared humanity and their repeated, habitual behavior. This close observation draws the readers into the characters' emotions to share the experience of their pain and fear, and to laugh at their foibles.

Because she was Jewish, World War II forced Sarraute into hiding, and she spent the war years posing as a governess to her children. It was after the war that Sarraute's real career began. Jean-Paul Sartre wrote an introduction to her novel *Portrait of a Man Unknown* in which he coined the expression "anti-novel" to describe the rejection of nineteenth century concepts of plot and character found in her work. Although Sarraute's writing is highly innovative, she compares herself with Fyodor Dostoevski, Gustave Flaubert, and Virginia Woolf, all exceptional creators of character and all experts in the use of irony.

Another important aspect of Sarraute's writing, introduced in *The Planetarium*, is her *sous-conversations* (sub-conversations), in which there is a disjunction between the spoken words of interrupted sentences and the tropistic movements beneath. This novel serves as a good introduction to Sarraute's work. In subsequent novels, Sarraute developed her notion that humanity consists of the observers and the observed, which are constantly interchanging; her self-conscious approach to writing, in which narrators critique the novel in which they function; and her interest in suspicion, dependence, and control.

In the early 1960's, Sarraute turned to playwriting; she succeeded in turning the preverbal tropisms into dialogue, first for the radio, then for the stage. Characters speak in banal, conversational language that reveals deeply hidden undercurrents in their relationships. Sarraute's theories of narrative method, clearly expressed in the collection of essays *The Age of Suspicion*, have influenced a generation of subsequent writers of the New Novel including Alain Robbe-Grillet and Michel Butor.

BIBLIOGRAPHICAL REFERENCES: For a clear, general analysis, see Gretchen Rous Besser, *Nathalie Sarraute*, 1979, although Sarraute's production since the publication of this work is considerable. Other full-length works are Valeri Minogue, *Nathalie Sarraute and the War of the Words: A Study of Five Novels*, 1981, and Helen Watson-Williams, *Novels of Nathalie Sarraute: Towards an Aesthetic*, 1981. Insightful and challenging is a study by French feminist critic Monique Wittig, "The Place of the Action," in *Three Decades of the French New Novel*, 1986. For an examination of Sarraute's plays, see Bettina Knapp, "Nathalie Sarraute: A Theatre of Tropisms," *Performing Arts Journal*, 1976, 15-27.

Joanne Butcher

MAY SARTON

Born: Wondelgem, Belgium
Date: May 3, 1912

PRINCIPAL WORKS

POETRY: *Encounter in April*, 1937; *Inner Landscape*, 1939; *The Lion and the Rose*, 1948; *The Land of Silence*, 1953; *In Time Like Air*, 1958; *Cloud, Stone, Sun, Vine*, 1961; *A Private Mythology*, 1966; *As Does New Hampshire*, 1967; *A Grain of Mustard Seed*, 1971; *A Durable Fire*, 1972; *Collected Poems, 1930-1973*, 1974; *Selected Poems of May Sarton*, 1978; *Halfway to Silence*, 1980; *Letters from Maine*, 1984; *The Silence Now*, 1989.

NOVELS: *The Single Hound*, 1938; *The Bridge of Years*, 1946; *Shadow of a Man*, 1950; *A Shower of Summer Days*, 1952; *Faithful Are the Wounds*, 1955; *The Birth of a Grandfather*, 1957; *The Fur Person*, 1957; *The Small Room*, 1961; *Joanna and Ulysses*, 1963; *Mrs. Stevens Hears the Mermaids Singing*, 1965; *Miss Pickthorn and Mr. Hare*, 1966; *The Poet and the Donkey*, 1969; *Kinds of Love*, 1970; *As We Are Now*, 1973; *Crucial Conversations*, 1975; *A Reckoning*, 1978; *Anger*, 1982; *The Magnificent Spinster*, 1985; *The Education of Harriet Hatfield*, 1989.

AUTOBIOGRAPHY: *I Knew a Phoenix: Sketches for an Autobiography*, 1959; *Plant Dreaming Deep*, 1968; *May Sarton: A Self-Portrait*, 1982.

JOURNALS: *Journal of a Solitude*, 1973; *The House by the Sea*, 1977; *Recovering: A Journal*, 1980; *At Seventy: A Journal*, 1984; *After the Stroke: A Journal*, 1988.

BIOGRAPHY: *Honey in the Hive: Judith Matlack, 1898-1982*, 1988.

OTHER NONFICTION: *A World of Light: Portraits and Celebrations*, 1976; *Writings on Writing*, 1980.

CHILDREN'S LITERATURE: *Punch's Secret*, 1974; *A Walk Through the Woods*, 1976.

One of the most prolific and distinguished of American women of letters, Eleanor May Sarton was born in Wondelgem, Belgium, on May 3, 1912, to a Belgian father and British mother. In 1916, she and her parents immigrated to the United States, settling in Cambridge, Massachusetts, where she was naturalized in 1924. George Sarton, her father, was a distinguished historian of science on the faculty at Harvard University. Her British mother, Mabel Elwes Sarton, was an artist and designer of furniture and textiles. Sarton was educated at the Shady Hill School in Cambridge, Massachusetts, attended the Institut Belge de Culture Française, and was graduated from the Boston High and Latin School in 1929. Preferring not to attend college, she was selected in 1930 as apprentice to Eva Le Galliene at New York's Civic Repertory Theatre, where she remained until 1936. In 1933, she founded the Apprentice Theatre at the New School for Social Research, and in 1936, she became the director of Associated Actors Theatre in Hartford, Connecticut.

Sarton has taught at the Stuart School in Boston (1937-1940), Harvard University (1950-1953), Bryn Mawr College (1953), and Wellesley College (1960-1964). She has received seventeen honorary degrees from American colleges and universities. Since 1964, Sarton has been writing full-time, as well as lecturing and reading her poetry at universities and conferences across the country. Her works include novels, poetry, journals, and memoirs, and several miscellaneous works, including two children's books. Her range thus extends across several distinctly different genres of literature; some of the same themes are addressed in a variety of forms.

Sarton explores several kinds of personal growth in her novels, including the miraculous flowering of unexpected or unconventional love and friendship. In some of the novels, unconventional love is repressed or denied, often with devastating consequences, as in *The Small Room* and in *As We Are Now.* In others, love powerfully transforms the lives of those who are open to it. In *Mrs. Stevens Hears the Mermaids Singing*, love for both men and women moves the protagonist, Hilary Stevens, to create works of art inspired by a personal

Muse (the theme of several of Sarton's best poems, as well as of several other novels). In *A Reckoning*, Laura Spelman, dying of cancer, remembers her mother, her daughter, and a beloved woman friend, memories that enable her to achieve a transcendent perspective on her life. Harriet Hatfield, sixty-year-old protagonist of *The Education of Harriet Hatfield*, also achieves a perspective on her past life, when she opens a feminist bookstore in a working-class neighborhood. Conversations with several younger friends help Harriet to understand some issues for lesbians and gay men she has never confronted before. In all of her novels, Sarton explores with sensitivity and courage the difficulties and joys of intense personal relationships in an often-hostile world.

In "The Writing of a Poem" (reprinted in *Writings on Writing*), Sarton called the making of a lyric poem a "holy game." The "game" is the intellectual crafting of effects; the "holiness" is a life discipline undertaken to keep the poet "perfectly open and transparent, so that he [sic] may meet everything . . . with an innocent 'eye.'" This combination of sacred calling and formal crafting is one of the principal themes of Sarton's poetry. "The Muse as Medusa," from *A Grain of Mustard Seed*, "The Sacred Wood" and "Because What I Want Most Is Permanence" from *The Land of Silence*, and "The Autumn Sonnets" from *A Durable Fire*, are among the finest of Sarton's poems in the *ars poetica* tradition. Other themes in Sarton's poetry include the power of passionate love, the magical beauty of the natural landscape, the difficult quest for self-knowledge, the relationship of art to issues of social justice, and the role of silence and solitude in the poet's life.

Sarton's journals and memoirs present more directly many of the issues addressed in her novels and poetry, especially the importance of friends and lovers in the poet's life, as well as the role of solitude and silence for the artist. Sarton has a gift for divining, in her personal experience, patterns of meaning common to women of all ages and from many different educational and economic backgrounds. These readers, to whom Sarton refers as "Friends of the Work," often find her journals and memoirs uncannily reminiscent of their own experience of love and family, as well as evoking the beauty and healing power of the natural world.

Sarton distinguishes between "journals," selective accounts of day-to-day experience, and "memoirs," distilled reflections on the past. The most powerful of the journals, such as *Recovering*, *Journal of a Solitude*, and *The House by the Sea*, achieve an aesthetic integrity seldom seen in the journal form. The most widely known of the memoirs, *Plant Dreaming Deep*, confirmed Sarton's reputation as a writer acutely sensitive to issues of aging, both as metaphor for human limitation, and, more important, as opportunity for positive growth. Sarton's literary career embraces more than a half-century of experimentation and achievement in a wide variety of literary forms. At the height of her power, she celebrates with style and profound insight the life of artist and lover.

BIBLIOGRAPHICAL REFERENCES: Agnes Sibley, *May Sarton*, 1972, the first full-length study of Sarton's poetry and prose, is a general introduction to the works, and a later treatment is available in Elizabeth Evans, *May Sarton Revisited*, 1989; both are volumes in the Twayne World Authors series. A more comprehensive treatment of Sarton's themes can be found in *May Sarton: Woman and Poet*, 1982, edited by Constance Hunting. This collection of essays also includes interviews with the poet and an annotated bibliography of primary and secondary sources prior to 1982. Since 1978, a number of perceptive articles have appeared in feminist journals, including Annis Pratt, "Aunt Jennifer's Tigers: Notes Toward a Preliterary History of Women's Archetypes," *Feminist Studies*, 1978, 163-194; Marlene Springer, "As We Shall Be: May Sarton and Aging," *Frontiers*, 1980, 46-49; and Kathleen Woodward, "May Sarton and Fictions of Old Age," *Women and Literature*, 1980, 108-127. In her book *Inspiring Women: Reimagining the Muse*, 1986, Mary DeShazer includes a chapter on Sarton's poetry, " 'Toward Durable Fire': The Solitary Muse of May Sarton."

Susan Swartzlander
Marilyn Mumford

JEAN-PAUL SARTRE

Born: Paris, France
Date: June 21, 1905

Died: Paris, France
Date: April 15, 1980

Principal Works

NOVELS: *La Nausée*, 1938 (*Nausea*, 1949); *Les Chemins de la liberté*, 1945-1949 (*The Roads to Freedom*, 1947-1950), includes *L'Âge de raison* (*The Age of Reason*), *Le Sursis* (*The Reprieve*), and *La Mort dans l'âme* (*Troubled Sleep*).

SHORT FICTION: *Le Mur*, 1939 (*The Wall and Other Stories*, 1948).

PLAYS: *Les Mouches*, pr., pb. 1943 (*The Flies*, 1946); *Huis-Clos*, pr. 1944 (*No Exit*, 1946); *Morts sans sépulture*, pr., pb. 1946 (*The Victors*, 1948); *La Putain respectueuse*, pr., pb. 1946 (*The Respectful Prostitute*, 1947); *Les Mains sales*, pr., pb. 1948 (*Dirty Hands*, 1948); *Le Diable et le Bon Dieu*, pr. 1951 (*The Devil and the Good Lord*, 1953); *Kean: Ou, Désordre et génie*, pb. 1952; *Nekrassov*, pr. 1955 (English translation, 1956); *Les Séquestrés d'Altona*, pr. 1959 (*The Condemned of Altona*, 1960); *Les Troyennes*, 1965 (*The Trojan Women*, 1967).

NONFICTION: *L'Imaginaire: Psychologie phénoménologique de l'imagination*, 1940 (*The Psychology of Imagination*, 1948); *L'Être et le néant*, 1943 (*Being and Nothingness*, 1956); *L'Existentialisme est un humanisme*, 1946 (*Existentialism*, 1947); *Réflexions sur la question juive*, 1946 (*Anti-Semite and Jew*, 1948); *Baudelaire*, 1946 (English translation, 1950); *Situations I-X*, 1947-1975; *Saint-Genet: Comédien et martyr*, 1952 (*Saint Genet: Actor and Martyr*, 1963); *Critique de la raison dialectique, I: Théorie des ensembles pratiques*, 1960 (*Critique of Dialectical Reason, I: Theory of Practical Ensembles*, 1976); *Les Mots*, 1963 (*The Words*, 1964); *L'Idiot de la famille: Gustave Flaubert, 1821-1857*, 1981; *Un Théâtre de situations*, 1972 (*Sartre on Theater*, 1976); *Les Carnets de la drôle de guerre*, 1983 (*The War Diaries of Jean-Paul Sartre: November, 1939-March, 1940*, 1985); *Le Scénario Freud*, 1984 (*The Freud Scenario*, 1985).

Philosopher, playwright, novelist, editor, and critic, Jean-Paul Sartre dominated European intellectual life for two decades following World War II. He was born in Paris on June 21, 1905, the son of a naval engineer, Jean-Baptiste, who died when the child was only fifteen months old. His mother, Anne-Marie, took the child with her to live with her parents, the Schweitzers, in Alsace, where, as later recounted in his autobiography *The Words*, the boy felt he was the center of the universe. Yet his idyll was dispelled when, at the age of ten, he was sent to a Paris school and, a year later, his adored mother was remarried.

A brilliant and contentious student of philosophy, Sartre was thirty-three years old when his first literary work was published. He taught philosophy in a *lycée* in provincial Le Havre, where, despondent over aging in obscurity, he began writing the meditation on solitude that evolved into the short, spare, and challenging novel *Nausea*. This fictive diary of a solitary, unsuccessful biographer traumatized by his discovery of the contingency of any life remained Sartre's greatest achievement in fiction; however, contemptuous of art's evasions, he was later to repudiate it, as well as the short stories in *The Wall and Other Stories* and the three completed volumes of a projected tetralogy entitled *The Roads to Freedom*.

Mobilized at the outbreak of World War II and captured by the Germans, Sartre wrote his first plays and began to develop ideas on solidarity and freedom while in prison camp. After his release, Sartre spent most of the war years in Paris, writing prolifically. As editor of *Les Temps modernes*, the leftist magazine he cofounded in 1944, and as literary and political gadfly, Sartre became the celebrated center of a group of influential Left Bank intellectuals. Not least of these was Simone de Beauvoir, the pioneer feminist he had met before the war who became his devoted companion for some fifty years, though they rejected marriage and each pursued affairs with others.

While France was still under the German occupation, Sartre wrote stage works that dramatized human beings in urgent situations requiring the enlightened exercise of freedom. Though it makes use of ancient myth, *The Flies*, for example, was a call to French audiences to take responsibility for their subjection to a foreign power. Also produced during the Occupation was Sartre's most frequently performed play, *No Exit*, a drama set in Hell about three characters who each choose an inauthentic identity. After the war, Sartre continued to use theater to promulgate his philosophical and political ideas.

A prominent public figure who eventually abandoned fiction and theater for polemics and political action, Sartre traveled throughout the world, arousing controversy with his attacks on Soviet and American policies. He supported Algerian and Israeli independence and condemned the Soviet invasion of Hungary, the American war in Vietnam, and South African apartheid. In 1964, shortly after publication of *The Words*, Sartre was awarded the Nobel Prize in Literature. Yet, in a dramatic gesture motivated by scorn for what he viewed as the coercive categories of bourgeois society, Sartre refused to accept the prestigious award. He courted controversy again in 1968, when, during the Paris student rebellion, Sartre defied arrest in supporting youthful radicals. In failing health for the last two decades of his life, Sartre became a living icon, though he was still at work on his massive, obsessive biography of Gustave Flaubert when he died, of uremia, on April 15, 1980.

Dubbed "the pope of existentialism," Sartre was the acknowledged leader of an extremely fashionable but elusive movement in modern philosophy. Raymond Aaron, Albert Camus, Arthur Koestler, and Maurice Merleau-Ponty were among others associated with the school, and they were also companions with whom the truculent Sartre eventually had a quarrel. *Being and Nothingness*, his most thorough and systematic statement of existentialist philosophy, is a forbiddingly dense, copious examination of key concepts, including those of contingency, consciousness, and bad faith. *Existentialism*, originally a lecture Sartre gave to defend and popularize his ideas, is a more accessible version of the existentialist credo. Existentialism attracted fierce devotion from acolytes and vehement rage from others, but Sartre refused to be typecast even in a philosophy opposed to categories. Others of his many writings also blended Marxist and Freudian ideas.

Sartre delighted in his own metamorphoses, his numerous shifts of approach, activity, and opinion. A stubborn man of enormous and varied energies arrayed in battle against the complacencies of middle-class conventions, he was proudly tendentious. Many others, including his detractors, saw him as he saw himself: as the conscience of a nation and an era. Beyond Sartre's seminal work in fiction, philosophy, and theater, the cunning dialectician and official dissident will be remembered for the range of his accomplishments and for the awesome role of intellectual that he defined for himself and for others.

BIBLIOGRAPHICAL REFERENCES: Annie Cohen-Solal, *Sartre: A Life*, 1987, draws on a wealth of documentary materials and interviews with hundreds of the author's acquaintances to produce the most thorough and absorbing biography of Sartre. Also useful, Ronald Hayman, *Sartre: A Life*, 1987. Axel Madsen, *Hearts and Minds: The Common Journey of Jean-Paul Sartre and Simone de Beauvoir*, 1977, traces the parallel and converging lives of Sartre and his longtime companion; *Adieux: A Farewell to Sartre*, 1984, is de Beauvoir's own memoir of Sartre's daily routine during the last decade of his life as well as a transcription of valedictory conversations between the two authors. Catharine Savage Brosman, *Jean-Paul Sartre*, 1983, provides a short and accessible but incisive overview of Sartre's career and of secondary work about him, while Peter Caws, *Sartre*, 1979, offers a more formidably technical study that concentrates on Sartrean philosophy. That philosophy is approached from several perspectives in the essays collected in *The Philosophy of Jean-Paul Sartre*, 1981, edited by Paul A. Schilpp. Max Charlesworth, *The Existentialists and Jean-Paul Sartre*, 1976, examines when and whether Sartre was an "existentialist," and Germaine Brée, *Camus and Sartre: Crisis and Commitment*, 1972, compares and contrasts Sartre to another important French author usually associated with that movement. Steven G. Kellman, "*La Nausée*," in *The Self-*

Begetting Novel, 1980, studies Sartre's most influential novel as an example of reflexive fiction. Dorothy McCall, *The Theatre of Jean-Paul Sartre*, 1969, examines Sartre as playwright. For additional overviews, see Hazel E. Barnes, *Sartre*, 1973; Simon Glynn, *Sartre: An Investigation of Some Major Themes*, 1987; and Brian Masters, *Sartre: A Study*, 1974.

Steven G. Kellman

FERDINAND DE SAUSSURE

Born: Geneva, Switzerland
Date: November 26, 1857

Died: Geneva, Switzerland
Date: February 22, 1913

PRINCIPAL WORKS

LINGUISTICS AND PHILOLOGY: *Mémoire sur le système primitif des voyelles dans les langues indo-européennes*, 1879; *Cours de linguistique générale*, 1916 (*Course in General Linguistics*, 1959).

Ferdinand de Saussure is regarded by most scholars as the creator of modern linguistics—the scientific, objective study of language. Although he published only a few papers and no major works during his lifetime, the lecture notes of his students have been collected and edited into one of the most influential texts of modern linguistics, *Course in General Linguistics*. His major accomplishment was to establish the systematic study of language as an objective subject; he also pointed the way to the development of the discipline of semiology, or the study of signs and the system of signs.

Born into a family distinguished for its intellectual achievements, Saussure was introduced to the study of language at an early age. By the time he was fifteen, he had mastered Greek, Latin, French, German, and English. In 1875 he entered the University of Geneva, first intending to study physics and chemistry; after one year he transferred to the University of Leipzig and switched to the study of language. It was an apt choice in schools, for Leipzig was the center of the *Junggrammatiker* (young grammarians), who were attempting to bring to language study something of the rigor and objectivity of the natural sciences.

In 1879, Saussure published *Mémoire sur le système primitif des voyelles dans les langues indo-européennes* (memoir on the primitive system of vowels in the Indo-European languages), a breathtaking work of scholarship that won immediate and widespread attention and acclaim. Completing his doctorate at Leipzig, Saussure moved to Paris, where he taught at the École Pratique des Hautes Études until 1891, when he returned to the University of Geneva as a professor. At Geneva Saussure taught a number of courses, but most notable were the classes in general linguistics that he gave from 1906 through 1911. The lecture notes of his students from these classes were gathered by Charles Bally and Albert Sechehaye and edited into *Course in General Linguistics*. Saussure himself published no complete or comprehensive view of his theories; he died at the relatively young age of fifty-five, in February, 1913.

Saussure's central accomplishment was to place the study of language on a scientific basis, and this he accomplished through a logical series of steps that provided the proper foundation for all future examinations. First, Saussure admitted that language was a complex phenomenon, and the initial task was to determine how to approach it. He noted that language is a system of signs, in which the individual units of a particular language make sense (that is, communicate) only as part of an overall system. The smallest unit in this system is the linguistic sign. Often (but not always) a word, the linguistic sign is the smallest unit of meaning in a language. It is composed of two parts, the *signifiant*, or signifier, and the *signifie*, or the signified. In the broadest sense, these might be called sound and meaning, respectively. When they are linked together (as the sounds of *d-o-g* are with the concept of a certain animal), a linguistic sign is created.

The linguistic sign is arbitrary; that is, there is no natural link between the two parts. This point is of key importance to Saussure, because it forces the realization that the linguistic sign is part of a system and must fit into a pattern; it has no independent existence. Saussure used the analogy of language and chess: It matters not whether a knight is made of wood, marble, or metal, only that it moves in certain ways in relation to all the other chess pieces. Like the knight, the individual units of a language are part of a system.

The system of language is expressed through the medium of sound, but there is a fundamental difference between the system and its physical expression. The expression is the substance of language, but the system is its form, and Saussure pointed out that form must take precedence over substance in language study. He demonstrated this by his emphasis on two essential dichotomies in language.

First, language can be synchronic or diachronic. That is, language can be studied at a single moment in time (synchronic) or as it develops across time (diachronic). While a diachronic examination will reveal that languages change their sounds and substances—for example, Latin became French, Spanish, and Italian—it also demonstrates that the languages always retained a coherent system that allowed speakers to communicate at any given moment. Furthermore, the sound changes that take place across time happen without apparent reason and without exception. This reinforces the central concepts that the particular linguistic sign is arbitrary and that the overall pattern is the key to language.

Second, Saussure made a critical distinction between *la langue* and *parole*. *La langue* is the overall system of language, while *parole* is its realization in actual speech. There will be differences in pronunciation, vocabulary choice, and other items between different speakers of a language—an inevitable aspect of *parole*. Yet as long as the pattern remains consistent, understanding and communication will be maintained, which is the strength of *la langue*. The existence of these two aspects of language explains why a single language can have greatly differing dialects and yet remain a coherent whole.

Reviewed after their enunciation by Saussure, these fundamentals of linguistics might seem simple, even obvious; yet they represented a startling breakthrough in the study of language and made possible the achievements of modern linguistics.

BIBLIOGRAPHICAL REFERENCES: The essential English-language work is Saussure's *Course in General Linguistics*, 1959, edited by Charles Bally and Albert Sechehaye, with Albert Reidlinger, and translated by Wade Baskin. It must be kept in mind that this book is a collection and edited version of the lecture notes of Saussure's students, and its organization and emphasis are that of the compilers, not Saussure himself. Still, it is probably the central text for all modern linguistics—a truly seminal work. The best starting place for study of Saussure and his theories is Jonathan Culler, *Ferdinand de Saussure*, 1986 (rev. ed.). This slim volume is clear, accurate, and perceptive. Culler's study moves beyond linguistics to relate Saussure to broader developments in modern philosophy, science, and even art. Hans Aarsleff's essay "Taine and Saussure," in *From Locke to Saussure: Essays on the Study of Language and Intellectual History*, 1982, provides more depth and detail and also places Saussure within the context of developments in linguistics, helpful in revealing how novel his thoughts were. More of this theme is explored in Roy Harris' well-written work *The Language Makers*, 1980. An in-depth review of the subject can be found in E. F. K. Koerner, *Ferdinand de Saussure: Origin and Development of His Linguistic Thought in Western Studies of Language*, 1973. For an overview of Saussure, two works by Robert Robins are available: *General Linguistics*, 1965, provides the necessary background knowledge of the discipline, while *A Short History of Linguistics*, 1967, is, as the title implies, a review of changes and developments in the field. Together with Philip Davis, *Modern Theories of Language*, 1973, these works give the reader the knowledge needed to appreciate Saussure and his thought.

Michael Witkoski

DOROTHY L. SAYERS

Born: Oxford, England
Date: June 13, 1893

Died: Witham, England
Date: December 17, 1957

PRINCIPAL WORKS

MYSTERY AND DETECTIVE FICTION: *Whose Body?*, 1923; *Clouds of Witness*, 1926; *Unnatural Death*, 1927; *The Unpleasantness at the Bellona Club*, 1928; *Lord Peter Views the Body*, 1928; *The Documents in the Case*, 1930 (with Robert Eustace); *Strong Poison*, 1930; *The Five Red Herrings*, 1931; *The Floating Admiral*, 1931 (with others); *Have His Carcase*, 1932; *Murder Must Advertise*, 1933; *Hangman's Holiday*, 1933; *Ask a Policeman*, 1933 (with others); *The Nine Tailors*, 1934; *Gaudy Night*, 1935; *Six Against the Yard*, 1936 (with others); *Busman's Honeymoon*, 1937; *Double Death: A Murder Story*, 1939 (with others); *In the Teeth of the Evidence and Other Stories*, 1939; *A Treasury of Sayers Stories*, 1958; *Lord Peter: A Collection of All the Lord Peter Wimsey Stories*, 1972; *Striding Folly*, 1972.

PLAYS: *Busman's Honeymoon*, pr. 1936 (with Muriel St. Clare Byrne); *The Zeal of Thy House*, pr., pb. 1937; *The Devil to Pay, Being the Famous History of John Faustus*, pr., pb. 1939; *Love All*, pr. 1940; *The Just Vengeance*, pr., pb. 1946; *The Emperor Constantine: A Chronicle*, pr. 1951 (revised as *Christ's Emperor*, 1952).

RADIO PLAYS: *He That Should Come: A Nativity Play*, pr. 1938; *The Man Born to Be King: A Play-Cycle on the Life of Our Lord and Saviour Jesus Christ*, pr. 1941-1942.

POETRY: *Op. 1*, 1916; *Catholic Tales and Christian Songs*, 1918; *Lord, I Thank Thee—*, 1943; *The Story of Adam and Christ*, 1955.

NONFICTION: *The Mysterious English*, 1941; *The Mind of the Maker*, 1941; *Unpopular Opinions*, 1946; *Creed or Chaos? and Other Essays in Popular Theology*, 1947; *The Days of Christ's Coming*, 1953, revised 1960; *The Story of Easter*, 1955; *The Story of Noah's Ark*, 1955; *Christian Letters to a Post-Christian World*, 1969; *Wilkie Collins: A Critical and Biographical Study*, 1977.

Dorothy Leigh Sayers is one of the world's most admired mystery writers and her detective, Lord Peter Wimsey, one of its most celebrated fictional sleuths. Sayers was the only child of an Anglican clergyman and his wife; her childhood was spent in Oxford and in England's bleak Fen country, both of which would later serve as settings for her novels. Educated at home until she was fifteen, she attended the Godolphin School in Salisbury and later entered the University of Oxford, where she studied modern languages and became one of the first women to receive a degree. In the years that followed, she worked as a teacher and as a reader and editor for Blackwell's, an Oxford company that published two volumes of her religious poetry, before taking a job in 1922 with a London advertising firm. She continued to work as an advertising copywriter for nearly a decade, until the success of her novels permitted her to devote herself full-time to her writing.

In 1923, Sayers embarked on her career as a mystery writer with *Whose Body?*, the first of the Lord Peter Wimsey books. Wimsey is an amateur sleuth; the witty, brilliant second son of the fifteenth Duke of Denver, he wears a monocle, collects rare books, quotes liberally from the classics, and occasionally undertakes a bit of detective work, assisted by his manservant, Bunter. Yet Wimsey's outwardly frivolous manner masks an inner depth of character that Sayers would develop as the series continued, allowing him to grow and change in a manner unlike most fictional detectives. Although Wimsey initially undertakes crime solving as little more than a diverting hobby, by the third book, *Unnatural Death*, Sayers is exploring her detective's moral qualms over the resolution of the case. Later books find Wimsey, who suffered a nervous breakdown following his service in World War I, falling into deep depression after bringing a criminal to justice.

Sayers herself was living a far from conventional life during the early years of the Wimsey series; as a member of London's bohemian artistic society, she entered into several brief love affairs and secretly bore an illegitimate son, who was reared by her cousin. Although she married Oswald Arthur Fleming in 1926, her earlier experiences would find their way obliquely into *Strong Poison*, the novel that introduces Harriet Vane. Like her creator, Harriet is a brilliant onetime Oxford scholar, a writer of detective fiction, and a member of London's bohemian subculture; when Wimsey encounters her, she is on trial for the murder of her former lover. The Wimsey-Vane romance would stretch over seven years, four novels—*Strong Poison*, *Have His Carcase*, *Gaudy Night*, and *Busman's Honeymoon*—and two short stories, causing several critics to note with amusement that their author appeared to have fallen in love with her own detective and effectively written herself into his life. Wimsey gradually drops the aristocratic mannerisms that mark his style in the series' earlier entries as he examines himself through Harriet's eyes and sets about reshaping his life with a new determination and purpose.

Interspersed with the four "Harriet Vane" novels are three Wimsey books and several short-story collections, including *Murder Must Advertise*, which draws on Sayers' years in advertising as Lord Peter takes a job at an agency while investigating a murder, and *The Nine Tailors*, a book praised by many critics as not only the best of the Wimsey novels but also one of the best mysteries ever written. Set in a small country village, the story is an elaborate puzzle that hinges on the art of bell ringing, and its well-drawn characters, vividly evoked setting, and intricate plotting offer ample proof of Sayers' talents as a writer.

Despite her popularity as a mystery writer, Sayers abandoned the form in the late 1930's to devote herself entirely to religious writings and scholarship. During the last twenty years of her life, she published several collections of essays, including *Creed or Chaos? and Other Essays in Popular Theology* and *Unpopular Opinions*, which analyze the moral and ethical dilemmas of the modern world. Her work *The Mind of the Maker* explores Christianity through the idea of God as a creative artist. She also enjoyed success as a dramatist, both on the radio with *The Man Born to Be King*, a twelve-part series on the life of Christ, and on the stage with *The Devil to Pay* and *The Emperor Constantine*. In her later years, Sayers published several translations of classic works.

It is as a mystery writer, however, that Sayers remains best known, and she is often credited with helping to bring the genre into the twentieth century through her well-developed, three-dimensional characters and her experimentations in plotting and criminal methodology. Sayers' wide-ranging interests and traditional education in the classics make her novels among the most literate of the genre, although her detractors—who include authors Rex Stout and Julian Symons—describe her books as snobbish and socially conservative and Wimsey as an aristocratic prig. Her fluidity and skill as a writer, however, have won praise from her many admirers, including mystery author P. D. James. Certainly Sayers' work has stood the test of time; her books remain continually in print, and her name appears repeatedly on lists of influential mystery writers.

BIBLIOGRAPHICAL REFERENCES: James Brabazon, *Dorothy L. Sayers: The Life of a Courageous Woman*, 1981, offers a well-researched and interesting portrait of Sayers' life. Janet Hitchman, *Such a Strange Lady*, 1975, combines biographical information with a literary analysis of Sayers' work, as does Ralph E. Hone, *Dorothy L. Sayers: A Literary Biography*, 1979. Trevor H. Hall, *Dorothy L. Sayers: Nine Literary Studies*, 1980, adopts a historical perspective in analyzing Sayers' work and also contains reminiscences by her acquaintances. *As Her Whimsey Took Her: Critical Essays on the Work of Dorothy L. Sayers*, 1979, edited by Margaret P. Hannay, contains a collection of critical essays as well as a listing of collections containing letters and unpublished manuscripts. Nancy M. Tischler, *Dorothy L. Sayers: A Pilgrim Soul*, 1980, focuses specifically on Sayers' religious writing and is useful for those with an interest in her nonfiction. See also SueEllen Campbell, "The Detective Heroine and the Death of Her Hero: Dorothy Sayers to P. D. James," *Modern Fiction Studies*, XXIX

(Autumn, 1983), 497; Donald G. Marshall, "Gaudy Night: An Investigation of Truth," *VII: An Anglo-American Literary Review*, IV (1983), 98; and Lionel Basney, "God and Peter Wimsey," *Christianity Today*, XVII (September 14, 1973), 27.

Janet E. Lorenz

ARTHUR SCHNITZLER

Born: Vienna, Austria
Date: May 15, 1862

Died: Vienna, Austria
Date: October 21, 1931

PRINCIPAL WORKS

PLAYS: *Anatol*, pr., pb. 1893 (English translation, 1911); *Liebelei*, pr. 1895 (*Light-O'-Love*, 1912); *Freiwild*, pr. 1896 (*Free Game*, 1913); *Der grüne Kakadu*, pr., pb. 1899 (*The Green Cockatoo*, 1913); *Reigen*, pb. 1900 (*Hands Around*, 1920); *Der einsame Weg*, pr., pb. 1904 (*The Lonely Way*, 1915); *Der tapfere Kassian*, pr. 1904 (*Gallant Cassian*, 1914); *Komtesse Mizzi: Oder, Der Familientag*, pb. 1907 (*Countess Mizzi*, 1907); *Professor Bernhardi*, pr., pb. 1912 (English translation, 1913).

SHORT FICTION: *Sterben*, 1895; *Leutnant Gustl*, 1900 (*None but the Brave*, 1925); *Der blinde Geronimo und sein Bruder*, 1900 (*The Blind Geronimo and His Brother*, 1913); *Frau Bertha Garlan*, 1901 (*Bertha Garlen*, 1913); *Die Hirtenflöte*, 1911 (*The Shepherd's Pipe*, 1922); *Der Mörder*, 1911 (*The Murderer*, 1922); *Frau Beate und ihr Sohn*, 1913 (*Beatrice*, 1926); *Viennese Idylls*, 1913; *The Shepherd's Pipe and Other Stories*, 1922; *Fräulein Else*, 1924 (English translation, 1925); *Traumnovelle*, 1926 (*Rhapsody*, 1927); *Little Novels*, 1929; *Viennese Novelettes*, 1931.

NOVELS: *Der Weg ins Freie*, 1908 (*The Road to Open*, 1923); *Casanovas heimfahrt*, 1918 (*Casanova's Homecoming*, 1921); *Spiel im Morgengrauen*, 1927 (*Daybreak*, 1927); *Therese*, 1928 (*Theresa: The Chronicle of a Woman's Life*, 1928); *Flucht in die Finsternis*, 1931 (*Flight into Darkness*, 1931).

AUTOBIOGRAPHY: *Jugend in Wien*, 1968 (*My Youth in Vienna*, 1970).

Arthur Schnitzler was one of the most prominent writers living in the city of Vienna during the highly productive and creative late-nineteenth, early-twentieth century era that produced individuals such as Sigmund Freud, Ludwig Wittgenstein, and Johannes Brahms. Born in that city on May 15, 1862, he was the son of a famous Jewish professor of medicine and became himself a practicing physician upon graduation from the University of Vienna in 1885. For a time he was involved in studies in depth psychology. He was, however, more interested in a literary career and rather unsuccessful as a man of medicine. Schnitzler was somewhat of a dandy and a compulsive seducer but was at the same time always a keen observer of his own and his contemporaries' behavior. He married in 1903 and had several children, one of whom, his daughter Lili, committed suicide in 1928. Schnitzler died on October 21, 1931, in Vienna and is buried there.

From 1888 to 1891, Schnitzler worked on the *Anatol* cycle of loosely connected dialogue sketches centering on the romantic obsessions of the young and frivolous bachelor Anatol, who, like a social butterfly, becomes infatuated with a new woman—and attempts to seduce her—in every scene. The overwhelming mood of the sketches is one of a melancholy boredom, as Anatol, in repetitive but vain attempts, seeks to gain some sense of the authentic experience of himself and others. He is never able to penetrate to his true emotions and remains fixed in an illusory vision of life. *Light-O'-Love* depicts two young frivolous women, Mizi and Christine, working girls from the outskirts of Vienna, who pursue love affairs with men of higher social status, in the vain illusion that they might elevate their class position. They are the prototypes of Schnitzler's frequent character figures, the "sweet girl" (*süsses Mädel*), a kind of young, lower-class woman common to Viennese social circles and with whom the author was very familiar in his personal life. The young men of the play take such affairs and seductions lightly and the ending is inevitably tragic. One of the men, Fritz, is killed in a duel because he has seduced a married woman. *The Green Cockatoo* is another of Schnitzler's well-known one-act plays and takes place in France at the time of the 1789 revolution. As in many of his works, the action of this play revolves around the differences between reality and appearance, the typically Austrian theme of the theatricality of life.

Hands Around is the best known of Schnitzler's plays and depicts a series of ten separate scenes involving a group of characters who have sex and go on to exchange partners in a cycle that links them to each other like a daisy chain. The series involves individuals from all levels of Viennese society. Because the scenes center so unabashedly on the sex act—the couples have nothing else to share except superficial talk—the play was banned from performance and publication in Germany and was involved in a court trial in Berlin in 1921. As in the earlier pieces, Schnitzler gives a devastating portrait of a decadent society in which people pursue fleeting sensations and in which true human interaction is reduced to a mere game of vanity and sexual conquest. The primacy of sexuality in Schnitzler's plays and his keen observations of its role in motivating behavior once prompted Freud—who was doing his scientific work on sexuality and the psyche at the same time Schnitzler was writing his plays—to call the author his "double." Both men seemed to be commenting on the same psychological phenomena from different perspectives.

The play *Professor Bernhardi* treats the issue of anti-Semitism, a common social and political experience in Vienna during Schnitzler's time. A young Austrian, Adolf Hitler, was preaching his message of racial hatred at the time Schnitzler was working on the play. A Jewish doctor, Bernhardi, refuses to disturb the peace of a young Catholic girl, who is unaware that she is dying, by calling in a priest. An ugly incident ensues, and Bernhardi loses his position and is sent to prison. Schnitzler pointedly exposes a largely Christian society that, despite its commitment to brotherly love, is motivated by racial hatred, envy, and blatant stupidity. Schnitzler was also a prolific writer of narrative literature. *None but the Brave* is one of his most often read stories and deals with the young Lieutenant Gustl, who, after an opera performance, has a small confrontation in the lobby with a man of the lower classes. Since Gustl feels that his precious honor has been besmirched, he agonizes over the essentially trivial event, even considering suicide. Gustl is much like Schnitzler's other male characters, a basically frivolous and vain personality who courts more the appearance than the substance of life. He manages to rationalize away the seriousness of the event and talk himself out of suicide. The text is written in an innovative narrative style that attempts to record Gustl's flighty thought processes. *The Road to the Open* presents a critical vision of Vienna during Schnitzler's life. The novel examines a young artist and aesthete who undergoes a spiritual transformation when his lover sacrifices herself for his career.

Casanova's Homecoming depicts the aging lover in his obsessive search for a final conquest. He murders a young man who is a youthful version of himself. Like *None but the Brave*, the well-known story *Fräulein Else* also uses a narrative technique of recording the often nonlinear strains of the character's consciousness. It deals with an event in the life of a somewhat psychologically unstable young woman who becomes the victim of the sexual manipulations of an older man. The vain pursuit of sexuality and sensation versus the quest for authentic meaning in life characterizes these later narrative texts, as they do the majority of Schnitzler's writings.

BIBLIOGRAPHICAL REFERENCES: For interpretive studies in English, see Martin Swales, *Arthur Schnitzler: A Critical Study*, 1971; *Arthur Schnitzler*, 1973, translated by Reinhard Urbach and Donald G. Daviau; and *Arthur Schnitzler and His Age*, 1984, edited by Petrus W. Tax and Richard H. Lawson. Excellent studies written in German are Reinhard Urbach, *Arthur Schnitzler*, 1968; Renate Wagner, *Frauen um Schnitzler*, 1980; *Arthur Schnitzler in neuer Sicht*, 1981, edited by Hartmut Scheible; Rolf Allerdissen, *Arthur Schnitzler: Impressionistisches Rollenspiel und skeptischer Moralismus un seinen Erzählungen*, 1985. See also Richard Plaut, "Notes on Schnitzler's Literary Technique," *The Germanic Review*, XXV (1950), 13-25; Heinz Politzer, "Arthur Schnitzler: Poetry of Psychology," *Modern Language Notes*, LXXVIII (1963), 353-372; Martin Swales, "Arthur Schnitzler as a Moralist," *Modern Language Review*, LXII, no. 3 (1967), 462-475; Robert O. Weiss, "The Psychoses in the Works of

Arthur Schnitzler," *The German Quarterly*, XLI (1968), 377-400; Marie Grote, "Themes and Variations in the Early Prose Fiction of Arthur Schnitzler," *Modern Austrian Literature*, III, no. 4 (1970), 22-47; Maria P. Alter, "Schnitzler's Physician: An Existential Character," *Modern Austrian Literature*, IV, no. 3 (1971), 7-23; Wolfgang Nehring, "Schnitzler, Freud's Alter Ego?" *Modern Austrian Literature*, X (1977), 179-194; and Theodor W. Alexander, "Arthur Schnitzler's Use of Mirrors," *Seminar*, XIV (1978), 187-194.

Thomas F. Barry

BRUNO SCHULZ

Born: Drohobycz, Poland
Date: July 12, 1892

Died: Drohobycz, Soviet Union
Date: November 19, 1942

Principal Works

SHORT FICTION: *Sklepy cynamonowe*, 1933 (*The Street of Crocodiles*, 1963); *Sanatorium pod klepsydrą*, 1936 (*Sanatorium Under the Sign of the Hourglass*, 1978).

MISCELLANEOUS: *Proza*, 1964; *Księga listów*, 1975 (*Letters and Drawings of Bruno Schulz, with Selected Prose*, 1988); *Listy, fragmenty, wspomnienia o pisarzu*, 1984.

Bruno Schulz is one of the greatest figures in Polish modernist literature of the period between world wars and one of the most original European fiction writers in the first half of the twentieth century. He was born in the small town of Drohobycz in the Polish province of Galicia (then part of the Austro-Hungarian Empire; today part of the Soviet Ukraine), the son of a Jewish merchant, Jakub Schulz, and his wife, Henrietta Schulz. His family's faith was Mosaic, but the language they mostly spoke was Polish. Schulz himself went a step further than his parents toward cultural assimilation by not adhering to any specific religious creed and writing exclusively in Polish (except for one short story written in German, which unfortunately has not survived). A morbidly shy and reticent man, tormented all of his life by an inferiority complex and a sense of inadequacy, Schulz was also burdened with all the psychological consequences of his status as an outsider. He entered Polish literature as a member of an ethnic minority, a first-generation intellectual, and a newcomer from a remote province. This fact perhaps explains why from the very beginning he cared so much about the stylistic mastery of his prose: In order to be taken seriously, he had no choice but to dazzle the critics with an unquestionable brilliance.

One of the most striking characteristics of Schulz is the contrast between his rich, fertile, unbridled imagination and the fact that he spent virtually all of his life in his backwater hometown of Drohobycz. After being graduated from the local high school in 1910, he did spend five years in Lvov and Vienna, studying architecture and painting; however, for the rest of his life he resided mainly in Drohobycz, toiling as an underpaid, overworked high school teacher of arts and crafts. Drohobycz finally became the place and cause of his death as well. Schulz was caught there by the Soviet invasion in 1939 and the Nazi one in 1941. Under the German occupation, he survived for a while thanks to a Gestapo agent who hired him to decorate his house. During a roundup on November 19, 1942, however, he was shot by another Gestapo agent, who held some grudge against Schulz's protector.

As his surviving letters show, throughout his life Schulz was painfully aware that his creative potential was being constantly stifled by the pressure of everyday reality. Another paradox of his career is the contrast between his remarkable accomplishment as a writer and the meagerness of his output: His entire oeuvre consists of two slender collections of short stories, along with a few volumes of letters and essays. Indeed, everything in his life, from his poverty to his pathological shyness, seemed to conspire to keep his productivity at a minimum level and delay his recognition as much as possible. He began to write rather late in his life, in the mid-1920's, switching to literature from graphic arts. In fact, his first publication was a portfolio of etchings he distributed as a limited edition in the early 1920's. Characteristically, Schulz's beginnings as a writer stemmed from his correspondence, which for him was the principal way to maintain contact with the external world. His early short stories were originally written as postscripts to his letters to a female friend, the writer Debora Vogel. Collected as *The Street of Crocodiles*, the stories were published thanks to the enthusiastic support of the influential novelist Zofia Nałkowska. (As legend has it, she had agreed reluctantly to read the manuscript of this unknown author only because the request had come from a mutual friend.)

Schulz's first book met with critical acclaim, even though its success was limited to the circles of the literary avant-garde. Significantly, the two authors who wrote the most penetrating analyses of Schulz's work in the 1930's were two other representatives of what was then most innovative in Polish literature: the novelist and playwright Stanisław Ignacy Witkiewicz and the novelist Witold Gombrowicz. In 1936, buoyed by the favorable reception of *The Street of Crocodiles*, Schulz published *Sanatorium Under the Sign of the Hourglass*, another collection of short stories composed in part of his earlier writings. These two collections differ only slightly. Both are written in lyrical and stylistically luxuriant prose, and both use the setting of a Drohobycz-like provincial town as the point of departure for a complex interplay of realism and fantasy. The only difference is perhaps that *The Street of Crocodiles* is a more tightly knit collection of stories sharing the same characters, whereas *Sanatorium Under the Sign of the Hourglass* has a much looser composition. Its longer and more complex fictional constructions (including the full short story "The Spring") apparently foreshadowed Schulz's only novelistic undertaking.

Since 1934 he had been working intermittently on his novel "Mesjasz" (messiah); apart from two fragments included as separate stories in his second collection, though, the text of this novel, in all probability never completed, perished during the war. Besides short stories, drawings, and letters (the latter preserved only in small part), Schulz's surviving output also includes a number of brilliant essays and book reviews, scattered in prewar Polish periodicals. Most of these critical works, such as the essay "The Mythologizing of Reality," show him as a perspicacious and profound theorist with a clear, consistent set of original ideas concerning the role and significance of literature.

Schulz's name is often mentioned in one breath with those of two other great innovators in prewar Polish literature, Witkiewicz and Gombrowicz. Yet his singular achievement is a combined result of his innovation and his dependence on a specific tradition. He owes much to the spirit of modernist literature of the last decades of the Austro-Hungarian Empire. In his own way, Schulz continued the tradition of expressing the fundamental problems of human existence in the language of myth or subconscious symbolism. In order to reach back to this language's original sources, he often explores the materials of dream, childlike imaginings, erotic fantasy, or popular culture. Metaphor is the chief device that enables him to imitate the peculiar poetics of these layers of imagination and reproduce mythologized reality's constant metamorphoses. Schulz's metaphors, however, create rather than reproduce. In his work, the author-narrator emerges as a demiurgic maker of the world represented. While burdening him with a sense of sinful transgression and guilt, this kind of usurpation of divine prerogative also results in his ironic detachment, adding to the semantic complexity of his prose.

BIBLIOGRAPHICAL REFERENCES: The Penguin editions of *The Street of Crocodiles*, 1977, and *Sanatorium Under the Sign of the Hourglass*, 1979, both translated by Celina Wieniewska, contain the entirety of Schulz's work published in book form in his lifetime. They are complemented by a highly illuminating collection, *Letters and Drawings of Bruno Schulz, with Selected Prose*, 1988, edited by Jerzy Ficowski and translated by Walter Arndt with Victoria Nelson, which brings together Schulz's surviving correspondence, his essays and book reviews, a selection of his graphic works and photographs, and three short stories originally published in periodicals. Unfortunately, there is not much criticism on Schulz available in English. John Updike's introduction to *Sanatorium Under the Sign of the Hourglass* (1979) may serve as a basic introductory work. A more specialized analysis is Colleen M. Taylor, "Childhood Revisited: The Writings of Bruno Schulz," *Slavic and East European Journal*, XIII (1969), 455-471. Louis Iribarne, "On Bruno Schulz," *Cross Currents*, VI (1987), 173-177, is a brief but useful piece introducing Iribarne's translation of five short texts by Schulz; also included are two of Schulz's drawings.

Stanislaw Baranczak

E. F. SCHUMACHER

Born: Bonn, Germany
Date: August 16, 1911

Died: Zurich, Switzerland
Date: September 4, 1977

PRINCIPAL WORKS

SOCIAL CRITICISM: *Roots of Economic Growth*, 1962; *Small Is Beautiful: Economics As If People Mattered*, 1973; *Good Work*, 1977.

PHILOSOPHY: *A Guide for the Perplexed*, 1977.

Ernst Friedrich (Fritz) Schumacher, a British economist and social philosopher, was born on August 16, 1911, in Bonn, Germany, where his father was a professor of economics at the university. In 1917, the elder Schumacher accepted a post at the University of Berlin, and young Fritz was reared in the comfortable middle-class atmosphere of the cosmopolitan German capital. In 1929, Schumacher enrolled at the University of Bonn, where he was influenced to study economics by Joseph Schumpeter, who later taught at Harvard University. In 1930, he continued his studies at the London School of Economics and attended lectures at the University of Cambridge, given by the famous British economist John Maynard Keynes. In October, 1930, he was awarded a Rhodes scholarship and enrolled at New College, Oxford. In late 1932, he went to New York, where he did research and lectured on economics at Columbia University during the 1933-1934 term. Returning to Germany, he was effectively blocked from an academic career by his opposition to the Nazi regime but finally found employment as a financial investment consultant to a director of the Unilever Corporation in England. In October, 1936, he married and immediately left Germany for his new job in London, resolved never to return while the Nazi regime remained in power.

When World War II started, Schumacher and his wife were interned as enemy aliens and assigned to work on a farm, an experience which led to a lifelong interest in organic farming and conservation. (He became president of the British Soil Association in 1970.) His friends came to his aid, and in March, 1942, he was hired by the Institute of Statistics at Oxford and began to contribute articles on economic matters to various journals and newspapers. During this period, Schumacher became a socialist and supported such socialist policies as state-controlled central planning of the economy and nationalization of industries. Though worried about abuses of personal freedom in the Soviet Union, he looked forward to the socialization of postwar Germany. He also abandoned his Christian religious heritage and became a militant atheist.

Professionally, an article Schumacher published in the spring of 1942 in the journal *Economica* on multilateral international payments was incorporated into an important postwar planning report authored by Lord Keynes. In 1944, Schumacher was asked to assist William Beveridge in planning postwar employment policies for the British government. Lord Beveridge's economic policies were dominated by his moral principles, an attitude that Schumacher, a scientific rationalist, despised. Yet he was moved by Lord Beveridge's liberal insistence that the state's power be used for the social benefit of the powerless.

In 1945, Schumacher returned to Germany as a member of an Allied team, headed by American economist John Kenneth Galbraith, that was investigating the effectiveness of Allied bombing of industrial targets. In 1946, he was granted British citizenship and joined the Labour Party. While working as an economic adviser for the British Control Commission for Germany, he began a systematic program of reading in philosophy and history. Particularly influenced by the Spanish philosopher José Ortega y Gasset, he became convinced that many of the world's problems were created by a lack of clear philosophical thinking.

In 1950, Schumacher was appointed as economic adviser to the National Coal Board, his principal occupation for the next twenty years. His reading program now turned to the study of Oriental civilizations and new ways of viewing reality. He became convinced that the extreme rationalism of the Western culture was a disease leading to personal and societal disaster and that the spiritual dimension of life was the primary element in human existence. Under the influence of G. I. Gurdjieff, Gurdjieff's disciple Maurice Nicholl and the English Buddhist Edward Conze, his whole way of thinking began to change. He studied Buddhism and began to practice yoga. In 1954, a mystical breakthrough while meditating confirmed his new faith in the spiritual dimensions of reality. In 1955, he served as economic adviser to the Burmese government, an experience that led him to write his most famous essay, on Buddhist economics, a social critique of Western economic science, subsequently published in his collected essays *Small Is Beautiful*. Upon returning to England, Schumacher declared himself a Buddhist and then, paradoxically, began to study the works of Saint Thomas Aquinas and other Catholic mystics and philosophers. Eventually, he found the philosophical framework he was seeking in Thomism and in 1971 converted to Catholicism.

In 1959, Schumacher lectured on the nature of man and the meaning of life in the Extramural Studies Department of London University and later at Imperial College. When his first wife died in 1960 leaving him with four children, he married again a year later; he had four more children with his second wife.

In the 1960's, Schumacher turned his attention to the economic problems of development in the Third World. He criticized Western foreign aid advisers for promoting large-scale, capital-intensive, high technology for Third World peoples who suffered massive under-employment, low levels of technical education, and a shortage of local capital. He advocated the use of "appropriate technology," that which would promote employment, utilize actual levels of skills, and improve the living standards of the poor. In 1965, he founded the Intermediate Technology Development Group, designed to offer practical advice to under-developed nations on the kinds of intermediate technology that were practical, cheap, and sufficient for their needs at their present stage of economic development. While he traveled and lectured in India, South Africa, Zambia, Peru, and Tanzania, in England his attacks on the prevailing development theories of his fellow economists created a furor and much discussion.

After he was retired in 1970 from the National Coal Board, Schumacher decided to publish his essays on economics and social organization in *Small Is Beautiful*, which appeared in 1973. The book was received with little interest in England, but when published in the United States, it became a huge success, selling more than a million copies. Its author toured the United States, speaking to some sixty thousand people. Schumacher was profiled and interviewed, and his books were reviewed widely in the American media.

Many of the lectures given in America were published in *Good Work*. Schumacher expressed concern about the role of work in the development of the individual. He saw work as necessary not only to produce goods and services but also to develop the individual's full talents to make one better able to serve one's neighbors—liberating one from the inborn human tendency toward egocentricity. He proposed that people be educated to understand that work served a moral and spiritual role in the development of personhood. Quoting Saint Thomas Aquinas, Schumacher pointed out that there can be no joy in life without the joy of work. Modern utilitarianism and materialism treat work as a burden, an unpleasant necessity, and the worker as a "factor of production" to be used and discarded as profits or efficiency dictate, but neither good work nor good men could flourish in such an atmosphere. Schumacher's arguments were drawn from both Catholic social thought and his personal experience as a director of the Scott-Bader Company, a British plastics company owned and managed by its entire working force, famous as a model of a creative, humane socio-economic community.

Schumacher's last work, *A Guide for the Perplexed*, expressed his belief that the modern experiment to live without religion had failed and that in the postmodern era each person must engage in new philosophical "mapmaking," the old philosophy of scientific materialism and positivism having failed. Based on his own philosophical and religious study and experience, *A Guide for the Perplexed* sets forth the philosophical foundations of Schumacher's social, ethical, and economic theories.

BIBLIOGRAPHICAL REFERENCES: *E. F. Schumacher: His Life and Thought*, 1984, was written by Schumacher's daughter, Barbara Wood. An examination of actual applications of Schumacher's theories on intermediate technology is given by his protégé George McRobie, *Small Is Possible*, 1981. Schumacher was an editor of the British magazine *Resurgence*, which continues to reflect Schumacher's social and economic philosophy. After his death, Schumacher's English admirers founded the Schumacher Society, which sponsors an annual lecture series in his honor. S. Kumar edited the first series, *The Schumacher Lectures*, 1981. For reviews of Schumacher's work, see Asher Brynes, *The Nation*, CCXVIII (June 8, 1974), 725, and Peter Barnes, *The New Republic* CLXX (June 15, 1974), 29. See also the interview by Sam Love, "We Must Make Things Smaller and Simpler: An Interview with E. F. Schumacher," *Futurist*, VIII (December, 1974), 281-284.

Joseph R. Peden

DELMORE SCHWARTZ

Born: Brooklyn, New York
Date: December 8, 1913

Died: New York, New York
Date: July 11, 1966

PRINCIPAL WORKS

POETRY: *Genesis: Book One*, 1943; *Vaudeville for a Princess and Other Poems*, 1950; *Summer Knowledge: New and Selected Poems, 1938-1958*, 1959; *Last and Lost Poems of Delmore Schwartz*, 1979.

SHORT FICTION: *The World Is a Wedding*, 1948; *Successful Love and Other Stories*, 1961.

PLAY: *Shenandoah*, pb. 1941.

ESSAYS: *Selected Essays of Delmore Schwartz*, 1970.

TRANSLATION: *A Season in Hell*, 1939, revised 1940 (by Arthur Rimbaud).

MISCELLANEOUS: *In Dreams Begin Responsibilities*, 1938; *In Dreams Begin Responsibilities and Other Stories*, 1978.

Delmore Schwartz was one of the poets of the Middle Generation, so called by critic Bruce Bawer, who took his cue from some lines by Robert Lowell. That generation of poets included Lowell, Randall Jarrell, and John Berryman, as well as Schwartz, who in some ways led the group into poetry. It was he who first published a book, and it was he who showed the way in contemporary American poetry during the years before and during World War II.

Born in New York City of parents whose families had emigrated from Romania when they were very young, Schwartz was reared in an unhappy household. His autobiographical poem *Genesis* recounts some of his experiences as a child and his reactions to his parents, who were eventually divorced when Schwartz was a teenager. Educated at the University of Wisconsin and New York University, Schwartz later taught at Harvard University, where he undertook graduate work in philosophy. He had already begun writing poetry as a student in George Washington High School, where he was encouraged by his teacher, Mary J. J. Wrinn, who included some of his work in her book *The Hollow Reed* (1935). During his college years Schwartz wrote criticism as well as poetry, and by the time his first book appeared he was being hailed as "the American Auden."

In Dreams Begin Responsibilities is a collection of poetry and prose, including the title story and some of the poems that had earlier appeared in magazines and journals, such as *Poetry* and *The Partisan Review*. In his early work, Schwartz was clearly influenced not only by W. H. Auden but also by poets of the older generation—William Butler Yeats, T. S. Eliot, and Ezra Pound—and by writers who were very much discussed in the 1930's, Karl Marx and Sigmund Freud. In fact, his autobiographical poem *Genesis* is heavily influenced by Freudian psychology, which was not, however, to remain a lasting influence any more than Marxist philosophy was. Some of his finest poems, frequently anthologized ever since, nevertheless reflect a new voice. "The Heavy Bear That with Me Walks" and "In the Naked Bed, in Plato's Cave" are remarkable for their attempt to make the abstract concrete, and for an idiom that directly reflects the epigraph from Alfred North Whitehead that prefaces "The Heavy Bear": "the withness of the body." Indeed, it is Schwartz's ability in these and other poems to communicate the physicality of experience while at the same time rendering lines of lyric grace and mellifluousness that is one of his greatest accomplishments.

Not that Schwartz's early poems are easy reading: They are not. They are very much in key with the modernist attitude that required mental exertion as opposed to rhapsodic response (although such rhapsodic verse came later in Schwartz's career, as many of the poems in *Summer Knowledge* reveal). Unsurprisingly, given Schwartz's reading in philosophy, philosophical ideas also permeate his poetry. Like the work of Eliot, for whom he had a kind of love-hate regard, Schwartz's poetry invites, even requires, the reader to think as well as feel. The trap of time is a frequent theme in these early poems, and its solution is love, however difficult. Fear and guilt, of which Schwartz like other poets of his generation had an abundant share, form another theme, for which Schwartz offers confrontation, not evasion, as a solution, as in the poem "Father and Son."

Whether it was the early acclaim he received, which he could not sustain, or the failures in his personal life that damaged him (his first marriage ended in divorce in 1944, as did his second in 1955), the work in *Vaudeville for a Princess and Other Poems* shows a growing sense of defeat and is mostly unsuccessful. Only three of the poems were reprinted along with verse from *In Dreams Begin Responsibilities* in *Summer Knowledge*, which includes some of his best later poetry. Somehow, the oppressiveness of his long early guilt seems to have found release, and the poems of the 1950's soar with newfound energy. "The First Morning of the Second World," for example, shows a new acceptance and a new poetic mode. Walt Whitman, not Eliot, is the presiding spirit in this poetry, as evidenced by longer lines with broader cadences. The sprung rhythms of Gerard Manley Hopkins and the rhapsodic verse of Dylan Thomas are also influences, but again the voice is Schwartz's own. There are lapses, but the poetry as a whole seemed to presage a resurgence of poetic inspiration and delight.

Unfortunately, the inspiration and delight did not endure, and by the early 1960's Schwartz's personal and professional difficulties reasserted themselves. Drinking became an ever increasing problem, and he quarreled with friends and colleagues. Schwartz's superb critical writing, like his poetry, began to decline, and he also wrote fewer short stories. He died of a heart attack in one of the shabby hotels in midtown New York in July, 1966, leaving behind much unpublished and unfinished work, some of which has been collected, edited, and published by scholars and friends, many of whom still recognize the genius that was Delmore Schwartz.

BIBLIOGRAPHICAL REFERENCES: Richard McDougall, *Delmore Schwartz*, 1974, in the Twayne series, was the first critical biography of Schwartz. It is succeeded by James Atlas' longer and more definitive *Delmore Schwartz*, 1977, the standard biography. In *The Middle Generation: The Lives and Poetry of Delmore Schwartz, Randall Jarrell, John Berryman, and Robert Lowell*, 1986, Bruce Bawer treats Schwartz and his work in the context of his contemporaries. A number of useful articles and reviews have appeared over the years on Schwartz's poetry and fiction. See, for example, Sister Hilda Bonham, "Delmore Schwartz: An Idea of the World," *Renascence*, XIII (1961), 132-135, for an analysis of "The Heavy Bear"; Jay L. Halio, "Delmore Schwartz's Felt Abstractions," *The Southern Review*, n.s. I (1965), 803-819, for a discussion of the development of the imagery and style in Schwartz's poetry; Philip Rahv, "Delmore Schwartz: The Paradox of Precocity," *The New York Review of Books*, May 20, 1971, 19-22, for a memoir by a friend and colleague that discusses Schwartz as a critic as well as a personality. Schwartz is also supposed to be a model for the character of Von Humboldt Fleisher in Saul Bellow's novel *Humboldt's Gift*, 1975, although Bellow has said the fictional character is actually a composite of several personalities.

Jay L. Halio

ANDRÉ SCHWARZ-BART

Born: Metz, France
Date: May 23, 1928

Principal Works

NOVELS: *Le Dernier des Justes*, 1959 (*The Last of the Just*, 1961); *Un Plat de porc aux bananes vertes*, 1967 (with Simone Schwarz-Bart); *La Mulâtresse Solitude*, 1972 (*A Woman Named Solitude*, 1973).

André Schwarz-Bart is one of the most important French writers of the post-Holocaust period. He was born in Metz, in eastern France, on May 23, 1928, of Jewish parents who had emigrated from Poland in 1924. In the close-knit community of their Jewish neighborhood, they followed Orthodox tradition (the father had prepared for the rabbinate), told and retold Hebrew stories and legends, and spoke only Yiddish. In fact, it was not until he attended public school that Schwarz-Bart learned French and associated with gentile children, although he had already been subjected to anti-Semitic insults and violence. On days off from school, he helped his father sell stockings in the open-air markets. In 1940, with the outbreak of war in France, the family was evacuated first to the Island of Oléron, off the Atlantic coast, then to Angoulême, where Schwarz-Bart studied metalworking. There, the Germans arrested his parents, two brothers, and a sister. At age fourteen, left to care for three younger brothers, he hired out as a farm laborer, until the four boys were shipped to Paris in early 1943.

In Paris, Schwarz-Bart became a member of the Communist Youth League and, lying about his age, also joined the Resistance movement. He was thus able to smuggle his brothers into the so-called Free Zone, as well as his sister, whom he coolly had taken out of a children's home. After his arrest in Limoges and subsequent escape, he continued his underground activities until the Liberation. Back in Paris, he learned that his parents and brothers would never return from their concentration camp. Devastated, he willingly accepted his responsibilities as head of household. He was seventeen years old. During the day he worked in a foundry, while at night he devoured detective and mystery novels borrowed from the public library. Among these, he borrowed Fyodor Dostoevski's *Crime and Punishment* (1866) and thereby discovered great literature.

Spurred by a subconscious need to relate his experience to others, Schwarz-Bart now devoted all of his spare time to improving his written and spoken French, completely neglected during his wandering war years, and passed the *baccalauréat* examinations in 1948. After a discouraging semester at the Sorbonne, he dropped out of university, but he resumed his studies in 1950, earning a certificate in philosophy. To pay for his tuition, he successively worked as a counselor at a Jewish orphanage, secretary of the Jewish Student Association, and instructor at the Jewish Refuge in Neuilly. In the meantime, influenced by Dostoevski, Leo Tolstoy, Stendhal, Georges Bernanos, Lautréamont, Thomas Mann, and above all the Old Testament, he wrote short stories in which he incorporated not only their ideas and themes but also the accounts of Nazi terror he heard from his young charges.

One of these narratives is the somewhat autobiographical "La Fin de Marcus Libnitzki" (the end of Marcus Libnitzki), published in 1953. It relates the death of a young Jewish Resistance fighter shot by the Germans in Limoges, as told to Marcus' brother by various witnesses. To explain further how the Jews had let themselves be exterminated, Schwarz-Bart planned a vast novel that would use the past in order to illuminate the present. Dissatisfied with a first draft, he reworked the entire premise, having a fictional biographer discover a manuscript concerning a family of Jewish spiritual leaders, beginning in 1819 and ending on a French train bound for a concentration camp. An early excerpt, "La Légende des Justes" (the legend of the Just Men), appeared in 1956 as part of the yet unpublished "biography of Ernie Levy." Still displeased, however, he rewrote this version three more times. The final text, much expanded and tightened, used a more conventional linear time sequence, from the 1185 pogrom in York, England, to the 1943 destruction in the ovens of Auschwitz of Ernie Levy, his young "bride" Golda, and the children they are shepherding. In 1959, when the novel, now entitled *The Last of the Just*, was critically acclaimed and won the prestigious Goncourt Prize, it became a worldwide success.

Two years later, Schwarz-Bart married Simone, a student from Guadeloupe who has become a novelist in her own right and with whom he would have two sons. Next, he and his wife collaborated on a novel about the desperate struggle of black women in the French Antilles and of their ancestors in precolonial Africa. Taking its title from the old heroine's memory of the day she took a plate of pork with green bananas to her mother's lover, *Un Plat de porc aux bananes vertes* was published in 1967 and was awarded the Jerusalem Prize. *A Woman Named Solitude*, which Schwarz-Bart wrote alone, re-creates the beauty and joy of African life and folklore, contrasting them to the cruelty of West Indian plantation owners and the humiliation of the slaves. Throughout his three novels, Schwarz-Bart emphasizes the dignity and grandeur of the victims, as they try to live ethically and well in spite of the horror.

André Schwarz-Bart was not himself a witness to the Nazi genocide or to the enslavement of Africans, but the Holocaust and the inhuman treatment of blacks in the Caribbean colonies are evident in his novels. It is as one of the modern epic poets of Jewish martyrdom that he is best known, although much controversy arose on the publication of *The Last of the Just*. This controversy resulted partly from the fact that he had made several important historical and interpretive mistakes and was especially a result of the fact that he had refused to portray Jews as ready and willing to resist and fight against their oppressors, including the Germans. Instead, as he had already explained in his 1956 excerpt, he wanted to present the continuity of Jewish suffering exemplified in the Talmudic tradition of the *Lamed-Vov*, the thirty-six Just Men, who through their conduct may help redeem humanity.

BIBLIOGRAPHICAL REFERENCES: A book-length study of Schwarz-Bart's work is the excellent analysis by Francine Kaufmann, *Pour relire "Le Dernier des Justes,"* 1986. See also "Three Goncourt Prizes: Romain Gary, Roger Ikor, André Schwarz-Bart," in Charles C. Lehrmann, *The Jewish Element in French Literature*, 1971; "Of Time and Atrocity," in Lawrence L. Langer, *The Holocaust and the Literary Imagination*, 1975; "André Schwarz-Bart: The Last Passion," in Sidra DeKoven Ezrahi, *By Words Alone: The Holocaust in Literature*, 1980; Charlotte H. Bruner, "A Caribbean Madness: Half Slave and Half Free," *Canadian Review of Comparative Literature*, XI (June, 1984), 236-248; and Seymour Menton, "*The Last of the Just*: Between Borges and García Márquez," *World Literature Today*, LIX (Autumn, 1985), 517-524.

Pierre L. Horn

LEONARDO SCIASCIA

Born: Racalmuto, Sicily
Date: January 8, 1921

Principal Works

NOVELS: *Gli zii di Sicilia*, 1958; *Il giorno della civetta*, 1961 (*Mafia Vendetta*, 1963); *Il consiglio d'Egitto*, 1963 (*The Council of Egypt*, 1966); *Morte dell'inquisitore*, 1964 (*Death of the Inquisitor*, 1969); *A ciascuno il suo*, 1966 (*A Man's Blessing*, 1968); *Candido: Ovvero, Un sogno fatto in Sicilia*, 1977 (*Candido: Or, A Dream Dreamed in Sicily*, 1979).

SHORT FICTION: *Il mare colore del vino*, 1973 (*The Wine-Dark Sea*, 1985).

PLAY: *L'onorevole*, pb. 1965.

ESSAYS: *Le parrocchie di Regalpetra*, 1956 (*Salt in the Wound*, 1969); *Cruciverba*, 1983.

NONFICTION: *Pirandello e la Sicilia*, 1961; *Feste religiose in Sicilia*, 1965; *La scomparsa di Majorana*, 1975; *I Siciliani*, 1977 (with Dominique Fernandez); *L'affaire Moro*, 1978; *Kermesse*, 1982.

Leonardo Sciascia was born in Racalmuto, Sicily, on January 8, 1921. He has lived much of his life in Sicily, where, before his success as a novelist and public figure in the 1960's, he was a teacher. More than any other Italian author of the late twentieth century, Sciascia has occupied himself with the problems of Sicilian society. His grim chronicles of the Mafia's infestation of Sicily, including the political corruption of Sicilian government, present a grimly realistic picture of life on the island.

Sciascia was educated in the Istituto Magistrale in Caltanissetta, where he received his teacher's diploma. From 1949 to 1957, he taught at an elementary school in the same city. In 1957, he moved to Palermo, where he taught until his writing enabled him to live on his literary earnings. He began writing in the neorealist style, chronicling the misery and poverty of the average Italian in the postwar era. His first success, *Salt in the Wound*, reflects his experiences as a schoolteacher, describing the depressing task of trying to teach tough, unruly twelve-year-old children. It goes on to portray life in the mythical town of Regalpetra. This book foreshadows Sciascia's later efforts to show that the corruption of society (especially in Sicily) sometimes overwhelms all attempts to reform it. Sciascia's pessimism, one of his hallmarks, is everywhere present in this early work.

In *Mafia Vendetta*, Sciascia brings into focus one of Sicily's major problems: organized crime at a level that pervades all strata of society. By the time this novel appeared, Sciascia was already recognized as one of Italy's most courageous writers. He had received the Premio Libera Stampa Lugano, the Premio Prato, and the Premio Crotone. Novels such as *A Man's Blessing* further developed Sciascia's societal views, portraying characters who are all, more or less, in bondage to political and criminal corruption. Sciascia condemned the corruption of Sicilian society not only through his writings but also through his political activities as a deputy of the Radical Party at the European Parliament, beginning in 1979. He has also written books denouncing conditions in Italy, such as *L'affaire Moro*, about the murder of Aldo Moro by the Red Brigades. Sciascia's style is relatively simple. His novels are brief, seldom more than 150 pages. Rather than outrage, he voices bitter irony at the apparently hopeless morass of Sicilian society. Sciascia will remain one of Italy's most respected and powerful novelists.

BIBLIOGRAPHICAL REFERENCES: An excellent and comprehensive study of Sciascia's work is Giovanna Jackson, *Leonardo Sciascia, 1956-1976: A Thematic and Structural Study*, 1981. See also Verina Jones, "Leonard Sciascia," in *Writing and Society in Contemporary Italy: A Collection of Essays*, 1984, edited by Michael Caesar and Peter Hainsworth; Gore Vidal, "Sciascia's Italy," in *The Second American Revolution and Other Essays*, 1982; Jo Ann

Cannon, "The Detective Fiction of Leonardo Sciascia," in *Modern Fiction Studies*, XXIX, no. 3 (1983), 523-534.

Philip Brantingham

OUSMANE SEMBÈNE

Born: Ziguinchor, Senegal
Date: January 1, 1923

PRINCIPAL WORKS

NOVELS: *Le Docker noir*, 1956; *Ô pays, mon beau peuple!*, 1957; *Les Bouts de bois de Dieu*, 1960 (*God's Bits of Wood*, 1962); *L'Harmattan, livre I: Référendum*, 1964.

NOVELLAS: *Véhi-Ciosane: Ou, Blanche-Genèse, suivi du Mandat*, 1965 (*The Money-Order, with White Genesis*, 1972); *Xala*, 1973 (English translation, 1976).

SHORT FICTION: *Voltaïque*, 1962 (*Tribal Scars*, 1974).

SCREENPLAYS: *Borom-Sarret*, 1962; *La Noire de . . .* , 1966; *Mandabi*, 1968 (also known as *Le Mandat*); *Emitaï*, 1972; *Xala*, 1974; *Ceddo*, 1977.

Ousmane Sembène's fiction treats the tensions in a society attempting to break with tradition and colonialism simultaneously. He was born at Ziguinchor, Casamance, in the south of Senegal, on January 1, 1923. (Some sources reverse the order of his given name and surname and indicate January 8 as his date of birth.) His family of fishermen spoke the Wolof language, but he would eventually begin to write in French. Therefore, the complex problems associated with tradition and colonialism arose early in his own life. French was the language of the white man, but to write in Wolof would deprive his work of a significant audience. Sembène spent three years at a technical school at Marsassoum, near the place of his birth. He then worked at a variety of trades and was laying brick at Dakar when World War II began. He joined the Free French forces and participated in the invasion of Italy. He later served in France, working as a stevedore at the port of Marseilles, and in Germany. After his discharge in 1946, he returned to Dakar to work as a fisherman but was soon back on the docks of Marseilles, working this time as a civilian stevedore. He read widely and became active in his trade union, soon rising to a position of authority. His years as a laborer and a union representative gave him a sympathy for the working man which is evident throughout his fiction. Sembène's first novel, *Le Docker noir* (the black docker), grew out of his waterfront years. It is the story of a black stevedore who writes a novel, only to have the manuscript stolen by a white woman who publishes it under her name. The problems of race, class, and expatriation are intermingled in the novel.

Sembène's next novel, *Ô pays, mon beau peuple!* (O my country, my beautiful people), further explores the same themes. A young expatriate Senegalese returns to his homeland with a white wife and ideas about modernized, cooperative farming. He is quickly estranged from both black and white societies, even from his own family, and is eventually murdered. Sembène traveled throughout Africa and Europe, and his proletarian sympathies and anti-capitalist views soon led him to the Soviet Union, China, and Cuba as well. He studied at Moscow's Gorki Film Studios for a year. His third novel, *God's Bits of Wood*, is larger in scope and more optimistic in tone than the first two. It is based upon the successful strike of railroad workers on the Dakar-Niger line in 1947-1948.

Tribal Scars is a collection of twelve stories emphasizing the plight of the common man and, especially, the common woman. *L'Harmattan, livre I* (the storm, book 1) treats Charles de Gaulle's referendum on French rule in colonial West Africa. The novel is the first in a projected trilogy. Sembène next published two novellas together under the title *The Money-Order, with White Genesis*. These won for Sembène the literature prize of the 1966 Festival of Negro Arts in Dakar. In the early 1960's, Sembène had embarked upon his second artistic career, that of filmmaker. His short films *Borom-Sarret* and *La Noire de . . .* (black girl) were followed by *Mandabi*, his first full-length film, an adaptation of *The Money-Order*. *Mandabi* portrays the bourgeoisie's exploitation of the poor, in the form of educated civil servants who cheat a simple Muslim out of the proceeds of a large money order he has received from Paris. The film was a significant turning point for Sembène. It employed his native language of Wolof in an attempt to reach an African audience never exposed to his written works. In addition, it was a great critical success, winning for Sembène the special jury prize at the 1968 Venice Film Festival and the award as the best foreign film at the 1970 Atlanta Film Festival.

From the 1970's onward, Sembène has concentrated primarily on filmmaking. *Emitaï*, set in his native Casamance, dramatizes the clash of tribal customs and colonial military power. Sembène wrote *Xala* as a novella and as a film at virtually the same time. It satirizes the colonial attitudes that persist in independent Senegal, through the story of an acquisitive Senegalese businessman who suffers from the *xala*, impotence, immediately after adding a third wife to his household. *Ceddo* (the common people) is Sembène's most ambitious and controversial film. The history of the film's difficulties with the censors reads like a satire of Sembène's own devising. It has been banned in Senegal—not because it criticizes African complicity in the slave trade, the subjugation of women, and Islamic colonialism, but because the government balked at the spelling of the title. The official government position is that the Wolof term should be spelled *cedo*. Sembène, who had earlier returned to make his permanent home at Dakar, argued that African filmmakers must be free to express their own vision of their native land. Sembène founded and edits *Kaddu*, the first Wolof monthly. His satires, marked by a realistic presentation, show that he rejects both the rationalizations for colonialism and the sentimentality and chauvinism of *négritude*, a "black is beautiful" movement launched in Senegal during the 1930's. He is widely regarded as the finest film director Africa has produced.

BIBLIOGRAPHICAL REFERENCES: See A. C. Brench's discussion of Sembène in *The Novelists' Inheritance in French Africa*, 1967. Brench also edited *Writing in French from Senegal to Cameroon*, 1967. Each of the following contains an entry for Sembène: O. R. Dathorne, *African Literature in the Twentieth Century*, 1976; Shatto Arthur Gakwandi, *The Novel and Contemporary Experience in Africa*, 1977; *African Authors: A Companion to Black African Writing*, Vol. 1, *1300-1973*, 1973, edited by D. E. Herdeck; *African Writers on African Writing*, 1975, edited by G. D. Killam; *The Writer in Modern Africa*, 1969, edited by Per Wästberg; *A Reader's Guide to African Literature*, 1971, edited by Hans Zell and Helene Silver; and *World Authors: 1970-1975*, 1980, edited by John Wakeman. See the following regarding Sembène's work as screenwriter and director: "*Mandabi*: Review, New York Film Festival," *The New York Times*, September 30, 1969, 41; "Sembène Interview, New York City," *The New York Times*, November 2, 1969, 2; "*Ceddo*: Ousmane Sembène, Director, Interview," *The New York Times*, January 27, 1978, 3; and "*Ceddo*: Review," *The New York Times*, February 17, 1978, 3.

Patrick Adcock

MARY LEE SETTLE

Born: Charleston, West Virginia
Date: July 29, 1918

PRINCIPAL WORKS

NOVELS: *The Love Eaters*, 1954; *The Kiss of Kin*, 1955; *O Beulah Land*, 1956; *Know Nothing*, 1960; *Fight Night on a Sweet Saturday*, 1964; *The Clam Shell*, 1971; *Prisons*, 1973 (also known as *The Long Road to Paradise*); *Blood Tie*, 1977; *The Scapegoat*, 1980; *The Killing Ground*, 1982; *Celebration*, 1986.

MEMOIRS: *All the Brave Promises: Memories of Aircraft Woman Second Class 2146391*, 1966.

CHILDREN'S LITERATURE: *The Story of Flight*, 1967; *Water World*, 1984.

NONFICTION: *The Scopes Trial: The State of Tennessee vs. John Thomas Scopes*, 1972.

Mary Lee Settle is a distinguished American writer who has had to be periodically rediscovered; both her life and her career exhibit a series of ups and downs. She was born July 29, 1918, in Charleston, West Virginia. Her father and mother, Joseph Edward and Rachel Tompkins Settle, were from the small circle of enterprising West Virginia families who helped establish industry and coal mining. When Settle was around the age of two, the family moved deeper into the Appalachian hinterlands, to Pineville, Kentucky, near where her father owned a coal mine on Straight Creek in Harlan County. When Settle was about seven years old, the coal business failed, and the family moved to Orlando, Florida. There her father, a civil engineer, worked in the land boom—designing, for example, the layout of Venice, Florida. When the Florida boom fizzled in 1928, the family returned to live with Settle's maternal grandmother in Cedar Grove, West Virginia. Eventually, the family settled in Charleston, where it struggled through the Depression. Despite hard times, there was money for Settle's elocution lessons and, later, attendance at Virginia's Sweet Briar College.

After two years at Sweet Briar College, Settle rebelled and left. On the basis of her acting credentials—a summer at Virginia's Barter Theater and an audition for the role of Scarlett O'Hara—Settle went to New York. There, after working as a model, she married an Englishman, Rodney Weathersbee, in 1939. They moved to Canada, where Weathersbee enlisted in the Canadian army and their son Christopher was born. Settle herself joined the World War II struggle in 1941: Leaving her son with her parents in West Virginia, she traveled to Great Britain and enlisted in the Women's Auxiliary Air Force (WAAF) branch of the Royal Air Force (RAF). Her service with the WAAF, recounted in *All the Brave Promises*, was a watershed period in her life, forcing her to confront the British class system and quickly lose her genteel ways. She was on control tower duty for thirteen months, until overcome by "signals shock" from constantly listening for radioed pilots' voices through enemy jamming. Settle then transferred to the Office of War Information in London; there, among a coterie of excellent writers and editors, she herself began to write.

After World War II, Settle faced a major decision. She landed a good editing job with *Harper's Bazaar* magazine in New York, but after a brief stint, she decided to devote herself to her own writing. In 1946, already divorced from Weathersbee, Settle returned to Britain with her son and married Douglas Newton, a British poet. They lived the romantic life of struggling writers in England and in Paris. For funds, Settle took on free-lance journalistic assignments—for example, writing an etiquette column for *Woman's Day* under the name Mrs. Charles Palmer and serving as English correspondent for *Flair* magazine. Meanwhile, she wrote six plays and four film scripts without finding a producer or publisher. Finally, in 1954, she published her first novel, *The Love Eaters*, about an amateur play production in a West Virginia town. Her second novel, *The Kiss of Kin*, a reworking of one of her plays also set in West Virginia, soon followed. Enthusiastic reviewers praised Settle as a sophisticated novelist of small-town manners.

Unhappily, Settle's hard-earned success soon turned sour. There were strains on her marriage, and in 1955, she left her second husband (they were divorced in 1956) and returned to Charleston with her son. Here she slowly sank into poverty while publishing *O Beulah Land* and *Know Nothing*, two volumes in the Beulah Quintet, considered by some to be her major work. A third volume, *Fight Night on a Sweet Saturday*, suffered so much editorial cutting that she later rewrote it as *The Killing Ground*. In 1961, she worked in New York as an editor for American Heritage; in 1965, she began teaching one semester a year at Bard College; and in 1969, she began living abroad to protest Richard Nixon's election as president. Two of her novels—*The Clam Shell*, an autobiographical work based on her Sweet Briar years, and *Prisons*, another volume in the Beulah Quintet—appeared without benefit of New York reviews. She had trouble finding a publisher for her next novel, *Blood Tie*, which drew on her three-year stay in Turkey.

Eventually published, *Blood Tie* won for Settle the 1978 National Book Award in Fiction. Though critics at first howled that Settle was "unknown," the award marked a dramatic upswing in her career. Her subsequent novels, including *The Scapegoat* (the best volume in the Beulah Quintet), *The Killing Ground*, and *Celebration*, have been published to major reviews. Meanwhile, Settle returned to the United States in 1974 to live in Charlottesville, Virginia, where she acquired a circle of friends, and in 1978, she married William Littleton Tazewell, a journalist and historian. Both taught writing at the University of Virginia but have since retired to their home in Norfolk, Virginia, to concentrate on their own work.

In part, the mixed response to Settle's fiction reflects her association with the South and in particular Southern Appalachia. She has been sometimes scornfully dismissed, sometimes proudly claimed as a "regional" writer. No writer, however, more easily exposes the limited meaning of such labels; for her, "regional" in effect means "international." She has lived abroad for long periods, and her two best novels, *Blood Tie* and *Celebration*, have international settings. Even her monumental Beulah Quintet, with its great theme of the search for freedom, begins in seventeenth century Great Britain with the symbolically entitled *Prisons* (*O Beulah Land*, *Know Nothing*, *The Scapegoat*, and *The Killing Ground* follow in chronological order). Critical reception of Settle's work has also been shaped by prevailing attitudes toward historical fiction, often dismissed as a genre, as if tainted by association with popular sagas. Critical fashions change, however, and Settle is one of a number of writers—including figures as diverse as Larry McMurtry and Thomas Flanagan—who have contributed to a modest renaissance of the historical novel.

BIBLIOGRAPHICAL REFERENCES: A book-length critical study of Settle's work is George Garrett, *Understanding Mary Lee Settle*, 1988. Comprehensive information on her life appears in "Mary Lee Settle," *Contemporary Authors: Autobiography Series*, Vol. 1, 1984, edited by Dedria Bryfonski. A slightly dated but still informative survey of her life and work is George Garrett, "Mary Lee Settle," in *Dictionary of Literary Biography*, Vol. 6: *American Novelists Since World War II*, 1980, edited by James E. Kibler, Jr. Several fine articles have appeared on the Beulah Quintet. Besides Roger Shattuck's introduction to the Ballantine paperback edition, these include William J. Schafer, "Mary Lee Settle's Beulah Quintet: History Darkly, Through a Single-Lens Reflex," *Appalachian Journal*, X (Autumn, 1982), 77-86; Nancy Carol Joyner, "Mary Lee Settle's Connections: Class and Clothes in the Beulah Quintet," *The Southern Quarterly*, XXII (Fall, 1983), 33-45 (reprinted in *Women Writers of the Contemporary South*, 1984, edited by Peggy Whitman Prenshaw); and Jane Gentry Vance, "Mary Lee Settle's *The Beulah Quintet*: History Inherited, History Created," *Southern Literary Journal*, XVII (Fall, 1984), 40-53. See also J. D. O'Hara, "What Rogue Elephants Know," *The Nation*, May 20, 1978, 605-606; E. L. Doctorow, "Mother Jones Had Some Advice," *The New York Times Book Review*, October 26, 1980, 1; Peggy Bach, "The Searching Voice and Vision of Mary Lee Settle," *The Southern Review*, XX (Autumn, 1984), 842-850; and Joyce

Coyne Dyer, "Embracing the Common: Mary Lee Settle in World War II," *Appalachian Journal*, XII (Winter, 1985), 127-134.

Harold Branam

PETER SHAFFER

Born: Liverpool, England
Date: May 15, 1926

PRINCIPAL WORKS

PLAYS: *Five Finger Exercise*, pr., pb. 1958; *The Private Ear*, pr., pb. 1962; *The Public Eye*, pr., pb. 1962; *The Merry Roosters Panto*, pr. 1963; *The Royal Hunt of the Sun: A Play Concerning the Conquest of Peru*, pr., pb. 1964; *Black Comedy*, pr. 1965; *A Warning Game*, pr. 1967; *The White Liars*, pb. 1967; *It's About Cinderella*, pr. 1969; *The Battle of Shrivings*, pr. 1970; *Equus*, pr., pb. 1973; *Amadeus*, pr. 1979; *Yonadab: The Watcher*, pr. 1985; *Lettice and Lovage*, pr. 1987.

SCREENPLAYS: *Lord of the Flies*, 1963 (with Peter Brook); *Follow Me!*, 1971; *The Public Eye*, 1972; *Equus*, 1977; *Amadeus*, 1984.

TELEPLAYS: *The Salt Land*, 1955; *Balance of Terror*, 1957.

RADIO PLAY: *The Prodigal Father*, pr. 1955.

NOVELS: *Woman in the Wardrobe*, 1951 (with Anthony Shaffer); *How Doth the Little Crocodile?*, 1952 (with A. Shaffer); *Withered Murder*, 1956 (with A. Shaffer).

Peter Levin Shaffer is one of the most important playwrights of the twentieth century. He was born in Liverpool, England, on May 15, 1926, the son of Jack Shaffer, a realtor, and his wife, Reka Fredman Shaffer. He was educated at St. Paul's School, London. In wartime, he was conscripted for service in the coal mines, where he served from 1944 to 1947. He then completed his education, receiving a B.A. from Trinity College, Cambridge, in 1950. With his twin brother Anthony, Peter Shaffer then began to write mystery novels. In 1951, *Woman in the Wardrobe* was published under the joint pseudonym "Peter Antony" and it was followed the next year by *How Doth the Little Crocodile?* Meanwhile, Peter Shaffer was living in New York, where he worked in the New York Public Library from 1951 to 1954, when he returned to England and got a job with a firm of music publishers in London, where he worked for a year. He had now turned his efforts to drama, and in 1955, the British Broadcasting Corporation (BBC) produced a radio play which he had written; that same year, an independent television company produced his first television play, *The Salt Land*. In 1956, Shaffer published one more murder mystery.

It was clear to Shaffer, however, that his genre was dramatic writing, whether for stage or screen. After writing another teleplay, *Balance of Terror*, produced in 1957 by the BBC, Shaffer wrote his first stage play, *Five Finger Exercise*, which opened at the Comedy Theatre in London's West End on July 16, 1958, where it ran for a year before moving to New York in December, 1959. Although the play was conventional in form, in it Shaffer's fascination with psychology was already evident: The story traces the effects which a German tutor has on various members of a household. From 1961 to 1962, Shaffer served as a music critic for *Time and Tide*, while continuing to explore various possibilities in drama. In 1962, Shaffer moved toward comedy of the absurd, with two one-act plays performed together, *The Private Ear* and *The Public Eye*. The following year, Shaffer collaborated on the screenplay for *Lord of the Flies*, thus gaining valuable experience for later adaptations of his own plays.

Shaffer's first major success was the historical play *The Royal Hunt of the Sun*, which was highly stylized, with elements of the Japanese Kabuki theater. Although critics differed about the effectiveness of Shaffer's dialogue and his realization of character, no one questioned the high quality of the play as spectacular theater. With *Equus* in 1973, Shaffer proved his quality as a thinker, as well as his ability in theatrical invention. The play is the story of a psychiatrist, Martin Dysart, who is attempting to treat a boy named Alan Strang by discovering why he blinded several horses in a north England stable. As the play proceeds, Dysart concludes that curing the boy means depriving him of his contact with divinity, which Alan had found in the horses. At the end of the play, the tragedy is not only Alan's, but Dysart's as well, and probably that of the whole modern world, which cannot reconcile sanity and faith. *Equus* brought Shaffer the Tony Award, the Outer Critics Circle Award, and the New York Drama Critics Circle Award. When the play was made into a film in 1977, Shaffer wrote the screenplay.

Two years later came the play which many consider Shaffer's masterpiece. *Amadeus* is the story of the composer Antonio Salieri's obsessive jealousy of the young musical genius Wolfgang Amadeus Mozart. Shaffer based his play on a rumor that Salieri had poisoned Mozart. Using that story, he writes of a second-rate artist whose anger is directed at the God who denied him genius, to bestow it upon a foolish boy; unable to revenge himself upon God, he turns his fury on Mozart himself. *Amadeus* was acclaimed by the critics and embraced by the public. It won for Shaffer the Tony Award and the Best Play of the Year award from *Plays and Players*. When it was made into a film, with Shaffer writing the screenplay, it received the New York Film Critics Circle Award and the Los Angeles Film Critics Association Award. In 1985, the play won an Academy Award for Best Picture, and Shaffer was given an Academy Award for Best Screenplay Adaptation. Although the two plays which followed *Amadeus* were less successful, Shaffer continues to hold his place as one of the most interesting playwrights and filmwriters of the century. In 1987, the British government recognized his achievements by naming him Commander of the British Empire.

Although some of Shaffer's best plays have been set in the past, for example, *The Royal Hunt of the Sun*, placed in the sixteenth century, and *Amadeus*, in the eighteenth, his themes arise from what he sees as the tragic elements in modern life. In *The Royal Hunt of the Sun*, for example, the central character, Martin Ruiz, is portrayed by two actors, who split the role between them, one playing the young Martin, who sees the conqueror of Peru, Francisco Pizarro, as a hero, and the other assuming the role of the older Martin, who realizes that when Pizarro brought Christianity and civilization to Peru, he brought the infidelity and the uncertainty of modern life. In *Equus*, again the loss of faith is a central theme. The rational psychiatrist Dysart, appalled by Alan's seemingly senseless cruelty to the horses, comes to realize that even though Alan's religion is allied to madness, the boy has experienced a contact with divinity which Dysart himself has never known. For all his rationality, Dysart feels a terrible sense of emptiness.

The mystery of genius is one of the themes of *Amadeus*, yet it is related to the eternal quest of believing man for some understanding of God's actions. Shaffer explores the character of Salieri, a Job without God's favor, who dies as miserably as he lived. If Salieri had not had faith, he could have endured the blind judgments of fate, which denied him genius; because he does believe in God, he is tortured by the evidence of God's injustice. Ironically, the only gift God gives Salieri is the power to perceive the genius of his rival. In the play *Yonadab*, Shaffer went to the Old Testament for the story of Amnon's rape of his sister Tamar, which eventually led to Absalom's murder of Amnon and his rebellion against his father David. In Shaffer's version of the story, he has the rape orchestrated by a court hanger-on, the title character of the play, who honestly believes a legend that incest in the royal family is good, rather than evil. Here once again Shaffer poses a question which is essentially religious: How does man decide among competing systems, whether of faith or of ethics based on faith? Shaffer's success is based on the fact that, as he himself has said, he does not repeat himself, in setting, in theatrical technique, or in theme. Certainly his audiences are spellbound by his plays. The literal-minded are delighted by the pure spectacle; the thoughtful find that every play Shaffer writes, in the tradition of the best drama from Aeschylus on, poses more questions than it answers.

BIBLIOGRAPHICAL REFERENCES: John Russell Taylor, *Peter Shaffer*, 1974, is an excellent critical treatment. See also his earlier *Anger and After*, 1962. Other helpful books are Gene Plunka, *Peter Shaffer: Roles, Rites, and Rituals in the Theater*, 1988; Robert Brustein, *The Third The-*

atre, 1969; Frederick Lumley, *New Trends in Twentieth Century Drama*, 1967; and *Behind the Scenes*, 1971, edited by J. F. McCrindle. On the making of the film *Amadeus*, see Peter Shaffer, "Mostly Mozart: Making the Screen Speak," *Film Comment*, XX (September/October, 1984), 50-51. See also Richard Combs's excellent review of *Amadeus*, *Monthly Film Bulletin*, LII (January, 1985), 14-15. For further study, see Joan F. Dean, "Peter Shaffer's Recurrent Character Type," in *Modern Drama*, 1978; Dennis A. Klein, "Breaking Masculine Stereotypes: The Theatre of Peter Shaffer," *University of Dayton Review* (Winter/Spring, 1986/1987), 49-55; C. J. Gianakaris, "A Playwright Looks at Mozart: Peter Shaffer's *Amadeus*," *Comparative Drama*, XV (Spring, 1981), 37-53; and the same writer's "Drama into Film: The Shaffer Situation," *Modern Drama*, XXVIII (March, 1985), 83-98.

Rosemary M. Canfield Reisman

VARLAM SHALAMOV

Born: Vologda, Russia
Date: July 1, 1907

Died: Moscow, Soviet Union
Date: January 17, 1982

Principal Works

SHORT FICTION: *Kolymskie rasskazy*, 1978 (*Kolyma Tales*, 1980, and *Graphite*, 1981).

POETRY: *Ognivo*, 1961; *Shelest list'ev*, 1964; *Doroga i sud'ba*, 1967; *Moskovskie oblaka*, 1972; *Tochka kipeniia*, 1977.

MEMOIRS: *Chetvertaya Vologda*, 1985; *Dvadtsatye gody*, 1987.

Varlam Tikhonovich Shalamov was a prose writer, poet, and essayist, whose seventeen-year imprisonment in Soviet labor camps provided him with the material for a remarkable set of short stories, known collectively as *Kolyma Tales*. He was born on July 1, 1907 (June 18, according to the Julian calendar used in prerevolutionary Russia), the fifth child of a Russian Orthodox priest. Vologda, Shalamov's home town, is a provincial city some 250 miles to the northeast of Moscow. Shalamov continued to live in Vologda through World War I and the revolution that brought the Bolsheviks to power; soon afterward, though, his family began to come apart. The first blow was material: Under the new, officially atheist government, Shalamov's father lost his pension. Then, in 1920, one brother was killed in the civil war between the regime and its opponents, and his father went blind from glaucoma.

In 1924 Shalamov left Vologda for Moscow, where he first worked as a tanner at a leather factory; in 1926 he enrolled in the law department of Moscow State University. Throughout the late 1920's he was very much caught up in Moscow's cultural life, with its rapidly evolving literary groups and the fierce polemics that raged in the press. While a student, he came into contact with circles that opposed the emerging Stalinist direction in the Soviet Union's political life. In February of 1929, he was arrested during a raid on an underground printing press and was sentenced to three years of hard labor in the northern Urals. He was freed a year early, in 1931, and by 1932 he had returned to Moscow, where he worked for the next five years as a journalist, critic, and writer, publishing several articles and stories in some of the more prestigious literary journals. He was rearrested in 1937, at the beginning of the purges, and that year he was sent to hard labor in the Kolyma region, one of the coldest inhabited places on earth. In 1942, when his original five-year sentence should have ended, his term was extended until the end of the war, and in 1943, after having been denounced for remarking upon the quality of German armaments, he was sentenced to ten more years. (According to one story, he was also condemned for referring to Ivan Bunin—the 1933 Nobel laureate who had emigrated from the Soviet Union—as a classic Russian writer.) On several occasions Shalamov narrowly escaped execution, and he was often close to death from cold, hunger, and exhaustion. Somehow he survived his ordeal, and during the 1950's he returned once more to Moscow to resume his literary career.

Shalamov's subsequent writings can be grouped into four categories. He wrote a handful of essays on literature, primarily on poetry; to the general Soviet reader, though, he was best known as a poet of moderate talent, with five collections of poetry appearing between 1961 and 1977. He had begun to publish his poems in 1957, but before that—beginning in the late 1930's and continuing until 1956—he wrote the poems that made up the unpublished collection "Kolymskie tetradi" (the Kolyma notebooks). These works represented a first attempt to detail the horrors of Kolyma and to reflect upon his experience. The third type of work, and that for which he is most likely to be remembered, comprises the more than one hundred short prose pieces that deal with his imprisonment. He appears to have written the vast majority of them during the late 1950's and early 1960's. Some were smuggled out to the West and published abroad, but even during the relatively liberal Khrushchev years his writing on Kolyma was too graphic to be printed in the Soviet Union. In 1972 Shalamov was forced to denounce the publication of his works abroad, though the statement he issued was not without its ambiguities. Under the policy of *glasnost* instituted by Mikhail Gorbachev, Shalamov's stories still were not published immediately; only in June, 1988, did the highly regarded literary journal *Novy mir* print a major selection of the *Kolyma Tales*. The fourth category of Shalamov's writing, his memoirs, remained unpublished during his lifetime. During the 1970's, his health gradually began to fail. He died on January 17, 1982, with his major achievements yet to be recognized in his homeland.

For many years the Soviet public knew Shalamov only through the verse that he could publish openly. Much of it deals with nature; some of it is about poetry itself. Running through nearly all of his poems is a reflective mood—he seems less interested in capturing a moment than in conveying ideas that have been given time to mature. On the surface the poems seem simple and direct, and they are often classical in their form. Yet their quiet exterior conceals a second meaning that no doubt escaped readers unfamiliar with Shalamov's life or with his other works. Thus in the poem "Stlannik" (dwarf cedar) he describes how that tree grasps the earth and seeks only a drop of warmth, how it nurtures life though seemingly dead, and how it rises from the snow in the spring. Readers of *Kolyma Tales* would readily see the poem as an allegory of the survival of prisoners in the far north.

Shalamov's greatest achievement is clearly *Kolyma Tales*. The stories' power derives in part from their understatedness: Their form is laconic and often seemingly artless, their emotional tone neutral. Shalamov wants to convey a physical suffering and spiritual despair so great that at times his characters are beyond feeling anything at all except perhaps an animal instinct to survive or a blind desire to end their misery. While some writers—Aleksandr Solzhenitsyn, for example—have remarked that people could grow stronger as a result of their experiences in the camps, Shalamov has stated that nothing good ever came to anybody from Kolyma, and his stories illustrate that conviction. Yet he also believed that human qualities can survive in the camps, even if they must remain dormant.

Shalamov manages to remove the usual narrative distance between the reader and the events that he describes; thus, his audience comes into direct contact with a world in which the usual values have been turned upside down or have lost their meaning entirely. His brief pieces powerfully condemn the modern totalitarian state's oppression of the individual.

BIBLIOGRAPHICAL REFERENCES: Shalamov's stories were collected abroad and published as *Kolymskie rasskazy*, 1978; two generous selections from this book have been translated by John Glad as *Kolyma Tales*, 1980; and *Graphite*, 1981. Works that came to light later, including *Chetvertaya Vologda*, can be found in the volume *Voskreshenie listvennitsy*, 1985. Shalamov has received very little critical attention. Brief comments can be found in Edward J. Brown, *Russian Literature Since the Revolution*, 1982 (rev. ed.); and in David Lowe, *Russian Writing Since 1953: A Critical Survey*, 1987. John Glad has provided useful forewords to his two volumes of translations, while a comparison between Aleksandr Solzhenitsyn and Shalamov is made in Geoffrey Hosking, "The Ultimate Circle of the Stalinist Inferno," *New Universities Quarterly*, XXXIV, no. 2 (1980), 161-168. For remarks on Shalamov's poetry as well as his short fiction, see Vera Dunham's review of Glad's translations in *Slavic Review*, XLI (1982), 534-537.

Barry P. Scherr

NTOZAKE SHANGE
Paulette Williams

Born: Trenton, New Jersey
Date: October 18, 1948

PRINCIPAL WORKS

PLAYS: *for colored girls who have considered suicide when the rainbow is enuf*, pr., pb. 1976; *Where the Mississippi Meets the Amazon*, pr. 1977; *From Okra to Greens: A Different Kinda Love Story*, pr. 1978; *Black & White Two-Dimensional Planes*, pr. 1979; *Boogie Woogie Landscapes*, pr. 1979; *Spell No. 7*, pr. 1979; *Mother Courage and Her Children*, pr. 1980.

POETRY: *Nappy Edges*, 1978; *A Daughter's Geography*, 1983; *Ridin' the Moon in Texas: Word Paintings*, 1987.

NOVELS: *Sassafrass, Cypress, and Indigo*, 1982; *Betsey Brown*, 1985.

ESSAYS: *See No Evil: Prefaces, Essays, and Accounts, 1976-1983*, 1984.

The works of poet, playwright, and novelist Ntozake Shange are an essential part of black contemporary literature. Her first popularly successful work, *for colored girls who have considered suicide when the rainbow is enuf*, is poetry brought to the stage and expressed by dance and music. This work was Shange's initial step toward a prolific and innovative literary career.

Shange's intellectual and cultural environment as a child affected her artistic development. Shange was born Paulette Williams in Trenton, New Jersey, on October 18, 1948, to Paul T. Williams, a surgeon, and Eloise Williams, a psychiatric social worker and educator. An eclectic combination of popular music and various types of literature shaped her artistic development. In a self-interview in her poetry *Nappy Edges*, Shange said that her mother read to her from such diverse writers as the Scottish poet William Dunbar, William Shakespeare, T. S. Eliot, and the American poet Countée Cullen. Her musical sense was influenced by Dizzy Gillespie, Chuck Berry, Charlie Parker, Miles Davis, and Josephine Baker, who were frequent guests at her parents' home.

Although the combination of diverse literary and musical influences nourished her literary aspirations, Shange felt oppressed by society because of her race and gender. While she was an undergraduate, she attempted suicide and struggled with the reality of life as a black and a woman. She attempted to resolve her feelings of oppression by changing her name while working toward her master's degree at the University of Southern California. She changed her name to the Zulu words Ntozake, "she who comes with her own things," and Shange, "she who walks like a lion." By changing her name, Shange replaced a name that had nothing to do with her sense of her own reality (Paulette is derived from a man's name, Paul, and Williams is an Anglo-Saxon name) with a name that identified and clarified her identity as a black woman.

Shange's creative aspirations became clearer and more productive during her teaching years. She taught humanities, women's studies, and Afro-American studies at Sonoma State College, Mills College, and at University of California extension classes between 1972 and 1975. During this period, she created interdisciplinary and improvisational works that were performed in bars from San Francisco to New York. These acts were poetry readings accompanied by dance and music. Shange strives to create a sense of movement in her poetry, and music and dance are the elements by which she attempts to bring the written word alive.

After moving to New York in 1975, Shange's creative integration of music, dance, and poetry moved from the bar to the stage. Seven women dressed as the colors of the rainbow enacted Shange's poetry in what she calls a choreopoem: *for colored girls who have considered suicide when the rainbow is enuf. The New York Times* praised Shange's effort, noting that it was "a play to be seen, savored, and treasured." Official recognition is evidenced by its many subsequent productions in the United States, England, Brazil, and the West Indies, and Shange was awarded the Obie Award, the Outer Critics Circle Award, and the *Mademoiselle* Award.

Shange's success with her poetry led her to experiment with other genres of literature. In 1978, Shange wrote a prose piece entitled *Sassafrass, Cypress, and Indigo*, which explores the aspirations, beliefs, and personal turmoil of three black girls from Charleston, South Carolina, and follows their dreams to different American cities. Shange's continual stress on the importance of the black female voice is evident in her poetry in *Nappy Edges*. She discusses the responsibility of the black poet in "things i wd say," of black heritage, and of the subjugation of women by men. In *See No Evil*, Shange explains her creative and political voice. Shange's travels to the Caribbean, South and Central America, and the South Pacific exposed her to different theater communities and to the cultural aggression she found in women around the world. In her collection of poems *A Daughter's Geography*, Shange poetically describes her travels "from the indigo moods of Harlem streets to the sun-drenched colors of the Caribbean," and she emphasizes her belief in the power of women to improve and revolutionize societies.

Shange continues to experiment with language and form in her works. *Ridin' the Moon in Texas* is a book of "word paintings." Her poetry is combined with visual aids such as photographs and paintings by other artists. The subject of the black woman and the style of implementing and combining different art forms are characteristic of Shange's work. Shange celebrates the black woman in her poetry, novels, and performance pieces. She uses music and dance, psychology and sociology, politics, and ordinary household items to exercise her black female voice. Although Shange has been criticized for her "worn-out feminist clichés" and her failure to develop her characters adequately, she expresses an honesty and sincerity in her work. Her works are woman-centered. She presents vulnerability, fear, and joy by using dance and music to capture the vitality of women and by using politics and the oppressive aspects of society to capture the thoughts and attitudes of women. Shange's works are an important part of contemporary literature because she strives to represent the beauty and importance of a particular voice within society.

BIBLIOGRAPHICAL REFERENCES: *Interviews with Contemporary Women Playwrights*, 1987, compiled by Kathleen Betsko and Rachel Koenig, includes a candid interview with Shange; *Dictionary of Literary Biography*, Vols. 38, 1985, includes an extensive biography of Shange written by Elizabeth Brown; *Contemporary Authors*, Vols. 85-88, 1980, edited by Frances Carol Locher, includes a biography; and see *Contemporary Literary Criticism*, Vol. 8, 1976, for essays by John Simon and Michele Wallace. For the feminist viewpoint, see Carolyn Mitchell, "'A Laying On of Hands': Transcending the City in Ntozake Shange's *for colored girls who have considered suicide when the rainbow is enuf*," in *Women Writers and the City: Essays in Literary Criticism*, 1984, edited by Susan Merrill Squier. For further study, see also *Black Women Writers at Work*, 1983, edited by Claudia Tate; Carol P. Christ, *Diving Deep and Surfacing: Women Writers on Spiritual Quest*, 1980; and Sandra L. Richards, "Conflicting Impulses in the Plays of Ntozake Shange," *Black American Literature Forum*, XVII (Summer, 1983), 73-78.

Kathleen M. Ermitage

GEORGE BERNARD SHAW

Born: Dublin, Ireland
Date: July 26, 1856

Died: Ayot St. Lawrence, England
Date: November 2, 1950

PRINCIPAL WORKS

PLAYS: *Widowers' Houses*, pr. 1892, revised 1898; *Arms and the Man*, pr. 1894; *Candida: A Mystery*, pr. 1897; *The Devil's Disciple*, pr. 1897; *The Man of Destiny*, pr. 1897; *You Never Can Tell*, pb. 1898; *Mrs. Warren's Profession*, pb. 1898; *Captain Brassbound's Conversion*, pr. 1900; *Caesar and Cleopatra*, pb. 1901; *The Admirable Bashville*, pr. 1902; *Man and Superman*, pb. 1903; *How He Lied to Her Husband*, pr. 1904; *John Bull's Other Island*, pr. 1904; *Passion, Poison, and Petrifaction*, pr., pb. 1905; *Major Barbara*, pr. 1905; *The Doctor's Dilemma*, pr. 1906; *The Interlude at the Playhouse*, pr., pb. 1907; *Getting Married*, pr. 1908; *The Shewing Up of Blanco Posnet*, pr. 1909; *Press Cuttings*, pr., pb. 1909; *Misalliance*, pr. 1910; *The Dark Lady of the Sonnets*, pr. 1910; *Fanny's First Play*, pr. 1911; *Overruled*, pr. 1912; *Androcles and the Lion*, pr. 1913; *Pygmalion*, pr. 1913 (in German), pr., pb. 1914 (in English); *Great Catherine*, pr. 1913; *The Music Cure*, pr. 1914; *The Inca of Perusalem*, pr. 1916; *Augustus Does His Bit*, pr. 1917; *O'Flaherty, V.C.*, pr. 1917; *Annajanska, the Bolshevik Empress*, pr. 1918; *Heartbreak House*, pb. 1919; *Back to Methuselah*, pb. 1921; *Jitta's Atonement*, pr. 1923; *Saint Joan*, pr. 1923; *The Apple Cart*, pr. 1929; *Too True to Be Good*, pr. 1932; *On the Rocks*, pr. 1933; *Village Wooing*, pr., pb. 1934; *The Six Men of Calais*, pr. 1934; *The Simpleton of the Unexpected Isles*, pr., pb. 1935; *The Millionairess*, pr., pb. 1936; *Cymbeline Refinished*, pr. 1937; *Geneva*, pr. 1938; *In Good King Charles's Golden Days*, pr., pb. 1939; *Buoyant Billions*, pb. 1947 (in German), pr. 1949 (in English); *Shakes Versus Shaw: A Puppet Play*, pr. 1949; *Far-Fetched Fables*, pr., pb. 1950; *Passion Play: A Dramatic Fragment*, pb. 1971.

NOVELS: *An Unsocial Socialist*, 1884, 1887; *Cashel Byron's Profession*, 1886, revised 1889, 1901; *Love Among the Artists*, 1900; *The Irrational Knot*, 1905; *Immaturity*, 1930; *An Unfinished Novel*, 1958.

SHORT FICTION: *The Adventures of the Black Girl in Her Search for God*, 1932.

LITERARY CRITICISM: *The Quintessence of Ibsenism*, 1891, revised 1913; *The Perfect Wagnerite: A Commentary on "The Ring of the Niblungs,"* 1898, revised 1907; *Dramatic Opinions and Essays*, 1906; *The Sanity of Art*, 1908; *Pen Portraits and Reviews*, 1931; *Our Theatre in the Nineties*, 1931; *The Nondramatic Literary Criticism of Bernard Shaw*, 1972.

POLITICS: *Common Sense About the War*, 1914 (expanded as *What I Really Wrote About the War*, 1930); *How To Settle the Irish Question*, 1917; *Ruskin's Politics*, 1921; *The Intelligent Woman's Guide to Socialism and Capitalism*, 1928, revised 1937; *Everybody's Political What's What*, 1944.

AUTOBIOGRAPHY: *Shaw Gives Himself Away: An Autobiographical Miscellany*, 1939; *Sixteen Self Sketches*, 1949; *Shaw: An Autobiography*, 1969-1970; *Shaw 1914-1918: Journey to Heartbreak*, 1973.

CORRESPONDENCE: *Collected Letters, 1874-1897*, 1965; *Collected Letters, 1898-1910*, 1972; *Collected Letters, 1911-1925*, 1985; *Collected Letters, 1926-1950*, 1988.

EDITED TEXT: *Fabian Essays in Socialism*, 1889, revised 1908, 1931, 1948.

One of the greatest British dramatists, perhaps the greatest dramatist of his generation, George Bernard Shaw revitalized the moribund English stage with a body of work that continues to entertain and challenge audiences around the world. Born in Dublin, Ireland, on July 26, 1856, to a family in financial decline, he was reared in a household that might have come from one of his plays. His father, George Carr Shaw, was a good-natured drunkard somewhat in the manner of Alfred Doolittle in *Pygmalion*, while his mother, the former Lucinda Elizabeth Gurly, was a strong-willed woman who in 1874 abandoned her family to go to London with her voice teacher, George John Vandeleur Lee, to pursue a musical career.

Largely self-taught, Shaw left school early. From 1874 to 1876 he worked as an office boy, cashier, and rent collector for Charles Townsend, a Dublin real estate agent. Here as well as at home he saw the evil effects of poverty and social injustice that he would repeatedly attack in his plays.

In 1876 Shaw joined his mother in London. After a brief stint with the Edison Telegraph Company (1879-1880), he devoted himself entirely to literature, writing five mediocre novels; he observed that anyone who would read *An Unsocial Socialist* would read anything. A lecture by Henry George in 1882 converted Shaw to Socialism; two years later he helped Beatrice and Sidney Webb found the Fabian Society, an organization of bourgeois Socialists who favored gradual reform. Shaw's "desperate days," as he called this period, ended when William Archer asked him to become a music critic for the *Star.* Under the pseudonym Corno di Bassetto, he wrote readable, astute analyses of performances, always advocating innovation and excellence. These qualities also characterize his art and music criticism for the *World* and his theater criticism for the *Saturday Review.*

His 1890 lecture to the Fabian Society on Henrik Ibsen led not only to his book *The Quintessence of Ibsenism* but also to a private performance of *Gengangere* (pb. 1881; *Ghosts*, 1885). The Independent Theatre Company then asked Shaw for a play of his own. He revised *Widowers' Houses*, an attack on slumlords, which he had begun in 1885 with Archer. By 1901 he had written nine more plays, the best of them mingling wit with social criticism. His first major success, *The Devil's Disciple*, came not in London but in New York; not until Harley Granville-Barker produced eleven of his plays at the Royal Court Theatre, largely funded by Shaw himself (he was married to the Irish heiress Charlotte Payne Townsend in 1898), did his reputation become secure. Awarded the Nobel Prize in Literature in 1925, largely for his brilliant *Saint Joan*, he continued to write until his death at age ninety-four.

Like Ibsen, like many English playwrights of the seventeenth and eighteenth centuries, Shaw wanted to use the stage as a pulpit to reform society by forcing audiences to see the disparity between reality and conventional wisdom. In *Major Barbara* it is the munitions factory owner, Andrew Undershaft, not the Salvation Army, that helps the poor. *Pygmalion* points to the folly of class distinctions, since accent, not character or merit, determines one's station. Joan of Arc is canonized, but if she returned to earth she would once again be executed for her refusal to accept any authority beyond personal revelation.

Shaw was less concerned with specific political or social reforms—though he did want these—than with the evolution of mankind from its present state of weak imperfection to a condition approaching the divine. Like the serpent in *Back to Methuselah*, Shaw did not so much examine present conditions and ask why things were that way. Rather, he imagined a different future and asked why things could not be so ordered. He believed in an irresistible "life force" that would lead to a better world if only people linked their wills to its power. Significantly, Shaw's women are more aware of this evolutionary force, more in harmony with it, than his male characters—Major Barbara, Candida, and, most clearly, Saint Joan come immediately to mind.

Rejecting the notion of his contemporary Oscar Wilde that art should exist solely for its own sake, Shaw sometimes went to the opposite extreme of writing tracts rather than plays. The early dramas are especially didactic. Act 3 of *Man and Superman* is little more than a Platonic discourse on the life force. Yet Shaw realized that to educate he first had to entertain, and his best comedies delight and instruct. *Major Barbara*'s wit rivals Wilde's in *The Importance of Being Earnest* (pr. 1895); the exposure of the hypocrisy of organizations dedicated to doing good is at once pointed and funny. *John Bull's Other Island*, Shaw's exploration of the Irish question, made King Edward VII laugh so hard that he broke his chair. *Pygmalion* is highly enjoyable, but audiences cannot miss the implied criticism of England's class system. Always a gadfly, often a butterfly, Shaw created among his fifty plays at least a dozen that will remain staples of the dramatic repertoire, inviting the spectator to laugh at the same time that they compel him to think.

BIBLIOGRAPHICAL REFERENCES: The literature on Shaw is extensive. Elsie R. Adams and Donald C. Haberman, *G. B. Shaw: An Annotated Bibliography of Writings About Him*, 1986-1987, contains 2,677 entries arranged chronologically through 1978. Among the biographies are Hesketh Pearson, *Bernard Shaw: A Full-Length Portrait*, 1942, revised 1951; Stephen Winsten, *Jesting Apostle: The Life of Bernard Shaw*, 1956, based partly on research, partly on firsthand acquaintance; and J. Percy Smith, *The Unrepentant Pilgrim: A Study of the Development of Bernard Shaw*, 1965. B. C. Rosset, *Shaw of Dublin: The Formative Years*, 1964, examines the dramatist's early life (to 1886), as does the first volume of Michael Holroyd, *Bernard Shaw*, 1988, which covers the period 1856-1898. Stanley Weintraub, *The Unexpected Shaw: Biographical Approaches to G. B. S. and His Work*, 1982, uses the life to understand the writings. Eldon C. Hill, *George Bernard Shaw*, 1978, presents the typical Twayne survey of the life and works. Good studies of the plays include Charles A. Berst, *Bernard Shaw and the Art of the Drama*, 1973; Louis Crompton, *Shaw the Dramatist*, 1969; John A. Mills, *Language and Laughter: Comic Dialectic in the Plays of Bernard Shaw*, 1969, which analyzes Shaw's linguistic virtuosity; Maurice J. Valency, *The Cart and the Trumpet: The Plays of George Bernard Shaw*, 1973; Robert F. Whitman, *Shaw and the Play of Ideas*, 1977, which argues that the drama derives its power from the conflict between idealism and reality. Keith M. May, *Ibsen and Shaw*, 1985, considers Shaw's debt to the Norwegian playwright. Harold Bloom has edited a collection of critical essays on the plays: *George Bernard Shaw*, 1987; Elsie B. Adams, "Heartless, Heartbroken, and Heartfelt: A Recurrent Theme in the Plays of Bernard Shaw," *English Literature in Transition (1880-1920)*, XXV (1982), 4-9, treats the role of emotion in the plays. For a study of the fiction, see R. F. Dietrich, *Portrait of the Artist as a Young Superman*, 1969.

Joseph Rosenblum

IRWIN SHAW

Born: New York, New York
Date: February 27, 1913

Died: Davos, Switzerland
Date: May 16, 1984

PRINCIPAL WORKS

NOVELS: *The Young Lions*, 1948; *The Troubled Air*, 1951; *Lucy Crown*, 1956; *Two Weeks in Another Town*, 1960; *Voices of a Summer Day*, 1965; *Rich Man, Poor Man*, 1970; *Evening in Byzantium*, 1973; *Nightwork*, 1975; *Beggerman, Thief*, 1977; *The Top of the Hill*, 1979; *Bread upon the Waters*, 1981; *Acceptable Losses*, 1982.

SHORT FICTION: *Sailor off the Bremen and Other Stories*, 1939; *Welcome to the City and Other Stories*, 1942; *Act of Faith and Other Stories*, 1946; *Mixed Company*, 1950; *Tip on a Dead Jockey and Other Stories*, 1957; *Selected Short Stories of Irwin Shaw*, 1961; *Love on a Dark Street*, 1965; *Short Stories of Irwin Shaw*, 1966; *God Was Here, but He Left Early*, 1973; *Short Stories: Five Decades*, 1978.

PLAYS: *Bury the Dead*, pr. 1936; *The Gentle People*, pb. 1939; *Sons and Soldiers*, pb. 1944; *The Assassin*, pr. 1944; *Children from Their Games*, pb. 1962.

NONFICTION: *Report on Israel*, 1950 (with Robert Capa); *In the Company of Dolphins*, 1964; *Paris! Paris!*, 1976 (with Ronald Searle).

Irwin Shaw has been most widely acclaimed as a writer of ironically urbane short stories, which in large measure helped to define what many know to be "*The New Yorker* story," and for *The Young Lions*, which remains one of the most noteworthy American novels about World War II. Shaw was born in New York City, on February 27, 1913, to William Shaw and Rose (Tompkins) Shaw. He attended public schools in Brooklyn before enrolling in Brooklyn College. After his freshman year, however, he was forced to withdraw from college because of academic difficulties. For the next several years, he worked in a variety of jobs in local factories and retail stores in order to make his reenrollment financially feasible. In 1934, he was graduated from Brooklyn College with a B.A. degree, having distinguished himself by writing several plays for the college dramatic society and a regular column for the college newspaper; he also played quarterback for the varsity football team.

After graduation, Shaw helped to support his family by writing radio scripts for the serials *Dick Tracy* and *The Gumps*. In 1936, he submitted *Bury the Dead* to the New Theater League, and after several Off-Broadway performances, it was produced on Broadway, establishing Shaw as an important new voice in the American theater. The play concerns the refusal of six ordinary soldiers to be buried after they have been killed in battle. In technique, it owes much to the experimental German theater of the 1920's; in tone and theme, it is distinctly American, resembling much of the antiwar literature that followed World War I.

The success of *Bury the Dead* led to a Hollywood contract, and for financial reasons, Shaw wrote occasional screenplays. His second stage play, *The Gentle People*, was produced on Broadway by the Group Theater. Also during this time he published his first collection of short stories, *Sailor off the Bremen and Other Stories*. *The Gentle People* had more commercial success than *Bury the Dead*, but the critical response was more lukewarm. When *The Assassin* was dismissed for its fairly conventional technique and structure and for its seemingly propagandist acceptance of conventional views of the war, Shaw responded bitterly in the 1946 preface to the published play, denouncing the narrow ideological range afforded by the major Broadway critics to political plays and, in effect, ending his career as a dramatist.

Still, Shaw's reputation as a writer of short stories became firmly established, with his stories being included regularly in the O. Henry Prize collections and with several, such as "Walking Wounded" in 1944, being awarded first prize. This war story appeared in *Act of Faith and Other Stories*, published in 1946, which along with *Sailor off the Bremen and Other Stories* and *Welcome to the City and Other Stories*, published in 1942, established

Shaw's range as a writer of short stories. The much-anthologized "The Girls in Their Summer Dresses" and "The Eighty-Yard Run" deftly treat the sexual and social ironies that often undercut the success seemingly inherent in upper-middle-class American life. "Second Mortgage" and "Main Currents of American Thought" are notable explorations of the effects of economic turmoil on the urban family struggling to avoid poverty. "Residents of Other Cities," "Act of Faith," and "Medal from Jerusalem" are notable for their treatments of Jewish issues.

In 1948, Shaw published *The Young Lions*, his first and still most highly regarded novel. The first American novel to attempt a panoramic treatment of the European theater of World War II (and still generally acknowledged as the most successful of all such treatments), *The Young Lions* presents the eventually interconnected experiences of three soldiers, two Americans and one German. The structure of the novel depends on very elaborate parallels between events and characters and on a subtle pattern of interrelated symbols. It has been criticized for being structurally too contrived, but it has been praised for its precise depiction of incidents and its memorable characterizations.

Shaw subsequently published many other works of both short and long fiction. In general, the short stories have been much more highly regarded than the novels, which have been seen as relying too much on melodramatic structural devices. This impression of the novels has been reinforced by the publication of "entertainments" such as *Nightwork* and *The Top of the Hill*. In addition, the television adaptation of the Jordache novels, *Rich Man, Poor Man* and *Beggerman, Thief*, has done much to increase Shaw's commercial success at the expense of his critical reputation.

In almost all Shaw's work, there is an underlying pessimism about the horrors of experience, represented as "accidents" that dramatically alter a character's circumstances and attitudes. This pessimism is balanced only by a restrained faith in the basic goodness of some individuals who can by their actions somewhat mitigate the effects of those horrors. The critical consensus is that the balance is maintained effectively by the ironic detachment that Shaw finds possible in the short stories, but that the balance is undercut by the melodramatic structuring that he finds necessary in the novels. Nevertheless, the response to Shaw's last two novels, *Bread upon the Waters* and *Acceptable Losses*, has suggested to some critics that a serious reevaluation of Shaw's importance is necessary.

BIBLIOGRAPHICAL REFERENCES: James R. Giles, *Irwin Shaw*, 1983, is a useful book-length study of Shaw's work. John W. Aldridge, *After the Lost Generation*, 1951, and Leslie Fiedler, "Irwin Shaw: Adultery, the Last Politics," *Commentary*, XXII (1956), 71-74, are the two most influential attacks against Shaw and have established the critical justifications for ignoring his work. Cleanth Brooks and Warren French, *Understanding Fiction*, 1959 (2d ed.), provides a succinct analysis of "The Girls in Their Summer Dresses," and Bergen Evans, "Irwin Shaw," *English Journal*, XL (1951), 485-491, is a positive appraisal of *The Young Lions*. See also William Startt, "Irwin Shaw: An Extended Talent," *Midwest Quarterly*, II (1961), 325-337, and James R. Giles, "Irwin Shaw's Original Prologue to *The Young Lions*," *Resources for American Library Study*, XI (1981), 115-119.

Martin Kich

SAM SHEPARD
Samuel Shepard Rogers

Born: Fort Sheridan, Illinois
Date: November 5, 1943

Principal Works

PLAYS: *Cowboys*, pr. 1964; *Rock Garden*, pr. 1964; *Icarus's Mother*, pr. 1965; *Red Cross*, pr. 1966; *La Turista*, pr. 1966; *Melodrama Play*, pr. 1967; *Forensic and the Navigators*, pr. 1967; *The Holy Ghostly*, pr. 1969; *The Unseen Hand*, pr. 1969; *Operation Sidewinder*, pr., pb. 1970; *Mad Dog Blues*, pr., pb. 1971; *Cowboy Mouth*, pr., pb. 1971 (with Patti Smith); *Back Bog Beast Bait*, pr. 1971; *The Tooth of Crime*, pr. 1972; *Geography of a Horse Dreamer*, pr., pb. 1974; *Action*, pr. 1974; *Angel City*, pr., pb. 1976; *Suicide in B-Flat*, pr. 1976; *Curse of the Starving Class*, pb. 1976; *Seduced*, pr. 1978; *Buried Child*, pr. 1978; *True West*, pr. 1980; *Fool for Love*, pr., pb. 1983; *A Lie of the Mind*, pr. 1985.

SCREENPLAYS: *Me and My Brother*, 1968 (with Robert Frank); *Zabriskie Point*, 1969 (with Michelangelo Antonioni and others); *Paris, Texas*, 1984 (with L. M. Kit Carson); *Fool for Love*, 1985.

MISCELLANEOUS: *Hawk Moon: A Book of Short Stories, Poems, and Monologues*, 1973; *Rolling Thunder Logbook*, 1977; *Motel Chronicles*, 1982.

Samuel Shepard Rogers has been compared to Eugene O'Neill in theatrical range and power. He was born in Fort Sheridan, Illinois, on November 5, 1943, the son of Army Air Force bomber pilot Samuel Shepard Rogers and Jane Schook Rogers. Between 1943 and 1955, the family moved often from army post to army post, including a stay in Guam. They finally settled in California, residing during Shepard's teenage years on an avocado and sheep ranch in Duarte. Shepard found some aspects of the ranching life attractive but chafed against the ordinariness of his relationship with his parents and the tedium of rural society. He became enamored of motion pictures and their heroes, took up jazz drumming, and read Beat poets Lawrence Ferlinghetti and Gregory Corso. In 1962, he auditioned for the Bishop's Company Repertory Players and began a six-month tour as an itinerant actor, ending up in New York City's East Village in 1963. There, he secured a job at the Village Gate, which introduced him to the country's best jazz musicians and to Ralph Cook. Cook launched the Theatre Genesis, as well as Sam Shepard's career, in the 1960's.

The atmosphere of East Village and the impetus of Off-Off-Broadway theater perfectly nurtured Shepard's eclectic talent. In 1964, he made his debut as a playwright with *Cowboys* and *Rock Garden*, two one-act plays that introduced several of his themes and stylistic techniques. In *Rock Garden*, he presents a father who revels in his lifeless arrangement of rocks, whereas the son builds a counterpointed description of his sexual techniques with women until it subsumes the father's drone in an explosion of metaphors. This conflict of generations, brought forth through metaphorical language that rises from a dark, nearly bare stage, is typical of Shepard's early plays. The open stage requires audience members to exercise their imaginations in order to "complete" Shepard's dramatic scenes, thus contributing to his expansion of time and space.

Taking his lead from the Beat generation and from jazz improvisation, Shepard creates "transformational" characters, who act themselves out through disruptions, explosions, contradictions, and shifting realities. Often, they fear the loss of their individuality because of some unnameable force, and they move and talk rapidly in an attempt to invent themselves as larger-than-life figures. Thus, Shepard is preoccupied in his early plays with various mythic models—the cowboy, the Indian, the rock star, the gangster, the film star, the gothic monster, the business magnate—who suggest possibilities for people wishing to escape the traps of body, geography, or system.

Many of Shepard's characters do escape or transform themselves on the stage. For example, several in *Operation Sidewinder* emerge to a "fifth world" of Hopi legend, as the corrupt "fourth world" comes to final destruction. The mythical figures of *Mad Dog Blues* join hands and exit dancing through the audience. In *La Turista*, Kent ends the play by swinging from a rope at the back of the theater, crashing through the set, and leaving only his outline behind. These attempts at escape stem from the playwright's serious concern that America was "cracking open and crashing into the sea"—an outlook that led him to rely on apocalyptic endings, not necessarily motivated or prepared for by the dramatic plot. They also reflect his personal restlessness.

Eventually, however, Shepard began to recognize that escape is not always possible. In *The Tooth of Crime*, for example, an established rock star, Hoss, dreams of shucking off his responsibilities and his retinue to strike out like a "gypsy killer" into open territory. Instead, his personality and reputation are usurped by Crow, a young challenger, and he finally kills himself as a last act of independence. *Curse of the Starving Class* portrays a family one member describes as having "nitroglycerine in the blood"—a condition that leads to their destruction and the loss of their ranch. *Buried Child*, for which Shepard won the Pulitzer Prize in 1979, is a dramatization of blighted family relationships, brought forth by incest between mother and son. So long as the dead child of that union remains buried on their property, no crops grow, and the family members are mentally or physically crippled. Only a violent intrusion by an outsider can unearth their secret and make their farm, as well as their lives, productive again.

A major concern in Shepard's work, hinted at in the plays discussed above, is that the nuclear family may be bankrupt—that power struggles, conflicts, and obligatory role-playing destroy most family relationships. *True West*, *Fool for Love*, and *A Lie of the Mind* all illustrate the playwright's preoccupation with the family's decay and the fragility of modern love. In Shepard's family conflicts, women appear to have the lesser voice, seeming only to support the males in their macho strivings. Yet as Florence Falk points out, Shepard's women are resilient survivors, whereas the men often remain empty inside their macho images. Later plays, such as *Fool for Love* and *A Lie of the Mind*, have countered critics' complaints about his female characters by presenting women who work through their debilities and establish themselves as equal or even superior to their men.

Shepard's dramatic imagination and power have been widely recognized, but opinion is unsettled as to his eventual stature in American drama. Yet the sheer volume of his work—more than forty plays, three volumes of prose, and several screenplays—commands attention. That he has received the Pulitzer Prize as well as more than a dozen Obie awards for dramatic excellence and international recognition for his screenplays, adds luster to his reputation. These accomplishments make him, at the very least, one of the leading lights in American arts and letters.

BIBLIOGRAPHICAL REFERENCES: No complete edition of Shepard's plays exists, but several of his better-known works are in *Seven Plays*, 1981, with an introduction by Richard Gilman, and in *Four Two-Act Plays*, 1980. Two good critical biographies are Ron Mottram, *Inner Landscapes: The Theater of Sam Shepard*, 1984, and Ellen Oumano, *Sam Shepard: The Life and Work of an American Dreamer*, 1986. For analyses of plays produced before 1981, see *American Dreams: The Imagination of Sam Shepard*, 1981, edited by Bonnie Marranca. Other studies include Doris Auerbach, *Shepard, Kopit, and the Off Broadway Theater*, 1982; Herbert Blau, "The American Dream in American Gothic: The Plays of Sam Shepard and Adrienne Kennedy," *Modern Drama*, XXVII (1984), 520-539; Dennis Carroll, "The Filmic Cut and 'Switchback' in the Plays of Sam Shepard," *Modern Drama*, XXVIII (1985), 125-138; Sheila Rabillard, "Sam Shepard: Theatrical Power and American Dreams," *Modern Drama*, XXX (1987), 58-71; and W. W. Demastes, "Understanding Sam Shepard's Realism," *Comparative Drama*, XXI (1987), 229-248. Two articles on individual plays reflect larger concerns in Shepard's work and are therefore especially valuable: Tucker Orbison, "Mythic Levels in Shepard's *True West*," *Modern Drama*, XXVII (1984), 506-519; and Leonard Wilcox, "Modernism vs. Postmodernism: Shepard's *The Tooth of Crime* and the Discourses of Popular Culture," *Modern Drama*, XXX (1987), 560-573.

Perry D. Luckett

VIKTOR SHKLOVSKY

Born: St. Petersburg, Russia
Date: January 18, 1893

Died: Moscow, Soviet Union
Date: December 8, 1984

Principal Works

CRITICISM: *Voskresheniye slova*, 1914 (*Resurrection of the Word*, 1972); *Svintsovyy zhrebiy*, 1914; *Rozanov*, 1921 (English translation, 1982); *Khod konya*, 1923; *Literatura i kinematograf*, 1923; *O teorii prozy*, 1925; *Udachi i porazheniya Maksima Gor'kogo*, 1926; *Ikh nastoyashcheye*, 1927; *Motalka, knizhka ne dlya kinematografov*, 1927; *Pyat' chelovek znakomykh*, 1927; *Tekhnika pisatel'skogo remesla*, 1927; *Gamburgskiy schyot*, 1928; *Mater'yal i stil' v romane L'va Tolstogo "Voyna i mir,"* 1928; *Matvey Komarov, zhitel' goroda Moskvy*, 1929; *Podenshchina*, 1930; *Poiski optimizma*, 1931; *Kak pisat' tsenarii*, 1931; *Chulkov i Levshin*, 1933; *Zametki o proze Pushkina*, 1937; *Dnevnik*, 1939; *Zametki o proze russkikh klassikov*, 1953; *Za i protiv: Zametki o Dostoyevskom*, 1957; *Khudozhestvennaya proza: Razmyshleniya i razbory*, 1959; *Za sorok let: Stat'i o kino*, 1965; *Staroye i novoye: Kniga statey o detskoy literatury*, 1966; *Povesti o proze: Razmyshleniya i razbory*, 1966; *Tetiva: O neskhodstve skhodnogo*, 1970; *Energiya zablyuzhdeniya: Kniga o syuzhete*, 1981; *Za 60 let: Raboty o kino*, 1985.

NOVELS: *Sentimental'noye puteshestviye: Vospominaniya 1917-1922*, 1923 (*A Sentimental Journey: Memoirs 1917-1922*, 1970); *Zoo: Ili, Pis'ma ne o lyubvi*, 1923 (*Zoo: Or, Letters Not About Love*, 1971); *Tret'ya fabrika*, 1926 (*Third Factory*, 1977); *Kratkaya no dostovernaya povest' o dvoryanine Bolotove*, 1930; *Zhitiye arkhiyereyskogo sluzhi*, 1931; *Kapitan Fedotov*, 1936; *Marko Polo*, 1936; *Povest' o khudozhnike Fedotove*, 1955.

BIOGRAPHY: *Room, zhizn' i rabota*, 1929; *O Mayakovskom*, 1940 (*Mayakovsky and His Circle*, 1972); *Lev Tolstoy*, 1963 (English translation, 1978); *Eyzenshteyn*, 1973.

SHORT FICTION: *O masterakh starinnykh, 1714-1812*, 1951; *Istoricheskiye povesti i rasskazy*, 1958.

SCREENPLAYS: *Bukhta smerti*, 1926; *Kryl'ya kholopa*, 1926; *Po zakonu*, 1926; *Predatel'*, 1926 (with Lev Nikulin); *Prostitutka*, 1927; *Schastlivye cherepki*, 1927; *Tret'ya meshchanskaya*, 1927 (with Abram Room); *Dva bronevika*, 1928; *Dom na trubnoy*, 1928 (with others); *Ivan da Marya*, 1928 (with B. Altshuler and V. Sirokov); *Kazaki*, 1928 (with Vladimir Barskiy); *Kapitanskaya dochka*, 1928; *Ledyanoy dom*, 1928 (with Georgiy Grebner and Boris Leonidov); *Ovod*, 1928 (with Konstantin Mardzhanov); *Ukhaby*, 1928; *Posledniy attraktsion*, 1929; *Turksib*, 1929 (with Aleksandr Macheret, E. Aron, and V. Turin); *Ochen' prosto*, 1931; *Mërtvyy dom*, 1932; *Gorizont*, 1933; *Zhit'*, 1933; *Zolotye ruki*, 1933; *Minin i Pozharskiy*, 1939; *Alisher Navoi*, 1947; *Dalëkaya nevesta*, 1948 (with E. Pomeshchikov and N. Rozhkov); *Chuk i Gek*, 1953; *Dokhunda*, 1957; *Kazaki*, 1961.

JOURNALISM: *Vstrechi*, 1944.

MEMOIRS: *Zhili-byli*, 1964.

TRAVEL SKETCH: *Gornaya Gruziya: Pshaviya, Khevsuretiya, Mukheviya*, 1930.

CHILDREN'S LITERATURE: *Puteshestviye v stranu kino*, 1926; *Nandu II*, 1928; *Turksib*, 1930; *Marko Polo, razvedchik*, 1931; *Skazka o tenyakh*, 1931; *Zhizn' khudozhnika Fedotova*, 1936; *Rasskaz o Pushkine*, 1937.

ANTHOLOGIES: *Sobraniye sochineniy v trekh tomakh*, 1973-1974; *Izbrannoye v dvukh tomakh*, 1983.

Because of the energy, imagination, and versatility manifested in his numerous writings, Viktor Borisovich Shklovsky won recognition as the most durable and possibly the most prominent critic and writer affiliated with the Russian Formalist movement. His father was a mathematics teacher of Jewish ancestry, and his mother was of Latvian descent; he was born in St. Petersburg on January 18, 1893, and was reared in a household which included an older half-brother and a sister. Apparently even during his adolescent years, Shklovsky had a proclivity for literary disputation. He published a short article in 1908, and while he enrolled at the University of St. Petersburg in 1913, problems of critical theory evidently interested him more than academic matters; in 1914, an important essay, *Resurrection of the Word*, appeared, which presented his assessment of the challenging new ideas advanced by Russian Futurist writers. In order to promote innovative approaches to art and literary style, he took a leading part in the formation of Opoyaz, a society for the study of poetic language.

During World War I, Shklovsky enlisted in the army and served with Russian forces stationed in Galicia and the Ukraine. For a certain time, he also was employed in the capital as an instructor for armored car personnel. His political leanings led to complications after the Russian Revolutions of 1917. In connection with his official duties, he spent time on the Austrian front and also in Iran; while in Petrograd, he took part in a plot to restore parliamentary government at the expense of the Bolshevik regime. He escaped to Kiev, but upon his return, he was exonerated of political charges. In Petrograd Shklovsky married Vasilisa Georgievna Kordi, who became the mother of his two children, Varvara and Nikita. Shklovsky assisted young writers, such as the Serapion brothers, and he became a member of Lef, an association of Futurist and Formalist authors. Once more to avoid arrest on political grounds, he emigrated and remained abroad for more than a year, first in Finland and then in Germany; in the autumn of 1923, under the terms of a general amnesty, he returned to his native country and settled in Moscow. Highly idiosyncratic views of his personal travails during this period were presented in semiautobiographical works such as *A Sentimental Journey*, *Zoo*, and *Third Factory*, which have the appearance of novels but, because of their unusual patterns of discursive narration and odd ways of designating the author's point of view, elude precise classification. Shklovsky's penchant for experimentation also was demonstrated in curious traits, such as the frequent use of one-sentence paragraphs; in places, he employed an erratic mixture of high-sounding phrases and colloquial expressions.

In major theoretical efforts such as *O teorii prozy*, Shklovsky formulated distinctions which posed in forthright terms the criteria that were important for literary analysis as he conceived of it. Contending that form rather than content should be regarded as the proper standard by which fictional works should be understood, he maintained that devices such as obstruction, parallelism, retardation, and contact were the essential elements of narrative writing. In arguing that the sum total of such means determined the nature and quality of literary works, Shklovsky posited an approach to criticism that, while supported by many examples, struck some readers as extreme and was viewed by others as a bold and innovative method. The notion of estrangement (*ostranenie*), which later was cited by many others in a variety of contexts, was probably the most influential of the conceptions that Shklovsky developed.

A sizable part of Shklovsky's writing had to do with the cinema, and indeed, he wrote and collaborated in the composition of many screenplays; his views about film were presented in theoretical works and biographical studies. Among the exemplars he cited as vital in the development of modern cultural ideas was Sergei Eisenstein, the director whose seemingly plotless techniques in some ways resembled Shklovsky's prose conceptions. At times other literary figures, both major and relatively little known, were discussed in the course of critical investigations that were meant to illustrate the interdependence of genres. Works dealing with historical figures in their turn were followed by fictional narratives that were set in past centuries. During periods when, under Soviet premier Joseph Stalin, ideological constraints imposed severe limitations on the nature and scope of creative activity, Shklovsky turned to outwardly more innocuous forms of writing. In 1930, in a newspaper article, he renounced his earlier views in an effort to mollify critics in official circles. Nevertheless, when subsequently his memoir *Mayakovsky and His Circle* appeared, Shklovsky was taken to task for his positive stance toward Futurism. Concerns of a different sort also affected his life; during World War II, he served as a correspondent and furnished reports from areas where fighting had taken place. In February, 1945, his son Nikita was killed in action; some time later, Shklovsky was divorced from his wife and was married to Serafima Gustavovna Narbut.

Although further difficulties with his literary efforts arose during the later years of Stalin's government, Shklovsky subsequently was honored as an important Soviet author. His biographical study *Lev Tolstoy*, which presented an extensive though somewhat uneven interpretation of the great writer, was well received; he was awarded the State Prize of the Soviet Union for his work on Sergei Eisenstein. The continuing vitality of Formalist conceptions in his thought was demonstrated in *Tetiva*, where he enlarged upon his earlier views to set forth a balanced version of his theories. Even during the last years of his life, further works, as well as new editions of his writings, appeared; and at the time of Shklovsky's death, at the age of ninety-one, he was generally regarded as one of the most significant literary theorists of the twentieth century.

BIBLIOGRAPHICAL REFERENCES: On a general level, there are a variety of studies dealing with theoretical issues, such as Victor Erlich, *Russian Formalism: History, Doctrine*, 1955; Krystyna Pomorska, *Russian Formalist Theory and Its Poetic Ambiance*, 1968; and Peter Steiner, *Russian Formalism: A Metapoetics*, 1984; these differ as to matters of emphasis and judgment. Mikhail Mikhailovich Bakhtin and Pavel Nikolayevich Medvedev, *The Formal Method in Literary Scholarship: A Critical Introduction to Sociological Poetics*, 1978, translated by Albert J. Wehrle, presents the limitations discerned by two leading Soviet thinkers, in a work which originally appeared in 1928. Tony Bennett, *Formalism and Marxism*, 1979, is a British writer's attempt to reconcile two approaches to literature. Wider issues are handled well in Ewa M. Thompson, *Russian Formalism and Anglo-American New Criticism: A Comparative Study*, 1971. One of the most celebrated tenets of Shklovsky's theories has also been considered separately in studies such as Robert H. Stacy, *Defamiliarization in Language and Literature*, 1977; W. Wolfgang Holdheim, "The Concept of Poetic Estrangement," *Comparative Literature Studies*, XI (1974), 320-325; Daniel Laferrière, "Potebnja, Šklovskij and the Familiarity/Strangeness Paradox," *Russian Literature*, IV (1976), 175-198; Peter Rossbacher, "Šklovskij's Concept of *Ostranenie* and Aristotle's *Admiratio*," *Modern Language Notes*, XCII (1977), 1038-1043; Donald R. Riccomini, "Defamiliarization, Reflexive Reference, and Modernism," *Bucknell Review*, XXV, no. 2 (1980), 107-113; and Lawrence Crawford, "Viktor Shklovskij: *Différance* in Defamiliarization," *Comparative Literature*, XXXVI (1984), 209-219. Shklovsky's position in relation to other writers is discussed in several of the contributions to *Russian Formalism, a Retrospective Glance: A Festschrift in Honor of Victor Erlich*, 1985, edited by Robert Louis Jackson and Stephen Rudy. For sympathetic comments by a Soviet observer, see Vladimir Ognev, "Viktor Shklovskii Teaches Us to Think," *Soviet Studies in Literature*, XX, no. 1 (1983/1984), 3-20. On the emergence of Shklovsky's ideas, there is Richard Sherwood, "Viktor Shklovsky and the Development of Early Formalist Theory on Prose Literature," in *Russian Formalism*, 1973, edited by Stephen Bann and John E. Bowlt. Various stages in Shklovsky's career have been traced in articles by Richard Sheldon, including "Shklovsky, Gorky, and the Serapion Brothers," *The Slavic and East European Journal*, XII (1968), 1-13; "The Formalist Poetics of Viktor Shklovsky," *Russian Literature Tri-Quarterly*, II (1972), 351-371; and "Shklovskii and Mandelshtam," in *Russian and Slavic Literature*, 1976, edited by Richard Freeborn, R. R. Milner-Gulland, and Charles A. Ward. Sheldon's study "Viktor Shklovsky and the Device of Ostensible Surrender," *Slavic Review*, XXXIV (1975), 86-108, provoked a rejoinder from Victor Erlich, "On Being Fair to Viktor Shklovsky: Or, The Act of Hedged Surrender," *Slavic Review*, XXXV (1976), 111-118, which was followed by Sheldon's "Reply to Victor Erlich," 119-121, in the same journal and issue. The relationship between fiction, criticism, and film in some of Shklovsky's endeavors is discussed in the first part of N. M. Lary, *Dostoevsky and Soviet Film: Visions of Demonic Realism*, 1986. The unusual hybrid genre developed in Shklovsky's autobiographical novels has been dealt with from the standpoint of certain well-known works; see Malgorzata Pruska-Carroll, "Fragmentation and Unity in Šklovskij's *Žili byli* and *Sentimental'noe putešestvie*," *Russian Langauge Journal*, XXXIII (1979); Carol Avins, "Emigration and Metaphor: Viktor Shklovsky, *Zoo: Or, Letters Not About Love* (1923)," in *Border Crossings: The West and Russian Identity in Soviet Literature, 1917-1934*, 1983; and Robert Augustin Smart, "Viktor Shklovsky and *Sentimental Journey*," in *The Nonfiction Novel*, 1985. Fyodor Solomonovich Grits, *The Work of Viktor Shklovsky (An Analysis of "Third Factory")*, translated by Richard Sheldon, was published in 1977 as an appendix to the English-language version of *Third Factory*; the Russian edition originally appeared in 1927. Further references, including a large number of works in Russian and other languages, may be found in Richard Sheldon, *Viktor Shklovsky: An International Bibliography of Works By and About Him*, 1977.

J. R. Broadus

LESLIE MARMON SILKO

Born: Albuquerque, New Mexico
Date: March 5, 1948

Principal Works

POETRY: *Laguna Woman*, 1974.
NOVEL: *Ceremony*, 1977.
SHORT FICTION: *Storyteller*, 1981.
CORRESPONDENCE: *The Delicacy and Strength of Lace: Letters Between Leslie Marmon Silko and James A. Wright*, 1986.

Leslie Marmon Silko is one of the most acclaimed writers of the American Indian literary renaissance of the 1970's—along with N. Scott Momaday and Louise Erdrich. Born March 5, 1948, in Albuquerque, New Mexico, Silko was reared on the Laguna Pueblo Reservation, in the house where her father, Lee H. Marmon, was born. During her childhood, she spent much time with her great-grandmother, A'mooh, who lived next door. A'mooh and Silko's Aunt Susie, Mrs. Walter K. Marmon, were among the people who taught her the Laguna traditions and stories which would become the primary resource for her poetry and fiction. Silko has Laguna, Mexican, Plains Indian, and Anglo ancestry. Her great-grandfather, Robert Gunn Marmon, was a trader who was elected to one term as governor of the pueblo. Nevertheless, the family, which lived at the edge of the village, occupied a marginal place in the community. Silko attended schools at Laguna until high school. After she was graduated from high school in Albuquerque, she attended the University of New Mexico. In 1969, she was graduated magna cum laude with a B.A. in English. She then entered law school and attended three semesters before deciding to devote herself to writing. Silko has taught at Navajo Community College, Many Farms, Arizona, at the University of New Mexico, and at the University of Arizona. Formerly married to attorney John Silko, she has two sons, Robert and Cazimir.

The poetry in Silko's first book, *Laguna Woman*, established many of the themes that she would develop in her later work. Laguna myth, culture, and ceremony are embodied in the contemporary experience of these poems. She refers to one of the Laguna creation myths in "Prayer to the Pacific": "Thirty thousand years ago/ Indians came riding across the ocean/ carried by giant sea-turtles." The poem conveys a cyclic concept of nature, in which the landmass of North America is separated from, but also connected to, China by the ocean. In her novel *Ceremony* the central character, Tayo, a veteran of World War II, remembers refusing to kill a Japanese soldier, who looked like his uncle, Josiah. Weather patterns in the Philippine jungles and at Laguna are also shown as related to each other and to the people living in these places. Other poems, such as "When Sun Came to River Woman," reveal nature as both the setting and the result of copulation. Human intercourse, the rain and sun, and the ceremonial songs are all necessary in the bringing of new life—they are interconnected and interdependent. An essential part of Tayo's recovery in *Ceremony* is his relationship with T'seh Montaño, a medicine woman who revives his sexuality and who teaches him how to use and protect medicinal plants growing in the natural locale.

In *Ceremony* the prose narrative, set in the aftermath of World War II, is juxtaposed with ancient myths, told in centered verse. The nonchronological prose narrative is told in segments with many flashbacks, similar to the structure of Momaday's *House Made of Dawn* (1969). The nearly five-hundred-year existence of Laguna at its present location has made it possible for Silko to write out of a cultural tradition intricately tied to the natural environment. Yet it is a place that has suffered severe trauma in the second half of the twentieth century. The atom bomb was developed at nearby Los Alamos, and the first atom bomb exploded just 150 miles from Laguna. In the early 1950's, the Anaconda Company opened a large, open-pit uranium mine on Laguna land. The danger of nuclear war is a central concern in *Ceremony*. Tayo comes to understand that this threat has the effect of uniting all of the world's people into one clan again.

Silko collected her short fiction, nonfiction prose, and poetry, including the poems from *Laguna Woman* and the centered verse in *Ceremony*, in *Storyteller*. The selections in the book vary greatly in content and form—from the directly autobiographical poetry at the beginning to the title piece, "Storyteller" set in Alaska, to "Lullaby," the story of a Navajo woman who, like most Native Americans, has suffered devastating cultural and personal losses. Out of these diverse selections emerges a central idea—that all live in relation to the earth, and one's physical, mental, and spiritual survival depends on an awareness of that relationship.

In August of 1978, poet James Wright wrote a letter to Silko saying that *Ceremony* was "one of the four or five best books" he had read about America. Silko responded, and a correspondence began that was to last until Wright's death in March of 1980. Anne Wright edited the letters in *The Delicacy and Strength of Lace*, and they were published in 1986. These letters reveal Silko's spontaneity and talent; perhaps more important, they chronicle a literary friendship between a white, male, mainstream poet and a Native American female writer. Dialogues such as theirs prepare the way for the long overdue acceptance of literature by Native Americans in the American literary canon.

BIBLIOGRAPHICAL REFERENCES: Bertha P. Dutton and Miriam A. Marmon, *The Laguna Calender*, 1936, provides useful background information on Laguna culture. A chapter on Silko's *Ceremony* is included in Alan R. Velie, *Four American Indian Literary Masters*, 1982. There is also a discussion of *Ceremony* in Charles R. Larson, *American Indian Fiction*, 1978. Per Seyersted discusses her work in general in *Leslie Marmon Silko*, 1980, a brief introductory study in the Boise State University Western Writers series. In *Native American Literature*, 1985, Andrew Wiget discusses Silko's poetry and fiction, providing many insightful interpretations and statements of her major themes. Paula Gunn Allen's commentary on Silko's work in *The Sacred Hoop: Recovering the Feminine in American Indian Traditions*, 1986, is particularly helpful, since Allen is part Laguna and thus capable of pointing out many cultural references not apparent to the general reader. Silko's work is also discussed in H. David Brumble III, *American Indian Autobiography*, 1988, which emphasizes the continuing influence of the oral tradition. See also Leslie Silko's essay, "An Old-Time Indian Attack Conducted in Two Parts," in *The Remembered Earth*, 1979, edited by Geary Hobson, and Dexter Fisher's interview of Leslie Silko in *The Third Woman*, 1980.

Norma C. Wilson

ALAN SILLITOE

Born: Nottingham, England
Date: March 4, 1928

Principal Works

NOVELS: *Saturday Night and Sunday Morning*, 1958; *The General*, 1960; *Key to the Door*, 1961; *The Death of William Posters*, 1965; *A Tree on Fire*, 1967; *A Start in Life*, 1970; *Travels in Nihilon*, 1971; *The Flame of Life*, 1974; *The Widower's Son*, 1976; *The Storyteller*, 1979; *Her Victory*, 1982; *The Lost Flying Boat*, 1983; *Down from the Hill*, 1984; *Life Goes On*, 1985; *Out of the Whirlpool*, 1987.

SHORT FICTION: *The Loneliness of the Long-Distance Runner*, 1959; *The Ragman's Daughter*, 1963; *Guzman Go Home and Other Stories*, 1968; *A Sillitoe Selection*, 1970; *Men, Women, and Children*, 1973; *The Second Chance and Other Stories*, 1981.

POETRY: *Without Beer or Bread*, 1957; *The Rats and Other Poems*, 1960; *A Falling Out of Love and Other Poems*, 1964; *Shaman and Other Poems*, 1968; *Love in the Environs of Voronezh and Other Poems*, 1968; *Poems* (with Ted Hughes and Ruth Fainlight), 1971; *Barbarians and Other Poems*, 1974; *Storm: New Poems*, 1974; *Snow on the North Side of Lucifer*, 1979; *Sun Before Departure*, 1984.

TRAVEL SKETCHES: *The Road to Volgograd*, 1964; *Mountains and Caverns*, 1975.

PLAYS: *All Citizens Are Soldiers*, pb. 1969 (translated and adapted with wife Ruth Fainlight from a play by Lope de Vega); *Three Plays*, pb. 1978.

CHILDREN'S LITERATURE: *The City Adventures of Marmalade Jim*, 1967; *Marmalade Jim at the Farm*, 1980; *Marmalade Jim and the Fox*, 1984.

MEMOIRS: *Raw Material*, 1972.

OTHER NONFICTION: *Every Day of the Week*, 1987.

SCREENPLAYS: *Saturday Night and Sunday Morning*, 1960; *The Loneliness of the Long-Distance Runner*, 1961; *Che Guevara*, 1968; *The Ragman's Daughter*, 1971.

Alan Sillitoe is England's best writer of proletarian fiction and the spokesman for the English working class of the 1950's and 1960's. He was born in Nottingham, England, the setting for much of his fiction, on March 4, 1928, to Sylvia and Christopher Sillitoe, the latter a tannery worker. Through his family's struggle for economic survival during the Depression of the 1930's, he gained the subject matter and the political beliefs that later found expression in his literary work. Though an avid student, he left school at the age of fourteen and between 1942 and 1946 worked, like his Nottingham protagonists, at a variety of factory jobs. He worked as a controller at the Langar Airfield in Nottingham before serving with the Royal Air Force in Malaya in 1947-1948.

While in Malaya, Sillitoe began writing but destroyed the poems, short stories, and first draft of a novel that he completed while recuperating from tuberculosis. In 1949, following his convalescence, he returned to Nottingham and then traveled to France and Majorca, where, at Robert Graves's suggestion, he began to write about what he knew best, Nottingham. *Saturday Night and Sunday Morning* was awarded the Authors' Club Prize as the best English first novel of 1958; the following year, Sillitoe won the Hawthornden Prize for *The Loneliness of the Long-Distance Runner.* The Nottingham novels and books of poetry that followed his initial success reflected his leftist political views, which were also the subject of *The Road to Volgograd*, a topographical and ideological journey to Russia.

After 1970, Sillitoe completed his Nottingham trilogy and, while returning sporadically to his Nottingham settings, would use more diverse settings (including Antarctica in *The Lost Flying Boat*). He has also experimented with narrative strategies (as in *The Storyteller* and *Down from the Hill*) and has written fiction about the writing of fiction. Despite the change in setting and style, Sillitoe's fiction has remained consistent in his criticism of the English establishment and of capitalism generally, though increasingly his focus has been on the individual rather than society. *The Widower's Son*, for example, attests the failure of the human heart to survive society's conditioning and to sustain human relationships.

Sillitoe's reputation rests on his Nottingham novels and short stories, with their proletarian protagonists, their struggle between the authority figures and the working class, and their condemnation of social and political institutions. Sillitoe's early protagonists, Smith in "The Loneliness of the Long-Distance Runner" and Arthur Seaton of *Saturday Night and Sunday Morning*, embrace their working-class status and refuse to bow to a coercive and alienating society. Their behavior is at odds with the ambitious social climbing of Joe Lampton, the working-class hero of *Room at the Top* (1957), by John Braine, with whom Sillitoe is often compared. With *Key to the Door*, however, Sillitoe's switch of protagonists meant a new focus—the plight of the working-class intellectual with literary interests in a repressive society (the tie to Sillitoe is obvious). When Brian Seaton refuses to fire on the Malayan communists, his action is more overtly political than his brother's or Smith's. Similarly, Frank Dawley, the protagonist of Sillitoe's trilogy (*The Death of William Posters*, *A Tree on Fire*, and *The Flame of Life*), joins the struggle to free Algeria from colonialism and learns to channel his anger into a worthwhile course of action.

Some of Sillitoe's later fiction (*Out of the Whirlpool* and a few of the stories included in *The Second Chance and Other Stories*) are set in Nottingham and do involve the working class, but Sillitoe has extended his range and become more concerned with the contemporary fixation on narration. *Life Goes On*, a sequel to *A Start in Life*, continues the earlier novel's account of the improbable adventures of lower-class outcasts, but it becomes more focused on literary technique and incorporates a novel-within-a-novel. The same concern with the writing of fiction occurred earlier in *The Storyteller*, which depicts a working-class protagonist who tells stories to survive. As the protagonist's stories begin to merge with his life, Sillitoe allegorically poses questions about the nature and motivation of the writer/creator. *Down from the Hill*, a memory novel, depicts the storyteller-protagonist first as an apolitical youth, then as a politicized screenwriter. *The Widower's Son*, on the other hand, concerns a more mainstream subject, the institutionalizing of the human heart, which produces a military success but a domestic failure.

Though *The Widower's Son* and *Her Victory* seem closely related to the work of D. H. Lawrence, another Nottingham writer with an underprivileged background, it is only in the later novels that Sillitoe has been able to get any Lawrentian distance from his subject, so closely has he been tied to his characters in the past. In fact, he has been more often associated with the "angry young men" of the generation of John Osborne. Despite his movement from the Nottingham working-class jungle to a more inclusive English society, a more detached stance, and a less overtly political subject matter, Sillitoe will be remembered as the proletarian novelist of the 1950's and the 1960's, the spokesman whose career parallels the rise of the New Left in England. Although his novels made his reputation, he was more at home with the short story, which does not require the structural skill critics found wanting in his episodic novels. His style was also poetic, and had he not written fiction so appropriate to his time, he certainly would be remembered for his several books of poems.

BIBLIOGRAPHICAL REFERENCES: Allen Richard Penner, *Alan Sillitoe*, 1972, provides a short biography, a selected bibliography, and an overview of Sillitoe's work. A later evaluation is Stanley S. Atherton, *Alan Sillitoe: A Critical Assessment*, 1979. A more narrowly focused study is Ronald Dee Vaverka, *Commitment as Art: A Marxist Critique of a Selection of Alan Sillitoe's Political Fiction*, 1978. See also Frederick R. Karl, *The Contemporary British Novel*, 1962; Anthony Burgess, *The Novel Now: A Student's Guide to Contemporary Fiction*, 1967; John Hurrell, "Alan Sillitoe and the Serious Novel," *Critique: Studies in Modern Fiction*, IV (1960/1961), 3-16; Stanley S. Atherton, "Alan Sillitoe's Battleground," *Dalhousie Review*, XLVIII (1968), 324-333; Allen Richard Penner, "*The General*: Exceptional Proof of a Critical

Rule," *Southern Humanities Review*, IV (1970), 135-143; Saul Maloff, "The Eccentricity of Alan Sillitoe," in *Contemporary British Novelists*, 1965, edited by Charles Shapiro; J. R. Osgerby, "Alan Sillitoe's *Saturday Night and Sunday Morning*," in *Renaissance and Modern Essays*, 1966, edited by G. R. Hibbard; Anna R. Nardella, "The Existential Dilemmas of Alan Sillitoe's Working-Class Heroes," *Studies in the Novel*, V (1973), 469-482; John A. Byers, "The Initiation of Alan Sillitoe's *Loneliness of the Long-Distance Runner*," *Modern Fiction Studies*, XXII (1976/1977), 584-591; Michael Wieding, "Alan Sillitoe's Political Novels," in *Cunning Exiles: Studies of Modern Prose Writers*, 1975, edited by Don Anderson and Stephen Knight; Keith Wilson, "Arthur Seaton Twenty Years On: A Reappraisal of Sillitoe's *Saturday Night and Sunday Morning*," *English Studies in Canada*, VII (1981), 414-426; Kurt Schluter, "The Time and Life of Arthur Seaton in Alan Sillitoe's *Saturday Night and Sunday Morning*," *Anglia*, CI (1983), 99-116; William Hutchings, "The Work of Play: Anger and the Expropriated Athletes of Alan Sillitoe and David Storey," *Modern Fiction Studies*, XXXIII (1987), 35-47; and David Craig, "The Roots of Sillitoe's Fiction," in *The British Working-Class Novel in the Twentieth Century*, 1984, edited by Jeremy Hawthorn. There are two interesting interviews with Sillitoe: John Halperin, "Interview with Alan Sillitoe," *Modern Fiction Studies*, XXV (1979), 175-189; and Joyce Rothschild, "The Growth of a Writer: An Interview with Alan Sillitoe," *Southern Humanities Review*, XX (1986), 127-140.

Thomas L. Erskine

GEORGES SIMENON

Born: Liège, Belgium
Date: February 13, 1903

Principal Works

MYSTERY AND DETECTIVE FICTION: *Pietr-le-Letton*, 1931 (*Maigret and the Enigmatic Lett*, 1963); *M. Gallet, décédé*, 1931 (*Maigret Stonewalled*, 1963); *Le Pendu de Saint-Pholien*, 1931 (*Maigret and the Hundred Gibbets*, 1963); *Le Charretier de la Providence*, 1931 (*Maigret Meets a Milord*, 1963); *La Tête d'un homme*, 1931 (*A Battle of Nerves*, 1940); *Le Chien jaune*, 1931 (*A Face for a Clue*, 1940); *La Nuit du carrefour*, 1931 (*Maigret at the Crossroads*, 1964); *Un Crime en Hollande*, 1931 (*A Crime in Holland*, 1940); *Au rendez-vous des terre-neuves*, 1931 (*The Sailors' Rendez-vous*, 1970); *La Danseuse du Gai-Moulin*, 1931 (*At the Gai-Moulin*, 1940); *La Guingette à deux sous*, 1931 (*The Guingette by the Seine*, 1940); *Le Port des brumes*, 1932 (*Death of a Harbour Master*, 1942); *L'Ombre chinoise*, 1932 (*Maigret Mystified*, 1964); *L'Affaire Saint-Fiacre*, 1932 (*Maigret Goes Home*, 1967); *Chez les Flamands*, 1932 (*The Flemish Shop*, 1940); *Le Fou de Bergerac*, 1932 (*The Madman of Bergerac*, 1940); *Liberty-Bar*, 1932 (English translation, 1940); *L'Écluse numéro un*, 1932 (*The Lock at Charenton*, 1941); *Maigret*, 1934 (*Maigret Returns*, 1941); *Les Nouvelles Enquêtes de Maigret*, 1944 (*The Short Cases of Inspector Maigret*, 1959); *Les Vacances de Maigret*, 1948 (*No Vacation for Maigret*, 1959); *Maigret et son mort*, 1948 (*Maigret's Special Murder*, 1964); *La Première Enquête de Maigret*, 1949 (*Maigret's First Case*, 1970); *Mon Ami Maigret*, 1949 (*My Friend Maigret*, 1969); *Maigret et la vieille dame*, 1950 (*Maigret and the Old Lady*, 1965); *L'Amie de Mme Maigret*, 1950 (*Madame Maigret's Friend*, 1960); *Les Mémoires de Maigret*, 1950 (*Maigret's Memoirs*, 1963); *Maigret au Picratt's*, 1950 (*Maigret in Montmartre*, 1963); *Maigret en meublé*, 1950 (*Maigret Takes a Room*, 1965); *Maigret et la grande perche*, 1951 (*Maigret and the Burglar's Wife*, 1969); *Maigret, Lognon, et les gangsters*, 1952 (*Maigret and the Gangsters*, 1974); *Le Révolver de Maigret*, 1952 (*Maigret's Revolver*, 1969); *Maigret et l'homme du banc*, 1953 (*Maigret and the Man on the Bench*, 1975); *Maigret a peur*, 1953 (*Maigret Afraid*, 1961); *Maigret se trompe*, 1953 (*Maigret's Mistake*, 1964); *Maigret à l'école*, 1954 (*Maigret Goes to School*, 1964); *Maigret et la jeune morte*, 1954 (*Maigret and the Dead Girl*, 1965); *Maigret chez le ministre*, 1954 (*Maigret and the Calame Report*, 1969); *Maigret et le corps sans tête*, 1955 (*Maigret and the Headless Corpse*, 1967); *Maigret tend un piège*, 1955 (*Maigret Sets a Trap*, 1965); *Un Échec de Maigret*, 1957 (*Maigret's Failure*, 1962); *Maigret s'amuse*, 1957 (*Maigret's Little Joke*, 1965); *Maigret voyage*, 1957 (*Maigret and the Millionaires*, 1974); *Les Scrupules de Maigret*, 1957 (*Maigret Has Scruples*, 1959); *Maigret et les témoins récalcitrants*, 1959 (*Maigret and the Reluctant Witnesses*, 1964); *Une Confidence de Maigret*, 1959 (*Maigret Has Doubts*, 1968); *Maigret aux assises*, 1960 (*Maigret in Court*, 1961); *Maigret et les vieillards*, 1960 (*Maigret in Society*, 1962); *Maigret et le voleur paresseux*, 1961 (*Maigret and the Lazy Burglar*, 1963); *Maigret et les braves gens*, 1962 (*Maigret and the Black Sheep*, 1976); *Maigret et le client du samedi*, 1962 (*Maigret and the Saturday Caller*, 1964); *Maigret et le clochard*, 1963 (*Maigret and the Bum*, 1973); *La Colère de Maigret*, 1963 (*Maigret Loses His Temper*, 1967); *Maigret et le fantôme*, 1964 (*Maigret and the Apparition*, 1975); *Maigret se défend*, 1964 (*Maigret on the Defensive*, 1968); *La Patience de Maigret*, 1965 (*The Patience of Maigret*, 1966); *Maigret et l'affaire Nahour*, 1966 (*Maigret and the Nahour Case*, 1967); *Le Voleur de Maigret*, 1967 (*Maigret's Pickpocket*, 1968); *Maigret à Vichy*, 1968 (*Maigret in Vichy*, 1969); *Maigret hésite*, 1968 (*Maigret Hesitates*, 1970); *L'Ami de l'enfance de Maigret*, 1968 (*Maigret's Boyhood Friend*, 1970); *Maigret et le tueur*, 1969 (*Maigret and the Killer*, 1971); *Maigret et le marchand du vin*, 1970 (*Maigret and the Wine Merchant*, 1971); *La Folle de Maigret*, 1970 (*Maigret and the Madwoman*, 1972); *Maigret et l'homme tout seul*, 1971 (*Maigret and the Loner*, 1975); *Maigret et l'indicateur*,

1971 (*Maigret and the Informer*, 1973); *Maigret et M. Charles*, 1972 (*Maigret and Monsieur Charles*, 1973).

NOVELS AND NOVELLAS: *Le Relais d'Alsace*, 1931 (*The Man from Everywhere*, 1942); *Le Passager du Polarys*, 1932 (*Danger at Sea*, 1954); *Les Gens d'en face*, 1933 (*The Window over the Way*, 1966); *La Maison du canal*, 1933 (*The House by the Canal*, 1948); *Les Fiançailles de M. Hire*, 1933 (*Mr. Hire's Engagement*, 1956); *Le Coup de lune*, 1933 (*Tropic Moon*, 1942); *Le Haut Mal*, 1933 (*The Woman in the Gray House*, 1944); *L'Homme de Londres*, 1933 (*Newhaven-Dieppe*, 1944); *Le Locataire*, 1934 (*The Lodger*, 1943); *Les Suicidés*, 1934 (*One Way Out*, 1943); *Faubourg*, 1937 (*Home Town*, 1944); *L'Assassin*, 1937 (*The Murderer*, 1963); *Chemin sans issue*, 1938 (*Blind Alley*, 1946); *L'Homme qui regardait passer les trains*, 1938 (*The Man Who Watched the Trains Go By*, 1958); *Monsieur la Souris*, 1938 (*The Mouse*, 1950); *Les Inconnus dans la maison*, 1940 (*Strangers in the House*, 1954); *Il pleut, bergère . . .* , 1941 (*Black Rain*, 1965); *Le Voyageur de la Toussaint*, 1941 (*Strange Inheritance*, 1958); *L'Âińe des Ferchaux*, 1945 (*Magnet of Doom*, 1948); *La Fuite de Monsieur Monde*, 1947 (*M. Monde Vanishes*, 1967); *Le Clan des Ostendais*, 1947 (*The Ostenders*, 1952); *Lettre à mon juge*, 1947 (*Act of Passion*, 1952); *La Neige était sale*, 1948 (*The Stain in the Snow*, 1964); *Le Fond de la bouteille*, 1949 (*The Bottom of the Bottle*, 1954); *Les Fantômes du chapelier*, 1949 (*The Hatter's Ghosts*, 1956); *Les Quatres Jours du pauvre homme*, 1949 (*Four Days in a Lifetime*, 1953); *Les Volets verts*, 1950 (*The Heart of a Man*, 1951); *Une Vie comme neuve*, 1951 (*A New Lease on Life*, 1963); *Antoine et Julie*, 1953 (*The Magician*, 1955); *Feux rouges*, 1953 (*The Hitchhiker*, 1967); *Crime impuni*, 1955 (*The Fugitive*, 1955); *Le Grand Bob*, 1955 (*Big Bob*, 1972); *Les Témoins*, 1955 (*The Witnesses*, 1956); *Les Complices*, 1956 (*The Accomplices*, 1963); *En cas de malheur*, 1956 (*In Case of Emergency*, 1958); *Dimanche*, 1958 (*Sunday*, 1966); *L'Ours en peluche*, 1960 (*Teddy Bear*, 1972); *Betty*, 1961 (English translation, 1975); *Le Train*, 1961 (*The Train*, 1966); *La Port*, 1962 (*The Door*, 1964); *Les Anneaux de Bicêtre*, 1963 (*The Bells of Bicêtre*, 1964); *La Chambre bleue*, 1964 (*The Blue Room*, 1964); *Le Petit Saint*, 1965 (*The Little Saint*, 1965); *Le Confessional*, 1966 (*The Confessional*, 1968); *La Mort d'Auguste*, 1966 (*The Old Man Dies*, 1967); *Le Chat*, 1967 (*The Cat*, 1967); *La Prison*, 1968 (*The Prison*, 1969); *La Main*, 1968 (*The Man on the Bench in the Barn*, 1970); *Novembre*, 1969 (*November*, 1970); *La Disparition d'Odile*, 1971 (*The Disappearance of Odile*, 1972); *La Cage de verre*, 1971 (*The Glass Cage*, 1973); *Les Innocents*, 1972 (*The Innocents*, 1973).

AUTOBIOGRAPHY: *Quand j'étais vieux*, 1970 (*When I Was Old*, 1971); *Lettre à ma mère*, 1971 (*Letter to My Mother*, 1976); *Mémoires intimes*, 1981 (*Intimate Memoirs*, 1984).

George Joseph Christian Simenon is a master of the contemporary psychological novel. Perhaps best known for his detective stories featuring Inspector Maigret, he is also internationally celebrated for his other novels, which—like the Maigret works—deal with guilt and innocence, flight and return, and the search for home.

Simenon's parents were a mismatched couple; his father was a petit bourgeois accountant, while his mother came from a family known for pretentiousness and instability. The contrast between his parents' values became a lifelong preoccupation reflected in his stories, which often satirize the upper middle class while affirming the integrity of the rural working class. Simenon dropped out of school at sixteen to help augment the family income, and after finding himself inept at menial jobs he became a successful reporter. His writing career was fully launched by age seventeen, when he wrote his first novel. At this time he also began writing fiction pieces for all the Paris journals. At the time of his marriage to Regine Renchon in 1923 he was writing hundreds of short stories a year. Since the early 1920's Simenon has written more than four hundred books and more than two thousand separately published short stories.

Simenon began writing thrillers and romances for an audience of shopgirls and secretaries, but he soon found his forte in the detective story. Inspector Jules Maigret made his debut in

Maigret and the Enigmatic Lett in 1931. Intuitive, fatherly, as much against the inhumane criminal justice system as against crime itself, Maigret was an instant success. Over the next four years, Simenon produced some twenty novels featuring his popular pipe-smoking detective and then turned to writing "straight" novels, many of which were also well received. Yet by the late 1930's Maigret fans mourned the lack of new Maigret novels, and Simenon found himself forced to satisfy the public. In 1939 he began a new Maigret series, and he continued writing these along with other novels for the duration of his career. At about the time he began the new series, he was divorced from his wife and married Denise Ouimet. The second group of Maigret novels is informed by Simenon's experiences in the United States and even includes episodes in which Maigret collaborates with the American police. In the early 1970's Simenon gave up writing novels entirely; one of his late works, *Intimate Memoirs*, is an account of the factors which led to the suicide of his daughter, Mary-Georges, in 1978.

Like Graham Greene, Simenon has placed his works into two categories, the "Maigrets" and the series novels. (Greene called his thrillers "entertainments.") Yet Simenon's Maigrets and his other stories share the same themes of flight and disappointed search. His characters often undertake desperate searches for lost Edens, unspoiled families, and a sense of their own self-worth. In the Maigrets they commit crimes in their desperation. Maigret unravels the problems with a mixture of intuition and empathy. When he finally hears the criminal's confession, he experiences a catharsis, such as that at the end of a tragic drama. For Maigret, "to understand all is to forgive all," and in understanding and forgiving he takes some of the criminal's pain upon himself. In the non-Maigret novels, the characters undertake the same sorts of hopeless quests, but there is no father figure to understand their predicaments and restore the violated worlds. Often these stories are more pessimistic and even nihilistic in their conclusions. The two kinds of novels share a milieu. The main difference is the presence or absence of Maigret himself.

Maigret is a very human detective, subject to error; in fact, he is most often blinded by his own desire to believe in innocence and Eden. In *Maigret and the Old Lady*, for example, he is deceived by the woman's childlike femininity; in *Maigret at the Crossroads*, again, he sees at first openness and innocence and causes damage through his unwillingness or inability to look past the surface. The theme of many of the Maigrets and of the others as well is that each adult carries with him an idealized image of childhood and home which he seeks to reestablish, at whatever cost to himself and others.

What makes the novels memorable, though, is not their characters, which are sometimes sketchily developed, or their themes, which lack variety. It is Simenon's detailed observation, which makes these novels so realistic that they could easily serve the sociologist as well as the fiction reader. Nearly every conceivable milieu within the French social structure is reproduced in most minute detail—the details of ordinary houses of prostitution, furniture factories, shipping firms, petit bourgeois and haute bourgeoise households, fishing vessels, and boarding houses. These places and their occupants are briefly but convincingly described, as if by a longtime inhabitant. Moreover, the details of dress, weather, and furnishings are not only exact but also suggestive, even symbolic. This evocative use of the concrete permeates all the novels, giving Simenon the reputation of a novelist of ambience. Simenon's major contribution to literature may well be in the detective field. He has joined the hard-boiled American school of detective fiction with the gentler, more descriptive British school to create an enactment of the ritual of crime and investigation which is both realistic and mythic.

BIBLIOGRAPHICAL REFERENCES: Stanley G. Eskin, *Simenon*, 1987, is the definitive critical biography. Its account of Simenon's life and its interpretations of his works are unmatched, and it contains a complete primary bibliography up to 1987. Its bibliography of secondary sources is, however, limited. Also good is Lucille Becker, *Georges Simenon*, 1977, which is a sound critical work that also includes some biographical material. It contains a good annotated bibliography. A readable biography is Fenton Bresler, *The Mystery of Georges Simenon*, 1983. See also John Raymond, *Simenon in Court*, 1968; Thomas Narcejac, *The Art of Simenon*, 1942; Julian Symons, *Mortal Consequences: A History from the Detective Story to the Crime Novel*, 1972; Gavin Lambert, *The Dangerous Edge*, 1975; and Trudee Young, *Georges Simenon: A Checklist of His "Maigret" and Other Mystery Novels and Short Stories in French and English*, 1976. Also useful are Brendan Gill, "Profile," *The New Yorker*, XXVIII (January 24, 1953), 35-36; Carvel Collins, "The Art of Fiction IX: Georges Simenon," *The Paris Review*, IX (Summer, 1955), 71-90; and Charles J. Rolo, "Simenon and Spillane: The Metaphysics of Murder for the Millions," in *New World Writing*, 1952.

Janet McCann

CLAUDE SIMON

Born: Tananarive, Madagascar
Date: October 10, 1913

PRINCIPAL WORKS

NOVELS: *Le Tricheur*, 1945; *Gulliver*, 1952; *Le Sacre du printemps*, 1954; *Le Vent: Tentative de restitution d'un rétable baroque*, 1957 (*The Wind: Attempted Restoration of a Baroque Altarpiece*, 1959); *L'Herbe*, 1958 (*The Grass*, 1960); *La Route des Flandres*, 1960 (*The Flanders Road*, 1961); *Le Palace*, 1962 (*The Palace*, 1963); *Histoire*, 1967 (English translation, 1968); *La Bataille de Pharsale*, 1969 (*The Battle of Pharsalus*, 1971); *Les Corps conducteurs*, 1971 (*Conducting Bodies*, 1974); *Triptyque*, 1973 (*Triptych*, 1976); *Leçon de choses*, 1975 (*The World About Us*, 1983); *Les Géorgiques*, 1981.

JOURNAL: *La Corde raide*, 1947.

OTHER NONFICTION: *La Chevelure de Bérénice*, 1983.

One of the principal French writers of the New Novel, Claude Simon has combined the exploration of new modes of novelistic discourse with a trenchant view of the human condition to create a unique fictional universe. He was born in Tananarive, Madagascar (then a French possession), on October 10, 1913. He left the African island one year later when, with the onset of World War I, his father, an army officer, was called up for active military service. After his father was killed in the war, Simon spent his childhood in Perpignan, a small town in the eastern Pyrenees. Simon received his secondary education at the Collège Stanislas in Paris and later studied at both the Universities of Oxford and Cambridge. He then began to train as a painter with André Lhote, who had been one of the early cubist painters. Paintings of various kinds appear in several of Simon's novels. Simon spent the years 1936 to 1939 traveling in Europe. His peregrinations included a brief stay in Spain, where he participated in the Civil War on the Republican side. When World War II started, Simon was drafted into a cavalry regiment. After the French defeat at the Battle of the Meuse, he was captured by the Germans but managed to escape from his prison camp. Simon's reflections on the two wars in which he took part appear in *La Corde raide* (the tightrope), a journal that he published in 1947. War is a major theme in many of Simon's novels, for, in addition to its specific devastation, it exposes the chaos underlying the apparent order of existence as well as emphasizes humankind's lack of progress. After the war, Simon returned to the Pyrenees region, settling in the village of Salses and becoming a winegrower. He later moved to Paris, where he has resided since.

Simon's first novel, *Le Tricheur* (the cheater), was published in 1945. The works that he produced during the 1940's and 1950's, which constitute his first phase, present many of the themes that appeared in later, better-known novels but are largely traditional in form. Yet *The Wind* and, to a lesser extent, *The Grass* already point toward the more innovative fictions of Simon's second period with respect to such matters as narrative perspective, temporality, and the nature of representation. The anonymous narrator of *The Wind* attempts to restore the reality of a series of incidents in a small town in southern France. The ceaselessly blowing wind is a metaphor of the destructive passage of time that blurs events and characters. The narrator succeeds in establishing a pattern of criminal activities but begins to suspect that his discovery is an invention created by his desire to give meaning to the events he is investigating, by language that has imposed its own particular order. What is baroque in this novel and in so many of the later novels is the tension between the work of art as an illusion and the self-consciousness of the processes that engendered it.

Simon's first recognition as a novelist came with the publication of *The Flanders Road* in 1960, which won for him the Prix de l'Express and placed its author among the foremost practitioners of the New Novel. These writers, among them Alain Robbe-Grillet, Nathalie

Sarraute, and Michel Butor, were attempting to elaborate a new poetics of the novel by calling into question its traditional structures. In *The Flanders Road*, considered by many to be Simon's best work, the protagonist Georges had been a soldier in World War II and was captured by the Germans after most of his unit had been killed. After the war, Georges spends a night with Corinne, his dead captain's wife, about whom he had fantasized while a prisoner. During the course of this night, Georges pursues his memories of the war, in the hope of determining the true nature of the events with which he was involved and thereby seizing his own identity. Georges discovers that he cannot adequately separate fact from imagination, however, and that his memories have become mental images, re-presentations that have lost their spatio-temporal coordinates as they have combined with one another in associative patterns. The self, fragmented in proliferating language, becomes a fictional construct.

Triptych ushered in the third phase of Simon's novelistic production. Simon eliminates the central narrative consciousness of his earlier works in order to emphasize further the novel as text. Like a piece of cloth, a textile, the work becomes an interweaving of many strands. As its title implies, the novel consists of three principal stories, which become progressively interconnected through various processes of association and generation. A particular element may function in a variety of contexts, within one or several stories. For example, a couple making love in a barn is linked to a nude woman in another story. She resembles a woman on a strip of film in the possession of two boys spying on the couple in the barn—and that figure is linked to a film being shown locally and, in another story, to a film being made. *Les Géorgiques* (the Georgics) creates a complex polyphony through its interweaving of three historical events—the French Revolution, the Spanish Civil War, and the defeat of France in 1940. Yet given Simon's concept of the cyclical nature of history, the convergence of these moments tends to restore the unifying narrative consciousness more typical of Simon's earlier works.

The awarding of the Nobel Prize in Literature to Simon in 1985 was met with some opposition in both France and the United States. Simon's detractors felt that his experimental writing had impoverished the novel instead of enriching it. Unlike the works of some of the writers with which he is associated, however, Simon's novels are never arid intellectual exercises reflecting solipsistically on their own elaboration. For Simon, the activity of writing is inseparable from an exploration of the human condition. Simon's vision of the human condition is, admittedly, a relatively pessimistic one. The specious order of everyday existence is easily shattered by war, crime, and passion. History is cyclical, belying apparent progress and imposing predetermined roles on the actors who occupy its stage. The demarcation between the real and the imaginary is illusory. Enmeshed in the labyrinthine web of language, the pursuit of identity and meaning generates other fictions. This apprehension of reality is coextensive with the creation of new novelistic forms and with the assumption by Simon's readers of a greater share in the creative process.

BIBLIOGRAPHICAL REFERENCES: J. A. E. Loubère, *The Novels of Claude Simon*, 1975; Salvador Jimenez-Fajando, *Claude Simon*, 1975; and John Fletcher, *Claude Simon and Fiction Now*, 1978, are general, introductory studies that examine the themes and structures of Simon's work. Loubère's is the most insightful of the three. Karen Gould, *Claude Simon's Mythic Muse*, 1979, focuses on a variety of symbols and archetypes, with relatively little attention to form. Doris Kadish has written an excellent but limited study on Simon as a New Novelist in *Practice of the New Novel in Claude Simon's "L'Herbe" and "La Route des Flandres,"* 1979. *Orion Blinded: Essays on Claude Simon*, 1981, edited by Randi Birn and Karen Gould, examines the three phases of Simon's writings from a variety of critical perspectives. Two later volumes that include an examination of *Les Géorgiques* are the collection of essays edited by Alastair B. Duncan, *Claude Simon: New Directions*, 1985, and the volume by Celia Britton, *Claude Simon: Writing the Visible*, 1987. The second of these appeals to a more sophisticated audience given its Lacanian perspective on Simon's fictions. Maria Minich Brewer has edited a special number of *L'Esprit créateur* devoted to Claude Simon, XXVII (1987), whose essays focus on *The Flanders Road*, *The World About Us*, and *Les Géorgiques*. A more sophisticated collection of articles can be found in the Claude Simon issue published by *The Review of Contemporary Fiction*, V (1985). In addition to several excellent essays on Simon's use of painting and on intertextuality in *Les Géorgiques*, it contains two interviews with the author. See also the chapters on Claude Simon in John Sturrock, *The French New Novel*, 1969, and Stephen Heath, *The Nouveau Roman*, 1979.

Philip H. Solomon

NEIL SIMON

Born: New York, New York
Date: July 4, 1927

PRINCIPAL WORKS

PLAYS: *Adventures of Marco Polo: A Musical Fantasy*, pb. 1959 (with William Freiberg); *Heidi*, pb. 1959; *Come Blow Your Horn*, pr. 1960; *Little Me*, pr. 1962; *Barefoot in the Park*, pr. 1963; *The Odd Couple*, pr. 1965; *Sweet Charity*, pr., pb. 1966; *The Star-Spangled Girl*, pr. 1966; *Plaza Suite*, pr. 1968; *Promises, Promises*, pr. 1968; *Last of the Red Hot Lovers*, pr. 1969; *The Gingerbread Lady*, pr. 1970; *The Prisoner of Second Avenue*, pr. 1971; *The Sunshine Boys*, pr. 1972; *The Good Doctor*, pr. 1973; *God's Favorite*, pr. 1974; *California Suite*, pr. 1976; *Chapter Two*, pr. 1977; *They're Playing Our Song*, pr. 1978; *I Ought to Be in Pictures*, pr. 1980; *Brighton Beach Memoirs*, pr. 1982; *Biloxi Blues*, pr. 1984; *Broadway Bound*, pr. 1986.

SCREENPLAYS: *After the Fox*, 1966 (with Cesare Zavattini); *Barefoot in the Park*, 1967; *The Odd Couple*, 1968; *The Out-of-Towners*, 1970; *Plaza Suite*, 1971; *Last of the Red Hot Lovers*, 1972; *The Heartbreak Kid*, 1972; *The Prisoner of Second Avenue*, 1975; *The Sunshine Boys*, 1975; *Murder by Death*, 1976; *The Goodbye Girl*, 1977; *The Cheap Detective*, 1978; *California Suite*, 1978; *Chapter Two*, 1979; *Seems Like Old Times*, 1980; *Brighton Beach Memoirs*, 1985; *Biloxi Blues*, 1987.

Since the early 1960's, Marvin Neil Simon has dominated the popular theater in America; his seemingly endless string of well-made comedies has provided him with both popular recognition and tremendous wealth. He was born in the Bronx on July 4, 1927, the son of Irving Simon, a garment salesman, and Mamie Simon. As a young child, Simon remembers sitting on a stone ledge watching a Charlie Chaplin film. He laughed so hard that he fell off the ledge and had to be taken to the doctor's office. This incident would define for Simon the true meaning of comedy: "to make a whole audience fall onto the floor." Simon graduated from DeWitt Clinton High School in 1943 and entered New York University as an engineering student under the U.S. Army Air Force Reserve training program. Leaving the service in 1946, Simon went to work in the mailroom of the New York office of Warner Bros. Then, Goodman Ace, a veteran Columbia Broadcasting System (CBS) comedy writer, asked Simon and his brother, Daniel Simon, to submit a comic sketch. Ace read their work and hired the pair immediately. For the next fifteen years, the Simon duo wrote for a variety of radio and television shows, including the *Phil Silvers Arrow Show* (1948), the *Tallulah Bankhead Show* (1951), the *Sid Caesar Show* (1956-1957), and the *Garry Moore Show* (1959-1960).

After his brother ended their collaboration to become a television director, Simon turned his attention to writing full-length plays. *Come Blow Your Horn* premiered on Broadway in 1960. Based on his own experiences as a young man leaving the Bronx to live with his brother in Manhattan, this autobiographical work contains many of the now well-recognized Simon hallmarks: quick, witty dialogue, vivid characterizations, and plot complications. After writing the book for *Little Me*, Simon wrote *Barefoot in the Park*, a play that enjoyed 1,532 performances on Broadway. One of Simon's most popular plays, its theme, that relationships can only succeed if individuals learn to be tolerant and to compromise, became another central feature of the playwright's work.

Simon followed this success with a series of Broadway hits. *The Odd Couple* was a humorous look at the attempt of two opposites, the now-famous Oscar and Felix, to live together. *The Star-Spangled Girl*, a rare Simon flop, was the story of radical protest in the late 1960's. In *Plaza Suite*, Simon abandoned strict comedy and engineered three delicate one-act segments around more serious themes. This tragicomic blend worked well both on the stage and for the audience, and Simon continued to incorporate these poignant moments of pathos in his future work. Simon followed *Plaza Suite* with *Last of the Red Hot Lovers*. A dark work, the play marked an advance in Simon's writing from the polite comedy of his early plays to a more harsh, black humor.

Simon's next play, *The Gingerbread Lady*, almost closed before its Broadway opening. A drama focusing on the career of an alcoholic cabaret singer, the play failed to attract the same enthusiastic reviews and large audiences that his earlier plays had enjoyed; however, Simon's next two comedies, *The Prisoner of Second Avenue* and *The Sunshine Boys*, were extremely successful. Simon's next project was *The Good Doctor*, a series of dramatic vignettes based on Anton Chekhov's short stories. That same year Simon's wife, Joan Baim, a former dancer, died, and the playwright married actress Marsha Mason. Simon wrote about this period of his life in *Chapter Two*, perhaps his most autobiographical work and one of his most acclaimed plays. After the failure of *God's Favorite*, Simon returned to the one-act structure of *Plaza Suite* to write *California Suite*. The four playlets in this work examine both the comic and serious consequences of life's difficulties. In the following years, Simon wrote two musicals, *They're Playing Our Song* and *Little Me*, a revision of the 1962 musical comedy, and two more comedies, *I Ought to Be in Pictures* and *Fools*. Simon's most fully realized work in later years has been the highly autobiographical trilogy that began with *Brighton Beach Memoirs*, first produced in 1982. Treating Simon's own childhood and family, the play traces the painful transition of a young Jewish adolescent, Eugene, into confusing manhood. The second play, *Biloxi Blues*, follows Eugene as he undergoes basic training in Biloxi, Mississippi, in 1943. The cycle is completed by *Broadway Bound*.

Despite the variety of Simon's comedies, several recurring themes and features remain at the heart of each work. Simon tends to write about the close and often-difficult relationships between husbands and wives and within families. Beyond the witty dialogue and the masterful comic episodes, Simon captures, with both sensitivity and depth, the many conflicts that characterize these groupings. His finely drawn characters are middle class, sometimes Jewish, but always searching for balance in their lives. Simon's central message is a plea for moderation and for people to make meaningful commitments and to learn to adapt to the needs and insecurities of others. Perhaps because of his tremendous commercial success, critical opinion about Simon's work is divided. Some critics argue that Simon is a superficial playwright, that his plays are mere "vehicles" for gags and one-liners. Others have identified a growing maturity in his work and have effectively challenged those who are dismissive of Simon's work. Whatever the case, Simon enjoys a popularity with audiences that no other contemporary American playwright can match.

BIBLIOGRAPHICAL REFERENCES: Robert K. Johnson's *Neil Simon*, 1983, is one of the best general critical introductions to Simon's work. See also Edythe M. McGovern, *Neil Simon: A Critical Study*, 1979, and John Simon, *Uneasy Stages: A Chronicle on the New York Theater*, 1975. For a good encyclopedic reference, see Sheila Ennis Geitner, "Neil Simon," in *Dictionary of Literary Biography*, Vol. 7: *Twentieth Century Dramatists, Part 2 K-Z*, 1981, edited by John MacNicholas. See also Richard Watts, Jr., "The Girl Patriot and the Rebels," *New York Theatre Critics' Reviews*, XXVII (1966/1967), 194; Norman Nadel, "*Star-Spangled Girl*: Funny—For One Act," *New York Theatre Critics' Reviews*, XXVII (1966/1967), 196; Richard Watts, "The New York of Neil Simon," *New York Theatre Critics' Reviews*, XXXII (1971), 191; Gerald M. Berkowitz, "Neil Simon and His Amazing Laugh Machine," *Players Magazine*, XLVII (1972), 110-113; Clive Barnes, "*Memoirs* Is Simon's Best Play," *New York Theatre Critics' Reviews*, XLIV (1983), 345; John Simon, "Journeys into Night," *New York Magazine*, XVI (1983), 55-58; Daniel Walden, "Neil Simon's Jewish-Style Comedies," in *From Hester Street to Hollywood: The Jewish-American Stage and Screen*, 1983, edited by Sarah Blaher Cohen; and Douglas Watt, "It's Taps for *Biloxi Blues*," *New York Theatre Critics' Reviews*, XLVI (1985), 323.

Michael John McDonough

ISAAC BASHEVIS SINGER

Born: Leoncin, Poland
Date: July 14, 1904

PRINCIPAL WORKS

SHORT FICTION: *The Spinoza of Market Street*, 1961; *Gimpel the Fool and Other Stories*, 1963; *Short Friday and Other Stories*, 1964; *The Séance and Other Stories*, 1968; *A Friend of Kafka and Other Stories*, 1970; *A Crown of Feathers and Other Stories*, 1973; *Passions and Other Stories*, 1975; *Old Love*, 1979; *The Collected Stories*, 1982; *The Image and Other Stories*, 1985; *The Death of Methuselah and Other Stories*, 1988.

NOVELS: *Sotan in Goray*, 1935 (*Satan in Goray*, 1955); *Di Familie Muskat*, 1950 (*The Family Moskat*, 1950); *Der Hoyf*, 1953-1955 (*The Manor*, 1967, and *The Estate*, 1969); *Der Kunstnmakher fun Lublin*, 1959 (*The Magician of Lublin*, 1960); *Der Knekht*, 1961 (*The Slave*, 1962); *Sonim, de Geshichte fun a Liebe*, 1966 (*Enemies: A Love Story*, 1972); *Neshome Ekspeditsyes*, 1974 (*Shosha*, 1978); *Der Bal-Tshuve*, 1974 (*The Penitent*, 1983); *Der Kenig vun di Felder*, 1988 (*The King of the Fields*, 1988).

CHILDREN'S LITERATURE: *Zlateh the Goat and Other Stories*, 1966; *The Fearsome Inn*, 1967; *Mazel and Shlimazel: Or, The Milk of a Lioness*, 1967; *When Shlemiel Went to Warsaw and Other Stories*, 1968; *A Day of Pleasure: Stories of a Boy Growing Up in Warsaw*, 1969; *Elijah the Slave*, 1970; *Joseph and Koza: Or, The Sacrifice to the Vistula*, 1970; *Alone in the Wild Forest*, 1971; *The Topsy-Turvy Emperor of China*, 1971; *The Wicked City*, 1972; *The Fools of Chelm and Their History*, 1973; *Why Noah Chose the Dove*, 1974; *A Tale of Three Wishes*, 1975; *Naftali the Storyteller and His Horse, Sus, and Other Stories*, 1976; *The Power of Light: Eight Stories*, 1980; *The Golem*, 1982; *Stories for Children*, 1984.

PLAYS: *The Mirror*, pr. 1973; *Yentl, the Yeshiva Boy*, pr. 1974 (with Leah Napolin); *Shlemiel the First*, pr. 1974; *Teibele and Her Demon*, pr. 1978.

AUTOBIOGRAPHY: *Mayn Tatn's Bes-din Shtub*, 1956 (*In My Father's Court*, 1966); *A Little Boy in Search of God: Mysticism in a Personal Light*, 1976; *A Young Man in Search of Love*, 1978; *Lost in America*, 1980.

Perhaps the greatest Yiddish writer, Isaac Bashevis Singer skillfully employs modernist fictional techniques to pose questions about man, God, and existence. Born in Leoncin, Poland, in 1940, Singer reveals in his writing the conflicting elements of his upbringing. His father, Pinchas Mendel Singer, was a Hasidic rabbi who told his son stories of demons and spirits. His mother, Bathsheba Zylberman Singer, whose first name he eventually adopted in its Yiddish form, was on the contrary a rationalist who talked of their Bilgoray relatives. This difference in temperament between his parents is evident in "Why the Geese Shrieked," one of the Tales in *A Day of Pleasure*. When a woman brings two dead geese to Rabbi Singer because they have continued to make strange noises, he seeks a supernatural explanation. His wife remarks that the sound is merely air passing through the severed windpipe and that if the woman removes the windpipe, the shrieking will cease, as indeed it does.

Singer's two older siblings also influenced him. His sister Hende Esther, thirteen years his senior, enjoyed telling him love stories. Most important to his literary growth was his brother, Israel Joshua Singer, who became an important author; for many years Singer was better known as Israel's brother than as a writer himself. When Singer was four, the family moved to 10 Krochmalna Street, Warsaw, which serves as the setting for *Shosha* and some of Singer's best short fiction. In 1917, he and his mother left the Polish capital for Bilgoray to escape the hunger and disease caused by World War I. During the four years he remained in the hamlet, he observed the rural Jewish life that plays so large a role in his writing. Singer remarked that without that experience he never could have written *Satan in Goray.*

After a brief attempt at rabbinical training at the Tachkemoni Seminary, Warsaw (1921-

1922), he returned to Bilgoray, then went to Dzikow, where his father was serving as rabbi. In this village he found the Hasidic tales of Rabbi Nachman of Bratzlav. One may regard Singer's fiction as the inverse of Rabbi Nachman's: Both are haunted by the supernatural, but while Rabbi Nachman's always have a happy ending directed by God, Singer's reveal doubt about Divine Providence.

In 1923, Singer began his literary career when his brother invited him to become proofreader for the Yiddish magazine he was coediting in Warsaw, *Literarische Bletter.* To supplement his income, Singer also translated various popular works into Yiddish. He also began to write, publishing his first story in 1925 in his brother's periodical. When Israel Joshua left for America, Singer worked for a time as associate editor of *Globus* magazine. Soon, however, he realized the danger of Nazism; in 1935, he followed his brother to New York, where he began his long and fruitful association with the *Jewish Daily Forward*.

Singer's first large-scale recognition in the United States came in 1950, with the English-language publication of *The Family Moskat*, a family saga modeled on his brother's work. Saul Bellow's masterful translation of "Gimpl Tam" (1945) as "Gimpel the Fool" in the *Partisan Review* three years later added to a reputation that has continued to grow. Singer has won virtually every literary prize available—Newbery Awards for his children's stories (which he did not begin writing until he was sixty-two years old), National Book Awards, and the Nobel Prize in Literature in 1978.

In presenting the Nobel Prize to Singer, Lars Gyllensten of the Swedish Academy remarked that in his works "the Middle Ages seem to spring to life again . . . , the daily round is interwoven with wonders, reality is spun from dreams, the blood of the past pulsates in the present." Seven of Singer's novels and most of his successful short stories are set in the vanished world of Eastern European Jewry, a world he neither sentimentalizes nor romanticizes. Since his first stories appeared, his chief attackers have been Yiddishists who see him as pessimistic and irreligious. Singer has replied that he is merely realistic: Not all Polish Jews were honest, God-fearing, and chaste; tragedy was their lot at least as often as comedy.

Mingling with this realistic world which reflects his mother's rationalism is the surrealistic realm of demons, dybbuks, and other supernatural beings, the legacy of his father. Whether they are external representations of unconscious drives or actual beings—Singer maintains that they are real—they reveal the perils that threaten one's body and soul. Further, they point to the unfathomable nature of the universe, which does not lend itself, at least not totally, to logical explication.

Therefore, Singer does not attempt to solve the mysteries of existence. One of the reasons he gives for his delight in writing for children is that young readers want a good story, not a message. His writing instead highlights the unfathomable nature of the world. How can the existentially isolated individual survive? How should he live? How can he relate to the rest of suffering humanity? "If God is wisdom," Haiml Chentshiner asks in *Shosha*, "how can there be foolishness? And if God is life, how can there be death?" Cybula in *The King of the Fields* wonders why any creature must suffer. As puzzling as these questions are, they must be faced. Characters such as Jacob and Wanda/Sarah (*The Slave*) or Gimpel the Fool are saved because they are willing to believe in a Providence they cannot see. Recognizing their divorce from God, the source of wisdom, they still reveal a sense of compassion for His creation and so are redeemed.

Whether set in upper West Side Manhattan or primitive Poland, Singer's fiction portrays the ongoing struggle between the forces of good and evil, between humankind's highest aspirations and deepest sensuality. Like his fellow modernists, he sees chaos, not cosmos, and he provides neat, happy endings only in his children's stories (and not always in them). Yet he believes that one has no choice but to exercise free will and seek the truth, even if one ends up, like *Shosha*'s Aaron Greidinger and Haiml Chentshiner, sitting in a silent, dark room waiting, waiting for an answer.

BIBLIOGRAPHICAL REFERENCES: Two biographies of Singer are Paul Kresh, *Isaac Bashevis Singer: The Magician of West Eighty-sixth Street*, 1979, and Dorothea Straus, *Under the Canopy*, 1982. Irving Buchen, *Isaac Bashevis Singer and the Eternal Past*, 1968, the first book-length study of Singer, remains an important work. Edward Alexander, *Isaac Bashevis Singer*, 1980, provides a useful introduction; most of the book is devoted to the novels. *Critical Views of Isaac Bashevis Singer*, 1969, edited by Irving Malin, presents fourteen essays on the writer and concludes with an extensive bibliography of primary and secondary sources in English. *The Achievement of Isaac Bashevis Singer*, 1969, edited by Marcia Allentuck, offers another twelve essays. David Neal Miller, *Fear of Fiction: Narrative Strategies in the Works of Isaac Bashevis Singer*, 1985, deals largely with untranslated works that mix fictional and nonfictional elements. The first number of *Studies in American Jewish Literature*, 1981, is devoted entirely to Singer. Irving Howe's introduction to the Modern Library edition of *Selected Stories of Isaac Bashevis Singer*, 1966, presents an excellent overview of the short fiction. Other useful articles include Janet Hadda, "The Double Life of Isaac Bashevis Singer," *Prooftexts*, V (May, 1985), 165-181; Susan Moire, "The World of Isaac Bashevis Singer," *Quadrant*, XXVI (March, 1982), 69-71; Judith Rinde Sheridan, "Isaac Bashevis Singer: Sex as Cosmic Metaphor," *Midwest Quarterly*, XXIII (Summer, 1982), 365-379; and Michael Fixler, "The Redeemers: Themes in the Fiction of Isaac Bashevis Singer," *The Kenyon Review*, XXVI (1964), 371-386. Richard Burgin and Isaac Bashevis Singer have assembled *Conversations with Isaac Bashevis Singer*, 1985, a collection of interviews in which the author discusses his views on life and literature. An earlier interview appeared in *The Paris Review* (Fall, 1968); it has been reprinted in *Writers at Work*, 1981, 5th series, edited by George Plimpton.

Joseph Rosenblum

ANDREI SINYAVSKY

Born: Moscow, Soviet Union
Date: October 8, 1925

Principal Works

NOVELS AND NOVELLAS: *Sud idyot*, 1960 (*The Trial Begins*, 1960); *Lyubimov*, 1963 (*The Makepeace Experiment*, 1965); *Kroshka Tsores*, 1980; *Spokoynoy nochi*, 1984.

SHORT FICTION: *Fantasticheskie povesti*, 1961 (*Fantastic Stories*, 1963).

LITERARY CRITICISM: *Chto takoe sotsialisticheskii realizm*, 1959 (*On Socialist Realism*, 1960); *For Freedom of Imagination*, 1971; *Progulki s Pushkinym*, 1975; *V teni Gogolya*, 1975; *"Opavshie listya" V. V. Rozanova*, 1982.

NONFICTION: *Mysli vrasplokh*, 1965 (*Unguarded Thoughts*, 1972); *Golos iz khora*, 1973 (*A Voice from the Chorus*, 1976).

Andrei Donatovich Sinyavsky is the godfather of the post-Stalin renaissance in Russian literature. Born on October 8, 1925, into the family of an ineffectual radical idealist, Sinyavsky was reared as a true believer in the Communist system. Although well-educated, his parents held menial white-collar jobs. In his late teens Sinyavsky served in the Soviet army. Demobilized, he entered Moscow University in 1947, where he defended his dissertation on Maxim Gorky, the father of Socialist Realism, in 1952. Two friendships of his student years would have enormous consequences for Sinyavsky: Hélène Pelletier, the daughter of the French naval attaché who was permitted to attend Moscow University, and Yuli Daniel, whose bohemian apartment became a center for young intellectuals. Soon after graduation Sinyavsky was married to Mariya Rozanova, a student of art history. Although Sinyavsky had acquired some exposure to Western literature and art, he remained a fervent believer in the moral integrity of the Communist system. The first doubt arose when his father was arrested in 1951 on preposterous charges. In the early 1950's Sinyavsky worked as a lecturer at Moscow University and then as a researcher at the Institute of World Literature. His articles were bringing him a degree of renown, but he wished to write fiction as well. Sinyavsky's first story, "At the Circus" (1955), already reflects his love of the phantasmagoric and his persistent identification of the artist with the criminal.

Nikita Khrushchev's historic 1956 denunciation of Stalin's twenty-year reign of terror shattered Sinyavsky's illusions. His new friendship with Boris Pasternak, who had sent his suppressed novel, *Doktor Zhivago* (1957; English translation, 1958), abroad, perhaps inspired him to ask Hélène Pelletier to smuggle his work abroad for publication. Under the pseudonym Abram Tertz, two long works appeared in France in 1959; a theoretical essay, *On Socialist Realism*, decrying the sterility of Socialist Realism and calling for a new "phantasmagoric" literature, and a novella, *The Trial Begins*, which illustrated the essay's literary thesis and was a powerful indictment of the Stalinist dictum that the end justifies the means. In 1961, his story collection *Fantastic Stories* appeared in the West, followed two years later by *The Makepeace Experiment*, an anti-utopian political fantasy. Sinyavsky's reflections on many themes, especially religious ones, appeared in a collection of aphoristic notes entitled *Unguarded Thoughts*. These Western publications created a sensation and endless speculation about the identity of their author. Sinyavsky/Tertz successfully led his double life for nearly six years. Pressure mounted after the fall of the relatively liberal Khruschev in 1964. In late 1965, the Soviet government learned the identity of "Tertz," and Sinyavsky and his fellow writer Yuli Daniel were arrested. Wishing to preserve the appearance of legality in the eyes of Western public opinion, Soviet officials orchestrated a show trial in February, 1966. Although the trial was closed to the Western press, the defendants' wives smuggled out their own handwritten transcripts, which were published abroad. Sinyavsky was sentenced to seven years.

Sinyavsky was released in June of 1971, and two years later he was permitted to emigrate to France with his wife and child. The camp years had not been wasted. During his sentence he had utilized his bimonthly letters to his wife to pour out his thoughts on many subjects. Once in Paris, these letters, totaling some fifteen hundred pages, became the nuclei of three books. *A Voice from the Chorus* is a gathering of reflections inspired both by camp life and by the author's philosophical and artistic interests. The other two volumes, *V teni Gogolya* (in the shadow of Gogol) and *Progulki s Pushkinym* (strolls with Pushkin), are irreverent and highly personal meditations on two giants of Russian literature. Sinyavsky resumed his career as a creative writer with *Kroshka Tsores* (little Tsores), a brief novella exploring the theme of guilt and the artist. The major work of the emigration is *Spokoynoy nochi* (good night), a long, highly fragmented, phantasmagoric memoir-novel about Sinyavsky's life as a Soviet intellectual and secret dissident writer, his betrayal, his trial, and his years in a labor camp.

Sinyavsky, who holds a teaching position at the Sorbonne, is widely known and translated into many languages, but his life in emigration has not been easy. Just as he found himself in conflict with Soviet society, he has found himself odd man out in émigré circles. Émigré journals at first welcomed Sinyavsky to their pages, where he published penetrating essays on the Soviet scene. His brilliantly eccentric views proved unacceptable to opinionated editors, and he soon found himself without an outlet for his writings. Partially in response, Sinyavsky and his wife established their own small journal. Since 1978, *Sintaksis* has served as a forum for the views of Sinyavsky and other émigré writers who urge a "pluralist" outlook in opposition to those who favor more traditional, if not authoritarian approaches to art and society.

Spokoynoy nochi is a distillation of Sinyavsky's approach to fiction. Densely metaphoric and richly allusive, it makes heavy demands on the reader's knowledge of culture and history (especially Russian), as well as of the author's own life. Each of the memoir-novel's five chapters centers on the events of a particular night. The biographic fact serves as a point of departure for numerous seemingly unrelated vignettes that ultimately form a sort of ornate, surrealist mosaic depicting one man's life during the nightmare of Stalinism.

In spite of the structural and stylistic complexity of Sinyavsky's writings, his themes are simple: Stalinist tyranny and the nature of art and the artist. Stalinism very nearly destroyed a nation and its culture—all in the name of an ideal, Communism. The means perverted the goal. So bizarre was that world that it could be rendered only by an equally bizarre, phantasmagoric art. Sinyavsky's other theme is the transcending power of art and the inherently subversive character of the free artist. These two interconnected themes unite Sinyavsky's oeuvre from *The Trial Begins* through *Spokoynoy nochi* and his critical and journalistic writings.

Andrei Sinyavsky (re-)introduced a fantastic, modernist, aesthetically oriented prose into a literature which had been stifled by a primitive, dogmatic Socialist Realism. Although the realistic strain remains dominant in Russian letters, Sinyavsky's seminal essay *On Socialist Realism* and his subsequent fiction blazed a path for the revival of the fantastic. Both Vassily Aksyonov and Sasha Sokolov, the most important younger writers to emerge in the 1960's and 1970's (and later both émigrés), have heeded Sinyavsky/Tertz's phantasmagoric imperative. With the advent of Mikhail Gorbachev's "openness," a new generation of Soviet authors may choose to follow in his footsteps.

BIBLIOGRAPHICAL REFERENCES: The best eyewitness account of the young Sinyavsky/Tertz is written by Hélène Zamoyska, "Sinyavsky, the Man and the Writer," in Leopold Labedz and Max Hayward, *On Trial: The Case of Sinyavsky (Tertz) and Daniel (Arzhak): Documents*, 1967, which also contains a transcript of the trial. Book-length studies of the pre-1966 writings include Margaret Dalton, *Andrei Siniavskii and Julii Daniel': Two Soviet "Heretical" Writers*, 1973, and Richard Lourie, *Letters to the Future: An Approach to Sinyavsky-Tertz*, 1975. Deming Brown provides a good overview in "The Art of Andrei Sinyavsky," in his *Soviet Literature Since Stalin*, 1978. Donald Fanger, "Conflicting Imperatives in the Model of the Russian Writer: The Case of Tertz/Sinyavsky," in *Literature and History: Theoretical Problems and Russian Case Studies*, 1986, edited by Gary S. Morson, surveys work through 1984. See also M. J. Leatherbarrow, "The Sense of Purpose and Socialist Realism in Tertz's *The Trial Begins*," *Forum for Modern Language Studies*, XI (1975), 268-279. *Kroshka Tsores* is examined in Vera Dunham, "Serenity: A Note on Sinyavsky's Style," in *The Third Wave: Russian Literature in Emigration*, 1984, edited by Olga Matich and Michael Heim. *Spokoynoy nochi* is treated in Olga Matich, "*Spokoinoj no i*: Andrej Sinjavskij's Rebirth as Abram Terc," *Slavic and East European Journal*, XXXIII, no. 1 (1989), 50-63. The short stories are separately treated in Andrew Durkin, "Narrator, Metaphor, and Theme in Sinjavskij's *Fantastic Tales*," *Slavic and East European Journal*, XXIV (1980), 133-144. On Sinyavsky's critical writings, see Czesław Miłosz's introduction to *On Socialist Realism* in Abram Tertz, *The Trial Begins and On Socialist Realism*, 1965. Sinyavsky's "official" literary criticism of the Soviet period is examined in Walter F. Kolonosky, "Andrei Siniavskii: The Chorus and the Critic," *Canadian-American Slavic Studies*, IX (1975), 352-360; Max Hayward, "Sinyavsky's *A Voice from the Chorus*" and "Pushkin, Gogol, and the Devil," in *Writers in Russia: 1917-1978*, 1983, treat Sinyavsky's books from the camp years, while the literary and social criticism of the émigré period is surveyed in Catherine Theimer Nepomnyashchy, "Sinyavsky/Tertz: The Evolution of the Writer in Exile," *Humanities in Society*, VII, nos. 3/4 (1984), 123-142.

D. Barton Johnson

JOSEF ŠKVORECKÝ

Born: Náchod, Czechoslovakia
Date: September 27, 1924

PRINCIPAL WORKS

NOVELS AND NOVELLAS: *Zbabělci*, 1958 (*The Cowards*, 1968); *Legenda Emöke*, 1963; *Bassaxofon*, 1967 (*The Bass Saxophone: Two Novellas*, 1977; includes *Legenda Emöke*); *Farářuv Konec*, 1969; *Lvíče*, 1969 (*Miss Silver's Past*, 1973); *Tankový prapor*, 1971; *Mirákl: Politická detectivka*, 1972; *Prima sezońa*, 1974 (*The Swell Season: A Text on the Most Important Things in Life*, 1982); *Příběh inženýra lidských duší*, 1977 (*The Engineer of Human Souls: An Entertainment on the Old Themes of Life, Women, Fate, Dreams, the Working Class, Secret Agents, Love and Death*, 1984); *Scherzo capriccioso*, 1983 (*Dvorak in Love: A Light-Hearted Dream*, 1987).

MYSTERY AND DETECTIVE FICTION: *Smutek poručíka Boruvky*, 1966 (*The Mournful Demeanor of Lieutenant Boruvka*, 1974); *Konec poručíka Boruvky*, 1975; *Návrat poručíka Boruvky*, 1980; *Hříchy pro pátera Knoxe*, 1973 (*Sins for Father Knox*, 1988).

CRITICISM: *O nich—o nás*, 1968; *All the Bright Young Men and Women: A Personal History of the Czech Cinema*, 1971; *Jiri Menzel and the History of CLOSELY WATCHED TRAINS*, 1982.

Josef Valcav Škvorecký, long one of Czechoslovakia's best-known novelists, has established a distinguished international literary reputation since his exile in 1968. He was born in Náchod, Bohemia, on September 27, 1924, son of Josef Škvorecký, a bank clerk, and Anna Kurazova Škvorecký, an actress. After he was graduated from high school in the midst of the Nazi occupation of his homeland, between 1943 and 1945, Škvorecký was impressed into labor at Messerschmitt factories first in Náchod and then in Nové Město. These experiences are vividly depicted in several of his major novels. During the final months of the war, he spent time digging trenches and working in a cotton mill. Although he entered the Faculty of Medicine at Prague's Charles University in 1945, after beginning to write fiction he transferred to the Faculty of Philosophy, was graduated in 1949, and received his Ph.D. in 1951. During this time, he became an active member of the Prague underground community of writers and artists resisting the censorship imposed by the postwar Communist regime. When he was drafted, Škvorecký served in the elite tank division at a military post near Prague from 1951 to 1953.

During the next decade, Škvorecký built a substantial literary reputation as a translator and editor of American writers such as Stephen Crane, Ernest Hemingway, and Edgar Allan Poe. His early short stories and an early novel, however, were censored before publication. Although written in 1948 at the age of twenty-four, Škvorecký's first published novel, *The Cowards*, did not appear until 1958. Here Daniel Smiricky, also the protagonist of several other Škvorecký novels, is full of youthful preoccupation with self, jazz, and girls as he moves through eight days at the beginning of the dramatic May, 1945, transition from German occupation to Soviet occupation of Czechoslovakia. The novel's depictions of both German and Soviet military men were found offensive; the book was banned and confiscated, and the author removed from his post as editor of the journal *Světová Literatura*. Suppression made the book even more popular, and its author became a national literary figure. Subsequent fluctuations in political climate permitted occasional publication of some of his shorter fictions such as *Legenda Emöke*, but the greater part of Škvorecký's work during this period was film and television screenplays. Two books in English on the history of Czech cinema and Škvorecký's associations with famed director Jiri Menzel and other luminaries of the screen attest Škvorecký's passion for film.

In spite of continued censorship of his work, Škvorecký published several more short-story collections between 1964 and 1968, as well as a detective novel, *The Mournful Demeanor of Lieutenant Boruvka*. He has won several awards for translation and fiction and has served actively in film, television, and literary organizations. August 21, 1968, the Soviet invasion of Czechoslovakia, marked a radical break in Škvorecký's career. He and his wife of ten years, Zdena Salivarová, a singer, actress, and novelist, emigrated to Toronto, Canada, where Škvorecký became a professor in the English department at Erindale College of the University of Toronto. He and his wife also established Sixty-Eight Publishers, which they dedicated to distributing the works of Czechoslovakian writers both in Czechoslovakia and in exile.

In 1970, translation of *The Cowards* first made Škvorecký's work available to English-speaking audiences. Other notable translations followed, including *Miss Silver's Past* and *The Bass Saxophone*. Continuous contributions to the literary community as political commentator, critic, editor, publisher, and translator earned for Škvorecký international visibility. In 1980, he was awarded the Neustadt International Prize for Literature. One of the most notable of Škvorecký's novels, *The Engineer of Human Souls*, was published in 1984 and received the Canadian Governor General's Literary Award in the same year. In *The Engineer of Human Souls*, Daniel Smiricky, the semiautobiographical young protagonist of *The Cowards*, *Tankový prapor* (the tank corps), *Mirákl* (miracle in Bohemia), and *The Swell Season*, appears once more. Smiricky's adventures as he matures, from girl chasing to teaching English at a Canadian college, are chronicled in these novels. He seems to have been the inspiration for Škvorecký's protagonists in *The Bass Saxophone*, *Miss Silver's Past*, and *Dvorak in Love*.

Škvorecký's foray into mystery and detective fiction produced a continuing series of novels with Lieutenant Boruvka as their central character. In a context of ever-alert and powerful political and social censors, mystery fiction allowed a writer to continue his profession. At the same time, he could, perhaps, incorporate subtle commentary on politics and society, as Škvorecký does in *Miss Silver's Past*. Škvorecký ranks among such distinguished Eastern European, post-World War II, exiled writers as his fellow countryman Milan Kundera, Polish Nobel Prize winner Czesław Miłosz, and Russians Joseph Brodsky and Aleksandr Solzhenitsyn. *The Engineer of Human Souls* and *The Cowards* have met with great critical acclaim. Škvorecký's works transcend national borders and ideologies to address a truly international audience.

BIBLIOGRAPHICAL REFERENCES: *World Literature Today: A Literary Quarterly of the University of Oklahoma*, LIV (1980), is devoted solely to Škvorecký. Sam Solecki, "The Laughter and Pain of Remembering," *Canadian Forum*, XXXIX (1984), 39-41, terms *The Engineer of Human Souls* "one of the most important novels ever written in Canada." Terrie Goldie, "Political Judgments," *Canadian Literature*, CIV (1985), 165-167, sparked a controversy when he accused Smiricky, and Škvorecký by implication, of being right wing, anti-Communist, antifemale, anti-Arab, antiunion, antisocial and suffering from a general "failure of humanity." This view was extended in Stephen Henighan, "Josef Škvorecký and Canadian Cultural Cringe," *Canadian Literature*, CXVI (1988), 253-259. Defenses of *The Engineer of Human Souls* in response to Goldie include Škvorecký, "A Judgment of Political Judgments," *Canadian Literature*, CX (1986), 171-176, and Marketa Goetz-Stankiewicz, "Forum on Škvorecký Reviewed: Literary Mirrors," *Canadian Literature*, 110 (1986), 165-171. *Czech Literature Since 1956: A Symposium*, 1980, edited by William E. Harkins and Paul I. Trensky, contains analyses of Škvorecký's influence and role in contemporary Czech literary history in several of its essays.

Virginia Crane

AGNES SMEDLEY

Born: Campground, Missouri
Date: February 23, 1892

Died: Oxford, England
Date: May 6, 1950

Principal Works

JOURNALISM: *Chinese Destinies: Sketches of Present-Day China*, 1933; *China's Red Army Marches*, 1934; *China Fights Back: An American Woman with the Eighth Route Army*, 1938; *Battle Hymn of China*, 1943.

NOVEL: *Daughter of Earth*, 1929.

BIOGRAPHY: *The Great Road: The Life and Times of Chu Teh*, 1956.

Agnes Smedley wanted to be known, and primarily is known, as an independent American radical, a working-class feminist, and a writer who served the causes in which she believed. She was born in Campground, Missouri, on February 23, 1892, the daughter of a farmer and jack-of-all-trades, Charles Smedley, and his wife, Sarah Ralls. Smedley's lifelong commitment to the causes of the poor and to feminism were fueled by the wretched life she experienced as a child. Her family moved constantly. Their constant financial instability caused both parents to suffer, something they, at times, passed on to their children. Her mother died at an early age from the cumulative effects of poverty and overwork.

With the help of relatives, Smedley escaped from this life by getting an eighth-grade education and becoming a schoolteacher. At one of these jobs she met the sister of Ernest Brundin, who would later become her first husband, and she moved with the two of them to California, where they all became involved in radical political movements. She learned about the anti-imperialist Indian national independence movement, about anarchism and Socialism from Emma Goldman, and about Margaret Sanger's birth control movement. While she admired the cultural sophistication of the Brundins, transplanted New Yorkers, she remained throughout her life a rough, earthy, outspoken person. Eventually she married Ernest Brundin, but they were temperamentally unsuited to each other. After their divorce, Smedley moved to New York City, where she lived among that first generation of radicals and artists that made Greenwich Village famous.

In New York, Smedley became deeply involved in politics. She helped to establish birth control clinics, studied Indian culture, and worked at establishing herself as a journalist. There, too, she met Virendranath Chattopadhyaya, who was to become her teacher and, later, her common-law husband for many years. With him she traveled to Germany and the Soviet Union and worked in exile for Indian independence from England.

In 1927, Smedley left "Chatto" for good, taking refuge in Denmark, where she wrote her first book, *Daughter of Earth*, a thinly disguised autobiographical novel. It essentially summarizes her life powerfully and melodramatically, but in unsophisticated language. She continues this story in her later book *Battle Hymn of China*. In fact, Smedley did reorient her life, shifting her attention from India to China. In 1928 she went to China as a special correspondent for the *Frankfurter Zeitung*, and it was there that she did her most important work between 1929 and 1942.

During this time Smedley was one of a few foreign visitors who recognized the power, popularity, and, consequently, the importance of the Chinese Communist forces in the war against Japan. In China, Smedley, always an independent leftist in politics, immediately identified with the causes of the poor industrial workers in Shanghai and with the even poorer peasants in the countryside. She believed that the Communist revolutionaries were nationalists who fought against Western and Japanese imperialism and for agrarian land reform and democracy.

Like most Western journalists in China, Smedley spent most of her early years in Shanghai and other cities controlled by the Nationalist government. Unlike many journalists, however, she was immediately and continuously involved in social and political work. Her first book on China, *Chinese Destinies*, is a collection of articles which has Shanghai for its background. Her next, *China's Red Army Marches*, depicts the struggles of the Communist forces in Jiangxi province to regroup after their early defeats by the Nationalists. Although Smedley never visted Jiangxi, her description of this battle between good and evil forces is based on information she gathered from refugees whom she sheltered and helped.

After a visit to Moscow and a brief stay in the United States, Smedley returned to China and gained fame as the reporter who broadcast news of the "Xian incident," when Chiang Kaishek was kidnapped and forced to agree to a united front with the Communist forces against the Japanese. Living in Hankow (now the city of Wu-han), Smedley also helped to smuggle medical supplies through Japanese territory to Communist forces at their headquarters in Yen-an.

During this period, Smedley (along with the more famous Edgar Snow) spent long periods of time with Communist forces. She was able to interview leaders of the revolutionary armies, especially Mao Tse-tung and Chu Teh. These experiences formed the basis for her last three books. *China Fights Back* and *Battle Hymn of China* are eyewitness reports designed to tell Americans about China's struggles against the Japanese, especially about the Red Army, its leaders, its organization and tactics, and its own attempts to shed the feudal culture with which China had, so to speak, bound its own feet. Her last book, the biography of Chu Teh, was an attempt to introduce the West to China's most important military figure. It was published posthumously, and, like all Smedley's books, it was highly partisan and a bit oversimplified. Nevertheless, Smedley was a highly respected authority on the Chinese situation who advised both the civilian and military arms of the American government on Chinese matters.

With the end of World War II and the onset of the Cold War, Smedley quickly became, like other journalists, military men, and diplomats who did not support Chiang Kaishek, a victim of smear campaigns and political witch-hunts. At the time of her death, Smedley had been accused of spying for the Soviet Union and being a member of the Communist Party. Neither of these accusations proved to be true. Smedley was always an independent radical, and her major writings belong to that tradition of opinionated journalism, popular in the nineteenth century, which was practiced by writers as diverse as Horace Greeley, Jack London, Upton Sinclair, John Reed, and H. L. Mencken.

BIBLIOGRAPHICAL REFERENCES: Janice R. and Stephen R. MacKinnon, *Agnes Smedley: The Life and Times of an American Radical*, 1988, is the first study of Smedley's life and work. This labor of love took fourteen years to research and write. It has the only complete bibliography of Smedley's books and articles and presents an exhaustively researched biography as well as careful descriptions of Smedley's books and major works. See also Harold L. Ickes, "Death by Association," *The New Republic*, CXXII (May 29, 1950), 16-17, and "Agnes Smedley's 'Cell-Mates,'" *Signs*, III (Winter, 1977), 531-539, edited by Janice and Stephen MacKinnon.

Michael Helfand

C. P. SNOW

Born: Leicester, England
Date: October 15, 1905

Died: London, England
Date: July 1, 1980

PRINCIPAL WORKS

NOVELS: *Death Under Sail*, 1932; *New Lives for Old*, 1933; *The Search*, 1934; *Strangers and Brothers*, 1940 (also known as *George Passant*); *The Light and the Dark*, 1947; *Time of Hope*, 1949; *The Masters*, 1951; *The New Men*, 1954; *Homecomings*, 1956; *Conscience of the Rich*, 1958; *The Affair*, 1960; *Corridors of Power*, 1964; *The Sleep of Reason*, 1968; *Last Things*, 1970; *The Malcontents*, 1972; *In Their Wisdom*, 1974; *Coat of Varnish*, 1979.

BIOGRAPHY: *Variety of Men*, 1967; *Trollope: His Life and Art*, 1975; *The Realists: Portraits of Eight Novelists*, 1978; *The Physicists: A Generation That Changed the World*, 1981.

NONFICTION: *Richard Aldington: An Appreciation*, 1938; *The Two Cultures and the Scientific Revolution*, 1959 (revised as *Two Cultures and a Second Look*, 1964); *The Moral Un-Neutrality of Science*, 1961; *Science and Government*, 1961.

Charles Percy Snow—British novelist, scientist, and literary critic—is notable for both his realistic fiction and his commentaries about the "two cultures" of science and literature. He was born October 15, 1905, in the lower-middle-class district of Leicester. His father, William Edward Snow, a clerk in a shoe factory, was an amiable but remote figure in Snow's early life, who seems to have neither helped nor hindered his son's intellectual growth. Snow's doting mother, Ada Sophia Robinson, on the other hand, encouraged her son's precocity and, despite the family's poverty, sent Snow to private grammar schools until the age of sixteen. In 1925, he entered Leicester University College, where he received his B.Sc. in chemistry in 1927 and M.Sc. in physics in 1928. Having determined from his youth to become a novelist, Snow nevertheless chose science for a career, following his own pragmatic instincts and aversion to poverty. In 1928, he gained acceptance into the Ph.D. program in physics at Christ's College, Cambridge, and its prestigious research core, the Cavendish Laboratory. This pivotal event in Snow's life marked his entry into the "corridors of power" (a phrase he coined), as the University of Cambridge was clearly the exuberant center of a new "heroic age" of scientific discovery, where men such as Lord Ernest Rutherford, J. D. Bernal, John Cockroft, and P. M. S. Blackett were revolutionizing physics and biochemistry. Upon completing his doctorate in 1930, Snow, who wore thick horn-rimmed glasses and looked well beyond his twenty-five years, was elected a Fellow at Christ's College. Now comfortable in science, he turned his attentions to his first interest, fiction writing.

Snow began writing in deliberate reaction against the purely aesthetic mode of fiction typified by writiers such as James Joyce and Virginia Woolf. This antirealistic trend, he believed, was self-indulgent and pernicious, and it threatened the breakdown in society of morality and individual responsibility. His early novels are apprentice works: *Death Under Sail*, an intriguing detective story intended for a popular audience; *New Lives for Old*, a story about rejuvenation, for which he was compared with H. G. Wells; and *The Search*, a weightier novel about the ambitions of research scientists, the fruit of Snow's close observations of the academic power structure and the brilliant, temperamental scientists who controlled it.

On holiday in Marseilles in 1935, Snow was suddenly struck by the idea of a *roman fleuve*, a series of novels to be connected by a central protagonist (Lewis Eliot) whose private pursuits would intertwine, and often clash, with his public actions. Snow's objective was to examine the actions of man alone and man in society, and his inner design was to create a "resonance" between what Lewis Eliot sees in observing men and events outside himself and what he feels as similar experiences enter his own life. The first novel, *Strangers and Brothers*, was completed in 1940; however, between 1940 and 1944, Snow's war job as technical director for the Ministry of Labour retarded his progress on the series. His second and third novels, *The Light and the Dark* and *Time of Hope*, earned for Snow wider recognition; *The Masters*, by consensus his most exquisitely constructed novel, intrigued many with its behind-the-scenes analysis of committee politics and personal ambition. *The New Men*, *Homecomings*, *Conscience of the Rich*, and *The Affair* all helped to establish Snow's international reputation as the preeminent novelist of man in society.

In 1959, Snow delivered the time-honored Rede Lecture at the University of Cambridge, an event that sparked one of the most heated debates of the decade between scientific and literary intellectuals. In the lecture, entitled "The Two Cultures and the Scientific Revolution," Snow warned that a "gulf of mutual incomprehension" between the literary culture and scientific community threatened Western society and implied that this ignorance of science by nonscientists was irresponsible. Rebuttal followed, the most scathing of which came from Cambridge professor of English and literary critic F. R. Leavis. Snow weathered these attacks as well as bouts of ill health in the 1960's, produced one of his most widely admired novels, *Corridors of Power*, and finished his series with *Last Things* in 1970.

Like his literary predecessors Anthony Trollope and Matthew Arnold, Snow assumed a humanitarian stance with an insistence upon the moral function of art. His thematic landscape is marked by polarities that create the central tension in the novels, for example, power and responsibility, private ambition and social ethics, personal suffering and public performance, and redemptive love and possessive love. Underlying the series is the moral directive that a man should do what he can to improve the human condition, that even though the individual life may be tragic, the social life need not be so. Most readers detect a darkening of moral vision in *The Sleep of Reason* and *Last Things*. An aging protagonist here records the effects wrought by a permissive, affluent society in which individual social responsibility has been abdicated. Snow was once anachronistically referred to as the greatest living nineteenth century novelist. When the mood of the country was predominantly antiexperimental, Snow's literary reputation soared. All tallied, however, the critical reception of Snow's novels has never been strongly positive, there being several persistent complaints, such as a failure to integrate the personal and external experiences of the protagonist from one novel to the next, the plain and functional prose style that many find dull, and the lack of empathy for the protagonists.

BIBLIOGRAPHICAL REFERENCES: One of the earliest book-length studies of Snow's writing was prepared by fellow novelist and personal friend William Cooper (Harry Hoff), *C. P. Snow*, 1959. Frederick R. Karl has written several pieces on Snow's fiction, notably *C. P. Snow: The Politics of Conscience*, 1963, a favorable appraisal, and his reassessment, "C. P. Snow: The Unreason of Reason," in his *Contemporary British Novelists*, 1965. See also Robert Gorham Davis, *The World of C. P. Snow*, 1962, which has coverage of the Snow-Leavis affair and novels up to 1960; Jerome Thale, *C. P. Snow*, 1965, which covers the series up to and including *Corridors of Power*. Two later studies cover the entire series: David Shusterman, *C. P. Snow*, 1975, and Suguna Ramanathan, *The Novels of C. P. Snow: A Critical Introduction*, 1978, the latter a perceptive and sympathetic critique of Snow's themes, character delineation, style, and intelligence in depicting the drama of management. F. R. Leavis' notorious *ad hominem* attack on Snow, *Two Cultures? The Significance of C. P. Snow*, 1962, is a must-read for insight into the two-cultures debate. A serious analysis and indictment of Snow as literary critic and as novelist is Rubin Rabinovitz, *The Reaction Against Experiment in the English Novel, 1950-1960*, 1967. Snow's brother, Philip Snow, has written an epistolary biography of the author, *Stranger and Brother: A Portrait of C. P. Snow*, 1983. An edition of Snow's letters by Caroline Nobile Gryta, *Selected Letters of C. P. Snow: A Critical Edition*, 1988 (dissertation), spans fifty years of the novelist's correspondence. No serious study of Snow should begin without first consulting Paul Boytinck, *C. P. Snow: A Reference Guide*, 1980. Important articles on Snow's work include Patrick Swinden, "The World of C. P. Snow," *Critical Quarterly*, XV (1973), 297-313. See also Michael Millgate, "Structure and Style in the Novels of C. P. Snow," *Research in English Literature*, I (1960), 34-41, and Alfred Kazin, "A Brilliant Boy from the Midlands," in his *Contemporaries*, 1962. Nancy Poland, "A Conversation with C. P. Snow," *Harvard Magazine*, LXXVII (1975), 40-47, and Roy Newquist, "C. P. Snow," in his *Counterpoint*, 1964, are both very revealing interviews with the author. Lionel Trilling, "Science, Literature, and Culture: A Comment on the Snow-Leavis Controversy," *Commentary*, XXXIII (1962), 461-477, offers objective and rational views on the two cultures and should be read in response to Leavis' assessment of the "significance" of Snow (above).

Caroline Nobile Gryta

SASHA SOKOLOV

Born: Ottawa, Canada
Date: November 6, 1943

PRINCIPAL WORKS

NOVELS: *Shkola dlia durakov,* 1976 (*A School for Fools*, 1977); *Mezhdu sobakoi i volkom*, 1980; *Palisandriia*, 1984 (*Astrophobia*, 1989).

Sasha Sokolov is the most critically acclaimed modernist author to appear on the Russian literary scene during the 1970's and 1980's. Aleksandr Vsevolodovich Sokolov was born November 6, 1943, in Ottawa, where his father was a Soviet military diplomat. Departing Canada following an espionage scandal, the family returned to Moscow, where their dreamy son drifted through an unsatisfactory career in the public schools. In 1962 Sokolov entered the Military Institute of Foreign Languages. Army life was not to his liking, and he ended first in jail for being absent without leave and then in a mental hospital as part of a ploy to gain his military discharge. After a period on the fringes of Moscow's literary bohemia, the aspiring author entered the journalism department at Moscow State University. Completing an internship on a provincial newspaper, Sokolov returned to the capital, where he worked for *Literary Russia*. When he received his university degree in 1971, Sokolov abandoned Moscow for a job as a gamekeeper on the remote upper Volga, where he would be free to write. Here, over a two-year period, he completed *A School for Fools*, a modernist tour de force that then had little chance of appearing in the Soviet Union. Smuggled abroad with the help of an Austrian woman whom Sokolov subsequently married, the novella appeared in the United States in 1976. Growing out of Sokolov's youthful encounters with Soviet institutions and the sheer dreary duplicity of Soviet life, the novella depicts that world through the innocent eyes of its schizophrenic narrator, a student at a "special" school. Translated into several languages, *A School for Fools* became the only novel by a living Russian author to win the praise of Vladimir Nabokov.

While the novel was making its way toward publication abroad, Sokolov launched a campaign to emigrate, which brought him into conflict with the government. Following a hunger strike and extensive publicity, he was allowed to join his bride-to-be in Vienna in late 1975. The following year he arrived in North America, where he was able to claim his Canadian citizenship. While still in Russia, Sokolov had started a novel based upon an unsolved murder he had heard about during his years as a gamekeeper. *Mezhdu sobakoi i volkom* (between dog and wolf) is a novel of startling originality and daring. Its metaphorical title refers to twilight, when the normally distinct becomes blurred. The plot emerges from the drunken narrator's inability to distinguish between a real dog and wolf—a failure that results in his murder for the killing of a hunting dog. As a result of its structural and stylistic complexity, the novel gained much critical acclaim but few readers. The unofficial Leningrad journal *Chasy* awarded it its 1981 Andrey Bely Prize.

Sokolov has been peripatetic during his years in the United States and Canada. He has held a variety of short-term jobs ranging from language teacher and radio writer to Vermont ski instructor. He has also held grants from the Canadian government and has been Regents' Lecturer at the University of California, as well as giving numerous literary readings and conference talks that are actually highly polished essays of great wit and charm.

Sokolov's work was banned in the Soviet Union of Leonid Brezhnev, although it was known to literary cognoscenti through smuggled copies and radio broadcasts. With the rise of Mikhail Gorbachev's *glasnost*, Sokolov became recognized as a major literary figure in his homeland, as he already was in the West.

Astrophobia, Sokolov's third novel, is a radical departure from his earlier, more involuted work. *Astrophobia* is a comic, picaresque work that lampoons many popular genres: the sensational memoir, the political espionage thriller, the futurological fantasy, and the pornographic novel. Its hero(ine), the bizarre Palisander/Palisandra, recounts his/her life story from privileged Kremlin orphan to penniless exile, ending with a triumphant return to his/her rightful position as the ruler of Russia. The novel is parody raised to the level of high art.

A School for Fools is representative of Sokolov's work. It is a first-person account of the mental landscape of a nameless, schizophrenic adolescent. There is little or no plot, and the work is composed of a small number of scenes that occur and recur in evolving variants. It is difficult to determine whether events occur in the past, present, or future, or whether they are real or imaginary. The boy's disordered perceptions literally shape the language, the manner, and the content of the story, which deals with his attempts to come to terms with the elemental experiences of love, sex, and death in his small, oppressive universe. The novella progresses largely through a complex pattern of phonetic associations and recurrent images. The language is of great wit and beauty.

The central theme that runs throughout Sokolov's novels is ambiguity. Traditional fiction, like life, rests on certain unconscious and unquestioned assumptions. Time is linear and is divided into past, present, and unknown future; it is constant for all. Memory recalls the past, not the future. People are either male or female, not both. Personal identity is fixed. Incest is avoided. One is either dead or alive. These assumptions are implicitly called into question in Sokolov's novels. Everything takes place in a twilight zone where nothing is certain. Sokolov replaces the usual coordinates of existence with a richly woven web of words which arises from the world of the subconscious and replaces mundane reality. Sound texture and wordplay are the heart of his lyrical style, which tends to displace content. One critic has aptly remarked that Sokolov's prose is not merely a stream of consciousness, but rather an inundation of consciousness.

The mainstream of Russian literature in both the nineteenth and twentieth centuries has been realistic in form, socially and morally committed in content. Sokolov belongs to a brilliant, minor line in Russian literary history which was inaugurated by the modernist Andrey Bely in the early years of this century. That tradition, suppressed in the early years of the revolution in favor of a sturdy, simple-minded Socialist Realism, was reinvoked by Andrei Sinyavsky (as Abram Tertz), whose 1956 samizdat essay "On Socialist Realism" called for a "phantasmagoric art." Sokolov's work is the most brilliant response to Sinyavsky's modernist imperative.

BIBLIOGRAPHICAL REFERENCES: One of the best introductory surveys is D. Barton Johnson, "Sasha Sokolov: The New Russian Avant-Garde," *Critique: Studies in Contemporary Fiction*, XXX (1989). An extensive literary biography and a bibliography of works by and about Sokolov may be found in a special Sokolov issue of *Canadian-American Slavic Studies*, XXII, nos. 1/2, 1988, which contains essays on many aspects of Sokolov's work. Of particular note are John Freedman, "Memory, Imagination, and the Liberating Force of Literature in Sasha Sokolov's *School for Fools*"; Olga Matich, "Sasha Sokolov and His Literary Context"; and Leona Toker, "Gamesman's Sketches (found in a bottle): A Reading of Sasha Sokolov's *Between Dog and Wolf*." See also D. Barton Johnson, "Sasha Sokolov's Twilight Cosmos: Themes and Motifs," *Slavic Review*, XLV (1986), 639-649, and "Sasha Sokolov and Vladimir Nabokov," *Russian Language Journal*, CXXXVIII/ CXXXIX (1987), 415-426. Good discussions of *A School for Fools* may be found in Alexander Boguslawski, "Sokolov's *A School for Fools*: An Escape from Socialist Realism," *Slavic and East European Journal*, XXVII (1983), 91-97; Fred Moody, "Madness and the Pattern of Freedom in Sasha Sokolov's *A School for Fools*," *Russian Literature Triquarterly*, XVI (1979), 7-32. For a more theoretically oriented discussion, see D. Barton Johnson, "A Structural Analysis of Sasha Sokolov's *School for Fools*: A Paradigmatic Novel," in *Fiction and Drama in Eastern and Southeastern Europe: Evolution and Experiment in the Postwar Period*, 1980, edited by Henrik Birnbaum and Thomas Eekman. On the untranslated *Mezhdu sobakoi i volkom*, see D. Barton Johnson,

"Sasha Sokolov's *Between Dog and Wolf* and the Modernist Tradition," in *Russian Literature in Emigration: The Third Wave*, 1984, edited by Olga Matich with Michael Heim. *Astrophobia* is treated in Olga Matich, "Sasha Sokolov's *Palisandriia*: History and Myth," *The Russian Review*, XLV (1986), 415-426, and D. Barton Johnson, "Sasha Sokolov's *Palisandrija*," *Slavic and East European Journal*, XXX (1986), 389-403.

D. Barton Johnson

ALEKSANDR SOLZHENITSYN

Born: Kislovodsk, Soviet Union
Date: December 11, 1918

Principal Works

NOVELS AND NOVELLAS: *Odin den' Ivana Denisovicha*, 1962 (*One Day in the Life of Ivan Denisovich*, 1963); *Rakovy korpus*, 1968 (*Cancer Ward*, 1968); *V kruge pervom*, 1968 (*The First Circle*, 1968); *Avgust chetyrnadtsatogo*, 1971 (*August 1914*, 1972); *Lenin v Tsyurikhe*, 1975 (*Lenin in Zurich*, 1976); *Krasnoye koleso: Uzel I, Avgust chetyrnadtsatogo*, 1983.

SHORT FICTION: *Dlya pol'zy dela*, 1963 (*For the Good of the Cause*, 1964); *Dva rasskava: Sluchay na stantsii Krechetovka i Matrënin dvor*, 1963 (*We Never Make Mistakes*, 1963); *Krokhotnye Rasskazy*, 1970.

PLAYS: *Olen' i shalashovka*, pb. 1968 (*The Love Girl and the Innocent*, 1969; also known as *Respublika truda*); *Svecha na vetru*, pb. 1968 (*Candle in the Wind*, 1973).

NONFICTION: *Les Droits de l'écrivain*, 1969; *Nobelevskaya lektsiya po literature 1970 goda*, 1972 (*The Nobel Lecture*, 1973); *A Lenten Letter to Pimen, Patriarch of All Russia*, 1972; *Solzhenitsyn: A Pictorial Autobiography*, 1972; *Arkhipelag GULag, 1918-1956: Opyt khudozhestvennogo issledovaniya*, 1973-1975 (*The Gulag Archipelago, 1918-1956: An Experiment in Literary Investigation*, 1974-1978); *Pis'mo vozhdyam Sovetskogo Soyuza*, 1974 (*Letter to Soviet Leaders*, 1974); *Bodalsya telënok s dubom*, 1975 (*The Oak and the Calf*, 1980); *Amerikanskiye rechi*, 1975; *Warning to the West*, 1976; *The Mortal Danger: How Misconceptions About Russia Imperil America*, 1980.

MISCELLANEOUS: *Sochineniya*, 1966; *Stories and Prose Poems by Alexander Solzhenitsyn*, 1971; *Six Etudes by Aleksandr Solzhenitsyn*, 1971; *Mir i nasiliye*, 1974; *Prusskiye nochi i poema napisannaya v lagere v, 1950*, 1974.

Aleksandr Isayevich Solzhenitsyn is widely regarded as the most significant Russian writer of the twentieth century. Many critics see in his writings a revival of nineteenth century Russian realist literature. He was born on December 11, 1918, in Kislovodsk, Soviet Union. His father, an artillery officer in the Russian army, died six months before Aleksandr's birth. His mother worked as a typist and stenographer. As a youth, Solzhenitsyn felt a desire to become a writer but did not receive any encouragement. From 1939 to 1941, he studied mathematics at the University of Rostov. He was drafted into the army in 1941, where he served with distinction. In February, 1945, the Soviet secret police (KGB) intercepted a letter from Solzhenitsyn to a friend. The letter allegedly contained comments critical of Soviet premier Joseph Stalin. Solzhenitsyn was promptly arrested on February 9, and he was sentenced to eight years of imprisonment. From 1945 to 1953, he was confined in several prisons and labor camps. Solzhenitsyn's experiences during those years provided the inspiration for the bulk of his subsequent literary output.

Following his release from prison in 1953, Solzhenitsyn was sentenced to internal exile in Kazakhstan in the Asian portion of the Soviet Union. In 1956, he was declared "rehabilitated" and allowed to settle in Riazan, not far from Moscow. Nikita Khrushchev's rise to power in 1956 and his subsequent de-Stalinization program (1962-1963) created a climate in which Solzhenitsyn was able to experience his first success as a writer. *One Day in the Life of Ivan Denisovich*, Solzhenitsyn's first short novel, appeared in the November 20, 1962, issue of *Novy mir.* It was an immediate success. Its portrayal of the horrors of a labor camp during Stalin's tenure in power complemented Khrushchev's criticism of the former dictator. Two other short novels were published by *Novy mir* in January, 1963. With Khrushchev's fall from power, individuals less willing to condemn Stalin's memory publicly came to power and with them, a return to stricter censorship. After 1963, Solzhenitsyn was unable to have any more of his writings approved for publication. He soon became known as one of the Soviet Union's leading dissidents. His works circulated in the Soviet Union in handwritten or typed samizdat copies; in the West, they appeared in print, although unauthorized.

The publication abroad of *The First Circle* and *Cancer Ward* in 1968, his being awarded the Nobel Prize in Literature in 1970, and the publication of *August 1914* in 1971 all intensified his problems with the state. In 1973, the KGB discovered a manuscript of *The Gulag Archipelago*, Solzhenitsyn's exposé of the origins and nature of the Soviet labor camp system. The discovery prompted him to authorize its publication abroad. The immediate popularity of *The Gulag Archipelago* in the West led to Solzhenitsyn's arrest on February 12, 1974. The following day, he was stripped of his citizenship and expelled from the Soviet Union.

Solzhenitsyn's fictional works are both historical and autobiographical. Common themes are the basic injustice of the Soviet system that purports to liberate, while enslaving the Russian people; the heroic struggle of the individual to keep a sense of human dignity while being subjected to the injustice and brutality of the prison or labor camp; and the ironic fact that the police state succeeds in creating a socialist society in the prison or labor camp, while failing to do so in society at large.

Solzhenitsyn's first novel, *One Day in the Life of Ivan Denisovich*, is set in a Siberian labor camp during January, 1951. It chronicles a single day in the life of Ivan Denisovich Shukov, sentenced to ten years for having survived a German prisoner-of-war camp. His life consists of a struggle for survival, in which individual cunning and teamwork are the means to that end. For those who felt that *One Day in the Life of Ivan Denisovich* was only a recollection of Solzhenitsyn's own nightmare, he later wrote the massive documentary *The Gulag Archipelago*. Solzhenitsyn used the letters, memoirs, and oral testimony of 227 survivors to demonstrate that the prison camp system was an intrinsic part of the Soviet system dating back to the 1917 Revolution. The brutality and dehumanization of the gulag is not an aberration but an inevitable by-product of Marxist-Leninism.

Using imagery from Dante's *Inferno* (c. 1320), Solzhenitsyn in *The First Circle* depicts the Soviet system as a series of increasingly tight circles of Hell. Marvino Prison on the outskirts of Moscow is a model in miniature of the Soviet state. Stalin and his immediate lieutenants, like the "privileged" prisoners in Marvino, occupy the first circle. With one false move, anyone can slip down to the next circle in a spiraling descent into Hell. In *Cancer Ward*, the locale is the cancer ward of a hospital somewhere in a central Asian city. There, a group of people from all walks of life, including both opponents and proponents of the Soviet system, are brought together by a common enemy, cancer. The ever-present threat of death gives to each of them the freedom to discuss frankly otherwise forbidden subjects, such as the individual and the state, ideology, morality, and humaneness. Despite a feeling of gloom and despair in Solzhenitsyn's novels, a glimmer of hope seems to shine through. It is evident in the indestructible spirit of the individual, like Ivan Denisovich, who refuses to give up hope or to surrender his human dignity and be crushed by the system. It also appears in the person of the Baptist, Alyoshka, in *One Day in the Life of Ivan Denisovich*, who sees Jesus Christ as the lord of all situations, or the Christian woman among the patients in *Cancer Ward*. Both possess an inner peace that those around them cannot comprehend.

After his expulsion in 1974, Solzhenitsyn went first to West Germany, where he was received by Germany's leading postwar writer, Heinrich Böll. Solzhenitsyn then resided briefly in Zurich, Switzerland, where he was joined by his second wife, Natalya Svetlova, and their children. After 1976, he made his home in Vermont. To his continued criticism of the Soviet system, Solzhenitsyn added an equally harsh criticism of Western materialism. Some Western intellectuals were disillusioned and disappointed to find that Solzhenitsyn's struggle for freedom was rooted in his love for Russia and his deep Christian faith, rather than Western liberalism and rugged individualism.

BIBLIOGRAPHICAL REFERENCES: Michael Scammell, *Solzhenitsyn: A Biography*, 1984, a massive work, is an outstanding source on Solzhenitsyn's life. It has received wide scholarly acclaim.

For a brief introduction for the general reader, consult Andrej Kodjak, *Alexander Solzhenitsyn*, 1978. Christopher Moody, *Solzhenitsyn*, 1973, contains two chapters of biography, followed by analysis of his most important works. Solzhenitsyn's career has stimulated a wealth of critical attention. Donald M. Fiene has compiled a list of 2,465 critical works in thirty-eight languages, many in English, in *Alexander Solzhenitsyn: An International Bibliography of Writings By and About Him*, 1973. *Aleksandr Solzhenitsyn: Critical Essays and Documentary Materials*, 1973, edited by John B. Dunlop, Richard Haugh, and Alexis Klimoff, contains a wide range of critical essays by various international scholars. Fourteen deal with the whole corpus of Solzhenitsyn's works; twenty-one focus on specific works. A follow-up volume, *Solzhenitsyn in Exile: Critical Essays and Documentary Materials*, 1985, edited by John B. Dunlop, Richard S. Haugh, and Michael Nicholson, is similar in makeup. Of particular importance in both volumes are the extensive annotated bibliographies. Since his exile from the Soviet Union, increasing attention has been given to Solzhenitsyn's Christian faith as the basis of his moral judgment. Niels C. Nielsen, Jr., *Solzhenitsyn's Religion*, 1975; Olivier Clément, *The Spirit of Solzhenitsyn*, 1976; and Edward E. Ericson, Jr., *Solzhenitsyn: The Moral Vision*, 1980, all examine Solzhenitsyn's literary works with a view toward understanding how his Christian faith has influenced their moral themes. Ericson's volume complements the other two by documenting the changing attitude of Western journalists toward Solzhenitsyn as he began to criticize Western materialism. Of related interest is *Solzhenitsyn at Harvard*, 1980, edited by Ronald Berman, which contains Solzhenitsyn's controversial Harvard commencement address, together with six responses. See also Stephen Carter, *The Politics of Solzhenitsyn*, 1977, which attempts to explain Solzhenitsyn's political position from an examination of his writings and public statements; Zhores A. Medvedev, *Ten Years After Ivan Denisovich*, 1974, translated by Hilary Sternberg, which chronicles the persecution of Solzhenitsyn by the Soviet authorities; and Vladimir Lakshin, *Solzhenitsyn, Tvardovsky, and "Novy Mir,"* 1980, translated by Michael Glenny, a defense of *Novy mir* and its editor in the light of Solzhenitsyn's negative criticism in *The Oak and the Calf*.

Paul R. Waibel

SUSAN SONTAG

Born: New York, New York
Date: January 16, 1933

PRINCIPAL WORKS

LITERARY CRITICISM: *Against Interpretation and Other Essays*, 1966; *Styles of Radical Will*, 1969; *On Photography*, 1977; *Illness as Metaphor*, 1978; *Under the Sign of Saturn*, 1980; *AIDS and Its Metaphors*, 1989.

JOURNALISM: *Trip to Hanoi*, 1968.

NOVELS: *The Benefactor*, 1963; *Death Kit*, 1967.

SHORT FICTION: *I, etcetera*, 1978.

SCREENPLAYS: *Duet for Cannibals*, 1969; *Brother Carl*, 1972; *Promised Lands*, 1974; *Unguided Tour*, 1983.

EDITED TEXTS: *Selected Writings*, 1976 (by Antonin Artaud); *A Barthes Reader*, 1982.

MISCELLANEOUS: *A Susan Sontag Reader*, 1982.

Although Susan Sontag has written novels and short fiction and thinks of herself as a creative writer, her work as a critic is what has established her as one of the most important American writers of her time. She was born in New York City but grew up in Tucson, Arizona, and Los Angeles, California. She was a precocious student, thinking herself a writer at the age of eight and attending college by the time she was fifteen years old. Her bachelor's degree in philosophy at the University of Chicago is reflective of her desire to understand the principles behind the subject matter she studies.

Sontag's forte is the extended essay, in which she examines her subject as a phenomenon, a gestalt, around which her perceptions and insights arrange themselves. *On Photography* is a characteristic title for her. The book is neither a history of photography nor an interpretation of specific photographs. Rather it is an inquiry into what photography means. What is the significance of the medium as an art form? What are photographs supposed to prove or to show? Such questions are epistemological; that is, they are about ways of knowing. Sontag asks how photography knows the world. She does not pursue her subject as a scholar (although her books are full of scholarship) because the subject in and of itself is not what matters to her most. Instead, her focus is on the subject as it relates to such fundamental questions as the nature of art and the representation of reality.

Similarly, when Sontag investigates the way cancer has been used as metaphor, her attention is drawn to the integrity of the disease and to what it means to have cancer. She has hard words for writers who simply use the cancer metaphor to describe various species of corruption. To do so, she argues, is to cloud what it means to have an illness, to insert a moral factor in the metaphor of disease in order to describe social phenomena.

When Sontag says in a famous essay that she is "against interpretation," she has in mind the kind of criticism that dissects a subject and robs it of its vitality. The critic or commentator has to grasp a subject in its entirety, see it as a living totality, in order to convey its intricate structure and style. One of the reasons she has favored films and made some of her own is that people still seem to be able to respond to them in a holistic way and are willing to take this art form in all of its immediacy by surrendering themselves to it. She has been inspired by the French New Novel and has patterned her own fiction after its destruction of logical plots and psychological characterization. She aims, instead, for sensory pleasure, an erotics of art, that destroys hard categorizations. She favors suggestiveness over precision.

In virtually all of her writing, Sontag has presented herself as a cutting-edge intellectual, deeply engaged with the politics and aesthetics of her time. Her work appears in influential periodicals such as the *Partisan Review* and *The New York Review of Books*, and she travels widely, appearing at many important public forums and lecture series. *Trip to Hanoi* is an autobiographical account of her visit to North Vietnam during the United States' war against it. Whether it is a new trend in world history (such as the advent of Solidarity in Poland), a new illness (such as acquired immunodeficiency syndrome, AIDS), or a trendy term (such as "camp"), Sontag is likely to be the critic who will articulate public consciousness of these developments. Many of her essays have become classics.

Sontag has spent much time in Europe and has been heavily influenced by such thinkers as Walter Benjamin and Roland Barthes. Like them, she has not confined herself to any particular kind of criticism. She has been interdisciplinary, drawing upon art history, literary theory, and political philosophy. Like Barthes, she reflects, with keen curiosity, on a society's signs, on the language that is elaborated to describe phenomena. Like Benjamin, she is enough of a historian to want to know the conditions out of which art arises. Although she writes as an intellectual, her criticism is insistent on the primacy of feeling, on a form of knowing that transcends analysis of particular elements. If she can examine only aspects of her subjects, she nevertheless implies that they must be seen as no more than representative parts of a larger whole.

BIBLIOGRAPHICAL REFERENCES: Two interviews provide insight into Sontag's life and work: Robert Boyers, "Women, the Arts, and the Politics of Culture: An Interview with Susan Sontag," *Salmagundi*, XXXI/XXXII (1975), 29-48, and Charles Simmons, "Sontag Talking," *The New York Times Book Review*, LXXXII (December 18, 1977), 7. There have been several articles assessing Sontag's criticism; see Richard Gilman, "Susan Sontag and the Question of the New," *The New Republic*, CLX (May 3, 1969), 23, and Cary Nelson, "Soliciting Self-Knowledge: The Rhetoric of Susan Sontag's Criticism," *Critical Inquiry*, VI (Summer, 1980), 707-726. For shrewd appraisals of *On Photography*, see William H. Gass, "A Different Kind of Art," *The New York Times Book Review*, LXXXII (December 18, 1977), 7, and Larry Hickman, "Experiencing Photographs: Sontag, Barthes, and Beyond," *Journal of American Culture*, VII (Winter, 1984), 69-73. *Illness as Metaphor* receives careful study in Peter Brooks, "Death of/as Metaphor," *Partisan Review*, XLVI (1979), 438-444. Sontag's fiction and films have not been accorded much detailed attention, but a few studies are worth consulting: John Wain, "Song of Myself," *The New Republic*, CXLIX (September 21, 1963), 26; Tony Tanner, "Space Odyssey," *Partisan Review*, XXXV (Summer, 1968), 446-451; Joe David Bellamy, *The New Fiction: Interviews with Innovative American Writers*, 1974; Theodore Solotaroff, *The Red Hot Vacuum and Other Pieces on the Writing of the Sixties*, 1970; and Sharon Smith, *Women Who Make Movies*, 1975.

Carl Rollyson

WOLE SOYINKA

Born: Near Abeokuta, Nigeria
Date: July 13, 1934

PRINCIPAL WORKS

PLAYS: *The Swamp Dwellers*, pr. 1958; *The Invention*, pr. 1959; *The Lion and the Jewel*, pr. 1959; *The Trials of Brother Jero*, pr. 1960; *A Dance of the Forests*, pr. 1960; *The Strong Breed*, pb. 1963; *Three Plays*, pb. 1963; *Five Plays*, pb. 1964; *Kongi's Harvest*, pr. 1964; *Before the Blackout*, pr. 1964; *The Road*, pr., pb. 1965; *Madmen and Specialists*, pr. 1970; *Jero's Metamorphosis*, pb. 1973; *The Bacchae*, pr., pb. 1973; *Collected Plays*, pb. 1973, 1974; *Death and the King's Horseman*, pb. 1975; *Opera Wonyosi*, pr. 1977; *A Play of Giants*, pb. 1984; *Requiem for a Futurologist*, pb. 1985.

RADIO PLAY: *Comwood on the Leaves*, pr. 1960.

POETRY: *Idanre and Other Poems*, 1967; *Poems from Prison*, 1969; *A Shuttle in the Crypt*, 1972; *Ogun Abibiman*, 1976; *Mandela's Earth and Other Poems*, 1988.

NOVELS: *The Interpreters*, 1965; *Season of Anomy*, 1973.

TRANSLATION: *The Forest of a Thousand Daemons*, 1968 (by D. O. Fagunwa).

AUTOBIOGRAPHY: *The Man Died*, 1972; *Aké: The Years of Childhood*, 1981.

LITERARY CRITICISM: *Myth, Literature, and the African World*, 1976; "Nobel Lecture 1986: This Past Must Address Its Present," 1987.

ESSAYS: *Art, Dialogue, and Outrage: Essays on Literature and Culture*, 1988.

Akinwande Oluwole Soyinka, awarded the Nobel Prize in Literature in 1986, is arguably the most important African man of letters. His unique work exemplifies his vision as a Yoruba, an African, and a world citizen. His knowledge of oral and written literature is a fusion of his traditional Yoruba and his Western and world literary heritage. He was born at Isara, Ijebu Remo, near Abeokuta, Nigeria, on July 13, 1934, the son of a catechist elementary principal father and a businesswoman mother who provided a stimulating home environment in Abeokuta richly described in *Aké*. Both of his parents were Christians, and on both sides of the family were three generations of distinguished relatives. He attended the local school on the family Bishops Court compound, Abeokuta Grammar School, and Ibadan Government College forty-five miles away. Though not permitted to be initiated into manhood in the traditional Yoruba manner until after years of family discussions with Isara relatives, he overheard relatives speak of *òrò* uncles as well as British rule; the young Wole also observed the rise of the women's movement begun by his mother and women friends to help inform illiterate young women about children, family, health, and business care. When yet another market tax was imposed, the women marched on the Alake until the District Officer secured a withdrawal of the tax. Early observation of leadership by family women enabled Soyinka to portray women with independence whether urban professionals and businesswomen, village traditionalists, or earth-mothers. The importance of the earth or fertility is central to Soyinka's cyclical view of the past, present, and future, wherein those living are in touch with ancestors and are the vehicles for spirits to be reborn, ensuring the future.

From 1954 to 1957, Soyinka studied English literature at Leeds University in West Yorkshire, England, where he earned a B.A. In London in 1958, *The Swamp Dwellers* started Soyinka's stage career, which then continued as a play reader. He also taught, wrote, acted, and finally directed for the Royal Court Theatre, which in 1959 produced his first play about South Africa, *The Invention*, and then the comedy *The Lion and the Jewel* (also performed in Lagos with *The Swamp Dwellers*, which is considered one of his most important works). In 1960, Soyinka traveled widely in Nigeria on a Rockefeller grant before writing the commissioned play *A Dance of the Forests*, perhaps his most complex work, along with *Madmen and Specialists*, for Independence Day, October 1.

Nearly every year for more than two decades, Soyinka has prodigiously produced poetry, drama, prose, and criticism and always with a clear moral pattern. Each work in each genre has proved to be significant. His views have ranged from traditional (*The Strong Breed*, *Idanre and Other Poems*, *Ogun Abibiman*, *The Road*, and *A Dance of the Forests*) to colonial (*The Interpreters* and *Death and the King's Horseman*) to postcolonial ("October Poems" in *Idanre and Other Poems, Madmen and Specialists*, *A Shuttle in the Crypt*, and *Season of Anomy*) to international (*Opera Wonyosi, Ogun Abibiman*, and *A Play of Giants*) to pro-black diaspora (*Ogun Abibiman*, *Myth*, *Literature, and the African World*, and most of his literary criticism). His plays have been produced in numerous cities, and he has lectured on numerous campuses. Always, he speaks out against apartheid and affirms African life; for Soyinka, to write is to be both political and religious as part of the African character. The artist, in performing dramatically and verbally, is to be like Ogun, to Soyinka the most admirable god in the Yoruba pantheon. He chose to emulate Ogun because to act physically, which includes speech, is to cross the abyss of transition between the visible and invisible worlds. Each of Soyinka's works reflects his devotion to Ogun, as he explains in *Myth, Literature, and the African World*.

Soyinka's *The Man Died*, the autobiography in which he recounts his treatment in isolation during the Nigerian Civil War, stridently criticizes the atrocities to which he was witness during that time. This denunciation of leaders who abuse their power runs throughout Soyinka's canon, from *The Swamp Dwellers* through *Season of Anomy* and beyond: The purpose of art is as much a moral one, to denounce the perpetrators of oppression, as it is a celebratory one in service of the Dionysian qualities embodied in Ogun. It is this spiritual dimension of Soyinka's art that makes his work unique.

BIBLIOGRAPHICAL REFERENCES: See *African Literature Association Bulletin* and *African Studies Association* for current titles of papers, reviews, and many articles in international journals. In particular, *Research in African Literatures* is a good source for notes and articles on Soyinka. Also consult *Ariel: A Review of International English Language*, IV, no. 1 (1973); XII, no. 3 (July, 1981); and October, 1982; *Ba Shiru*, X, no. 1 (1979), and XI, no. 1 (1980); *Commonwealth Literature Today*; *Journal of Commonwealth Literature*, IX, no. 3 (April, 1975), and X, no. 3 (1976); *Journal of Modern African Studies*, XXVI, no. 3 (September, 1988), 517-548; *World Literature Today*, LV, no. 1 (1981); and *World Literature Written in English*, Autumn, 1981; November, 1981; Spring, 1982; Autumn, 1982; Summer, 1984; and Autumn, 1985. For a view of Soyinka by a fellow African writer, see Chinua Achebe, *The Trouble with Nigeria*, 1983. Detailed analyses of Soyinka's work can be found in Martin Banham, *"The Lion and the Jewel": A Critical View*, 1981; Bonnie J. Barthold, "*Season of Anomy*," in *Black Time: Fiction of Africa, the Caribbean, and the United States*, 1981; Eldred Durosimi Jones, *The Writing of Wole Soyinka*, 1973; Ketu H. Katrak, *Wole Soyinka and Modern Tragedy: A Study of Dramatic Theory and Practice*, 1986; Bernth Lindfors, "Wole Soyinka and the Horses of Speech," in *Folklore in Nigerian Literature*, 1973; Obi Maduakor, "Soyinka's Animystic Poetics," *The African Studies Review*, XXV (March, 1982), 37-48; "Soyinka's *Season of Anomy*: Ofeyi's Quest," in *Design and Intent in African Literature*, 1982, edited by David F. Dorsey and Stephen H. Arnold; and James Gibbs, *Wole Soyinka*, 1985. The political and religious aspects of Soyinka's works are discussed in William Bascom, *Ifa Divination: Communication Between Gods and Man in West Africa*, 1969; James Booth, *Writers and Politics in Nigeria*, 1981; Onwuchekwa Jemie Chinweizu, *Toward the Decolonization of African Literature*, 1983; and *Black Literature and Literary Theory*, 1984, edited by Henry Louis Gates, Jr. Other aspects of Soyinka's work are covered in Greta Avery-Coger, *Index of Subjects, Proverbs, and Themes in the Writings of Wole Soyinka*, 1988. Also useful is the collection of writings compiled as a tribute to Soyinka on the occasion of his Nobel Prize in Literature: *Before Our Very Eyes: Tribute to Wole Soyinka*, 1987, edited by Dapo Adelugba.

Greta McCormick Coger

MURIEL SPARK

Born: Edinburgh, Scotland
Date: February 1, 1918

PRINCIPAL WORKS

NOVELS: *The Comforters*, 1957; *Robinson*, 1958; *Memento Mori*, 1959; *The Ballad of Peckham Rye*, 1960; *The Bachelors*, 1960; *The Prime of Miss Jean Brodie*, 1961; *The Girls of Slender Means*, 1963; *The Mandelbaum Gate*, 1965; *The Public Image*, 1968; *The Driver's Seat*, 1970; *Not to Disturb*, 1971; *The Hothouse by the East River*, 1973; *The Abbess of Crewe: A Modern Morality Tale*, 1974; *The Takeover*, 1976; *Territorial Rights*, 1979; *Loitering with Intent*, 1981; *The Only Problem*, 1984; *A Far Cry from Kensington*, 1988.

SHORT FICTION: *The Go-Away Bird and Other Stories*, 1958; *Voices at Play*, 1961; *Collected Stories I*, 1967.

PLAY: *Doctors of Philosophy*, 1963.

POETRY: *The Fanfarlo and Other Verse*, 1952; *Collected Poems I*, 1967.

NONFICTION: *Child of Light: A Reassessment of Mary Wollstonecraft Shelley*, 1951; *Emily Brontë: Her Life and Work*, 1953 (with Derek Stanford); *John Masefield*, 1953; *Letters of John Henry Newman*, 1957 (with Stanford).

EDITED TEXTS: *Tribute to Wordsworth*, 1950 (with Derek Stanford); *Selected Poems of Emily Brontë*, 1952; *My Best Mary: The Selected Letters of Mary Shelley*, 1953 (with Stanford); *The Brontë Letters*, 1954.

CHILDREN'S LITERATURE: *The Very Fine Clock*, 1958.

Muriel Spark is one of the most critically acclaimed of contemporary novelists. Born Muriel Sarah Camberg in Edinburgh, Scotland, on February 1, 1918, Spark was educated at James Gillespie's School for Girls (which appears fictionally as the Marcia Blaine School in *The Prime of Miss Jean Brodie*) and wrote poetry from the age of nine. At age nineteen, Muriel moved to Rhodesia and married S. O. Spark; they would have a son, Robin. Many of Spark's short stories (such as "Bang-Bang You're Dead," "The Go-Away Bird," and "The Curtain Blown by the Breeze") can be linked to this period of her life.

In 1944, divorced from her husband and having returned to England, Spark began work with the Political Intelligence Office of the British Foreign Office, which was concerned with anti-Nazi propaganda. There, she gained an appreciation for the paradoxes of fact made into fiction and fiction presented as fact that figure in many of her novels. After the war, Spark was appointed General Secretary of the Poetry Society in London, and between 1948 and 1949 she served not only as editor of *Poetry Review* but also as coeditor and cofounder (with Derek Stanford) of *Forum Stories and Poems*. In the early 1950's, Spark's interests turned to biography with her studies of Mary Shelley and John Masefield.

Although a critic, poet, and short fiction writer (she has also written radio plays, a full-length drama, and a children's book), Spark's primary genre is the novel. Acknowledging no religious faith between her Presbyterian school days and 1952, Spark converted to Roman Catholicism in 1954 and began her career as a novelist when Macmillan and Company commissioned her to write a novel the same year. Spark has said that her conversion, which was preceded by an illness and followed by several months of Jungian therapy, enabled her to write longer fiction, which she has published consistently ever since. Although her novels during the 1970's (particularly *Not to Disturb, The Driver's Seat*, and *The Abbess of Crewe*) reflect a bleaker view of the human condition, Spark's work is generally satiric, focusing on the frauds, murders, blackmailings, and terrorism that representatives of the modern secular world practice upon one another. Drawing from the techniques of the Metaphysical poets, Spark forces the reader to join disparate ideas with a resulting effect that is close to what T. S. Eliot calls, in his 1921 essay "The Metaphysical Poets," a "dissociation of sensibility."

That is, one is never quite certain in a Spark novel where the reality ends and the illusion begins.

The themes with which Spark is concerned have remained consistent since the publication of her first novel in 1957. A modern woman and a Roman Catholic, Spark demonstrates an ambivalence toward the contemporary secular world in general and the Roman Catholic community in particular. Her novels are filled with lies and deceptions and those who scheme and blackmail through their use. As a novelist, Spark is herself a plotter, and her stories place the reader in a position not unlike that occupied by her characters. In *The Comforters*, for example, Caroline Rose finds herself manipulated by an agency outside the frame of the novel (a "typing ghost") which is, like the novelist herself, a manipulator of plot. Fond of conjoining seen and unseen worlds, Spark often forces her characters (and readers) to accept the inexplicable: messages from Death (*Memento Mori*), novels coming to life (*Loitering with Intent*), and the existence of malevolent spirits (*The Ballad of Peckham Rye*, *A Far Cry from Kensington*, and *The Bachelors*). These examples allude to one of Spark's primary themes: an acceptance of the existence of evil and the problem of human suffering (a theme explicitly treated in *The Only Problem*).

Alan Bold has said that Spark's "singular achievement as a novelist" has been "to synthesize the linguistic cunning of poetry with the seeming credibility of prose." In general, critics have agreed, praising Spark for her wit and the economy of her prose style. While some reviewers believe Spark's concerns as a Catholic interfere with her aims as a novelist, most see a connection between her faith and satiric vision, considering her one of the most important novelists of the second half of the twentieth century. Spark's work appeals not only to critics but also to general readers. Several of her novels have been made into films (*The Prime of Miss Jean Brodie* perhaps the most successfully), and her work often appears among book club selections.

BIBLIOGRAPHICAL REFERENCES: Several excellent book-length studies and collections of essays about Spark's work have appeared in the 1980's. Among the best are Alan Bold, *Muriel Spark*, published in 1986 as part of the Contemporary Writers series; *Muriel Spark: An Odd Capacity for Vision*, 1984, a collection of essays covering a wide variety of approaches to Spark's work and edited by Alan Bold; Ruth Whittaker, *The Faith and Fiction of Muriel Spark*, 1982, which has many valuable and previously unpublished interviews and letters; and Dorothea Walker's concise *Muriel Spark*, 1988. Older studies worth consulting are Derek Stanford, *Muriel Spark: A Biographical and Critical Study*, 1963, still one of the best sources for biographical material; Patricia Stubbs, *Muriel Spark*, 1973; and Allan Massie, *Muriel Spark*, 1979. See also Alan Kennedy's chapter on Spark, "Cannibals, Okapis, and Self-Slaughter in the Novels of Muriel Spark," in *The Protean Self: Dramatic Action in Contemporary Fiction*, 1974; Frank Kermode's comments in *The Sense of an Ending: Studies in the Theory of Fiction*, 1967, and his interview with Spark in "The House of Fiction: Interviews with Seven English Novelists," *Partisan Review*, Spring, 1963, 30; and Judy Little, *Comedy and the Woman Writer: Woolf, Spark, and Feminism*, 1983.

Jennifer L. Randisi

STEPHEN SPENDER

Born: London, England
Date: February 28, 1909

PRINCIPAL WORKS

POETRY: *Nine Experiments, by S. H. S.: Being Poems Written at the Age of Eighteeen*, 1928; *Twenty Poems*, 1930; *Poems*, 1933; *Vienna*, 1935; *The Still Centre*, 1939; *Ruins and Visions*, 1942; *Poems of Dedication*, 1947; *Returning to Vienna: Nine Sketches, 1947*, 1947; *The Edge of Being*, 1949; *Collected Poems, 1928-1953*, 1955; *The Generous Days*, 1971; *Collected Poems, 1928-1985*, 1985.

CRITICISM: *The Destructive Element: A Study of Modern Writers and Beliefs*, 1935; *The Creative Element: A Study of Vision, Despair, and Orthodoxy Among Some Modern Writers*, 1953; *The Struggle of the Modern*, 1963.

AUTOBIOGRAPHY: *World Within World: The Autobiography of Stephen Spender*, 1951.

PLAYS: *Trial of a Judge*, pr. 1938; *To the Island*, pr. 1951.

ESSAYS: *Forward from Liberalism*, 1937; *Life and the Poet*, 1942; *Citizens in War and After*, 1945; *Shelley*, 1952; *The Making of a Poem*, 1955; *The Year of the Young Rebels*, 1969; *Love-Hate Relations: A Study of Anglo-American Sensibilities*, 1974; *Eliot*, 1975; *The Thirties and After: Poetry, Politics, People, 1933-1970*, 1978; *Henry Moore: Sculptures in Landscape*, 1979.

SHORT FICTION: *The Burning Cactus*, 1936.

NOVELS AND NOVELLAS: *The Backward Son*, 1940; *Engaged in Writing and The Fool and the Princess*, 1958; *The Temple*, 1988.

TRAVEL SKETCHES: *European Witness*, 1946; *Learning Laughter*, 1952; *Sirmione Peninsula*, 1954; *China Diary*, 1982.

CORRESPONDENCE: *Letters to Christopher: Stephen Spender's Letters to Christopher Isherwood, 1929-1939*, 1980.

JOURNALS: *Journals, 1939-1983*, 1986.

MISCELLANEOUS: *In Irina's Garden, with Henry Moore's Sculpture*, 1986.

Stephen Harold Spender, one of the best lyrical poets and most ardent political writers of the 1930's, later became an important literary critic, essayist, and journalist. He was born in London, England, on February 28, 1909, the second of four children. Because both of his parents, Edward Harold Spender and Violet Hilda Schuster Spender, died when he was a teenager, his maternal grandmother, Hilda Schuster, played a significant role in his upbringing. In his perceptive autobiography, *World Within World*, Spender characterized his unhappy youth as a "humorless adolescence." In 1928, Spender published his first volume of poetry, *Nine Experiments*, and entered University College, Oxford. There he felt like an outsider, cut off from the "hearties and aesthetes" who populated his college. He fell in love with one of the "hearties," I. A. R. Hyndman. Perhaps because of Spender's unhappy youth, his work is characterized by its onlooker's viewpoint and its sympathy for the underdog.

The verses that Spender wrote between 1928 and 1930 (published under the title *Twenty Poems* in 1930) show the influence of his Oxford environment, especially that of his friend W. H. Auden and the members of his literary circle, which included Cecil Day Lewis, Louis MacNeice, Christopher Isherwood, and Edward Upward. Because Spender had an inherited income of three hundred pounds a year, he was financially independent and, therefore, able to travel and write without the awkward necessity of earning a living. In the summer of 1930, he left Oxford without a degree in order to join Isherwood in Germany. Spender's talent blossomed in the politically explosive, *Sturmfrei* (permissive) atmosphere of Berlin, where he wrote some of his best verse, collected in the 1933 volume *Poems*. He then moved to Austria, where he attempted to blend poetry with political ideology in *Vienna*, a long poem about the savage suppression of the February, 1934, socialist insurrection by the right-wing Dollfuss government. In 1936, after publishing *The Burning Cactus*, a volume of carefully crafted short stories, and ending long affairs with Hyndman and an Austrian woman, Spender met and married Agnes (Inez) Pearn, an Oxford student.

Like many of his generation, Spender thought Marxism was the only viable alternative to Fascism. Because the Communists were aiding the Republicans in the Spanish Civil War, Spender joined the Party in order to take a personal stand against Fascism. The Spenders went to Spain in 1937, an odyssey Spender described in his autobiography and in an important volume of his poetry, *The Still Centre*. In Spain, he broke with the Communists over the question of the atrocities committed by both sides. The same year that *The Still Centre* was published, Spender's childless marriage to Pearn was dissolved. In April, 1941, he married the well-known pianist Natasha Litvin, a union which produced a son and a daughter. During World War II, from 1941 to 1944, Spender served with the London Auxiliary Fire Service.

In the postwar era, Spender had almost abandoned poetry to concentrate on prose. In 1954, he published *The Creative Element*, a work of criticism which, along with *The Destructive Element* and *The Struggle of the Modern*, represents his finest critical work. From 1953 to 1967, he coedited *Encounter* magazine, but when he learned that the Central Intelligence Agency (CIA) helped to fund it, he immediately resigned his position. Although Spender has written in a variety of literary forms, several themes permeate his literary canon. The most important of these is the proper relationship of the individual to society and its corollary concept, the merger of the public self with the private soul. Other topics emphasized by Spender include the nature of sexuality, the role of belief in the modern world, and the relationship of poetry and the poet to politics. In *Trial of a Judge*, Spender's struggle to merge poetry and politics is expressed through the moral and legal dilemmas faced by a liberal judge (representing Spender's authorial voice) who realizes that both Communism and Fascism, though ideologically antithetical, will ultimately strangle individual freedom. Much of Spender's poetry and some of his most important prose (for example, *The Destructive Element*) are concerned with the nature of faith in the modern world. In *The Creative Element*, he argued that poetry was the proper vehicle to provide a connection between people's private and public lives by using it to transform the realities of the external world into symbols representing the individual's inner experience.

While his works have a remarkable lyrical quality, Spender cannot be considered either a great poet or a great prose writer. He is, nevertheless, an important figure in both genres. His works express the concerns of a self-critical and compassionate man, uncompromisingly honest and dedicated to truth, attempting to reconcile his natural inclination for individualism with his social concerns.

BIBLIOGRAPHICAL REFERENCES: Perhaps the most useful annotated bibliography on Stephen Spender is Hemant Balvantrao Kulkarni, *Stephen Spender: Works and Criticism*, 1976, a reliable guide to selecting secondary sources about both Spender's life and his work. Kulkarni also wrote an excellent study of Spender, *Stephen Spender: Poet in Crisis*, 1970. A handy reference for Spender's poetry is A. T. Tolley, *The Early Published Poems of Stephen Spender: A Chronology*, 1967. Also useful are the essays, autobiographies, and novels of Spender's friend Christopher Isherwood. See Isherwood's essay, "Stephen Spender" in *Exhumations*, 1966, and his autobiographies, *Christopher and His Kind*, 1977, and *Lions and Shadows*, 1938. One of the best studies of Spender's early works is Andrew Kingsley Weatherhead, *Stephen Spender and the Thirties*, 1975, particularly useful in interpreting Spender's poems and motives. A. T. Tolley, *The Poetry of the Thirties*, 1975, examines the early poetry. It is complemented by Surya Nath Pandey, *Stephen Spender: A Study in Poetic Growth*, 1982, which compares Spender's early and mature work. For Spender's political and social ideals, see Elton E. Smith, *The Angry Young Men of the Thirties*, 1975. A fascinating study of the connection between Spender's poetry and politics is J. J. Connors, *Poetry and Politics: A Study of the Careers of C. Day Lewis, Stephen Spender, and W. H. Auden in the*

1930's, 1976. See also Derek Stanford, *Stephen Spender, Louis MacNeice, Cecil Day Lewis: A Critical Essay*, 1969.

Nancy E. Rupprecht

JEAN STAFFORD

Born: Covina, California
Date: July 1, 1915

Died: White Plains, New York
Date: March 26, 1979

Principal Works

NOVELS: *Boston Adventure*, 1944; *The Mountain Lion*, 1947; *The Catherine Wheel*, 1952.

NOVELLA: *A Winter's Tale*, 1954.

SHORT FICTION: *Children Are Bored on Sunday*, 1953; *The Interior Castle*, 1953; *Bad Characters*, 1964; *Selected Stories of Jean Stafford*, 1966; *Collected Stories*, 1969.

CHILDREN'S LITERATURE: *Arabian Nights: The Lion and the Carpenter, and Other Tales from the Arabian Nights*, 1959; *Elephi: The Cat with the High I.Q.*, 1962.

NONFICTION: *An Etiquette for Writers: 1952 Writers' Conference in the Rocky Mountains*, 1952; *A Mother in History*, 1966.

Jean Stafford was a novelist and short-story writer of considerable distinction. Born to John and Mary McKillop Stafford on July 1, 1915, in Covina, California, Jean was the youngest of four children in a family beset by poverty. Her father, who held many jobs, also wrote stories and opinionated essays which he regularly read aloud to his children. The Stafford family moved from Covina to San Diego, then to a succession of small towns in Colorado, finally settling in Boulder in 1925. At age six, Jean began to write poems and stories, and she completed her first novel by age eleven. She also began to read the dictionary simply for pleasure and, even as a child, displayed an incredible command of language. From 1925 to 1932, Stafford attended University Hill School and State Preparatory School in Boulder. In 1932, she enrolled in the University of Colorado, Boulder, financing her education by scholarships and part-time work, and was graduated with both A.B. and A.M. degrees in 1936. After graduation, she studied philology at the University of Heidelberg on a one-year fellowship.

Shy and intellectual, Stafford was a misfit in both high school and college. Returning from Germany, she attended a writing school in Boulder and was introduced to poet Robert Lowell, a man with a very different background from her own, whom she would later marry. She spent one unhappy year as an instructor at Stephens College and, in 1938, taught briefly at the Writers' Workshop in Iowa. There, she decided to write, not teach, and left abruptly in midsemester for Boston, arriving with one-third of a manuscript under her arm. In Boston, Stafford renewed her acquaintance with Robert Lowell. One night, returning home from an evening of drinking at a Boston nightclub, Lowell lost control of the car in which they were driving and Stafford was seriously injured. Despite the accident and the lawsuit which followed, a courtship blossomed and the two were married on April 2, 1940, in New York City.

Stafford's first novel, published in 1944, was a best-seller and was praised by reviewers for its traces of Marcel Proust and Henry James. *Boston Adventure* deals with a young woman's realization that discovery of self requires rejection of society's limitations and introduces concerns that would reoccur in Stafford's later work: human motivations, instincts, relationships, and the complexities and incongruities of being alive, especially of being alive as a woman. In 1945, Stafford received a Guggenheim Fellowship for fiction and a National Institute of Arts and Letters grant. In that year, she also bought her first home in the small village of Damariscotta Mills, Maine, and she was at work on her second novel, *The Mountain Lion*.

Stafford's and Lowell's marriage had always been stormy, even violent, and they were separated in 1946. The subsequent months were difficult for Stafford. She traveled, spent a few days in a mental hospital, then stayed in a run-down Greenwich Village hotel. In 1947, she committed herself to the Payne Whitney Clinic in New York and spent a year there under treatment for hysteria and deep depression. Also in 1947, Stafford's masterpiece second novel was published. Unlike the first, *The Mountain Lion* was written out of her own experience in the West rather than her imaginings of an East she hardly knew. It explored this geographical dichotomy as well as the complexities of childhood, themes that appear in many of Stafford's stories. The style was also more naturally her own in this work, reflecting her ability to find the most appropriate word for her creative expression, no matter how unusual it might be.

In 1948, Stafford obtained a divorce from Lowell. In that same year, she was awarded another Guggenheim Fellowship for fiction and the National Book Club Award. In 1950, Stafford married Oliver Jensen, a second unhappy marriage that lasted only a few months. In 1952, Stafford's third novel, *The Catherine Wheel*, was published. In what is considered her most carefully structured novel, Stafford again deals with psychological motivation and alienation and explores the major theme of her work: women and their situation in society. In 1953, Stafford was divorced from Jensen and, as before, experienced psychological collapse, this time complicated by physical ill health. While recuperating with friends in the Virgin Islands, she wrote "In the Zoo," which received the First Prize O. Henry Award in 1955.

Stafford is best known for her more than fifty short stories, which, like her novels, are largely autobiographical. Almost all of her characters are girls and women; many are orphans, aged, or ill. Stafford deals with the powerlessness of women caught in social roles; for those who assert themselves in an attempt to develop identity, her stories suggest, the result is often madness. Her first collection, *Children Are Bored on Sunday*, appeared in 1953. In 1959, Stafford married A. J. Liebling, critic and columnist for *The New Yorker*. During this four-year marriage, she published no fiction, except for two juvenile books, and explained that perhaps it was because she was happy for the first time in her life. Nevertheless, Stafford and Liebling began to drift apart before Liebling's death. They quarreled over Stafford's drinking, which was a problem throughout her life, and they were frequently separated.

Although very much a part of the New York literary world, Stafford had often felt ill at ease with the New York intellectuals. Thus, after Liebling's death in 1963, she made her home in Springs, Long Island. There, known as the Widow Liebling and in failing health, Stafford became increasingly reclusive. Her second collection of short stories, *Bad Characters*, was published in 1964. In 1965 she contracted for an autobiographical novel, "The Parliament of Women," which remained unpublished at her death. Another collection, *Selected Stories of Jean Stafford*, was published in 1966. During the 1960's and 1970's, Stafford wrote nonfiction for popular magazines and, in 1969, her *Collected Stories* was published. In 1970, Stafford received the Pulitzer Prize for *Collected Stories* and was also made a member of the National Academy of Arts and Letters. As she aged, Stafford grew more and more to resemble the ill-tempered old women in her fiction. Her life—beset by physical and mental illness, unhappiness, lack of deserved recognition for her work, and lessening creativity—was further debilitated in 1977, when she suffered a stroke resulting in aphasia. The Jean Stafford who had read the dictionary for pleasure then found it difficult to speak even the simplest of thoughts. She died on March 26, 1979, at the Burke Rehabilitation Center in White Plains, New York.

Critics have suggested that Stafford's ironic vision allows for no clear-cut perspective on her work. Her preoccupation with language is reflected in a rich and complex style, rooted both in the formal, rhetorical tradition of Henry James and the more informal and colloquial of Mark Twain, and she has been compared with both. Stafford has been praised for her nonsentimental approach but perhaps more often criticized for emotional detachment from her characters, who are seldom able to resolve feelings of alienation. Ironically, this same detachment seems to suggest that the objective, intellectual viewpoint is the only way for individuals to rise above the inevitable difficulties of life to experience realization or knowledge, however short-lived.

Most critical analyses tend to view Stafford's treatment of women as a metaphor for the universal alienation in modern society, rather than as a commentary on the lives of women.

Stafford would probably approve of the lack of attention she has received from the feminist perspective, because she expressed strong disapproval of the feminist movement in articles written toward the end of her life. At the time of Stafford's death, her name was not familiar to most readers. Although she has to some extent been "rediscovered"—*The Catherine Wheel* was reissued in 1981 in a series called "Neglected Books of the 20th Century"—critics still suggest that she deserves more attention.

BIBLIOGRAPHICAL REFERENCES: Wanda Avila, *Jean Stafford: A Comprehensive Bibliography*, 1983, is a foundational reference that contains short summaries of Stafford's publications and critical works about her. Mary Ellen Williams Walsh, *Jean Stafford*, 1985, considers critical periods in Stafford's life in relation to her fiction and concludes with a review of her criticism. See also David Roberts, *Jean Stafford: A Biography*, 1988, and Maureen Ryan, *Innocence and Estrangement in the Fiction of Jean Stafford*, 1987. Other studies include Ihab Hassan, "Jean Stafford: The Expense of Style and the Scope of Sensibility," *The Western Review*, Spring, 1955, 185-202; Olga W. Vickery, "Jean Stafford and the Iconic Vision," *The South Atlantic Quarterly*, LXI (Autumn, 1962), 484-491; Blanche H. Gelfant, "Reconsideration: *The Mountain Lion*," *The New Republic*, May 10, 1975, 22-25; Jeannette Mann, "Toward New Archetypal Forms: *Boston Adventure*," *Studies in the Novel 8*, Fall, 1976, 291-303; and the Jean Stafford memorial issue of *Shenandoah*, XXX (1979).

William S. Haney II

CHRISTINA STEAD

Born: Rockdale, Australia
Date: July 17, 1902

Died: Sydney, Australia
Date: March 31, 1983

PRINCIPAL WORKS

NOVELS: *Seven Poor Men of Sydney*, 1934; *The Beauties and Furies*, 1936; *House of All Nations*, 1938; *The Man Who Loved Children*, 1940, 1965; *For Love Alone*, 1944; *Letty Fox: Her Luck*, 1946; *A Little Tea, a Little Chat*, 1948; *The People with the Dogs*, 1952; *Dark Places of the Heart*, 1966 (also known as *Cotter's England*); *The Little Hotel*, 1974; *Miss Herbert (The Suburban Wife)*, 1976; *I'm Dying Laughing: The Humourist*, 1986.

SHORT FICTION: *The Salzburg Tales*, 1934; *The Puzzleheaded Girl*, 1967; *Ocean of Story: The Uncollected Short Stories of Christina Stead*, 1985.

EDITED TEXTS: *Modern Women in Love: Sixty Twentieth-Century Masterpieces of Fiction* 1945 (with William Blake); *Great Stories of the South Sea Islands*, 1955.

TRANSLATIONS: *Colour of Asia*, 1955 (by Fernard Gigon); *In Balloon and Bathyscaphe*, 1956 (by Auguste Picard); *The Candid Killer*, 1956 (by Jean Giltène).

Until the 1960's, Christina Stead was either unmentioned in Australian literary histories or briefly alluded to as an expatriate writer who had inexplicably attracted the attention of British and American readers and critics. Her work had never been published in her own country. Now, however, she is regarded as the most important writer of fiction in the history of Australia after Patrick White.

Christina Stead was born in Rockdale, a working-class suburb of Sydney, and attended first St. George High School and then the academically selective Sydney Girls' High School; subsequently, she went to Sydney Teachers' College and later became a demonstrator in psychology at the university. She developed an interest in modern fiction and in writing at college, and her novels and short stories all attest a keen perception and understanding of psychological problems and their subtle manifestations. In this respect she has been compared with Leo Tolstoy and Fyodor Dostoevski, not without justification.

Seven Poor Men of Sydney was written in Europe, after Stead had left Australia in 1928. It is a study of poverty in an urban environment but (like almost all of her later writing) is directed at an understanding of interpersonal relationships rather than of political and social phenomena. Especially compelling is the treatment of the latent incestuous feelings of Catherine Bagenault and her illegitimate half brother Michael, a veteran who is unable to take action. The descriptions of various locations in Sydney are impressive both in natural detail and in evocation of atmosphere supportive of the story. *The Salzburg Tales* (which includes four stories written while Stead was training to be a teacher) and *The Beauties and Furies* (about a married Englishwoman who goes to live with a younger man, a student in Paris) cannot be said to have advanced Stead's art, though they do demonstrate her interest in certain character types: the prevaricator, the charmer, the domineering father, the doctrinaire, and the nascent feminist.

With *House of All Nations*, Stead entered a new area of fiction: the world of international finance, centered in Paris, and an almost journal-like narration of events. What results is a prolix account of the machinations of Jules Bertillon and his Banque Mercure that result in his personal wealth and the bank's failure. The novel uses as its epigraph Bertillon's observation, "No one ever made enough money," and a Balzacian array of minor characters shows mankind's attempt to overcome the shortfall with the aid of the charming confidence-man banker. Because the House of All Nations is a chic Parisian brothel, the novel's title suggests Stead's satiric intent. (Her husband, William Blake, was a stockbroker and banker, so the details of the financial manipulations are presumably reliable.) If the Great Depression made

House of All Nations a contemporary success, its interest has since diminished; its length and overcrowded canvas of minor characters are clear weaknesses.

Stead's next two books, *The Man Who Loved Children* and *For Love Alone*, are certainly her greatest achievements, though the former was not recognized fully until its republication in 1965 with a long and detailed appreciation by the respected critic Randall Jarrell. In many ways, *The Man Who Loved Children*, which is set in Washington, D.C., is a brutal picture of family life: Sam Pollitt, "A subaltern bureaucrat," and his second wife, Henrietta (Henny), a scion of a wealthy Baltimore family, yet one who could be "beautifully, wholeheartedly vile," have grown apart, and their children are the stakes in their bitter battles. The oldest child, Louisa (by Sam's first wife, now dead), aged twelve, is swept into the vortex of the parental conflict and exhibits extraordinary perceptiveness of the psychological forces at work. Yet she plans her parents' murder. Because of its study of family relationships, emotional shortcomings, and personal priorities, *The Man Who Loved Children* is an acute and meaningful study of modern bourgeois life.

Hardly less compelling and authoritative is *For Love Alone*, Stead's best exposition of the theme of personal discovery through casting off of family, unworthy models, and lovers. Teresa Hawkins (like Stead, a teacher trainee) seeks self-fulfillment—first through adoration of Jonathan Crow, a minor university teacher in Australia, then through attachment to James Quick, an American businessman in England—and escape from her insensitive father, who personifies the belief that women must accept a role of social and sexual dependency. Many readers assumed that this was an overtly feminist novel, but the author vehemently denied this, asserting that it was yet another exploration of the forces that motivate individuals to think and act. Indeed, Stead excels in the analysis of motivation, the description of passions, and the differentiation of male and female speech, particularly in dialogue. In almost every respect, Stead's art is advanced in *For Love Alone*: There is greater economy of plot and characters, the prose is more beautifully textured, and the theme is more clearly and effectively developed.

In Stead's next novel, *Letty Fox: Her Luck*, a study of free love, the texture of the prose and the pace of narration seem inharmonious with the subject and theme. Detail often buries interest and obscures the view. Some critics think this Stead's weakest novel, though others reserve that place for *A Little Tea, A Little Chat*, a quite untypical work that takes as its subject matter the search for money and the pursuit of sex of a middle-aged Wall Street manipulator, Robbie Grant.

The People with the Dogs is a book about an American family. The Massines, New York descendants of nineteenth century Russian liberals, live in a typical brownstone and yet own a thousand-acre unproductive farm. They accommodate their European culture and refinement to the haste and materialism of their immediate environment. As Stead has commented, "The Massines have joy and they love each other and live for each other." They personify, somewhat ironically, rootedness in transience, democracy in an aristocratic tradition, and rural simplicity amid urban sophistication. It is a compassionate study.

Dark Places of the Heart purports to be a proletarian novel about Nellie Cotter, a London journalist and bohemian from a Tyneside family who has incestuous impulses (like those of Catherine Bagenault in *Seven Poor Men of Sydney*) and who is married to and deserted by George Cook. Again, Stead details a search for love and friendship, for self. *The Little Hotel*, with its wider range of eccentrics and poseurs, is a more satisfactory fiction set in a nondescript Swiss pension: the genteel poor and their vanities are subjected to Horatian satiric study, and the examination is livened by an almost uncharacteristic levity.

One posthumous work, *I'm Dying Laughing: The Humourist*, set in the milieu of the American Left in the 1930's and 1940's, draws on the basic elements of all Stead's earlier works: political and social commitments, family feuds, sexual fantasies, political and personal infidelities, betrayals, and the search for love and self-realization. It suggests the impossibility of being both morally upright and rich. Her novels have established Stead as a major modern writer in English and not merely a major Australian author, and *The Man Who Loved Children* and *For Love Alone* remain her most successsful fictions.

BIBLIOGRAPHICAL REFERENCES: See Susan Sheridan, *Christina Stead*, 1988. Ronald G. Geering, in *Christina Stead*, 1969, and in an afterword to *Ocean of Story: The Uncollected Stories of Christina Stead*, provides a detailed and reliable introduction, together with defenses against critical attacks. Elizabeth Hardwick, "The Neglected Novels of Christina Stead," in *A View of My Own*, 1964, was the first appreciation from a major critic but focused principally on *The Man Who Loved Children*; Randall Jarrell, "An Unread Book," his forty-page introduction to the 1965 edition of that novel, remains a detailed and illuminating analysis of it. Other informative studies are Michael Wilding, "Christina Stead's Australian Novels," *Southerly*, XXVIII (1967), 20-33, and Colin Roderick, "Christina Stead," *Southerly*, VII (1946), 87-92, which is now dated, though it reveals an early insight into her technique and merits. Both Joan Lidoff, in *Christina Stead*, 1982, and Diana Brydon, in her study of the same name, 1987, offer feminist readings.

Marian B. McLeod

LINCOLN STEFFENS

Born: San Francisco, California
Date: April 6, 1866

Died: Carmel, California
Date: August 9, 1936

PRINCIPAL WORKS

JOURNALISM: *The Shame of the Cities*, 1904; *The Struggle for Self-Government*, 1906; *Upbuilders*, 1909; *Lincoln Steffens Speaking*, 1936.
PHILOSOPHY: *Moses in Red*, 1926.
AUTOBIOGRAPHY: *The Autobiography of Lincoln Steffens*, 1931.
CORRESPONDENCE: *The Letters of Lincoln Steffens*, 1938.

Joseph Lincoln Steffens, the most notable of the early twentieth century muckrakers and one of the most important journalists of his time, was born in San Francisco, on April 6, 1866. The son of Joseph Steffens, a prominent businessman, and his wife, English-born Elizabeth Symes, he grew up in Sacramento, where the family moved in 1870. Childhood explorations took precedence over schooling and discipline until his parents seized the initiative and enrolled him in a military academy. After an additional year with a private tutor, Steffens entered the University of California at Berkeley and earned his degree in 1889. Declining his father's offer to join his business, he decided to pursue a general interest in philosophy and began graduate study in Germany. There, his interests broadened to include ethics and psychology. When Steffens finally returned to New York City in 1892, his father discontinued financial support and forced him to seek work.

Steffens' first job was covering Wall Street as a reporter for the *New York Evening Post*. He quickly became disillusioned with big business. Steffens also worked as a police reporter. He soon discovered that police, criminals, politicians, and businessmen often worked together for mutual benefit—with the public usually the loser. He was beginning to piece together an understanding of interdependence among various social elements that he would later describe as a "System."

After a brief stint as a city editor, Steffens moved to *McClure's* magazine in 1901. There he gave his fascination with civic corruption a national scope. His "Tweed Days in St. Louis," which appeared in the October, 1902, *McClure's*, gave him the distinction of being the first "muckraker" and made him an influential figure in the emerging Progressive movement. Steffens continued his scientific search into the causes of municipal corruption and broadened his study to include other municipalities. He found a cycle of corruption that was pervasive and consistent. His articles, collected in *The Shame of the Cities*, confirmed his earlier suspicion that politics and business were inseparable. Yet Steffens was optimistic, hoping that an informed public would become righteously indignant, abandon its moral apathy, and work to make government more democratic.

As Progressivism moved from the city to the state level, Steffens followed. He soon published *The Struggle for Self-Government*, a series of investigative articles on state politics. Certain that corruption had become institutionalized and that a "System" did in fact exist, Steffens believed that civic awareness in itself would be insufficient to bring about meaningful reform unless coupled with strong progressive leadership. As his interest in the role of leadership in the cause of national reform grew, he completed *Upbuilders*. The book presented chapters on five individuals who had successfully applied the Golden Rule as a means of solving social and political problems. Steffens hoped to illustrate the potential of applied Christianity as an ethical basis for human relationships, but the Golden Rule appeared to be unobtainable for society as a whole. Middle-class hypocrisy prevented it.

Steffens became increasingly disillusioned. He suggested that perhaps the greatest evil in society was "privilege"—special legislation, "pull," and "protection." He analyzed this point in a series of articles he wrote in 1910 and 1911 entitled "It: An Exposition of the

Sovereign Political Power of Organized Business." His knowledge of the workings of the political economy was increasing, but so too was his belief that changes far more drastic than those sought by most Progressives were necessary. Steffens' pessimism increased after the death of his wife in 1911. Seeking rejuvenation, he moved to New York's Greenwich Village and joined Mabel Dodge's circle of writers, artists, and Socialists. The Mexican and Russian revolutions provided him with opportunities to observe violent social upheavals, and he began to flirt with the idea of historical determinism. In Russia, Steffens thought he had truly witnessed the future. Finally, the "System" had been destroyed. As a defender of the goals of the Russian Revolution and as an admirer of Vladimir Ilich Lenin, Steffens wrote *Moses in Red*. In comparing modern revolutions with the story of Moses in the Old Testament, Steffens hoped to show that revolution was a scientifically determinable phenomenon. If men chose to ignore the laws of nature and maintain outdated forms of economy (capitalism), then revolution was inevitable.

In the mid-1920's, Steffens began writing his autobiography. He thought that he could use his life as an instructive example of a process of "unlearning" the ingrained political and social processes of his society. He wanted to share his wisdom with a younger generation, in which he placed hope for the future. His last book, *Lincoln Steffens Speaking*, published after his death in 1936, was a collection of newspaper articles in which he attempted to explain the collapse of the economic system during the Great Depression.

Steffens' importance rests with his talent as a journalist and social thinker. His muckraking books provide insights into business, politics, and human nature that embody the liberal prescription for a truly democratic society. His autobiography is a classic recounting of a lifetime spent in search of a democratic-humanistic ideal. Steffens has been criticized for being superficial and for lacking an ideological center. The charges are somewhat unfair. He offered a fundamental critique of capitalism and the profit motive. He challenged the legitimacy of corporate and political elites and helped to generate a mass reaction to injustice. He appeared to wander intellectually because he never stopped asking questions; political analysis always seemed to take precedence over political commitment.

BIBLIOGRAPHICAL REFERENCES: *The Letters of Lincoln Steffens*, 1938, edited by Ella Winter and Granville Hicks, provides a useful list of Steffens' publications. Ella Winter, *And Not to Yield: An Autobiography*, 1963, is an excellent source for personal information on Steffens' later years written by his widow. Also helpful is *The World of Lincoln Steffens*, 1962, edited by Ella Winter and Herbert Shapiro, a collection of articles from Steffens' post-muckraking years. The standard work on muckraking is still Louis Filler, *Crusaders for American Liberalism*, 1939, which offers insightful comments on Steffens and places him in the context of the larger muckraking movement. Other studies include Russell M. Horton, *Lincoln Steffens*, 1974, an excellent, short, intellectual biography; Justin Kaplan, *Lincoln Steffens*, 1974, a detailed, popular account; P. F. Palermo, *Lincoln Steffens*, 1978, a brief analysis of Steffens' writings and career; and Robert Stinson, *Lincoln Steffens*, 1979, an account of Steffens as writer and journalist.

Steven L. Piott

WALLACE STEGNER

Born: Lake Mills, Iowa
Date: February 18, 1909

Principal Works

NOVELS: *Remembering Laughter*, 1937; *The Potter's House*, 1938; *On a Darkling Plain*, 1940; *Fire and Ice*, 1941; *The Big Rock Candy Mountain*, 1943; *Second Growth*, 1947; *A Shooting Star*, 1961; *All the Little Live Things*, 1967; *Angle of Repose*, 1971; *The Spectator Bird*, 1976; *Recapitulation*, 1979; *Crossing to Safety*, 1987.

SHORT FICTION: *The Women on the Wall*, 1950; *The City of the Living and Other Stories*, 1956.

ESSAYS: *The Sound of Mountain Water: The Changing American West*, 1969; *One Way to Spell Man*, 1982; *The American West as Living Space*, 1987.

BIOGRAPHY: *The Uneasy Chair: A Biography of Bernard DeVoto*, 1974.

OTHER NONFICTION: *Mormon Country*, 1942; *One Nation*, 1945; *Beyond the Hundredth Meridian: John Wesley Powell and the Second Opening of the West*, 1954; *Wolf Willow: A History, a Story, and a Memory of the Last Plains Frontier*, 1962.

In a varied career of more than half a century, Wallace Earle Stegner has earned an honored place in American letters and is one of the foremost authors to have been closely associated with western North American themes. He was born on February 18, 1909, in Lake Mills, Iowa, to George H. Stegner and his wife, Hilda (Paulson) Stegner, but his family soon moved from the Midwest to live in a succession of western locales ranging from southern Saskatchewan to Salt Lake City, Utah, where he entered the University of Utah in 1925. Stegner was a shy, quiet child, but he became both a fine athlete and scholar despite a domineering father and the displacements of his early family life. At the university, he became a student of the noted writer Vardis Fisher, whose work was an early influence upon him. Completing a B.A. there in 1930, Stegner then attended the University of Iowa, from which he received an M.A. in 1932 and a Ph.D. in 1935.

In his mid-twenties, Stegner was poised for a career either as a teacher or as a writer, but by 1937, he had chosen both, for in that year he gained the first of several university appointments and his first major fiction work, *Remembering Laughter*, was published. This novella is the story of an Iowa farmer, Alec Stuart, and his prim wife, Margaret, whose vital younger sister is drawn into an affair with Alec. The heart of the tale describes the affair's somber legacy of pregnancy, alienation, and death, relieved only at the end by the courageous departure of the fourteen-year-old son/nephew to find a new life. While *Remembering Laughter* is far surpassed by most of Stegner's later fiction, it is a well-wrought statement of many themes he would later explore, particularly that of conflicts within families. Stegner's next three novels describe other varieties of social, emotional, and physical isolation. *The Potter's House*, set in California, concerns a deaf-mute artisan and his family, whose life is upset by the meddling of the potter's brother. *On a Darkling Plain* is the story of a young Canadian soldier who, wounded by gas in the Great War, seeks recuperative isolation by homesteading in Saskatchewan, only to be brought back to a sense of community in joining with his neighbors to combat the deadly influenza epidemic of 1918. *Fire and Ice* forgoes the connection with the land seen in Stegner's first novels and concerns the struggles of a Midwestern college student caught in conflicts of ideology and personal conduct.

In these few years, Stegner had completed his novelist's apprenticeship, and in 1943, he achieved his first critical and popular success with *The Big Rock Candy Mountain*. This semiautobiographical novel is dominated by the character of the ambitious but erratic Bo Mason, a seeker after the American Dream whose search for prosperity pushes the limits of the law and family cohesion alike. The events of the novel closely parallel the Stegner family's years in Saskatchewan, Montana, Washington, and Utah as Wallace's father pursued a futile series of money-making schemes. In large measure, this first longer novel set the tone of Stegner's future writing, particularly in suggesting that the restless individualism of Bo Mason is the disabling, if not destructive, expression of an outworn frontier mythology.

After *The Big Rock Candy Mountain*, Stegner might conceivably have become identified exclusively with the West (and in fact he has remained, throughout his career, a spokesman for the West both as a writer and as a conservationist), but he chose New England as the locale of his next novel, *Second Growth*, a study of change and renewal in social values following World War II. Almost all the author's subsequent books have had Western locales, but Stegner has resisted easy classification as a "regional" writer by diversifying his themes and by examining their widest cultural implications. Stegner's Pulitzer Prize-winning novel *Angle of Repose*, perhaps the best known of all of his books, is a key example of his wish to examine major issues such as the relationship of the West and the East in American culture and the significance of history in personal and social life. The novel's narrator, Lyman Ward, is an ailing professor of history engaged in distilling the letters and diaries of his grandparents, whose married life in the nineteenth century West Lyman discovers to have been a web of misunderstanding. Susan Ward, his grandmother, regarded her marriage as an undeserved exile from the genteel East, while her husband, a visionary and idealistic mining engineer, suffered professional failure and Susan's incomprehension. The geological term "angle of repose," denoting the incline at which a landslide or talus slope achieves stability, serves as a metaphor of the uneasy stability of relationships maintained at cross-purposes. Stegner achieved a new level of thematic and structural richness in *Angle of Repose* by mingling past and present while maintaining control of the narrative through his alter ego Lyman Ward, who expresses Stegner's belief in "life chronological, not life existential."

In a short story, "Field Guide to the Western Birds," and in the novel *All the Little Live Things* Stegner developed the character Joe Allston, who, like Lyman Ward, is a vigorously ironic dissenter from contemporary American social and moral values. Allston reappeared in *The Spectator Bird*, a National Book Award winner which was well received by the public, though some critics found the older Allston tedious, if believable. *The Spectator Bird* is another retrospective novel but uses European locales and themes (surprisingly, the Danish writer Isak Dinesen is a minor character). The theme of remembrance was further explored in *Recapitulation*, which reintroduces the character of Bruce Mason of *The Big Rock Candy Mountain*, and a novel set in the Midwest and New England, *Crossing to Safety*. An account of Stegner's career as a novelist reveals chronological gaps that were largely taken up with work on short fiction and nonfiction writing. In his short stories, Stegner often rehearses material that he later explores in novels. For example, both "The Blue-Winged Teal" (perhaps his best short story) and "Maiden in a Tower" make an appearance, in altered form, in *Recapitulation* two decades after their publication in the collection *The City of the Living and Other Stories*. Similarly, within the body of his nonfiction, the commissioned documentary study *One Nation* anticipates *Second Growth*, and more indirectly, Stegner's scholarly historical study *Beyond the Hundredth Meridian* precedes *Angle of Repose* in its attention to the conflict of myth and reality in Western development.

While the acclaimed John Wesley Powell book is straight history, Stegner's *Wolf Willow*, subtitled *A History, a Story, and a Memory of the Last Plains Frontier*, combines autobiography, history, and two short stories, "Genesis" and "Carrion Spring." Widely admired in Canada as well as the United States, *Wolf Willow* is centered on the author's reminiscence of the part of his childhood spent in East End, Saskatchewan, at the foot of the Cypress Hills. Notwithstanding the fact that it was written before the midpoint of his literary career, the book draws together so many of Stegner's strengths as a writer, including his mastery of the short story, his use of evocative family chronicle, and his appreciation of the role of history and environment in daily life, that it may be taken as a paradigm of the work of this unusually versatile man of letters.

BIBLIOGRAPHICAL REFERENCES: Forrest G. Robinson and Margaret G. Robinson, *Wallace Stegner*, 1977, is a book-length reference on the author; the identically titled study by Merrill and Lorene Lewis, published in the Western Writers series in 1972, is an essay-length comprehensive survey. In *Conversations with Wallace Stegner on Western History and Literature*, 1983, Stegner's perceptive interlocutor is Richard W. Etulain. Much of the best scholarly commentary on Stegner has been collected in *Critical Essays on Wallace Stegner*, 1982, edited by Anthony Arthur, a tribute which includes nine representative reviews, dating from 1943 to 1977, and fourteen analytical articles; the editor's introduction summarizes Stegner's stature in American letters. Two of Arthur's contributors have elsewhere commented on aspects of Stegner's work: Kerry Ahern, "Heroes vs. Women: Conflict and Duplicity in Stegner," appears in *Women, Women Writers, and the West*, 1979, and Joseph M. Flora's article on Stegner is found in *A Literary History of the American West*. The index entry for Stegner in this survey is the largest for any individual. Stegner's activity—frequently literary—in environmental issues is chronicled in T. H. Watkins, "Typewritten on Both Sides: The Conservation Career of Wallace Stegner," *Audubon*, LXXXIX (September, 1987), 88-103.

C. S. McConnell

GERTRUDE STEIN

Born: Allegheny, Pennsylvania
Date: February 3, 1874

Died: Neuilly-sur-Seine, France
Date: July 27, 1946

Principal Works

NOVELS AND NOVELLAS: *Three Lives*, 1909; *The Making of Americans*, 1925; *Ida, a Novel*, 1941; *Brewsie and Willie*, 1946; *Blood on the Dining Room Floor*, 1948; *Things As They Are*, 1950; *Mrs. Reynolds and Five Earlier Novelettes, 1931-1942*, 1952; *A Novel of Thank You*, 1958.

PLAYS: *Geography and Plays*, pb. 1922; *Operas and Plays*, pb. 1932; *Four Saints in Three Acts*, pb. 1932; *In Savoy: Or, Yes Is for a Very Young Man (A Play of the Resistance in France)*, pr., pb. 1946; *The Mother of Us All*, pr. 1947; *Last Operas and Plays*, pb. 1949; *In a Garden: An Opera in One Act*, pb. 1951; *Lucretia Borgia*, pb. 1968; *Selected Operas and Plays*, pb. 1970.

ESSAYS: *Descriptions of Literature*, 1926; *Composition as Explanation*, 1926; *Useful Knowledge*, 1928; *How to Write*, 1931; *Lectures in America*, 1935; *Narration: Four Lectures*, 1935; *What Are Masterpieces*, 1940; *Motor Automatism*, 1969 (with Leon M. Solomons); *Look at Me Now and Here I Am: Writing and Lectures, 1909-1945*, 1971; *Reflections on the Atomic Bomb*, 1973; *How Writing Is Written*, 1974.

POETRY: *Tender Buttons: Objects, Food, Rooms*, 1914; *Two (Hitherto Unpublished) Poems*, 1948; *Bee Time Vine and Other Pieces: 1913-1927*, 1953; *Stanzas in Meditation and Other Poems: 1929-1933*, 1956.

MEMOIRS: *Matisse, Picasso, and Gertrude Stein, with Two Shorter Stories*, 1933; *The Autobiography of Alice B. Toklas*, 1933; *Everybody's Autobiography*, 1937; *Picasso*, 1938; *Wars I Have Seen*, 1945.

Gertrude Stein, who studied psychology under William James at Harvard University and went to medical school at The Johns Hopkins University, became one of the United States' most celebrated expatriates. Abandoning her medical studies just months short of graduation, Stein moved to Paris in 1903 and, except for occasional brief visits, she never returned to the United States.

Stein spent her childhood in Europe and until her teens was more comfortable speaking French and German than English. Her parents—Daniel Stein, a businessman who became vice president of the Omnibus Cable Company in San Francisco, and Amelia Keyser Stein—were both dead before Gertrude Stein went east in 1893. Stein left Oakland, California, where the family had lived, to enter Harvard's annex, later Radcliffe College. Stein's oldest brother, Michael, set up trust funds that assured Gertrude and her siblings life incomes sufficient to sustain them. Gertrude's closest family connection was with her brother Leo, two years her junior, whom she joined in Paris, where he lived, in 1903.

Stein was always interested in the essence of how people communicate. At Harvard, she had conducted experiments in automatic writing, and she was struck by the poetry and repetitiveness of what her subjects produced. In France, she came under the spell of Gustave Flaubert, whom she translated, and of the impressionist artist Paul Cézanne. From Cézanne, she imbibed the notion that everything in an artistic composition is as important as every other thing in the composition. Working with words, she began to transpose this idea into her writing, first in *Three Lives,* then in the rambling novel *The Making of Americans.* Such emerging cubists as Pablo Picasso, Henri Matisse, and Marcel Duchamp (frequent callers at 27 rue de Fleurus, where Gertrude lived from 1903 until 1938) gave Stein the idea of applying to writing principles the cubists were experimenting with in art.

Just as cubists used paint and form as their building blocks, so did Stein consciously strive to strip writing—which she approached as the universal poetry—to its essences: words, surfaces, rhythms, repetitions, and finally, entities. The last of these, her most significant literary achievement, is exemplified by her oft-quoted but little understood utterance that a rose is a rose is a rose, a categorical statement of her concept of absolute quintessence, which harks back to the interest in discovering universals with which William James had challenged her at Harvard. Stein, like the pre-Socratic philosophers, embarked on a quest for essences, seeking to discover them in words, the building blocks of thought.

Sitting for Picasso some ninety times in 1906 while he was painting her portrait, Stein talked extensively about cubism, with which Picasso was then experimenting, and about her notions that words have equal value and that people think continuously in seemingly chaotic and repetitive ways. She was beginning to formulate standards and methods of verbal portraiture that would defy current literary conventions and would result in such stylistically controversial works as *Three Lives* and "Portrait of Mabel Dodge at the Villa Curonia," as well as to such subsequent works as *Matisse, Picasso, and Gertrude Stein*, *Picasso*, and *Mrs. Reynolds and Five Earlier Novelettes, 1931-1942*.

Gertrude Stein lived from 1907 until her death with her friend and lover Alice B. Toklas. Stein's close relationship with her brother Leo deteriorated and came to an end around 1914, near the start of her literary career, which Leo disparaged. Stimulated by the composers, artists, and writers with whom she was regularly surrounded, Stein wrote profusely in every possible creative medium. During her lifetime, few academicians took Stein's work seriously.

Stein was, however, writing in an age when literary theorists such as Jacques Derrida, Roland Barthes, Harold Bloom, Norman Holland, Helen Vendler, Jane Tompkins, Fredric Jameson, Jacques Lacan, and others had begun to examine writing in the light of sophisticated theoretical constructs derived from psychology, linguistics, and rhetoric. Clearly, Stein was a monumental pioneer in language whose contributions to the understanding of literature have not yet been wholly appreciated.

BIBLIOGRAPHICAL REFERENCES: Since Stein's death, Yale University, to which Stein bequeathed her papers, has published the multivolume set *The Yale Edition of the Unpublished Writings of Gertrude Stein*, edited by Carl Van Vechten, 8 vols., 1951-1958. The shrewdest critical assessments of Stein are John Malcolm Brinnin, *The Third Rose: Gertrude Stein and Her World*, 1959; James R. Mellow, *Charmed Circle: Gertrude Stein and Company*, 1974; and Wendy Steiner, *Exact Resemblance to Exact Resemblance: The Literary Portraiture of Gertrude Stein*, 1978, which, more than any other assessment, penetrates the essence of what Stein accomplished with words. Among earlier assessments, Donald Sutherland, *Gertrude Stein: A Biography of Her Work*, 1951, remains useful. Alice B. Toklas, *What Is Remembered*, 1963, is tough-minded and revealing. The best succinct assessment of Stein's language is Marjorie Perloff, "Poetry As Word-System: The Art of Gertrude Stein," *The American Poetry Review*, VIII, no. 5 (1979), 33-35.

R. Baird Shuman

JOHN STEINBECK

Born: Salinas, California
Date: February 27, 1902

Died: New York, New York
Date: December 20, 1968

PRINCIPAL WORKS

NOVELS: *Cup of Gold*, 1929; *To a God Unknown*, 1933; *In Dubious Battle*, 1936; *Of Mice and Men*, 1937; *The Grapes of Wrath*, 1939; *The Moon Is Down*, 1942; *Cannery Row*, 1945; *The Wayward Bus*, 1947; *The Pearl*, 1948; *Burning Bright*, 1950; *East of Eden*, 1952; *Sweet Thursday*, 1954; *The Short Reign of Pippin IV*, 1957; *The Winter of Our Discontent*, 1961; *Acts of King Arthur and His Noble Knights*, 1976.

SHORT FICTION: *The Pastures of Heaven*, 1932; *Tortilla Flat*, 1935; *The Long Valley*, 1938.

NONFICTION: *Their Blood Is Strong*, 1938; *The Forgotten Village*, 1941; *Sea of Cortez*, 1941 (with Edward F. Ricketts); *Bombs Away: The Story of a Bomber Team*, 1942; *A Russian Journal*, 1948 (with Robert Capa); *Once There Was a War*, 1958; *Travels with Charley in Search of America*, 1962.

PLAY: *Burning Bright*, pb. 1951.

SCREENPLAY: *The Forgotten Village*, 1941.

CORRESPONDENCE: *Journal of a Novel: The "East of Eden" Letters*, 1969; *Steinbeck: A Life in Letters*, 1975.

Winner of the Nobel Prize in Literature for 1962, John Steinbeck secured his place in American literature largely on the basis of his inimitable novel, *The Grapes of Wrath*, which defined an epoch in American life by brilliantly combining the documentary quality of journalism with the superior insight of highly imaginative fiction. Steinbeck grew up in California, close to itinerant farm laborers and to the economic struggles brought on by the Depression. Although Steinbeck attended Stanford University intermittently in the early 1920's and supported himself with odd jobs, his earliest stories reflect his interest in the nature-oriented lives of simple workers and peasants, not intellectual matters. Based on his acute perceptions, this early fiction has a directness and immediacy that is sometimes lacking in his later work, where his prose is unduly burdened by his theories of nature.

By 1936, Steinbeck's focus shifted to incorporate the political conditions in which his proletarians lived. *In Dubious Battle*, published that year, centered on a strike of migratory fruit pickers who were identified as an exploited class of people. *Of Mice and Men* is one of his fullest explorations of biological determinism, the notion that men and women are shaped by nature in ways that practically ensure their fate. Lenny is a retarded giant of a man who depends on his friend, the smaller and smarter George, to protect him. Yet Lenny does not know his own strength. He crushes puppies when he means only to pet them; he breaks Curly's wife's neck when he means only to stroke her lovely blonde hair.

The Grapes of Wrath, Steinbeck's masterpiece, follows the fate of the Joad family, who are evicted from their foreclosed farm in Oklahoma and make their way to the "promised land" of California. Slowly they lose their illusions as they are forced to work for starvation wages and are treated as riffraff by the police and the landowners. Tom Joad becomes a labor organizer when he realizes that his family cannot survive by itself. Steinbeck does not take a specifically socialist point of view—although he does provide an admiring glimpse of a government camp where the Joads and their fellow workers are able to establish a harmonious community based on equality of opportunity and responsibility.

What makes *The Grapes of Wrath* such an impressive work is its panoramic view of society. While the Joads' story particularizes the events of an epoch, the novel contains beautifully written passages that evoke the spirit of the times and create large-scale pictures of the displacement felt by people who lose their jobs and their farms. Steinbeck's remarkable accomplishment is that he not only makes readers empathize with a single family but also makes them identify with whole classes of people who are thrust into chaotic conditions as the result of a devastated economy.

None of Steinbeck's subsequent work equals the breadth and the depth of *The Grapes of Wrath*. *East of Eden*, his next major novel, is turgid and too allegorical. Set in Southern California, from the Civil War to World War I, this family saga about two brothers and their stern father is a reenactment of the story of Cain and Abel with an overlay of psychologizing that attempts to explain the genesis of good and evil.

Except for *The Winter of Our Discontent*, a fine novel tracing the moral collapse of a descendant of an old New England family who cannot cope with the twentieth century, Steinbeck's best work as a writer in the postwar years is to be found in his lighthearted travel book *Travels with Charley in Search of America*, an account of his forty-state tour with his poodle.

BIBLIOGRAPHICAL REFERENCES: Richard Astro, *John Steinbeck and Edward F. Ricketts: The Shaping of a Novelist*, 1973, is strongly recommended for students of Steinbeck's ideas; Ricketts, a marine biologist, had a profound impact on the novelist's vision of life. Warren French, *John Steinbeck*, 1975, is one of the indispensable studies of Steinbeck's career; French includes a chronology, a biographical chapter, perceptive discussions of all Steinbeck's books, and an annotated bibliography. Howard Levant, *The Novels of John Steinbeck*, 1974, is an excellent critical study with a preface by Warren French that situates Levant's study in the context of Steinbeck criticism. See also Paul McCarthy, *John Steinbeck*, 1980; Louis Owens, *John Steinbeck's Re-Vision of America*, 1985; John H. Timmerman, *John Steinbeck's Fiction*, 1986; and issues of *Steinbeck Quarterly*, a journal containing articles, reviews, and brief biographical and bibliographical notes about Steinbeck.

Carl Rollyson

GEORGE STEINER

Born: Paris, France
Date: April 23, 1929

PRINCIPAL WORKS

CRITICISM: *Tolstoy or Dostoevsky: An Essay in the Old Criticism*, 1959; *The Death of Tragedy*, 1960; *Language and Silence: Essays on Language, Literature, and the Inhuman*, 1967; *Extraterritorial: Papers on Literature and the Language Revolution*, 1971; *In Bluebeard's Castle: Some Notes Toward the Redefinition of Culture*, 1971; *After Babel: Aspects of Language and Translation*, 1975; *On Difficulty and Other Essays*, 1978; *Heidegger*, 1978 (also known as *Martin Heidegger*); *Antigones*, 1984; *Real Presences: Is There Anything in What We Say?*, 1989.

NOVEL: *The Portage to San Cristóbal of A. H.*, 1979.

SHORT FICTION: *Anno Domini*, 1964.

ANTHOLOGY: *George Steiner: A Reader*, 1984.

EDITED TEXTS: *Homer: A Collection of Critical Essays*, 1962 (with Robert Fagles); *The Penguin Book of Modern Verse Translation*, 1966.

MISCELLANEOUS: *Fields of Force: Fischer and Spassky at Reykjavik*, 1974.

George Steiner, one of the most influential comparatists, critics, and translation theorists of the late twentieth century, was born on April 23, 1929, in Paris. His parents were both university professors, and, as the author notes in *After Babel*, his early youth was spent in multilingual surroundings—so much so that he is considered by some as a native speaker of English, French, and German. He studied at various universities and subsequently filled professorial positions at universities in Europe and the United States. After some time at Yale University, Steiner accepted a professorship in English and comparative literature at the University of Geneva, where he later became head of the comparative literature department. Steiner emerged as a critical force before his thirtieth birthday with his first long work, *Tolstoy or Dostoevsky*, published in 1959. This work is based on the premise that the function of the critic is distinguished from that of the reviewer in that the critic is to distinguish not between the good and the bad but between the good and the excellent. *Tolstoy or Dostoevsky*, as a gauntlet thrown in the face of the then-prevailing critical current of New Criticism, also proved that there was still much to say about literary greats through the employ of "old" critical methods, centering on the various nontextual forces which mold the literary work and which aid in its interpretation.

The Death of Tragedy was composed two years later. In this book, the author locates the tragic tradition solely in the classical world (and in truly classically oriented works), which regard the forces which govern the fate of man as blind. The decline of the dramatic tradition is necessarily paralleled by the waxing of the Christian worldview of justice and redemption, as well as by the artistic heritage of Romanticism, with its cult of genius. This interesting volume ends with the (optimistic?) hint that the twentieth century world, with its unspeakable cruelty and totalitarian systems, may see the rebirth of this ancient dramatic genre. Steiner's next book was a collection of essays entitled *Language and Silence*. This volume is an attempt to understand the scope, importance, and future of language and linguistic culture in the face of the antihumanistic history of twentieth century totalitarianism. Steiner speaks of a certain "retreat from the word"—the inability of modern language to function in the face of bestiality—as well as of the necessary role of the spoken and written word faced with inhumanity. Steiner was also working on his theories as editor of *The Penguin Book of Modern Verse Translation*. This anthology, with its enlightening introduction (published later as the essay "Poem into Poem"), became one of the most important texts in verse translation theory, and set translation into verse—the re-creation of a poem in one given language into another poem in another tongue—as the only viable and honest method of translating verse. The magisterial study *After Babel* was developed from this preliminary essay. Like the foregoing, it battles the notion that "what remains untranslated in verse translation is the poem itself." In *After Babel*, Steiner suggests that all linguistic interpretation—even in everyday conversation—is a type of translation, and delineates the re-creative process of the verse translator as a hermeneutic method, which he considers literary criticism of the highest caliber. (This idea is linked to Steiner's conviction that literary criticism should be vivid, engaging, and text- rather than theory-centered).

Steiner's volume entitled *Extraterritorial* continues in the vein of *Language and Silence*. Again, he speaks of the "lost center" of linguistic expression of the mid- and late-twentieth century. This collection of essays reexamines Steiner's earlier thesis of the deep relationship between poetry and linguistics, and deals with various linguists and their theories, including Roman Jakobson and Noam Chomsky. *On Difficulty and Other Essays* was published in 1978. By Steiner's own admission, the essays collected in this volume are "working papers" or "position papers," designed to provoke a response from his colleagues. *On Difficulty and Other Essays* addresses many of the same questions discussed in *After Babel*, though here the linguistic element is more pronounced. Among others, there may be found articles dealing with Chomsky and Benjamin Lee Whorf and their relationship to literature.

Unlike many contemporary critics, Steiner has always emphatically insisted on the distinction between creative work and the criticism, commentary, and theorizing that feeds on it. He has spoken frankly of the critic's envy of the great writer (with the implication that to be anything less than great is not worth the game). In 1964, Steiner published a collection of three long stories or novellas, *Anno Domini*; the book was respectfully received but created no stir. His only other venture into fiction was both more substantial and more controversial. *The Portage to San Cristóbal of A. H.*, a short novel first published in *The Kenyon Review* in 1979 and later issued in book form, tells of the capture of Adolf Hitler (who is supposed to have survived the war and who is in his nineties as the story takes place) in a South American jungle. Controversy over Steiner's portrait of Hitler dominated critical responses to the novel, which is in fact an engaging work written in a clean, poetic style with striking imagery. In this novel, Steiner dramatizes the almost magical power of the Word, which in the hands of an evil master can invest ghastly cruelty with a seductive charm.

In 1984, Steiner published *Antigones*, a wide-ranging critical study of the metamorphoses of Antigone in Western literature from Sophocles to the twentieth century. In 1985, Steiner was invited to deliver the annual Leslie Stephen Memorial Lecture at the University of Cambridge. That lecture, published in pamphlet form in 1986 under the title *Real Presences*, argues the thesis developed at greater length in Steiner's 1989 book of the same title. The title alludes to the "real presence" of the divine which has permeated world literature for thousands of years. In recent memory, Steiner suggests, modernism has denied the existence of God, and, in doing so, has left literature prey to the meaning-destructive methods of deconstruction. Although he does not foresee any large-scale reacceptance of the divine as an informing presence, Steiner defends this "outdated" approach to literature as a valid manifestation of the ideal toward which art strives, and offers a hopeful prediction for the regeneration of art. This current of hope, maintained in full knowledge of the horrors of the twentieth century, runs through the entirety of Steiner's work, and characterizes him not only as an important theorist (especially in this age of centerless deconstruction) but also as a humanist—which is, after all, more important.

BIBLIOGRAPHICAL REFERENCES: The most available resources on Steiner are interviews with him and reviews of his work. For general articles, see J. Parini, "George Steiner," *The Hudson Review*, XXXVIII (August, 1985), 496-502, and Otto Friedrich, "George Steiner," *Time*, CXIX (March 29, 1982), 70. For a more in-depth article, see Karen Kildahl, "George Steiner," *Critical Survey of Literary Theory*, 1987, edited by Frank N. Magill. For reviews, see

L. Lepschy, "*After Babel*," *Romance Philology*, XXXIII (Fall, 1980), 411-413; C. Norris, "*On Difficulty*," *The Modern Language Review*, LXXVI (January, 1981), 138-139; P. Lively, "*The Portage to San Cristóbal of A. H.*," *Encounter*, LVII (November, 1981), 84-85; and P. E. Easterling, "*Antigones*," *The Classical Review*, XXXVI, no. 1 (1986), 14-15.

Charles Kraszewski

RICHARD G. STERN

Born: New York, New York
Date: February 25, 1928

PRINCIPAL WORKS

NOVELS: *Golk*, 1960; *Europe: Or, Up and Down with Schreiber and Baggish*, 1961; *In Any Case*, 1962 (also known as *The Chaleur Network*); *Stitch*, 1965; *Other Men's Daughters*, 1973; *Natural Shocks*, 1978; *A Father's Words*, 1986.

SHORT FICTION: *Teeth, Dying, and Other Matters*, 1964; *1968: A Short Novel, an Urban Idyll, Five Stories, and Two Trade Notes*, 1970; *Packages*, 1980; *Noble Rot: Stories, 1949-1988*, 1989.

NONFICTION: *The Books in Fred Hampton's Apartment*, 1973; *The Invention of the Real*, 1982; *The Position of the Body*, 1986.

EDITED TEXTS: *Honey and Wax: The Powers and Pleasures of Narrative*, 1966; *American Poetry of the Fifties*, 1967.

Richard Stern is often referred to as a writer's writer, much honored by his peers but relatively neglected by the critics and (with a couple of exceptions) by the reading public. He was born Richard Gustave Stern on February 25, 1928, in New York City, the son of a dentist; both his parents were of German-Jewish descent. A brilliant and precocious student, Stern entered the University of North Carolina at the age of sixteen; he was graduated in 1947. He received an M.A. from Harvard University in 1949 and a Ph.D. from the University of Iowa in 1954. In 1955, he began teaching at the University of Chicago, where he would remain, with visiting stints at other universities. In 1950, Stern and Gay Clark were married; they had four children. The marriage ended in divorce; in 1985, Stern married the poet Alane Rollings.

With *Golk*, Stern made a strong debut as a novelist. Centering on a fictitious television program based on the then-popular *Candid Camera*, the 1960 work came at a time when television, though already all-pervasive in American life, had received little serious attention. The program, called *You're On Camera*, catches people unawares, exposing them to the laughter of viewers all over the country. The novel's protagonist, Herbert Hondorp, becomes involved in the program, but when he himself is trapped in embarrassing behavior, he decides to betray his employer. Involved in the plot is Hondorp's marriage, in which fidelity and betrayal become equally entwined—as in the television program. Fidelity and betrayal are recurring themes in Stern's fiction. *In Any Case*, Stern's third novel, is based on a historical incident during World War II. The protagonist seeks to prove that his son, who was killed during the war and who has been branded as a traitor, was in fact innocent. As a "spy novel," *In Any Case* is above the usual run of thrills-and-secrets fiction; its main intent is to focus on the father's unswerving loyalty to his son's memory. Ultimately, the father manages to prove that his son indeed was not a traitor; this discovery brings a modicum of fulfillment.

Fidelity and betrayal are also central to the autobiographical novel *Other Men's Daughters*, Stern's greatest popular success, which enjoyed a brief run on the best-seller list. The protagonist, a professor of biology at Harvard, is deeply unhappy in his marriage yet reluctant to leave his family. His hesitations are overcome when he forms a relationship with a student. *Other Men's Daughters* illustrates another defining characteristic of Stern's fiction: his intellectual curiosity. In *Other Men's Daughters*, one sees the world as a biologist sees it; the protagonist's profession is not mere window-dressing. Similarly, in *Natural Shocks* both style and theme are related to the profession of the protagonist, a globe-trotting journalist accustomed to the company of people who make things happen. In the course of the novel he must confront the unyielding reality of death.

The range and variousness of Stern's fiction—and his relative lack of self-absorption (compare his friend and fellow novelist Philip Roth)—have no doubt cost him readers, yet these are the very qualities that make his work stand out. His achievements have been recognized with Fulbright, Guggenheim, and Rockefeller fellowships; in addition, he has been honored by the American Academy and Institute of Arts and Letters.

BIBLIOGRAPHICAL REFERENCES: For Stern's views on writing, see Robert L. Raeder, "An Interview with Richard Stern," *Chicago Review*, XVIII (Summer, 1966), 170-175; see also an article by Hugh Kenner, "*Stitch*: The Master's Voice," in the same issue and immediately following the Raeder interview. Stern's late-blooming popular success is discussed in Molly McQuade, "Richard Stern: After More Than Thirty Years as a Writer and Teacher, He Is at Home with the Rewards and Hardships Posed by a Dual Career," *Publishers Weekly*, CCXXXV (January 20, 1989), 126. Earlier articles include Alan Gross, "Someplace to Be Somebody: A Look at Artists' Workplaces in Chicago," *Chicago*, XXXI (April, 1982), 158, and Richard Rosen, "Heirs to Maxwell Perkins," *Horizon*, XXIV (April, 1981), 50. See also James Sullivan, "Richard G. Stern," in *Critical Survey of Long Fiction Supplement*, 1987, edited by Frank N. Magill.

Philip Brantingham

ADALBERT STIFTER

Born: Oberplan, Bohemia
Date: October 23, 1805

Died: Linz, Austria
Date: January 28, 1868

PRINCIPAL WORKS

NOVELS AND NOVELLAS: *Studien*, 1844-1850 (includes *Der Condor*, *Die Mappe meines Urgrossvaters*, *Der Hochwald*, *Die Narrenburg*, *Brigitta*, *Der Hagestolz*, and *Abdias*); *Bunte Steine*, 1853 (includes *Bergmilch*, *Bergkristall*, *Kalkstein*, *Granit*, and *Turmalin*); *Der Nachsomer*, 1857 (*Indian Summer*, 1985); *Witiko*, 1865-1867; *Erzählungen*, 1869; *Julius*, 1950; *Limestone and Other Stories*, 1968 (includes *The Recluse*, *Limestone*, and *Tourmaline*).

Adalbert Stifter's literary fortunes have risen and fallen several times in the German-speaking world, but in America, he has remained nearly unknown outside the circle of scholars of German literature. Born October 23, 1805, in the village of Oberplan, in Czechoslovakia (then a part of the Austrian Empire), he was the son of a linen trader and small-scale farmer. His mother was the daughter of a butcher. After his father died in an accident in 1817, Stifter's maternal grandfather took him to the well-respected school of the Benedictine monastery of Kremsmünster, where he succeeded admirably. He left Kremsmünster in 1826 and entered the University of Vienna as a student of law. In Vienna, partly because he was often in financial difficulties, he experienced the sadness of being rejected as the suitor of Fanny Greipl, whose parents thought that he was beneath her. Supporting himself as a private tutor, often tutoring the children of prominent families, and occasionally selling a painting he had done, he married Amalia Mohaupt on November 15, 1837, even though he was still in love with Fanny.

In the 1840's, he began to succeed as a writer, but his gifts as a painter served him well in the moving descriptions of his native Austrian landscape found in his prose. The first novella he published, *Der Condor* (the condor), was well received, and it was soon followed by a number of others during a period of unusual creative activity. *Abdias* and *Brigitta* in particular secured for him great fame. By 1850, six volumes of his works, each volume appearing under the title *Studien*, had been published. In 1849, Stifter moved from Vienna to Linz and in 1850, was appointed as an inspector of schools for that part of Austria, a task that took away precious time from his writing. His reaction to the Revolution of 1848 was soon one of disenchantment with political action, and he sought in education a means of ennobling mankind.

His most cogent statement of aesthetic, moral, and philosophical principles is found in the preface to his 1853 collection of novellas, *Bunte Steine* (colorful stones). In his view, it is not the dramatic, cataclysmic events and emotions of life that are actually powerful, but rather the quiet, steady working of rational conduct. This philosophy, which he called the "gentle law," is reflected in the best-known novella from *Bunte Steine*, *Bergkristall* (rock crystal), and his most widely appreciated novel, *Indian Summer*. The latter work especially has been faulted for dwelling too much on the details of the scenes and characters portrayed, but for Stifter, the general is seen through the particular and the discrete is an embodiment of overarching principles. By means of the serene word, he hoped to embody the ideals of classical German humanism, although in his personal life he was not able, in an age of revolution and social change, to achieve the ideal to which his prose tends. After an unfortunate series of deaths of individuals who were close to him and after suffering from illnesses himself, he ended his life voluntarily in January of 1868.

His admirers have included such famous writers as Friedrich Nietzsche, Rainer Maria Rilke, Hugo von Hofmannsthall, Thomas Mann, and W. H. Auden. Since at least the 1850's, however, opinion has been divided in regard to Stifter's stature, with the earliest and most notorious attacks on him led by the German playwright Friedrich Hebbel. Stifter's supporters admit that his prose is one of loving devotion to the seemingly unspectacular, but they find in this devotion an atmosphere of rarest beauty and profundity.

BIBLIOGRAPHICAL REFERENCES: Much of the major Stifter criticism is in German, as is the standard bibliography by Eduard Eisenmeier, *Adalbert-Stifter-Bibliographie*, 1971. Book-length studies in English on Stifter include Eric Blackall's reliable and learned *Adalbert Stifter: A Critical Study*, 1948; Margaret Gump's brief but useful *Adalbert Stifter*, 1974; and Martin and Erika Swale's very fine *Adalbert Stifter: A Critical Study*, 1984. One further work, devoted specifically to *Indian Summer*, is Christine O. Sjögren, *The Marble Statue as Idea: Collected Essay on Adalbert Stifter's "Der Nachsommer,"* 1972. See also J. P. Stern, "Propitiations: Adalbert Stifter," and "On Some Criticisms of Stifter's work," in *Re-interpretations: Seven Studies in Nineteenth-Century Germany Literature*, 1964. The latter article reviews trends in Stifter studies since Stifter's death. Further articles on individual works are Christine O. Sjögren, "The Allure of Beauty in Stifter's *Brigitta*," *Journal of English and Germanic Philology*, LXXXI (1982), 47-54; John Whiton, "Symbols of Social Renewal in Stifter's *Bergkristall* (Rock Crystal)," *The Germanic Review*, XLVII (1972), 259-280; Margrit Sinka, "Unappreciated Symbol: The *Unglückssäule* in Stifter's *Bergkristall*," *Modern Austrian Literature*, XVI (1983), 1-17; and Eve Mason, "Stifter's *Turmalin* (Tourmaline): A Reconsideration," *The Modern Language Review*, LXXII (1977), 348-358.

Thomas P. Baldwin

FRANK R. STOCKTON

Born: Philadelphia, Pennsylvania
Date: April 5, 1834

Died: Washington, D.C.
Date: April 20, 1902

PRINCIPAL WORKS

NOVELS: *Rudder Grange*, 1879; *The Casting Away of Mrs. Lecks and Mrs. Aleshine*, 1886; *The Late Mrs. Null*, 1886; *The Dusantes*, 1888; *The Great War Syndicate*, 1889; *Ardis Claverden*, 1890; *Pomona's Travels*, 1894; *Mrs. Cliff's Yacht*, 1896; *The Great Stone of Sardis*, 1898; *Kate Bonnet: The Romance of a Pirate's Daughter*, 1902.

SHORT FICTION: *The Lady, or the Tiger? and Other Stories*, 1881; *The Christmas Wreck and Other Stories*, 1886; *Amos Kilbright: His Adscititious Experience, with Other Stories*, 1888; *The Rudder Grangers Abroad and Other Stories*, 1891; *The Clocks of Rondaine and Other Stories*, 1892; *The Watchmaker's Wife and Other Stories*, 1893; *Fanciful Tales*, 1894; *The Story Teller's Pack*, 1897; *A Vizier of the Two-Horned Alexander*, 1898; *The Magic Egg*, 1902; *John Gayther's Garden and Stories Told Therein*, 1902.

CHILDREN'S LITERATURE: *Ting-a-Ling*, 1870; *Roundabout Rambles in Lands of Fact and Fancy*, 1872; *Tales out of School*, 1875; *A Jolly Fellowship*, 1880; *The Floating Prince and Other Fairy Tales*, 1881; *The Bee Man of Orn and Other Fanciful Tales*, 1887.

Francis Richard Stockton was one of the most popular American humorists of the late nineteenth century, excelling in stories of whimsical fancy, in episodic novels of domestic comedy, and in tales of the occult and supernatural. A descendant of one of the signers of the Declaration of Independence, Stockton was the third son of William Smith Stockton and his second wife, Emily Drean Stockton. Because his physique was generally frail and because he had been born with one leg shorter than the other, young Frank was severely limited in his childhood activities. On his daily walks to school, however, he began to develop his imaginative faculties by orchestrating dramas in his mind, plotting serial tales for his personal diversion. He later noted, "I caused the fanciful creatures who inhabited the world of fairyland to act . . . as if they were inhabitants of the real world." Such creative strategy later came to characterize Stockton's most successful children's literature and science fiction.

At Central High School in Philadelphia, Stockton won a short-story contest, an achievement which encouraged his aspirations toward an eventual career in writing. In 1852, though, when he was graduated, Stockton was apprenticed to a wood engraver and for the next fourteen years, worked for a living at this craft, accumulating rejection slips for his occasional forays into fiction. By 1859, he had published only two short stories. In 1860, Stockton married Mary Anne (Marianne) Edwards Tuttle (her first name has also been spelled without the *e*'s). He then began to apply himself more vigorously to his writing, and he soon had a serialized tale accepted for publication in the prestigious *Southern Literary Messenger*, a journal at one time partially written and edited by Edgar Allan Poe. A brief, uncharacteristic political posture manifested itself at this time in Stockton's life: He published a pamphlet supporting the right of the South to secede from the Union. When Fort Sumter fell, however, Stockton, a genial, amiable gentleman who actually abhorred controversy, withdrew the slender publication and for the rest of his life, happily avoided any social or political dispute.

When Stockton published "Ting-a-Ling," a fairy tale about a giant and a dwarf, in *Riverside Magazine* in 1867, he came to the attention of Mary Mapes Dodge, soon to be recognized as a significant force in children's literature. Dodge hired Stockton as her assistant editor on *Hearth and Home*, a periodical for the juvenile market. He was now able to focus his complete attention on the literary arena, and when five years later Dodge assumed the editorship of the classic *St. Nicholas* magazine, she took Stockton along as her assistant editor once more. Stockton not only helped edit *St. Nicholas* but also contributed tales under his own name and under the pseudonyms Paul Fort and John Lewes as well.

In 1876, Stockton began experiencing eye difficulties, problems exacerbated by his increasingly heavy load of editorial work and his demanding writing schedule; by 1878, he was forced to resign his post at *St. Nicholas*. From then on, with his wife often acting as his amanuensis and reader, Stockton devoted himself to his own creative writing, with humor constituting his major orientation. He observed, "The discovery that humorous compositions could be used in journals other than those termed comic marked a new era in my life." Sitting comfortably in his New Jersey home, Stockton dictated stories and novels which, he insisted, were without hidden philosophic meaning or deep, critical implications. Success as an entertainer was his simple aim.

His best-known works now began to appear in book form as well as in such popular magazines of the day as *Cosmopolitan*, *Scribner's*, and the *Ladies' Home Journal*. A resounding success was the episodic novel *Rudder Grange*, vignettes chronicling the misadventures of a newly married couple who, with their shrewd but often miscalculating maid Pomona, settle on a houseboat. The audience demanded sequels, and Stockton delivered more sketches of the hapless group in *The Rudder Grangers Abroad and Other Stories* and *Pomona's Travels*.

Financial success afforded the Stocktons opportunity to travel, and voyages abroad continued to energize the abundant imagination of the acclaimed humorist, particularly directing him to compose another renowned success, *The Casting Away of Mrs. Lecks and Mrs. Aleshine*, a tale of two widows from a small town in Pennsylvania who, along with a formal gentleman, are shipwrecked but, nevertheless, find themselves in enviable circumstances: They are castaways on a tropical island, yet living in a charming home with a full larder. *The Dusantes* became the sequel demanded by Stockton's readership.

Stockton's most memorable piece, however, the one for which succeeding generations of readers have remembered and will continue to remember his name is "The Lady, or the Tiger?" a tale originally appearing in *Century's Magazine* for November, 1882. The story's challenging conclusion spawned much speculation as intrigued readers endeavored to disentangle the verbal clues in pursuit of a solution to this literary cipher that is timelessly intriguing. From time to time, Stockton exploited occultist worlds and other spiritualist manifestations in his imaginative prose. "The Lady in the Box," for example, a tale from *John Gayther's Garden and Stories Told Therein*, is strongly reminiscent of Poe and the elements of gothic mystery as a woman's cataleptic trance is controlled in history, a phenomenon enabling her to transcend forty years without aging. *The Great Stone of Sardis*, set in the New York of 1947, deals with materials virtually foreign to the pre-twentieth century sensibility: submarines, sophisticated communications systems, and the existence of a mammoth diamond located in the very center of the earth. The Jules Verne influence on Stockton's science fiction work is most clearly noticeable in this story.

The Stocktons retired to an estate they had purchased in West Virginia. In mid-April, 1902, Stockton attended the banquet of the National Academy of Sciences in Washington, D.C. While there, he was taken ill and carried to his hotel room, where he died April 20, 1902, of a cerebral hemorrhage. Stockton was buried in Woodland Cemetery, Philadelphia, not far from the spot where he had been born.

BIBLIOGRAPHICAL REFERENCES: For further study, see Henry L. Golemba, *Frank R. Stockton*, 1981, an informative study of the author's life and work, and Martin I. J. Griffin, *Frank R. Stockton: A Critical Study*, 1965, which contains a detailed examination of the author's life. Other useful commentary may be found in Jill P. May, "Frank R. Stockton," *Dictionary of Literary Biography*, Vol. 42: *American Writers for Children Before 1900*, 1985. See also Arthur H. Quinn, *American Fiction*, 1936, where Stockton's work is examined in the stream of historical criticism under "The Fiction of Fantasy." Arthur T. Quiller-Couch, *Adventures in Criticism*, 1926, offers a positive British assessment. For relevant evaluations of Stockton made by his contemporaries, see William Dean Howells, "Stockton's Novels and Stories,"

The Atlantic Monthly, LXXXVII (1901), 136-138; Hamilton W. Mabie, "Frank R. Stockton," *Book Buyer*, XXII (1902), 355-356; and Clarence Clough Buel, "The Author of 'The Lady, or the Tiger?' " *Century*, X (1886), 404-408.

Abe C. Ravitz

IRVING STONE

Born: San Francisco, California
Date: July 14, 1903

Died: Los Angeles, California
Date: August 26, 1989

PRINCIPAL WORKS

NOVELS: *Pageant of Youth*, 1933; *Lust for Life*, 1934; *Sailor on Horseback*, 1938; *The President's Lady*, 1951; *Love Is Eternal*, 1954; *The Agony and the Ecstasy*, 1961; *The Passions of the Mind*, 1971; *The Greek Treasure*, 1975; *The Origin*, 1980; *Depths of Glory*, 1985.

EDITED TEXT: *I, Michelangelo, Sculptor: An Autobiography Through Letters*, 1962 (with Jean Stone).

MISCELLANEOUS: *The Drawings of Michelangelo*, 1961; *The Story of Michelangelo's Pietà*, 1964.

Irving Stone was born July 14, 1903, in San Francisco, California, son of Charles Tennenbaum and Pauline Rosenberg Tennenbaum Stone. He legalized the surname of his stepfather. Educated at the University of California, Berkeley, Stone received his B.A. in 1923, taught economics at the University of Southern California from 1923 to 1924, when he was awarded his M.A., and then did postgraduate work at the University of California for two more years. In 1934, Stone married Jean Factor, who was to become his editor and researcher; the marriage produced a daughter and a son, Paula and Kenneth. Although Stone's *Pageant of Youth* was published in 1933, he first scored heavily with the biographical novel format in 1934 when he dramatically re-created the life of artist Vincent van Gogh. Spirited, colorful, and fact-filled, *Lust for Life* attracted a wide audience who wanted both livelier biographies and rewarding, factual novels. Traveling across Holland, Belgium, and France to recapture the life of the shy and awkward but compassionate artist driven to madness by his less feeling peers, Stone developed a special method of characterization by writing as if he were the character himself. The success of *Lust for Life* was enough to inspire a major film in 1956 starring Kirk Douglas.

In 1938, Stone won high praise from critics for *Sailor on Horseback*, which detailed the life of novelist Jack London. Armed with London's correspondence, family documents, and autobiographical writings, Stone produced a seamless amalgam, leaving the reader to wonder where London left off and Stone began. Vivid scenes that account for both London's actions and his dreams caused critics to hail Stone's portrait as full, skillful, and honest. Preferring to write about artists, authors, and political leaders, Stone moved close to the realm of romantic suspense when he chose Rachel Jackson, the wife of Andrew Jackson, as the center of *The President's Lady*. Scorned by the public because of doubt about her divorce from her first husband, Rachel was crafted as an undeniably appealing victim by the author, especially in those scenes where she was used as a political weapon against her husband. The couple's deep love and her untimely death before his presidency greatly moved women readers. The story was filmed in 1953.

In Mary Todd Lincoln, the protagonist of *Love Is Eternal*, Stone found an ideal subject, for he could merge an account of her vilification by the public with a solidly researched narrative of the Civil War period to deliver a heady mixture. Taking his title from the romantic inscription inside Mrs. Lincoln's wedding band, Stone wrote some of his most moving prose about the deepening love that comes to a couple—in this case a most unusual couple—who must grow and rebuild after defeat and remorse. *Love Is Eternal* was a popular success, broadening Stone's audience. Stone's next subject was the great sculptor Michelangelo. Although some critics regarded *The Agony and the Ecstasy* as simply a bad novel and believed the author to be better suited to historical nonfiction, an eager public pushed the work up the best-seller list. The story became a major motion picture in 1965. The four and a half years of research, including Stone's apprenticeship to a sculptor, his mix of letters, diaries, histories, and observations, as well as extensive editing by his wife, brought forth an accessible Michelangelo "purged not only of ambisexuality, but of egotism, fault-finding, harsh irony, and ill temper," as one reviewer noted, a simplistic view for a popular audience. Stone followed this triumph with nonfiction spin-offs such as *The Drawings of Michelangelo*, *I, Michelangelo, Sculptor*, and *The Story of Michelangelo's Pietà*.

By the time *The Passions of the Mind* was written, Stone was even more smitten with research. Sigmund Freud's psychoanalytical studies, his friends and their milieu—all this took Stone six and a half years of research and writing, only to produce a work considered ponderous and indiscriminate by most critics. Similarly, *The Greek Treasure*, the story of Heinrich and Sophia Schliemann and the discovery of ancient Troy, was poorly received by the critics and failed to attain the popular success of its predecessors. *The Origin*, about Charles Darwin's life and writings, garnered higher praise for Stone from most critics; Redmon O'Hanlon termed it "Stone's best researched and best written book to date." Stone compressed Darwin's early life in order to concentrate on the voyage of the *Beagle*, and he is especially fine at rendering the scientist's familial surroundings. Still, there were cavils over "the making of lists and the fussy accumulation of historical detail."

Stone's account of the Impressionist painter Camille Pissarro—*Depths of Glory*—received the most damning critiques of the author's career, ranging from one critic's comment on the less than ideal subject and the "arch drivel" of its dialogue to another's reflection that "it is filled with information—but so is the almanac," adding that "no one comes to life." The more Stone has written, the more he has fallen victim to his nemesis—too much history and not enough life. Nevertheless, two of his books—*Lust for Life* and *The Agony and the Ecstasy*—are among the most widely read biographical novels of the twentieth century.

BIBLIOGRAPHICAL REFERENCES: For further study, see these reviews: Susan Forrest, "The Agony of Irving Stone," *Fort Lauderdale News*, January 10, 1975, 455; Hassoldt Davis, *The New York Times*, September 18, 1938, 1; R. J. Clements, *Saturday Review*, XLIV (March 18, 1961), 18; Redmon O'Hanlon, "Tracking Down the Beagle," *The Times Literary Supplement*, June 19, 1981, 690; Peter Plagens, "Artist Novel," *Art in America*, February, 1986, 19; Susan Isaacs, "Painter and the Maid," *The New York Times Book Review*, October 20, 1985, 16. See also the interview with Stone by Jean W. Ross in *Contemporary Authors*, New Revision Series, Vol. 23, 1988, edited by Deborah A. Straub, and the book by Ray Newquist, *Counterpoint*, 1964.

Clifton L. Warren

ROBERT STONE

Born: New York, New York
Date: August 21, 1937

PRINCIPAL WORKS

NOVELS: *A Hall of Mirrors*, 1967; *Dog Soldiers*, 1974; *A Flag for Sunrise*, 1981; *Children of Light*, 1986.

SCREENPLAYS: *WUSA*, 1971 (with Judith Rascoe); *Who'll Stop the Rain*, 1978 (with Rascoe).

Robert Stone is one of the most important novelists of his generation. He was born in New York City on August 21, 1937, the son of C. Homer Stone and his wife, Gladys Catherine Grant. He was reared almost entirely by his mother in rather economically difficult circumstances. Because of his mother's emotional problems, Stone spent a number of years in a Catholic orphanage and attended Catholic schools. He left high school before his graduation and joined the Navy, serving from 1955 to 1958. He attended New York University from 1958 to 1959 while also working as an editorial assistant for the New York *Daily News*. In 1959, he married Janice G. Burr, with whom he has had two children. In 1962, he was a Stegner Fellow at Stanford University, where he met Ken Kesey and became involved with Kesey's Merry Pranksters and the drug-oriented counterculture, which Tom Wolfe describes in his book *The Electric Kool-Aid Acid Test* (1968). Stone has taught writing courses at a number of colleges and universities, including Princeton, Amherst, Stanford, Harvard, and New York universities. His first novel, *A Hall of Mirrors*, won for Stone the Faulkner Award for best first novel. His second novel, *Dog Soldiers*, won for Stone the National Book Award in 1975. *A Flag for Sunrise*, his third novel, won the John Dos Passos Prize for literature as well as the American Academy of Arts and Literature Award in 1982. He was a Guggenheim Fellow in 1971, a National Endowment for the Humanities Fellow in 1983, and he is a member of the International Association of Poets, Playwrights, Editors, Essayists and Novelists (PEN). In addition to novels, Stone writes reviews and essays and occasional stories for such journals as *Harper's Magazine*, *Esquire*, and *The Atlantic*.

Stone's fiction is deeply engaged with the complex issues and forces of the age. His fiction has virtually Tolstoyan ambitions: to show ideas and morality in action in darkly extreme circumstances and to probe the spiritual depths of the American experience. If Stone receives criticism for the unrelieved harshness of his portrayal of the human condition, he nevertheless earns praise for his uncompromising honesty and artistic integrity. "As a young man," Stone has noted, "I made it a point to be where things were happening." This concern is reflected in his fiction, to which he gives a strong sense of place. In his essay "The Reason for Stories: Toward a Moral Fiction," Stone writes: "I think the key is to establish the connection between political forces and individual lives." Accordingly, in each of his works, Stone casts rather beleaguered selves into situations of social and political crisis—New Orleans, in a time of racial strife and right-wing plots, forms the setting for *A Hall of Mirrors*; California at the end of the Vietnam War for *Dog Soldiers*; Central America in the late 1970's for *A Flag for Sunrise*; and Hollywood and a Mexican filmmaking location for *Children of Light*.

Stone's novels are chronicles of survivors, although rather unfit and undeserving ones. His protagonists are failed and lost pilgrims in a world dominated by corruption and betrayal. For Stone, modern American history is the history of moral failure and moral enfeeblement. At the heart of the moral failure is betrayal—of self, of others, of ideals, of beliefs. Stone lets his wounded characters work out their destinies in starkly extreme circumstances, portrayals offering only slim grounds for hope. The cynical Rheinhart, the protagonist of *A Hall of Mirrors*, betraying his artistic and humane sensibilities, comes to New Orleans and works as an announcer for a right-wing radio station spewing forth racism and jingoism. He barely survives an elaborate right-wing plot to foment racial conflict. John and Marge Converse are the feckless and reckless survivors of *Dog Soldiers*, who try to cash in on the moral corruption of the Vietnam War by trying to smuggle three kilograms of heroin out of Vietnam for a quick score in the States. Another moral burnout, encapsulated by his cynicism, an anthropologist and former Central Intelligence Agency (CIA) operative, is Frank Holliwell of *A Flag for Sunrise*, who betrays any sense of goodness to survive the murky political corruption of Central America in the late 1970's. Gordon Walker, of *Children of Light*, actor and screenwriter, fails miserably to recover a lost dream on a film set in Mexico. Recovering from his excesses, Gordon, at the end, decides to stop going with the flow, a decision which offers some hope for moral renewal.

Along with the survival of the morally unfit in Stone's fiction, there is the defeat and death of the morally decent. The actions of those characters who bear the burden of decency and caring are rendered futile and ineffectual by the corrupt social and political forces swirling about them. Thus, in *A Hall of Mirrors*, Morgan Rainy and Geraldine, Rheinhart's lover, are defeated, with Geraldine dying in jail. The Nietzsche-reading samurai figure, Ray Hicks, of *Dog Soldiers*, suffers death by corrupt American drug officials. The idealism of Sister Justin Feeney is exploited in *A Flag for Sunrise*, and she faces rape, torture, and death in the aftermath of a failed coup. In *Children of Light*, the lovely but schizophrenic actress Lu Anne Bourgeois commits suicide like the character Edna Pontellier from Kate Chopin's *The Awakening* (1899), whose role she is portraying. In each case, the moral weaknesses and failures of the protagonists directly or indirectly contribute to the defeat and death of the decent and morally sensitive. Stone's work shows great depth and insight in its treatment of the American experience. Following in the tradition of such writers as Theodore Dreiser and John Dos Passos, Stone is a realist who yet takes full advantage of modernist techniques in such things as point of view and narrative variety. He locates his stories in recognizable social and political contexts to probe a condition beyond politics—the moral and spiritual tenor of the twentieth century. The high critical success of his work is a tribute to the honesty and seriousness of his artistic commitments.

BIBLIOGRAPHICAL REFERENCES: Insight into Stone's work is provided in several published interviews: "A Talk with Robert Stone," *The New York Times*, October 18, 1981, 34-36; Maureen Karaguezian, "Interview with Robert Stone," *Tri-Quarterly*, VI, no. 1 (Fall, 1982), 91-115; E. J. Schroeder, "Interviews with Tim O'Brien and Robert Stone," *Modern Fiction Studies*, XXX (Spring, 1984), 135-164; W. C. Woods, "The Art of Fiction XC: Robert Stone," *The Paris Review*, XXVII (Winter, 1985), 25-57; and Jean W. Ross, *Contemporary Authors*, New Revision Series, Vol. 23, 1988, edited by Deborah A. Straub. For a discussion of individual works, see Joseph Epstein, "American Nightmares," *Commentary*, March, 1982, 42-45; Maureen Karaguezian, "Irony in Robert Stone's *Dog Soldiers*," *Critique: Studies in Modern Fiction*, XXIV, no. 2 (1983), 65-73; Frederick Karl, *American Fictions: 1940-1980*, 1983; Stephen H. Knox, "A Cup of Salt for an O.D.: *Dog Soldiers* and Anti-Apocalypse," *Journal of General Education*, XXXIV, no. 1 (Spring, 1982), 60-68; L. Hugh Moore, "The Undersea World of Robert Stone," *Critique: Studies in Modern Fiction*, XI, no. 3 (1969), 43-56; and Frank W. Shelton, "Robert Stone's *Dog Soldiers*: Viet Nam Comes Home to America," *Critique: Studies in Modern Fiction*, XXIV, no. 2 (1983), 74-81.

John G. Parks

TOM STOPPARD
Tomas Straussler

Born: Zlin (modern Gottwaldov), Czechoslovakia
Date: July 3, 1937

Principal Works

PLAYS: *A Walk on the Water*, televised pr. 1963, staged pr. 1964 (revised and televised as *The Preservation of George Riley*, 1964); *The Gamblers*, pr. 1965; *Rosencrantz and Guildenstern Are Dead*, pr. 1966; *Tango*, pr. 1966; *Enter a Free Man*, pr., pb. 1968 (revision of *A Walk on the Water*); *The Real Inspector Hound*, pr., pb. 1968; *After Magritte*, pr. 1970; *Dogg's Our Pet*, pr. 1971; *Jumpers*, pr., pb. 1972; *Travesties*, pr. 1974; *Dirty Linen and New-Found-Land*, pr., pb. 1976; *Every Good Boy Deserves Favour*, pr. 1977; *Night and Day*, pr., pb. 1978; *Dogg's Hamlet, Cahoot's Macbeth*, pr. 1979; *Undiscovered Country*, pr. 1979; *On the Razzle*, pr., pb. 1981; *The Real Thing*, pr., pb. 1982; *Rough Crossing*, pb. 1985; *Dalliance*, pb. 1986; *Hapgood*, pr., pb. 1988.

RADIO PLAYS: *If You're Glad I'll Be Frank*, 1965; *Albert's Bridge*, 1967; *Where Are They Now?*, 1970; *Artist Descending a Staircase*, 1972.

TELEVISION PLAYS: *A Separate Peace*, 1966; *Squaring the Circle*, 1984.

NOVELS: *Lord Malquist and Mr. Moon*, 1966.

Catapulted to fame in 1967 with the National Theatre's production of *Rosencrantz and Guildenstern Are Dead* (it was first produced in Edinburgh), Tom Stoppard emerged as a leading dramatist in the second of the two waves of new drama that arrived on the London stage in the mid-1950's and the mid-1960's, respectively. Writing high comedies of ideas with what critic Kenneth Tynan described as a hypnotized brilliance, Stoppard established a reputation almost immediately with dazzling displays of linguistic fireworks that evoked comparisons with Oscar Wilde, George Bernard Shaw, and James Joyce. His reinventions of William Shakespeare's *Hamlet* (pr. c. 1600-1601) in *Rosencrantz and Guildenstern Are Dead*, Wilde's *The Importance of Being Earnest* (pr. 1895) in *Travesties*, and August Strindberg's *Fröken Julie* (pb. 1888; *Miss Julie*, 1912) in *The Real Thing* are his masterpieces. His linguistic caprices and his creative plagiarisms join forces with a love of ideas with which his characters play as much as they do with language.

Born Tomas Straussler on July 3, 1937, to Eugene and Martha Straussler of Zlin (later Gottwaldov), Czechoslovakia, Stoppard was only two years old when, on the eve of Adolf Hitler's annexation of that country, his father, the company doctor for an international shoe company, was transferred to Singapore. Before the Japanese invasion of Singapore, Mrs. Straussler and her two sons were moved to Darjeeling, India, where she managed a company shoe shop. His father was killed during the invasion, and his mother later married Major Kenneth Stoppard, who moved his family to England in 1946. Bored by school, the young Stoppard chose not to go to university and, instead, became a news reporter in Bristol and later a drama critic for a short-lived magazine, *Scene*. His early writing included a novel, some short stories, and a series of short radio plays.

His major plays (*Rosencrantz and Guildenstern Are Dead*, *Jumpers*, *Travesties*, *Night and Day*, *The Real Thing*, and *Hapgood*), although scintillating in their language, ideas, and plots, were frequently criticized for the absence of emotionally credible characters and, as well, for their lack of social or political commitment. In later plays—*Every Good Boy Deserves Favour* (about political prisoners in central Europe), *Professional Foul* (also about freedoms in Czechoslovakia), and *Squaring the Circle* (about Poland's Solidarity movement)—Stoppard entered the political arena. Although active in the anticommunist human rights movement, he kept his distance from the many new playwrights whose political orientation was leftist, who protested economic injustices at home, and who opposed strongly the

English class system and the effects of England's colonial past.

In *Rosencrantz and Guildenstern Are Dead*, Shakespeare's two most insignificant characters take center stage and become metaphysicians of sorts as they ponder philosophical questions of existence and choice. Like Vladimir and Estragon in Samuel Beckett's *En attendant Godot* (pb. 1952; *Waiting for Godot*, 1954), Ros and Guil debate with each other and with the leader of the traveling players some of the same problems that plague Hamlet in Shakespeare's play. In *Jumpers*, debates on ethics take place between the traditional philosopher, George Moore (after a real life author, G. E. Moore, of a work entitled *Principia Ethica*, 1903), and a modern logical positivist, Archibald Jumper (patterned after an Oxford philosopher, Sir Frederick Ayer).

Theories of art are debated in *Travesties* by three characters: Lenin, James Joyce, and dadaist Tristan Tzara. Since all three were supposed to have been living in Zurich about the time of the Russian Revolution, Stoppard imagines their having met in a library in Zurich. The ingenious plot includes secretaries to Joyce and Lenin named Gwendolyn and Cecily and is structured on the kinds of confusion of identities found in Wilde's *The Importance of Being Earnest*.

The debate of ideas continues in *The Real Thing*, in which the subject of the debate again is art, but love as well. In *Hapgood*, Stoppard fuses debates on modern scientific theories of waves, a spy mystery, and romance, creating his usual brilliance of ideas, plot inventiveness, and character identities that remain confusing even at the end. The title of Irving Wardle's review of *The Real Thing*, "Cleverness with Its Back to the Wall," is a description that in varying degrees can be applied to Stoppard's plays, as the cleverness at times seems to get in the way of dramatic substance. To the critic, however, who applies Stoppard's own description of his plays as "ambushes for the audience" and his own rejection of "yes" and "no" answers to questions, the literate high comedies of ideas provide a refreshing contrast to the plays of the so-called committed dramatist.

Stoppard admires Beckett, who "picks up a proposition and then dismantles and qualifies each part of its structure as he goes along, until he nullifies what he started out with." Characterizing his play debates as a "series of conflicting statements made by conflicting characters who tend to play an infinite leapfrog," Stoppard writes about two types of characters: Moons and Boots. The former loses himself in his arguments, while the latter emerges victorious by means of his style, the controlling factor in his survival. Stoppard, deriving the name of Boot from a character in Evelyn Waugh's novel *Scoop* (1938), can, by virtue of his own identity as inventive stylist, be categorized as a Boot character. Many of his early plays contain characters with the names Moon and Boot.

Stoppard is not a philosopher—he is very definitely a playwright. He uses the world and that world's thought that he finds around him in something of the wild, dizzy, and exhilarating manner of a metaphysical poet. With Harold Pinter, Stoppard shares a reputation as the most inventive stylist of the two waves of revolution that swept the English stage in the second half of the twentieth century.

BIBLIOGRAPHICAL REFERENCES: Like Pinter, Stoppard enjoys the prestige of attention from both academic and theater critics in the many books that have been written about his plays. Ronald Hayman, *Tom Stoppard*, 1977, is one of the earliest and still one of the basic studies, although it does not include the later plays. *Tom Stoppard: An Assessment*, by C. W. E. Bigsby, 1979, is a short but incisive view of Stoppard's style. Victor Cahn, *Beyond Absurdity: The Plays of Tom Stoppard*, 1979, traces absurdist techniques through Stoppard's plays to that date. Joan Fitzpatrick Dean, *Tom Stoppard: Comedy as a Moral Matrix*, 1981, although insightful, lacks an index, bibliography, and other back matter. Felicia Londré, *Tom Stoppard*, 1981, is especially good in tracing the sources of the abundant allusions in Stoppard's writing. Jim Hunter, *Tom Stoppard's Plays*, 1982, is meant for performers, directors, and audiences. Tim Brassell, *Tom Stoppard: An Assessment*, 1985, is a solid analysis in the standard monograph format. The subtitle of Richard Corballis, *Tom Stoppard: The Mystery and the Clockwork*, 1985, suggests his approach to Stoppardian enigmas. Susan Rusinko, *Tom Stoppard*, 1986, traces the Moon and Boot characters from their most clearly defined treatment in Stoppard's only novel, *Lord Malquist and Mr. Moon*, through their development in the varied genres in which Stoppard has worked: fiction, original stage dramas, stage adaptations, radio and television plays, and screenplays. Anthony Jenkins, *The Theatre of Tom Stoppard*, 1987, brings to the subject the viewpoint of an actor, director, and drama teacher in his attempt to show that Stoppard's work is all of a piece.

Susan Rusinko

DAVID STOREY

Born: Wakefield, Yorkshire, England
Date: July 13, 1933

Principal Works

NOVELS: *This Sporting Life*, 1960; *Flight into Camden*, 1960; *Radcliffe*, 1963; *Pasmore*, 1972; *A Temporary Life*, 1973; *Saville*, 1976; *A Prodigal Child*, 1982; *Present Times*, 1984.

PLAYS: *The Restoration of Arthur Middleton*, pr. 1966; *In Celebration*, pr., pb. 1969; *The Contractor*, pr. 1969; *Home*, pr., pb. 1970; *The Changing Room*, pr. 1971; *The Farm*, pr., pb. 1973; *Cromwell*, pr., pb. 1973; *Life Class*, pr. 1974; *Mother's Day*, pr. 1976; *Sisters*, pr. 1978; *Early Days*, pr. 1980.

SCREENPLAYS: *This Sporting Life*, 1963; *In Celebration*, 1974.

Each of David Malcolm Storey's works is awaited in Great Britain as a major statement on his times by a novelist whom many consider to be the best of his generation. Born the third son of a coal miner, Storey was reared on a large urban housing estate in the provincial north of England. His life was complicated from the first by the fact that an elder brother died before his birth, leaving his mother in the grips of a suicidal grief. (Another brother, Anthony, is a minor novelist known for his melodramatic mixing of theology and eroticism.) The young Storey's sense of being an outsider was exacerbated by his being educated out of his class at Wakefield's Queen Elizabeth Grammar School, and by his decision, at age seventeen, to become an artist. This determination involved him in a class and family struggle. Two years at Wakefield College of Art were made more desolate by his teachers' pressuring him to become a commercial artist. Next, disappointed by his failure to train for a professional life, his parents refused to sign his application form to the Slade School of Fine Art in London. Then, in order to support himself fully while in school, Storey played professionally for Leeds Rugby League Club for four seasons. In a 1982 interview, he commented on the psychological strain of living in two opposing worlds: "When I played football the other players thought I was homosexual, and at the Slade, they thought I was a yob [hooligan]." Storey's move to London was final; his marriage to Barbara Rudd Hamilton in 1956 has brought him two sons and two daughters. His painting won for him several prizes, but it was to writing that Storey dedicated himself after leaving art school.

Storey's Leeds experiences are evident in *This Sporting Life*, the story of professional rugby footballer Arthur Machin's tender but abortive affair with his downtrodden landlady, and his discovery that material "success" (as defined by both the working and the middle classes of England in the newly prosperous late 1950's) cannot bring a sense of wholeness of belonging. The novel was the eighth that Storey had written (he has continued to write far more than he publishes) and went the rounds of more than a dozen publishers over a four-year period before it was finally accepted. Similarly, Storey's first play, *The Restoration of Arthur Middleton*, was written nine years before its first production. The difficulties of Storey's early years ended when in 1960 *This Sporting Life* won for him the Macmillan Fiction Award, the icing on the cake of widespread critical acclaim. Numerous other awards have included Great Britain's most prestigious literary award, the Booker-McConnell Prize, for his autobiographical *Saville* in 1976. Awards for his dramas, above all *The Contractor*, *Home* (set in an insane asylum), and *The Changing Room*, have included the *Evening Standard* Award in 1967, and the New York Drama Critics Circle Award in 1971, 1973, and 1974.

This Sporting Life also led to an intense and fruitful working friendship with the film and play director Lindsay Anderson, for whom Storey wrote screen versions of both his first novel and his play *In Celebration*, in which three "successful" sons briefly return home to their working-class family (*A Prodigal Child* is one of Storey's later explorations of this autobiographical theme of the return). *In Celebration* exemplifies how Storey's work balances on a knife-edge between black melodrama and stoic satire: The film, he has said, "came out as very remorseless, . . . whereas the audiences always laughed heartily at the live production" (*Mother's Day*, by way of analogy, is a farce about incest). Over the course of his career, Storey has moved away from the schematizing and allegorizing of his first three novels toward letting his material dictate his form. His hugely ambitious third novel, *Radcliffe* (compared by critics to Emily Brontë's *Wuthering Heights*, 1847; though also condemned as morbid Gothic fantasy), had been predicated on what Storey sees as the original sin of decadent Western society—the division between soul and body, which in *Radcliffe* is paralleled by the division between an enfeebled upper class and a vigorous but philistine lower class, figured in the destructive homosexual relationship of Leonard Radcliffe and "Vic" Tolson, a working-class giant drawn with demoniac energy. A similar decadence of society breeds the breakdowns of the central characters in *Pasmore* and *A Temporary Life*.

Storey's plays, unlike his novels, are loosely plotted, poetic evocations of situations and relationships, far more psychological in method and intent than the novels, although frequently intimately related to them: *The Contractor*, for example, dramatizes and expands one episode from *Radcliffe*, the erecting of a huge show marquee for a wedding; *The Changing Room* picks up on the last scene of *This Sporting Life* (a climactic rugby match), focusing on what Storey has called the "rituals" of men gathered into groups, where their individual personalities, as well as their clothes, may undergo "change"; *In Celebration* dramatizes psychological material Storey decided mostly to leave out of *Saville*, and was written during a period when work on the novel had ground to a halt.

Storey's slowly written novels, and his swiftly written plays, also share a quality of distance: The dialogue of both often has a very British quality of unemotional understatement, difficult to read for some Americans; indeed, all communication in *Home* takes place in evasive euphemisms. A similar distance informs Storey's use of autobiographical material: Clearly, his work depends on it, but his imagination transforms it. Lastly, both plays and novels are powerfully visual. Storey has said that he envisages his plays as moving paintings, with the proscenium arch as a "picture frame." Similarly, much of the enormous and disturbing energy of his novels is stored in their imagery and descriptions: Landscapes can become Kafkaesque states of mind.

BIBLIOGRAPHICAL REFERENCES: William Hutchings, *The Plays of David Storey: A Thematic Study*, 1988, is a comprehensive analysis, drawing on an extensive interview with Storey for useful background information. John Russell Taylor's 1974 pamphlet *David Storey* is useful but somewhat dated. Mary Eagleton and David Pierce, *Attitudes to Class in the English Novel*, 1979, has a sensitive account of *Pasmore*; *The Uses of Fiction: Essays on the Modern Novel in Honour of Arnold Kettle*, 1987, edited by Douglas Jefferson and Martin Graham, includes David Craig's interesting account, "David Storey's Vision of the Working Class." Randall Stevenson, *The British Novel Since the Thirties: An Introduction*, 1986, is useful for its brief contextualization of Storey's work. An excellent introduction to his work as a whole is his 1982 interview with John Haffenden, published in Haffenden's *Novelists in Interview*, 1985. On the plays, see also Phyllis R. Randall, "Division and Unity in David Storey," in *Essays on Contemporary British Drama*, 1981, edited by Hedwig Rock and Albert Wertheim; Lewis F. Shelton, "David Storey and the Invisible Event," *Midwest Quarterly*, XXII (1981), 397-406; William J. Free and Lynn Page Whittaker, "The Intrusion Plot in David Storey's Plays," *Papers on Language and Literature*, XVIII (1987), 151-165; and Austin E. Quigley, "The Emblematic Structure and Setting of David Storey's Plays," *Modern Drama*, XXII (1979), 259-276.

Joss Marsh

RANDOLPH STOW

Born: Geraldton, Australia
Date: November 28, 1935

PRINCIPAL WORKS

NOVELS: *A Haunted Land*, 1956; *The Bystander*, 1957; *To the Islands*, 1958; *Tourmaline*, 1963; *The Merry-Go-Round in the Sea*, 1965; *Visitants*, 1979; *The Girl Green as Elderflower*, 1980; *The Suburbs of Hell*, 1984.

POETRY: *Act One*, 1957; *Outrider*, 1962; *A Counterfeit Silence: Selected Poems*, 1969.

Randolph Stow was born in 1935 in Geraldton, Western Australia, where his father was a lawyer. The largely autobiographical novel *The Merry-Go-Round in the Sea* gives an account of his childhood experiences there. His first novel, *A Haunted Land*, and most of the poems in *Act One* were written while he was an undergraduate at the University of Western Australia. He spent his years there studying English and French literature and avidly reading in other European literatures. The reading of these years shows in a number of his novels, but especially in the rich allusiveness of *To the Islands*. *The Bystander*, Stow's second novel, was written after he was graduated. In 1957, Stow worked for some months on an Aboriginal mission in the northwestern corner of Australia, and from his experiences there was born his masterpiece, *To the Islands*, one of the best Australian novels of the twentieth century. *Tourmaline*, too, in the geographical isolation of its setting, reflects his sense at the mission of being at the world's end, as if he were at a remote settlement within the remote settlement of Western Australia.

After studying anthropology at the University of Sydney, Stow worked as an assistant anthropologist in the Trobriand Islands off northeastern New Guinea until he underwent a physical and emotional collapse there. Written twenty years later, *Visitants* is based upon these experiences. In 1960, Stow traveled to England, where, with some interruptions, he has continued to reside. Soon after arriving in England, Stow was awarded a Harkness Fellowship in the United States, where he wrote *The Merry-Go-Round in the Sea*, a rather happy account of his childhood. The next fourteen years were nonproductive from a literary viewpoint, but *Visitants* was quickly followed by *The Girl Green as Elderflower*. In the ten years after *The Girl Green as Elderflower*, Stow published only one book, *The Suburbs of Hell*. *Outrider*, Stow's second book of verse, was published after he moved to England. The main book of his verse, however, is *A Counterfeit Silence*. Although much of his best work is in his poetry, Stow has not written poetry with any regularity since the 1960's.

Stow is one of the earliest of a group of Australians who during the period of the 1960's to the 1980's have written both fiction and poetry—writers such as Bruce Beaver, David Malouf, Roger McDonald, and Rodney Hall. That association of genres is especially a phenomenon of this time, an expression perhaps of the breakdown of formal distinctions between genres. Few of these writers, however, have written novels strong in narrative content; their novels, like Stow's, tend to be elusive, impalpable. In addition, Stow, as a number of critics have remarked, has always had difficulty in harmonizing romantic and realistic elements in his novels. The works which are freest of that difficulty are *To the Islands*, in which the level of poetic intensity is steadily maintained, and *The Merry-Go-Round in the Sea*, a warm and relaxed record of childhood years.

It is difficult to generalize about Stow, for each of his novels is different from the other; change rather than development characterizes his literary career. One finds in his work not so much recurrent themes as areas of interest: a penchant for the romantic (whether medieval or nineteenth century Romantic), the anthropological, and the modern French symbolists. Linear narrative and realism do not appeal to him. There are fewer restraints operating upon his poetry than upon his fiction, and the best of his poetry, especially his love poems (a rarity in the emotionally inhibited literature of Australia), is more accessible than his novels. Stow's works, like the man himself, are elusive and, except in the case of the two novels mentioned, have a withheld quality about them. The events and personages of his novels are always seen at a distance and are obscured underneath the technical experimentation. As early as in the epigraph to *A Counterfeit Silence*, Stow betrayed an ambivalence toward writing, a reluctance to communicate in words. The quotation is from Thornton Wilder: "Even speech was for them a debased form of silence; how much more futile is poetry, which is a debased form of speech." Since *The Merry-Go-Round in the Sea*, Stow seems to be temporizing, unwilling to let go an admiring public and a substantial reputation but unwilling, too, to commit himself to a work of serious import.

BIBLIOGRAPHICAL REFERENCES: Ray Willbanks, *Randolph Stow*, 1978, is a good introduction to Stow's career and major work. Anthony Hassall, *Strange Country: A Study of Randolph Stow*, 1986, is a more academic study and covers Stow's later work. See also Helen Watson-Williams, "Randolph Stow's Suffolk Novel," *Westerly*, XXV (December, 1980), 68-72; John Beston, "The Theme of Reconciliation in Stow's *To the Islands*," *Modern Fiction Studies*, XXVII (1981), 95-107; S. A. Ramsey, "The Silent Griefs: Randolph Stow's *Visitants*," *Critical Quarterly*, XXIII (1981), 73-81; George Moore, "Island of Ascent: The Australasian Novels of Randolph Stow," *International Fiction Review*, XIII (1986), 61-68; Derek Wright, "The Mansren Myth in Randolph Stow's *Visitants*," *International Fiction Review*, XIII (1986), 82-86; Bruce King, *Antipodes* (Dallas), I (1987), 75-78; and George Moore, "Randolph Stow's *Tourmaline* and *To the Islands*," *International Fiction Review*, XIV (1987), 68-74.

John B. Beston

BOTHO STRAUSS

Born: Naumburg an der Saale, Germany
Date: December 2, 1944

PRINCIPAL WORKS

PLAYS: *Peer Gynt: Nach Henrik Ibsen*, pb. 1971; *Die Hypochonder*, pr. 1971; *Prinz Friedrich von Homburg: Nach Heinrich von Kleist*, pb. 1972; *Bekannte Gesichter, gemischte Gefühle*, pb. 1974; *Sommergäste: Nach Maxim Gorky*, pb. 1974; *Trilogie des Wiedersehens*, pr. 1975 (*Three Acts of Recognition*, 1981); *Gross und Klein: Szenen*, pb. 1978 (*Big and Little*, 1979); *Kalldewey: Farce*, pb. 1981; *Der Park*, pb. 1983.

POETRY: *Unüberwindliche Nähe*, 1976; *Diese Erinnerung an einen, der nur einen Tag zu Gast war*, 1985.

NOVELS: *Schützenehre*, 1974; *Marlenes Schwester*, 1975; *Die Widmung*, 1977 (*Devotion*, 1979); *Rumor*, 1980; *Paare, Passanten*, 1981; *Der junge Mann*, 1984 (*The Young Man*, 1989); *Die Fremdenführerin*, 1986.

Botho Strauss was born on December 2, 1944, to middle-class parents in the Ruhr region of Germany. He attended school in that area and went on to study German literature, theater history, and sociology at the University of Cologne and the University of Munich during the early 1960's. From 1967 to 1970, he served as critic and editor of the well-known West German journal, *Theater heute*. Since 1970, he has worked as a producer with the theatrical group Schaubühne am Hallischen Ufer and resides as an independent author in Berlin. Strauss has received a number of literary prizes and awards, and several of his works have been made into films.

Strauss's writings present examples of the style that has been termed the "New Subjectivity," a trend that emerged in German literature during the early 1970's. The works of Peter Handke and Karin Struck are also included in this movement. Many of the writers of the 1960's had focused on political themes and had sought to promote a socially committed literature. Authors such as Strauss and Handke, however, began to write about more personal themes of the individual's existential and psychological alienation. Strauss's texts seek to uncover not the political factors that shape the individual's existence but rather the unconscious and irrational forces that seem to determine so much of the conscious personality. This focus is motivated, in part at least, by the belief that true social change must first begin within the self.

Strauss's first major play, *Die Hypochonder* (the hypochondriacs), is set in Amsterdam in 1901 and involves a rather complicated murder-mystery plot. The traditional conventions of this genre—open questions concerning the identity of the murderer and the motivation for the act—make the concepts of interpretation, meaning, and a transcendent order to events problematic. Strauss's deliberately convoluted plot confounds notions of "reality" and forces the viewer to confront his subjectivity and the essential impenetrability of experience. *Three Acts of Recognition*, one of Strauss's better-known plays, presents a series of characters who are visiting an art exhibition and who, as they come and go on the stage, make observations on topics such as art, love and marriage, careers, and friendships. The plot serves as a vehicle for Strauss's comments on the complex and alienating nature of modern life and the various types of personalities that modern society has produced. Many of the characters suffer from a profound sense of isolation and an inability to establish true communication with others. The play moves along on a disturbing note of pessimism about the nature of human relationships.

The play *Big and Little* is written in the manner of many expressionist dramas such as the *Stationendramen* of Georg Kaiser. It consists of ten connected but not continuous scenes involving the life of a woman named Lotte. Her husband has left her for another woman and, disillusioned, she tries to promote an idealistic message of love and forgiveness to those she sees. The people that she meets in the various scenes are all representative of the existential emptiness, the essential lack of spiritual significance, that Strauss sees as characteristic of modern life. Lotte becomes deeply emotionally disturbed by what she encounters and the play ends on this pessimistic note. The novel *Devotion* deals with a man, Richard Schroubek, who is writing a chronicle of his love affair with Hannah Beyl, who has recently left him. Such moments of loss, abandonment, and dislocation all mark the experience of Strauss's characters and initiate their reflections upon the self and others. Schroubek's document of self-examination, which is at times rather morbid and ironic, has a therapeutic effect and he believes that he has put his emotions in perspective. When he finally sees her again, however, he is disillusioned and the whole affair no longer seems to make any sense. Strauss's figures are all involved at some level in a quest to make sense of their feelings. *Rumor* (noise) is another novel in which the main character, Bekker, is extremely isolated from others and, as a result, prone to anger and violence. He reacts strongly against a world in which power games dictate the nature of relationships. Bekker's experience of himself and others becomes gradually more fragmented and frustrated.

The Young Man consists of several sections held together by the ironic reflections of the narrator, Leon Pracht. It is a somewhat autobiographical "novel of education" and also bears a faint resemblance to the eighteenth century German novels of that same genre, Novalis' *Heinrich von Ofterdingen* (1802; *Henry of Ofterdingen*, 1842) and Johann Wolfgang von Goethe's *Wilhelm Meisters Lehrjahre* (1795-1796; *Wilhelm Meister's Apprenticeship*, 1824). As is common with Strauss's works, this text is an extended rumination on the quality of life in the depersonalized and anonymous modern world. The introduction contains the narrator's reflections on the romantic form of his novel and his "poetic" journey. In the first section, Leon has left his work in the theater world and has become a writer. He is obsessed with ideas about life in the nuclear era. In the novel's second section, he observes an alternative society—the "Synkreas"—in which man's creative and artistic faculties would be wholly utilized. The third section deals with a businesswoman who has a profound spiritual experience after a series of horrible visions and nightmares. She commits herself to a life of love and unselfish activity. Strauss suggests that the compulsive pursuit of material goods so prevalent in Western culture is motivated by an existential fear of death. In the section entitled "The Tower," Leon meets with the film producer Ossia in a high-technology hotel, and they discuss theories of art. The novel ends with Leon alone since his girlfriend, Yossica, has left him to pursue her own artistic career.

Strauss's writings present a critical view—an often ironic unmasking—of life in twentieth century postindustrial society and can best be understood as a necessary counterpoint to the political and sociological preoccupations of German authors during the 1960's. They produce a profound and rather bleak vision of the psychological stresses and existential alienation that define the modern individual's sense of self: plagued by crippling neuroses and a spiritual vacuum that limit one's capacity for self-knowledge and stifle the ability to establish genuine intimacy with other human beings.

BIBLIOGRAPHICAL REFERENCES: For background information and a section on Strauss's works, see Linda C. DeMeritt, *New Subjectivity and Prose Forms of Alienation: Peter Handke and Botho Strauss*, 1987. Leslie Adelson, *Crisis of Subjectivity: Botho Strauss's Challenge to West German Prose of the 1970's*, 1984, presents an excellent introduction in English. For reviews of Strauss's most representative work, *Devotion*, see Lore Dickstein, *Saturday Review*, VI (July 21, 1979), 50; Inge Judd, *Library Journal*, CIV (July, 1979), 1487; and Nicholas Shrimpton, *New Statesman*, XCIX (February 29, 1980), 325.

Thomas F. Barry

ARKADY STRUGATSKY and BORIS STRUGATSKY

Arkady Strugatsky

Born: Batumi, Georgia, Soviet Union
Date: August 28, 1925

Boris Strugatsky

Born: Leningrad, Soviet Union
Date: April 15, 1933

Principal Works

NOVELS: *Izvne*, 1960; *Strana bagrovykh tuch*, 1960; *Popytka k begstvu*, 1962 (*Escape Attempt*, 1982); *Dalekaya raduga*, 1964 (*Far Rainbow*, 1964); *Khishchnye veshchi veka*, 1965 (*The Final Circle of Paradise*, 1976); *Ponedel'nik nachinayetsya v subbotu*, 1965 (*Monday Begins on Saturday*, 1977); *Trudno byt' bogom*, 1966 (*Hard to Be a God*, 1973); *Ulitka na sklone*, 1966-1968 (*The Snail on the Slope*, 1980); *Skazka o troyke*, 1968 (*Tale of the Troika*, 1977); *Vtoroe nashestvie Marsian*, 1968 (*The Second Invasion of Mars*, 1979); *Obitayemyy ostrov*, 1969 (*Prisoners of Power*, 1977); *Malysh*, 1971; *Gadkie lebedi*, 1972 (*The Ugly Swans*, 1979); *Piknik na obochine*, 1972 (*Roadside Picnic*, 1977); *Za milliard let do knotsa sveta*, 1976-1977 (*Definitely Maybe: A Manuscript Discovered Under Unusual Circumstances*, 1978); *Zhuck v muraveinike*, 1979-1980 (*Beetle in the Anthill*, 1980); *Volny gasyat veter*, 1985-1986 (*The Time Wanderers*, 1987); *Khromaya sud'ba*, 1986.

SHORT FICTION: *Put' na Amal'teyu*, 1960 (*Destination Amalthea*, 1962); *Vozvrashchenie (polden', XXII vek)*, 1962 (*Noon: Twenty-second Century*, 1978).

Arkady Natanovich and Boris Natanovich Strugatsky are the best-known Russian science-fiction writers in America, and are honored for their wit and imagination. The older of the brothers, Arkady Strugatsky, was born on August 28, 1925, in Batumi, Georgia; Boris' birth followed almost eight years later on April 15, 1933, when the family of Natan Strugatsky, a bibliographer, and Aleksandra Litvinchova, a teacher, had moved to Leningrad. After World War II, both brothers went to university; their different degrees make them an ideal team as science-fiction writers, and, in consequence, all of their work is written together.

Arkady is the "linguist" of the team, and uses his degree from the Russian Institute of Foreign Languages, which he earned in 1949, to work joyfully at coining futuristic jargon, describing aliens, or mimicking the language of bureaucracies all over the known (and unknown) cosmos. Married to Elena Oshanina, a sinologist, in 1955, Arkady worked as an editor and translator of English and Japanese until 1964, when the brothers decided to become full-time writers. With a degree in astronomy from Leningrad University (earned in 1956), Boris Strugatsky is the team's "resident scientist"; his position was perhaps reinforced by his 1957 marriage to Adelaida Karpeliuk, a fellow astronomer. Because Boris worked in his field until 1964, he has brought experience at first hand of the world—and the frustrations—of a scientist to the brothers' literary creations; they focus on grotesque struggles with bureaucracy, such as those depicted with a perfect satiric pen in *The Snail on the Slope*, in which the last order of the day, issued by the chief scientist (and now director), requires the "eradication" of the "Eradicators."

When the Strugatskys began writing science fiction in the early 1960's, their short pieces, which are collected in *Noon: Twenty-second Century* and *Destination Amalthea*, were the Soviet equivalents of the "space operas" of American writers such as Robert A. Heinlein and Arthur C. Clarke; typically, the Strugatskys' forecast follows the prescriptions of Marxism-Leninism. Thus, the society of their award-winning tale of a Venus exploration, *Strana bagrovykh tuch* (the country of the purple clouds), sees the death-pangs of capitalism, and the further time advances, the closer to universal acceptance Communism comes. In the mid-1960's, however, the Strugatskys turned away from such orthodoxy. *Hard to Be a God* features a protagonist whose desire to accelerate class warfare on an alien planet leads to something of a disaster, and the 1969 novel *Prisoners of Power* portrays a despairing hero in a strange country which clearly resembles Stalinist Russia.

Such critical elements brought the Strugatskys into disfavor during the Leonid Breshnev era, and most of their work in the 1970's could be published only in magazines. After their brilliant satire *The Snail on the Slope*, however, the Strugatskys turned to more straightforward science fiction. The 1972 novel *Roadside Picnic*, wherein scientists and rogues try to utilize alien "leftovers," stands at the beginning of an overhaul of the Strugatskys' universe. Arraigned around the central enigma of "the Wanderers," story after story traces the effects of this old, alien race on future humans.

In 1981, the Strugatskys were awarded the prestigious Aelita Prize by the Union of Soviet Writers for their novel *Beetle in the Anthill*. Here, the plot asks whether the quest to decipher an alien master plan for man's fate is pure paranoia or a legitimate search for higher powers (the aliens standing in for dead gods), whose schemes would come as close to giving existence a purpose as is possible in a postmodern universe. As these questions are explored further in their later novels such as *The Time Wanderers*, the Strugatskys continue to touch upon issues of man's destiny and moral responsibility and to shed sarcastic light on the modus operandi of an Earth-wide bureaucracy which bears both universal and specifically Soviet traits.

BIBLIOGRAPHICAL REFERENCES: A good source is Patrick L. McGuire, "Future History, Soviet Style: The Work of the Strugatsky Brothers," in *Critical Encounters II*, 1982, edited by Tom Staicar; McGuire is one of the brothers' translators, and his chapter analyzes development and change in the texts which share a common future world. McGuire's article "Arkady and Boris Strugatsky," in *Anatomy of Wonder: A Critical Guide to Science Fiction*, 1987, edited by Neil Barron, has a comprehensive bibliography. Darko Suvin, "The Literary Opus of the Strugatskii Brothers," *Canadian-American Slavic Studies*, VIII (1974), 454-463, is a thorough and intelligent presentation. For further study, see also Istvan Csicsery-Ronay, "Toward the Last Fairy Tale: On the Fairy-Tale Paradigm in the Strugatskys' Science Fiction," *Science Fiction Studies*, XIII (1986), 1-41; Vladimir Gakov, "A Test of Humanity: About the Work of the Strugatsky Brothers," *Soviet Literature*, VIII (1982), 154-161; S. Simonetta and R. M. Philmus, "The Science Fiction Films of Andrei Tarkovsky," *Science Fiction Studies*, XIV (1987), 294-306; "A Talk with Arkadi Strugatsky," *Soviet Literature*, XII (1986), 36-40; Diana Greene, "Male and Female in *The Snail on the Slope* by the Strugatsky Brothers," *Modern Fiction Studies*, XXXII (1986), 97-108; Raphael Aceto and R. M. Philmus, "The Ambiguous Miracle in Three Novels by the Strugatsky Brothers," *Science Fiction Studies*, XI (1984), 291-303; Stanisław Lem and Elsa Schieder, "About the Strugatskys' *Roadside Picnic*," *Science Fiction Studies*, X (1983), 317-332; and Alexander Fyodorov, "Arkadi Strugatsky: 'Man Must Always Be Man,'" *Soviet Literature*, IX (1983), 113-123.

Reinhart Lutz

JESSE STUART

Born: W-Hollow, Riverton, Kentucky
Date: August 8, 1907

Died: W-Hollow, Riverton, Kentucky
Date: February 17, 1984

PRINCIPAL WORKS

NOVELS: *Trees of Heaven*, 1940; *Taps for Private Tussie*, 1943; *Mongrel Mettle*, 1944; *Foretaste of Glory*, 1946; *Hie to the Hunters*, 1950; *The Good Spirit of Laurel Ridge*, 1953; *Daughter of the Legend*, 1965; *Mr. Gallion's School*, 1967; *The Land Beyond the River*, 1973.

SHORT FICTION: *Head o' W-Hollow*, 1936; *Men of the Mountains*, 1941; *Tales from the Plum Grove Hills*, 1946; *Clearing in the Sky and Other Stories*, 1950; *Plowshare in Heaven*, 1958; *My Land Has a Voice*, 1966; *The Best-Loved Short Stories of Jesse Stuart*, 1982.

POETRY: *Harvest of Youth*, 1930; *Man with a Bull-Tongue Plow*, 1934; *Album of Destiny*, 1944; *Kentucky Is My Land*, 1952; *Hold April*, 1962; *The World of Jesse Stuart: Selected Poems*, 1975.

AUTOBIOGRAPHY: *Beyond Dark Hills*, 1938; *The Thread That Runs So True*, 1949; *The Year of My Rebirth*, 1956; *God's Oddling*, 1960; *To Teach, To Love*, 1970; *My World*, 1975; *The Kingdom Within: A Spiritual Autobiography*, 1979.

ESSAYS: *Lost Sandstones and Lonely Skies and Other Essays*, 1979; *If I Were Seventeen Again and Other Essays*, 1980.

Jesse Stuart is one of the more remarkable and original writers in American literature. Amazingly prolific, with more than sixty books in a variety of genres, Stuart produced work that was largely uneven. It has been as much admired by a broad popular audience as it has been maligned, or ignored, by the mainstream of literary opinion. Born in a log cabin in W-Hollow in the hills of eastern Kentucky, Stuart was the first in his family to finish high school. He worked his way through Lincoln Memorial University, a small mountain college in Tennessee, from which he was graduated in 1929.

After two years of teaching and administrative experience in his native region, he attended Vanderbilt University, where he pursued but did not complete an M.A. in English. He was particularly drawn to Vanderbilt because of the presence there of the Fugitive-Agrarians, such poets, writers, and teachers as Donald Davidson, John Crowe Ransom, and Robert Penn Warren. Although Stuart sometimes seemed to confuse the moral, aesthetic, and philosophical bases of Nashville Agrarian thought with mere farming, he was certainly influenced profoundly by what he took to be the group's back-to-the-farm and anti-industrial arguments, as well as by its emphasis on the Southern sense of place, family, community, and language. The best record of Stuart's vision of these years is found in his first and finest autobiographical volume, *Beyond Dark Hills*, which was originally submitted as a term paper at Vanderbilt.

Man with a Bull-Tongue Plow, Stuart's first important book, appeared in 1934. This rough collection of 703 sonnets is a work of genuine force and energy. Stuart begins the volume with an announcement: "I am a farmer singing at the plow." He then carries the reader through the cycles of the seasons, the land, and the lives, loves, and deaths of the mountain country and people. The stance he assumes here, the primitive mountain bard, the poet of Appalachia, would remain his typical persona and most effective voice throughout his career. He had been profoundly influenced by the work of Robert Burns, and, with the appearance of this volume, Stuart was hailed as the American Burns. His later volumes of poetry never lived up to the power and freshness of this work.

With the publication of *Head o' W-Hollow*, Stuart's first collection of stories, he was hailed as an important writer of fiction with substantial gifts of humor, observation, and creative use of language based on mountain dialect and idiom. Through many volumes over the next four decades Stuart's fiction evoked this hillbilly world, until W-Hollow seemed, to some observers, to have earned a place akin to William Faulkner's Yoknapatawpha County in the literary geography of America. *Trees of Heaven*, his first novel, renders this world fully as it works out a love story between a squatter's daughter, Subrinea Tussie, and a landowner's son, Tarvin Bushman, against the thematic background of the squatter-landowner conflict. Through the patriarchal landowner Anse Bushman, Stuart powerfully renders what may be his single great theme: love of land, of farming, of drawing strength from the earth. *Taps for Private Tussie*, Stuart's next novel, continues the hilarious chronicle of the Tussies, the indolent hill clan committed to avoiding work, to eating, drinking, and dancing all night long. Immensely popular, this comic novel was a best-seller and received the Thomas Jefferson Award for the best Southern book of 1943.

Much of his life Stuart was a teacher, in the country schools of Kentucky and in colleges and universities as far afield as Egypt, where he taught for a year at the University of Cairo. Stuart thought teaching "the greatest profession under the sun," and in *The Thread That Runs So True* he paid tribute to the profession. This award-winning autobiographical hymn to teaching has at its center the dramatic presence of a man who walked twenty miles to carry a suitcase loaded with books to his poor mountain students. It was declared "the best book on education" written in the twentieth century by the president of the National Education Association, and it remains Stuart's most popular book.

In 1954, Stuart was named poet laureate of Kentucky. In the same year he suffered a severe heart attack. *The Year of My Rebirth* is his journal of the struggle back to life from his near-fatal heart attack. It is also a spiritual autobiography which weaves together his love of place and a motif of resurrection. Another strong presence in this meditation on life and death is his father, who had died shortly after Stuart's heart attack. A few years later, in *God's Oddling*, Stuart paid moving tribute to his father as farmer, earth poet, "giant of the earth."

Conservationist, farmer, teacher, and writer, Jesse Stuart lived a rich, eventful life. He imprinted W-Hollow deeply in the literary imagination of millions of readers. As a farmer-conservationist who eventually owned one thousand acres of his beloved valley, he planted thousands of trees, leaving his mark on the landscape of Kentucky. After his death in 1984, Stuart's bequest to the people established the Jesse Stuart Nature Preserve. Balanced assessment of Stuart's literary achievement was complicated during his lifetime by his insistent personal legend and by the uncritical enthusiasm of the popular press. His position as a major twentieth century local colorist is secure, but he may, with the passage of time, come to be seen in a more positive and less limited sense as a genuine voice of Appalachian consciousness and as one of the more important regional writers in American literature.

BIBLIOGRAPHICAL REFERENCES: Ruel E. Foster, in *Jesse Stuart*, 1968, provides one of the best overall assessments of Stuart's life and work, although this volume does not cover the complete career. H. Edward Richardson, *Jesse: The Biography of an American Writer*, 1984, is a complete chronicle of Stuart's life and contains useful insights into Stuart's prose and poetry. Mary Washington Clarke, *Jesse Stuart's Kentucky*, 1968, stresses aspects of folklore and folk life in Stuart's work and refines the definition of Stuart as regionalist. See also Wade Hall, *The Truth Is Funny: A Study of Jesse Stuart's Humor*, 1970; *Jesse Stuart: Essays on His Work*, 1977, edited by J. R. LeMaster and Mary Washington Clarke; and J. R. LeMaster, *Jesse Stuart: Kentucky's Chronicler-Poet*, 1980, and *Jesse Stuart: A Reference Guide*, 1979.

H. R. Stoneback

WILLIAM STYRON

Born: Newport News, Virginia
Date: June 11, 1925

Principal Works

NOVELS AND NOVELLAS: *Lie Down in Darkness*, 1951; *The Long March*, 1956; *Set This House on Fire*, 1960; *The Confessions of Nat Turner*, 1967; *Sophie's Choice*, 1979.
PLAY: *In the Clap Shack*, pr. 1972.
ESSAYS: *This Quiet Dust*, 1982.

William Styron has been described as the greatest Southern writer since William Faulkner. An only child, he was born in Newport News, Virginia, on June 11, 1925, to William Clark Styron and Pauline Margaret Styron, the latter of whom died when the author was a teenager. As a student at a private boys' school in Virginia, Styron performed miserably. His initial college studies were at Davidson College in North Carolina; he subsequently enlisted in the Marines in 1943 for two years of noncombative service. Following military duty, he received training in creative writing at Duke University, from which he was graduated in 1947. He then went to New York and worked several months for the publisher McGraw-Hill, an experience recaptured in the early chapters of *Sophie's Choice*. At that time, he started seriously working on his first novel, and he has continued to produce serious fiction since. He and his wife, Rose Burgunder Styron, have lived most of their adult lives in Roxbury, Connecticut.

Only two characteristics of Styron's fiction can be readily discerned, and they have to do with the Southern tradition and his style. Styron, somehow, at once is and is not a Southern writer. His fiction is grounded in the regionalism it transcends: The usual attributes of Southern literature, such as longing for the past and the guilt about slavery, are consistently present, but his works are not derivative of the usual formula. The style of his writing conveys a delicacy and a sensitivity to life, as well as a perception about what it means to be human, that is not found in the other Southern works. Yet Styron's subject matter and plots tend to center on the violent. His women characters, even Sophie Zawistowska of *Sophie's Choice*, seem weak, and his works are methodically set in a historical context the significance of which can only be guessed through interpretation.

Styron published his first novel, *Lie Down in Darkness*, in 1951. Winner of that year's Pulitzer Prize, *Lie Down in Darkness* is one of the most accomplished first novels ever written. It tells of the suicide of Peyton Loftis (Styron's version of Temple Drake and Blanche DuBois) which occurs as the first atom bombs are set off in Japan; radio reports of the destruction are received the day of her burial. Styron's novella *The Long March* opens with the pointless deaths of eight Marines who are killed when shells fall short of a target. This external violence is matched by the internal violence of Captain Mannix, who decides to resist the determination of Colonel Templeton that the surviving soldiers march the thirty-six miles back to their headquarters. The tension between Mannix and Templeton becomes an allegory of humankind's suffering as it struggles against the gods and fate. Styron revisited the conflict between Mannix and Templeton when he wrote *Set This House on Fire*. Cass Kinsolving is an infinitely suffering individual coping with inescapable, all-powerful, nonhuman forces represented by Mason Flagg. The violence of the novel has two main components: Francesca, an Italian peasant girl, is raped by Mason, who is then, in turn, murdered by Cass. The house to be set on fire is Cass himself, who comes to symbolize the world. From a news report, Cass learns that scientists have made yet another advanced nuclear bomb; thus the potential for man's self-destruction correlates with Cass's ability to destroy Flagg and thereby his own morality, and the murder he commits convincingly foretells nuclear holocaust.

In 1967, one of the most controversial novels of the decade appeared. *The Confessions of*

Nat Turner precipitated an immediate uproar. The work is based on an actual slave rebellion in Virginia in the early 1800's; Styron took a historical document, some twenty pages of "confessions" of Nat Turner, the leader of the rebellion, and extensively fictionalized the account. The work won for Styron the Pulitzer Prize, and he received both critical and popular acclaim. At the same time, a number of black readers strenuously objected to the work for several reasons: They did not approve of Styron's characterization of Nat Turner, who, they asserted, was emasculated and ineffectual and generally inaccurately portrayed. They also found the character too motivated by the desire to rape a white woman rather than to correct the evils of slavery. Styron was accused of writing for profit and sensation, not out of commitment to racial equity; historical inaccuracies in the narrative were pointed out and magnified. Styron responded to these charges in part by quoting from the "Author's Note" to the novel, in which he had written that *The Confessions of Nat Turner* was meant to be "less an 'historical novel' in conventional terms than a meditation on history."

The same methodology was at once apparent a dozen years later when Styron published *Sophie's Choice*. The slave plantation which had been the metaphor for suffering and inhumanity is revisited in the German torture and death camps in Poland, including Auschwitz. Violence, crime, and brutality—common denominators of existence—define humanity; a Nazi officer forces Sophie to choose which one of her two children will live and which will die. Subsequently, Sophie herself must choose whether to live or die—the son she had earlier chosen for survival disappears, as does the other main character of the novel, Stingo, Styron's persona. Some Jewish readers faulted the author's use of the Holocaust, but the objections did not match, either in number or in substance, those voiced about his previous novel.

Despite the controversy surrounding some of his writing, Styron's novels have lasted the test of time—and place. Throughout his career, Styron has methodically worked to escape being labeled a regional writer, and works such as *The Confessions of Nat Turner* and *Sophie's Choice* have enabled him to do just that.

BIBLIOGRAPHICAL REFERENCES: Styron's works have received a large amount of critical attention. Book-length studies treating the fiction written up to the date of their own publication include two collections of essays: *The Achievement of William Styron*, 1974, edited by Robert K. Morris and Irving Malin, and *Critical Essays on William Styron*, 1982, edited by Arthur D. Casciato and James L. W. West III. Marc L. Ratner wrote *William Styron*, 1972, for the Twayne series; he presents an excellent discussion of the first four novels. Another useful book is John Kenny Crane, *The Root of All Evil: The Thematic Unity of William Styron's Fiction*, 1984. Richard Foster published a discussion of *Set This House on Fire* in "An Orgy of Commerce: William Styron's *Set This House on Fire*," *Critique: Studies in Modern Fiction*, III (Summer, 1960), 59-70. *William Styron's "Nat Turner": Ten Black Writers Respond*, 1968, edited by John Henrik Clarke, is a collection which expresses sundry responses, mostly objections, to *The Confessions of Nat Turner* by black thinkers. Also helpful to understanding that work is George Core, "*The Confessions of Nat Turner* and the Burden of the Past," *The Southern Literary Journal*, II (Spring, 1970), 117-134, and Nancy M. Tischler has compiled "*The Confessions of Nat Turner*: A Symposium," *Barat Review*, VI (1971), 3-37. *Sophie's Choice* has been well discussed by Frederick C. Stern in "Styron's Choice," *The South Atlantic Quarterly*, LXXXII (Winter, 1983), 19-27, and Richard L. Rubenstein, "The South Encounters the Holocaust: William Styron's *Sophie's Choice*," *Michigan Quarterly Review*, XX (Fall, 1981), 425-442. Robert Coltrane discusses Styron's critical essays in "The Unity of *This Quiet Dust*," *Papers on Language and Literature*, XXIII (Fall, 1987), 480-488. Additionally, Jackson R. Bryer and Mary Beth Hatem have prepared *William Styron: A Reference Guide*, 1978. Bibliographies have been prepared by Philip W. Leon, published as *William Styron: An Annotated Bibliography of Criticism*, 1978, and by James L. W. West III, published as *William Styron: A Descriptive Bibliography*, 1977. An excellent overview of Styron's life and writings and criticism of his writings is provided by Melvin J. Friedman in *Fifty Southern Writers After 1900*, 1987, edited by Joseph M. Flora and Robert Bain.

Carl Singleton

ITALO SVEVO
Ettore Schmitz

Born: Trieste, Austria
Date: December 19, 1861

Died: Motta di Livenza, Italy
Date: September 13, 1928

PRINCIPAL WORKS

NOVELS: *Una vita*, 1892 (*A Life*, 1963); *Senilità*, 1898 (*As a Man Grows Older*, 1932); *La coscienza di Zeno*, 1923 (*Confessions of Zeno*, 1930).

SHORT FICTION: *La novella del buon vecchio e della bella fanciulla*, 1930 (*The Nice Old Man and the Pretty Girl and Other Stories*, 1930); *Corto viaggio sentimentale e altri racconti inediti*, 1949 (*Short Sentimental Journey and Other Stories*, 1966); *Further Confessions of Zeno*, 1969.

ESSAYS: *Saggi e pagini sparse*, 1954.

Italo Svevo is an important author whose works have never quite achieved popular success. He was born Ettore Schmitz in Trieste, in what was then Austria, in 1861, the fifth child of Jewish parents Francesco and Allegra Moravia Schmitz. The household was affluent, and Svevo's childhood was a happy one. His father, more through diligence than astuteness, had become a prosperous businessman, a feat of which he was intensely proud. Hoping that his sons would follow in his footsteps, in 1873 he sent Ettore and his brother Adolfo to business school in Germany, where Ettore displayed utter indifference to commerce, preferring philosophy and literature. Several years later, however, he found himself forced into the business world when his father's business dealings suddenly failed and Francesco, who had taken such pride in being self-made, spiraled into depression and senility. This event left a great mark on Svevo, who as a writer was to imbue his characters with a sort of self-induced senility. As a result of this catastrophe, Svevo went to work as a bank clerk to help support the family, and this job provided the inspiration for his first novel, *A Life*. Published in 1892 at his own expense, the book recounted, with the ironic character analysis that would be Svevo's stock-in-trade, the day-to-day existence of a daydreaming bank clerk. Six years later, he published a second novel, *As a Man Grows Older*, which describes a man's attempts to aggrandize his unremarkable love affair. Both books were ignored.

Svevo's marriage to his cousin Livia Veneziani in 1895 eventually afforded him a position in his father-in-law's very successful paint manufacturing company. Daydreaming and writing seemed inextricably bound for Svevo, so when he went to work for Livia's parents, he swore to abandon writing in order to concentrate on his job and, amazingly, kept his vow for more than two decades, indulging his creative desire only to the extent of producing an occasional article or short story for his own amusement. During these years, however, at least one person provided encouragement. Svevo had engaged an English tutor, a struggling Irish writer named James Joyce, to whom he gave copies of his books. To Svevo's surprise, Joyce responded enthusiastically, yet the books remained in oblivion until the paint factory temporarily closed during World War I and, twenty years after the publication of his last novel, Svevo's thoughts again returned to serious literature. He began to compose what is today generally acknowledged as his masterpiece, *Confessions of Zeno*, which he had published, again at his own expense, in 1923. This third book fell as flat as its predecessors had, and Svevo, who had entertained great hopes for it, became very depressed. His depression was soon alleviated. Joyce, now a well-respected writer, admired the novel and was able to get it reviewed by several prominent European critics who were almost unanimous in their praise. To say that Svevo became the toast of Europe would be an exaggeration; however, he was feted by the Parisian literary society, and he returned to Italy to find himself something of a mentor to a new generation of Italian writers. After so many years of public indifference, he enjoyed his newfound recognition tremendously. He died as the result of an automobile accident two years later, in 1928.

It seems natural that Svevo, with his interest in character analysis, would be intrigued by psychology, and *Confessions of Zeno* is one of the first significant novels to incorporate Freudian analysis. Zeno's "confessions" begin when a psychoanalyst suggests that Zeno write his memoirs in order to understand his compulsive cigarette smoking. The ensuing memoirs reflect Zeno's daydreams, delusions, neuroses, and rationalizations, and the reader finds himself thrust into the position of playing Zeno's therapist, trying to sort out the truth.

Svevo's novels are not primarily plotted works so much as slices of life designed to shed light upon the main character's unconscious motivations. His protagonists are willing victims of what Svevo called "senility"—habitual daydreaming leading to an inability to respond lucidly and directly to real life. Some of Svevo's early critics thought that his characters were weak and contemptible, implying that they did not represent the average man; yet the Svevian hero has emerged a successful portrait precisely because Svevo managed to depict a universal human tendency. Unlike his "healthy" characters, who take life in stride, Svevo's heroes seem to regard life as an immense project requiring much cerebral management. Even the smallest detail is absorbed and made self-conscious. When a man in a *caffè* tells Zeno how many muscles are used in the simple act of walking, Zeno finds, when he rises to leave, that he has acquired a slight limp. Emilio Brentano, in *As a Man Grows Older*, cannot relax and enjoy his love affair because he is too busy neurotically trying to "improve" his dull but beautiful mistress. Far from being contemptible, Svevo's heroes actually elicit the empathy of the reader, who is given to understand that all this neurosis and anxiety merely add up to a strange kind of *joie de vivre*.

Svevo's early detractors criticized not only the insignificance of his heroes but the insignificance of his prose style as well. Accustomed to beautiful prose, Italian critics regarded Svevo's style as mundane and lacking in poetry. Most modern critics, while admitting Svevo's style lacks distinction, do not perceive this as a major failing (some find that it actually complements his subject matter) and cite as Svevo's strengths his irony, his accuracy and integrity of perception, and his originality. As a result of the recognition of *Confessions of Zeno* as a major literary contribution, Svevo's first two books were resurrected and reevaluated. Today, *As a Man Grows Older* is regarded as a brilliant but somewhat lesser novel than *Confessions of Zeno*, while *A Life* is viewed as a flawed but exceedingly Linnovative first attempt. Two volumes of short stories, *Short Sentimental Journey and Other Stories* and *The Nice Old Man and the Pretty Girl and Other Stories*, as well as a collection of essays, were published posthumously and were well received. Yet Svevo has never reached the popular appeal it would seem he deserves, considering many critics regard two of his books as literary milestones. In Italy, he is very well known, more sporadically so in the rest of Europe, but in the United States, he remains virtually unknown.

BIBLIOGRAPHICAL REFERENCES: John Gatt-Rutter, *Italo Svevo: A Double Life*, 1988, is a comprehensive biographical study of Svevo. Beno Weiss, *Italo Svevo*, 1987, a volume in the Twayne series, offers a compact survey. P. N. Furbank, *Italo Svevo: The Man and the Writer*, 1966, is an extremely enjoyable account of Svevo's life and offers a thorough critique of almost all of his works. John Freccero, "Italo Svevo: Zeno's Last Cigarette," in *From "Verismo" to Experimentation: Essays on the Modern Italian Novel*, 1969, edited by Sergio Pacifici, provides detailed commentary on the central metaphor of Svevo's most important novel. Domenico Vittorini, "The Reaction to Naturalism," in *The Modern Italian Novel*, 1930, provides a brief contemporary assessment of Svevo. The introduction to *The Nice Old Man and the Pretty Girl and Other Stories*, 1930, is particularly illuminating, as it was penned by Eugenio Montale, an Italian critic who was an admirer and good friend of Svevo. Also of interest is "A Man Grows Older," in the March 30, 1962, edition of *The Times Literary Supplement*.

Susan Davis

GRAHAM SWIFT

Born: London, England
Date: May 4, 1949

PRINCIPAL WORKS

NOVELS: *The Sweet-Shop Owner*, 1980; *Shuttlecock*, 1981; *Waterland*, 1983; *Out of This World*, 1988.

SHORT FICTION: *Learning to Swim and Other Stories*, 1982.

Graham Swift is one of England's important contemporary novelists. Born in London on May 4, 1949, he did not directly experience the momentous events of the Depression-ridden 1930's, the world war of the early 1940's, or the difficult postwar problems of social and economic recovery, but his work has consistently concerned itself with history and its subtle influences. Swift, whose father was a government civil servant, attended Dulwich College in London, where he had been preceded half a century before by two other noted writers, Raymond Chandler and P. G. Wodehouse. He was graduated with a bachelor's degree from the University of Cambridge in 1970 and received his master's from the same university in 1975. He also attended the University of York. From the mid-1970's until the success of his third novel, *Waterland*, published in 1983, he was a part-time English instructor in London. His first novel, *The Sweet-Shop Owner*, was published in 1980, and his subsequent work has won for Swift much praise and many awards. *Waterland* was one of the finalists for the prestigious Booker Prize and was named by *The Guardian* as the best English novel of 1983.

The Sweet-Shop Owner contains a number of themes which have continued to occupy Swift. Willy Chapman, the protagonist, is the long-standing proprietor of a small London shop. His wife, now dead, married Willy to spite and to escape her family and provided the funds and the initial discipline that made the shop successful. The novel takes place on the last day of Chapman's life, and Swift illuminates Chapman's story by a series of flashbacks to his own history and to the relations with his wife and his estranged daughter, all governed by the long-established currents and rhythms of his ordered existence. On his last day, Willy—suffering from heart disease—rebels against those rhythms in the futile hope and expectation that his daughter will return. Personal history rather than the usual history of war and politics infuses the story; family relationships, or the lack of them, provide the story's focus; and alienation, personal and familial, and its unrequited quest for healing, is the overriding theme.

These concerns continue to dominate Swift's work. His second novel, *Shuttlecock*, published in 1981, is also a history of personal and familial alienation. Prentis, like Chapman, is a cog in society's machine, working as an archivist or researcher in the police bureaucracy; as Willy was dominated by his wife, so Prentis is subjected to his superior. Prentis' relations with his wife and son are also strained and convoluted. Again history and its permeability play a part in the story of Prentis' father, ostensibly a war hero who in reality was perhaps the opposite. There is no resolution to the problems raised in the novel, however, and the questions asked remain unanswered. In 1982 Swift published a series of short stories in *Learning to Swim and Other Stories*. "Learning to Swim" relates the tale of an unsatisfactory marriage, and in "The Watch" Swift tells a magic story of time and history. Some critics complained that the overall tone of the collection was too negative, that the lives portrayed were too painful. Nevertheless, many of them linger in the memory as archetypes of some aspects of the human condition.

Waterland was the novel that captured the attention of the critics. Swift's tale of Tom Crick, a history teacher, and Crick's story of his present life and past history—including the saga of his own ancestors—has been compared to the works of Charles Dickens, William Faulkner, and James Joyce. As often happens in Swift's writings, Crick's relationship with his childhood, his students, his wife, and the headmaster of the school where he teaches is difficult, consuming, and fated. Crick, in his fifties, is being made redundant: History is being cut back and merged with something called general studies. Yet the headmaster and the educational establishment are not being merely philistine; Crick himself has abandoned formal history—the history of the French Revolution—in order to relate the more intimate, personal history of himself, his ancestors, and the Fens, the waterlands of the title, of Eastern England. In addition, Crick's wife, unable to have a child of her own, had kidnapped an infant, was apprehended, and is in a mental institution. The Fens—flat but always changing from land to water and back again—become a metaphor for the convolutions between past and present, between sons and fathers, husbands and wives, reality and imagination, history and fiction. Crick and his worlds reflect the themes that Swift had earlier explored: the impact of an earlier time, the aloneness and alienation of the individual, and the difficulty if not impossibility of relating to others.

Swift followed *Waterland* with *Out of This World*, published in 1988. Here the author again works with generational relationships, this time between a sixtyish photographer, Harry Beech, currently photographing from the air the prehistoric remains of England, and his daughter Sophie, who is undergoing analysis in New York. Experiences, the past, and history itself have all come between them, and Swift explores the attempt to restitch the rift, to transcend, somehow, what has occurred before. The chapters generally alternate between the first-person narratives of Harry and Sophie, with other voices remaining muted in the background. *Out of This World* is very much a Swiftian story in its themes of past happenings and insufficient love but nevertheless differs from *Waterland*. The historical context is not rooted in such a concrete geography as in the Fens of Norfolk. The title reflects the worlds of the photographer, capturing his pictures from above the earth, and his daughter, trying to reintegrate the remembrances of her story on the psychologist's couch.

In regard to his constant references to history and its echoes and its relationship to his novels and short stories, Swift has written, "Fiction is not fact, but it is not fraud. The imagination has the power of sheer, fictive invention, but it also has the power to carry us to truth, to make us arrive at knowledge we did not possess and even, looked at from a common point of view, thought we had no right to possess." If the real present is caught in the past of history, it might well be fiction that allows an escape from history.

BIBLIOGRAPHICAL REFERENCES: In "Throwing Off Our Inhibitions," *The Times*, March 5, 1988, 20, Swift has discussed the craft of writing. His use of history has been explored by John Brewer and Stella Tillyard, "History and Telling Stories: Graham Swift's *Waterland*," *History Today*, XXXV (January, 1985), 49-51. See also the following reviews of his work: Alan Hollinghurst, "Falling Short," *The Times Literary Supplement*, August 27, 1982, 920, and "Of Time and the River," *The Times Literary Supplement*, October 7, 1983, 1073; Michael Gorra, "Silt and Sluices," *The Nation*, CCXXXVIII (March 31, 1984), 392-394, and "When Life Closes In," *The New York Times Book Review*, XC (June 23, 1985), 11-12; Peter S. Prescott, "Faulkner of the Fens," *Newsweek*, April 30, 1984, 75-76; Walter Clemons, "A Swift Arrival," *Newsweek*, June 24, 1985, 74; William H. Pritchard, "The Body in the River Leem," *The New York Times Book Review*, LXXXIX (March 25, 1984), 9; Michael Wood, "Haunted Places," *The New York Review of Books*, XXXI (August 16, 1984), 47-48; Linda Gray Sexton, "The White Silence of Their Lives," *The New York Times Book Review*, XCIII (September 11, 1988), 14; Anne Duchene, "By the Grace of the Teller," *The Times Literary Supplement*, March 11-17, 1988, 275; and Philip Howard, "Camera Ergo Sum," *The Times* (London), March 10, 1988, 19.

Eugene S. Larson

JUN'ICHIRŌ TANIZAKI

Born: Tokyo, Japan
Date: July 24, 1886

Died: Yugawara, Japan
Date: July 30, 1965

Principal Works

NOVELS AND NOVELLAS: *Chijin no ai*, 1924 (*Naomi*, 1985); *Manji*, 1928-1930; *Tade kuu mushi*, 1928-1929 (*Some Prefer Nettles*, 1955); *Bushūkō hiwa*, 1931-1932 (*The Secret History of the Lord of Musashi*, 1982); *Sasameyuki*, 1943-1948 (*The Makioka Sisters*, 1957); *Shōshō Shigemoto no haha*, 1950 (*The Mother of Captain Shigemoto*, 1956); *Kagi*, 1956 (*The Key*, 1960); *Fūten rōjin nikki*, 1961-1962 (*Diary of a Mad Old Man*, 1965).

SHORT FICTION: "Kirin," 1910; "Shisei," 1910 ("The Tattooer," 1963); "Shōnen," 1910; "Hōkan," 1911; "Akuma," 1912; "Kyōfu," 1913 ("Terror," 1963); "Otsuya goroshi," 1913; "Watakushi," 1921 ("The Thief," 1963); "Aoi Hano," 1922 ("Aguri," 1963); "Mōmoku monogatari," 1931 ("A Blind Man's Tale," 1963); "Ashikari," 1932 (English translation, 1936); "Shunkinshō," 1933 ("A Portrait of Shunkin," 1936); *Hyofu*, 1950; "Yume no ukihashi," 1959 ("The Bridge of Dreams," 1963); *Yume no ukihashi*, 1960; *Kokumin no bungaku*, 1964; *Tanizaki Jun'ichirō shu*, 1970; *Seven Japanese Tales*, 1981.

MEMOIRS: *Yōshō-jidai*, 1957 (*Childhood Years: A Memoir*, 1988).

ESSAYS: *In'ei raisan*, 1934 (*In Praise of Shadows*, 1955).

Jun'ichirō Tanizaki explored Japanese traditionalism and the male infatuation with dominant women in a wide-ranging body of work embracing novels, novellas, short stories, plays, and essays. He was the son of the struggling owner of a printing establishment and spent his childhood growing up in the Nihonbashi section of Tokyo. His mother was quite attractive, and the young Tanizaki, as later autobiographical statements attest, was enthralled by her beauty. He was a handsome youth, often bullied by his classmates. In primary school, his precociousness was recognized by a teacher who guided him in exploring the Japanese and Chinese classics, giving him an early appreciation of traditions and literary aesthetics. At the First Municipal High School in Tokyo, he was an outstanding student and went on to study in the Japanese literature department at Tokyo Imperial University, where he joined the student literary magazine *Shinshichō* (new thought tides). Since he could not pay his university fees, he did not finish his degree studies, choosing instead to pursue writing as a career.

The first substantial works were two plays published in 1910, but it was "The Tattooer," an erotic short story describing the coming to life of a spider etched on the back of a drugged courtesan and the enraptured entrapment of the tattooer in the transformed beauty of his "victim," that launched his literary career. In 1911, this Poe-like creation and other works won for Tanizaki the praise of Nagai Kafū, a writer-critic whom Tanizaki admired and who characterized Tanizaki as a fellow struggler against the prevailing naturalist school of writing and its emphasis on describing reactions to real-life situations. Many of his early works—"Shōnen" (children), "Akuma" (demon), and "Kyōfu" (terror)—reflecting *fin de siècle* influences of Charles Baudelaire, Oscar Wilde, and Edgar Allan Poe and his personal infatuation with the hedonistic macabre, are characterized by "diabolism" (*akumashugi*), his preoccupation with the perverse and deviant.

Tanizaki was married for the first time in 1915, but this marriage, which ended in divorce in 1930, was complicated by a liaison between his wife and his friend, the writer Haruo Satō, and Tanizaki's fascination for his sister-in-law Seiko. The writer's involved personal life received autobiographical treatment in "Itansha no kanashimi" (sorrows of a heretic), about a gifted writer and the sadistic carnal attentions of his prostitute lover, and "Haha o kouru ki" (yearnings for my mother), published a year after his mother died, concerning the narrator's dream quest for his departed mother. These and other stories, serialized in magazines and newspapers, developed Tanizaki's fixation on female characters representative of the idealized mother or the domineering sexual siren ministering to the lustful desires of emotionally repressed men. Other important writings from this period include an autobiographical novel, a two-act play set in Edo, and a rare political novel, perhaps inspired by the Russian Revolution. Tanizaki also wrote plays in the early 1920's, exploring the theme of guilt and happiness involving two men competing for the love of one woman, and dallied with filmmaking. Important short stories from this period include "The Thief" and "Aguri."

On September 1, 1923, the great Kantō earthquake devasted the Tokyo-Yokohama region, prompting Tanizaki to move to the Osaka region. This move interrupted the writing of *Naomi*, a long work (reminiscent of *Pygmalion*) about the effort to change a Japanese bar girl into a sophisticated woman capable of mingling in refined circles with foreigners. For some years, Tanizaki had been intrigued by the West, considering Europe to be a more vibrant civilization than the Orient. Though his early stories explored dissolute Japanese themes shrouded in the native past, he had, nevertheless, an admiration for things Western, as seen in *Naomi*.

He continued a flirtation with a Western life-style while residing near the port city of Kobe with its large foreign enclave, but gradually he discovered in the more traditional ways of the Kansai region (especially as characterized by the softspoken women of the area) an appreciation for vestiges of a fading past which rekindled childhood memories of what was no longer available in a Tokyo being rebuilt into a modern city. This interest in the customs, language, and style of the Osaka-Kyoto-Nara region became manifest in his writings, particularly the serialized novels *Manji* and *Some Prefer Nettles*. The former explored the intertwined relationship of two men and two women who relate to shared events from their different perspectives. Tanizaki had the dialogue translated into the Kansai dialect to give the story a sense of location. *Some Prefer Nettles* went beyond the contemporary localism of *Manji* to mark a complete return to the author's nativist roots. Kaname, the main character, in the midst of a failing marriage complicated by a Eurasian prostitute who merely satisfies him and a wife Misako who is leaving him for her lover, becomes captivated by the harmonious traditional relationship between his father-in-law and his young mistress Ohisa. In exploring what is lacking in his own "modern" relationships and discovering what his in-law has in his, Kaname comes to an appreciation of old Japan.

Tanizaki married a young Kansai woman in 1931, but he soon became infatuated with Matsuko Morita (who became his third and last wife), the wife of a wealthy merchant, who inspired him to write "The Blind Man's Tale" and *The Secret History of the Lord of Musashi*. Other important works from this time are "Ashikari" and "A Portrait of Shunkin." These writings reflected what Tanizaki described in his 1934 essay *In Praise of Shadows* as a preference for the traditional aesthetic over glaring modernism.

The Makioka Sisters, a novel chronicling the history of a declining Osaka family in the prewar years, was banned by the wartime military authorities for its acceptance of Westernisms; when the book was fully published in the late 1940's, it won for him several awards and reestablished his reputation. Tanizaki returned to Heian Japan for inspiration in *The Mother of Captain Shigemoto* to reconstruct fictitiously the perverse romance of a famous courtier and her lover. The story of an aged professor's sexual dalliances related in his and his wife's diaries in *The Key*, published in the *Chūō Kōron* journal, was a huge success. "The Bridge of Dreams" once again delved into the theme of mother fixation. *Diary of a Mad Old Man*, a humorous account of love in old age, was his last major work. Analyses of Tanizaki's literary career usually focus on the transitions in his life and the resulting effects on his writings. The decadent fascination with fetishes, sadism, excreta, and other perversities found in his early fiction are attributed to personal sexual ambivalances stemming from his childhood maternal fixation and adult marriage problems, expressed in a writing style liberated by exposure to Western writers. With his move to the Kansai region and ensuing disenchantment with occidental modernity, Tanizaki is said to have turned to the Japanese past as a new source of exoticism. During this middle period, he eschewed current events, returning to the classical and medieval ages for inspiration. With the completion of *The Makioka Sisters*, he turned to the recent but disappearing past while accepting the modernity of the times. His postwar writings were freed from an obsession with the past, and his lifelong exploration of sensual idealism was resuscitated in his final works.

The shifts from occidentalism to orientalism or from diabolism to classicism that many see in Tanizaki's oeuvre are debatable. What transcends these speculations is the indisputable quality of literary craftsmanship shown in Tanizaki's mastery of language and sensory detail (smells, tastes, sounds, colors) employed in an exploration of the hedonistically decadent. Weak men sexually enraptured by demonic femmes fatales and haunting mother figures provide the motifs for delving into tradition and history. In 1927, the novelist Ryūnosuke Akutagawa criticized Tanizaki for his fixation on the fanciful and depraved at the cost of artistic value. Tanizaki rejected this critique, defending the "architectural beauty" of his writings. Indeed, despite the infatuation with prurient elements, his fiction captures an elemental Japaneseness expressed in an aesthetic of sensuality indelibly stamped with the author's personality.

BIBLIOGRAPHICAL REFERENCES: Donald Keene's chapter on Tanizaki in *Dawn to the West: Japanese Literature of the Modern Era (Fiction)*, 1984, combines a fine biographical study with an analysis of his works. A probing essay exploring Tanazaki's themes and comparing him with Osamu Dazai and Yukio Mishima is Donald Keene, "Three Modern Novelists," in *Landscapes and Portraits: Appreciations of Japanese Culture*, 1971. Edward G. Seidensticker, "Tanizaki Jun-ichirō, 1886-1965," *Monumenta Nipponica*, XXI, nos. 3/4, 249-265, critiques his writings and evaluates his standing among modern Japanese writers. Gwenn Boardman Peterson, *The Moon in the Water: Understanding Tanizaki, Kawabata, and Mishima*, 1979, contains interpretive chapters on Tanizaki plus a useful chronology and list of English translations. Hisaaki Yamanouchi discusses the theme of "eternal womanhood" as it relates to Tanizaki and Yasunari Kawabata in *The Search for Authenticity in Modern Japanese Literature*, 1978, and Makoto Ueda probes Tanizaki's literary concepts in *Modern Japanese Writers and the Nature of Literature*, 1976. Tanizaki's place in the aesthetic school is discussed in a 1968 work by Mitsuo Nakamura, *Modern Japanese Fiction, 1868-1926*. Arthur G. Kimball, *Crisis in Identity and Contemporary Novels*, 1973, analyzes *Diary of a Mad Old Man* as a representative work. Brief references to Tanizaki are in Irena Powell, *Writers and Society in Modern Japan*, 1983.

William M. Zanella

PETER TAYLOR

Born: Trenton, Tennessee
Date: January 8, 1917

PRINCIPAL WORKS

SHORT FICTION: *A Long Fourth and Other Stories*, 1948; *The Widows of Thornton*, 1954; *Happy Families Are All Alike*, 1959; *Miss Leonora When Last Seen and Fifteen Other Stories*, 1963; *The Collected Stories of Peter Taylor*, 1968; *In the Miro District and Other Stories*, 1977; *The Old Forest and Other Stories*, 1985.

PLAYS: *Tennessee Day in St. Louis*, pr. 1956; *A Stand in the Mountains*, pb. 1965; *Presences: Seven Dramatic Pieces*, pb. 1973.

NOVELS: *A Woman of Means*, 1950; *A Summons to Memphis*, 1986.

Though he has published several plays and novels, Peter Matthew Hillsman Taylor is best known as one of America's finest short-story writers. From the 1930's to the 1980's, his prizewinning narratives have continued to be regarded as major achievements in a golden age of short fiction writing. During an era of great social change, Taylor's publication record was amazingly steady.

The settings of his fiction and his focus on upper-middle-class Southern culture have roots in Taylor's own Tennessee background. Born in the country (in Trenton, Tennessee, on January 8, 1917), Taylor at age seven moved with his family to Nashville, two years later to St. Louis, and then in 1932 to Memphis, where, after graduation from high school and a brief trip abroad, he enrolled at Southwestern at Memphis and became acquainted with Allen Tate, who was his freshman English instructor. In the next few years, in the course of transferring to Vanderbilt University and then to Kenyon College, Taylor met the significant critic-teachers and nascent poets who would prove to be not only major literary influences but lifelong friends—Tate, John Crowe Ransom, Randall Jarrell, and Robert Lowell. The formalist strain in these associations, as well as Taylor's Southern consciousness, was enhanced by his brief encounters as a graduate student at Louisiana State University with Robert Penn Warren and Cleanth Brooks.

Taylor was one of the American writers of the post-World War II period who was nurtured by academia and the critical support it gave to a generation of creative artists. In turn, many of the writers, like Taylor, reciprocated by becoming themselves teachers in creative writing programs at various universities. Throughout his writing career, Taylor taught at universities as varied as the Women's College of the University of North Carolina at Greensboro, the University of Chicago, Ohio State University, the University of Virginia, Harvard University, and Memphis State University. As well as affording him an economic base, these involvements with higher education provided Taylor with consistent contact with American youth during a period of cultural turmoil. Yet there is little evidence in his work that he was influenced by the radicalism manifested in the 1960's and 1970's. His fiction instead seems to reflect the steadiness of his personal life. While friends such as Tate, Lowell, and Jarrell underwent the anguish of divorce, had mental breakdowns, or committed suicide, Taylor's life progressed along more conventional lines. He remained married to Eleanor Lilly Ross, whom he had wed in 1943, and together they shared (in addition to rearing their two children) an interest in restoring old houses and in pursuing their respective writing careers. Eleanor Ross Taylor has published several volumes of poetry.

The family and its different generations and extended branches form the central matter of Peter Taylor's fiction and serve to structure his elaborate intertwining of social, psychological, and historical materials. Typically, the stories are tightly crafted, reflecting the influence of Taylor's early teachers and his poet friends. At times, Taylor himself has worked from poetry to prose in composing his stories and several of his later narratives have been published in verse form. Throughout his career, Taylor's stories have evidenced his formalist roots; they are invariably carefully articulated character dramas, modulated by his own delicate taste, demonstrating a controlled and complex set of implications. In one of his earliest and most successful pieces, "A Spinster's Tale," the narrator's sense of being the only woman in the family is amplified and irritated by the idea of the town drunk, Mr. Speed, as the symbolic embodiment of what she believes is an uninhibited and untrustworthy masculine world surrounding her. In her ultimate encounter with this pathetic drunk at the story's conclusion, she not only discovers that she has the emotional strength to summon the police but also begins to sense, with some fear, the cruelty that has been inextricably mixed in her newfound strength.

More typical of Taylor's domestic analysis is "Guests," a story examining the visit of country cousins, the Kincaids, to their city relatives, the Harpers. On the surface, the narrative presents a social comedy in which Henrietta Harper's insistent social hospitality is adamantly resisted by a defensively proud Annie Kincaid, much to the discomfort of Johnny Kincaid, whose shifting dispositions seem so often the social prizes over which the women struggle. The hidden pathos of the growing personal distance created by different social histories is suggested in the speculations of the narrator, Edmund Harper, about his cousin Johnny: "Here is such a person as I might have been, and I am such a one as he might have been." While Taylor's characters do not often seem uniquely striking, the sense of the self weighing its enhanced or diminished social power creates a vividly convincing picture of the domestic history of an era. "The Old Forest," a story set in the 1930's, sketches, through the puzzled desperation of the narrator, Nat Ramsey, the very different feminine possibilities of his working-class date, Lee Ann Deehart, and his upper-middle-class fiancée, Caroline Braxley. In the search for the mysteriously vanished Lee Ann, the characters seem to gain insights that result in their being established more firmly in their respective social roles.

At its finest, Taylor's fiction is an acute mixture of psychological insight tempered by acceptance and, at times, forgiveness, with a feeling of history as the inevitable weight of social facts. As his characters interact, they often endeavor to experience other social possibilities, only at last to see in what they are not the labyrinthian cultural depths of their own social being. While their imaginative participation in the lives of others traces a broadening of social consciousness, the movement back to an awareness of what they are and what they are not leads most often to a bittersweet recognition of social limits.

BIBLIOGRAPHICAL REFERENCES: Robert Penn Warren's introduction to *A Long Fourth and Other Stories*, 1948, is an insightful brief statement on Taylor's achievement. Albert J. Griffith, *Peter Taylor*, 1970, a volume in the Twayne series, is a helpful introductory study. *Conversations with Peter Taylor*, 1987, edited by Hubert H. McAlexander, is a useful collection of interviews. Stuart Wright, *Peter Taylor: A Descriptive Bibliography, 1934-87*, 1988, is an indispensable resource. See also James Curry Robinson, *Peter Taylor: A Study of the Short Fiction*, 1988. Among articles exploring particular themes are Morgan Blum, "Peter Taylor: Self-Limitation in Fiction," *The Sewanee Review*, LXX (1962), 559-578; Ashley Brown, "The Early Fiction of Peter Taylor," *The Sewanee Review*, LXX (1962), 588-602; Barbara Schuler, "The House of Peter Taylor," *Critique: Studies in Modern Fiction*, IX (1967), 19-30; Jan Pinkerton, "The Non-Regionalism of Peter Taylor," *The Georgia Review*, XXIV (1970), 432-440; William Peden, "A Hard and Admirable Toughness: The Stories of Peter Taylor," *The Hollins Critic*, VII (1970), 1-9; Jane Barnes Casey, "A View of Peter Taylor's Stories," *The Virginia Quarterly Review*, LIV (1978), 213-230; Alan Williamson, "Identity and the Wider Eros: A Reading of Peter Taylor's Stories," *Shenandoah*, XXX (1978), 71-84; Zachery Leader, "Old Times in the New South," *The Times Literary Supplement*, January 22, 1982, 75-76. Articles on Taylor's plays include Brainard Cheney, "Peter Taylor's Plays," *The Sewanee Review*, LXX (1962), 579-587; and Richard Howard, "'Urgent Need and Unbearable Fear,'" *Shenandoah*, XXIV (1973), 44-47.

Walter Shear

PAUL THEROUX

Born: Medford, Massachusetts
Date: April 10, 1941

PRINCIPAL WORKS

NOVELS AND NOVELLAS: *Waldo*, 1967; *Fong and the Indians*, 1968; *Girls at Play*, 1969; *Murder in Mount Holly*, 1969; *Jungle Lovers*, 1971; *Saint Jack*, 1973; *The Black House*, 1974; *The Family Arsenal*, 1976; *Picture Palace: A Novel*, 1978; *The Mosquito Coast*, 1982; *Half Moon Street: Two Short Novels*, 1984; *O-Zone*, 1986; *My Secret History*, 1989.

SHORT FICTION: *Sinning with Annie and Other Stories*, 1972; *The Consul's File*, 1977; *World's End and Other Stories*, 1980; *The London Embassy*, 1982.

TRAVEL SKETCHES: *The Great Railway Bazaar: By Train Through Asia*, 1975; *The Old Patagonian Express: By Train Through the Americas*, 1979; *The Kingdom by the Sea: A Journey Around Great Britain*, 1983; *Sailing Through China*, 1984; *The Imperial Way*, 1985 (with Steve McCurry); *Sunrise with Seamonsters: Travels and Discoveries 1964-1984*, 1985; *Patagonia Revisited*, 1986 (with Bruce Chatwin); *Riding the Iron Rooster: By Train Through China*, 1988.

LITERARY CRITICISM: *V. S. Naipaul: An Introduction to His Work*, 1972.

PLAY: *The Autumn Dog*, pr. 1981.

SCREENPLAY: *Saint Jack*, 1979 (with Peter Bogdanovich and Howard Sackler).

CHILDREN'S LITERATURE: *A Christmas Card*, 1978; *London Snow: A Christmas Story*, 1979.

Paul Edward Theroux is the primary delineator in fiction of Americans in exile and is the best-known American travel writer of his time. He was born in Medford, Massachusetts, on April 10, 1941, the son of Albert Eugene and Anne Dittami Theroux. His father was a shoe-leather salesman, and his mother had been a teacher. Among his six siblings is novelist Alexander Theroux. Young Theroux sought privacy from his large family by reading and decided to become a writer when he was fourteen years old.

After high school, he attended the University of Maine for one year and was graduated from the University of Massachusetts in 1963. He then briefly went to graduate school at Syracuse University before joining the Peace Corps. He taught English at Soche Hill College in Limbe, Malawi, until October, 1965, when he was arrested and deported for spying and aiding revolutionaries attempting to overthrow the country's dictator. Theroux had volunteered to be a messenger for the dictator's leading opponent, not realizing that the man was plotting an assassination. Expelled from the Peace Corps, he lectured at Makerere University in Kampala, Uganda, until 1968. His first novel, *Waldo*, was published in 1967, and that same year, he married Anne Castle, a fellow teacher; they have two sons. Theroux taught Jacobean drama at the University of Singapore from 1968 until 1971, when he decided to write full-time. Since then, he has lived primarily in his wife's native country, England.

Theroux's fiction reflects his experiences since most of it deals with exiles, usually Americans, in Africa, Asia, Latin America, and England. *Fong and the Indians* presents a Chinese Catholic living in Kenya and subjected to the prejudice of Africans, Americans, and the British. *Jungle Lovers* chronicles two Americans trying to improve the lives of the citizens of Malawi and discovering strong resistance to change. Since Theroux's fiction is ironic and skeptical, the Americans' motives are ambiguous. The hero of *Saint Jack*, perhaps Theroux's best novel, is a middle-aged American hustler and pimp in Singapore. *The Black House*, a subtle horror tale, concerns an English anthropologist who returns to England after years in Uganda to find himself so alienated that he has an affair with a beautiful woman created by his imagination.

In 1975, Theroux's career entered a new phase with the publication of *The Great Railway Bazaar.* Always in love with trains and travel, he took a four-month trip through Asia and turned his impressions into a surprise best-seller. Such travel writing had not been popular since the 1930's, but Theroux's book, a distinctive blend of colorful details, decadence, wit, and anger, almost single-handedly created a new readership, paving the way for his books about Latin America, England, and China, as well as similar works by writers such as Bruce Chatwin and Jonathan Raban. Before his first travel book, Theroux's novels were generally well received by reviewers and ignored by readers. Afterward, such novels as *The Family Arsenal* and *The Mosquito Coast* became best-sellers.

Theroux writes realistic fiction, almost comedies of manners, earning for him comparisons with Anthony Trollope, Henry James, W. Somerset Maugham, and Evelyn Waugh. On another level, his works are darkly ironic, violent explorations of the nature of evil similar to the fiction of Joseph Conrad, Graham Greene, and V. S. Naipaul. Although most of his protagonists are Americans, his view of the world is said by many commentators to be Anglicized: It is concerned with the decline of the international influence of the writers from his adopted country. Also, his writings about England, as with the short-story collection *The London Embassy* and the travel book *The Kingdom by the Sea*, emphasize the economic and social decay of Great Britain.

Theroux's infatuation with the expatriate experience is also in the English tradition, an approach to fiction that allows him, as does his travel writing, to contrast cultures. His characters often find themselves at the mercy of social, political, and natural forces over which they have no control. They fail all the more when they fool themselves into thinking that they have complete control over their circumstances. In *Doctor Slaughter*, one of two short novels in *Half Moon Street*, an American scholar in London enjoys exerting power over men as a high-class prostitute only to be devastated when she realizes that she has become merely a pawn in international politics. The protagonist of *The Mosquito Coast* uproots his family from Massachusetts because he despises what America has become, but once in the Honduran jungle, he tries to turn it into another version of what he has fled, leading to madness and death. The protagonist of *Saint Jack*, a corrupt version of Conrad's Lord Jim, considers himself a tainted saint, unselfishly devoted to his clients. Still, he is the least self-deluded of Theroux's characters, recognizing the individual's responsibility not to make the world any worse than it need be. Theroux seems torn between a cynicism about human nature and an almost Dickensian belief in the possibilities of individual goodness beneath society's decadent, violent surface.

BIBLIOGRAPHICAL REFERENCES: For a fellow author's view of Theroux's choice of subject matter, see Martin Amis, "Paul Theroux's Enthusiasms," in *The Moronic Inferno*, 1987. For two articles investigating the symbolism in Theroux's fictions, see Samuel Coale, "'A Quality of Light': The Fiction of Paul Theroux," *Critique: Studies in Modern Fiction*, XXII (1981), 5-16, and in the same issue, Robert F. Bell, "Metamorphoses and Missing Halves: Allusions in Paul Theroux's *Picture Palace*," 17-30. See also the interview "America: A Destination for an Enormous Part of the World," *U.S. News and World Report*, July 15, 1985, 34. When Theroux published *The Kingdom by the Sea*, he provoked strong feelings with his sometimes negative portrayal of Great Britain; see Arthur Lubow, "Paul Theroux: Casting a Cold Eye on the Land Where He Lives; an American Writer Makes Waves in Great Britain," *People Weekly*, XX (December 12, 1983), 124. Reviews of Theroux's books include Vernon Young, "End of the Voyage," *American Scholar*, LI (Winter, 1982), 83; William J. Schafer, "The Imagination of Catastrophe," *North American Review*, CCLXVIII (September, 1983), 61-66; Susan Lardner, "Perfect Stranger (the Novels of Paul Theroux)," *The New Yorker*, LX (January 7, 1985), 72; John Rothfork, "Technology and the Third World: Paul Theroux's *The Mosquito Coast*," *Critique: Studies in Modern Fiction*, XXVI (Summer, 1985), 217-227; Mark Salzman, review of *Riding the Iron Rooster*, *The New York Times Book Review*, XCIII (June 19, 1988), 17; and Sybil Steinberg, review of *My Secret History*, *Publishers Weekly*, CCXXXV (March 31, 1989), 44.

Michael Adams

LEWIS THOMAS

Born: Flushing, New York
Date: November 25, 1913

PRINCIPAL WORKS

ESSAYS: *The Lives of a Cell: Notes of a Biology Watcher*, 1974; *The Medusa and the Snail: More Notes of a Biology Watcher*, 1979; *Late Night Thoughts on Listening to Mahler's Ninth Symphony*, 1983.

MEMOIRS: *The Youngest Science*, 1983.

POETRY: *Could I Ask You Something? Notes of a Medicine Watcher*, 1984.

Lewis Thomas is one of the most important contemporary American essayists and science writers. He was born in Flushing, New York, on November 25, 1913, the son of Dr. Joseph Thomas, a successful general practitioner who later became a surgeon, and Grace (Peck) Thomas, a nurse. Dr. Thomas often took his son Lewis along with him while he made house calls. In his memoir, *The Youngest Science*, Thomas describes growing up in a medical family at a time when a general practitioner was still expected to make house calls but, beyond accurate diagnosis, could do little to cure ordinary diseases. This therapeutic nihilism gradually changed by World War II, with the discovery of penicillin, sulfadiazine, and other new miracle drugs. In his essays, Thomas traces the transformation of modern medicine into a clinical science through discoveries in immunology and biochemistry.

Thomas was a precocious student who skipped several grades, was graduated from the McBurney School in Manhattan at age fifteen, majored in biology at Princeton University, and then entered Harvard Medical School in 1933. After completing his clinical training in neurology, pathology, and immunology, he served with the Navy as a virologist in the Pacific and afterward embarked on a brilliant career in biomedical research and administration. He served as Dean of the New York University and the Yale University schools of medicine, and as Chancellor of the Sloan-Kettering Cancer Institute in New York. For most of his career, Thomas was a medical researcher and administrator, at the Rockefeller Institute, The Johns Hopkins University, Tulane University, the University of Minnesota, New York University and Bellevue Hospital, and Yale University. He became a successful essayist in his fifties almost by accident.

Though Thomas wrote some poetry as an undergraduate, and later published more than two hundred articles for professional journals, he only started writing essays for *The New England Journal of Medicine* in 1971. His monthly column there, "Notes of a Biology Watcher," proved so successful that Viking Press published his first essay collection, *The Lives of a Cell*, in 1974. Much to Thomas' surprise, it became a best-seller and won for him a National Book Award in 1975. Thomas continued writing for *The New England Journal of Medicine* until 1978, collecting additional essays for a second collection, *The Medusa and the Snail*. He has appeared as a regular columnist for *Discover* magazine, publishing a third essay volume, *Late Night Thoughts on Listening to Mahler's Ninth Symphony* the same year as his memoir, *The Youngest Science*.

In his essays, Thomas employs an informal discursive style—brief, factual, witty, and optimistic. His mastery of the short essay form resulted from the editorial constraints on his monthly columns. One of Thomas' recurrent themes throughout his essays is the importance of symbiosis, the tendency of organisms to link together to create mutually beneficial relationships. Partnerships are essential in nature, where everything is interdependent. Organicism is the root metaphor in Thomas' writing, beginning with *The Lives of a Cell*. He imagines that Earth's biosphere is an integrated whole, with the human community functioning as a kind of global nervous system. In *The Medusa and the Snail*, he argues that symbiosis and altruism are the driving forces behind this global cooperation, evident everywhere, from the ecology of the cell to the behavior of social insects to a multitude of host-parasite partnerships throughout nature. Nothing exists absolutely alone. The ultimate symbiont is planet Earth, seen by Thomas as a gigantic living cell, surrounded by a self-regulating atmosphere. In his third essay volume, *Late Night Thoughts on Listening to Mahler's Ninth Symphony*, Thomas tempers his optimistic sense of the promise of science with an increased awareness of the risks of unrestrained militarism and the threat of nuclear war.

Thomas' memoir, *The Youngest Science*, is divided between personal reminiscence and medical history, with the early chapters describing Thomas' childhood and education and the later chapters recounting his medical career. In his discussion of the development of modern medicine, Thomas is preoccupied with the trade-offs between high-quality bedside care and high technology in the practice of medicine. The Whitney Museum has published a limited edition of Thomas' poetry, *Could I Ask You Something?*, with illustrations by Alfonso Ossorio.

Perhaps Thomas' most important accomplishment has been his ability to reach a broad public audience, touching upon a wide range of scientific and general topics and using the concise, familiar essay form to articulate his unique personal vision. His literary success has been an inspiration to other physicians and medical scientists to maintain the tradition of medical humanism in an age of overspecialization.

BIBLIOGRAPHICAL REFERENCES: Andrew J. Angyal, *Lewis Thomas*, 1989, is the first full-length study of Thomas' life and work. For a complete listing of Thomas' medical publications, see the bibliography in *Cellular Immunology*, LXXXII (November, 1983), 7-16. For an accurate introduction to Thomas' career, see Jeremy Bernstein, "Profiles: Biology Watcher," *The New Yorker*, January 2, 1978, 27-46 (reprinted in his *Experiencing Science: Profiles in Discovery*, 1978). Another good source is the interview by David Hellerstein, "The Muse of Medicine," *Esquire*, CI (March, 1984), 72-77. See also Steven Weiland, "'A Tune Beyond Us, Yet Ourselves': Medical Science and Lewis Thomas," *Michigan Quarterly Review*, XXIV (Spring, 1985), 293-306; Howard Nemerov, "Lewis Thomas, Montaigne, and Human Happiness," in *New and Selected Essays*, 1985; "Biological Musings," *The New York Times Book Review*, May 6, 1979, 1, and "Calling Dr. Thomas," *The New York Review of Books*, XXX (July 21, 1983), 12-13, both by Stephen Jay Gould; Joyce Carol Oates, "Beyond Common Sense: *The Lives of a Cell*," *The New York Times Book Review*, May 26, 1974, 2-3; and John Updike, "Books: A New Meliorism," *The New Yorker*, July 15, 1974, 83-86.

Andrew J. Angyal

JAMES THURBER

Born: Columbus, Ohio
Date: December 8, 1894

Died: New York, New York
Date: November 4, 1961

PRINCIPAL WORKS

HUMOR: *Is Sex Necessary?*, 1929 (with E. B. White); *The Owl in the Attic and Other Perplexities*, 1931; *My Life and Hard Times*, 1933; *The Middle-Aged Man on the Flying Trapeze*, 1935; *Let Your Mind Alone!*, 1937; *My World—and Welcome to It*, 1942; *The Thurber Carnival*, 1945; *The Beast in Me and Other Animals*, 1948; *Thurber Country*, 1953; *Thurber's Dogs*, 1955; *Alarms and Diversions*, 1957; *Lanterns and Lances*, 1961; *Credos and Curios*, 1962.

FANTASY: *Fables for Our Times and Famous Poems Illustrated*, 1940; *Many Moons*, 1943; *The Great Quillow*, 1944; *The White Deer*, 1945; *The 13 Clocks*, 1950; *Further Fables for Our Time*, 1956; *The Wonderful O*, 1957.

PLAYS: *The Male Animal*, pb. 1940 (with Elliott Nugent); *A Thurber Carnival*, pr. 1960.

AUTOBIOGRAPHY: *The Thurber Album*, 1952; *The Years with Ross*, 1959.

CORRESPONDENCE: *Selected Letters of James Thurber*, 1981.

MISCELLANEOUS: *The Seal in the Bedroom and Other Predicaments*, 1932; *The Last Flower*, 1939; *Men, Women, and Dogs*, 1943; *Thurber and Company*, 1966.

Generally considered the greatest American humorist since Mark Twain, James Grover Thurber was born on December 8, 1894, in Columbus, Ohio, the setting for many of his comic reminiscences. His father was active in local politics; his mother had a histrionic gift of comic impersonation that gave his mind "a sense of confusion that . . . never left it." When Thurber was six, his older brother accidentally shot him with an arrow in the left eye, which was replaced with a glass one. In Columbus, Thurber attended the public schools and Ohio State University, where he wrote for the campus paper and for the student monthly, of which he became editor in chief.

In June, 1918, Thurber left Ohio State University without taking a degree. He had tried to enlist in the armed forces but was rejected because of his eyesight. Instead, he became a code clerk for the State Department, first in Washington, D.C., then at the American embassy in Paris. In the summer of 1920, Thurber returned to Columbus, where for the next four years he was a reporter and columnist for the Columbus *Dispatch*. In 1922, Thurber married Althea Adams of Columbus. Two years later, he resigned from the *Dispatch* to try his hand at free-lance writing. In 1925 he went to France to write a novel, which never materialized. Instead, he became a reporter for the Paris and later the Riviera edition of the *Chicago Tribune*. After a year in France, the Thurbers returned to the United States, and Thurber began work as a reporter for the New York *Evening Post*.

In February, 1927, Thurber finally began his real career when he met E. B. White, the celebrated writer for *The New Yorker*, and its editor, Harold Ross, who hired him. Thurber contributed to "The Talk of the Town" column and submitted his own comic stories and essays. In 1929, he and White collaborated on what was for both a first book, *Is Sex Necessary?*, which spoofed books on sex therapy. Here Thurber found one of his recurring themes, "the melancholy of sex," which he would develop into a full-scale mock war between men and women. *Is Sex Necessary?* also introduced Thurber as a cartoonist and illustrator. White found that he had been filling wastebaskets with penciled drawings, which White rescued, inked in, and persuaded the publishers to include as illustrations. All Thurber's subsequent books except four fairy-tale and fantasy books were illustrated by the author, and his cartoons and drawings soon became a hallmark of *The New Yorker*.

In 1931, Thurber published his first book alone, *The Owl in the Attic and Other Perplexities*. The first section, a series of eight stories about Mr. and Mrs. Monroe, deals with the sort of matrimonial relationship that was to become a major subject of his later work. The domination of the American male by the American female and the innocence of animals figure in *The Seal in the Bedroom and Other Predicaments*, Thurber's first book of cartoons and drawings. A self-taught draftsman, Thurber developed a unique and instantly recognizable style that renders people and objects in linear outline, flowing gracefully but without shading or cross-hatching. In 1933, Thurber published *My Life and Hard Times*, a comic autobiography that many readers consider his most amusing. In it, Thurber carries to burlesque extremes some of the episodes of his boyhood and college days. It is a prime example of his definition of his humor as "emotional chaos told about calmly and quietly in retrospect."

Thurber's men and his own personae in his writings are often suffering from hesitation, neuroses, hypochondria, apprehension, and fragmentation of character. The real Thurber bore little resemblance to these characters; friends and interviewers noted that far from being shy and trapped, Thurber was confident and assured. The antihero features in *The Middle-Aged Man on the Flying Trapeze*, one of Thurber's best collections of stories and essays, published in 1935. In their subdued way, Thurber's protagonists are often frustrated romantics, like Walter Mitty. Thurber objected to any attempts to regiment the freewheeling imagination, and *Let Your Mind Alone!* includes a number of pieces satirizing inspirational and self-help books, which Thurber believed were trying to discipline readers into a pedestrian conformity to a dull norm.

Despite the birth of his daughter Rosemary in 1931, Thurber's marriage had been troubled for a long time, and in 1935, he was divorced. Several stories written around this time—"One is a Wanderer" and "The Evening's at Seven"—are serious, poignant studies of loneliness. That same year, however, Thurber married Helen Wismer, a magazine editor, and this marriage endured for the rest of his life. As for the battle of the sexes, Thurber said that it was a gimmick, that he admired vibrant and intelligent women. His is a mock misogyny: He truly believed that women could manage things better than men.

During the late 1930's and early 1940's, the war years, Thurber produced several successful books, both serious and humorous, that pointedly denounced or mocked human behavior: *The Last Flower*, a poignant book-length cartoon denouncing war; *The Male Animal*, a play written in collaboration with college friend Elliott Nugent (later a successful actor and director), which continued the battle-of-the-sexes theme and championed academic freedom while it attacked right-wing witch-hunting on the campus of a Midwestern university; *Men, Women, and Dogs*, his second book of cartoons; and *My World—and Welcome to It*, which contains his best-known short story, "The Secret Life of Walter Mitty," featuring a protagonist who triumphs over a nagging wife by retreating into a fantasy world in which he is the superhero he wishes to be.

While Thurber was having all these artistic successes, the sight in his remaining eye began to deteriorate, and despite a series of operations, he gradually became blind. After 1951, he had to give up drawing altogether, his later books are illustrated by earlier drawings, sometimes reversed or rearranged. Fortunately for his writing, he had total recall and could memorize several entire versions of a story or essay before dictating it. During his operations, Thurber wrote a few stories reflecting frustration and rage—"The Cane in the Corridor" and "The Whip-poor-will," for example. Thurber's reaction was usually more positive, and he soon turned to writing fairy tales that entertain with a gentle and humane moral. The first two of these, *Many Moons* and *The Great Quillow*, are children's books; the third and best tale, *The White Deer*, is for adults as well.

In 1945 Thurber had his biggest success, with *The Thurber Carnival*, an anthology of his best work up to that time. One obstacle to recognition of Thurber as a serious and significant artist was the fact that his work was in miniature—short stories, essays, cartoons, and drawings—but *The Thurber Carnival* provided an overview that allowed a more appreciative focus on his entire body of work. By 1948, Thurber was receiving the recognition he deserved. In 1949, Columbia University gave him the Laughing Lions Award for humor, and over the next four years he received honorary doctorates from Kenyon College, Williams College, and Yale University.

The Thurber Album appeared in 1952—a departure from Thurber's usual humor, being a series of well-researched biographical sketches of family members, friends, and Ohio State University professors who offered positive role models for American values. In 1956, *Further Fables for Our Time* satirized intellectual and political intolerance, rumor, and vicious innuendo, winning the American Library Association's Liberty and Justice Award. In 1957, another book-length fantasy, *The Wonderful O*, told the story of a pirate whose mother tries to ban the letter *o* on an island, only to have the islanders rebel and reaffirm the *o* in "love," "valor," and "freedom." Thurber visited England in 1958 and was the first American since Mark Twain to be "called to the table" for *Punch*'s Wednesday luncheon. In 1959, he published *The Years with Ross*, a book-length sketch of his time with the founder of *The New Yorker.* He won a Tony Award for adapting some of his short pieces into a revue, *A Thurber Carnival*, which was produced successfully in New York in 1960. In September, Thurber joined the cast, playing himself for eighty-eight performances in a sketch entitled "File and Forget." The next year, 1961, he revisited Europe and published another collection, *Lanterns and Lances*. On October 4, Thurber was stricken with a blood clot in the brain, underwent emergency surgery, and rallied—but he died of pneumonia on November 4. He is buried in Columbus, Ohio.

Though Thurber is now firmly established as the major American humorist of the twentieth century, admired by writers such as T. S. Eliot, Dylan Thomas, and Edmund Wilson, his work, like that of all great humorists, has an underlying seriousness in its satire on war, failed communication between the sexes, political intolerance and extremism, thought control and linguistic degeneration; it offers an astute commentary on human nature, addressing the predicaments and perplexities of modern time.

BIBLIOGRAPHICAL REFERENCES: Robert E. Morsberger, *James Thurber*, 1964, the first book-length study of Thurber, examines the romantic imagination in Thurber's works, the war between men and women, the role of animals as a commentary on human folly in Thurber's prose and drawings, Thurber's political satire, and the subtleties in his use of language. Richard C. Tobias, *The Art of James Thurber*, 1970, analyzes Thurber's use of a comic masque, his fairy tales, and his prose style. Charles S. Holmes, *The Clocks of Columbus: The Literary Career of James Thurber*, 1972, is an excellent biographical and critical study, though handicapped by lack of permission to quote from Thurber's letters. *Thurber: A Collection of Critical Essays*, 1974, edited by Charles S. Holmes, contains twenty-five essays, including articles by E. B. White, Dorothy Parker, W. H. Auden, Peter De Vries, Malcolm Cowley, and John Updike. Edwin T. Bowden, *James Thurber: A Bibliography*, 1969, is the definitive bibliography of primary writings and drawings. Burton Bernstein, *Thurber: A Biography*, 1975, is a complete biography, drawing upon letters that Holmes could not use; it is, however, at times a slanted and overly dark portrait. Catherine McGehee Kenney, *Thurber's Anatomy of Confusion*, 1984, analyzes Thurber's wordplay, picture of society, portraits of perplexed individuals, and tragic awareness of mutability and mortality. Sarah Eleanora Toombs, *James Thurber: An Annotated Bibliography of Criticism*, 1987, is a thoroughly researched source for critical writing about Thurber. See also interviews such as George Plimpton and Max Steele, "James Thurber," in *Writers at Work*, 1959; "James Thurber in Conversation with Alistair Cooke," *The Atlantic Monthly*, CXCVIII (August, 1956), 36-40; Henry Brandon, "The Tulle and Taffeta Rut," in *As We Are*, 1961; and "Salute to Thurber," *Saturday Review*, XLIV (November 25, 1961), 14-18.

Robert E. Morsberger

WALLACE THURMAN

Born: Salt Lake City, Utah
Date: August 16, 1902

Died: New York, New York
Date: December 21, 1934

PRINCIPAL WORKS

NOVELS: *The Blacker the Berry*, 1929; *Infants of the Spring*, 1932.

EDITED TEXTS: *Fire!! A Quarterly Devoted to the Younger Negro Artists*, 1926; *Harlem: A Forum of Negro Life*, 1928.

PLAY: *Harlem*, pr. 1929 (with William Jourdan Rapp).

Wallace Henry Thurman may have seen the death of the Harlem Renaissance after *Infants of the Spring*, but while the renaissance was alive his imagination and critical attention helped to keep it healthy. Thurman was born on August 16, 1902, in Salt Lake City, Utah, to Beulah and Oscar Thurman. His parents soon separated and he was reared by his maternal grandmother, Emma Jackson, to whom he dedicated his first novel, *The Blacker the Berry.* He enrolled briefly at the University of Utah, then moved to California and started a premedical curriculum at the University of Southern California. He did not finish his premedical studies because he became involved in the type of work that was to absorb his energies for the rest of his brief life: He began to write a column for a black Los Angeles newspaper, and he edited a magazine. The magazine lasted six months, the longest any of his independent editorial projects would last.

Thurman arrived in Harlem in 1925 and worked for meals as a jack-of-all-trades on a small magazine whose editor knew the staff of the black-radical magazine *The Messenger*; Thurman was later hired as managing editor of *The Messenger.* Editorial and administrative work suited Thurman, and he continued in it throughout the renaissance; he was, in fact, one of the few younger renaissance figures who had a steady, predictable source of income.

By the time he began work on *The Messenger,* he had been around Harlem enough that he knew everyone worth knowing. His most important acquaintance was poet/novelist/playwright Langston Hughes, who roomed across the hall from him in the boarding house that served as the model for "Niggerati Manor" in *Infants of the Spring*. Hughes brought to Thurman in 1927 a request to serve as editor of a new magazine for publishing experimental and unconventional literature by younger black writers. Black magazines which published art and literature (the National Association for the Advancement of Colored People's *The Crisis* and the Urban League's *Opportunity,* for example) were not primarily literary magazines, and the idea of Hughes and his friends was that a strictly literary magazine with solely artistic criteria was necessary. The new magazine, *Fire!!*, was visually stunning (designed by Afro-American artist Aaron Douglas) and editorially adventurous, a tribute to Thurman's abilities. Unfortunately the magazine was too adventurous for most of the readers who bought that first issue (more than one short story, for example, contained sexually unorthodox characters), and the final, ironic blow for the project was that the remaining copies of the first issue were destroyed by a fire in the apartment where they were stored. With no inventory and no income, the group could not continue publication. Thurman took it upon himself to repay the debt for the paper, printing, and binding of this high quality publication; repayment took about four years.

The next year Thurman founded a general interest magazine, which he called *Harlem*. Again the magazine was well designed and edited; moreover it was not so controversial as *Fire!!*, but it too failed after one issue. Thurman did not have time to mourn the failure because he was busy writing and working on the editorial staff of Macauley Publishing Company, the company that published *The Blacker the Berry* in 1929. This novel, which details the effects of color prejudice and self-hatred among Afro-Americans, received mixed reviews. Thurman was more successful in February, 1929, with a production of the play

Harlem, written with William Jourdan Rapp and based on one of the controversial short stories in the defunct *Fire!!* The play ran at the Apollo Theatre in New York City for ninety-three performances, had successful road company tours, and was revived on Broadway in October of 1929.

Thurman briefly tried his hand at writing "social problem" screenplays for an independent filmmaker in Hollywood, then came back to Harlem where he wrote his most important work, *Infants of the Spring*, also published by his employer, Macauley Publishing Company. The title is taken from a passage in William Shakespeare's *Hamlet* which summarizes Thurman's view of the Harlem Renaissance; he believed that it had been killed before it had flowered. He also believed that the "canker" was internal: The Harlem Renaissance, in his opinion, died of too much self-consciousness and self-indulgence. This harsh evaluation was not fully accepted in 1932 when the novel was published, nor has it been fully accepted since, but the novel itself has been accepted as a skillfully satirical *roman à clef*. The novel, which follows the lives of black writers and artists living in a rooming house called "Niggerati Manor," includes deftly drawn (and quartered) characters such as "Tony Crews" (Langston Hughes) and "Sweetie Mae Carr" (Zora Neale Hurston).

Thurman contracted tuberculosis in the early 1930's and died of it in New York City on December 21, 1934. In his autobiography, *The Big Sea* (1940), Langston Hughes affectionately and critically limns Thurman as a man whose critical bent caused him to see flaws in everything, including his own writing. According to Hughes, Thurman wanted to be a great literary figure and believed that he was "merely" a journalist. With *Infants of the Spring*, Thurman's literary ambitions and his journalistic talent work together; the result is a satirical novel that is still read with enjoyment, long after both the satirist and the objects of his satire have passed from the scene. Posterity seems to have judged Thurman more kindly than he judged himself.

BIBLIOGRAPHICAL REFERENCES: Langston Hughes, in his autobiography *The Big Sea*, 1940, presents a fascinating character sketch of Wallace Thurman. For discussions of Thurman's literary career and novels in the context of Afro-American literary history, see Robert Bone, *The Negro Novel in America*, 1965, and Hugh M. Gloster, *Negro Voices in American Fiction*, 1948. For a closer look at Thurman's life, see Dorothy West, "Elephant's Dance: A Memoir of Wallace Thurman," *Black World*, XX (1970), 77-85. Huel D. Perkins' reevaluation, "Renaissance 'Renegade'? Wallace Thurman," *Black World*, XXV (1976), 29-35, is worth reading. See also Daniel Walden, "The Canker Galls . . . Or, The Short Promising Life of Wallace Thurman," in *The Harlem Renaissance Re-Examined*, 1987.

Isaac Johnson

J. R. R. TOLKIEN

Born: Bloemfontein, South Africa
Date: January 3, 1892

Died: Bournemouth, England
Date: September 2, 1973

PRINCIPAL WORKS

FICTION: *The Hobbit: Or, There and Back Again*, 1937; *Farmer Giles of Ham*, 1949; *The Lord of the Rings*, 1954-1955 (includes *The Fellowship of the Ring, The Two Towers*, and *The Return of the King*); *Tree and Leaf*, 1966; *The Tolkien Reader*, 1966; *Smith of Wootton Major*, 1967; *The Father Christmas Letters*, 1976; *The Silmarillion*, 1977; *Unfinished Tales of Numenor and Middle-Earth*, 1980; *The Book of Lost Tales*, 1983-1984; *The Lays of Beleriand*, 1985; *The Shaping of Middle-Earth*, 1986; *The Lost Road and Other Writings*, 1987; *The Return of the Shadow: The History of "The Lord of the Rings," Part One*, 1988.

PLAY: *The Homecoming of Beorhtnoth Beorhthelm's Son*, pb. 1953.

POETRY: *Songs for the Philologists*, 1936 (with others); *The Adventures of Tom Bombadil and Other Verses from the Red Book*, 1962; *The Road Goes Ever On: A Song Cycle*, 1967; *The Lays of Beleriand*, 1985.

NONFICTION: *A Middle English Vocabulary*, 1922; *The Letters of J. R. R. Tolkien*, 1981.

TRANSLATIONS: *Sir Gawain and the Green Knight, Pearl, and Sir Orfeo*, 1975; *The Old English Exodus*, 1982.

EDITED TEXTS: *Sir Gawain and the Green Knight*, 1925 (with E. V. Gordon); *Ancrene Wisse: The English Text of the Ancrene Riwle*, 1962.

MISCELLANEOUS: *The Tolkien Reader*, 1966; *Pictures by J. R. R. Tolkien*, 1979; *Finn and Hengest: The Fragment and the Episode*, 1983; *Tree and Leaf*, 1988 (includes the poem "Mythopoeia").

John Ronald Reuel Tolkien was born in Bloemfontein, South Africa, one of two sons of Arthur Reuel and Mabel Suffield Tolkien. When he was four years old, his father died and his mother returned to England, to a town near Birmingham. The verdant English countryside to which he was moved made an immediate impression on the boy; for it was to become the locale for his now-famous fantasy world. Tolkien's first teacher was his mother, and from her he acquired a love of languages and fantasy. Following her death in 1904, he and his brother were reared by Father Francis Xavier Morgan, a Roman Catholic priest. Tolkien received his secondary education at King Edward VI School in Birmingham and then attended Exeter College, Oxford, where he received his bachelor's degree in 1915. He then joined the Lancashire Fusiliers and served on the Western Front until the end of World War I. In 1916 he married Edith Mary Bratt; together they would have a daughter and three sons.

After the war, he returned to the University of Oxford and earned his master's degree in 1919. His love of language led him to work for two years as an assistant on the *Oxford English Dictionary*. Between 1920 and 1925 he taught English at the University of Leeds. In 1925 he returned to Oxford as a professor of Anglo-Saxon at Pembroke College, soon becoming the Rawlinson and Bosworth Professor of Anglo-Saxon. He was elected a Fellow of Pembroke College in 1926 and was Merton Professor of English Language and Literature from 1945 until his retirement, in 1959. During these years he continued his work in Anglo-Saxon and medieval literature and lore, publishing monographs and articles on works such as *Beowulf* and Geoffrey Chaucer's *The Canterbury Tales* (1387-1400).

When he was forty-five years old, *The Hobbit*, a novel for children, was published. It became an immediate success. Ostensibly based upon stories which he had created for the amusement of his children, *The Hobbit*, a heroic tale of dragons, giants, and heroes, appealed to both children and adults. Far more profound was *The Lord of the Rings* trilogy, which occupied him for fifteen years. These works, which described the fantastic secondary world of Middle-Earth, which had its own languages, history, customs, people, and geography, became enormously popular. Tolkien fan clubs and fan magazines emerged and flourished. During these years Tolkien received numerous awards and honors, ranging from children's book awards to honorary doctorates.

Although he officially retired from his professorship in 1959, Tolkien continued to write about Middle-Earth. At his death in 1973, he left behind many notes and partially completed manuscripts. Some of these were collated by his son, Christopher Tolkien, and published in 1977 as *The Silmarillion*, the story of the creation of Middle-Earth. *The Book of Lost Tales*, a collection of Tolkien's stories, was edited and published by his son in 1983 and 1984. Other posthumous works have followed.

Tolkien made his fictional world come alive. Because his fantasy world was firmly rooted in the medieval tradition, Tolkien's professional specialty, and because he was a perfectionist regarding detail, his descriptions of Middle-Earth are consistent and absorbing. Within this world, heroic adventures could and did take place. That too was part of the medieval epic literary tradition. Tolkien used many of the traditional characteristics of the epic in his works: heroes, quests, visits to the underworld, and noble deaths in battle. His variation on the theme was his unheroic hero. Middle-Earth had to be saved by ordinary and even humble heroes. Moreover, the effort had to be commensurate with the result; good could not triumph without hardship and suffering.

While Tolkien stated that his works were neither allegorical nor topical, his stories have strong applications for the modern world. His experiences in the trenches of World War I, as well as the totalitarianism of the pre- and post-World War II era, affected him deeply and often surface in his work. Tolkien was concerned with the problem of power—whether it be political, spiritual, or personal. All of his characters are forced to choose whether to accept or to reject power. Tolkien was also concerned with the theme of good versus evil. Although he has been criticized as simplistic, his attitude was not only medieval but also modern. Tolkien created a world in which dignity is alive and good can triumph over evil.

Tolkien's significance lies in his ability to write literature which appeals to all ages. At the simplest level, his stories appeal to children. At a higher level, the heroic tales are delightful fiction. At a still higher level, the work enters the realm of ethical philosophy. Tolkien's fantasy world provides a place where moral values exist and quests can still be achieved.

BIBLIOGRAPHICAL REFERENCES: For a succinct introduction to Tolkien the person, his work, and critical reception, see A. M. Kolich, "J. R. R. Tolkien," in *Dictionary of Literary Biography*, Vol. 15, *British Novelists, 1930-1959*, 1983, edited by Bernard Oldsey. *Tolkien Criticism: An Annotated Checklist, Revised Edition*, 1981, compiled by Richard C. West, is an excellent compendium of Tolkien criticism. For biographical material, see Humphrey Carpenter, *Tolkien: A Biography*, 1977; Daniel Grotta-Kurska, *J. R. R. Tolkien: Architect of Middle-Earth*, 1976; Deborah Rogers, *J. R. R. Tolkien*, 1980; and Catharine R. Stimpson, *J. R. R. Tolkien*, 1969. For further critical analysis, see T. A. Shippey, *The Road to Middle-Earth*, 1983; Lin Carter, *Tolkien: A Look Behind "The Lord of the Rings,"* 1969; *Shadows of Imagination: The Fantasies of C. S. Lewis, J. R. R. Tolkien, and Charles Williams*, 1979, edited by Mark R. Hillegas; *Tolkien and the Critics*, 1968, edited by Neil Isaacs and Rose Zimbardo; Paul Kocher, *Master of Middle-Earth: The Fiction of J. R. R. Tolkien*, 1972; Jane Nitzche, *Tolkien's Art: A Mythology for England*, 1979; Ruth Noel, *The Mythology of Middle-Earth: A Study of Tolkien's Mythology and Its Relationship to the Myths of the Ancient World*, 1977; Anne Cotton Petty, *One Ring to Rule Them All: Tolkien's Mythology*, 1979; William Ready, *Understanding Tolkien and "The Lord of the Rings,"* 1969; and Gunnar Urang, *Shadows of Heaven: Religion and Fantasy in the Writing of C. S. Lewis, Charles Williams, and J. R. R. Tolkien*, 1971. Useful introductions to Tolkien's fantasy world are Robert Foster, *The Complete Guide to Middle-Earth*, 1978; Randel Helms, *Tolkien's World*, 1974; and *A Tolkien Compass*, 1975, edited by Jared Lobdell, which includes a guide by Tolkien.

William S. Brockington, Jr.

LEO TOLSTOY

Born: Yasnaya Polyana, Russia
Date: September 9, 1828

Died: Astapovo, Russia
Date: November 20, 1910

PRINCIPAL WORKS

NOVELS AND NOVELLAS: *Detstvo*, 1852 (*Childhood*, 1862); *Otrochestvo*, 1854 (*Boyhood*, 1886); *Yunost'*, 1857 (*Youth*, 1886); *Semeynoye schast'ye*, 1859 (*Family Happiness*, 1888); *Kazaki*, 1863 (*The Cossacks*, 1872); *Voyna i mir*, 1865-1869 (*War and Peace*, 1886); *Anna Karenina*, 1875-1877 (English translation, 1886); *Smert' Ivana Il'icha*, 1886 (*The Death of Ivan Ilyich*, 1887); *Kreytserova sonata*, 1891 (*The Kreutzer Sonata*, 1890); *Voskreseniye*, 1899 (*Resurrection*, 1899); *Khadzi-Murat*, 1911 (*Hadji Murad*, 1911).

SHORT FICTION: *Sevastopolskiye rasskazy*, 1855-1856 (*Sebastopol*, 1887); *The Kreutzer Sonata, The Devil, and Other Tales*, 1940; *Notes of a Madman and Other Stories*, 1943; *Tolstoy Tales*, 1947.

NONFICTION: *Ispoved'*, 1884 (*A Confession*, 1885); *V chem moya vera*, 1884 (*What I Believe*, 1885); *Chto takoye iskusstvo?*, 1898 (*What Is Art?*, 1898); *O Shekspire i o drame*, 1906 (*Shakespeare and the Drama*, 1906).

Among the world's greatest novelists, Leo Nikolayevich Tolstoy also wrote an important body of nonfiction advocating pacifism and social justice. The fourth son of Princess Marya Nikolayevna Volkonsky and Nikolay Ilyich Tolstoy, a retired lieutenant colonel and gentleman farmer, Tolstoy was born on the family estate of Yasnaya Polyana, Tula Province, Russia, on September 9 (August 28 according to the Russian Julian calendar), 1828. His mother died two years later in giving birth to her fifth child; her death may explain why Tolstoy, who fathered thirteen children, developed a terror of childbirth and in his novels portrayed it as a harrowing experience. Although he could not have remembered much about his mother, he drew on accounts of her to create Princess Marya in *War and Peace*. His father, who died when Leo was nine years old, served as the model for Nikolay Rostov in that work, and many of Tolstoy's other relatives and acquaintances provided him with characters for his fiction, as he himself was the model for Levin in *Anna Karenina*.

Tolstoy's youth was carefree and dissipated. In 1846, he enrolled in Kazan University to prepare for a diplomatic career but left after a year of studying Oriental languages. He would later become adept at Greek (which he claimed he taught himself in three months), Hebrew, German, French, and English, all of them represented in his fourteen-thousand-volume library. Despite a rigorous program of self-improvement that he established for himself after leaving the university, he spent the next four years as a typical Russian aristocrat (Tolstoy was a count), traveling between his country estate and the cities of St. Petersburg and Moscow. Though he eventually abandoned this social milieu, his experiences in high society allowed him to paint vivid portraits of its members. Bored, in 1851 he joined the army and served in the Caucasus and in the Crimean War. He would reject this life, too, but he learned at first hand what war was like. In *War and Peace*, he presents the Battle of Austerlitz not as a grand panorama of clashing armies and heroic encounters but rather from the limited perspective of a soldier engaged in the action. As an officer, he would also have met characters like Count Vronsky and his circle, so well depicted in *Anna Karenina*. More immediately, he used his observations to create a series of sketches that appeared as *Sebastopol*; many of these stories contrast the quiet bravery of common soldiers with the vainglorious posturing of their officers.

Resigning his commission in 1856, Tolstoy turned his attention to improving the lot of his peasants, setting up a school, publishing textbooks, and traveling to Western Europe to observe teaching methods. In 1862, he married the eighteen-year-old Sofia Andreyevna Bers, sixteen years his junior. The next decade and a half, in which he created his two monumental novels, *War and Peace* and *Anna Karenina*, would be the happiest and most productive of his life. In his later years, he became increasingly concerned with religion, pacifism, and social issues, writing a large number of tracts attacking the established church, war, and injustice. Like Levin, he worked alongside the peasants. He also made his own shoes, became a vegetarian, and refused to allow others to serve him. He wrote his last novel, *Resurrection*, to raise money for the Dukhobars, a group of pacifists seeking to emigrate to Canada. Like much of his writing in this period, the novel attacks the Russian Orthodox church, which excommunicated him in 1901. Several times he attempted to abandon Yasnaya Polyana and the trappings of aristocracy. In November, 1910, he made the last of these efforts, dying in a railway station in Astapovo on his way to his beloved Caucasus.

Tolstoy not only produced two of the world's greatest novels but also revolutionized the genre. In 1851, he tried in "A History of Yesterday" to re-create a typical day in his life. Rejecting the Romantic fiction popular at the time, he sought to describe life in all of its contradictions and complexity while at the same time depicting the psychological motivations of his characters as they revealed themselves through subtle gestures and simple expressions. From this literary experimentation came works of epic proportions and epic stature. *War and Peace* contains more than 550 characters, at least fifty of them significant; *Anna Karenina* treats 143, and again some fifty play important roles in the work. Both are social histories, the one of the period 1805 to 1814, the other of the 1860's, and while Tolstoy focuses on the aristocratic world he knew so intimately, he shows a keen understanding of the common people as well. In his work, Tolstoy combines psychological probing with the novel of manners on a grand scale. Although he writes in the third person as an omniscient author, he allows his characters to reveal themselves.

Tolstoy's preeminence as a writer of fiction is unquestioned. John Galsworthy and E. M. Forster are only two of the many who have called *War and Peace* the greatest novel ever written, and another critic has commented that if God wrote a novel, it would be *Anna Karenina*. More problematic is Tolstoy's position as a reformer. Yet even here he has been influential. In his own day, he was regarded as the conscience of the nation as he pleaded for the lives of revolutionaries condemned to death, and Mahatma Gandhi found his works deeply inspirational. Though Tolstoy often adopted extreme positions, he has come to be recognized as a serious thinker, even if his religious and social tracts pale before the brilliance of his novelistic achievement.

BIBLIOGRAPHICAL REFERENCES: David R. Egan and Melinda A. Egan, *An Annotated Bibliography of English Language Sources to 1978*, 1979, lists more than two thousand studies and provides useful annotations. Tolstoy's life has been described repeatedly by his own family. Alexander Tolstoy, *Tolstoy: A Life of My Father*, 1953, and his *The Tragedy of Tolstoy*, 1933, offer a sympathetic view. Ilya Tolstoy, *Tolstoy by His Son*, 1914, 1971 (rev. ed.); Leo L. Tolstoy, *The Truth About My Father*, 1924; and Sergei Tolstoy, *Tolstoy Remembered*, 1962, all reveal much about life in Yasnaya Polyana. Sofia Tolstoy, *The Autobiography*, 1922, and her diaries give a more negative view. Ernest J. Simmons, *Leo Tolstoy*, 1946, is a balanced, close study of the life and works; a shorter version of this book appeared as *Tolstoy*, 1972. Henri Troyat, *Tolstoy*, 1967, is a vivid popular biography. A. N. Wilson, *Tolstoy*, 1988, is a fresh account of Tolstoy's life and work, drawing on later scholarship and making use of Wilson's own considerable experience as a novelist. Richard F. Gustafson, *Leo Tolstoy: Resident and Stranger*, 1986, is a revisionist study that emphasizes the religious current in Tolstoy's writings, particularly as it reflects the distinctives of Russian Orthodox theology. General studies of Tolstoy's fiction include John Bayley, *Tolstoy and the Novel*, 1966, which devotes about half its space to *War and Peace*; Ruth I. Benson, *Women in Tolstoy: The Ideal and the Erotic*, 1973, the title summarizing the book's contents; and Thomas G. S. Cain, *Tolstoy*, 1977, which stresses the autobiographical elements in the fiction. Reginald Frank Christian, *Tolstoy: A Critical Introduction*, 1969, concentrates on the literary qualities of the novels; Ronald Hagman, *Tolstoy*, 1970, also looks closely at fictional techniques. For a good introductory survey, see William Woodin Rowe, *Leo Tolstoy*, 1986. For an outstanding study of *War and Peace*, see Gary Saul Morson, *Hidden in Plain View: Narrative and Creative Potentials in "War and Peace,"* 1987. Isaiah Berlin, *The Hedgehog and the Fox: An Essay on Tolstoy's View of History*, 1953, is a classic examination of the author, who, according to Berlin, sought a unified vision but was by nature a fox, pursuing many diverse ideas. Sarla Mittal, *Tolstoy: Social and Political Ideas*, 1966, praises his vision of nonviolent reform. *New Essays on Tolstoy*, 1978, edited by Malcolm Jones, offers a collection of pieces on all aspects of this multidimensional writer.

Joseph Rosenblum

CHARLES TOMLINSON

Born: Stoke-on-Trent, Staffordshire, England
Date: January 8, 1927

Principal Works

POETRY: *Relations and Contraries*, 1951; *The Necklace*, 1955; *Seeing Is Believing*, 1958; *A Peopled Landscape*, 1963; *Poems: A Selection*, 1964; *American Scenes and Other Poems*, 1966; *The Way of a World*, 1969; *Words and Images*, 1972; *Written on Water*, 1972; *The Way In, and Other Poems*, 1974; *Selected Poems, 1951-1974*, 1978; *The Shaft*, 1978; *The Flood*, 1981; *Notes from New York and Other Poems*, 1984; *Collected Poems*, 1985; *The Return*, 1987.

NONFICTION: *Some Americans: A Personal Record*, 1981; *Poetry and Metamorphosis*, 1983.

EDITED TEXT: *The Oxford Book of Verse in English Translation*, 1980.

MISCELLANEOUS: *In Black and White: The Graphics of Charles Tomlinson*, 1976.

Alfred Charles Tomlinson is a contemplative poet in the tradition of William Wordsworth and Wallace Stevens. Mindful of the transience and interdependence of all natural things, he focuses on the concrete, sensible world and its relationship to human knowledge and morality. The bulk of his work consists of rhapsodic meditations on the gorgeous transformations of natural forms and the changing truths one intuits as one experiences the flux of nature. Reality and truth, the poet asserts, must be sought "not in concrete" but instead "in space made articulate" ("The Necklace").

Tomlinson was born on January 8, 1927, in Staffordshire, England, and educated at Queens College, Cambridge, where he received a B.A. in 1948, and London University, where he received an M.A. in 1955. In 1956, he joined the faculty of the University of Bristol, where he has taught for many years; he has also, over the years, traveled widely and held several visiting professorships, including some in the Southwestern United States. A painter as well as a poet, he has had numerous one-man shows, and he has continued to receive many literary awards. He married Brenda Raybould in 1948, becoming the father of two daughters. They made their permanent home in Gloucestershire, England.

Tomlinson's favorite subjects are rocks, mountains, water, light, and the moon and sun; as he paints his subjects, he captures gradations of coloration as well as volume, shape, and texture. While recording such changeable appearances, he addresses the predicament of locating meaning, of fixing on essentials, in a world of flux. Can one, he asks in the early poem "Written on Water," gain a hold and thus generalize a basis for morality? Can one discern a universal ethic in a world of constant change? In *Relations and Contraries*, he decides to fix upon "meaning" in metaphor and analogy, which will bring together at least two planes of disparate experience. In the famous "Poem I," a horse pulls a wagon filled with farm goods. As the poet listens to the "hooves describe an arabesque on space," he reflects on the intermingling and interdependence of the external and internal worlds.

Seeing Is Believing, like *A Peopled Landscape*, expresses Tomlinson's deep respect for English history, but once again, the poet deals with the relativity of knowledge and perception; he also utilizes familiar images of light and dark in sequences of movement and space. The mind, the imagination, and the eye work in unison to perceive the world and to discern meaning, as his title *Seeing Is Believing* suggests. Indeed, to translate seeing into meaning entails moral responsibility; one must always respect the separateness, the individuality, indeed, the autonomy, of the perceived object. "I leave you," he writes of a tree he has just described, "to your own meaning, yourself alone." Elsewhere, he speaks of Paul Cézanne with high praise, for Cézanne knew to paint his mountains "unposed," to accept the object as it always "is"—separate and ultimately indefinable, autonomous, and mysterious. *The Flood* continues Tomlinson's concern with the "fineness of relationships," and the poet describes locales that have held continuing fascination for him, including New Mexico, France, Italy, and England. Once again, poetry is based upon sensation, but sensation is never an end in itself; it involves a reaching out for significance, an active stretching out to the universe.

The Return reiterates many of his characteristic themes and includes some of his most skilled poems. "February" focuses on a piece of glass that has been frozen in a stream of water. The metamorphic processes of nature have mesmerized the poet, and he celebrates the transmutations wrought by the exquisite shimmering of the glass. In "Night Ferry," the poet struggles within the flux of nature. Aware of his ultimate ignorance, he cries: "We hang in the balance of fathoms, chart and stars/ Where mountains on mountains stand round us and only the/ water stirs." Perhaps the only comfort one can attain is that if there is a heaven, it exists in human terms, to be imaginatively perceived and understood through the individual will.

Stylistically, Tomlinson's verse is characterized by random end rhythms and echo effects, assonance, dissonance, and roving alliteration, all organized within alternating indented lines and visually marked line divisions which attenuate his intended voice inflections. His syntax is elaborate, although the poems are markedly free of rhetoric. Given his subject, it is understandable that the "I" is restrained. All these effects of language, rhythm, image, and sound reinforce the relativistic nature of observed experience and knowledge—that all experience depends upon the inderdependence of mind and object, and object and the universal flux.

BIBLIOGRAPHICAL REFERENCES: The best starting place is *Charles Tomlinson: Man and Artist*, 1988, edited by Kathleen O'Gorman. An excellent essay on Tomlinson is Calvin Bedient, "Charles Tomlinson," in *Eight Contemporary Poets*, 1974. See Edward Hirsch, "The Meditative Eye of Charles Tomlinson," *The Hollins Critic*, XV (April, 1978), 1-12, for a discussion of the poet's use of surfaces and landscapes. See also Michael Schmidt, "In the Eden of Civility," *The Times Literary Supplement*, December 1, 1978, 1406, for a provocative article on Tomlinson's rhythms, images, and influences, particularly that of Edward Thomas. Also interesting is Donald Hall, "Poet's Progress," *The New York Times Book Review*, March 1, 1981, 12, on Tomlinson's sensitivity to nature and the uniqueness of his poetry written in America. Michael Hennessy, "Perception and Self in Charles Tomlinson's Early Poetry," *Rocky Mountain Review of Language and Literature*, XXXVI (1982), 91-102, is an excellent study of human egotism, temptation, and the compelling morality of the natural world. William S. Saunders, "Artifice and Ideas," *Delta*, LIX (1979), 35-40, treats the difficult balance of the inner (human) and outer (natural) worlds, essential to Tomlinson's aesthetic. Writing about Tomlinson as a Symbolist concerned with nature, not social issues, is Sidney Bolt, "Not the Full Face," *Delta*, XL (1967), 4-9, and discussing his "American" characteristics, particularly his affinities with Ezra Pound, is Alfred Corn, "Fishing by Obstinate Isles," in *The Metamorphoses of Metaphor*, 1987. Tomlinson's affinities with William Carlos Williams are discussed in Paul L. Mariani, "Charles Tomlinson," in *A Usable Past*, 1984. A superior essay on Tomlinson is Octavio Paz, "The Graphics of Charles Tomlinson: Black and White," in *On Poets and Others*, 1986, which treats the interpenetration of the objective and subjective in the poet's vision and craft. Hugh Kenner, an early champion of Tomlinson, includes an appreciative overview of his work in *A Sinking Island: The Modern English Writers*, 1988.

Lois Gordon

JOHN KENNEDY TOOLE

Born: New Orleans, Louisiana
Date: 1937

Died: Biloxi, Mississippi
Date: March 26, 1969

PRINCIPAL WORKS

NOVELS: *A Confederacy of Dunces*, 1980; *The Neon Bible*, 1989.

John Kennedy Toole will perhaps always be touted more for his potential than for his accomplishments, for his first published novel, *A Confederacy of Dunces*, was not printed until eleven years after his death. Born in 1937 in New Orleans, Louisiana, Toole was the son of John Toole, a car salesman, and Thelma Ducoing Toole, a teacher. The author, who had written his first novel at the age of sixteen, received a B.A. from Tulane University in 1958 and an M.A. in English from Columbia University the following year. Afer teaching at the University of Southwestern Louisiana, Toole served in the army, writing *A Confederacy of Dunces* while stationed in Puerto Rico from 1962 to 1963. Later Toole returned to New Orleans, where he worked toward a Ph.D. at Tulane University and taught at Saint Mary's Dominican College. In late 1968, he left New Orleans to travel and a few months later committed suicide in his car in Biloxi, Mississippi. He was thirty-one years old.

The Neon Bible, which Toole wrote at the age of sixteen, was finally cleared for publication in 1989, following legal battles among the author's heirs. The novel is set in a small Southern town in the 1940's and focuses on young David, who must deal with eccentric family members and the rigid, unforgiving religious fanaticism of the small-town community. David's crisis occurs when his father departs to fight in the war, his favorite aunt leaves town, and the preacher takes his mother away.

The publication of *A Confederacy of Dunces* has a unique history. Between 1963 and 1966, Toole negotiated with the publishing house Simon & Schuster, which, after commanding numerous revisions, finally rejected the work in 1966. Toole apparently gave up hope of the novel's ever being published. After Toole's death, however, his mother sent the worn, nearly illegible carbon copy to eight more publishers during the next seven years. In 1976, she began repeated efforts to persuade novelist Walker Percy, teaching at Loyola University in New Orleans, to read her son's novel. In the novel's foreword, Percy describes his unsuccessful attempts to dodge Thelma Toole, as well as his eventual determination to see the novel through to its publication by Louisiana State University Press in 1980. Despite the many rejections by publishers, *A Confederacy of Dunces* was a surprising critical success, selling forty-five thousand hardcover copies in five printings and later appearing on *The New York Times* paperback best-seller list for more than a month. The novel was awarded the 1980 Pulitzer Prize for fiction and was honored with a nomination for the prestigious Faulkner Award in 1981.

A Confederacy of Dunces is about thirty-year-old Ignatius J. Reilly, obese, educated, and lazy, who sponges off his garish, alcoholic mother, in the colorful city of New Orleans. Ignatius, whose name recalls Saint Ignatius Loyola, the founder of the Jesuit Order, is a proponent of medieval philosophy and values. He reads the work of the Roman Christian philosopher Boethius, who advocates passive acceptance of life's events. Ignatius records his thoughts and observations in Big Chief Tablets, which are strewn around his dank, monk's-cell of a room. He practices celibacy and upholds the ideals of theology and geometry and of taste and decency. Meanwhile, he escapes into the worlds of television and film while verbalizing his disgust at the vulgarity of such forms of entertainment; he consumes massive quantities of junk food and Dr. Nut soda despite a pyloric valve that causes intestinal distress when he is emotionally upset.

Ignatius' search for employment at his mother's insistence generates several subplots. At first he tries to work at the Levy Pants Company, a dying business in which almost no one, not even the owner, takes an interest. Ignatius decorates the office with hand-painted signs, rids the business of its problem of a backlog of files by discarding them, and incites unenthusiastic factory workers to riot in legitimate protest of squalid working conditions. He also befriends Miss Trixie, a senile octogenarian who shows up for work in her nightgown, mumbles incessantly about a Christmas turkey she was promised but never received, and begs to be allowed to retire. Ignatius' next job as a hot dog salesman for Paradise Vendors is even less profitable, for he eats more hot dogs than he sells and often slips away to the cinema.

In frequent correspondence with Myrna Minkoff, a New York political reformist whom he met in college and with whom he shares a love-hate relationship, Ignatius rebuffs her suggestions that all of his problems are sexual and organizes a group of French Quarter homosexuals in a plan to reform the world. Other subplots involve Ignatius' mother, who declares independence from her son and becomes socially active, and the proprietress of a strip joint, The Night of Joy, who peddles pornography and exploits her employees.

A Confederacy of Dunces has received much critical praise for the ingenuity of its characters and for the intricacy of its plot but mostly for its unique humor and the vividness of its language and local color. Some critics have been made uneasy by the overreliance on coincidence in the novel, but perhaps more disturbing to some has been the difficulty in categorizing the work. Ignatius J. Reilly is so repulsive, his treatment of his mother is so insensitive and cruel, that it is misleading to label him a comic hero. The title of the novel is from Jonathan Swift's writing: "When a true genius appears in the world, you may know him by this sign, that the dunces are all in confederacy against him." The novel is also in the mold of a Swiftian satire. Toole's hero is roguish, but the reader finds that this unpleasant character casts aspersions that likely echo the reader's own sentiments against the crassness, the materialism, and the decadence of society. Unlike the protagonist in traditional satires, however, Ignatius embraces many of the very hypocrisies, obscenities, and insensitivities against which he rails.

BIBLIOGRAPHICAL REFERENCES: See Lloyd Daigrepont, "Ignatius Reilly and the Confederacy of Dunces," *New Orleans Review*, IX (1981), 74-80, for a sound and thorough analysis of the incongruity of the protagonist of *A Confederacy of Dunces* with his society as the major source of the novel's comedy. For further study into the humor of the novel, William Nelson, "The Cosmic Grotesque in Recent Fiction," *Thalia*, V (1982/1983), 36-40, examines the novel's grotesque elements which nullify expectations of convention and resolution. Particularly insightful is David McNeil, "*A Confederacy of Dunces* as Reverse Satire: The American Subgenre," *Mississippi Quarterly*, XXXVIII (1984/1985), 33-47, which emphasizes the novel's place in the literary tradition of reverse satire, in which the protagonist hypocritically exemplifies the very ideals he criticizes. See also Edward C. Reilly, "Batman and Ignatius J. Reilly in *A Confederacy of Dunces*," *Notes on Contemporary Literature*, XII (1982), 10-11; Richard F. Patteson, "Ignatius Goes to the Movies: The Films in Toole's *A Confederacy of Dunces*," *Notes on Modern American Literature*, VI (1982), 14; Katherina M. Wilson, "Hrotsvit and the Tube: John Kennedy Toole and the Problem of Bad TV Programming," *Germanic Notes*, XV (1984), 4-5.

Lou Thompson

JEAN TOOMER

Born: Washington, D.C. *Died:* Doylestown, Pennsylvania
Date: December 26, 1894 *Date:* March 30, 1967

PRINCIPAL WORKS

SHORT FICTION: *Cane*, 1923.

PHILOSOPHY: *Essentials: A Philosophy of Life in Three Hundred Definitions and Aphorisms*, 1931.

RELIGION: *An Interpretation of Friends Worship*, 1947.

MISCELLANEOUS: *The Wayward and the Seeking: A Collection of Writings by Jean Toomer*, 1980.

Jean Toomer published only a single work of lasting literary importance, *Cane*, but that one volume has earned for him a distinguished place in American literary history. He was born Nathan Eugene Toomer in Washington, D.C., on December 26, 1894. His father, Nathan Toomer, abandoned his wife, Nina Pinchback, before their son was born. Reared in his maternal grandparents' home, Toomer was influenced by his grandfather, Pinckney Benton Stewart Pinchback, a proud and once-powerful man who had served as lieutenant governor of post-Civil War Louisiana during Reconstruction. Through much of his adolescence, the young man was known as Eugene Pinchback, and it was only when he began to pursue a literary career that he adopted his father's surname and changed Eugene to Jean.

Light-skinned and racially mixed, P. B. S. Pinchback had made his political career as a black; however, during Toomer's childhood the family lived in an exclusive white neighborhood on Washington's Bacon Street. Racial identity was an issue that Toomer considered carefully, and by the time he went to college, he had rejected identification with either race; instead, he embraced the label "American."

When Toomer was a teenager, the family moved to a black neighborhood, where he finished high school at the segregated M Street High School. After graduation, he attended a series of colleges: the University of Wisconsin, Massachusetts College of Agriculture, the American College of Physical Training, the University of Chicago, and the City College of New York. He never stayed at any school long enough to earn a degree, and he switched his academic interests several times.

Toomer's early interest in literature was inspired by his Uncle Bismark, who spent hours in bed surrounded by an eclectic array of books. It was not, however, until Toomer was studying at the City College of New York and had begun to meet literary figures such as E. A. Robinson, Waldo Frank, and Van Wyck Brooks that he thought seriously of writing as a career. Disappointed by his first efforts, Toomer returned to Washington and accepted an invitation to manage a school in Sparta, Georgia, for a few months. In Georgia, Toomer shared the life of the poor blacks who were served by the school, and he was moved by this introduction to rural black life. Encouraged by Frank after his return to New York in 1922, Toomer turned his experience in Georgia into *Cane*. The manuscript, which was finished by the spring of 1923, showed the influence of contemporary prose experimentation, combining prose and poetry in a three-part structure that begins in the rural South, moves to the urban North, and then returns to the South. In *Cane*, Toomer attempted to bridge the gap between the rural black heritage and the New Negro of the 1920's, creating a complex intermingling of black and white, rural and urban, primitive and civilized. *Cane* did not sell well, but it was a striking critical success, particularly among the other young black intellectuals who were forming the basis of the Harlem Renaissance.

Much of the critical reaction angered Toomer because it focused on his role as a black writer, a racial limitation that Toomer rejected. In reaction, he cut himself off from the literary crowd that had fostered his career. Although he published a few stories during the

1920's and a long narrative poem in 1936, he was unable to find a publisher for his other literary work. In the summer of 1924, Toomer traveled to George Ivanovitch Gurdjieff's Institute for Harmonious Development of Man in Fontainebleau, France. From that time until his marriage to Margery Latimer in 1932, Toomer worked as a teacher of the Gurdjieff philosophy, first in Harlem and then in Chicago. In 1934, after the death of his first wife in childbirth, he married Marjorie Content, and they settled in Doylestown, Pennsylvania. In 1940 he joined the Society of Friends, for whom he wrote several pamphlets. After 1950, he was generally incapacitated by illness, and he died in 1967 in Doylestown. Interest in Toomer was revived after *Cane* was reprinted in 1967. The general recognition that *Cane* is one of the outstanding achievements of the Harlem Renaissance guarantees Toomer a continuing place in American literary history.

BIBLIOGRAPHICAL REFERENCES: The most authoritative biography of Jean Toomer is Cynthia Earl Kerman and Richard Eldridge, *The Lives of Jean Toomer: A Hunger for Wholeness*, 1987, an exhaustive study that establishes the facts of Toomer's life. Brian Joseph Benson and Mabel Mayle Dillard, *Jean Toomer*, 1980, and Nellie McKay, *Jean Toomer, Artist: A Study of His Literary Life and Work, 1894-1936*, 1984, are important book-length studies that combine biography and literary analysis. Two collections of critical essays on *Cane* are *The Merrill Studies in Cane*, 1971, edited by Frank Durham, and *Cane*, 1988, edited by Darwin T. Turner. See also Arna Bontemps, "The Negro Renaissance: Jean Toomer and the Harlem of the 1920's," in *Anger and Beyond: The Negro Writer in the United States*, 1966, edited by Herbert Hill; Fritz Gysin, *The Grotesque in American Negro Literature: Jean Toomer, Richard Wright, and Ralph Ellison*, 1975; John M. Reilly, "The Search for Black Redemption: Jean Toomer's *Cane*," *Studies in the Novel*, II (1970), 312-324; Charles Scruggs, "Jean Toomer: Fugitive," *American Literature*, XLVII, 84-96; and Darwin T. Turner, "Jean Toomer: Exile" in *In a Minor Chord: Three Afro-American Writers and Their Search for Identity*, 1971.

Carl Brucker

SUSAN ALLEN TOTH

Born: Ames, Iowa
Date: June 24, 1940

PRINCIPAL WORKS

AUTOBIOGRAPHY: *Blooming: A Small-Town Girlhood*, 1981; *Ivy Days: Making My Way Out East*, 1984.

ESSAYS: *How to Prepare for Your High-School Reunion and Other Midlife Musings*, 1988.

Susan Allen Toth is an important Midwestern chronicler of the life of the common person. Her writing shows how a relatively ordinary life may seem uncommon and intriguing if it is told with a sensitivity and sympathy for humanity. Born on June 24, 1940, in Ames, Iowa, where she was also reared, she had a quiet and happy childhood with her mother, Hazel Erickson Allen Lipa, an English teacher at Iowa State University, and her sister, Karen, a year older than Toth. Her father, Edward Douglas Allen, a promising economist at Iowa State, died when she was seven years old, and her mother remained single until remarriage during Toth's college years.

Toth's childhood and adolescence are recorded in detail in her first book, *Blooming*, which is a thematic collection of reminiscences from her grade-school years to her arrival at Smith College. The book depicts incidents and people, apprehensions and successes, that shape the person she would become in adulthood. *Blooming* also describes Toth's early propensity for omnivorous reading, her immersion in the Protestant work ethic (from baby-sitting to detasseling corn), and the social and psychological importance of cultivating many girlfriends and boyfriends.

Blooming's eleven chapters explore Toth's early interests and involvements: the town swimming pools and her family's summer lake retreat, her friends and classes and parties, holiday celebrations, and preparations for and departure to college. *Ivy Days*, a memoir of Toth's four years at Smith College and her first two years of graduate school at the University of California at Berkeley, has seven chapters which tell of Toth's alliance with and adjustments to all sorts of other women, her fledgling attempts at the social customs of drinking and smoking, her embarrassments and boredom on uninteresting or threatening dates, her apprehensions and successes in college classes, and her enchantment with campus scenery and with East Coast families of her friends.

Ivy Days is not only more mature chronologically than her first book but also tighter in its writing, with more extended metaphors. Apples packed in a bag for lunch on the train home from college symbolize freedom and health, a quilt made by her aunt signifies solace and love in her claustrophobic dormitory room in Lawrence House, and six-foot long college scarves curled on other girls' shoulders broadcast popularity and romantic involvement. *Ivy Days* is a book at once universal and particular in its topics of uprooting, moving, homesickness, and making new friends.

Ivy Days is also about charting direction for life. Toth embarks on a history major after considering art history and economics, but two months later she finds governmental abstractions and legislative acts uninteresting when compared with the writing of Henry David Thoreau and Thomas Carlyle, which delights her. That her experiences as an English major are not all positive, however, is proved by a devastating comment from a creative writing instructor, which caused her to give up writing short stories for eighteen years.

After one summer working in Boston for the *Harvard Business Review* and another going to summer school in London, she was graduated from college, not with the summa cum laude distinction for which she had strived (illness having caused her to do poorly on the last qualifying examination) but with magna cum laude distinction and with her mother and stepfather in attendance at the ceremony. The last dozen pages of the book cover her

Berkeley years and her meeting and falling in love with Larry Toth, whom she married in 1963.

Toth's third book, *How to Prepare for Your High-School Reunion and Other Midlife Musings*, chronicles her feelings and concerns at the stage of mid-life, following her divorce in 1974 and remarriage to architect James Stageberg in 1985. Here she presents emotions and insights about single parenting, adult dating, adjustments in a happy remarriage, college teaching, tranquillity in nature, and fascination with material things. In one essay, childhood reminiscence about an inappropriate gift purchased for her mother concerns, more important, parental love. In other essays, she recommends five steps of preparation for attending a class reunion, offers suggestions and encouragement to would-be writers, shows how she combats an emotional crisis, and shares fears of violence and crime in an urban neighborhood. In three of the final essays, Toth hypothesizes about her maternal grandmother's life and the lessons Toth learned from her without ever meeting her.

Toth has said that she has been influenced by E. B. White's varied sentence structure, his use of surprising image, and his zest for life amid his own fear and self-doubt. She is an avid admirer of Henry David Thoreau, for his spare and strong style and his moral philosophy. From Sarah Orne Jewett she learned to write about small things and the quiet, domestic life.

In her personal revelations, Toth is unpretentious, self-deprecating, and unembarrassed. Her books are domestic writing about small things that concern humanity in general, and she uses commonplace subjects, such as picking raspberries or buying knee socks, to illustrate truths about life. Her style is modest and matter-of-fact, and her prose reveals universal experience in three important stages of growing and changing in life. Many critics have noted that her work is so well-received because her vivid memories spark similar reminiscences in her readers.

BIBLIOGRAPHICAL REFERENCES: See *Dictionary of Literary Biography*, 1986, where Patricia L. Skarda's comprehensive essay on Toth's works, influences, and life is followed by an interview with Toth. Many reviews of Toth's books have been published in newspapers and journals. Among the most useful are Susan Bolotin, "Growing Up in Ames," *The New York Times Book Review*, May 24, 1981, 4; Barbara Creaturo, "An Innocent from Iowa," *The New York Times Book Review*, June 17, 1984, 31; Elizabeth R. Baer, "Slinkies, Cold Cream, Compacts, and Pincushions," *Belles Lettres*, Fall, 1988, 19; and Robert Bartley, "Remembrance of Growing Up in America's Heartland," *The Wall Street Journal*, June 11, 1981, 26.

Jill B. Gidmark

MICHEL TOURNIER

Born: Paris, France
Date: December 19, 1924

PRINCIPAL WORKS

NOVELS: *Vendredi: Ou, Les Limbes du Pacifique*, 1967 (*Friday: Or, The Other Island*, 1969); *Le Roi des Aulnes*, 1970 (*The Ogre*, 1972); *Les Météores*, 1975 (*Gemini*, 1981); *Gaspard, Melchior, et Balthazar*, 1980 (*The Four Wise Men*, 1982); *Gilles et Jeanne*, 1983 (*Gilles and Jeanne*, 1987); *La Goutte d'or*, 1985 (*The Golden Droplet*, 1987).

SHORT FICTION: *Le Coq de Bruyère*, 1978 (*The Fetishist and Other Stories*, 1983).

TRAVEL SKETCH: *Canada: Journal de voyage*, 1977.

ESSAYS: *Le Vent Paraclet*, 1977 (*The Wind Spirit*, 1988).

CHILDREN'S LITERATURE: *Vendredi: Ou, La Vie sauvage*, 1971 (*Friday and Robinson: Life on Esperanza Island*, 1972).

CRITICISM: *Le Vol du vampire: Notes de lecture*, 1981.

OTHER NONFICTION: *Le Vagabond immobile*, 1984 (with Jean-Max Toubeau).

Michel Tournier is one of the most widely read, most honored, and certainly most controversial and thought-provoking writers on the contemporary European scene. He was born in Paris on December 19, 1924, thc son of Alphonse and Marie-Madeleine (Fournier) Tournier, who had met while studying German at the Sorbonne. Alphonse's educational career was curtailed by World War I; after being wounded, he abandoned professional ambitions and founded an international bureau which dealt with musicians' copyrights. Tournier's favorite toy was the phonograph; from childhood on, he enjoyed music, but even more the power of the spoken word. Marie-Madeleine's legacy was equally formative. While she gave up her teaching plans for child-rearing, she never lost her love for Germany, which she passed on to her children. Tournier's maternal great-uncle, Gustave Fournier, had taught German in Dijon, and tales about Gustave and Edouard, Tournier's grandfather, during the Prussian occupation of the 1870's form the basis of some of Tournier's autobiographical vignettes in *The Wind Spirit*. His own childhood was laced with train excursions to the Black Forest; these happy occasions took place within the growing shadow of Nazism. Tournier was not a diligent student nor was he a prodigious reader. Yet he was attracted to writers such as Hans Christian Andersen, whose works combine fantasy with reality. Tournier has said that he wishes his own works to be comprehensible to any twelve year old. His stories in *The Fetishist and Other Stories*, his rewriting of Daniel Defoe's *Robinson Crusoe* (1719) in *Friday*, and the novel *The Four Wise Men* reflect his early reading.

When he was four years old, Tournier underwent a routine tonsillectomy. To the nervous and hypersensitive young boy, the operation was a nightmare, an invasion. It gave Tournier a sense of alienation and a mistrust of other people. This feeling of solitude and separation was furthered by his experiences during World War II. Too young for active service, Tournier first saw the war from a perspective of youthful exuberance. At the beginning of the Occupation, his family lived in the Parisian suburbs, but their home was soon commandeered by German officers, and the Tourniers were socially categorized by their *germanistik* sympathies. The family moved to an apartment in Neuilly while Tournier stayed at a summer cottage in Villers-sur-Mer and, later on, in the village of Lusigny. In spring, 1944, by chance he was away from Lusigny when his foster family was deported to Buchenwald for having helped the Maquis. Tournier's love of German culture made Nazi excesses even more intolerable to him, but he admits that he, like the majority of the French, never considered joining the Resistance. From 1942 to 1945, Tournier studied philosophy at the Sorbonne under Gaston Bachelard and Jean-Paul Sartre. He also was influenced by fellow student Gilles Deleuze. In 1946, Tournier went to the university in Tübingen for a proposed three-week study of German philosophers; he stayed there for four years. In July, 1949, however, Tournier suffered the setback which ended his academic career: He failed his Sorbonne doctoral exam. It was a bitter blow, and yet it may also be seen as the beginning of his literary vocation.

From 1949 to 1958, Tournier worked in radio and television production, first for a French station, and than as an announcer for Europe No. 1. He lived in a Parisian hotel with other painters and writers. He also worked as a translator of contemporary German texts, most notably those of Erich Maria Remarque, into French, and he took courses from Claude Lévi-Strauss. In 1958, he became head of literary services for Editions Plon, where he worked until 1968. As a writer, Tournier is an anomaly. Already leading a reasonably comfortable intellectual life, he published *Friday* in 1967 at the age of forty-three. A study of human isolation and sensuality, it enjoyed immediate critical success, winning the Grand Prix de Roman of the Académie Française. The novel was a popular success as well; in fact, Tournier's novels generally top the French best-seller lists for weeks, even months.

The 1970's were a time of artistic development for Tournier. In 1970, *The Ogre* won the Prix Goncourt. Set against a background of World War II, its portrayal of Fascism, pederasty, and alienation is both repulsive and compelling. Tournier's personal background has led critics to speculate extensively on the novel's verisimilitude and *roman à clef* qualities. Tournier was elected to the Académie Goncourt in 1972, and throughout the early 1970's he traveled extensively; among the places he visited were Japan, Iceland, Canada, and Northern Africa. These trips were reflected in his own favorite work, *Gemini*, a study of twinship and solitude, sublimation and desire. Unfriendly critics have denounced *Gemini* as morally reprehensible, yet more favorable readers applaud its candid and intellectual approach to questions of sexual identity and power. During the 1970's, Tournier also devoted time to writing children's stories and to his hobby of photography. In 1975, Tournier was honored as a Chevalier de la Légion d'Honneur.

Tournier has frequently remarked upon the importance of the maturation process. His novels of the 1980's, *The Four Wise Men*, *Gilles and Jeanne*, and *The Golden Droplet*, and his more personal writings, *Le Vol du vampire* (vampire's flight) and *Le Vagabond immobile* (the stationary nomad), all reflect his earlier preoccupations, yet they also develop profound questions of responsibility, biblical interpretation, illusion and reality. Tournier's texts have been taken to task for lacking the structural complexity of the New Novel, yet he has deliberately chosen to focus his narratives on philosophical ideas and the portrayal of the human dilemma. Perhaps that is the very core of his appeal.

BIBLIOGRAPHICAL REFERENCES: A comprehensive study of Tournier available in English is Colin Davis, *Michel Tournier: Philosophy and Fiction*, 1988. For a solid introduction to Tournier's life and works, see William Cloonan, *Michel Tournier*, 1985, a volume in the Twayne World Authors series; Maura Daly, "An Interview with Michel Tournier," *Partisan Review*, LII (1985), 407-413; and Roger Shattuck, "Locating Michel Tournier," in *The Innocent Eye: On Modern Literature and the Arts*, 1984. For interpretations of Tournier's religious vision, consult Susan Petit, "The Bible as Inspiration in Tournier's *Vendredi*," *French Forum*, IX (1984), 343-354, and William Cloonan, "The Spiritual Order of Michel Tournier," *Renascence*, XXXVI (1983/1984), 77-87. A comparison of Tournier's work with contemporary American writing can be found in Katherine C. Kurk, "Narration as Salvation: Textual Ethics of Michel Tournier and John Barth," *Comparative Literature Studies*, XXV (1988), 251-262. For other critical commentary, see William Cloonan, "Word, Image, and Illusion in *La Goutte d'or*," *The French Review*, LXII (1989), 467-475, and Susan Petit, "*Gilles et Jeanne*: Tournier's *Le Roi des Aulnes* Revisited," *Romanic Review*, LVI (1985), 309-315.

Katherine C. Kurk

WILLIAM TREVOR
William Trevor Cox

Born: Mitchelstown, County Cork, Ireland
Date: May 24, 1928

PRINCIPAL WORKS

NOVELS: *A Standard of Behaviour*, 1958; *The Old Boys*, 1964; *The Boarding-House*, 1965; *The Love Department*, 1966; *Mrs. Eckdorf in O'Neill's Hotel*, 1969; *Miss Gomez and the Brethren*, 1971; *Elizabeth Alone*, 1973; *The Children of Dynmouth*, 1976; *Other People's Worlds*, 1980; *Fools of Fortune*, 1983; *The Silence in the Garden*, 1988.

SHORT FICTION: *The Day We Got Drunk on Cake and Other Stories*, 1967; *The Ballroom of Romance and Other Stories*, 1972; *The Last Lunch of the Season*, 1973; *Angels at the Ritz and Other Stories*, 1975; *Lovers of Their Time and Other Stories*, 1978; *The Distant Past*, 1979; *Beyond the Pale and Other Stories*, 1981; *The Stories of William Trevor*, 1983; *The News from Ireland and Other Stories*, 1986; *Nights at the Alexandra*, 1987.

PLAYS: *The Girl*, pr., pb. 1968; *The Old Boys*, pr., pb. 1971; *A Night with Mrs. da Tanka*, pr., pb. 1972; *Going Home*, pr., pb. 1972; *A Perfect Relationship*, pr. 1973; *Scenes from an Album*, pr., pb. 1981.

RADIO PLAYS: *Going Home*, pr. 1970; *A Perfect Relationship*, pr. 1973; *Scenes from an Album*, pr. 1975; *Beyond the Pale*, pr. 1980.

TELEPLAYS: *The Girl*, 1967; *A Night with Mrs. da Tanka*, 1968; *Broken Homes*, 1985.

NONFICTION: *Old School Ties*, 1976; *A Writer's Ireland: Landscape in Literature*, 1984.

William Trevor's fertile imagination can scarcely be summed up in two adjectives, but if one were so limited, then "gothic" and "elegiac" would do very well. Though not an experimentalist, he has developed a flexible narrative form that conveys a wide variety of attitudes, shifts of tone, speaking voices, and descriptive passages that, while not pretending to rival the accomplishments of his master, James Joyce, have succeeded in establishing Trevor as a leading fiction writer on both sides of the Atlantic. Born William Trevor Cox in a small town in County Cork, Ireland, Trevor was educated in a haphazard way until he entered St. Columba's College in Dublin in 1942. In 1950, he earned his baccalaureate from Trinity College and for the next decade or so eked out a living teaching school while working as a sculptor. Although one of his sculptures won a prize in 1952, he gave up sculpting a few years afterward in favor of writing. Meanwhile, he had left Ireland for England, where he eventually made his home in Devonshire after teaching in Rugby and Taunton and then working in advertising in London.

Moving to England was motivated strictly by economics, as work was hard to find in Ireland after graduation from Trinity College. Nevertheless, Trevor evidently found the English social and intellectual climate congenial, which explains his continued residence. More important, he found there a singular advantage to his writing, the advantage one enjoys as an acute observer of a culture different from one's own. Hence, his early stories and novels treat English subjects and involve English men and women; only later did he begin to focus upon his native Ireland. Perhaps the advantage of living away from his homeland for an extended period gave him the perspective he felt he needed. In any event, while books such as *The Old Boys* and *The Children of Dynmouth* deal impressively with English themes and English characters, short stories such as "Attracta" in *Lovers of Their Time and Other Stories* and the title story in *The News from Ireland and Other Stories* reveal Trevor's sure handling of Irish subjects, in both historical and contemporary settings.

The gothic aspect of Trevor's imagination shows itself in the assemblage of misfits, oddballs, and eccentrics that populate almost all of his fiction. Studdy and Nurse Clock in *The Boarding-House* also demonstrate its sinister side. Bitter rivals and indeed enemies, they link up in an unholy alliance to become the sole beneficiaries of an unusual bequest, but they are ultimately thwarted by their own greed and a failure to grasp the warped intelligence of those they are trying to cheat. Young Timothy Gedge, by contrast, seems to understand only too well the weaknesses of his victims, as he tries to insinuate himself into their lives. If like Studdy he is a confidence man, his youth and his loneliness combine to make him finally a creature more pathetic than wicked, though Trevor does not underestimate the potential—and real—evil of which Gedge is capable.

The presence of evil in the world and the inability of many human beings to communicate effectively with one another explain the sadness, or the elegiac quality, that colors so much of Trevor's work. *Nights at the Alexandra* develops this quality to an extraordinary degree. The keynote sounds with the opening short paragraph: "I am a fifty-eight-year-old provincial. I have no children. I have never married." This statement is the unintended legacy that Alexandra Messinger, an Englishwoman married to a German, leaves young Harry. She and her husband have fled from Nazi Germany and are living in a small Irish town during the "Emergency" (as the Irish called World War II). Told from the vantage point of many years later, *Nights at the Alexandra* recounts the story of a youngster who, badly misunderstood by his parents and siblings, becomes a loner. Much taken by the beautiful, mysterious but kindly woman many years her husband's junior, Harry defies parental orders not to visit with the strangers and ultimately elects to work in Herr Messinger's newly erected cinema instead of his father's lumberyard. Built despite wartime shortages and named for Frau Messinger, the cinema is her husband's gift to her and to the town. When it finally opens, however, Frau Messinger has died and her husband leaves the town and Cloverhill, the home where Harry visited them, forever. The illness is never named or explained, but it doubtless derives in part from an early heartbreak Frau Messinger experienced, the inability to give her husband a child, her deep sense of gratitude to him for his love and devotion, and in general the profound isolation she finds in these alien surroundings. "We can live without anything but love, Harry," she says at one point. "Always remember that." Yet though she has love, she dies, and dying, she takes with her any chance Harry may have to love, though he lives on.

Trevor has written plays for stage and television, many of them adapted from his own stories or novels. He believes short stories lend themselves better to films than novels do, but he has adapted both for radio and television, including "Beyond the Pale," "Voices from the Past," "The Love of a Good Woman," "Matilda's England," *Elizabeth Alone*, and "The Ballroom of Romance."

BIBLIOGRAPHICAL REFERENCES: For an extended discussion of Trevor's life and work, see Jay L. Halio and Paul Binding's essay in *British Novelists Since 1960*, 1981, edited by Jay L. Halio, and Halio's article in *Contemporary Novelists*, 1986, edited by D. L. Kirkpatrick. An interview with Trevor is in *The Writer's Place: Interviews on the Literary Situation in Contemporary Britain*, 1974, edited by Peter Firchow. See also Mark Ralph-Bowman, "William Trevor," *Transatlantic Review*, XLIII/XLIV (1976), 5-12; Tim Heald, "Beneath the Mask of Gentility," *The Times* (London), June 18, 1980, 13; Julian Gitzen, "The Truth Tellers of William Trevor," *Critique: Studies in Modern Fiction*, XXI (1979), 59-72; Mark Mortimer, "William Trevor in Dublin," *Etudes Irlandaises* (Lille), IV (1975), 77-85; and Janet Watts, "William Trevor's Little Irk," *The Observer* (London), June 11, 1980.

Jay L. Halio

YURY TRIFONOV

Born: Moscow, Soviet Union
Date: August 28, 1925

Died: Moscow, Soviet Union
Date: March 28, 1981

PRINCIPAL WORKS

NOVELS: *Studenty,* 1950 (*Students*, 1953); *Utoleniye zhazhdy,* 1963 (*Thirst Acquenched*, 1964); *Otblesk kostra*, 1965; *Neterpenie*, 1973 (*The Impatient Ones*, 1978); *Drugaya zhizn'*, 1975 (*Another Life*, 1983); *Dom na naberezhnoy,* 1976 (*The House on the Embankment*, 1983); *Starik*, 1978 (*The Old Man*, 1984); *Vremya i mesto*, 1981; *Ischeznoveniye*, 1987.

NOVELLAS: *Obmen*, 1969 (*The Exchange*, 1978); *Predvaritel'nye itogi*, 1970 (*Taking Stock*, 1978); *Dolgoe proshchaniye*, 1971 (*The Long Goodbye*, 1978).

SHORT FICTION: *Pod solntsem*, 1959; *V kontse sezona*, 1961; *Fakely na Flaminio*, 1965; *Igry v sumerkakh*, 1970; *Oprokinutyy dom*, 1981.

ESSAYS: *Kak slovo nashe otzovetsiya . . .* , 1985.

Yury Valentinovich Trifonov was one of the Soviet Union's leading prose writers of the 1960's and 1970's. He was born in Moscow on August 28, 1925, the son of Valentin Trifonov, a longtime revolutionary activist. The elder Trifonov, who had joined the Bolshevik Party in 1904, had suffered imprisonment and exile under the czarist regime. By the time of the 1917 Revolution, Valentin Trifonov was a member of the revolutionary council in Petrograd, and during the Civil War of 1918-1921, he helped to organize units of the Red Army. His prominent position allowed him to obtain an apartment in the "house on the embankment," a large gray structure in Moscow for high government officials and, later, the setting for Trifonov's novel of that name. In 1937, during the purges ordered by Joseph Stalin, Trifonov's father was arrested, and the following year, he was executed. An important influence on Trifonov's career was the effort to come to terms both with the revolutionary activities of his father and with his father's disappearance while Trifonov was still very young.

In 1938, Trifonov's mother was also arrested; until her release in 1946, he and his sister were reared by his grandmother. At the beginning of World War II, he was briefly evacuated to Central Asia, but then he returned to Moscow, where he worked at an airplane factory. In 1944, Trifonov, who had written both poetry and prose throughout his youth, entered the Gorky Literary Institute—Russia's leading writers' school. There he concentrated on prose, publishing his first stories, which were based on travels to Armenia and to the Kuban region, in 1947. He was graduated from the institute in 1949; his thesis was the novel *Students*, which deals with academic life during the postwar years. The book was awarded a Stalin Prize and brought Trifonov early renown. There was then a thirteen-year hiatus until the appearance of his next novel, *Thirst Acquenched*, which deals with the construction of an irrigation canal in Turkmenistan. His travels to the area resulted as well in the volume of stories *Pod solntsem* (under the sun). During the 1960's Trifonov also wrote numerous stories and sketches on sports, which formed the basis for several collections.

The first signs of Trifonov's later interests can be found in the factually based narrative *Otblesk kostra* (the fire's gleam), an account of Valentin Trifonov's role in the revolution and its aftermath. Although inspired by actual documents and memoirs, the book is less a conventional biography than an attempt on the part of the narrator to understand several key moments in his father's life. Even when Trifonov is simply describing actual events, he allows himself to manipulate the material to create an artistically more satisfying work; hence, while he resisted the efforts to assign this story of his father to any one genre, many critics persist in calling it a novel. Trifonov's interest in the biography of revolutionaries can also be seen in *The Impatient Ones*, a portrayal of Andrey Zhelyabov, who, as a member of the People's Will Party, conspired to assassinate Alexander II in 1881.

Trifonov gained renewed fame not so much through his historically based writings as through a series of stories and novellas from the late 1960's and early 1970's, in which he depicted a spiritual malaise within the urban middle and upper classes that had grown up in the shadow of Stalinism. Patricularly important in this regard is his "Moscow cycle," which originally consisted of the novellas *The Exchange*, *Taking Stock*, and *The Long Goodbye* but which most would extend to include the majority of his subsequent novels as well. While the three novellas are not overtly political, they offer an implicit critique of Soviet society by showing an entire generation of people who no longer believe, or are even interested, in revolutionary ideals. Their lives are totally occupied with efforts to achieve success, but they have discovered that neither acclaim from their peers nor material possessions provide satisfaction. In his later novels, Trifonov combined his portrayals of contemporary society with investigations into the events that formed his characters. By the end of the 1970's, Trifonov was attaining new heights with each work; thus his sudden death at age fifty-five, from a heart attack following a routine kidney operation, came as a great shock to all who follow Russian literature.

Trifonov's writing did not so much broaden as deepen. During the final decade of his life, he again and again returned to situations that he had treated earlier, exploring similar situations from different angles and trying to gain a deeper understanding of his characters, of the eras that he had lived through, and ultimately of both his father and of himself. Trifonov served as a spokesman for his generation. During the time that Leonid Brezhnev governed the Soviet Union, when most writers were too timid to examine the Stalinist legacy, Trifonov pushed back the limits of what was permissible within Soviet literature. He did not only treat once-forbidden topics, however, his works are notable most of all for their honesty, an honesty that does not allow for easy judgments. His villains are ususally deserving of some sympathy, and his protagonists elicit more pity than praise. Those whose outlook was formed during the Revolution find themselves ill-equipped for life afterward, while their descendants, those of Trifonov's age, have compromised all too often. Perhaps his most lasting achievement, then, was to chronicle the moral void sensed by many of his contemporaries, who no longer believed in the exemplars of the past and could find no heroes in the present.

BIBLIOGRAPHICAL REFERENCES: An overall introduction to Trifonov's late work can be obtained by reading N. N. Schneidman, *Soviet Literature in the 1970's: Artistic Diversity and Ideological Conformity*, 1979, and his "The New Dimensions of Time and Place in Iurii Trifonov's Prose of the 1980's," *Canadian Slavonic Papers*, XXVII (1985), 188-195. For detailed comments on the three Moscow novellas as well as on *Another Life* and *The House on the Embankment*, see B. Pankin, "A Circle or a Spiral? On Iurii Trifonov's Novels," *Soviet Studies in Literature*, XIV, no. 4 (1978), 65-100. Other general studies of Trifonov's mature period include Caroline de Maegd-Soëp, "The Theme of 'Byt'—Everyday Life—in the Stories of Iurii Trifonov," in *Russian Literature and Criticism*, 1982, edited by Evelyn Bristol; Paul M. Austin, "From Helsingfors to Helsinki: Jurij Trifonov's Search for His Past," *Scando-Slavica*, XXXII (1986), 5-15; and S. Paton, "The Hero of his Time," *Slavonic and East European Review*, LXIV (1986), 506-525. Studies of individual works include Andrew Durkin, "Trifonov's 'Taking Stock': The Role of Čexovian Subtext," *Slavic and East European Journal*, XXVIII (1984), 32-41; Josephine Woll, "Trifonov's *Starik*: The Truth of the Past," *Russian Literature Triquarterly*, XIX (1986), 243-258. Particularly informative are two studies by Sigrid McLaughlin: "Jurij Trifonov's *House on the Embankment*: Narration and Meaning," *Slavic and East European Journal*, XXVI (1982), 419-433, and her "Antipov's *Nikiforov Syndrome*: The Embedded Novel in Trifonov's *Time and Place*," *Slavic and East European Journal*, XXXII (1988), 237-250. See also the passing remarks on *Students* in Vera Dunham, *In Stalin's Time: Middleclass Values in Soviet Ficition*, 1976. See also Geoffrey Hosking, *Beyond Socialist Realism: Soviet Fiction Since "Ivan Denisovich,"* 1980; Nina Kolesnikoff, "Jurij Trifonov as a Novella Writer," *Russian Language Journal*, XXXIV, no. 118

(1980), 137-144; Edward Brown, *Russian Literature Since the Revolution*, 1982 (rev. ed.); and Richard L. Chapple, "Yury Trifonov and the Maturation of Soviet Literature," *Midwest Quarterly*, XXIX (1987), 40-54.

Barry P. Scherr

LIONEL TRILLING

Born: New York, New York
Date: July 4, 1905

Died: New York, New York
Date: November 5, 1975

PRINCIPAL WORKS

LITERARY CRITICISM: *Matthew Arnold*, 1939; *E. M. Forster*, 1943; *The Liberal Imagination: Essays on Literature and Society*, 1950; *The Opposing Self*, 1955; *A Gathering of Fugitives*, 1956; *Beyond Culture: Essays on Learning and Literature*, 1965; *Sincerity and Authenticity*, 1972; *Speaking of Literature and Society*, 1980.

NONFICTION: *Freud and the Crisis of Our Culture*, 1955; *Mind in the Modern World*, 1973; *Prefaces to "The Experience of Literature,"* 1979; *The Last Decade, Essays and Reviews, 1965-1975*, 1979.

NOVEL: *The Middle of the Journey*, 1947.

SHORT FICTION: *Of This Time, of That Place, and Other Stories*, 1979.

EDITED TEXTS: *The Portable Matthew Arnold*, 1949; *The Selected Letters of John Keats*, 1951; *The Experience of Literature: A Reader with Commentaries*, 1967; *The Life and World of Sigmund Freud*, 1970; *Literary Criticism: An Introductory Reader*, 1970; *The Oxford Anthology of English Literature*, 1973 (with others).

Lionel Trilling grew up in a Jewish neighborhood in New York City. Except for some of his youthful writing, he shunned specifically Jewish themes and identified his work with the great traditions of literature in Europe and the United States. His initial plan was to become a novelist, but he enrolled in Columbia University and became an astute student and critic, eventually obtaining his Ph.D. In fact, Trilling's dissertation, on Matthew Arnold, became a highly acclaimed book. Like Arnold, Trilling became not only a literary critic but also a critic of culture. Along with Edmund Wilson, Trilling has come to be regarded as perhaps the pivotal critic of his generation, defining the dominant character of American literature and assessing the literature itself in profoundly moral and historical terms.

Trilling's elegant, sober style helped to shape the literary tastes of a generation. In an enormously influential collection of essays, *The Liberal Imagination*, for example, he praises Henry James for his style, point of view, sensitivity, and complexity while deploring Theodore Dreiser's well-meaning but clumsy and vapid rhetoric. Trilling maintains that in novels, such as *The Princess Casamassima* (1886), James exhibited a political sensitivity and shrewdness that was every bit as valuable as Dreiser's—more so, since the literary value of James's work was so much greater. The point of such evaluations for Trilling's generation was that they rectified the rather provincial bias of earlier critics who were wary of James's European biases and too eager to elevate new American writers such as Dreiser to canonical status.

Trilling was particularly interested in the relationship between works of art and culture. As a result, he drew on a number of different academic disciplines, such as history, philosophy, and psychology. He was especially curious as to how Sigmund Freud's ideas about the mind might be applied to the study of literary works. While he had enormous respect for works of art, he thought that they were open to analysis using the vocabulary of the modern social sciences.

In *The Liberal Imagination*, Trilling articulates his stance as a critic heavily involved in determining the character of the age while assessing its roots in the past. In *Beyond Culture*, he extends his range by looking closely at the quality of American education. He is troubled by the way modern literature has been absorbed into the college curriculum, even though the producers of that literature had been against the institutionalization of knowledge. What will be the fate of the great modern works of literature in a setting that is itself conventionalized? Trilling seeks, in other words, to remind his readers (many of whom are academics) of the subversive value of literature which questions, rather than supports, the status quo. Implicit in

Trilling's argument is the notion that revolutionary ideas of modern literature should not be allowed to be domesticated. Somehow teachers have to give students a feel for the iconoclasm of art.

In "Some Notes for an Autobiographical Lecture," Trilling explains how he first became engaged with Matthew Arnold and then how the example of Arnold turned Trilling toward the writing of an intellectual biography that was to have a profound impact on all of his criticism. In the beginning, Arnold represented the poet as the passive vehicle through which the stresses and strains of his culture get expressed. In the end, the poet became a rebel defiant of culture, someone who wanted to change it. That is also the kind of critic Trilling became: Never sure that literature, the teaching of literature, or the writing of literary criticism were self-justifying activities, he actively took on the point of view of society and argued for and against it. In an autobiographical lecture, Trilling calls his stance "novelistic," by which he seems to mean that all of his assumptions have to be tested against experience and that ideas are not sacrosanct—they have no permanent truth—but must be constantly revaluated in a changing environment. While many critics might echo Trilling's sentiments, very few have embedded this novelistic imagination in their prose. Trilling's work, read in its entirety, confirms that his views of literature and society continued to develop in response to the changing times.

BIBLIOGRAPHICAL REFERENCES: Edward J. Shoban, Jr., *Lionel Trilling: Mind and Character*, 1981, is a general study of Trilling's complete works. It provides important biographical information as well as a study of Trilling's influential novel, *The Middle of the Journey*. William M. Chace, *Lionel Trilling: Criticism and Politics*, 1980, and Mark Krupnick, *Lionel Trilling and the Fate of Cultural Criticism*, 1986, are primarily concerned with Trilling's influence and his merit as a literary critic. *Art, Politics, and Will: Essays in Honor of Lionel Trilling*, 1977, edited by Quentin Anderson, Stephen Donadio, and Steven Marcus, is a valuable collection of essays by scholars, some of whom knew Trilling well and taught with him at Columbia University.

Carl Rollyson

FRANK TUOHY

Born: Uckfield, England
Date: May 2, 1925

PRINCIPAL WORKS

NOVELS: *The Animal Game*, 1957; *The Warm Nights of January*, 1960; *The Ice Saints*, 1964.

SHORT FICTION: *The Admiral and the Nuns, with Other Stories*, 1962; *Fingers in the Door and Other Stories*, 1970; *Live Bait and Other Stories*, 1978; *The Collected Stories of Frank Tuohy*, 1984.

TRAVEL SKETCH: *Portugal*, 1970.

BIOGRAPHY: *Yeats*, 1976.

John Francis Tuohy's writing is distinguished by two qualities: the excellence of his craft and the pessimism of his outlook. He was born May 2, 1925, in Uckfield, England, the son of Patrick Gerald Tuohy and Dorothy Annandale Tuohy. After graduation from the University of Cambridge in 1946, he embarked on a career teaching English language and literature in foreign countries, including Finland, Brazil, Poland, Japan, and the United States. His travels provided him with the settings for his novels and many of his stories, which center on the lives of expatriates and their interaction with one another and with foreign nationals. *The Animal Game* concerns a love affair between a Brazilian woman of the upper class and a crude English film director. The action is described mostly through the eyes of a well-educated Englishman, Robin Morris, the employee of a British oil company. A second novel, *The Warm Nights of January*, is also set in Brazil. In this story, a French artist falls in love with a Brazilian man. Tuohy's prizewinning third novel, *The Ice Saints*, is generally considered his best.

The Ice Saints, set in Poland, tells the story of a Polish professor, his wife, and their son, who inherits a fortune from his mother's English relatives. Rose Nicholson, the boy's aunt, goes to Poland in the guise of a tourist, visits her sister's family, and tries to persuade the boy, Tadeusz, to return to England, where he can enjoy his fortune. During her visit, Rose has an affair with a Polish government agent, who reveals the family's secret to the government, spoiling any hope they may have had to get Tadeusz out of the country. Without descending to propaganda, *The Ice Saints* paints a grim picture of life behind the Iron Curtain. Tuohy's vision of the Polish is of a people condemned to secrecy and duplicity. On the other hand, his English heroine is condemned by her own lack of discretion. The net effect is one of hopelessness, alleviated only by Tuohy's dry humor.

Tuohy's short stories can be categorized handily with respect to their settings: English tales and foreign tales. His three collections mix both kinds. The stories set in England tend to focus on comedy of manners, in the tradition of E. M. Forster and Angus Wilson. The stories set abroad tend to be more dramatic, if more cynical. *The Admiral and the Nuns, with Other Stories* features pieces set in Brazil and Poland, as well as in England. The title story features the character of the daughter of a British admiral educated in English convent schools, married to a Polish pioneer living in the Brazilian jungle. Another story in this collection tells the tale of an aged Polish nobleman reduced to working as a courier in a cocaine smuggling operation. *Fingers in the Door and Other Stories* features exclusively English settings, and some critics have disparaged it for lack of conflict and contrast. In *Live Bait and Other Stories*, Tuohy adds Japan and America to his stable of settings, both for the same purpose of showing the discomfort created for the characters by the confrontation of cultures.

"The Candidate," a story in the *Live Bait and Other Stories* collection, may serve as the model for an explanation of Tuohy's method. In this story, George Brady, lecturer at a provincial Polish university, is pressured by party officials and relatives to pass a young woman candidate for the English exam. The university administrators are themselves under pressure from a neighboring industrial collective, which wants to open its own university. Even some local nuns take up the cause of Krystyna Nowalek, so that during the exam Brady imagines he hears angels hovering over Krystyna as she writes her answers. In the oral examination, however, a change in the order of the candidates, intended to cause the examiners to mistake a brighter student for Krystyna, results in the embarrassment of one of the deans, a high party official, who consequently refuses to approve Krystyna's admission to the university. In the final twist, one of the departmental assistants reveals that the brighter student has connections that would assure her admission, regardless of the outcome of the exam. The assistant implies that Brady has knowingly bowed to this influence, rather than to the weaker pressure of Krystyna's supporters.

A story such as "The Candidate" reveals the deftness of Tuohy's narrative irony, characterization, and settings. The action of the tale, which takes only one day, gives the subtle sense that Brady's interest in passing or failing candidates on their merit alone is hopelessly naïve, given the realities of Polish politics. At the same time, the eight or ten characters in the story are drawn with clear, economical strokes. Even incidental characters, such as an aging former princess who approaches Brady in a public garden with an appeal for Krystyna, become vivid for the reader. Finally, Tuohy contrasts the drabness of the workers' suburb where Brady lives with both the decaying grandeur of the old medieval city and with the beauty of the Polish springtime. He renders all these aspects of the story in understated, terse, elegant prose.

Besides his novels and stories, Tuohy has also written a travelogue, *Portugal*, and a biography of the Irish poet William Butler Yeats. This latter work, called simply *Yeats*, has been praised for its concise, straightforward treatment of the poet's life and works. The book is notable for its intelligent use of photographs and illustrations. Although he makes some claim to be a man of letters, Tuohy will be remembered primarily as a fine craftsman of short stories with a firm place in twentieth century literature.

BIBLIOGRAPHICAL REFERENCES: A full account of Tuohy's career can be found in Lindsey Tucker, "Frank Tuohy," in *Dictionary of Literary Biography*, Vol. 14, 1983, edited by Jay L. Halio. For reviews of *The Collected Stories of Frank Tuohy*, see Jay Cantor, *The New York Times Book Review*, LXXXIX (January 6, 1985), 20; Peter Prescott, *Newsweek*, CV (February 4, 1985), 78; and Rhoda Koenig, *New York*, XVIII (February 18, 1985), 104. An analysis of the short story "The Admiral and the Nuns" can be found by Michael Adams, *Masterplots II: Short Stories Series*, Vol. 1, 1986, edited by Frank N. Magill.

James T. Jones

AMOS TUTUOLA

Born: Abeokuta, Nigeria
Date: 1920

Principal Works

NOVELS: *The Palm-Wine Drinkard*, 1952; *My Life in the Bush of Ghosts*, 1954; *Simbi and the Satyr of the Dark Jungle*, 1955; *The Brave African Huntress*, 1958; *Feather Woman of the Jungle*, 1962; *Ajaiyi and His Inherited Poverty*, 1967; *The Witch-Herbalist of the Remote Town*, 1981; *The Wild Hunter in the Bush of Ghosts*, 1983.

Amos Tutuola's reputation has been the subject of much controversy. The majority of African writers who write in English have been educated at a university; they borrow their formal structures from British literature and often employ their second language with as much skill as a native speaker. Tutuola had none of this academic preparation. He began school at the age of twelve, was trained as a blacksmith, and, finding no opportunity for plying his trade, became a government messenger in Lagos. It could hardly be imagined that he might become a recognized author. Yet he is given the distinction of having written the first major modern African novel in English.

The history of his achievement is extraordinary. Attracted by an advertisement from the United Society for Christian Literature, Tutuola worked feverishly on a draft of *The Palm-Wine Drinkard*. Clearly, the novel was unsuitable for this group. Yet it was provocative, and an intelligent reader saw its potential; it was sent to Faber and Faber in London, whose editors agreed to publish it. The result established Tutuola's career at the cost of much debate, which generally separated British and African critics. The basic argument was whether Tutuola's natural style was brilliantly innovative or embarrassingly incompetent. Dylan Thomas called the novel "a thronged, grisly, and bewitching story," and he admired its unusual style. Educated Africans protested that Faber's determination to publish the work without the usual editorial corrections indicated a patronizing colonial attitude that showed a preference for a childish quality in an African writer.

This debate, once so impassioned, cooled with Tutuola's subsequent publication. He came to be seen as a writer who does not meet conventional expectations but opens up a rare world, simultaneously original and naïve. The title of his first novel is indicative of the issue: Is "drinkard" an accidental error, or is the usage calculatingly ingenious in its subtle modification of the expected term "drunkard"? Regardless of such questions, Tutuola's book has achieved a fame he has not been able to equal since. After nine printings in the United States, it was translated into languages as different as Finnish, Japanese, and Serbian. It was developed into an opera and dramatized as a play repeatedly performed by the University of Ibadan's Travelling Theatre, both in English and in a version using Yoruba, Tutuola's native language.

The story tells of a "drinkard" whose liquor supplies are cut off when his tapster, responsible for extracting his daily ration of palm wine, falls from a tree to his death. Driven by deprivation, the drinkard determines to follow him down to "the land of the Deads" and effect his release so that he may again serve his thirsty needs. This situation establishes that archetypal pattern, familiar in all continents, of the visitor venturing into the shades to rescue one whom death had stolen. The actual incidents are wildly imaginative, with the traveler experiencing punishments and excitements before returning with a healing and reconciling benefice to all in his village.

Tutuola continued to write novels in a similar vein. The pattern was the telling of Yoruba myth but in a manner that allowed him to incorporate a mixture of modern experience, Greek legend, Nordic monsters, and pure imagination into a unique narrative form. There are magic, bizarre transformations, and ghosts. One of the ghosts in *My Life in the Bush of*

Ghosts has multiple television sets in her fingertips. The plots of all Tutuola's books are remarkable and outrageous. The stories remain compelling and the language ingenious, though there is some sense of repetition when the novels are read in succession; the astounding originality of the first book is reduced to the expected through familiarity.

There is some evidence that in his later novels Tutuola exhibits greater facility and calculation in the way he handles structure and dialogue. Yet his is a natural, instinctive talent for the most part; if he had learned any more sophisticated contrivances they would have undermined the native ingenuity of this remarkable storyteller.

BIBLIOGRAPHICAL REFERENCES: For background on African literature and to place Tutuola in context, see *An Introduction to African Literature*, 1967, edited by Ulli Beier; Bernth Lindfors, *Early Nigerian Literature*, 1982; and Oyekan Owomoyela, *African Literature*, 1978. Works which specifically address Tutuola's unique style include H. R. Collins, *Amos Tutuola*, 1969; Gerald Moore, *Seven African Writers*, 1962; and Bernth Lindfors, *Critical Perspectives on Amos Tutuola*, 1975. See also H. R. Collins, "Founding a New National Literature: The Ghost Novels of Amos Tutuola," *Critique: Studies in Modern Fiction*, IV (Fall, 1960/Winter, 1961), 17-28; Bernth Lindfors, "Amos Tutuola's Television-Handed Ghostess," in *Folklore in Nigerian Literature*, 1973; and Elijah Nyang'Aya, "The Freakish Tutuola," in *Standpoints on African Literature*, 1973.

John F. Povey

MARK TWAIN
Samuel Langhorne Clemens

Born: Florida, Missouri
Date: November 30, 1835

Died: Redding, Connecticut
Date: April 21, 1910

PRINCIPAL WORKS

LONG FICTION: *The Gilded Age*, 1873 (with Charles Dudley Warner); *The Adventures of Tom Sawyer*, 1876; *The Prince and the Pauper*, 1882; *The Adventures of Huckleberry Finn*, 1884; *A Connecticut Yankee in King Arthur's Court*, 1889; *The American Claimant*, 1892; *The Tragedy of Pudd'nhead Wilson*, 1894; *Tom Sawyer Abroad*, 1894; *Tom Sawyer, Detective*, 1896; *King Leopold's Soliloquy: A Defense of His Congo Rule*, 1905; *The Mysterious Stranger*, 1916; *Simon Wheeler, Detective*, 1963; *Three Thousand Years Among the Microbes*, 1967; *Which Was It?*, 1967; *The Chronicle of Young Satan*, 1969.

SHORT FICTION: *The Celebrated Jumping Frog of Calaveras County, and Other Sketches*, 1867; *The Curious Republic of Gondour and Other Whimsical Sketches*, 1919; *The Adventures of Thomas Jefferson Snodgrass*, 1928; *The Complete Short Stories of Mark Twain*, 1957; *Mark Twain's Satires and Burlesques*, 1967; *Mark Twain's Hannibal, Huck and Tom*, 1969; *Mark Twain's Fables of Man*, 1972; *The Comic Mark Twain Reader*, 1977; *Mark Twain at His Best: A Comprehensive Sampler*, 1986.

ESSAYS: *Sketches, Old and New*, 1876; *Sketches of the Sixties*, 1927 (with Bret Harte); *Hors de Combat*, 1938; *Washington in 1868*, 1943; *The Forgotten Writings of Mark Twain*, 1963; *Mark Twain on the Lecture Circuit*, 1960.

PLAY: *Ah Sin, the Heathen Chinee*, pb. 1961 (with Bret Harte).

TRAVEL SKETCHES: *The Innocents Abroad*, 1869; *Roughing It*, 1872; *A Tramp Abroad*, 1880; *Life on the Mississippi*, 1883; *Following the Equator*, 1897; *Europe and Elsewhere*, 1923; *Letters from the Sandwich Islands*, 1938; *Letters from Honolulu*, 1939; *Mark Twain's Travels with Mr. Brown*, 1940.

AUTOBIOGRAPHY: *Mark Twain's Autobiography*, 1924, expanded 1959.

CORRESPONDENCE: *Mark Twain's Letters*, 1917; *Mark Twain to Mrs. Fairbanks*, 1949; *The Love Letters of Mark Twain*, 1949; *Mark Twain's Letters to Mary*, 1961; *Mark Twain's Letters to His Publishers, 1867-1894*, 1967; *Mark Twain's Correspondence with Henry Huttleston Rogers, 1893-1909*, 1969.

JOURNALISM: *Mark Twain: San Francisco Correspondent*, 1957; *Mark Twain of the Enterprise, 1862-1864*, 1957; *Clemens of the Call: Mark Twain in San Francisco*, 1969.

LITERARY CRITICISM: *Is Shakespeare Dead?*, 1909.

PHILOSOPHY: *What Is Man?*, 1906; *Christian Science*, 1907; *Letters from the Earth*, 1962.

MISCELLANEOUS: *The Writings of Mark Twain*, 1922-1925; *Mark Twain's Notebook*, 1935; *Mark Twain's Notebooks and Journals*, 1975-1979.

Mark Twain is both the greatest humorist American literature has produced and one of its most important novelists. Born Samuel Langhorne Clemens, the son of John Marshall and Jane Lampton Clemens, in the small town of Florida, Missouri, he spent his boyhood in nearby Hannibal on the banks of the Mississippi River, a setting which would figure prominently in many of his best works. Twain's father died when he was twelve, and the young boy went to work as a printer's apprentice. At seventeen, he published his first humorous sketch, "The Dandy Frightening the Squatter," in a Boston magazine. A year later, he left Hannibal and found work as a printer in several cities before deciding, at the age of twenty-two, to set out for South America. While traveling down the Mississippi River by steamboat, however, he altered his plans and convinced an amenable riverboat captain to teach him his trade.

Twain's career as a steamboat pilot was cut short by the Civil War, and after a two-week stint in the Confederate Army he deserted and joined his brother in Nevada. There, he made unsuccessful forays into silver mining and adopted the pseudonym Mark Twain—a riverboat phrase meaning "two fathoms deep"—while working for a Virginia City newspaper. Twain moved to San Francisco, where he wrote the story that would win him national recognition, "The Celebrated Jumping Frog of Calaveras County." The story shows Twain already a master of the deadpan, Western-flavored "tall tale," and its use of dialect introduces the idiomatic style that would help earn for Twain a place among the giants of American literature.

As a reporter for the *Sacramento Union*, Twain traveled to Hawaii and sent home humorous travel sketches in the form of letters. In 1867, he embarked for Europe and the Holy Land as a newspaper travel correspondent, and his collected sketches were published in 1869 as *The Innocents Abroad*. The book's immense popularity with the reading public soon made its author a familiar figure on the lecture circuit. In 1870, Twain married Olivia Langdon, who would come to act as his editorial censor and with whom he had four children. The couple eventually moved to Hartford, Connecticut, where they would remain for twenty years. *Roughing It*, Twain's comical recollections of his sojourns in the West, was published in 1872 and was followed the next year by *The Gilded Age*, a social and political satire he cowrote with his friend Charles Dudley Warner.

In 1875, Twain published what would become one of his best-loved novels, *The Adventures of Tom Sawyer*. Drawing on his memories of his childhood in Hannibal, Twain created a rollicking portrait of an American boyhood characterized by high spirits, a thirst for adventure, and an irrepressible talent for mischief. The book became a classic.

In 1884, Twain completed a novel he had begun eight years earlier. Generally acknowledged as his greatest work, *The Adventures of Huckleberry Finn* is a scathing social satire disguised as a young boy's adventure. During the course of Huck's trip downriver with the runaway slave Jim, he encounters the hypocrisy, greed, and cruelty of "civilized" society and notes, in the book's famous final passage, "I reckon I got to light out for the territory ahead of the rest, because Aunt Sally she's going to adopt me and sivilize me, and I can't stand it. I been there before." Criticized as crude and vulgar by some at the time of its publication, *The Adventures of Huckleberry Finn* has since entered the ranks of the most important and influential American novels and was praised by Ernest Hemingway as the beginning of modern American fiction.

Although his final years were marked by sorrow (the deaths of his wife and two daughters), Twain found himself a celebrated and much-beloved public figure, recognized throughout the world and a legend in his own lifetime. His last years were devoted to philosophical works, often dark and bitter in tone, and to his autobiography, which was edited and published after his death by his devoted secretary—and later biographer—Albert Bigelow Paine. Twain died of heart disease in 1910.

Mark Twain's reputation as a writer has grown in the years since his death as the richness of his legacy has come to be appreciated by subsequent generations of readers and critics. Twain is often credited with giving American literature its first uniquely American voice, and the color and vibrancy of his work stand in stark contrast to the elegant language and seriousness of tone that mark other nineteenth century novels. Yet Twain's command of language was one of his chief strengths, and his genius lay in his ability to make even the roughest of dialects serve his purposes as eloquently as the most refined and educated of accents. Twain brought the energy and truth-stretching humor of the West to his work and used it to entertain society with an account of its own foibles and vices.

BIBLIOGRAPHICAL REFERENCES: A multivolume scholarly edition of Twain's works was published by University of California Press in the early 1980's. Among the most important of the many Twain biographies are Justin Kaplan, *Mr. Clemens and Mr. Twain*, 1966, which focuses on Twain's adult life and work; *Mark Twain: God's Fool*, 1973, by Hamlin Hill, an illuminating examination of the writer's last decade; and the three-volume *Mark Twain: A Biography:*

The Personal and Literary Life of Samuel Langhorne Clemens, 1912, by Twain's private secretary, Albert Bigelow Paine, who provides a detailed and valuable account of the writer's life. Personal accounts of Twain are offered in *My Mark Twain*, 1910, by writer and longtime friend William Dean Howells; daughter Clara Clemens' *My Father, Mark Twain*, 1931; and *Mark Twain: Businessman*, 1946, a memoir edited by Twain's grandnephew, Samuel Charles Clemens, which includes family letters and reminiscences. DeLancey Ferguson, *Mark Twain: Man and Legend*, 1943, and Louis J. Budd, *Our Mark Twain: The Making of His Public Personality*, 1983, both explore the contrasts between Clemens the man and Twain the legend. Justin Kaplan, *Mark Twain and His World*, 1974, is an interesting, illustrated biography of Twain and his time, and John Lauber, *The Making of Mark Twain: A Biography*, 1985, is a good, general biography. Two interesting essay collections are *The Mythologizing of Mark Twain*, 1984, edited by Sara deSaussure Davis and Philip D. Beidler, which examines the growth of Twain's public persona, and *Mark Twain: A Sumptuous Variety*, 1985, edited by Robert Giddings, which offers essays on a wide variety of aspects of Twain's career.

Janet E. Lorenz

ANNE TYLER

Born: Minneapolis, Minnesota
Date: October 25, 1941

PRINCIPAL WORKS

NOVELS: *If Morning Ever Comes*, 1964; *The Tin Can Tree*, 1965; *A Slipping-Down Life*, 1970; *The Clock Winder*, 1972; *Celestial Navigation*, 1974; *Searching for Caleb*, 1976; *Earthly Possessions*, 1977; *Morgan's Passing*, 1980; *Dinner at the Homesick Restaurant*, 1982; *The Accidental Tourist*, 1985; *Breathing Lessons*, 1988.

Although Anne Tyler's books have always been popular with general readers, acclaim from critics came more slowly. With *Dinner at the Homesick Restaurant*, however, Tyler's position in American literature was firmly established. In addition to having written more than forty short stories and eleven novels, Tyler is much in demand as a book reviewer. She has achieved her greatest success and recognition as a witty yet serious and compassionate observer of human nature, with a polished style, a strong sense of irony, and an uncanny ability to create memorable characters and to reproduce their speech as if she had actually heard it.

Tyler was born on October 25, 1941, in Minneapolis, Minnesota, the only daughter of Lloyd Parry and Phyllis (Mahon) Tyler; there were also four boys in the family, a circumstance that appears in reverse in Tyler's first novel, *If Morning Ever Comes*, in which the main character is an only son with six sisters. Tyler denies that her novels are autobiographical. Although she was reared in North Carolina, she does not consider herself a Southern writer, despite the repeated statement to that effect on the jackets of most of her books. Nor does she consider herself a feminist writer; she is more interested in people than in movements.

Tyler was graduated from Duke University in 1961, having begun college at the age of sixteen. A course on the short story taught by the writer Reynolds Price had a great impact on her, though not on her style. After doing graduate study in Russian at Columbia University, she married Taghi Modarressi, a psychiatrist, in 1963, and the couple had two daughters, Tezh and Mitra.

A longtime resident of Baltimore, Maryland, Tyler set most of her novels in various parts of that city, using other locations only briefly and secondarily as her plots required; such locales include small towns in North Carolina and Pennsylvania and such cities as New York, New Orleans, and Paris. She once said that what she was doing in her novels was populating a town—not with people she knew, but with people about whom she had written. Such comments are rare, however, as Tyler shuns publicity, does not give readings, and almost never grants interviews.

Winner of the National Book Critics Circle Award in 1986, *The Accidental Tourist* was filmed in 1987; the film also won awards, though the reviews were mixed. Critics responded to Tyler's next book, *Breathing Lessons*, in much the same way; while the book remained on best-seller lists for several months and won the Pulitzer Prize for fiction in 1989, some critics found it sentimental, slapstick, and banal, while others were unreserved in their enthusiastic praise, suggesting that it was her best book.

All Tyler's novels draw on a family or a family-like community as a context in which to observe how the characters play out their lives and their relations with one another. The author's viewpoint varies over a whole range of possibilities: a young boy in *If Morning Ever Comes*, a teenaged girl in *A Slipping-Down Life*, a wife in *Earthly Possessions*, and an elderly, dying mother in *Dinner at the Homesick Restaurant*, in which parts of the story are also told by each of the woman's three children. These examples should serve to show how Tyler varies her narrative voice, which is always sure and credible. The characters are often eccentric and quirky, but they are just as often, in the same book, pitiable in their idiosyncrasies, misunderstandings, and failures. The vicissitudes of marriage and the stresses of close relationships are the very stuff of Tyler's novels. Yet the novels contain as much diversity in both situation and characterization as life itself. One critic has commented that when she opens a Tyler novel she expects to meet friends but finds only relatives.

BIBLIOGRAPHICAL REFERENCES: See *Dictionary of Literary Biography*, Vol. 6, 1980 and 1982, and *American Women Writers*, Vol. 4, 1982, for appraisals of Tyler's work. Outstanding articles in periodicals can be found in *The Times Literary Supplement*, October 29, 1982; M. E. Gibson, "Family as Fate: The Novels of Anne Tyler," *The Southern Literary Journal*, Fall, 1983; and F. W. Shelton, "The Necessary Balance: Distance and Sympathy in the Novels of Anne Tyler," *The Southern Review*, October, 1984; J. Mathewson, "Taking the Anne Tyler Tour," *Horizon*, 1985; and M. Ferry, "Recommended: Anne Tyler," *English Journal*, February, 1987.

Natalie Harper

MIGUEL DE UNAMUNO Y JUGO

Born: Bilbao, Spain
Date: September 29, 1864

Died: Salamanca, Spain
Date: December 31, 1936

PRINCIPAL WORKS

NOVELS: *Paz en la guerra*, 1897 (*Peace in War*, 1983); *Amor y pedagogía*, 1902; *Niebla*, 1914 (*Mist*, 1928); *Abel Sánchez: Una historia de pasión*, 1917 (*Abel Sánchez*, 1947); *San Manuel Bueno, mártir*, 1931 (*Saint Manuel Bueno, Martyr*, 1954).

CRITICISM: *En torno al casticismo*, 1895; *La vida de Don Quijote y Sancho según Miguel de Cervantes Saavedra, explicada y comentada por Miguel de Unamuno*, 1905 (*The Life of Don Quixote and Sancho According to Miguel de Cervantes Saavedra Expounded with Comment by Miguel de Unamuno*, 1927); *L'Agonie du Christianisme*, 1925 (*The Agony of Christianity*, 1928); *Cómo se hace una novela*, 1927 (*How to Make a Novel*, 1976).

POETRY: *Poesías*, 1907; *Rosario de sonetos líricos*, 1911; *El Cristo de Velázquez*, 1920 (*The Christ of Velázquez*, 1951); *Teresa*, 1924; *Cancionero, diario poético*, 1953.

PLAYS: *La esfinge*, pr. 1909; *La difunta*, pr. 1910; *La venda*, pb. 1913; *Fedra*, pr. 1918 (*Phaedra*, 1959); *El otro*, pr., pb. 1932 (*The Other*, 1947); *El hermano Juan: O, El mundo es teatro*, pb. 1934.

ESSAYS: *Mi religión y otros ensayos breves*, 1910; *Del sentimiento trágico de la vida en los hombres y en los pueblos*, 1913 (*The Tragic Sense of Life in Men and Peoples*, 1921).

Miguel de Unamuno y Jugo is one of the most significant and controversial figures in the history of modern thought. Known primarily as an essayist at the beginning of his career, later criticism has focused on his renovation of the novel and on his poetry. Although he has become inseparably associated with the area of Castile, especially Salamanca, Unamuno was a Basque, born in Bilbao on September 29, 1864. His father, a baker, who died when Unamuno was only six years old, had settled in that city upon his return from Mexico, where he had hoped to win fame and fortune. In his first novel, *Peace in War*, Unamuno admittedly describes himself in his portrayal of the young orphan, Pachico, some of whose most vivid memories were of the 1874 Carlist siege and bombardment of Bilbao. A philologist by training, in 1891, Unamuno accepted the post of professor of Greek and Romance philology at the University of Salamanca. Except for his years in exile, Unamuno would never leave the university, which he considered one of the two safe and stable components of his life. The other was his marriage to Concepción (Concha) Lizárraga which lasted for forty-three years and produced nine children.

Unamuno was one of the leaders of the famous literary group known as the Generation of '98. Utilizing Spain's defeat in the Spanish-American War as a rallying point, writers such as Antonio Machado, Pío Baroja, José Martínez Ruiz, and Unamuno tried to analyze the reasons underlying Spain's decline and provide a philosophical framework for her regeneration in the twentieth century. In *En torno al casticismo* (on authenticity), Unamuno first developed his theory of "intrahistory," the cultural, unchanging base of a people, its authentic identity as compared with the trivial facts and figures of recorded "history." Spain as a theme dominates Unamuno's early essays and poetry, but in 1904, the prolonged illness and death of his son Raimundo provoked a spiritual crisis that was to influence profoundly all Unamuno's life and later work. Long branded as a political troublemaker, Unamuno now became known as a religious heretic as his inner doubts and fears became the obsession of his public writings. *The Tragic Sense of Life in Men and Peoples*, praised as one of the masterworks of twentieth century thought, is Unamuno's manifesto of a philosophy of struggle in a world where humankind's longing for meaning and faith clashes with cold rationality and science. This preoccupation with the metaphysical dilemmas of the twentieth century has led to Unamuno's inclusion as a precursor of existentialism.

In his search for an effective vehicle in which to describe the essence of humankind, Unamuno turned to the narrative and the stage. Novels such as *Abel Sánchez* and *Mist*, which in its famous confrontation scene between character and creator anticipated Luigi Pirandello's *Sei personaggi in cerca d'autore* (pr., pb. 1921; *Six Characters in Search of an Author*, 1922) by eighteen years, not only solidified Unamuno's place in vanguard literary circles but also earned for him a steadily growing reading public. Therefore, his deportation from Spain in 1924, motivated by his strident criticism of the dictatorship of Miguel Primo de Rivero, caused an immediate outcry in the international literary and diplomatic community. His return in 1930, after more than five years in exile, was a personal triumph. He was reappointed rector of Salamanca and elected as deputy to the Cortes, the Spanish parliament. In 1934, he was named lifetime rector of the University of Salamanca but suffered the double blow of the death of his wife and one of his closest children. Critical of the indecisiveness of the Republic, at first he had supported General Francisco Franco, but he soon became one of the general's most outspoken critics. Dismissed from his post, Unamuno died, during virtual house arrest by the angered Franco, on December 31, 1936.

Unamuno's plays consist of philosophy set into dialogue. A reading of them is better than their performance. His best-known drama, *The Other*, with identical twins as protagonists, reveals his complete rejection of any final answer even in a work of fiction. One brother kills another and, driven to suicide by remorse, takes to the grave the secret of his own identity and that of his victim. Unamuno believed that humankind was adrift in a sea of contradictions and that in order to arrive at the vital core, it was necessary to strip away all the layers of pseudocivilization and intellectualism. The constant conflicts between death and immortality, reason and faith, science and life, reality and illusion torment Unamuno's man of flesh and blood (*carne y hueso*). Such dualities can never be resolved, and Unamuno's work, therefore, is a study in unanswered questions and contradiction. Labeled a heretic, he yet could write one of the finest religious poems in the Spanish language, *The Christ of Velázquez*, a series of meditations on aspects of the famous painting of the crucified Christ. Frustrated at his country's apparent inertia and subjugation to the past, in 1898 Unamuno exclaimed that Don Quixote must die so that Spain, rid of madness, could be set free to face the future, but, almost immediately, he completely reversed his opinion and eulogized the knight as the authentic living symbol of Spain's past, present, and future. In *Saint Manuel Bueno, Martyr*, the philosopher who scorned unquestioning acceptance presents a hero-priest who, himself unable to believe, strives to preserve the innocent faith of his people.

Unamuno's place as one of the dominant thinkers of twentieth century literature and philosophy has never seriously been challenged, though there has been harsh criticism of the quality of his fiction and his poetry, and of the relevance of his philosophic writings. Intense and relentless, Unamuno himself was never objective, and the same can be said of much of the early evaluation of his work. Critics, many of them supporters of Unamuno's contemporary José Ortega y Gasset, charged that Unamuno was devoted only to a cult of his own personality and that what had the appearance of learned commentary was, in reality, anarchic indulgence. Criticism also was divided along lines of political affiliation. Called a "bad son of Spain" by those who resented his constant attacks, after his death he became a symbol of resistance to the Franco dictatorship. Detractors also derided the harshness and lack of musicality of his verse and ridiculed its drumming cadence, devoid of any pretense of polish. Yet Unamuno believed that he would be remembered primarily as a poet, and recent criticism has indeed affirmed the value of his verse. His sonnets, above all, have come to be regarded as examples of the finest in all Hispanic poetry. A growing awareness of Unamuno's role in the development of existentialism has encouraged a revival of interest in his novels and essays, and his reputation has been enhanced by the number of major writers, such as James Baldwin and Jorge Luis Borges, who have confessed their debt to him. It must be admitted, however, that alongside the positive reevaluation, there still exists vehement criticism. This debate would have pleased Unamuno, who wrote to provoke and incite and who abhorred indifference.

BIBLIOGRAPHICAL REFERENCES: *Bibliografía crítica de Miguel de Unamuno (1888-1975)*, 1976, edited by Pelayo H. Fernández, is an excellent compendium of editions, translations, and criticism. The most widely used collection is *Obras completas*, 1950-1964, edited by Manuel García Blanco. The English translations of the Bollingen Series LXXXV, Princeton University Press, 1976, edited by Anthony Kerrigan, Allan Lacy, and Martin Nozick, contain valuable introductions, for example, Salvador de Madariaga's introduction to *The Tragic Sense of Life in Men and Peoples*. A widely known but criticized biography is Margaret Rudd, *The Lone Heretic*, 1963. Martin Nozick, *Miguel de Unamuno*, 1971, is a better introduction to the man and his work. For further study, see Allan Lacy, *Miguel de Unamuno: The Rhetoric of Existence*, 1967; Julian Marias, *Miguel de Unamuno*, 1966, translated by Frances M. López-Moullas; and an excellent collection of essays, *Unamuno*, 1967, edited by José Rubia Barcia. See also Lucille V. Braun, "*The Intertextualization* of Unamuno y Jugo and Juan Goytisolo's *Reivindicación de Conde Julián*," *Hispanofila*, XXX (1987), 39-56; Debra Harper Love, "Whitman and Unamuno: Language for Immortality," *Walt Whitman Review*, XXV (1979), 66-72; David G. Turner, *Unamuno's Web of Fatality*, 1974; Frances Wyers, *Miguel de Unamuno: The Contrary Self*, 1976; Paul Ibe, *Unamuno: An Existential View of Self and Society*, 1967; Demetrios Basdekis, *Unamuno and Spanish Literature*, 1967; Luis Portello, "Unamuno's Last Lecture," in *The Golden Horizon*, 1953, edited by Cyril Connolly; and José Feneter Mora, *Unamuno: A Philosophy of Tragedy*, 1962, translated by Philip Silver.

Charlene Suscavage

JOHN UPDIKE

Born: Shillington, Pennsylvania
Date: March 18, 1932

PRINCIPAL WORKS

NOVELS: *The Poorhouse Fair*, 1959; *Rabbit, Run*, 1960; *The Centaur*, 1963; *Of the Farm*, 1965; *Couples*, 1968; *Rabbit Redux*, 1971; *A Month of Sundays*, 1975; *Marry Me: A Romance*, 1976; *The Coup*, 1978; *Rabbit Is Rich*, 1981; *Bech Is Back*, 1982; *The Witches of Eastwick*, 1984; *Roger's Version*, 1986; *S.*, 1988.

SHORT FICTION: *The Same Door*, 1959; *Pigeon Feathers and Other Stories*, 1962; *Olinger Stories: A Selection*, 1964; *The Music School*, 1966; *Bech: A Book*, 1970; *Museums and Women and Other Stories*, 1972; *Problems and Other Stories*, 1979; *Too Far to Go: The Maples Stories*, 1979; *Trust Me*, 1987.

POETRY: *The Carpentered Hen and Other Tame Creatures*, 1958 (also known as *Hoping for a Hoopoe*); *Telephone Poles and Other Poems*, 1963; *Midpoint and Other Poems*, 1969; *Tossing and Turning*, 1977; *Facing Nature*, 1985.

ESSAYS: *Assorted Prose*, 1965; *Picked-Up Pieces*, 1975; *Hugging the Shore: Essays and Criticism*, 1983.

PLAY: *Buchanan Dying*, pb. 1974.

AUTOBIOGRAPHY: *Self-Consciousness*, 1989.

John Updike is widely acclaimed as one of the most accomplished stylists and prolific writers of his generation; his fiction represents a penetrating chronicle of the changing morals and manners of American society. He was born in Shillington, Pennsylvania, on March 18, 1932, the only child of Wesley and Linda Grace Hoyer Updike. His father was a mathematics teacher at the high school and supported the family in lean times, first in the old parental home in Shillington, and later on a farm in Plowville, ten miles outside Shillington. A number of short stories, such as "Flight," and the novels *The Centaur* and *Of the Farm* draw upon this experience. After attending schools in Shillington, Updike went to Harvard University in 1950 on a full scholarship, majoring in English. He was editor of the Harvard *Lampoon* and was graduated in 1954 with highest honors. In 1953, he married Radcliffe student Mary Pennington, the daughter of a Unitarian minister; they were to have four children.

In 1954, Updike sold the first of many stories to *The New Yorker.* After a year in Oxford, England, where Updike studied at the Ruskin School of Drawing and Fine Art, he returned to the United States to a job as a staff writer with *The New Yorker*, for which he wrote the "Talk of the Town" column. In April of 1957, fearing the city scene would inhibit his writing, Updike and his family left New York for Ipswich, Massachusetts. He continued to sell stories to *The New Yorker* while working on longer fiction. His first book was a collection of verse, *The Carpentered Hen and Other Tame Creatures*, published in 1958. The next year, he published his first novel, *The Poorhouse Fair*, set in a retirement home. The novel received favorable reviews and won the Rosenthal Award. His first collection of short stories, *The Same Door*, also appeared in 1959. During this time, Updike was active in Ipswich community life and attended the Congregational Church—a setting depicted in a number of works. In 1974, the Updikes were divorced. In 1977, Updike remarried to Martha Bernhard.

During this same period—the late 1950's and early 1960's—Updike faced a crisis of faith prompted by his consciousness of death's inevitability. The works of such writers as Søren Kierkegaard and, especially, Karl Barth, the Swiss neoorthodox theologian, helped Updike come to grips with this fear and to find a basis for faith. Many of Updike's works explore theological and religious issues. In a real sense, Updike has become a kind of late twentieth century Nathaniel Hawthorne, whose works, like Hawthorne's, are saturated with religious and theological concerns. In fact, three of his novels, *A Month of Sundays*, *Roger's Version*, and *S.*, form an updated version of Hawthorne's *The Scarlet Letter* (1850).

Updike's work published during the 1960's established him as one of America's important serious writers. In 1960, he published *Rabbit, Run*, the first in a series of novels about a middle-class man and his family set in a small city in Pennsylvania. He returned to this character at intervals of a decade with *Rabbit Redux* and *Rabbit Is Rich*; the latter won the Pulitzer Prize for fiction in 1981. Each of these novels deals seriously with a man interacting with his changing culture, adapting but not fully capitulating to it, seeking always for something certain, if not transcendent. In 1962, Updike's second story collection, *Pigeon Feathers and Other Stories*, appeared, and in 1963, another collection of verse, *Telephone Poles and Other Poems*, was published. His novel *The Centaur*, also published in 1963, earned for Updike the National Book Award and election to the National Institute of Arts and Letters, the youngest man ever to be so elected. In 1966, *The Music School*, his third collection of stories, appeared.

In 1964-1965, Updike traveled to Eastern Europe as part of a cultural exchange program. A number of works reflect that experience, in particular his collection *Bech*. In 1973, Updike traveled, under State Department auspices, to Africa; his novel *The Coup* reflects that journey. With three collections of essays and reviews—*Assorted Prose*, *Picked-Up Pieces*, and *Hugging the Shore*—Updike has shown himself to be an excellent literary critic and cultural commentator as well as a gifted writer of fiction.

Updike's mature fiction has been concerned with the fate of eros in the upper-middle-class suburbs of the eastern United States. His fiction provides a vivid chronicle of the sexual mores and strained and broken marriages of contemporary America. Most of his protagonists are enmeshed in the compromises of modern life, in the horizontal, while yet yearning for the transcendent, the recovery of the vertical dimension. For many of his characters, sexual ecstasy, even with its attendant disappointments, replaces the passions of faith. In such works as *Couples*—a best-seller gaining for Updike favorable treatment in *Time* and *Life* magazines and a large sum for the film rights—the Rabbit books, *Marry Me*, and the story collections *Museums and Women* and *Problems and Other Stories*, Updike focuses upon marriage and its discontents, especially the various stages of marital disintegration. If innocence, real or imagined, is irrecoverable in Updike's fiction, if his characters often seem engulfed by moral squalor, they yet possess a lively and admirable energy, a spiritual striving, and a vital resistance to entropy that points to something quite other than defeat. Inseparable from the energy of his characters' striving is the astonishing variety and richness of Updike's narratives, reflecting a conviction that the vocation of writing, as with Henry James, constitutes a necessary assault upon the precincts of death. Thus, in both thematic seriousness and narrative range, Updike has produced a body of writings of the highest order.

BIBLIOGRAPHICAL REFERENCES: A large number of articles and book-length studies offer wide-ranging discussion of Updike's work. See Rachel C. Burchard, *John Updike: Yea Sayings*, 1971; Robert Detweiler, *John Updike*, 1984; David Galloway, *The Absurd Hero in American Fiction*, 1981; Donald J. Greiner, *The Other John Updike: Poems, Short Stories, Prose, Play*, 1981; Donald J. Greiner, *John Updike's Novels*, 1984; Donald J. Greiner, *Adultery in the American Novel: Updike, James, and Hawthorne*, 1985; Margaret M. Gullette, *Safe At Last in the Middle Years: The Invention of the Midlife Problem Novel—Saul Bellow, Margaret Drabble, Anne Tyler, and John Updike*, 1988; Alice and Kenneth Hamilton, *The Elements of John Updike*, 1970; Howard M. Harper, Jr., *Desperate Faith: A Study of Bellow, Salinger, Mailer, Baldwin, and Updike*, 1967; Josephine Hendin, *Vulnerable People: A View of American Fiction Since 1945*, 1978; George W. Hunt, *John Updike and the Three Great Secret Things: Sex, Religion, and Art*, 1980; *Critical Essays on John Updike*, 1982, edited by William R. McNaughton; Joyce B. Markle, *Fighters and Lovers: Theme in the Novels of John Updike*, 1973; "John Updike Number," *Modern Fiction Studies*, XX (Spring, 1974); Charles Thomas Samuels, *John Updike*, 1969; Tony Tanner, *City of Words: American Fiction 1950-*

1970, 1971; Larry E. Taylor, *Pastoral and Anti-Pastoral Patterns in John Updike's Fiction*, 1971; Suzanne Henning Uphaus, *John Updike*, 1980; Edward P. Vargas, *Rainstorms and Fire: Ritual in the Novels of John Updike*, 1973; and Ralph C. Wood, *The Comedy of Redemption: Christian Faith and Comic Vision in Four American Novelists*, 1988.

John G. Parks

LEON URIS

Born: Baltimore, Maryland
Date: August 3, 1924

PRINCIPAL WORKS

NOVELS: *Battle Cry*, 1953; *The Angry Hills*, 1955; *Exodus*, 1958; *Mila 18*, 1960; *Armageddon*, 1964; *Topaz*, 1967; *QB VII*, 1970; *Trinity*, 1976; *The Haj*, 1984; *Mitla Pass*, 1988.

SCREENPLAYS: *Battle Cry*, 1955; *Gunfight at the OK Corral*, 1957.

NONFICTION: *Exodus Revisited*, 1959 (with Dimitrios Harissiadis); *Ireland, a Terrible Beauty: The Story of Ireland Today*, 1975 (with Jill Uris).

Leon Marcus Uris endures as one of the most popular—and controversial—American novelists. Born August 3, 1924, in Baltimore, the son of Wolf William and Anna Blumberg Uris, he was educated in the Baltimore and Philadelphia city schools before enlisting in the United States Marine Corps in 1942. He served with the Marines in the Pacific and in Northern California and was honorably discharged in 1946. In 1945, while stationed near San Francisco, he met and married Marine Sergeant Betty Katherine Beck, with whom he had three children: Karen, Mark, and Michael. To support his family while struggling to publish, he worked as a home delivery manager for the *San Francisco Call-Bulletin*. When he finally sold an article on football to *Esquire* in 1950, he decided to work on a novel about World War II because "the real Marine story had not been told." That novel was *Battle Cry*, and its astonishing success in 1953 established him as a full-time writer. This realistic account of World War II introduced the formula that Uris would follow throughout his canon: rather stereotyped characters whose personal drama is played out against a background of international crisis.

The triumph of *Battle Cry*, made into a successful film in 1955 with a script by the novelist, was not to be repeated with Uris' second novel, *The Angry Hills*. Published in 1955, it is a less ambitious and less appealing story of Greek resistance fighters during the Nazi Occupation. The novel repeated the Uris approach, however, having been loosely based on the diary of an uncle who had fought in Greece as a volunteer in the Palestinian brigade. In the late 1950's, Uris' fortunes soared once again. In addition to writing the screenplay for the very successful Western *Gunfight at the OK Corral*, he published *Exodus*, a novel which not only stands as the author's greatest literary accomplishment but also entered mass culture as the definitive popular work on the birth of modern Israel. This success, coupled with the equivalent popularity of the film, which starred Paul Newman, established Uris as the unofficial historian of modern Judaism. It is because of his treatment of Jews and Arabs that he has engendered much controversey.

In *Exodus Revisited*, a work of photojournalism published with Dimitrios Harissiadis, a picture of Hasidic children is contrasted to a full-length photograph of a "modern" young woman: "A very few Jews cling to the ways of the ghetto. But Israel pins her hopes on her tough and wonderful sabras." It is this obvious polarization that has bothered even Jewish critics. Throughout his works, Uris is uncompromising in his treatment of Arabs as primitive and misled in politics.

After four more novels, a second marriage, and a six-year hiatus (during which he researched the background of modern Ireland), Uris produced his second greatest work. *Trinity* is a sprawling novel which dramatizes the background of modern Ireland from the potato famine to the Easter Rebellion of 1916. Very much like *Exodus* in theme, characterization, and structure, the novel was both a critical and a popular success. To do research for the novel, he and his third wife, Jill Peabody Uris, a professional photographer whom he had married in 1970, spent nearly a year traveling throughout Ireland. This expedition resulted in another photographic essay, *Ireland, a Terrible Beauty*, which actually appeared a year before the novel, in 1975.

It was not until 1984 that the Uris name again appeared on the best-seller lists, but when it did, it accompanied the most controversial work of his controversial career: *The Haj*. In what appeared to many critics and readers as a classic example of chutzpah, this champion of Zionism chose to write the modern history of the Palestinians from an Arab point of view. Perhaps because the novel seems to conclude that the Jews are the Arabs' "bridge out of darkness," the novel was generally savaged by the critics.

In *Mitla Pass*, published in 1988, Uris turned again to the familiar subjects of Zionism and Israeli-Arab conflict, this time the 1956 struggle over the Suez Canal. Although the structure of the story follows the traditional Uris formula of individuals caught up in conflicts of global significance, there is a different emphasis. The book seems much more personal, more of an "author's life" than the other novels.

It is perhaps surprising that Uris has not done more in the area of motion pictures, considering his early success and the cinematic quality of his narratives. The majority of his novels have been filmed, but when Uris has worked on the screenplays, his strong personality has clashed with those of the filmmakers. As Sharon Downey and Richard Kallan have observed, Leon Uris "remains a reader's writer and a critic's nightmare." Yet when his material meshes with his abilities, he becomes a dramatic chronicler of the events that have shaped the modern world.

BIBLIOGRAPHICAL REFERENCES: See Sharon D. Downey and Richard A. Kallan, "Semi-Aesthetic Detachment: The Fusing of Fictional and External Worlds in the Situational Literature of Leon Uris," *Communication Monographs*, XLIX (September, 1982), 192-204. Downey and Kallan analyze the first eight novels by examining the ways in which Uris blends real events with the lives of his fictional characters. See also Merle Miller, "The Backdrop Is Victory," *Saturday Review*, April 25, 1953, 16-17; Pat Frank, "Tough Story of Transition from Hometown Boys to Men Trained to Kill," *New York Herald Tribune Book Review*, May 3, 1953, 5; David Dempsey, "Unwitting Go-Between," *The New York Times Book Review*, October 16, 1955, 32-33; Maxwell Geismar, "Epic of Israel," *Saturday Review*, September 27, 1958, 22; Christopher Lehmann-Haupt, "How to Write a Leon Uris," *The New York Times*, December 2, 1970, 45; Pete Hamill, review of *Trinity, The New York Times Book Review*, March 14, 1976, 5; and review of *Mitla Pass*, *Library Journal*, November 1, 1988, 112.

Daniel J. Fuller

LUIS MIGUEL VALDEZ

Born: Delano, California
Date: June 26, 1940

Principal Works

PLAYS: *The Theft*, pr. 1961; *The Shrunken Head of Pancho Villa*, pr. 1965; *Las dos caras del patroncito*, pr. 1965; *La quinta temporada*, pr. 1966; *Los vendidos*, pr. 1967; *Dark Root of a Scream*, pr. 1967; *La conquista de México*, pr. 1968; *No saco nada de la escuela*, pr. 1969; *The Militants*, pr. 1969; *Vietnam campesino*, pr. 1970; *Huelguistas*, pr. 1970; *Bernabé*, pr. 1970; *Soldado razo*, pr., pb. 1971; *Actos*, pr. 1971 (includes *Las dos caras del patroncito, La quinta temporada, Los vendidos, La conquista de México, No saco nada de la escuela, The Militants, Vietnam campesino, Huelguistas*, and *Soldado razo*); *Las pastorelas*, pr. 1971; *La Virgen del Tepeyac*, pr. 1971; *Los endrogados*, pr. 1972; *Los olivos pits*, pr. 1972; *La gran carpa de los rasquachis*, pr. 1973; *Mundo*, pr. 1973; *El baille de los gigantes*, pr. 1973; *El fin del mundo*, pr. 1975; *Zoot Suit*, pr. 1978; *Bandido!*, pr. 1981; *"I Don't Have to Show You No Stinking Badges!*," pr. 1986.

SCREENPLAYS: *Zoot Suit*, 1981; *La Bamba*, 1987.

MISCELLANEOUS: *Pensamiento Serpentino: A Chicano Approach to the Theatre of Reality*, 1973.

Luis Miguel Valdez, political activist, playwright, director, essayist, and founder of El Teatro Campesino, is the most prominent figure in contemporary Chicano theater. Born on June 26, 1940, to migrant farm workers, he was second in a family of ten brothers and sisters. In spite of working in the fields from the age of six, Valdez completed high school and received a scholarship to San Jose State College, where he developed his early interest in theater. *The Shrunken Head of Pancho Villa* was written while Valdez was a student there. After receiving a bachelor's degree in English and drama in 1964, he joined the San Francisco Mime Troupe, whose work was based on *commedia dell'arte* and Bertolt Brecht. These experiences heavily influenced Valdez' work, especially in terms of style and production.

A 1965 meeting with César Chavez, who was organizing migrant farm workers in Delano, California, led to the formation of El Teatro Campesino, the cultural and propagandistic arm of the United Farm Workers Union. Valdez created short improvisational pieces for the troupe, called *actos*. All the *actos* are characterized by the use of masks, stereotyped characters, farcical exaggeration, and improvisation. *Las dos caras del patroncito* (the two faces of the boss) and *La quinta temporada* (the fifth season) are *actos* from this early period that highlight the plight of the farm workers and the benefits of unionization. Valdez left the union in 1967, bringing El Teatro Campesino with him to establish El Centro Campesino Cultural. He wanted to broaden the concerns of the troupe by fostering Chicanos' pride in their cultural heritage and by depicting their problems in the Anglo culture. *Los vendidos* (the sellouts), for example, satirizes Chicanos who attempt to assimilate into a white, racist society, and *La conquista de México* (the conquest of Mexico) links the fall of the Aztecs with the internal dissension of the Chicano activists. In 1968, El Teatro Campesino moved toward producing full-length plays, starting with Valdez' *The Shrunken Head of Pancho Villa*. Expressionistic in style, the play explores the conflict between two brothers—an assimilationist and a *pachuco*, a swaggering street kid—and the impact this extremism has on the tenuous fabric of the Chicano family. *Bernabé*, the next full-length play, marked the beginning of Valdez' search for meaning in Aztec and Mayan legends, history, and philosophy.

In 1971, Valdez moved his company permanently to the small town of San Juan Bautista in California. There they produced one of their major works, *La gran carpa de los rasquachis* (the great tent of the underdogs). Detailing the life of an "underdog" who crosses the

Mexican border to find "the promised land," only to die of grief and poverty, the play is a synthesis of the various styles that Valdez had used before, including *actos*, musical narration, and expressionism. The group's next effort, *El fin del mundo* (the end of the world), presents a bleak view of the end of the world by juxtaposing figures from the religious holiday El Día de los Muertos (day of the dead), characterized by stylized costumes and settings, and the dwindling resources of a contemporary world in urban decay. Unlike the earlier farm worker-oriented *actos*, there are no easy solutions offered. Fame came with *Zoot Suit*, the first Chicano play to reach Broadway. Although its run was relatively brief, owing to negative criticism, the play was very popular on the West Coast and was made into a film in 1981, with Valdez both the director and the writer of the screenplay.

During the 1980's, Valdez and El Teatro Campesino continued to tour at home and abroad, presenting works by Valdez and collectively scripted pieces that interpret the Chicano experience. The 1986 comedy *"I Don't Have to Show You No Stinking Badges!"* is about the political and existential implications of acting, both in theater and in society. In 1987, Valdez wrote the screenplay for the successful film *La Bamba*, the story of Ritchie Valens, a young Chicano pop singer, who died in an airplane crash in the late 1950's. This work reached a large audience.

Valdez' contributions to contemporary Chicano theater are extensive. Writing individually and with others, he has redefined the cultural forms of the barrio: the *acto*, a short comic piece intended to move the audience to political action; the *mito* (myth), which characteristically takes the form of an allegory based on Indian ritual, in an attempt to integrate political activism and religious ritual; and the *corrido*, a reinvention of the musical based on Mexican American folk ballads. He has placed the Chicano experience onstage in all of its political, cultural, and religious complexity in works that are revolutionary in technique as well as in content.

BIBLIOGRAPHICAL REFERENCES: For an excellent examination of Valdez' contributions within the context of Chicano theater, see Jorge A. Huerta, *Chicano Theatre: Themes and Forms*, 1982. See also Françoise Kourilsky, "Approaching Quetzalcoatl: The Evolution of El Teatro Campesino," *Performance*, II (1973), 37-46; Carlos Morton, "Teatro Campesino," *The Drama Review*, XVIII (1974), 71-76; John Harrop and Jorge Huerta, "The Agitprop Pilgrimage of Luis Valdez and El Teatro Campesino," *Theatre Quarterly*, XVII (1975), 30-39; Juan García, "Bertolt Brecht and Luis Valdez: The Relation Between the Self and the Techniques in Their Theatre," *De Colores*, V (1978-1980), 93-101; Jorge Huerta, "From the Temple to the Arena," in *The Identification and Analysis of Chicano Literature*, 1979, edited by Francisco Jiménez; Francisco Jiménez, "Dramatic Principles of The Teatro Campesino," in *The Identification and Analysis of Chicano Literature*, 1979, edited by Francisco Jiménez; Carlota Cárdenas de Dwyer, "The Development of Chicano Drama and Luis Valdez' *Actos*," in *Modern Chicano Writers*, 1979, edited by Joseph Sommers and Tomás Ybarra-Frausto; Edward G. Brown, "The Teatro Campesino Vietnam Trilogy," *Minority Voices*, IV (1980), 29-38; Dieter Herms, "Luis Valdez, Chicano Dramatist: An Introduction," in *Essays on Contemporary American Drama*, 1981, edited by Hedwig Bock and Albert Wertheim; Ruby Cohn, *New American Dramatists, 1960-1980*, 1982; Laura Martin, "Language Form and Language Function in *Zoot Suit* and *The Border*," *Studies in Latin American Popular Culture*, III (1984), 57-69; and an interview in David Savran, *In Their Own Words*, 1988.

Lori Hall Burghardt

LUISA VALENZUELA

Born: Buenos Aires, Argentina
Date: November 26, 1938

Principal Works

NOVELS: *Hay que sonreír*, 1966 (*Clara*, 1976); *El gato eficaz*, 1972; *Como en la guerra*, 1977 (*He Who Searches*, 1979); *Libro que no muerde*, 1980; *Cola de lagartija*, 1983; *El señor de Tacuru*, 1983 (*The Lizard's Tail*, 1983).

SHORT FICTION: *Los heréticos*, 1967 (*Clara: Thirteen Short Stories and a Novel*, 1976); *Aquí pasan cosas raras*, 1975 (*Strange Things Happen Here: Twenty-six Short Stories and a Novel*, 1979); *Cambio de armas*, 1982 (*Other Weapons*, 1985); *Donde viven las águilas*, 1983.

Luisa Valenzuela, Argentine novelist, short-story writer, journalist, and scriptwriter, is one of Argentina's most significant authors to emerge since the boom in Latin American literature during the 1960's. As the daughter of Luisa Mercedes Levinson, a prominent Argentinian writer, Valenzuela was initiated at an early age into the world of the written word. Her father, Pablo Francisco Valenzuela, was a doctor. She was reared in Belgrano and received her early education from a German governess and an English tutor. In 1945, she attended Belgrano Girls' School and then an English high school. She began writing for the magazine *Quince Abriles* in 1953 and completed her studies at the National Preparatory School Vincente López in 1955. Subsequently, she was graduated with a bachelor of arts degree from the University of Buenos Aires. She wrote for the Buenos Aires magazines *Atlántida*, *El Hogar*, and *Esto Es* and worked with Jorge Luis Borges in the National Library of Argentina. She also wrote for the Belgrano Radio and was a tour guide in 1957. It was during this time that her first short stories were published, in the magazine *Ficción*.

In 1958, when she was twenty years old, Valenzuela left Buenos Aires to become the Paris correspondent for the Argentine daily newspaper *El Mundo*. There she wrote programs for Radio Télévision Française and participated in the intellectual life of the then-famous *Tel Quel* group of literary theorists and structuralists. She married French Merchant Marine Theodore Marjak, resided in Normandy, and gave birth to a daughter, Anna-Lisa, in 1958. Three years later, she returned to Buenos Aires and joined Argentina's foremost newspaper, *La Nación*, where she became assistant editor. After she was divorced from her husband in 1965, she went to the University of Iowa's Writers' Workshop on a Fulbright grant in 1969. In 1972, she received a scholarship to study pop culture and literature in New York. She then became an avid traveler, living in Spain, Mexico, New York, and Buenos Aires; participating in conferences; continuing her journalism; and cultivating her fiction.

Her first novel, *Clara*, presents a naïve country girl turned prostitute in Buenos Aires; the girl's picaresque adventures in a male world alternate between the humorous and the sinister. As the novel progresses, the antiheroine's forthrightness slowly changes into a pathos under the constant attack of the city's anonymity, alienation, and male brutality. Valenzuela won the Instituto Nacional de Cinematografía Award in 1973 for the script "Hay que sonreír," based on her first novel. Her New York-Greenwich Village experience resulted in *El gato eficaz* (the efficient cat), an experimental novel sustained largely by the innovative use of language and an imaginative plot. In 1975, she returned to Buenos Aires and joined the staff of the journal *Crisis*. After participating in more workshops and conferences, she left Buenos Aires and settled in New York in 1978, where she conducted creative writing workshops and taught Latin American literature at Columbia University, as well as at other universities in the United States.

Although she has lived much of her life outside Argentina, Valenzuela, like other Argentine women writers, could not escape her involvement with an Argentine society torn by violence, class struggle, dictatorship, and dehumanization. Thus, much of her fiction, though written and published outside her native country, where it was banned, treats such themes as violence, political repression, and cultural repression, especially as they relate to women. Yet, as critics point out, her work continually undermines social and political myths while (unlike that of so many political writers) refusing to replace old mythic structures with new but equally arbitrary and authoritative ones.

BIBLIOGRAPHICAL REFERENCES: In *Women's Voices from Latin America*, 1985, edited by Evelyn Piccon Garfield, Valenzuela is one of six Latin American women writers interviewed. Garfield also gives a brief biography and a useful bibliography on each author. Sharon Magnarelli, *The Lost Rib: Female Characters in the Spanish American Novel*, 1985, contains a chapter entitled "Women, Language, and Cats in Luisa Valenzuela's *El gato eficaz*: Looking-Glass Games of Fire," in which Magnarelli gives an insightful and detailed critical analysis of Valenzuela's novel. *Contemporary Women Authors of Latin America*, 1983, edited by Doris Meyer and Margarite Fernandez Olmos, contains an insightful testimonial essay by Valenzuela and a short-story translation. See also Marie-Lise Gazarian Gautier, "The Sorcerer and Luisa Valenzuela: Double Narrators on the Novel/Biography, Myth/History," *Review of Contemporary Fiction*, VI (1986), 105-108; Edith Grossman, "To Speak the Unspeakable," *Center for Inter-American Relations Review*, XXXII (1984), 33-34; Sharon Magnarelli, "Luisa Valenzuela: From *Hay que sonreír* to *Cambio de armas*," *World Literature Today*, LVIII (1984), 9-13; Diane Marting, "Female Sexuality in Selected Short Stories by Luisa Valenzuela: Toward an Ontology of Her Work," *Review of Contemporary Fiction*, VI (1986), 48-54.

Genevieve Slomski

MARIO VARGAS LLOSA

Born: Arequipa, Peru
Date: March 28, 1936

PRINCIPAL WORKS

NOVELS: *La ciudad y los perros*, 1963 (*The Time of the Hero*, 1966); *La casa verde*, 1966 (*The Green House*, 1968); *Los cachorros*, 1967 (*The Cubs*, 1979); *Conversación en la catedral*, 1969 (*Conversation in the Cathedral*, 1975); *Pantaleón y las visitadoras*, 1973 (*Captain Pantoja and the Special Service*, 1978); *La tía Julia y el escribidor*, 1977 (*Aunt Julia and the Scriptwriter*, 1982); *La guerra del fin del mundo*, 1981 (*The War of the End of the World*, 1984); *La historia de Alejandro Mayta*, 1984 (*The Real Life of Alejandro Mayta*, 1986); *¿Quién mató a Palomino Molero?*, 1987 (*Who Killed Palomino Molero?*, 1987); *El hablador*, 1988.

SHORT FICTION: *Los jefes*, 1959; *The Cubs and Other Stories*, 1979.

PLAYS: *La señorita de Tacna*, pb. 1981; *Kathie y el hipopótamo*, pb. 1983; *La Chunga*, pb. 1987.

LITERARY CRITICISM: *Literatura en la revolución y revolución en literatura*, 1970 (with Julio Cortázar and Oscar Collazos); *La historia secreta de una novela*, 1971; *Gabriel García Márquez: Historia de un deicidio*, 1971; *La novela y el problema de la expresión literaria en Peru*, 1974; *La orgía perpetua: Flaubert y "Madame Bovary,"* 1975; *José María Arguedas: Entre sapos y halcones*, 1978; *La utopia arcaica*, 1978.

Peru's leading contemporary novelist, Mario Vargas Llosa, is regarded as one of the creators (along with such writers as Julio Cortázar, Gabriel García Márquez, and Carlos Fuentes) of the new Latin American novel. Born in the town of Arequipa in southern Peru, Mario Vargas Llosa was the son of Ernesto Vargas Maldonado and Dora Llosa Ureta. His parents were divorced before he was born, and he was taken by his mother to live at Cochabama, Bolivia, with her parents, who spoiled him. When he was nine, he and his mother left for Piura, in northwestern Peru; however, a year later, his parents remarried, and they moved the family to Lima.

The pampered and sensitive boy found himself no longer the center of attention. At the Catholic school he attended in Lima, he was younger than most of his classmates and was ridiculed for it. At home, his artistic activities had to be kept from his father, who (like many Peruvians) regarded writing as no work for a man. For Vargas Llosa, literature became an escape, and as he later described it, a way of justifying his existence. Intending to "make a man of him," Vargas Llosa's father sent his son to a military academy in Lima, the Leoncio Prado. Yet the machismo and brutality he encountered there proved highly traumatic for the young man.

This traumatic experience ended in 1952, when Vargas Llosa returned to Piura for his final year of secondary school. In Piura he worked part-time on the newspaper *La Industria* and wrote a play called "La huida" (the escape). Returning to Lima, Vargas Llosa studied for his degree in literature at the University of San Marcos, while being employed as a journalist with Radio Panamericana and the newspaper *La Crónica*. Then in 1955, he married Julia Urquidi, a Bolivian; the marriage ended in divorce. In 1965, he married his first cousin Patricia Llosa, with whom he had two sons and a daughter.

Vargas Llosa made a brief visit to Paris in 1958 and won a prize in a short-story competition sponsored by *La Revue française*. The winning story, "El desafío" (the challenge), was published in his first book of short stories, *Los jefes* (the leaders). The book won for Vargas Llosa the Premio Leopoldo Alas award in Spain, where it was published in 1959. That same year the author traveled to the University of Madrid on a scholarship but decided to move on to Paris without completing his doctoral dissertation. He lived there for seven years, working as a Berlitz teacher, as a journalist, and with URTF, the French radio and television network.

In Paris, Vargas Llosa met other Latin American and French writers and intellectuals but worked and wrote in relative isolation until the publication of his first novel, *The Time of the Hero*, a novel which caused a sensation throughout the Spanish-speaking world. Highly experimental in style, the novel portrays an educational institution that deliberately corrupts innocence and perverts idealism in its students (indicting both the Leoncio Prado and the Peruvian military regime which it represents). The Peruvian military authorities burned a thousand copies of the book on the grounds of the Leoncio Prado and dismissed the work as the product of a demented Communist mind. In Spain, however, it received the Premio de la Crítica Española, and has been translated into more than a dozen languages.

The Green House appeared three years later. The title refers both to a Piura brothel and to the rain forest. The social messages—the complicity between army and church, the horrors of human exploitation—coexist with the intense inner conflicts of the characters. Some critics disparaged the novel's characters as one-dimensional, failing to understand that for Vargas Llosa a novel is primarily a chronicle of action, not an inner revelation of the forces that motivate action. The book was awarded numerous prizes in Spain and Peru.

In 1966 Vargas Llosa left Paris for London, accepting an appointment as visiting lecturer in Latin American literature at the University of London; he also traveled and lectured throughout Great Britain and Europe. He then spent a semester as writer-in-residence at the University of Washington in Seattle.

After the publication of his third novel, *Conversation in the Cathedral*, a monumental two-volume indictment of Peruvian life under the corrupt dictatorship of Manuel Udria (1948-1956), Vargas Llosa lectured briefly at the University of Puerto Rico. The doctoral dissertation he had begun in 1959, a study of the fiction of his close friend, Gabriel García Márquez, was finally published in 1971. Two years later a fourth novel appeared: *Captain Pantoja and the Special Service*. While it once again attacked the unholy alliance of church, army, and brothel, it was written in a new farcical style. This comic vein continues in the author's next novel, *Aunt Julia and the Scriptwriter*, a satirical account of the discovery of a Bolivian genius in his genre: radio melodramas.

Besides being a writer of fiction, Vargas Llosa is also a prolific literary critic. He regards literary criticism as a creative act, not unlike that of writing a novel or a short story, in which the critic indulges in the same arbitrariness and fantasy as the author.

Finally, Vargas Llosa has taken an increasingly active role in Peruvian politics. As a spokesman for democratic centrism, he has been harshly criticized by his erstwhile colleagues on the left. Not only in speeches and journalistic pieces but also in novels such as *The Real Life of Alejandro Mayta*, Vargas Llosa has cast a skeptical eye on revolutionary ideology. Political controversy, however, has not diminished his reputation as one of the leading writers in Latin America.

BIBLIOGRAPHICAL REFERENCES: Luis A. Díez, in *Mario Vargas Llosa's Pursuit of the Total Novel*, 1970, offers an excellent and detailed study of Vargas Llosa's concept of the novel, along with illustrations from the author's works; Marvin A. Lewis, *From Lima to Leticia: The Peruvian Novels of Mario Vargas Llosa*, 1983, offers a brief but informative analysis of Vargas Llosa's novels. Bob M. Tusa, *Alchlemy of a Hero: A Comparative Study of the Works of Alejo Carpentier and Mario Vargas Llosa*, 1983, gives an illuminating comparative treatment of the form and content of the two writers' works. In *Mario Vargas Llosa: A Collection of Critical Essays*, 1978, edited by Charles Rossman and Alan Warren Friedman, a useful selection of in-depth analyses of the author's major works is presented, along with an interview, a chronology of events, and a bibliography. Raymond L. Williams, *Mario Vargas Llosa*, 1986, gives an overview of the author's life and work. See also Mark D. Larsen, "Religious Figures in Mario Vargas Llosa's *Los cachorros*," *Michigan Academician*, XVIII (1986), 375-382; Julie Jones, "Vargas Llosa's Mangacheria: The Pleasures of Community,"

Revista de estudios hispánicos, XX (1986), 77-89; and Sharon Magnarelli, "The Diseases of Love and Discourse: *La tía Julia y el escribidor* and Maria," *Hispanic Review*, LIV (1986), 195-205.

Genevieve Slomski

GORE VIDAL

Born: West Point, New York
Date: October 3, 1925

PRINCIPAL WORKS

NOVELS: *Williwaw*, 1946; *In a Yellow Wood*, 1947; *The City and the Pillar*, 1948; *The Season of Comfort*, 1949; *A Search for the King: A Twelfth Century Legend*, 1950; *Dark Green, Bright Red*, 1950; *Death in the Fifth Position*, 1952; *The Judgement of Paris*, 1952; *Death Before Bedtime*, 1953; *Death Likes It Hot*, 1954; *Messiah*, 1954; *Julian*, 1964; *Washington, D.C.*, 1967; *Myra Breckinridge*, 1968; *Two Sisters*, 1970; *Burr*, 1973; *Myron*, 1974; *1876*, 1976; *Kalki*, 1978; *Creation*, 1981; *Duluth*, 1983; *Lincoln*, 1984; *Empire*, 1987.

PLAYS: *Visit to a Small Planet*, pr. 1956; *The Best Man: A Play About Politics*, pr. 1960.

TELEPLAYS: *Visit to a Small Planet*, 1955; *The Indestructible Mr. Gore*, 1960.

SCREENPLAYS: *I Accuse*, 1958; *The Best Man*, 1964; *Last of the Mobile Hot-Shots*, 1970.

SHORT FICTION: *A Thirsty Evil: Seven Short Stories*, 1956.

ESSAYS: *Reflections upon a Sinking Ship*, 1969; *Homage to Daniel Shays: Collected Essays, 1952-1972*, 1972 (also known as *Collected Essays, 1952-1972*); *Matters of Fact and Fiction: Essays, 1973-1976*, 1977; *The Second American Revolution and Other Essays, 1976-1982*, 1982 (also known as *"Pink Triangle and Yellow Star" and Other Essays*).

EDITED TEXTS: *Best Television Plays*, 1956; *Views from a Window: Conversations with Gore Vidal*, 1980 (with Robert Stanton).

Regarded as one of the most promising novelists to come out of World War II, Gore Vidal has not only created an important body of fiction, but he has also become an influential man of letters, rivaling his contemporary John Updike in the scope and consistency of his work. Vidal was reared in Washington, D.C., and he has written novels and essays that have the authoritative character of one steeped in politics, but he first came to prominence with a war novel, *Williwaw.* Several novels on both contemporary and historical themes followed, but Vidal found himself unable to make enough money as a writer or to attract the critical praise that would ensure his career as a novelist. Consequently, he turned to writing for films and television, becoming one of the four or five best television writers before adapting his teleplay, *Visit to a Small Planet*, for a successful run on the Broadway stage. He would write numerous plays for stage, screen, and television.

Having achieved some degree of fame and financial security, Vidal returned to the novel in 1964, publishing *Julian*, a brilliant historical novel that re-creates the life of a fourth century Roman emperor who renounced Christianity. Vidal's reputation as a novelist recovered, he subsequently created a dazzling series of historical novels and contemporary satires. Of a piece with his acerbic and amusing essays, his fiction is distinguished by a disaffection with American history. *Burr*, for example, sides with one of history's losers, creating sympathy for a political leader who had none of the pomposity or hypocrisy of Alexander Hamilton, George Washington, or Thomas Jefferson. If Vidal has an American hero, it is Abraham Lincoln, the subject of what is perhaps Vidal's greatest novel. Lincoln is presented as a political genius who broke certain constitutional restraints in order to save the Union. *Lincoln*, when viewed in the context of Vidal's other historical novels, suggests that the president's very greatness may have contributed to the follies and abuses of power Vidal chronicles so entertainingly in *1876*.

Vidal's lucid prose stands in marked contrast to the baroque experimentalism of Norman Mailer and other celebrated contemporaries. In fact, in his essays Vidal has attacked much of contemporary American fiction, finding it esoteric and obscure, a literature produced for discussion in the American classroom, not a body of writing that will survive for a general audience. Vidal's models have been writers such as Edith Wharton, clear-eyed social critics and novelists of manners. In much of his fiction and nonfiction, Vidal has specialized as an analyst of political corruption and sexual mores. As early as *The City and the Pillar*, he produced a sympathetic study of a homosexual ostracized by society. *Myra Breckinridge* is a satire on the lurid adventures of a transsexual, and *Myron* is its sequel, set in Hollywood. Vidal has also satirized feminism in *Kalki*. The origins of his sardonic view of the Washington establishment are to be found in *Washington, D.C.*. Under the pseudonym Edgar Box, Vidal also tried his hand at mystery and detective fiction with novels such as *Death in the Fifth Position*, *Death Before Bedtime*, and *Death Likes It Hot*.

For many literary critics, Vidal the essayist predominates over Vidal the novelist. In some of his fiction, characterization seems weak, and he is apparently more interested in the points he has to make than in the people he has created. There are, however, major exceptions to this judgment. *Burr*, in which the historical figure's voice blends perfectly with Vidal's, is a triumph—as is *Lincoln*, in which Vidal restrains his sarcasm in favor of a sober yet lively narrative that reveals Lincoln's political intelligence in all of its magnificence.

BIBLIOGRAPHICAL REFERENCES: *Views from a Window*, 1980, edited by Robert J. Stanton and Gore Vidal, is a rather unusual collection of interviews with a contemporary author. Although the interviews are republished material taken from a variety of periodical sources, Vidal and his coeditor have trimmed some of the interviews and regrouped his comments by subject matter. Vidal has also included new commentary on old interviews. This is an extremely useful, well-indexed volume. Also of considerable importance in organizing a study of Vidal is *Gore Vidal: A Primary and Secondary Bibliography*, 1978, edited by Robert J. Stanton. Two books about Vidal written with his cooperation are Ray Lewis White, *Gore Vidal*, 1968, and Bernard F. Dick, *The Apostate Angel: A Critical Study of Gore Vidal*, 1974. Both books contain biographical and critical commentary, notes, and bibliographies. Dick, in particular, deals with academic prejudices against Vidal, while White writes a more conventional but no less helpful critique. See also Robert F. Kiernan, *Gore Vidal*, 1982. Vidal has been slighted in academic studies of fiction and nonfiction, but he is discussed in several standard literary histories and books of literary criticism: John Aldridge, *After the Lost Generation: A Critical Study of the Writers of Two Wars*, 1951; Walter Allen, *The Modern Novel in Britain and the United States*, 1964; Leslie Fiedler, *Love and Death in the American Novel*, 1966; and Theodore Ziolkowski, *Fictional Transfigurations of Jesus*, 1972.

Carl Rollyson

ELIO VITTORINI

Born: Syracuse, Sicily
Date: July 23, 1908

Died: Milan, Italy
Date: February 12, 1966

PRINCIPAL WORKS

NOVELS: *Conversazione in Sicilia*, 1937 (*In Sicily*, 1948; also known as *Conversations in Sicily*); *Uomini e no*, 1945 (*Men and Not Men*, 1985); *Le donne di Messina*, 1949 (*Women of Messina*, 1973).

NOVELLAS: *Il Sempione strizza l'occhio al Fréjus*, 1947 (*The Twilight of the Elephant*, 1951; also known as *Tune for an Elephant*); *La garibaldina*, 1950 (*La Garibaldina*, 1960).

TRAVEL SKETCH: *Nei morlacchi—Viaggio in Sardegna*, 1936 (also known as *Sardegna come un'infanzia*).

JOURNALISM: *Diario in pubblico*, 1957.

MISCELLANEOUS: *A Vittorini Omnibus*, 1960; *Opere*, 1974.

Elio Vittorini is remembered chiefly as one of Sicily's great twentieth century authors, although only two of his major works deal with that island: *In Sicily* and *La Garibaldina*. Vittorini was born on July 23, 1908, in Syracuse, Sicily, the son of a railway stationmaster and a simple countrywoman. He had little formal education, which contributed to his problems as a writer. In the 1930's, he worked as a newspaper editor and translator—he had taught himself English and translated a number of American authors, including Ernest Hemingway and John Steinbeck. It was when the Spanish Civil War began in 1936 and Germany and Italy began supporting the Franco forces that Vittorini rejected Italian Fascism and began working against it. His book *In Sicily*, serialized in 1937, is an anti-Fascist novel. It is couched in such ambiguous terms and situations, however, that at first it was permitted by the Fascist censors to be published. Later, after numerous complaints from Fascist officials, it was banned.

Vittorini joined the Communist Party of Italy, then underground, and worked with the Resistance. His novel *Men and Not Men* is the story of the Milan underground's fight in the winter of 1944, when Italy was occupied by German forces. Its style clearly borrows from the plain and repetitive style of Hemingway and other American authors. On the other hand, despite its stylistic failings, it signifies Vittorini's search for a poetic fiction. After the war, Vittorini continued working as an editor. His postwar works, such as *The Twilight of the Elephant* and *La Garibaldina*, were shorter than standard novels. His last long novel was *Women of Messina*, published in 1949. Of these works, only *La Garibaldina* has come close to the fame of *In Sicily*.

In his last years, Vittorini was influential chiefly for his editorial work for the publishers Einaudi, Bompiani, and Mondadori, where he continued to promote the translation of foreign authors and to edit an influential series of texts. He also issued several minor nonfiction works, which added little to his reputation; his creative period was over. He did not write much in his last years, although his importance in Italian literature was ensured by the continuing popularity of *In Sicily*, as well as *La Garibaldina*. In the United States and other English-speaking countries, both novels were translated and praised. The American edition of *In Sicily* boasts an introduction, full of praise, by Hemingway, while the British version had that honor done by Stephen Spender. Vittorini died in Milan, on February 12, 1966.

BIBLIOGRAPHICAL REFERENCES: Donald Heiney, *Three Italian Novelists: Moravia, Pavese, Vittorini*, 1968, is a clear and insightful study of Vittorini as an "operatic" novelist. For a view of Vittorini's place in contemporary Italian literature, see Sergio Pacifici, *The Modern Italian Novel: From Pea to Moravia*, 1979, and the text that he edited on the same subject, *From "Verismo" to Experimentalism: Essays on the Modern Italian Novel*, 1969. On a similar note, see *New World Journeys: Contemporary Italian Writers and the Experience of America*, 1977, edited by Angela Jeannet and L. K. Barnett. For a full-length study on Vittorini alone, see Joy Hambuechen Potter, *Elio Vittorini*, 1979, a volume in the Twayne World Authors series. See also Sergio Pacifici, "Understanding Vittorini 'Whole,'" *Italian Quarterly*, I (1958), 95-98; R. W. B. Lewis, "Elio Vittorini," *Italian Quarterly*, IV, no. 15 (1960), 55-61; and Glauco Cambon, "Elio Vittorini: Between Poverty and Wealth," *Wisconsin Studies in Contemporary Literature*, III (1962), 20-24.

Philip Brantingham

ERIC VOEGELIN

Born: Cologne, Germany
Date: January 3, 1901

Died: Palo Alto, California
Date: January 19, 1985

Principal Works

POLITICAL PHILOSOPHY: *The New Science of Politics*, 1952; *Order and History*, 1956-1987 (includes *Israel and Revelation*, *The World of the Polis*, *Plato and Aristotle*, *The Ecumenic Age*, and *In Search of Order*); *Anamnesis: Zur Theorie Geschiche und Politik*, 1966 (*Anamnesis*, 1978); *Science, Politics, and Gnosticism: Two Essays*, 1968; *From Enlightenment to Revolution*, 1975.

Eric Hermann Wilhelm Voegelin is one of the most important political philosophers and historians of the twentieth century. He was born in Cologne, Germany, on January 3, 1901, to Otto Stefan Voegelin, a civil engineer, and Elisabeth Ruchl Voegelin. In 1910, his family moved to Vienna, Austria. Voegelin entered a modified classical high school (*Realgymnasium*), which had a strong emphasis on ancient and modern languages and the sciences. He completed his Ph.D. in 1922 at the University of Vienna in the political science program of the law faculty. From 1923 to 1924, he was an assistant in the law faculty at the University of Vienna. In 1924, he received a Laura Spellman Rockefeller Fellowship, which allowed him to study in the United States and France for three years. In 1929, he was appointed as a *Privatdozent* and then, in 1936, as an associate professor of law at the University of Vienna. In 1932, he married Lissy Onken. In 1938, he was dismissed from his faculty position by the Nazis, largely because of his criticisms of their ideas on race. That same year, he fled to the United States to avoid arrest and imprisonment by the Nazis. From 1938 to 1939, he held short-term appointments at Harvard University and Bennington College. In 1939, he became an assistant professor in the political science department of the University of Alabama at Tuscaloosa. In 1942, he joined the political science department of Louisiana State University and was made Boyd Professor of Government in 1952. In 1958, he accepted an invitation from the University of Munich to hold its first chair in political science. In 1969, he returned to the United States as Henry Salvatori Distinguished Scholar at the Hoover Institution in Stanford, California. He spent the remainder of his career at Stanford.

Voegelin published five books in German before he was forced to leave Austria. Two of them dealt critically with the idea of racial superiority, and another examined the nature and character of the authoritarian state. Another introduced the concept of political religions, in other words, social and political orders that purport to save mankind from economic, social, and political disorder. The other examined American political and social theory. Voegelin's reputation, however, rests primarily on the work published after his forced emigration. In 1952, he published *The New Science of Politics*, a criticism of positivistic social science. The work also introduced his concept of modern Gnosticism, the pervasive belief in the soteriological power of knowledge. In 1956, he published the first volume of *Order and History*, his magnum opus. This volume, *Israel and Revelation*, examined the concept of political order and disorder in the Ancient Near East. The second and third volumes, *The World of the Polis* and *Plato and Aristotle*, appeared the following year. These works examined the experiential and theoretical developments in Greece that led to the creation of philosophy and political science as the cornerstone of the Western understanding of political order and disorder. Three more volumes were scheduled to appear in 1958 and 1959; the first, "Empire and Christianity," was to cover the rise of multicivilizational empires through the end of the Middle Ages. The other two, "The Protestant Centuries" and "The Crisis of Western Civilization," were to cover the twentieth century. The fourth volume, entitled *The Ecumenic Age*, did not appear until twenty years later, in 1976, and the fifth volume, *In Search of Order*, was published posthumously, in 1987.

Three important books did appear in the interval, however: *Anamnesis*, which appeared in 1966, contains a critical analysis of positivist science and a theoretical discussion of what a science of politics must encompass; *Science, Politics, and Gnosticism* develops the concept of later Gnosticism more fully; and *From Enlightenment to Revolution* provides a critical analysis of the eighteenth and nineteenth century efforts to establish a new science of society and history. When the last two volumes of *Order and History* did appear, Voegelin explained that civilizational data and theoretical changes had delayed the project. *The Ecumenic Age*, which appeared in 1974, examines the period of ecumenic empires, and *In Search of Order*, published in 1987, contains a series of essays on modern political philosophers, including Georg Wilhelm Friedrich Hegel.

Constant themes run through Voegelin's books from the earliest to the last. His primary concern was to understand the origins of the political disorders that convulsed the first half of the twentieth century. Voegelin was convinced that the prevailing positivistic, "value-free" approach could not address the crisis. His alternative was to develop a historical analysis of political order and disorder as a way of setting the current crisis in context. Voegelin's approach gained for him a wide audience in the United States and Europe. His criticisms of positivism drew sharp responses from advocates. On the whole, however, his work has been highly praised by leading scholars in philosophy and political science and has been compared to the work of Arnold Toynbee, Ernst Cassirer, and Pitirim Sorokin.

BIBLIOGRAPHICAL REFERENCES: *Eric Voegelin's Search for Order in History: Expanded Edition*, 1987, edited by Stephen A. McKnight, provides an interdisciplinary analysis of *The New Science of Politics* and *Order in History*. Ellis Sandoz, *The Voegelinian Revolution*, 1981, provides an intellectual biography; *Eric Voegelin's Thought: A Critical Appraisal*, 1982, edited by Sandoz, examines theoretical developments in Voegelin's later work. Eugene Webb, *Eric Voegelin, Philosopher of History*, 1982, examines developments in Voegelin's philosophy of history. Barry Cooper, *The Political Theory of Eric Voegelin*, 1986, contains a good discussion of historiogenesis. David Levy, *Political Order*, 1987, examines Voegelin's philosophical anthropology in relation to Max Scheler, Hans Jonas, and other leading scholars. Eugene Webb, *Philosophers of Consciousness*, 1988, contains an extended discussion of Voegelin's theory of consciousness in comparison to that of other thinkers.

Stephen A. McKnight

VLADIMIR VOINOVICH

Born: Stalinabad, Tadzhikistan, Soviet Union
Date: September 26, 1932

PRINCIPAL WORKS

NOVELS: *Zhizn' i neobychainye priklyucheniya soldata Ivana Chonkina*, 1975 (*The Life and Extraordinary Adventures of Private Ivan Chonkin*, 1977); *Pretendent na prestol: Novye priklyucheniya soldata Ivana Chonkina*, 1979 (*Pretender to the Throne: The Further Adventures of Private Ivan Chonkin*, 1981); *Moscorep*, 1986 (*Moscow 2042*, 1987).

NONFICTION: *Antisovetskiy Sovetskiy Soyuz*, 1985 (*The Anti-Soviet Soviet Union*, 1986).

SATIRE: *Ivan'kiada, ili rasskaz o vselenii pisatelya Voynovicha v novuyu kvartiru*, 1976 (*The Ivankiad: Or, The Tale of the Writer Voinovich's Installation in His New Apartment*, 1977).

MISCELLANEOUS: *Putem vzaimnoy perepiski*, 1979 (*In Plain Russian: Stories*, 1979).

Vladimir Voinovich is an outstanding Soviet satirist of the post-Stalin era. He joined the dissidents in the 1960's and himself emigrated to Munich in December, 1980, continuing his writing career abroad. According to his own account in "A Few Words About Myself" in *The Anti-Soviet Soviet Union*, he was born in Dushanbe (then Stalinabad), Tadzhikistan, on September 26, 1932. His father, of Serbian origin, was a journalist; his mother, who was Jewish, was a mathematics teacher. His distant ancestors served in the Russian navy, and nearer forebears were writers and scholars with Serbian focus. His father was arrested during the Stalinist purges in the late 1930's but was released, fleeing with his son to live with relatives in the Ukraine in time to participate in World War II.

Postwar conditions in the Ukraine did not allow his parents to support Vladimir, though he began school there and established the habit of reading with the same enthusiasm as his parents. The practice was fortunate, since further schooling was sporadic. At age eleven, he began to support himself, working at miscellaneous jobs—on collective farms, on the railroad, in factories, even a short time in radio. He spent about two years at the Moscow Pedagogical Institute from 1957 to 1959. He served in the army for four years and began writing poetry and songs there, achieving quick recognition. One of the songs, "Fourteen Minutes to Go," about Soviet cosmonauts became enormously popular; Premier Nikita Khrushchev himself sang it to greet Soviet astronauts as they returned from space. In 1960, Voinovich wrote his first story, "We Live Here," published in *Novy mir* in 1961, during the second "thaw" in Khrushchev's time. The story was well received by critics looking for new literature, but it was attacked by party-line critics for the "alien poetic of depicting life as it is." A campaign of attacking the writer's work began in earnest in 1963. Voinovich's support of Yuli Daniel and Andrei Sinyavsky in 1968 placed him with the dissidents as literary policy hardened and publication abroad was punishable.

It became clear to him that he would be unable to publish his first novel in the Soviet Union, *The Life and Extraordinary Adventures of Private Ivan Chonkin*, a hilarious satire about a loyal, good-hearted, but ordinary soldier who was sent to a conventionally corrupt and lazy collective farm on orders from a Stalinist army official who promptly forgot him. The book allowed the satire of army and collective farm inefficiency. In 1973, Voinovich sent part of the book abroad for publication, a practice sure to be censured; that year, he also signed a letter in support of Aleksandr Solzhenitsyn and wrote letters attacking literary practices of the time. Dismissal from the Writers' Union followed, making it impossible for him to earn his living as a writer. Unlike others of the so-called Third Wave of emigrating Russian writers, however, Voinovich stayed in the Soviet Union for another seven years "under constant KGB pressure, in an atmosphere of incessant threats, blackmail, and provocation." He continued to write and to send his work and comments abroad, and much of his work circulated in samizdat (illegal copies passed from hand to hand) in his own country.

In 1980, he addressed a satirical letter to the newspaper *Izvestiya* on the government's treatment of the dissident physicist Andrei Sakharov; with that he was allowed to emigrate to the West on December 21, settling in Munich, and six months later he was stripped of his Soviet citizenship by Premier Leonid Brezhnev. The first of the works he sent abroad before his exile were translated in 1977. The completed version of *The Life and Extraordinary Adventures of Private Ivan Chonkin* appeared in that year, a work which convinced Western readers that such a phenomenon as a riotously comical novel could emerge from the Soviet Union. The work made his reputation abroad, and *The Ivankiad* followed close on its heels. This autobiographical account of his mock-epic efforts to convince the Soviet bureaucracy of his right to a larger apartment (his wife was going to have a baby) exposed the dynamics of petty corruption in housing and literature, areas of continuing Soviet problems.

In Plain Russian followed in 1979, a collection of his open letters to various powers, together with short fiction published both in the Soviet Union and abroad but never available in a single volume. The year 1979 also brought *Pretender to the Throne*, the further adventures of Private Chonkin. This work is very bitter indeed about the brutal political system in the Soviet Union. After exile, Voinovich continued to publish. A collection of sketches about life in the Soviet Union, permeated with a fine sense of its ironies, came out in translation in 1986. The paradoxical title was *The Anti-Soviet Soviet Union*, the thesis being that the government of the country was the worst enemy of itself and its people. The sketches recalled works by Soviet satirists of the 1920's, but they aimed to supply information about the lives of the Soviet people, news of whose everyday life was during most of the Soviet period simply unavailable for interested Westerners. Scarcity and shoddiness of consumer goods, interference by secret police, censorship and prescription in literary life were some of the topics that came under Voinovich's knife. Voinovich noted at the end of this work that changes began under Premier Mikhail Gorbachev. The novel *Moscow 2042*, involves a flight from late twentieth century Munich by an expatriate Soviet writer to a Moscow of the future. This dystopian work increased the range of Voinovich's satire: The West as well as the Soviet Union came under his gaze.

Voinovich's novels and short works focus on ordinary life, as seen through the eyes of human types recognizable everywhere. The general decency, kindliness, and susceptibility to fear and guilt of his characters as they encounter the cruelties and absurdities of life in a dogma-dominated society sustain his view that he is not a political writer, but a writer, his political fate to the contrary. The gap between the power-mad rulers and the ordinary people, who only want to live ordinary lives and experience usual human pleasures, is the source not of tragedy (though at times tragic loss looms) but of a comedy that is humorous yet lands telling blows aimed at change. After his exile, Voinovich also published articles in the Western periodical press. He established himself as the outstanding satirist of his generation, moving because of his exile finally to a subject matter beyond the confines of his own country. Some critics have found his attitude toward women sexist, but the books have attained wide readership because of their pace and boisterous and savagely critical humor. Underlying the Gogolian satire, however, is the assertion of human claims and unregenerate orneriness in the face of the outrages of totalitarianism.

BIBLIOGRAPHICAL REFERENCES: *The Third Wave: Russian Literature in Emigration*, 1983, edited by Olga Matich and Michael Heim, contains discussion of issues by Soviet émigré dissidents, including Voinovich, as well as bio-bibliographical data. *Russian Literature and American Critics*, 1985, edited by Kenneth Brostrom, contains an article by John B. Dunlop, "Vladimir Voinovich's *Pretender to the Throne*." Wolfgang Kasack's article "Vladimir Voinovich and His Undesirable Satires," in *Fiction and Drama in Eastern and Southeastern Europe: Evolution and Experiment in the Postwar Period*, 1980, edited by Henrik Birnbaum and Thomas

Eekman, is worthy of attention and Voinovich receives notice in Geoffrey Hosking, *Beyond Socialist Realism: Soviet Fiction Since Ivan Denisovich*, 1980. See also Deming Brown, *Soviet Russian Literature Since Stalin*, 1978; Victor Terras, *Handbook of Russian Literature*, 1985; Edward J. Brown, *Russian Literature Since the Revolution*, 1982; P. S. Prescott, review of *Pretender to the Throne*, *Newsweek*, XCVIII (August 31, 1981), 63A; and R. Z. Sheppard, review of *The Life and Extraordinary Adventures of Private Ivan Chonkin*, *Time*, CIX (January 3, 1977), 80.

Martha Manheim

KURT VONNEGUT, JR.

Born: Indianapolis, Indiana
Date: November 11, 1922

PRINCIPAL WORKS

NOVELS: *Player Piano*, 1952; *The Sirens of Titan*, 1959; *Mother Night*, 1961; *Cat's Cradle*, 1963; *God Bless You, Mr. Rosewater: Or, Pearls Before Swine*, 1965; *Slaughterhouse-Five: Or, The Children's Crusade, a Duty-Dance with Death*, 1969; *Breakfast of Champions: Or, Goodbye Blue Monday!*, 1973; *Slapstick: Or, Lonesome No More!*, 1976; *Jailbird*, 1979; *Deadeye Dick*, 1982; *Galápagos*, 1985; *Bluebeard*, 1987.

SHORT FICTION: *Canary in a Cat House*, 1961; *Welcome to the Monkey House*, 1968.

ESSAYS: *Wampeters, Foma, and Granfalloons (Opinions)*, 1974; *Palm Sunday: An Autobiographical Collage*, 1981.

PLAY: *Happy Birthday, Wanda June*, pb. 1970.

TELEPLAY: *Between Time and Timbuktu: Or, Prometheus-5, a Space Fantasy*, 1972.

CHILDREN'S LITERATURE: *Sun Moon Star*, 1980 (with Ivan Chermayeff).

Few comic fiction writers since Mark Twain have achieved the combination of popularity and critical acclaim attained by social satirist Kurt Vonnegut, Jr. Born in Indianapolis, Indiana, on November 11, 1922, to Kurt Vonnegut, Sr., and the former Edith Lieber, Vonnegut was the youngest of three gifted children. His brother, Bernard, has made noteworthy contributions to the science of meteorology, and his sister, Alice, who died of cancer at age forty-one, showed talent as a sculptor. Vonnegut's father and paternal grandfather were architects, while the Liebers owned a prosperous local brewery. Unfortunately, anti-German prejudice inspired by World War I plus financial setbacks resulting from Prohibition and the Great Depression reversed the family's fortunes, and Kurt, Jr., grew up experiencing fewer economic advantages than his siblings.

A student in biochemistry at Cornell University from 1940 to 1942, Vonnegut wrote for the *Cornell Sun*, often expressing opposition to American involvement in World War II. Nevertheless, he enlisted in the U.S. Army early in 1943. The war years brought Vonnegut the double trauma of his mother's suicide, inspired at least in part by her family's continuing financial problems, and his own capture by German troops during the Battle of the Bulge. His experiences as a war prisoner in Dresden during that city's destruction by incendiary bombs in February in 1945 provide much of the material for *Slaughterhouse-Five*, his most acclaimed novel.

Soon after his repatriation, Vonnegut married Jane Marie Cox and became a student in anthropology at the University of Chicago, earning a pittance on the side as a police reporter. After the university's rejection of his master's thesis, Vonnegut, in 1947, accepted a job as a writer of public-relations copy for the General Electric Company. The years in Schenectady, the Ilium, New York, of Vonnegut's fictional universe, inspired him with a hatred of corporate insensitivity and an awareness of the destructive social impact of science and technology, themes of importance in *Player Piano*, his first novel, published in 1952, and much of the rest of his creative output. Technology is already the villain in his first accepted short story, "Report on the Barnhouse Effect," which appeared in the February, 1950, issue of *Collier's*. There, however, it is the military rather than industry which attempts to misuse the products of science.

By 1951, having moved from Schenectady to Cape Cod, Vonnegut had begun writing full time, relying mainly on the sale of short stories for his livelihood. When the short-story market weakened in the late 1950's, his desire to publish further novels became an urgent need. His second novel, *The Sirens of Titan*, appeared in 1959, attracting little immediate critical attention despite its eventual high reputation among Vonnegut's works. The book narrates the wanderings of a reluctant space traveler, Malachi Constant, whose life, like the lives of many of Vonnegut's characters, is determined not by will but by cosmic accident; Constant achieves some measure of fulfillment only when he discovers his capacity to love.

According to the introduction which Vonnegut added to his third novel, *Mother Night*, five years after its original publication, the book's point is that "We are what we pretend to be, so we must be careful about what we pretend to be." After agreeing to feign collaboration with the Nazis during World War II in order to pass along coded messages for the Allies, the novel's central character, Howard W. Campbell, Jr., plays his collaborationist role so well that he loses himself in his own and the world's duplicity, succumbing finally to a cynical despair.

Two more novels of the 1960's, *Cat's Cradle* and *God Bless You, Mr. Rosewater*, augmented Vonnegut's reputation among an increasingly devoted cult readership and anticipated themes which would receive definitive treatment in *Slaughterhouse-Five*, the book for which Vonnegut is best known. In *Slaughterhouse-Five*, the loving, unstable innocent is Billy Pilgrim, who evangelizes his consoling religious message despite having witnessed the technological marvel of incendiary warfare at Dresden and despite knowing precisely how technology will end the universe. The culmination of years of struggle to cope creatively with the horrors Vonnegut had experienced in World War II, *Slaughterhouse-Five* brought its author international acclaim.

Vonnegut's prolific output as novelistic social commentator has continued since the triumph of *Slaughterhouse-Five*, although none of his later works has caused quite the same critical stir. *Breakfast of Champions* gives a depressing picture of modern materialism and cultural inanity through the interconnected stories of Pontiac dealer Dwayne Hoover and Vonnegut's crude alter ego, science-fiction writer Kilgore Trout; *Slapstick* suggests the creation of extended families as a solution to the trauma of modern alienation; *Jailbird* describes the snares awaiting the unwary idealist in a world dominated by political and corporate power; *Deadeye Dick* explores the ambiguous nature of guilt in a world of bewildering complexity; *Galápagos* narrates the coming of millennial peace to the earth when evolutionary regression robs humanity of the capacity to commit evil; and *Bluebeard* tells of a Vonnegut-like artist's triumphant capitulation to his one true, if unfashionable, artistic talent, the ability to represent the panoramic littleness of human life in loving detail. One can hardly imagine a more accurate epitome of Vonnegut's own peculiar genius.

BIBLIOGRAPHICAL REFERENCES: An early book-length study of Vonnegut which remains useful for understanding the novels up to and including *Slaughterhouse-Five* is Peter J. Reed, *Kurt Vonnegut, Jr.*, 1972. David H. Goldsmith, *Kurt Vonnegut: Fantasist of Fire and Ice*, 1972, is another significant work on the first phase of Vonnegut's career. See also Stanley Schatt, *Kurt Vonnegut, Jr.*, 1976; Richard Giannone, *Vonnegut: A Preface to His Novels*, 1977; and Clark Mayo, *Kurt Vonnegut: The Gospel from Outer Space*, 1977. Schatt's study is also useful for its comments on the short fiction. Jerome Klinkowitz, *Kurt Vonnegut*, 1982, treats all the novels through *Jailbird*, suggesting a chronological development of Vonnegut's book-length fiction from the formulaic to the experimental to the personal. Two miscellaneous collections of Vonnegut scholarship which also deserve mention are *The Vonnegut Statement*, 1973, edited by Jerome Klinkowitz and John Somer, and *Vonnegut in America*, 1977, edited by Klinkowitz and Donald L. Lawler. Both volumes include excellent, even if outdated, Vonnegut bibliographies.

Robert H. O'Connor

LEV VYGOTSKY

Born: Orscha, Belorussia
Date: November 17, 1896

Died: Moscow, Soviet Union
Date: June 11, 1934

Principal Works

PSYCHOLOGY: *Myshlenie i rech: Psikhologicheskie issledovaniya,* 1934 (*Thought and Language*, 1962, 1986); *Umstvennoe razvitie detei v protsesse obucheniya*, 1935; *Izbrannye psikhologicheskie issledovaniya*, 1956; *Razvitie vysshykh psikhicheskikh funktsii*, 1960; *Psikhologiya iskusstvo*, 1965, 1968 (*The Psychology of Art*, 1971); *Mind in Society: The Development of Higher Psychological Processes*, 1978; *Sobranie sochinenii*, 1982-1984.

Lev Semenovich Vygotsky's pioneering work in psychology belatedly influenced the study of art, literature, linguistics, and education, as well as psychology. What little is known of his life comes from the accounts of his colleagues. He was born in 1896 in White Russia, the son of a small-town banker. He was educated by private tutors and later in the Jewish *Gymnasium*, where he developed an interest in Jewish history and culture. He attended medical school in Moscow in deference to his parents' practical concerns, but he later switched to the study of law, to be nearer humanistic subjects. While pursuing his studies at Moscow University, Vygotsky also attended Shanyavskii People's University, an unofficial institution established in reaction to government repression at the state universities. Following his graduation from Moscow University, Vygotsky returned to the provinces to teach literature and psychology. He attracted the notice of professional psychologists at a convention in 1924, at which he delivered a brilliantly original paper. His wife, Roza, accompanied him to Moscow in 1924, when he joined the staff of the Institute of Psychology there.

In the ten years following his appointment to the Psychological Institute, Vygotsky was extraordinarily productive. He founded a new institute for the study of children with physical handicaps and learning disabilities. While maintaining a heavy schedule as a researcher and lecturer, he produced a great number of articles and book-length studies. At the time of his death, of tuberculosis, in 1934, much of this work had not yet been published. As a result of the caprices of Stalinism, Vygotsky's approach to psychology fell out of favor, and it was not until the 1950's that his work began to appear again in the Soviet Union. Between the 1950's and the 1980's, many of his works were published for the first time, along with reissues of previously published material.

Vygotsky reacted against the work of such contemporaries as Ivan Pavlov, who, he believed, placed too much emphasis on reactions as the primary component of human behavior. In the early 1920's, Vygotsky developed his concept of "mediation," which distinguishes humans from other animals in their ability to connect stimuli and responses by means of various kinds of links, such as language. These means of mediation then become themselves stimuli of more complex responses, or "inner language," as Vygotsky called it. Vygotsky also assumed that language and thought developed independently, both in the individual and in the history of the human species. This presupposition led him to postulate that intelligence is a function of the ability to connect signs with concepts. On the basis of this presupposition, he developed the Vygotsky blocks, a test for schizophrenia which was the only one of Vygotsky's concepts widely known before the 1960's, when his works were first translated into English.

Vygotsky's first book, *The Psychology of Art*, unpublished even in Russian until 1965, was a revision of his doctoral thesis at the Moscow Institute of Psychology. This work, which reveals a broad interest in literature and philosophy, exhibits two important qualities of Vygotsky's thought: first, his notion that human psychology is a very complex phenomenon; and second, that psychology is a means to study culture, rather than an end in itself. In other works of the 1920's, Vygotsky addressed the divisions and schools of psychology in his day and outlined his own method, compatible with Marxism but not rigidly subject to it.

In the early 1930's, Vygotsky collected seven essays and fitted them together to compose his most important and influential work, *Thought and Language*. In this book, Vygotsky again surveys various approaches to the subject, focusing primarily on that of his contemporary Jean Piaget. He argues that speech and thought have different roots, and that the two are joined only at a given stage in the development of the individual, after which they exert a mutual influence on future development. The child, he showed, exhibits both speech without meaning and intellectual activity without words. It is the joining and subsequent interaction of the systems of language and thought that mark the maturation of the child. His natural interest in the learning process led Vygotsky to study children in educational settings. Here he observed that two forms of conceptual learning can be distinguished: one formal and systematic, the other spontaneous and loosely organized. This division led, in turn, to his theory of "inner speech," whereby the social function of communication in language is internalized as a set of psychological relations.

Vygotsky and his slightly younger colleague Alexander Luria undertook pioneering studies in cross-cultural psychology, comparing the reasoning processes of uneducated rural people with those of people who had varying levels of formal education. Luria, who went on to enjoy a long career and attained worldwide recognition as a neuropsychologist, always credited Vygotsky's influence and played a part in the revival of his work. Vygotsky's researches also led him into the field of psychopathology; one of his papers on mental illness, "Thought in Schizophrenia," was published in English in 1934.

Vygotsky left his mark not only on Soviet psychology—in his resistance to crudely dogmatic Marxist ideology and insistence on a pluralistic methodology, and in his influence on the work of his students—but also on the fields of art, literature, and linguistics. The belated translation of his works into English has brought increasing recognition of Vygotsky's immense contribution to twentieth century thought.

BIBLIOGRAPHICAL REFERENCES: A thorough study of Vygotsky in English is James V. Wertsch, *Vygotsky and the Social Formation of Mind*, 1985, which includes an extensive bibliography. Also particularly valuable is Alex Kozulin, "Vygotsky in Context," a long introductory essay in the revised and expanded edition of *Thought and Language*, 1986. A. R. Luria, *The Making of Mind: A Personal Account of Soviet Psychology*, 1979, edited by Michael Cole and Sheila Cole, includes a tribute to Vygotsky and a recollection of Luria's work with him. The 1962 edition of *Thought and Language* includes a supplement in which Piaget responds to Vygotsky's critique.

James T. Jones

JOHN WAIN

Born: Stoke-on-Trent, Staffordshire, England
Date: March 14, 1925

Principal Works

NOVELS: *Hurry on Down*, 1953 (also known as *Born in Captivity*); *Living in the Present*, 1955; *The Contenders*, 1958; *A Travelling Woman*, 1959; *Strike the Father Dead*, 1962; *The Young Visitors*, 1965; *The Smaller Sky*, 1967; *A Winter in the Hills*, 1970; *The Pardoner's Tale*, 1979; *Lizzie's Floating Shop*, 1981; *Young Shoulders*, 1982 (also known as *The Free Zone Starts Here*); *Where the Rivers Meet*, 1988.

POETRY: *Mixed Feelings: Nineteen Poems*, 1951; *A Word Carved on a Sill*, 1956; *A Song About Major Eatherly*, 1961; *Weep Before God: Poems*, 1961; *Wildtrack: A Poem*, 1965; *Letters to Five Artists*, 1969; *The Shape of Feng*, 1972; *Feng: A Poem*, 1975; *Poems for the Zodiac*, 1980; *Thinking About Mr. Person*, 1980; *Poems, 1949-1979*, 1981; *Twofold*, 1981; *Open Country*, 1987.

CRITICISM: *Gerard Manley Hopkins: An Idiom of Desperation*, 1959; *Essays on Literature and Ideas*, 1963; *The Living World of Shakespeare: A Playgoer's Guide*, 1964; *A House for the Truth: Critical Essays*, 1972; *Professing Poetry*, 1977; *Samuel Johnson 1709-84*, 1984 (with Kai Kin Yung).

AUTOBIOGRAPHY: *Sprightly Running: Part of an Autobiography*, 1962; *Dear Shadows: Portraits from Memory*, 1986.

BIOGRAPHY: *Arnold Bennett*, 1967; *Samuel Johnson*, 1974.

CHILDREN'S LITERATURE: *Lizzie's Floating Shop*, 1981.

SHORT FICTION: *Nuncle and Other Stories*, 1960; *Death of the Hind Legs and Other Stories*, 1966; *The Life Guard*, 1971; *King Caliban and Other Stories*, 1978.

PLAY: *Harry in the Night: An Optimistic Comedy*, pr. 1975.

RADIO PLAYS: *You Wouldn't Remember*, pr. 1978; *A Winter in the Hills*, pr. 1981; *Frank*, pr. 1982.

TELEPLAY: *Young Shoulders*, 1984 (with Robert Smith).

John Barrington Wain is a British man of letters of major importance, most famous for his early novel *Hurry on Down* and for his prizewinning biography of Samuel Johnson. He was born in Stoke-on-Trent, Staffordshire, England, on March 14, 1925, the son of Arnold A. Wain and Anne Wain. A man of humble background, Arnold Wain had become a dentist, the first professional person in his family. Generous and compassionate, he served as a preacher in the Church army, a city councillor, and a magistrate, and became a model for his son, who pays tribute to his father in *Dear Shadows*.

After attending the High School, Newcastle-under-Lyme, Wain, who had been rejected by the army for poor eyesight, went up to Oxford and entered St. John's College. At the University of Oxford, he met Charles Williams and was tutored by C. S. Lewis. He also came to know Richard Burton and with him participated in Shakespeare productions under the direction of the dynamic, unconventional don Nevill Coghill, who inspired his students to love Shakespeare and who, by acting on his convictions in the face of criticism from his peers, became another role model for Wain. In 1946, Wain received his B.A.; from 1946 to 1949, when he received his M.A., he was Fereday Fellow at the University of Oxford. Meanwhile, in 1947, he had married Marianne Urmston and had become a lecturer in English at the University of Reading, where he remained until 1955, when he resigned from his position to become a free-lance writer. The next year his marriage was dissolved.

With the publication of a book of poetry in 1951, *Mixed Feelings*, Wain's meteoric rise in reputation began. It was followed by another volume of poetry, which despite its conventionality was praised for voicing the anguish of twentieth century man. In 1953, he published the picaresque novel *Hurry on Down*, the story of an aimless university graduate who wanders through British society, seeking a niche where he can feel at home. Despite Wain's protests, this book brought him the label of "angry young man" (applied to those postwar writers who were attacking the English class structure). Critics predicted a bright future for Wain; many of them assumed that he would be the primary writer of his generation. During the decade, he produced two more novels and a critical work on Gerard Manley Hopkins. In 1953, he was chosen to edit a British Broadcasting Corporation (BBC) program featuring new writers. That same year, he edited two books of essays and a two-volume literary annual.

In 1960, Wain married Eirian James, with whom he eventually had three sons. His new happiness was reflected in what is probably his best book written during this period, *Sprightly Running*, which surveys the first thirty-five years of his life honestly and often joyfully. In the 1960's, Wain's energy was evidenced by a steady outpouring of work, including seven editions of works by writers as diverse as Alexander Pope, Fanny Burney, Thomas Hardy, and William Shakespeare and two books of criticism. As the decade proceeded, he published four volumes of poetry, which steadily became more experimental in form than his earlier works, as well as more concerned with social and political matters. He also brought out two collections of short stories and wrote three novels, which like the poetry were more serious and more pessimistic than his previously published fiction. Yet reviewers continued to be lukewarm about both his poetry and his fiction.

Despite the attractiveness of *Sprightly Running*, it was not until the 1970's that Wain attained the eminence which had been predicted for him. Although along with favorable comments critics continued to voice disappointment in his poetry and his fiction, which seemed to stop just short of brilliance, Wain was acknowledged as a distinguished man of letters. In 1973, he was honored with the place of Professor of Poetry at the University of Oxford. Then came a work which fulfilled Wain's early promise. Interestingly, it was a work of criticism, his perceptive biography of Samuel Johnson, which was universally admired and earned for Wain the James Tait Black Memorial Prize. It was followed by a novel, *The Pardoner's Tale*, which was admired by most critics, some of whom called it his best fictional work, and then by another well-reviewed novel, *Young Shoulders*, in 1982. In 1981, a work of another genre, *Lizzie's Floating Shop*, had been published; it won for Wain the Whitbread Award for children's literature. Readers also were delighted with another autobiographical volume, *Dear Shadows*, which, like its predecessor *Sprightly Running*, was not presumptuous but honest, warm, and frequently insightful.

Throughout the acclaimed Johnson biography, Wain had emphasized the need for courage in a tragic world, for reason in an irrational world, and for tradition in a world which is changing, not necessarily for the better. These Johnsonian themes are also Wain's themes. In *Dear Shadows*, Wain writes about eight people, four famous and four unknown, who were important in his life. In them, he saw the qualities he admires: his father's courage and sense of duty, the Stratford landlady's commonsense look at hasty passion, Nevill Coghill's determined revival of the Shakespearean tradition in twentieth century Oxford. Although none of Wain's imaginative works has quite fulfilled the expectations of the critics who so praised his first novel, the fact that year after year he has brought out works in various genres which are always respectable and often very good suggests that his place in literary history will be among the great men of letters. Like them, he has not limited himself to one area but has influenced his age through works of many kinds, not least of which is his scholarly biography of perhaps the greatest man of letters in English literature, Dr. Samuel Johnson.

BIBLIOGRAPHICAL REFERENCES: Dale Salwak, *John Wain*, 1981, and his bibliographical work, *John Braine and John Wain*, 1980, should be the starting points of any study of Wain. For comments on his early work, see Kenneth Allsop, *The Angry Decade*, 1958; James Gindin, *Postwar British Fiction*, 1962; Frederick R. Karl, "The Angries: Is There a Protestant in the House?" in *A Reader's Guide to the Contemporary English Novel*, 1962; and Walter Allen,

The Modern Novel, 1965. Other scholarly articles on Wain's novels include Angela Hague, "Picaresque Structure and the Angry Young Novel," *Twentieth Century Literature*, XXXII (Summer, 1986), 209-220; Wayne J. Douglass and Robert G. Walker, "'A Moralist Perchance Appears': John Wain's *Hurry on Down*," in *Renascence*, XXXI (1978), 43-50; and Edgin W. Mellown, "Steps Toward Vision: The Development of Technique in John Wain's First Seven Novels," *The South Atlantic Quarterly*, XVII (Summer, 1969), 330-342. See also Edmund Fuller, "The Unhappy Drifter," *The New York Times Book Review*, March 21, 1954, 5; D. J. Enright, "Strong Feelings," *New Statesman*, LXIV (September 14, 1962), 323; James Gray, "Never in Anger," *Saturday Review*, XLVI (May 18, 1963); David Littlejohn, "The Misfit at Home," *The Nation*, CXCVII (August 10, 1963), 75-76; Peter Lewis, "Rites of Passage," *The Times Literary Supplement*, October 15, 1982, 1141; Shirley Toulson, "Watching Wounded," *The Times Educational Supplement*, November 12, 1982, 23; Frank Kermode, "Past-Praiser," *London Review of Books*, June 5, 1986, 10; and Edward Blishen, "Dr. Johnson's Footsteps," *The Times Educational Supplement*, June 20, 1986, 20.

Rosemary M. Canfield Reisman

DEREK WALCOTT

Born: Castries, St. Lucia, West Indies
Date: January 23, 1930

Principal Works

POETRY: *25 Poems*, 1948; *Epitaph for the Young: XII Cantos*, 1949; *Poems*, 1951; *In a Green Night: Poems, 1948-1960*, 1962; *Selected Poems*, 1964; *The Castaway and Other Poems*, 1965; *The Gulf and Other Poems*, 1969 (also known as *The Gulf*); *Another Life*, 1973; *Sea Grapes*, 1976; *The Star-Apple Kingdom*, 1979; *The Fortunate Traveller*, 1981; *Selected Poetry*, 1981; *Midsummer*, 1984; *Collected Poems, 1948-1984*, 1986; *The Arkansas Testament*, 1987.

PLAYS: *Henri Christophe: A Chronicle*, pr., pb. 1950; *Harry Dernier: A Play for Radio Production*, pb. 1951; *Ione: A Play with Music*, pb. 1954; *Drums and Colours: An Epic Drama*, pr. 1958; *Ti-Jean and His Brothers*, pr. 1958; *Dream on Monkey Mountain*, pr. 1967; *In a Fine Castle*, pr. 1970; *The Charlatan*, pr. 1974; *The Joker of Seville*, pr. 1974; *O Babylon!*, pr. 1976; *Remembrance*, pr. 1978; *Pantomime*, pr. 1978; *Three Plays*, pb. 1985 (includes *A Branch of the Blue Nile*; *Beef, No Chicken*; and *The Last Carnival*).

Derek Alton Walcott may well be the most highly regarded poet writing in English, let alone from the English-speaking Caribbean. His prodigious talent and energy were recognized early in Castries, St. Lucia, and his mother, Alix Walcott, encouraged him and his twin brother, Roderick Walcott (also an accomplished playwright), in their art. Their father, Warwick Walcott, wrote and painted watercolors as an avocation and died at age thirty-five when the twin brothers were one year old. Derek Walcott has won numerous awards and fellowships for his writing, among them the Welsh Arts Council International Writers Prize (1980), the John D. and Catherine MacArthur Foundation Prize (1981), the *Los Angeles Times* Book Award (1986) for his *Collected Poems, 1948-1984*, and the Queen's Gold Medal for Literature (1989). He is a Fellow of the Royal Society of Literature (1966) and an Honorary Member of the American Academy and Institute of Arts and Letters (1979).

Walcott attended St. Mary's College in Castries and the University of the West Indies in Jamaica, earning a B.A. in English, French, and Latin in 1953. With his mother's financial help, he published his first volume of poems in 1948. His first play, *Henri Christophe*, was produced in 1954 by the student drama society at Jamaica. He taught Latin and other subjects in Grenada, St. Lucia, and Trinidad until 1959, when he founded the Little Carib Theatre Workshop (later known as the Trinidad Theatre Workshop). He worked with the company until 1976, writing many of his most important plays for actors he had trained. Among the plays premiered there were *Ti-Jean and His Brothers*, *Dream on Monkey Mountain* (which won an Obie Award in 1971), *The Joker of Seville*, and *O Babylon!* In that same period, he finished six volumes of poetry, including *Another Life*, the book-length autobiographical poem that, like its predecessor, William Wordsworth's *The Prelude* (1850), chronicles the growth of the poet's imagination.

In the late 1970's, Walcott began teaching at Yale, Columbia, Harvard, and New York universities before accepting a full-time post at Boston University in 1981. Dividing his time between teaching in the United States and living in St. Lucia and Trinidad has permitted the division within his African and European heritage (which he defined in "A Far Cry from Africa" and other early poems) to be elaborated in terms of the metropolitan state and the developing islands. The placing of his poetry in both halves of the New World reveals an ambitious effort to bring into creative tension the conflicts of his divided life as a part-black and part-white man of the postcolonial world of the Americas. That effort is mounted in a literary context—and thus his poetry raids the tradition within which he locates his work, that of Andrew Marvell, John Milton, Henry Vaughan, Thomas Traherne, John Donne, W. H. Auden, Dylan Thomas, William Butler Yeats, and many others, including Robert Lowell—

as well as in a historical context of a postslavery, postcolonial society.

The racial and political ironies of Walcott's West Indian situation are also the subject of his plays from the late 1970's, *Remembrance* and *Pantomime*. In the latter, a white Englishman and a black calypsonian from Trinidad exchange places in rehearsing a music-hall version of Robinson Crusoe, in which Crusoe is black and Friday is white. They play out their oppositions to reach a relationship that is nearly brotherhood, though Crusoe has to ask Friday for a raise. Walcott has been criticized for writing a self-indulgent, highly wrought poetic line, and he has been praised for a line that is Elizabethan in grandeur and richness. He has been accused of betraying the very people his poetry should speak to and for: the indigent, Creole-speaking West Indian who likely cannot read the poetry that Walcott writes. Such critics favor Jamaican "dub" and reggae-based poetry, while misconstruing the importance of the Trinidadian calypso in Walcott's work, and indeed in the East Caribbean. Walcott the lyric poet and narrative poet is also a dramatic poet, and his plays and poems elucidate one another. A thorough assessment of Walcott's work cannot be made without integrating the poet and playwright with the painter who swore on his eighteenth birthday to put his island into paint and words and who has been admirably at the task for decades. Walcott's best work may be those poems, such as *Another Life*, that, whatever the foregrounded subject, take as their realm the villages of St. Lucia—Anse La Raye, Dennery, Choiseul, Gros Islet, Vieuxfort, Soufriere, and the city of Castries—and the spectacular forests, mountains, and seas of the Caribbean.

BIBLIOGRAPHICAL REFERENCES: Irma E. Goldstraw, *Derek Walcott: An Annotated Bibliography of His Works*, 1984, is an exhaustive listing of his publications, including poems and variants, as well as uncollected journalistic essays written for Caribbean newspapers. Edward Baugh, *Derek Walcott: Memory as Vision: Another Life*, 1978, is an excellent reading of Walcott's long poem that is central to his other work. Robert Hamner, *Derek Walcott*, 1981, is a meticulously detailed biblio-biographical study. On the relation of Walcott's poetry to painting, see also Edward Baugh, "Painters and Painting in *Another Life*," *Caribbean Quarterly*, XXVI (1980), 83-93; Marian Stewart, "Walcott and Painting," *Jamaica Journal*, XLV (1981), 56-68; and Robert Bensen, "The Poet as Painter: Derek Walcott's *Midsummer*," *The Literary Review*, XXIX (1986), 257-268. The central positions on the controversy over Walcott and Edward Kamau Brathwaite as major West Indian poets are stated in Lawrence Breiner, "Tradition, Society, and the Figure of the Poet," *Caribbean Quarterly*, XXVI (1980), 1-12; Pat Ismond, "Walcott Versus Brathwaite," *Caribbean Quarterly*, XVII (1971), 54-71; and Anne Walmsley, "Dimensions of Song: A Comment on the Poetry of Derek Walcott and Edward Brathwaite," *Bim*, XIII (1970), 152-167. Valuable critical perceptions of Walcott's poetry may be found in Valerie Trueblood, "On Derek Walcott," *The American Poetry Review*, VII (May/June, 1978), 7-10; Seamus Heaney, "The Language of Exile," *Parnassus*, VIII (1979), 5-11; Andrew Salkey, "Inconsolable Songs of Our America: The Poetry of Derek Walcott," *World Literature Today*, LVI (1982), 51-53; Sven Birkerts, "Heir Apparent," *The New Republic*, CXCI (January 23, 1984), 31-33; Joseph Brodsky, "The Sound of the Tide," in *Less Than One*, 1986; and Peter Balakian, "The Poetry of Derek Walcott," *Poetry*, CXLIII (1987), 39-43. See also Susan Willis, "Caliban as Poet: Reversing the Maps of Domination," *The Massachusetts Review*, XXIII (1982), 615-630; Robert Bensen, "The New World Poetry of Derek Walcott," *Concerning Poetry*, XVI (1983), 29-42; and James McCorkle, "Re-Mapping the New World: The Recent Poetry of Derek Walcott," *Ariel*, XVII (1986), 3-14. Though Walcott's poetry has received more critical attention than his plays, several studies indicate fruitful directions for inquiry, including Robert Hamner, "Derek Walcott's Theater of Assimilation," *West Virginia University Philological Papers*, XXV (1979), 86-93, and his "Mythological Aspects of Derek Walcott's Drama," *Ariel*, VIII (1977), 35-58; Lloyd Brown, "Dreamers and Slaves: The Ethos of Revolution in Derek Walcott and Leroi Jones," *Caribbean Quarterly*, XVII (1971), 36-44; Theodore Colson, "Derek Walcott's

Plays: Outrage and Compassion," *World Literature Written in English*, XV (1973), 80-96; John Thieme, "A Caribbean Don Juan: Derek Walcott's *Joker of Seville*," *World Literature Written in English*, XXIII (1984), 62-75; Robert Hamner, "Exorcising the Planter-Devil in the Plays of Derek Walcott," *Commonwealth Essays and Studies*, VII (1985), 95-102; Patricia Ismond, "Walcott's Later Drama: From *Joker* to *Remembrance*," *Ariel*, XVI (1985), 89-101; Patrick Taylor, "Myth and Reality in Caribbean Narrative: Derek Walcott's *Pantomime*," *World Literature Written in English*, XXVI (1986), 169-177; and Jan R. Uhrbach, "A Note on Language and Naming in *Dream on Monkey Mountain*," *Callaloo*, IX (1986), 578-582. Walcott's interviews give valuable insight into his views on poetry, drama, and the politics and history of the New World. See Dennis Scott, "Walcott on Walcott," *Caribbean Quarterly*, XIV (1968), 77-82; Robert Hamner, "Conversation with Derek Walcott," *World Literature Written in English*, XVI (1977), 409-420; Edward Hirsch, "An Interview with Derek Walcott," *Contemporary Literature*, XX (1979), 279-292; and Ned Thomas, "Derek Walcott," *Kunapipi*, III (1981), 42-47.

Robert Bensen

ALICE WALKER

Born: Eatonton, Georgia
Date: February 9, 1944

Principal Works

NOVELS: *The Third Life of Grange Copeland*, 1970; *Meridian*, 1976; *The Color Purple*, 1982; *The Temple of My Familiar*, 1989.

SHORT FICTION: *In Love and Trouble: Stories of Black Women*, 1973; *You Can't Keep a Good Woman Down: Stories*, 1981.

POETRY: *Once: Poems*, 1968; *Five Poems*, 1972; *Revolutionary Petunias and Other Poems*, 1973; *Good Night, Willie Lee, I'll See You in the Morning: Poems*, 1979; *Horses Make a Landscape Look More Beautiful*, 1984.

CHILDREN'S LITERATURE: *Langston Hughes, American Poet*, 1974; *To Hell with Dying*, 1988.

ESSAYS: *In Search of Our Mother's Gardens: Womanist Prose*, 1983; *Living by the Word: Selected Writings, 1973-1987*, 1988.

EDITED TEXT: *I Love Myself When I Am Laughing . . . and Then Again When I Am Looking Mean and Impressive: A Zora Neale Hurston Reader*, 1979.

Alice Malsenior Walker identifies herself as a "womanist," that is, by her definition, a black feminist who seriously concerns herself with the double oppression of racism and sexism. These two themes dominate Walker's poetry, fiction, and prose. Born in 1944 to Georgia sharecroppers, Minnie Lue and Willie Lee (memorialized in *Goodnight, Willie Lee, I'll See You in the Morning*), Walker grew up in the small town of Eatonton. Her childhood was scarred, literally and figuratively, by a BB gun wound to her eye when she was eight years old. Although the scar and loss of sight were partially repaired by an operation when she was fourteen, Walker acknowledges the part played by this accident in her becoming a writer. It forced her to withdraw from social contacts, but it allowed her to retreat into a world of daydreams ("not of fairytales—but of falling on swords, of putting guns to my heart or head, and of slashing my wrists with a razor") and a world of reading and writing.

A scholarship for handicapped students sent Walker to Spelman College (a setting used in *Meridian*) in 1961; after two years, she transferred to Sarah Lawrence College, from which she was graduated in 1965. Here another painful personal experience precipitated her first volume of poetry, *Once*. Returning to college in the fall of 1964 from a summer in Africa, Walker faced the realization that she was pregnant, without money, without support. She seriously considered suicide before securing an abortion. After graduation Walker was awarded fellowships to both the Breadloaf Writers Conference and the MacDowell Colony, where she began writing her first novel, *The Third Life of Grange Copeland*, in 1967, the year she published her first short story, "To Hell with Dying." In that same year, Walker married Melvyn R. Leventhal, a civil rights lawyer whom she had met through her active involvement in the movement. They had one child, Rebecca Grant, before their divorce in 1976.

Walker has acknowledged the influence of Emily Dickinson, William Carlos Williams, E. E. Cummings, and Bashō on her verse, which she sees as having much in common with improvisational jazz. Her lines are of irregular length; the poems are frequently short. Walker's poetry is marked by an informal tone, a straightforward, unafraid, realistic approach to her subject matter—and her most effective subject is her own childhood. The clean, fresh, unadorned style of Walker's poetry also marks both volumes of her short fiction, *In Love and Trouble* and *You Can't Keep a Good Woman Down*. In the latter collection, Walker experiments with nonfiction fiction as she weaves a historical perspective into the fictional fabric. In "Coming Apart," the narrator forces her black husband to see how pornography, black and white, continues the exploitation begun in slavery by introducing him to inserted passages from black writers Audre Lord, Luisah Teish, and Tracy A. Gardner.

Walker's novels similarly illustrate consistency of theme—oppression—with variety of structure. Her first novel, *The Third Life of Grange Copeland*, is a chronologically ordered, realistic novel following its black sharecropper protagonist through three generations in pursuit of integrity and dignity.

Her second novel, *Meridian*, opens in Chicokemo, Mississippi, where ascetic Meridian Hill is working among the poor; the arrival of a friend and lover from her days as an activist in the Civil Rights movement throws the novel into a series of flashbacks. *The Color Purple* is an epistolary novel in which Celie, the young protagonist, overcome by physical and emotional abuse initiated by her father and continued by her husband, writes to God and to her sister, Nettie, exposing her painful life. It was this novel, adapted to the screen in 1985 under the direction of Steven Spielberg, which brought fame to Alice Walker. Although the film, a box-office success, was accused by many reviewers of having trivialized the novel, Walker herself was happy with the production, on which she was a consultant, because it brought a story of black women, told in authentic black speech, into the marketplace. The Washington Square paperback edition of *The Color Purple* sold more than a million copies.

Walker's own years of civil rights involvement grew out of a conviction that black writers must also be actively engaged in black issues: "It is unfair to the people we expect to reach to give them a beautiful poem if they are unable to read it." Her own activist stance is seen clearly in her *In Search of Our Mothers' Gardens*, as well as in her untiring efforts to reestablish the reputation of the neglected black writer Zora Neale Hurston (by editing a new collection of her short stories, *I Love Myself When I Am Laughing . . . and Then Again When I Am Looking Mean and Impressive*), and to make the black poet Langston Hughes more available to children (*Langston Hughes, American Poet*).

The crazy ("not patchwork") quilt has become an essential metaphor in Walker's work: It is the central symbol in her powerful short story, "Everyday Use"; it is the vehicle in *The Color Purple* which allows Sofia, while quilting with Celie, to give her the courage to be; and Walker has said that the enigmatic structure of her novel *Meridian* imitates the design of a quilt. In all the works of Alice Walker one finds a commitment to the preservation of the black heritage—the traditions, the culture, the family; to the necessity for putting an end to violence and injustice; to the relationship between individual dignity and community dignity; and to an insistence that women applaud their godliness.

BIBLIOGRAPHICAL REFERENCES: *Alice Malsenior Walker: An Annotated Bibliography: 1968-1986*, 1988, edited by Louis H. Pratt and Darnell D. Pratt, is comprehensive. Of the many interviews, several of the best are John O'Brien, *Interviews with Black Writers*, 1973, which is particularly useful on the writer's civil rights activities and on the black woman as writer; Mary Helen Washington, "Alice Walker: Her Mother's Gifts," *Ms.*, X (1982), 38; Sharon Wilson, "A Conversation with Alice Walker," *Kalliope*, 1984, 37-45; "Alice Walker" in *Black Women Writers at Work*, 1985, edited by Claudia Tate, is particularly insightful about *Meridian*. See also John F. Callahan, "Reconsideration: The Higher Ground of Alice Walker," *The New Republic*, CLXXI (1974), 21-22; Barbara Christian, "The Contrary Women of Alice Walker," *The Black Scholar*, XII (1981), 21; Martha J. McGowan, "Atonement and Release in Alice Walker's *Meridian*," *Critique: Studies in Modern Fiction*, XXIII (1981-1982), 25-36; Gloria Steinem, "Do You Know This Woman? She Knows You: A Profile of Alice Walker," *Ms.*, X (1982), 35; Sam Cornish, "Alice Walker: Her Own Woman," *The Christian Science Monitor*, February 3, 1984, B1; Houston A. Baker, Jr., and Charlotte Pierce-Baker, "Patches: Quilts and Community in Alice Walker's 'Everyday Use,'" *The Southern Review*, XXI (1985), 706-720; Susan Willis, "Alice Walker's Women," *New Orleans Review*, XII (1985), 33-41; Harold Hellenbrand, "Speech After Silence: Alice Walker's *The Third Life of Grange Copeland*," *Black American Literature Forum*, XX (1986), 113-128; Harris Trudier, "From Victimization to Free Enterprise: Alice Walker's *The Color Purple*," *Studies in American Fiction*, XIV (1986), 1-17; Marie H. Buncombe, "Androgyny as Metaphor in Alice Walker's Novels," *College Language Association Journal*, XXX (1987), 419-427.

Catharine F. Seigel

MARTIN WALSER

Born: Wasserburg, Germany
Date: March 24, 1927

Principal Works

PLAYS: *Überlebensgross Herr Krott: Requiem für einen Unsterblichen*, pr. 1913, pb. 1964; *Der Abstecher*, pr., pb. 1961 (*The Detour*, 1963); *Eiche und Angora*, pr., pb. 1962 (*The Rabbit Race*, 1963); *Der schwarze Schwan*, pr., pb. 1964; *Die Zimmerschlacht*, pr., pb. 1967; *Wir werden schon noch handeln*, pr. 1968 as *Der schwarze Flügel*, pb. 1968; *Ein Kinderspiel*, pb. 1970, pr. 1972; *Ein reizender Abend*, pr. 1971; *Aus dem Wortschatz unserer Kämpfe*, pb. 1971; *Das Sauspiel: Szenen aus dem 16. Jahrhundert*, pr., pb. 1975; *In Goethes Hand: Szenen aus dem 19. Jahrhundert*, pr., pb. 1982; *Die Ohrfeige*, pr. 1984; *Ein fliehendes Pferd*, pr. 1985.

NOVELS AND NOVELLAS: *Ehen in Philippsburg*, 1957 (*The Gadarene Club*, 1960; also known as *Marriage in Philippsburg*); *Halbzeit*, 1960; *Das Einhorn*, 1966 (*The Unicorn*, 1971); *Die Gallistl'sche Krankheit*, 1972; *Der Sturz*, 1973; *Jenseits der Liebe*, 1976 (*Beyond All Love*, 1982); *Ein fliehendes Pferd*, 1978 (*Runaway Horse*, 1980); *Seelenarbeit*, 1979 (*The Inner Man*, 1984); *Das Schwanenhaus*, 1980 (*The Swan Villa*, 1982); *Brief an Lord Liszt*, 1982 (*Letter to Lord Liszt*, 1985); *Brandung*, 1985 (*Breakers*, 1987); *Dorle und Wolf*, 1987 (*No Man's Land*, 1989); *Jagd*, 1988.

SHORT FICTION: *Messmers Gedanken*, 1985.

TRAVEL SKETCH: *Variationen eines Würgegriffs: Bericht über Trinidad und Tobago*, 1985.

ESSAYS: *Beschreibung einer Form: Versuch über Franz Kafka*, 1961; *Erfahrungen und Leseerfahrungen*, 1965; *Heimatkunde*, 1968; *Wie und wovon handelt Literatur*, 1973; *Wer ist ein Schriftsteller?*, 1979; *Selbstbewusstsein und Ironie*, 1981; *Heilige Brocken*, 1986.

Martin Walser is certainly to be ranked among the most prominent West German writers since 1945. Born on March 24, 1927, in the picturesque Bodensee area of southern Germany, Walser was the child of modest innkeepers. He attended a local school during the Nazi era and was graduated from secondary school in 1946. He went to several German universities and completed his studies in 1951 with an excellent dissertation on Franz Kafka. Still a student, he worked for a number of years with a southern German radio and television station and was married in 1950. Walser won the prestigious prize of the "Group 47" organization of German writers in 1955 and has since been an independent and prolific author. He has taught as a guest professor at a number of universities in the United States and in England. Walser has been the recipient of numerous prizes for literature.

Walser wanted to be a writer since childhood and his initial efforts were deeply influenced by his early reading of Kafka's works. He identified with the profound sense of isolation that pervades the latter's stories and the existential themes of the alienation, despair, and anxiety of the individual were prominent in his works. Much of his writing during the 1950's represents an attempt to come to terms with the literary and psychological influence of the renowned Prague author. For a number of reasons, Walser began to realize the crucial role played by social and economic factors in determining the individual's sense of self and the quality of interaction with others. Although Walser's works still touch upon existential themes such as aging, love and sexuality, and death, these "socialist" themes have come to predominate in his writings since the 1960's.

Walser's first novel, *The Gadarene Club*, suggests his efforts at emancipation from the influence of Kafka and his adoption of a critical stance toward German society. Written in a complex series of internal monologues, the novel focuses on several characters and their lives in the upper-middle-class social circles of a fictitious southern German city of Philippsburg. Walser levels a sharp and ironic critique of the shallow and egocentric social, sexual, and political machinations of his characters in a societal system that promotes the psychological estrangement of its members. The novels *Halbzeit* (halftime), *The Unicorn*, and *Der Sturz* (the fall) form a loose trilogy of texts that examine the character Anselm Kristlein and continue Walser's critical probing of the falsity and self-deception of middle-class German society from the economic boom period after the war until the beginning of the 1970's. Later texts such as *Die Gallistl'sche Krankheit* (the Gallistl illness), the story of Josef Gallistl's rejection of his upper-middle-class life and his adoption of socialist values, continue these themes. Other works, *Runaway Horse* and *Breakers* for example, examine love and marriage, sexuality and aging, and issues of male identity in modern industrial society.

Although known primarily for his narrative texts, Walser is also an acknowledged dramatist. His numerous plays also reveal an often ironic portrait of character types—from capitalists in *Überlebensgross Herr Krott* (larger-than-life Mr. Krott) and former Nazi doctors in *Der schwarze Schwan* (the black swan) to authoritarian bourgeois families in *Ein Kinderspiel* (a child's game)—of modern German society and they evidence, to a degree, the influence of Bertolt Brecht's satiric-didactic dramatic techniques and Friedrich Dürrenmatt's grotesque parodies. The play, *Die Ohrfeige* (the slap), depicts the situation of the unemployed, their anger and helplessness as well as their fundamental lack of comprehension of the industrial system that determines their lives.

Walser's writings, much like those of Heinrich Böll, present a critical vision of German society in the postwar period and as such they spring from a deeply humanistic and utopian sense of a kind of social organization that could be. His critique of modern capitalist societies and the kinds of personality distortion such societal structures produce in the individual suggest a romantic longing for a feeling of authentic community in which mutual cooperation (and not ruthless competition), self-respect, and love of others (and not neurotic self-doubt and veiled aggression) regulate human interaction. As a critic of modern social consciousness, Walser gives the reader a sadly accurate but nevertheless optimistic view of his contemporary situation.

BIBLIOGRAPHICAL REFERENCES: An invaluable source on Walser is the book published from the International Martin Walser Symposium, *Martin Walser International Perspectives*, 1987, edited by Jürgen E. Schlunk and Armand E. Singer. For further bibliographical references, consult Klaus Siblewski, *Martin Walser*, 1981. Earlier but still helpful sources are Anthony Edward Waine, *Martin Walser: The Development as Dramatist, 1950-1970*, 1978, and his *Martin Walser*, 1980. See also R. Hinton Thomas, "Martin Walser: The Nietzche Connection," *German Life and Letters*, XXXV (1982), 319-320; Stuart Parkes, "Martin Walser: Social Critic or *Heimatkünstler*," *New German Studies*, X (1982), 67-82; and Gerald A. Fetz, "Martin Walser's *Sauspiel* and the Contemporary German History Play," *Comparative Drama*, XII, no. 3 (1978), 249-265.

Thomas F. Barry

ROBERT WALSER

Born: Biel, Switzerland
Date: April 15, 1878

Died: Herisau, Switzerland
Date: December 25, 1956

Principal Works

SHORT FICTION: *Fritz Kochers Aufsätze*, 1904; *Aufsätze*, 1913; *Geschichten*, 1914; *Kleine Dichtungen*, 1914; *Prosastücke*, 1917; *Kleine Prosa*, 1917; *Der Spaziergang*, 1917 (*The Walk and Other Stories*, 1957); *Poetenleben*, 1917; *Seeland*, 1919; *Die Rose*, 1925; *Selected Stories*, 1982; *Aus dem Bleistiftgebiet: Mikragramme aus den Jahren 1924-1925*, 1985.

NOVELS: *Geschwister Tanner*, 1907; *Der Gehülfe*, 1908; *Jakob von Gunten*, 1909 (English translation, 1969); *Der "Raüber"-Roman*, 1972.

POETRY: *Gedichte*, 1909; *Unbekannte Gedichte*, 1958.

PLAYS: *Komödie*, pb. 1919.

MISCELLANEOUS: *Das Gesamtwerk*, 1966-1975, 1978; *Robert Walser Rediscovered: Stories, Fairy-Tale Plays, and Critical Responses*, 1985.

The prominent German publisher Siegfried Unseld has called Robert Walser "the greatest unknown author in the German language in [the twentieth] century." This prolific, dedicated, but very independent-minded writer of short prose, novels, playlets, and poems gained considerable recognition early in his career, most notably from Franz Kafka and Christian Morgenstern, Hugo von Hofmannsthal and Hermann Hesse. As time went on, however, his unconventional works never did appeal to a broader audience. Virtually forgotten for several decades, he was rediscovered in the 1960's and is viewed not only as a leading Swiss author of the twentieth century but also as one of the first modernist writers of self-conscious fiction.

Robert Otto Walser was born on April 15, 1878, in Biel, Switzerland, as the second youngest of eight children. His father, Adolf Walser, was a congenial man who tried his hand, although unsuccessfully, at a number of business ventures. His mother, Elisa Marti Walser, and two of his brothers suffered from mental instability. Robert was closest to his sister Lisa, a schoolteacher, and his successful brother Karl, who illustrated several of his books. At the age of fourteen, Walser left school and learned the banking trade. For some time, he toyed with the idea of becoming an actor but, having received no encouragement at all, turned to literature instead.

In 1896, Walser moved to Zurich, where he remained until 1905, constantly changing residences and clerical jobs, which was to become a pattern in his life. It was there that his first works, six poems, were published in the Swiss newspaper *Der Bund*, which in turn led to an invitation to publish additional poems, prose pieces, and playlets in the new literary journal *Die Insel* in Munich. Walser's big breakthrough came in 1904, when the publishing house of Insel in Leipzig published his first book, *Fritz Kochers Aufsätze* (Fritz Kocher's essays), supposedly the compositions of a gifted young schoolboy. This early work contains many themes, motifs, and narrative techniques that became the trademark of Walser's oeuvre. Although the slim volume with its amusing drawings by his brother Karl received high praise, it sold so poorly that the publisher reneged on his commitment to a second book of poems and dramas. It was to become an often repeated pattern. Received with initial enthusiasm, Walser was dropped quickly when his books failed to sell. In the spring of 1905, still convinced that his first book would be a great success, Walser joined his brother Karl in cosmopolitan Berlin to embark on a career as a free-lance writer. Soon thereafter, however, he enrolled in a school for domestic servants, an experience he later fictionalized in his novel *Jakob von Gunten*, and worked in a castle in Upper Silesia as a footman. He remained obsessed with the role of the servant for most of his life.

It was in his Berlin years (1905-1913) that Walser produced most of his novels in quick succession, notably *Geschwister Tanner* (the Tanner siblings), *Der Gehülfe* (the assistant), and *Jakob von Gunten*. These largely autobiographical novels with scant plots and shifting viewpoints all feature closely related central characters in lowly positions who engage in contradictory self-analysis. They are vaguely based on Walser's Zurich years and his experiences as the secretary of a Swiss inventor and as a student in the school for servants in Berlin. Although Walser had vowed that he would sooner join the army than become "a supplier to magazines," he continued to produce large numbers of short texts, many of which found their way into periodicals and newspapers throughout German-speaking Europe. During the later Berlin years, however, when his novels did not elicit the desired critical response and he found it more and more difficult to place his shorter prose pieces, his productivity began to suffer and he grew increasingly despondent.

In 1913, disappointed, nearly destitute, and convinced that he had failed as a novelist, Walser returned to his native Biel, where he was to spend the next seven years (1913-1921). For much of the time, he lived quietly in a spare attic room in the Hotel Blaues Kreuz (a temperance hostel) on what he described as "the periphery of bourgeois existence," forever in financial straits, forever struggling to find a publisher for his works. Several volumes of more traditional, almost neo-Romantic short prose appeared during the Biel period, much of it inspired during long walks in the environs of Biel: *Kleine Prosa* (short prose), for which he received a prize, *Prosastücke* (prose pieces), *Poetenleben* (poets' lives), and *Seeland* (lakeland). It was in Biel that Walser devised a new and rather peculiar method of writing, his "pencil system." He filled many large sheets of paper with increasingly small, seemingly illegible texts that were long thought to be written in a form of private shorthand. These "microgrammes" turned out to be first drafts of numerous prose pieces, playlets, and poems, many of which he wrote in Bern from 1924 to 1931. The novel *Der "Räuber"-Roman* (the "robber" novel), a witty novel about an artist in search of material, is now regarded as the most enduring narrative work in what have become known as Walser's microscripts.

In 1921, Walser moved to Bern, where, once again, he changed residences more than a dozen times. He was extremely productive but found few outlets for his works. Several manuscripts were rejected by publishers, and the last work that Walser was able to publish himself, *Die Rose* (the rose), a collection of demanding short texts, was poorly received. As the pieces he sent out to journals became more radical, they too were rejected with increasing frequency. By the late 1920's, Walser lived the life of a recluse. At times he drank heavily and suffered from severe bouts of anxiety. When he began hallucinating and hearing voices, he was committed to the mental hospital Waldau near Bern and diagnosed a schizophrenic, a diagnosis which is no longer believed to have been accurate. In Waldau, Walser continued to write sporadically, but after his involuntary transfer to a public institution in Herisau in 1933, he ceased writing altogether. Until he died of a heart attack on Christmas Day in 1956 at the age of seventy-eight, he performed simple manual work and took long solitary walks in the hills of eastern Switzerland. From 1936 until his death, he was visited several times a year by the Swiss critic and journalist Carl Seelig, who ultimately became Walser's legal guardian and literary executor. He recorded their conversations and published them in 1957 as *Wanderungen mit Robert Walser* (walks with Robert Walser), now regarded as a significant contribution to Walser scholarship. Walser, like several other unorthodox German-Swiss writers of his generation, gained wider public recognition only after his death. Many of his works were published posthumously. The rediscovery of Walser began, very slowly, in the late 1950's thanks to the efforts of Seelig. Interest in this author grew dramatically in the late 1970's, around the one hundredth anniversary of his birth, when a new edition of his collected works and several translations reached a broader, more diversified audience. Critical interest in Walser reached new heights in 1985 when the first volumes of his microscripts appeared.

BIBLIOGRAPHICAL REFERENCES: George C. Avery, *Inquiry and Testament: A Study of the Novels and Short Prose of Robert Walser*, 1968, although slightly dated, is still one of the best introductions to Walser, especially to his novels. More recent analyses of Walser's works are contained in *Robert Walser Rediscovered: Stories, Fairy-Tale Plays, and Critical Responses*, 1985, edited by Mark Harman, a book that grew out of a symposium held in 1983 at Dartmouth College. Equally important is Siegfried Unseld, "Robert Walser and His Publishers," in *The Author and His Publisher*, 1980. The first and definitive biography is Robert Mächler, *Das Leben Robert Walsers: Eine dokumentarische Biographie*, 1966. See also *Robert Walser: Leben und Werk in Daten und Bildern*, 1980, edited by Elio Fröhlich and Peter Hamm; Carl Seelig, *Wanderungen mit Robert Walser*, 1957; *Robert Walser-dossier*, 1984, edited by Elisabeth Pulver and Arthur Zimmermann; and *Briefe*, 1975, edited by Jörg Schäfer with Robert Mächler. For further study, see George C. Avery, "A Poet Beyond the Pale: Some Notes on the Shorter Works of Robert Walser," *Modern Language Quarterly*, XXIV (1963), 181-190; the special Walser issue of *Text und Kritik*, XII (1966), edited by Arnold Heinz; Malcolm Pender, "A Writer's Relationship to Society: Robert Walser's *'Räuber'-Roman*," *Modern Language Review*, LXXVIII (1983), 103-112; Susan Sontag, "Walser's Voice," foreword to *Selected Stories*, 1982, translated by Christopher Middleton; Guido Stefani, *Der Spaziergänger: Untersuchungen zu Robert Walser*, 1985; Guy Davenport, "A Field of Snow on a Slope of the Rosenberg," in his *DaVinci's Bicycle: Ten Stories*, 1979.

Judith Ricker-Abderhalden

SYLVIA TOWNSEND WARNER

Born: Harrow on the Hill, England
Date: December 6, 1893

Died: Maiden Newton, England
Date: May 1, 1978

Principal Works

SHORT FICTION: *Some World Far from Ours, and "Stay, Corydon, Thou Swain,"* 1929; *Elinor Barley*, 1930; *A Moral Ending and Other Stories*, 1931; *More Joy in Heaven, and Other Stories*, 1935; *Short Stories*, 1939; *The Cat's Cradle Book*, 1940; *A Garland of Straw and Other Stories*, 1943; *The Museum of Cheats*, 1947; *Winter in the Air, and Other Stories*, 1955; *A Spirit Rises*, 1962; *A Stranger with a Bag, and Other Stories*, 1966; *Swans on an Autumn River: Stories*, 1966; *The Innocent and the Guilty: Stories*, 1971; *Kingdoms of Elfin*, 1977; *Scenes of Childhood*, 1981; *One Thing Leading to Another: And Other Stories*, 1984.

POETRY: *The Espalier*, 1925; *Time Importuned*, 1928; *Opus 7*, 1931; *Rainbow*, 1932; *Whether a Dove or Seagull: Poems*, 1933 (with Valentine Ackland); *Two Poems*, 1945; *Boxwood*, 1957; *King Duffus and Other Poems*, 1968; *Azrael and Other Poems*, 1978; *Collected Poems*, 1983; *Selected Poems*, 1985.

NOVELS: *Lolly Willowes: Or, The Loving Huntsman*, 1926; *Mr. Fortune's Maggot*, 1927; *The True Heart*, 1929; *Summer Will Show*, 1936; *After the Death of Don Juan*, 1938; *The Corner That Held Them*, 1948; *The Flint Anchor*, 1954.

AUTOBIOGRAPHY: *Sketches from Nature*, 1963.

BIOGRAPHY: *The Portrait of a Tortoise: Extracted from the Journals and Letters of Gilbert White*, 1946; *T. H. White: A Biography*, 1967.

EDITED TEXT: *The Weekened Dickens*, 1932.

Sylvia Townsend Warner, though published often, has received sparse critical attention to assess her importance as a writer of short fiction, novels, poems, biographies, and translations. She was born in Harrow on the Hill, Middlesex, England, on December 6, 1893. Her father, George Townsend Warner, was a Harrow School housemaster, but Sylvia did not receive a formal education. Her mother, Eleanor (Hudleston) Warner, taught her to read, her father taught her history, and a governess tutored her in general subjects. By the age of ten, Sylvia was reading extensively in her father's library. She favored books on the occult, a subject that would later influence much of her writings. After her father died in 1916, she took a job in a munitions factory during World War I. She then moved to London to study music and was a member of the editorial committee that compiled the ten volumes of *Tudor Church Music* (1922-1929), which took ten years to complete.

Warner's first book of poetry, *The Espalier*, was published in 1925. Her first novel, *Lolly Willowes*, was printed in 1926 and was selected by the newly established Book-of-the-Month Club. Warner's second novel, *Mr. Fortune's Maggot*, published in 1927, was chosen by the Literary Guild. Despite this early popularity of her novels, Warner received little critical acclaim for them; she became best known for her short stories. From 1936 to 1978, *The New Yorker* published 144 of her stories. After her second book of poetry, *Time Importuned*, was published in 1928, Warner's first collection of short fiction came out in *Some World Far from Ours, and "Stay, Corydon, Thou Swain,"* in 1929. Her prose style was often praised for its conciseness, precise wording, fast-moving action, and ironic tone. In 1930, Warner and her friend Valentine Ackland moved to the country, where Warner wrote and Ackland opened an antique shop. Always active, Warner studied the black arts, elves, and mysticism. She also became an accomplished cook. She used much of this knowledge in her writings. In 1935, Warner became active in the Communist Party. In 1936, she and Ackland sailed to Barcelona, Spain, to volunteer their services to the Red Cross. (Warner and Ackland lived together until Ackland's death in 1969.) That same year, Warner's novel *Summer Will Show* was published. It is considered by some critics to be her best work.

In 1939 Warner published *Short Stories*, which was followed by another short-story collection, *The Cat's Cradle Book*, in 1940. Then her *A Garland of Straw and Other Stories* saw print in 1943. These stories show her continued interest in Spanish life, first shown in her novel *After the Death of Don Juan*. Some of these stories depict the effects of the Spanish Civil War on individuals and appear more angry than playful (as many of her earlier stories were). Warner's first biography, *The Portrait of a Tortoise*, appeared in 1946. It was followed by more short-story collections and novels over the next eight years until Warner's last novel, *The Flint Anchor*, appeared in 1954. After this publication, another book of short stories, *Winter in the Air, and Other Stories*, went on sale in 1955, and a collection of poems, *Boxwood*, was published in 1957.

In 1962, Warner's stories were collected in *A Spirit Rises*, and her autobiographical *Sketches from Nature* was published in 1963. In 1966, two short-story collections, *A Stranger with a Bag, and Other Stories* and *Swans on an Autumn River*, appeared. Warner's prolific output continued and her writings were still popular even when she was in her eighties. A short-story collection, *Kingdoms of Elfin*, and a collection of poems, *Azrael and Other Poems*, were published shortly before her death. Warner, though often published and highly praised for her style and insight into the human condition, has yet to have her works analyzed to judge her stature in the literary world; however, her witty writings will surely win for her a lasting place in twentieth century English literature.

BIBLIOGRAPHICAL REFERENCES: Barbara Brothers' biographical sketch "Sylvia Townsend Warner," in *Dictionary of Literary Biography*, Vol. 34, *British Novelists, 1890-1929: Traditionalists*, 1985, edited by Thomas F. Staley, provides a good overview of Warner's life and writings for readers not familiar with Warner. Claire Harmon, "Sylvia Townsend Warner, 1893-1978: A Celebration," *PN Review*, VIII, no. 23 (1981/1982), 30-61, contains some criticism, interviews, and Warner poetry. Also, John Updike, "The Mastery of Miss Warner," *The New Republic*, CLIV (March 5, 1966), 23-25, praises the writing and style of Warner.

Del Corey

ROBERT PENN WARREN

Born: Guthrie, Kentucky
Date: April 24, 1905

PRINCIPAL WORKS

POETRY: *Thirty-six Poems*, 1935; *Eleven Poems on the Same Theme*, 1942; *Selected Poems, 1923-1943*, 1944; *Brother to Dragons: A Tale in Verse and Voices*, 1953; *Promises: Poems, 1954-1956*, 1957; *Selected Essays*, 1958; *You, Emperors, and Others: Poems, 1957-1960*, 1960; *Selected Poems: New and Old, 1923-1966*, 1966; *Incarnations: Poems, 1966-1968*, 1968; *Homage to Theodore Dreiser on the Centennial of His Birth*, 1971; *Or Else—Poem/Poems 1968-1974*, 1974; *Selected Poems, 1923-1975*, 1976; *Now and Then: Poems, 1976-1978*, 1978; *Brother to Dragons: A New Version*, 1979; *Being Here: Poetry, 1977-1980*, 1980; *Ballad of a Sweet Dream of Peace*, 1981; *Rumor Verified: Poems, 1979-1980*, 1981; *Chief Joseph of the Nez Percé*, 1983; *New and Selected Poems, 1923-1985*, 1985.

NOVELS: *Night Rider*, 1939; *At Heaven's Gate*, 1943; *All the King's Men*, 1946; *World Enough and Time*, 1950; *Band of Angels*, 1955; *The Cave*, 1959; *Wilderness: A Tale of the Civil War*, 1961; *Flood: A Romance of Our Time*, 1964; *Meet Me in the Green Glen*, 1971; *A Place to Come To*, 1977.

SHORT FICTION: *Blackberry Winter*, 1946; *The Circus in the Attic and Other Stories*, 1947.

PLAY: *All the King's Men*, pb. 1947.

BIOGRAPHY: *John Brown: The Making of a Martyr*, 1929.

SOCIAL CRITICISM: *Segregation: Inner Conflict in the South*, 1956; *The Legacy of the Civil War: Meditations on the Centennial*, 1961; *Who Speaks for the Negro?*, 1965.

EDITED TEXTS: *An Approach to Literature: A Collection of Prose and Verse with Analysis and Discussions*, 1936 (with Cleanth Brooks and John Thibaut Purser); *Understanding Poetry: An Anthology for College Students*, 1938 (with Brooks); *Modern Rhetoric*, 1949 (with Brooks; better known as *Fundamentals of Good Writing: A Handbook of Modern Rhetoric*); *Understanding Fiction*, 1959 (with Brooks); *Faulkner: A Collection of Critical Essays*, 1966; *Randall Jarrell, 1914-1965*, 1967 (with Robert Lowell and Peter Taylor); *American Literature: The Makers and the Making*, 1974 (with R. W. B. Lewis); *Democracy and Poetry*, 1975.

Robert Penn Warren is the only American writer to win the Pulitzer Prize in both fiction and poetry. Indeed, he won the award three times: for *All the King's Men*, a novel based on the legend of Huey Long, the southern populist politician; for *Promises*, a mid-life resurgence of poetic power; and again for *Now and Then*, a demonstration of undiminished poetic skill published in the eighth decade of his life. As a college professor who wrote textbooks, Warren contributed significantly to changes in the teaching of literature in the United States. Warren has written excellent literary criticism, as well as social and historical commentary. In addition, he has produced a unique book-length poetic drama, *Brother to Dragons*, which combines philosophical comment with a horrifying true story of a murder perpetrated by a nephew of Thomas Jefferson.

Warren was born in Guthrie, a tiny community in southwestern Kentucky. As a young man, Warren's father aspired to become a poet and a lawyer, but he became a small-town banker instead. With three children of his own and a family of small half brothers and sisters inherited when his father died, he had no time to develop his taste for poetry. Robert felt as if he had stolen his father's life, since he realized the literary ambitions of which his father had only dreamed.

Warren's relationship to his father has had a profound effect on his fiction, which often concerns a young man with ambivalent feelings for a real or surrogate father. His early poetry, however, was more likely to reflect his beloved maternal grandfather, Gabriel Thomas Penn, a onetime Confederate cavalryman who had lived on a tobacco farm and had been an ardent reader of poetry and military history. On grandfather's farm in the summertime, the young Robert was steeped in stories of the Civil War and the local tobacco wars, both of which would find their way into his fiction. His first novel, *Night Rider*, dramatized the Kentucky tobacco war between growers and the monopolistic tyranny of the tobacco company. By the time Warren wrote *Wilderness*, he had a much less romantic view of that conflict than he had had as a child, when he believed that the Civil War was the great American epic.

Warren's talent for writing was discovered and fostered in his college years at Vanderbilt University by the poet John Crowe Ransom, who was teaching English there. Ransom encouraged him to write poetry, and Donald Davidson, who was teaching English literature, let Warren write imitations of *Beowulf* and Geoffrey Chaucer instead of the usual term papers. In 1924, Warren became the youngest member of a local literary society who called themselves the Fugitives and included Ransom, Davidson, and Allen Tate, who roomed with Warren.

After graduation from Vanderbilt, Warren earned a master's degree at the University of California at Berkeley in 1927. The next year he was doing postgraduate work at Yale University. In 1929, he published his first book, the biography *John Brown: The Making of a Martyr*, written with a distinctly Southern perception of that fanatic abolitionist.

Probably the most distinctive poem of Warren's early period—a period represented by his *Selected Poems, 1923-1943*—is the long poem based on a frontier legend, "The Ballad of Billie Potts." It displays themes that appear repeatedly in Warren's work—the theme of passage from the innocence of childhood into the fallen world of the fathers, the quest for identity with suggestions of an undiscovered self, an underlying mysticism implied in a return to the source of one's being.

At Louisiana State University, where Warren taught from 1934 to 1936, he absorbed the legends and the spectacle of Huey Long, who provided the germ of the character Willie Stark in *All the King's Men*. He also made the acquaintance of Cleanth Brooks, which resulted in one of the most fruitful partnerships in American letters. They cooperated at first to create and edit an excellent literary magazine, *The Southern Review*, but went on to produce literature textbooks such as *Understanding Poetry*, *Understanding Fiction*, and *Modern Rhetoric*, which did more than anything else to propagate the methods of the New Criticism.

BIBLIOGRAPHICAL REFERENCES: *Robert Penn Warren's "All the King's Men": A Critical Handbook*, 1966, edited by Maurice Beebe and L. A. Fields, provides a good introduction to Warren's most famous novel. A. Fred Sochatoff, *"All the King's Men": A Symposium*, 1957, offers a good sampling of the critical reception of this work, which endures as one of the most important of American political novels. To understand the context into which Warren must be placed, see Richard H. King, *A Southern Renaissance: The Cultural Awakening of the American South, 1930-1955*, 1980. The particular group at Vanderbilt has received considerable attention, as in *The Fugitives: A Critical Account*, 1958, by John M. Bradbury; *The Fugitive Group: A Literary History*, 1959, by Louise Cowan; and *The Burden of Time: The Fugitive and Agrarians*, 1965, by John L. Stewart. Two books by Victor Strandberg, *The Poetic Vision of Robert Penn Warren*, 1977, and *A Colder Fire: The Poetry of Robert Penn Warren*, 1965, are useful for understanding Warren's poetry. For other treatments of the lengthy Warren canon, see Charles H. Bohner, *Robert Penn Warren*, 1964; Leonard Casper, *Robert Penn Warren: The Dark and Bloody Ground*, 1960; Barnett Guttenberg, *Web of Being: The Novels of Robert Penn Warren*, 1975; James Justus, *The Achievement of Robert Penn Warren*, 1981; L. Hugh Moore, Jr., *Robert Penn Warren and History*, 1970; Katherine Snipes, *Robert Penn Warren*, 1983; and Marshall Walker, *Robert Penn Warren: A Vision Earned*, 1979.

Katherine Snipes

FRANK WATERS

Born: Colorado Springs, Colorado
Date: July 25, 1902

PRINCIPAL WORKS

NOVELS: *Fever Pitch*, 1930 (also known as *The Lizard Woman*); *The Wild Earth's Nobility*, 1935; *Below Grass Roots*, 1937; *The Dust Within the Rock*, 1940; *People of the Valley*, 1941; *The Man Who Killed the Deer*, 1942; *The Yogi of Cockroach Court*, 1947; *The Woman at Otowi Crossing: A Novel*, 1966; *Pike's Peak: A Family Saga*, 1971; *Flight from Fiesta*, 1986.

NONFICTION: *The Colorado*, 1946; *Masked Gods: Navaho and Pueblo Ceremonialism*, 1950; *Book of the Hopi*, 1963; *Leon Gaspard*, 1964; *Pumpkin Seed Point: Being Within the Hopi*, 1969; *Mexico Mystique: The Coming Sixth World of Consciousness*, 1975; *Mountain Dialogues*, 1981.

BIOGRAPHY: *Midas of the Rockies: The Story of Stratton and Cripple Creek*, 1937; *The Earp Brothers of Tombstone: The Story of Mrs. Virgil Earp*, 1960; *Robert Gilruth: Engineering Space Exploration*, 1963; *To Possess the Land: A Biography of Arthur Rochford Manby*, 1973.

Nominated for the Nobel Prize in Literature in 1985, Frank Waters has secured a place in American literature as a significant Western writer. He was born in Colorado Springs, Colorado, on July 25, 1902; his mother was from a prominent mining family, and his father was part Cheyenne Indian. Waters early became conscious of this duality in his parentage, especially after experiencing a mystical moment at his family's gold mine on Pikes Peak. This transcendental glimpse of the underlying unity of the earth became a pivotal experience in his life and work, reinforcing his need to reconcile dualities and leading him to a lifelong study of Oriental philosophy; primitive American Indian beliefs, myths, and rituals; and Jungian psychoanalysis. He studied engineering for three years at Colorado College before dropping out in 1924 to work, first in the oil fields of Wyoming and later as an engineer in California. Throughout his career he has expressed both the mystical and the rational sides of his experience in novels of poetic, intuitive insight and in essays, biographies, and anthropological studies of Native American cultures.

Two of Waters' initial attempts to give fictional form to his ideas, *The Yogi of Cockroach Court* (began in 1927 but not published until 1947) and *Fever Pitch*, reflect his early problem of blending idea and form while exploring such themes as the Yogic doctrines of Buddhism, the mystical experiences of wholeness and enlightenment, and the dynamic relationship of people to their environment. Driven by his own desire for reconciliation, Waters wrote an epical autobiographical trilogy that realistically tells the pioneer story of gold mining in the Rocky Mountains from 1870 to 1920: *The Wild Earth's Nobility*, *Below Grass Roots*, and *The Dust Within the Rock*. The first volume is based on his grandfather Dozier (renamed Rogier), who experiences moments of expanded consciousness and becomes obsessed to the point of madness by his effort to extract both gold and the hidden principle of existence from his Pikes Peak mine. The second book reflects Waters' emotionally divisive childhood, as Rogier's grandson, March Cable, is caught between his white mother and part-American Indian father, who fight for emotional dominance over their son. In the third book, March comes to terms with his own duality, achieving a symbolic synthesis of the Anglo (granite) and Native American (adobe) elements within his psyche. Waters later published a more focused, one-volume redaction of the trilogy as *Pike's Peak*.

After moving to Taos, New Mexico, in 1940 to study Pueblo culture, Waters wrote *People of the Valley*, the ethnic history of New Mexico as objectified in the pastoral life of Maria, a Hispano-Indian. The novel is a convincing inside view of the central character, who attains the wisdom of a seer, totally in harmony with her environment, a wild, natural, free product of the land whose life dramatizes the evolution of human consciousness. This work was followed by *The Man Who Killed the Deer*, Water's own favorite and arguably the best novel ever written about the American Indian. Artfully blending idea and form, Waters authentically portrays the Native American vision as he narrates the dilemmas of Martiniano, the protagonist. Changed by his "white" schooling and estranged from both cultures, Martiniano becomes physically and spiritually wounded when he violates the laws of each culture by killing a deer out of season and neglecting the prerequisite killing ceremony. Gradually he returns to the regenerative tribal rituals, finding healing and wholeness through the transforming power of the Cosmic Mother.

The Woman at Otowi Crossing, based on the real-life story of Edith Warner, is one of Waters' most admired novels. The protagonist, Helen Chalmers, opens a tearoom on the Rio Grande during World War II, adjacent to the Atomic City of Los Alamos and across the river from San Ildefonso Pueblo. An ordinary white woman, Chalmers unexpectedly has a transcendental experience of the timeless, which drives her toward self-fulfillment. Her "knowing" is deepened by her participation in the Pueblo Kiva rituals, where she experiences the essential unifying force of creation. A friend of both the American Indians and the atomic scientists, she becomes a bridge between two value systems at that point where the ancient and modern worlds touch. Although the novel is more explicitly didactic than Waters' earlier Native American novels, he convincingly portays metaphysical themes in a compelling, realistic narrative, enmeshed in the ordinary and commonplace. In *Flight from Fiesta*, Waters imaginatively dramatizes the purging of the old, atavistic hate between American Indian and white through the enigmatic relationship between Elsie, a ten-year-old girl in rebellion against her materialistic parents, and Inocencio, an old Pueblo Indian whose pottery she destroys in a tantrum. Set in Santa Fe during an annual fiesta in the 1950's, the novel portrays the adventures of the two characters who, mysteriously drawn to each other, flee from the fiesta, traveling through far-flung Western towns, mountains, deserts, and Pueblo dwellings. Their reconciliation clearly has allegorical implications, but Waters makes the abstractions palatable by rendering them through sharp, vivid images and evocative landscapes that authenticate the narrative.

In his novels and in such nonfiction works as *Masked Gods*, *Book of the Hopi*, *Mexico Mystique*, and *Mountain Dialogues*, Waters' primary concern has been the relationship of people to the land, the white and Native American races' conflicting relationship to the earth, and the evolution of human consciousness. Believing that mankind is one at the deepest level of consciousness, Waters speculates that, in the dialectical process of history, various cultures are, in their unique ways, traveling toward the realization of a great conscious unity. Waters' most important achievement is his artful, lifelike portrayal of these themes in his novels, of ideas that are thoroughly grounded in the actual circumstances of their Southwestern regional settings.

BIBLIOGRAPHICAL REFERENCES. Thomas J. Lyon, *Frank Waters*, 1973, is an invaluable literary biography; Martin Bucco, *Frank Waters*, 1969, is an earlier, but still useful, monograph; *Conversations with Frank Waters*, 1971, edited by John R. Milton, contains seven valuable taped television interviews; one very scholarly bibliography is Terence A. Tanner, *Frank Waters: A Bibliography, with Relevant Selections from His Correspondence*, 1983; *Frank Waters: A Retrospective Anthology*, 1985, edited by Charles L. Adams, is a useful collection of hard-to-find selections; there are ten volumes of the annual publication of *Studies in Frank Waters* from 1978 to 1988, which contain a number of excellent critical essays. See also William T. Pilkington, "Character and Landscape: Frank Waters' Colorado Trilogy," *Western American Literature*, II (1967), 183-193; James Peterson, "A Conversation with Frank Waters: Lessons from the Indian Soul," and "A Reverent Connection with the Earth," *Psychology Today*, VII (1973), 63-67; June Davis and Jack Davis, "Frank Waters and the Native American Consciousness," *Western American Literature*, XI (1974), 33-34; "Intuition and the Dance of Life: Frank Waters," in John R. Milton, *The Novel of the American West*, 1980;

Thomas J. Lyon, "Frank Waters," in *Fifty Western Writers: A Bio-Bibliographical Sourcebook*, 1982, edited by Fred Erisman and Richard W. Etulain; "Frank Waters: The Colorado College Symposium," *Writers' Forum*, II (1985), 164-221; "Frank Waters," in *A Literary History of the American West*, 1987, edited by Thomas J. Lyon et al.; and Charles L. Adams, "The Genesis of *Flight from Fiesta*," *Western American Literature*, XXII (1987), 195-200.

Clifford D. Edwards

JAMES WATSON

Born: Chicago, Illinois
Date: April 6, 1928

PRINCIPAL WORKS

MEMOIR: *The Double Helix: A Personal Account of the Discovery of the Structure of DNA*, 1968.

SCIENCE: *Molecular Biology of the Gene*, 1965, 1976, 1987 (with others); *The DNA Story: A Documentary History of DNA Cloning*, 1981 (with John Tooze); *Molecular Biology of the Cell*, 1983 (with others); *Recombinant DNA: A Short Course*, 1983 (with Tooze and David Kurtz).

James Dewey Watson played a pivotal role in the discovery of the structure of the deoxyribonucleic acid (DNA) molecule. He was born in Chicago on April 6, 1928, the son of James Dewey Watson, a businessman, and Jean (Mitchell) Watson. His parents, whose English and Scotch-Irish roots in the Midwest went back for several generations, provided their son and daughter Elizabeth with a comfortable childhood and an excellent education, beginning with nursery school at the University of Chicago. James was a child prodigy who developed the habit of reading widely, a practice that stood him in good stead when he was an ebullient member of the *Quiz Kids* radio show. He attended the Horace Mann Elementary School for eight years and the South Shore High School for two years. Aside from bird-watching, which he found a pleasant way to learn about ornithology, he had no special interest in science until he read Sinclair Lewis' *Arrowsmith* (1925), the story of a medical doctor's experiences with the joys and frustrations of research. This novel stimulated him to dream that he would make great scientific discoveries.

In the summmer of 1943, when he was only fifteen years old, he received a tuition scholarship to the University of Chicago's four-year experimental college. As an undergraduate, he was principally interested in birds and avoided taking any advanced chemistry and physics courses, although he did outstanding work in the courses of his program, obtaining A's even from professors who rarely gave A's. In 1947, he received a bachelor of science degree in zoology and a bachelor of philosophy degree. With a fellowship for graduate study in zoology at Indiana University, he went to Bloomington, where he came under the influence of the geneticist Hermann J. Muller and the microbiologist Salvador E. Luria. Watson's thesis, under the direction of Luria, was a study of the effect of high-energy X rays on the multiplication of bacteria-destroying viruses (bacteriophages). After receiving his Ph.D. in 1950, Watson, who had caught Luria's passion to understand the chemistry of viruses, was awarded a Merck Postdoctoral Fellowship by the National Research Council to continue his work in Copenhagen at the laboratories of the biochemist Herman Kalckar and the microbiologist Ole Maaløe. In the spring of 1951, Watson traveled with Kalckar to a symposium at Naples, where he met Maurice Wilkins, who was studying DNA crystals with X rays. This meeting stimulated Watson to change the direction of his research from bacteriophages to the structural chemistry of proteins and nucleic acids. Fortunately, Luria was able to arrange for Watson to work with John Kendrew, a molecular biologist at the Cavendish Laboratory of the University of Cambridge.

Watson arrived at Cambridge in the fall of 1951 and began to assist Kendrew with his X-ray studies of the protein myoglobin. Since the myoglobin molecule released the secrets of its structure only grudgingly, Watson grew bored with the hard work and modest results, and when he met Francis Crick, a physicist who was working desultorily on a doctoral thesis involving the X-ray diffraction of proteins, he discovered that they shared an enthusiasm about the gene and the way it replicated. Watson and Crick decided to collaborate. It seemed to both of them that the gene's secrets could be attacked only when its structure was known, which meant figuring out the structure of DNA.

With a fellowship from the National Foundation for Infantile Paralysis, Watson began his most productive period. The inspiration for the work of Watson and Crick was Linus Pauling, the American chemist who had deciphered the structures of numerous molecules, from the mineral molybdenite to the fibrous and globular proteins. Originally, Crick believed that solving DNA's structure was the job of Maurice Wilkins and Rosalind Franklin at King's College, London, but as time went on, Watson and Crick became impatient with the slow progress of the X-ray diffraction studies of the King's College group. The failure of Crick's colleagues at the Cavendish Laboratory to discover the structure of proteins before Pauling made a deep impression on Crick and Watson. Pauling had solved the structure by using his deep knowledge of structural chemistry to impose constraints on the molecular models he constructed. Watson and Crick believed that they could solve DNA's structure in the same way. Their experiments, with the help of findings by Franklin at King's College, resulted in their discovery of the double helix as the mechanism for the duplication of the DNA molecule. Watson and Crick described the double helix in their now-famous paper published in *Nature* on April 25, 1953.

Watson left the Cavendish Laboratory in the fall of 1953 to become a Senior Research Fellow in Biology at the California Institute of Technology. Watson had become interested in ribonucleic acic (RNA), and in Pasadena, he was able to work with Alexander Rich, a medical doctor who had collaborated with Pauling, in X-ray diffraction studies of RNA. In 1955, Watson returned to the Cavendish Laboratory to work again with Crick. During their year together, they published several papers on the general principles of viral structure. In 1956, Watson joined the Biology Department at Harvard University, where he quickly passed through the academic ranks, becoming full professor in 1961, and where he established a research laboratory in which many future leaders in molecular biology were trained. Watson's major interest in the late 1950's and early 1960's was the role of RNA in protein synthesis, and one of the important conclusions that he and his coworkers helped to establish was that protein synthesis requires the ordered interaction of three types of RNA. In 1962, Watson shared the Nobel Prize in Physiology or Medicine with Crick and Wilkins for his part in the discovery of the three-dimensional structure of DNA. With the prestige bestowed by the Nobel Prize, he became an effective spokesman for molecular biology. In 1965, he published a textbook, *Molecular Biology of the Gene*, which, through its successive editions, became the vade mecum for molecular biologists from college freshmen to practicing scientists.

The year 1968 marked several important events in Watson's life. On March 28, he married Elizabeth Lewis, a union that eventually produced two sons. Later in the year, he left Harvard to assume the directorship of the Cold Spring Harbor Laboratory on the North Shore of Long Island. According to some of his subordinates, he ran the laboratory as a benevolent despot, but he had a perceptive eye for important research problems and talented workers. In 1968, he also published *The Double Helix*, a controversial account of how the structure of DNA was discovered. Several reviewers thought that *The Double Helix* distorted the work of scientists into a race for prizes, but the book had its defenders, who praised Watson's honesty for depicting the confused motives and competitive personalities that comprise science as it is actually practiced. These reviewers believed that Watson's book was a much-needed amendment to the traditional picture of science as objective and impersonal.

During his early tenure at Cold Spring Harbor Laboratory, Watson initiated a large-scale study of how viruses can make cells cancerous, and in the process, he established the laboratory as a key site for studying the molecular biology of animal cells. In 1975, he was one of the founders and participants of the Asilomar Conference on the possible dangers of recombinant DNA research. He had a jaundiced view of what was accomplished, noting that the participants pretended to act responsibly but were actually irresponsible in approving recommendations that did not adversely affect anyone's work. In the 1980's, Watson became involved in a project, which had the potential to rival the size and scope of the Apollo moon-landing program, to map completely the genetic instructions for making a human being. Despite criticism, the National Institutes of Health began funding the Human Genome Project, and Watson became its director. He expressed great enthusiasm for the project's goals, and though the project's success would involve troubling ethical questions, Watson saw a mapped human genome as having the potential to do much good, for example, in helping to understand and eventually eliminate many genetic diseases.

Watson is most likely to be remembered among the wider public for *The Double Helix* because it frankly described for the first time the human circumstances behind a great scientific discovery. This book, which has been translated into many foreign languages and made into a major film, helped to shape a generation's view of science. Many scientists who were idealistic about their research regretted this influence. On the other hand, there is little doubt that Watson, who as a young man dreamed of scientific glory, achieved his dream.

BIBLIOGRAPHICAL REFERENCES: Much has been written about the double helix since its discovery. Watson's *The Double Helix* remains one of the best-known accounts, and the Norton Critical Edition of *The Double Helix*, 1980, edited by Gunther S. Stent, is the most useful version of the book, containing not only the text but also extensive commentaries and reviews. See also the review by Erwin Chargaff, "A Quick Climb Up Mount Olympus," *Science*, CLIX (March 29, 1968), 1448-1449. The best scholarly account of the discovery of DNA is Robert Olby, *The Path to the Double Helix*, 1974, with an excellent bibliography. A good popular treatment is Horace Freeland Judson, *The Eighth Day of Creation: Makers of the Revolution in Biology*, 1979, which deals with much more than the double helix. For other versions of the DNA story, see Anne Sayre, *Rosalind Franklin and DNA*, 1975, who writes from Franklin's perspective, and Francis Crick, *What Mad Pursuit: A Personal View of Scientific Discovery*, 1988, who writes from his own. For biographical details of Watson's life, see *Current Biography*, 1963, edited by Charles Moritz, and *Contemporary Authors*, 1977, edited by Christine Nasso. Watson's Nobel lecture, "The Involvement of RNA in the Synthesis of Proteins," in *Nobel Lectures, Physiology or Medicine, 1942-1962*, 1964, contains information about his scientific work in the years after the discovery of the double helix. Sheldon Krimsky, *Genetic Alchemy: The Social History of the Recombinant DNA Controversy*, 1982, discusses Watson's role in the debates about the development of recombinant DNA technology.

Robert J. Paradowski

EVELYN WAUGH

Born: London, England
Date: October 28, 1903

Died: Combe Florey, Somerset, England
Date: April 10, 1966

PRINCIPAL WORKS

NOVELS AND NOVELLAS: *Decline and Fall*, 1928; *Vile Bodies*, 1930; *Black Mischief*, 1932; *A Handful of Dust*, 1934; *Scoop*, 1938; *Work Suspended*, 1942; *Put Out More Flags*, 1942; *Brideshead Revisited: The Sacred and Profane Memories of Captain Charles Ryder, a Novel*, 1945; *Scott-King's Modern Europe*, 1947; *The Loved One: An Anglo-American Tragedy*, 1948; *Helena*, 1950; *Men at Arms*, 1952; *Love Among the Ruins: A Romance of the Near Future*, 1953; *Officers and Gentlemen*, 1955; *The Ordeal of Gilbert Pinfold: A Conversation Piece*, 1957; *Unconditional Surrender*, 1961 (also known as *The End of the Battle*); *Basil Seal Rides Again: Or, The Rake's Regress*, 1963.

SHORT FICTION: *Tactical Exercise*, 1954; *Charles Ryder's Schooldays and Other Stories*, 1982.

AUTOBIOGRAPHY: *A Little Learning*, 1964.

JOURNALS: *The Diaries of Evelyn Waugh*, 1976.

BIOGRAPHY: *Rossetti: His Life and Works*, 1928; *Edmund Campion*, 1935; *The Life of the Right Reverend Ronald Knox*, 1959.

CORRESPONDENCE: *The Letters of Evelyn Waugh*, 1980.

NONFICTION: *Labels: A Mediterranean Journal*, 1930; *Remote People*, 1931; *Ninety-two Days*, 1934; *Waugh in Abyssinia*, 1936; *Robbery Under Law: The Mexican Object-Lesson*, 1939; *The Holy Places*, 1952; *A Tourist in Africa*, 1960.

From the 1940's until his death in 1966, Evelyn Arthur St. John Waugh served as *bête noire* for left-wing critics on both sides of the Atlantic, a role he seemed to enjoy. He was born in London on October 28, 1903, the second son of Arthur Waugh, author and managing director of the publishing firm of Chapman and Hall, and Catherine Charlotte Raban. Evelyn's father and brother, Alec, had attended Sherborne School but Alec had been expelled and shortly thereafter published *The Loom of Youth* (1917), a sensational exposé of public school life. Sherborne was thus out of the question for Evelyn, so he attended Lancing College before going up to Oxford University.

In 1925, Waugh left Hertford College, Oxford, with a modest third-class degree in history. As a young man whose father and elder brother were firmly established as professional writers and editors, he might have been thought a natural candidate for a literary career himself. Instead, he tried several fields first—including art, to which he was strongly attracted—before finally turning to letters. He served brief tenures as a schoolmaster at two obscure public schools. The experience was a profoundly unhappy one, which led to Waugh's attempted suicide by drowning, yet it also furnished the material for his first novel. In the autumn of 1927, Waugh met Evelyn Gardner. The two were soon married, and Waugh's literary career was launched with two books: *Rossetti*, a commercial failure published in 1928, and *Decline and Fall*, a critical and commercial success appearing the same year. *Decline and Fall* is a madcap satire in the style of *Candide* (1759), with an ironic depiction of Oxford, spurious and neurotic schoolmasters, and the penal system (which Waugh likens to an English public school).

In 1930, his *Vile Bodies* satirized the Bright Young People, the English equivalent of America's flappers. This novel, like his first, was wildly funny, and he had found his audience. In contrast, his personal life was in ruins—just as he achieved literary success, his wife of fewer than two years deserted him for another man. That he peppered his novels with faithless young wives for the rest of his career testifies to the depth of his bitterness. He was received into the Roman Catholic church in September, 1930. The previous year, he had begun traveling in the Mediterranean with his wife. After his divorce, he traveled incessantly for three years—in Abyssinia, Africa, and South America. The results of this compulsive peregrination were the travel books *Labels*, *Remote People*, and *Ninety-two Days*, as well as considerable raw material for future novels.

Waugh's third novel, *Black Mischief*, appeared in 1932. It is certainly a satire of British colonialism, concluding with a scene in which the strains of a Gilbert and Sullivan composition go wafting out over the wacky African kingdom of Azania. A number of critics, though, purport to find the book racist and are extremely hostile to it. *Black Mischief* introduces Basil Seal, a lovable—and sometimes not so lovable—young rogue, who reappears in subsequent novels. Two years later, Waugh published his most pessimistic novel, *A Handful of Dust*. Its protagonist, Tony Last, like Paul Pennyfeather of *Decline and Fall* and Adam Fenwick-Symes of *Vile Bodies*, is an innocent wandering through a world of ravenous beasts. Tony's fate, unlike that of his predecessors, is tragic, while the novel's comedy is dark and its irony heavy. In 1935, Waugh was awarded the Hawthornden Prize for *Edmund Campion*, his study of Oxford's Jesuit martyr in the reign of Elizabeth I. In 1937, after a long and anxious wait for a dispensation from Rome, Waugh was finally free to marry Laura Herbert, who became the mother of his six children. Two years earlier, he had covered the Abyssinian war as a newspaper correspondent. The result was *Waugh in Abyssinia*, a book whose punning title he did not choose. His last novel of the 1930's, *Scoop*, recounts the hilarious adventures of unscrupulous journalists as they cover an absurd war in the primitive African nation of Ishmaelia.

At the outbreak of World War II, Waugh secured an Army commission, only after encountering considerable difficulty due to his age. In 1942, *Work Suspended* and *Put Out More Flags* were published. *Brideshead Revisited*, written while its author was on leave from active service, was published in May, 1945. The novel was easily Waugh's most popular. It also, for the first time, tied Waugh inextricably to the flaws of his first-person narrator. Charles Ryder is perceived as smug, snobbish, superficially attracted to the aristocracy, and contemptuous of the common man. Finally, *Brideshead Revisited* was the first novel in which Waugh placed the practice of Catholicism at the very heart of the narrative. It sold widely, especially in America, but most critics attacked its structure, its sentiments, or both. Waugh published several novellas during the postwar period. *Scott-King's Modern Europe* reflects Waugh's dismay at the postwar Europe that Great Britain had helped to fashion. *The Loved One*, which is on the surface a spoof of the American funeral industry, is, beyond that, a Juvenalian attack upon Anglo-American materialism in general. *Love Among the Ruins* is the bitter portrait of an arid and soulless Great Britain of the future. *Helena* is the only historical novel in the Waugh canon. *Helena*, fiction based upon scanty historical data, is the story of the mother of Constantine the Great, the first Christian emperor. She was canonized for her legendary discovery of the true cross. In the years following his return to civilian life, Waugh settled his family in the country, first at Piers Court, Stinchcombe, in Gloucestershire, later at Combe Florey in Somerset.

Four novels mark the final phase of Waugh's career. *The Ordeal of Gilbert Pinfold: A Conversation Piece* is an autobiographical novel based upon a psychotic episode Waugh had recently experienced. His war trilogy, *Men at Arms*, *Officers and Gentlemen*, and *Unconditional Surrender*, roughly parallels the author's own military service: the sometimes awkward training period of an aging subaltern, combat in the disastrous campaign on Crete, and service as liaison to partisans in Yugoslavia. Waugh's American publisher changed the title of the third novel to *The End of the Battle*, doubtless due to his awareness that the surrender cited was as much Great Britain's surrender to expediency as the Axis powers' surrender to the Allies. The trilogy was subsequently revised slightly and published in one volume under the title *Sword of Honour*. Waugh's last work of fiction was *Basil Seal Rides Again*, a very slight novella treating Basil in middle age. On Easter Sunday, April 10, 1966, shortly after returning home from Mass, Waugh fell dead from a massive heart attack. Even those critics who do not share his love for the past and his revulsion for the present have judged him one of the finest novelists and probably the foremost satirist of the twentieth century.

BIBLIOGRAPHICAL REFERENCES: Critical commentary as well as biographical information is found in Martin Stannard, *Evelyn Waugh: The Early Years 1903-1939*, 1986, the first volume of a projected two-volume work, and Christopher Sykes, *Evelyn Waugh: A Biography*, 1975. Other critical studies are Frederick J. Stopp, *Evelyn Waugh: Portrait of an Artist*, 1958 (slightly limited in scope since Waugh had not yet completed his career); Stephen J. Greenblatt, *Three Modern Satirists: Waugh, Orwell, and Huxley*, 1965; James F. Carens, *The Satiric Art of Evelyn Waugh*, 1966; William J. Cook, Jr., *Masks, Modes, and Morals: The Art of Evelyn Waugh*, 1971 (a valuable, though occasionally murky, examination of Waugh's use of narrative point of view); Gene D. Phillips, *Evelyn Waugh's Officers, Gentlemen, and Rogues: The Fact Behind His Fiction*, 1975; and George McCartney, *Confused Roaring: Evelyn Waugh and the Modernist Tradition*, 1987. For additional biographical details, see Alec Waugh, *My Brother Evelyn and Other Portraits*, 1967, and *Evelyn Waugh and His World*, 1973, edited by David Pryce-Jones. *A Bibliography of Evelyn Waugh*, 1986, edited by Robert Murray Davis et al., is an exhaustive listing of every known piece either by or about Waugh. See also R. Coppieters, "A Linguistic Analysis of a Corpus of Quoted Speech in Evelyn Waugh's Trilogy the *Sword of Honour*," *Studia Germanica Gandensia* (English language edition), XI (1969), 87-138; Patrick Adcock, "Basil Seal in America," *Evelyn Waugh Newsletter*, X (Autumn, 1976), 5-6; Jane Nardin, "The Myth of Decline in *A Handful of Dust*," *The Midwest Quarterly*, XVIII (1977), 119-130; and Patrick Adcock, "*Helena*: Waugh's Englishwoman on the Frontier of the Faith," *Publications of the Arkansas Philological Association*, XIV (Spring, 1988), 61-67.

Patrick Adcock

MAX WEBER

Born: Erfurt, Germany
Date: April 21, 1864

Died: Munich, Germany
Date: June 14, 1920

PRINCIPAL WORKS

SOCIAL STUDIES: *Gesammelte Ausätze zur Religionssociologie*, includes Vol. 1, *Die protestantische Ethik und der Geist de Kapitalismus. Die protestantischen Sekten und der Geist des Kapitalismus. Die protestantischen Weltreligion*, 1920 (*The Protestant Ethic and the Spirit of Capitalism*, 1930), Vol. 2, *Hinduismus und Buddhismus*, 1920 (*The Religion of India: The Sociology of Hinduism and Buddhism*, 1958), and Vol. 3, *Das antike Judentum*, 1920 (*Ancient Judaism*, 1952); *Die rationalen und soziologischen Grundlagen der Musik*, 1921 (*The Rational and Social Foundations of Music*, 1958); *Die Stadt*, 1921 (*The City*, 1958); *Wirtschaft und Gesellschaft*, 1922 (translations include *The Theory of Social and Economic Organization*, 1947; *Max Weber on Law in Economy and Society*, 1954; *The Sociology of Religion*, 1963; *Economy and Society: An Outline of Interpretive Sociology*, 1968); *Wirtschaftsgeschichte*, 1923 (*General Economic History*, 1927); *From Max Weber: Essays in Sociology*, 1946; *Max Weber on the Methodology of the Social Sciences*, 1949; *The Religion of China: Confucianism and Taoism*, 1951 (partial translation of *Gesammelte Ausätze zur Religionssociologie*, Vol. 1).

Max Weber was one of the founding fathers of modern social science. He was born in 1864 to a solidly established middle-class Prussian family. His father was a successful lawyer and parliamentarian, his mother a woman of culture and piety. Weber spent most of his first twenty-nine years in his parents' household, first in Erfurt, then in Berlin, where it became a meeting place for prominent politicians and celebrated scholars. In 1882, Weber began his studies in law at the University of Heidelberg, continuing at the universities of Berlin and Göttingen. He became a lecturer in law at the University of Berlin, where he was an enormously productive scholar. From 1894 to 1897, Weber taught economics at the Universities of Freiburg and Heidelberg.

In 1893, at age twenty-nine, Weber married and moved out of his parents' home. In 1897, his father died, only a few weeks after he and Max had quarreled violently. Believing that he had contributed to his father's death, Weber suffered a nervous breakdown. Chronically overburdened by his work and now suffering from exhaustion, remorse, and depression, Weber was forced to suspend his academic work over the next four years. From 1901 on, Weber began to recover and gradually resumed his scholarly work. He accepted a position as an associate editor of the *Archiv für Sozialwissenschaft und Sozialpolitik* (archives for social science and social welfare), which he helped build into the leading social science journal in Germany. Later in the decade, he cofounded, with Ferdinand Tönnies and Georg Simmel, the German Sociological Society.

In 1904, Weber published probably the best known of all of his works, *The Protestant Ethic and the Spirit of Capitalism*, which traced the contributions of Calvinism to the development of capitalism in the West. Seeking to steer between a vulgar Marxian economic determinism and an equally one-sided idealistic determinism, he offered the monograph as a modest illustration of "how ideas become effective forces in history." His subsequent analyses of the religions of China, India, and ancient Judaism extended the argument by examining the absence of full-blown capitalism where religious and cultural norms were not supportive.

In 1919, Weber accepted a chair at the University of Munich, where he delivered two classic lectures, "Science as a Vocation" and "Politics as a Vocation." These two lectures highlight the tensions in Weber's own life between scientific neutrality and political commitment. The years from 1918 to 1920 were a time of especially intense political activity for Weber: He helped found the German Democratic Party, served as adviser to the German delegation to the Versailles peace conference, helped draft the new Weimar Constitution, and unsuccessfully sought nomination to the newly constituted assembly. Throughout the war and postwar years, Weber labored on his never-to-be-completed magnum opus, *Economy and Society* (the incomplete three volumes were published posthumously). In June, 1920, Weber died of pneumonia; his last words were "The Truth is the Truth."

The unifying theme throughout Weber's diverse works was his preoccupation with the concept of "rationalization," the progressive shift from a world organized and legitimated on the bases of tradition, charisma, and sentiment, to one organized and legitimated on the basis of reason, logic, and efficiency. This "disenchantment of the world," rooted in ancient Judaism, the Enlightenment, and accelerated in later times by industrialization and urbanization, has found its highest expressions in the economic system of capitalism and the organizational system of bureaucracy. Weber's analysis of bureaucracy still dominates theory and research on the subject. Weber's contributions to the methodology of the social sciences have also been highly influential. He acknowledged that, in order to establish causality, both natural and human sciences must demonstrate an association among factors. He argued that, whereas in the natural world interactions mean nothing to the insentient objects and organisms involved, human interaction is based on intention, motivation, and shared symbols. Hence, no scientific explanation of human interaction is adequate without reference to this level of meaning, a methodological procedure and imperative he called *Verstehen* (understanding).

Originally trained as a student of law, Weber's interests and scholarship ranged across jurisprudence, political science, economics, sociology, comparative religions, and the histories of several nations and civilizations, both ancient and modern. Although he is chiefly regarded as a sociologist, his influence on all these fields has been decisive and enduring.

BIBLIOGRAPHICAL REFERENCES: Reinhard Bendix, *Max Weber: An Intellectual Portrait*, 1960, remains the single most comprehensive treatment of Weber's work. Also helpful is Julien Freund's commentary, *The Sociology of Max Weber*, 1968. Weber was introduced to the English-speaking world through Talcott Parsons, *The Structure of Social Action*, Vol. 2, 1937, and this work stands as a classic in its own right. For an excellent brief introduction, see "Max Weber," in Lewis Coser, *Masters of Sociological Thought: Ideas in Historical and Social Context*, 1971. See also the "Introduction: The Man and His Work" in *From Max Weber: Essays in Sociology*, 1946, translated and edited by H. H. Gerth and C. Wright Mills. For more personal views of Weber, see Marianne Weber's biography of her husband, *Max Weber: A Biography*, 1975, and Paul Honigsheim's memories of his friend and colleague, *On Max Weber*, 1968. An excellent collection of essays by noted authorities on Weber, assessing his impact on modern social science, is *Max Weber*, 1970, edited and with an introduction by Dennis Wrong. Reinhard Bendix and Guenther Roth, *Scholarship and Partisanship: Essays on Max Weber*, 1971, examines Weber's contribution and his place in intellectual and political history.

Robert B. Pettit

SIMONE WEIL

Born: Paris, France
Date: February 3, 1909

Died: Ashford, England
Date: August 24, 1943

PRINCIPAL WORKS

RELIGION AND PHILOSOPHY: *La Pesanteur et la grâce*, 1947 (*Gravity and Grace*, 1952); *Attente de Dieu*, 1950 (*Waiting for God*, 1951); *La Connaissance surnaturelle*, 1950; *Intuitions prechretiennes*, 1951; *Lettre à un Religieux*, 1951 (*Letter to a Priest*, 1953); *La Source grecque*, 1953; *Intimations of Christianity Among the Ancient Greeks*, 1957; *Leçons de philosophie de Simone Weil*, 1959 (*Lectures on Philosophy*, 1978); *Pensées sans ordre concernant l'amour de Dieu*, 1962; *On Science, Necessity, and the Love of God*, 1968.

SOCIAL CRITICISM: *L'Enracinement*, 1949 (*The Need for Roots*, 1952); *La Condition ouvrière*, 1951; *Oppression et liberté*, 1953 (*Oppression and Liberty*, 1958); *Écrits historiques et politiques*, 1960.

ESSAYS: *Selected Essays: 1934-1943*, 1962.

JOURNALS: *Cahiers I*, 1951; *Cahiers II*, 1953; *Cahiers III*, 1956; *The Notebooks of Simone Weil*, 1956; *First and Last Notebooks*, 1970.

CORRESPONDENCE: *Seventy Letters*, 1965.

PLAY: *Venise sauvée*, pb. 1955.

POETRY: *Poèmes*, 1968.

MISCELLANEOUS: *Écrits de Londres et dernières lettres*, 1957; *The Simone Weil Reader*, 1977; *Formative Writings, 1929-1941*, 1987.

Simone Adolphine Weil's writings have had significant influence on religious and political thought in the second half of the twentieth century. Born in Paris on February 3, 1909, Weil was the second child of Jewish agnostics Dr. Bernard and Selma Weil. Weil expressed social concerns at an early age—when only five years old, she steadfastly refused to eat sugar as long as French soldiers could not get it. The strain of humility which runs through Weil's adult writings also began early; the achievements of her brother André, a prodigy who went on to enjoy a distinguished career as a mathematician, eroded her self-confidence. Yet in this as in so much else Weil was a mixture of opposites, and her writings also reveal a strong consciousness of her intellectual powers and a morally judgmental tone bordering on arrogance. At the age of twelve Weil endured the first of the migraine headaches which tortured her throughout her life and from which she may have distilled some of her intense compassion for human suffering.

Weil was awarded her *baccalauréat* with distinction at the age of fifteen. After studies with the famed French philosopher Émile-Auguste Chartier (known by his pen name, Alain), she passed first in the extremely competitive entrance examination of the École Normale Supérieure. A brilliant and precocious student, she became deeply involved in social and political causes. Following her graduation in 1931, Weil began teaching philosophy at a girls' *lycée*. School boards shuffled her from one school to another, nervous at her picketing and her writing for leftist journals. By 1932, she was publishing in the *Révolution Prolétarienne* such articles as "Reflections on the Causes of Liberty and Social Oppression." In her notebooks of this period, Weil reflected on the social alienation caused by workers' increasing enslavement to industrial society.

To get experience of workers' lives at first hand, Weil left teaching in 1934 to work at a Renault auto factory. *The Need for Roots* presents her conclusions about the obligations of the state to the individual. Weil's anti-Fascist convictions led her in 1936 to join a unit training for the Spanish Civil War. Her pacifism kept her from battle—but not from injury: Working as a cook, she badly burned herself with oil and was forced to return after only two months. Weil's writing through the 1930's addressed the problems of economic depression, fanatical politics, and war. Her chief preoccupation became increasingly evident: how to reduce human suffering and to find meaning amid that suffering.

During leisure enforced by deteriorating health, Weil began reading the English metaphysical poets. George Herbert's "Love" (III) inspired the first of her mystical revelations. The religious concerns that came to dominate Weil's thought provide the thematic pulse of *Waiting for God*, a posthumously published collection of meditations and reflections. Weil criticizes the oversimplifying rationalism of Christian doctrine, insisting that God cannot be discovered through the senses or intellect.

On May 17, 1942, Weil and her family escaped to the United States, but America's complacency struck her as insensitive to the suffering of her embattled compatriots. In November, she went to England, where she wrote *The Need for Roots*, a response to the request of the Free French in London to report on possibilities for the regeneration of France. *The Need for Roots* is a passionate intellectual plea for the West to recover its spiritual heritage as the first step to solving political problems. Weil discusses the spiritual significance of physical labor, delineates the needs of the soul, and outlines the social principles upon which a truly Christian nation might be built. In the famous preface to the English translation of this book, also published posthumously, T. S. Eliot calls Weil "a woman of genius, of a kind of genius akin to that of the saints." The war notebooks include writing Weil did in America and England in 1942 and 1943, the last pages penned a few days before her death. Weil died on August 24, 1943, at the age of thirty-four, of pulmonary tuberculosis and starvation—she refused to eat more than what she assumed her people in occupied France were rationed.

Critics have pointed to contradictions in Weil's thought. Intensely religious, she rejected her Jewish background and refused baptism in the Christianity she adopted. She is both Marxist and mystical; in her writing, seventeenth century religious fervor stands side by side with twentieth century intellectualism. Yet it is the very inclusiveness of that paradoxical perspective which has drawn countless readers to her work. Weil has a rising reputation as a creative thinker, intensely realistic in her awareness of suffering, passionately idealistic in her hopes to lessen that suffering.

BIBLIOGRAPHICAL REFERENCES: For biography, Simone Pétrement, *Simone Weil: A Life*, 1976, first published in French in 1973, is the best source; Pétrement was a close friend of Weil, and her substantial, well-documented book provides a comprehensive account of Weil's life. The best guide to writings by and about Weil is J. P. Little, *Simone Weil: A Bibliography*, 1973, supplemented in 1980, although many books and articles on Weil have appeared since Little's bibliography was updated. Many of the book-length studies of Weil are introductory surveys of her life and work. Of these, one of the most accessible and insightful is Robert Coles, *Simone Weil: A Modern Pilgrimage*, 1987. Jacques Cabaud, *Simone Weil: A Fellowship in Love*, 1964, and Richard Rees, *Simone Weil: A Sketch for a Portrait*, 1966, also present Weil's thought in the context of her experiences. John Hellman, *Simone Weil: An Introduction to Her Thought*, 1982, offers helpful commentary on Weil in relation to her contemporaries. Betty McLane-Iles, *Uprooting and Integration in the Writings of Simone Weil*, 1987, gives special consideration to Weil's contributions to science. Peter Winch, *Simone Weil: "The Just Balance,"* 1989, is a sophisticated study that focuses on the uneasy mix of religion and philosophy in Weil's thought. *Simone Weil: Interpretations of a Life*, 1981, edited by George Abbott White, is an excellent and wide-ranging collection of essays. See also E. W. F. Tomlin, *Simone Weil*, 1954; David Anderson, *Simone Weil*, 1971; Dorothy Tuck McFarland, *Simone Weil*, 1983; Diogenes Allen, *Three Outsiders: Pascal, Kierkegaard, and Simone Weil*, 1983; John M. Dunaway, *Simone Weil*, 1984; and Eric Springsted, *Affliction and the Love of God: The Spirituality of Simone Weil*, 1986.

Steven C. Walker
Brandie Siegfried

PETER WEISS

Born: Nowawes, Berlin, Germany
Date: November 8, 1916

Died: Stockholm, Sweden
Date: May 10, 1982

PRINCIPAL WORKS

PLAYS: *Die Verfolgung und Ermordung Jean-Paul Marats, dargestellt durch die Schauspielgruppe des Hospizes zu Charenton unter Anleitung des Herrn de Sade*, pr., pb. 1964 (*The Persecution and Assassination of Jean-Paul Marat as Performed by the Inmates of the Asylum of Charenton Under the Direction of the Marquis de Sade*, 1965, best known as *Marat/Sade*); *Die Ermittlung*, pr., pb. 1965 (*The Investigation*, 1966); *Gesang vom lusitanischen Popanz*, pb. 1966 (*Song of the Lusitanian Bogey*, 1970); *Diskurs über die Vorgeschichte und den Verlauf des lang andauernden Befreiungskrieges in Viet Nam als Beispiel für die Notwendigkeit des bewaffneten Kampfes der Unterdrückten gegen ihre Unterdrücker sowie über die Versuche der Vereinigten Staaten von Amerika die Grundlagen der Revolution zu vernichten*, pb. 1967 (*Discourse of the Progress of the Prolonged War of Liberation in Viet Nam and the Events Leading Up to It as Illustration of the Necessity for Armed Resistance Against Oppression and on the Attempts of the United States of America to Destroy the Foundations of Revolution*, 1970, best known as *Vietnam Discourse*); *Dramen in zwei Bänden*, pb. 1968; *Trotski im Exil*, pr., pb. 1970 (*Trotsky in Exile*, 1971); *Hölderlin*, pr., pb. 1971; *Der neue Prozess*, pr. 1974.

NOVELS: *Der Schatten des Körpers des Kutschers*, 1960 (*The Shadow of the Coachman's Body*, 1969); *Abschied von den Eltern*, 1961 (*The Leavetaking*, 1966); *Fluchtpunkt*, 1962 (*Vanishing Point*, 1966); *Das Gespräch der drei Gehenden*, 1963 (*The Conversation of the Three Wayfarers*, 1970); *Die Ästhetik des Widerstands*, 1975-1981.

NONFICTION: *Notizbücher 1971-1980*, 1981; *Notizbücher 1960-1971*, 1982.

Peter Weiss is considered one of the most prominent playwrights and novelists of the German postwar era. Born in a suburb of Berlin to a Jewish family on November 8, 1916, he originally wanted to be a painter. When the Nazis came to power in the 1930's, Weiss's family emigrated to England, and he studied for several years at the art academy in Prague. He then finally moved to Sweden in 1939, where he spent the remainder of his life, becoming a Swedish citizen in 1945. Weiss began writing in 1946 at the age of thirty, and his first poetic efforts were written in Swedish. He was also involved at this time in making experimental films and documentaries. In 1952, Weiss began living with the Swedish artist Gunilla Palmstierna, who did the stage design for many of his later plays. A politically committed individual, he traveled to North Vietnam in 1968 to observe at first hand the effects of the war there. Throughout the course of his career, Weiss was the recipient of numerous literary prizes and honors. He died May 10, 1982, in Stockholm.

Weiss's first writings were highly experimental, surreal narratives. *The Shadow of the Coachman's Body* presents a first-person narrator who records his highly associative, almost hallucinatory impressions over a six-day period. Weiss's early interest in film is apparent in this text in which objects, events, and characters are recorded in a neutral fashion as they occur. *The Conversation of the Three Wayfarers* shares the same disjointed, surreal perspective as the author's first novel. It records the three narrators' conversations, which consist of fantasies, vaguely remembered events, and meandering observations on life. These texts suggest Weiss's attempt to come to terms with the discrepancies between the objective complexity of reality and his subjective perception of it. *The Leavetaking* and *Vanishing Point* are autobiographical novels in which Weiss seeks, here in a more personal way, to assess the nature of his reality. They deal with existential themes of personal alienation, the difficulty of authentic communication, and the individual's search for an identity separate from family and friends. These works represent Weiss's growing realization of the close interrelationship between self and society.

The dialectical play *Marat/Sade* brought Weiss international acclaim. It is a work about the history of ideas and political realities of revolution and social change. Its fictional premise is that of a play about the assassination of the progressive French revolutionary Jean-Paul Marat that is being staged and directed by the infamous sexual libertine Marquis de Sade within the Charenton mental asylum. This play-within-a-play becomes a dialogue between Marat and Sade on the nature of man, society, and the possibility of progress. Marat represents the optimistic Enlightenment position of the perfectibility of man, that the goals of the revolution—liberty, social equality, and brotherhood—can be realized. Sade presents a darker, more pessimistic picture of man in which perverse sexuality and repressed desire produce a society of irrational violence and destruction. Weiss's dramatic writing is strongly influenced by the practice of the Brechtian stage; that is, he uses songs and cabaret-style techniques to present his message. The dramatic oratorio *The Investigation* deals with the horror of the Nazi concentration camps and addresses in broad terms the issue of modern political oppression. The political plays *Song of the Lusitanian Bogey* and *Vietnam Discourse* present strongly propagandistic condemnations of the history of capitalist colonization and exploitation in Third World nations such as Angola and Vietnam. Weiss used, as he does in many of his works, extensive documentary sources in writing these plays.

The plays *Trotsky in Exile* and *Hölderlin* deal with the situation of the politically committed but alienated intellectual. In the former play, the socialist exile, who was at odds with the other early theoreticians of Marxism, reflects upon what he sees as the misguided course of the Russian revolution and speaks for the ideals of true socialism and the creative freedom of the visionary writer-intellectual. Weiss sees his own situation as a committed socialist author as being analogous in certain respects to that of Trotsky. In the latter play, based on the tragic life of the eighteenth century German poet Friedrich Hölderlin, Weiss again explores the fate of the socialist intellectual artist whose inspired visions of a just and equitable society place him both at the forefront of the revolutionary thought of his era and at odds with the less progressive spirit of the times. The play *Der neue Prozess* (the trial) is an adaptation of the novel *Der Prozess* (1925; *The Trial*, 1937) by Franz Kafka. Weiss did the original stage adaptation in 1974 and revised it in 1982. Kafka's novel deals with existential and psychological themes of the estranged personality which Weiss then transformed into a socialist critique of alienation in a capitalist society.

Weiss's last major work was the extended novel *Die Ästhetik des Widerstands* (the aesthetics of resistance). It is a mixture of fictional, autobiographical, and documentary materials in which the author speculates in the guise of the narrator about what his life might have been like had he been born into the lower classes. He discusses the socialist commitment that has been so significant in his life. Weiss's final literary work returns, in certain respects, to the autobiographical concerns of his first writings and summarizes the social concerns that had dominated his creative work throughout his career.

BIBLIOGRAPHICAL REFERENCES: For useful interpretive studies in English, see Ian Hilton, *Peter Weiss: A Search for Affinities*, 1970; Kathleen Vance, *The Theme of Alienation in the Prose of Peter Weiss*, 1981; and Roger Ellis, *Peter Weiss in Exile: A Critical Study of His Works*, 1987. See also the following important studies in German: Volker Canaris, *Über Peter Weiss*, 1970; Otto Best, *Peter Weiss: Vom existenzialistischen Drama zum marxistischen Welttheater*, 1971; Brigitte Keller-Schumacher, *Eine Interpretation des "Marat/Sade" von Peter Weiss*, 1973; Fred Müller, *Peter Weiss, Drei Dramen: Interpretationen*, 1973; Gerd Weinreich, *Peter Weiss' "Marat/Sade,"* 1974; Wolfgang Kehn, *Von Dante zu Hölderlin: Traditionswahl und Engagement im Werk Peter Weiss*, 1975; Manfred Haiduk, *Der Dramatiker Peter Weiss*, 1977; Ingeborg Schmitz, *Dokumentartheater bei Peter Weiss: Von der Ermittlung zu Hölderlin*, 1981; and Heinrich Vormweg, *Peter Weiss*, 1981. See also the following informative articles: John Milfull, "From Kafka to Brecht: Peter Weiss' Development Towards Marxism," *German Life and Letters*, XX (1966), 61-72; Robert Brustein, "Embarrassment of Riches," *The New*

Republic, XXII (1966), 23-28; William Oliver, "*Marat/Sade* in Santiago," *Educational Theatre Journal*, XX (1967), 486-501; and Siegfried Zielinski, "The New Weiss Investigation," *Theater*, XII (1980), 79-82.

Thomas F. Barry

DENTON WELCH

Born: Shanghai, China
Date: March 29, 1915

Died: Middle Orchard, Kent, England
Date: December 30, 1948

PRINCIPAL WORKS

NOVELS: *Maiden Voyage*, 1943; *In Youth Is Pleasure*, 1944; *A Voice Through a Cloud*, 1950.
SHORT FICTION: *Brave and Cruel and Other Stories*, 1948; *The Stories of Denton Welch*, 1985.
POETRY: *Dumb Instrument: Poems and Fragments*, 1976.
MISCELLANEOUS: *A Last Sheaf*, 1951; *The Denton Welch Journals*, 1952; *I Left My Grandfather's House: An Account of His First Walking Tour*, 1958; *Denton Welch: Extracts from His Published Works*, 1963; *The Journals of Denton Welch*, 1984.

For Dame Edith Sitwell, one of his earliest admirers, Denton Welch was "a born writer." For Maurice Cranston, he was "a born solipsist," for C. E. M. Joad, he was a latter-day decadent, and for Julian Symons, the harshest of his critics, he was "a pathetic rather than a tragic figure," whose writings betray the author's "complete narcissistic self-absorption" and "the poverty of his subjects." Welch saw himself as a monk dedicated to a single task, devoted not to God but to an art forged in his, Welch's, own image—an art that is not so much narcissistic as self-exploring, perhaps even self-creating. The intense and often intensely sensuous subjectivity of his writing, especially of the later works, is its most distinguishing feature. Situated at the very center of his writing and his world, his "I" exists as the author's attempt to reconstitute the self—both physical and psychological—that had been largely destroyed as a result of a near-fatal accident in 1935. His "I" exists less as a participant in the events described than as a spectator, as a presiding, recording consciousness. What distinguishes Welch's subjectivity from mere narcissism and his gaze from mere voyeurism is the manner in which he manages to transform them to narrative advantage. His preoccupation with his own subjective self constitutes his attempt to fill the emptiness he felt within. As he wrote in his journal, "Now I am alone here in the afternoon, with freezing mist outside, and nothing in me." Although his self-absorption may be traced to more or less specific physiological and psychological causes, the results extend well beyond the merely pathological to the forging of a decidedly new form of narrative art that is all the more surprising given just how derivative and unexceptional his poems and paintings are.

Maurice Denton Welch was born on March 29, 1915, in Shanghai, China. Never close to his father, a well-do-do businessman, he was devoted to his American-born mother, a Christian Scientist, from whose death in 1927 he never entirely recovered. Already an emotional cripple, in 1935 Welch became a physical cripple as well, sustaining injuries in a bicycle accident that eventually caused his death thirteen years later. Trained as an artist, Welch soon turned to writing and in 1940 published an article about a visit to painter Walter Sickert in Cyril Connolly's *Horizon*; in 1942, he began keeping a journal of considerable literary merit as well as biographical interest. His aptly entitled first novel appeared the following year. *Maiden Voyage* is, as are all Welch's novels and many of his stories, autobiographical in subject and episodic in form. "After I had run away from school," the novel begins, "no one knew what to do with me." The narrator-protagonist hardly knows what to do with himself. He leaves Repton, then leaves England for China, then leaves his father's house to explore this strange land, and then leaves China and returns to England, where he enrolls in art school. Written in a simple style suggestive of the narrator-protagonist's own youthfulness, *Maiden Voyage* proves a surprisingly mature work, one in which (as W. H. Auden has noted) "scientific objectivity" and "subjective terror" are strangely combined. Welch's second novel, *In Youth Is Pleasure*, was less well received. Only half as long as *Maiden Voyage*, its action and cast of characters more condensed, *In Youth Is Pleasure* focuses more narrowly and relentlessly on the sexual—or, rather, the homosexual—aspect of the protagonist's,

Orville Pym's, search for self-knowledge in a largely hostile, at times even terrifying, world surrounding the hotel where Pym goes between school terms with his father and two brothers. A number of reviewers found it difficult to sympathize with a character so narcissistic and "desperately miserable" as Pym. Yet the more important reason the novel fails is the use of a third-person narrator, which, as Maurice Cranston has pointed out, "demanded an interest in the external world which Denton Welch could not sustain."

Welch did not live to complete his third, and many contend, his best novel, *A Voice Through a Cloud*. In part the reason was physical: Pain began to make it difficult for him to write for more than a few minutes at a time. In part it may have been financial: He turned to the writing of short stories that would bring him the income he sorely needed following the death of his father. Many of these stories of failed sexual encounters Welch collected in *Brave and Cruel and Other Stories*, while others appear in *A Last Sheaf*, compiled by Eric Oliver, Welch's companion during his final years. Even in its unfinished state, *A Voice Through a Cloud* is a remarkable work. Narrated by "Maurice," the novel deals with Welch's accident and recovery, but in a way that is, as John Updike has pointed out, as much metaphorical as it is autobiographical. The novel proclaims man's "terrible fragility" and the author's painstaking effort "to reconstitute human experience particle by particle." Here the metaphorical maiden voyage from illness to recovery ends with yet another beginning as Maurice, well if not quite whole, goes to live on his own, no longer needing the help of Dr. Frawley, on whom he had come to depend both as patient and as son. Maurice is, as his journals show Welch was, free but unfulfilled, at least until he came to terms with his feelings for Oliver, at long last entering into precisely the kind of relationship that he, like so many of his narrators and characters, had previously only observed.

What Welch depicted in his writing—his novels and stories as well as his journals—is not a world such as one finds in the realistic fiction written by the majority of other English writers during the 1940's. It is instead a sensibility marked by the intensity of his perception, and marked, too, by its power to evoke rather than merely narrate or (despite the brilliance of Welch's startling imagery) describe. Freely mixing candor with guilt, subjective desire with clinical detachment, he broke free of the upper-middle-class prejudices and perspective for which his work has at times been attacked to forge in his writing what he could not in his life, a new form, one which (as Ruby Cohn has noted) prefigures the slightly later New Novel in France and the works of the Angry Young Men in England. If his scale was small—smaller in fact than that of Jane Austen, a writer he greatly admired—the intensity of his vision and the scrupulous honesty with which he portrayed his limited world were inversely great.

BIBLIOGRAPHICAL REFERENCES: Much of the criticism about Welch is in the form of reviews, general assessments of his work, and introductions. Robert Phillips, *Denton Welch*, 1974, part of Twayne's English Authors series, is thorough, informative, and authoritative, though its Freudian readings make it appear rather dated (despite Welch's susceptibility to psychoanalytical interpretation). Michael De-la-Noy, *Denton Welch: The Making of a Writer*, 1984, brings together a wealth of new material. De-la-Noy's introduction to his edition of *The Journals of Denton Welch* provides a useful summary of his findings. Jocelyn Brooke's introductions to his edition of *The Denton Welch Journals* and *Denton Welch: Extracts from His Published Works* cover much of critical and biographical ground. Brooke's "The Dual Role: A Study of Denton Welch as Painter and Writer," *Texas Quarterly*, VII (1964), 120-127, points to important differences between Welch's painterly and writerly subjects and visions. An important article about Welch as novelist is Ruby Cohn, "A Few Novel Techniques of Denton Welch," *Perspective*, X (Summer/Autumn, 1958), 153-159, in which she makes a strong case for Welch as a writer well ahead of his time. Concerning Welch's narrative technique in *A Voice Through a Cloud*, see John Updike, *Picked-Up Pieces*, 1975. Finally, Maurice Cranston's early essay, "Denton Welch," in *Spectator Harvest*, 1952, is similarly penetrating, touching on a number of issues (such as the "sinister quality in much of Denton Welch's work").

Robert A. Morace

FAY WELDON

Born: Alvechurch, Worcestershire, England
Date: September 22, 1931

Principal Works

NOVELS: *The Fat Woman's Joke*, 1967 (also known as *. . . And the Wife Ran Away*); *Down Among the Women*, 1971; *Female Friends*, 1974; *Remember Me*, 1976; *Words of Advice*, 1977 (also known as *Little Sisters*); *Praxis*, 1978; *Puffball*, 1979; *The President's Child*, 1982; *The Life and Loves of a She-Devil*, 1983; *The Shrapnel Academy*, 1986; *The Rules of Life*, 1987; *The Hearts and Lives of Men*, 1987; *Leader of the Band*, 1988; *The Heart of the Country*, 1988.

SHORT FICTION: *Watching Me, Watching You*, 1981; *Polaris and Other Stories*, 1985.

PLAYS: *Permanence*, pr. 1969; *Time Hurries On*, pb. 1972; *Words of Advice*, pr., pb. 1974; *Friends*, pr. 1975; *Moving House*, pr. 1976; *Mr. Director*, pr. 1978; *Action Replay*, pr. 1978 (also known as *Love Among the Women*); *I Love My Love*, pr. 1982; *After the Prize*, pr. 1981 (also known as *Word Worm*).

TELEPLAYS: *Wife in a Blonde Wig*, 1966; *The Fat Woman's Tale*, 1966; *What About Me*, 1967; *Dr. De Waldon's Therapy*, 1967; *Goodnight Mrs. Dill*, 1967; *The 45th Unmarried Mother*, 1967; *Fall of the Goat*, 1967; *Ruined Houses*, 1968; *Venus Rising*, 1968; *The Three Wives of Felix Hull*, 1968; *Hippy Hippy Who Cares*, 1968; *L133083*, 1968; *The Loophole*, 1969; *Smoke-screen*, 1969; *Poor Mother*, 1970; *Office Party*, 1970; *On Trial*, 1971 (in "Upstairs, Downstairs" series); *Old Man's Hat*, 1972; *A Splinter of Ice*, 1972; *Hands*, 1972; *The Lament of an Unmarried Father*, 1972; *A Nice Rest*, 1972; *Comfortable Words*, 1973; *Desirous of Change*, 1973; *In Memoriam*, 1974; *Poor Baby*, 1975; *The Terrible Tale of Timothy Bagshott*, 1975; *Aunt Tatty*, 1975; *Act of Rape*, 1977; *Married Love*, 1977 (in "Six Women" series); *Pride and Prejudice*, 1980; *Honey Ann*, 1980; *Watching Me, Watching You*, 1980 (in "Leap in the Dark" series); *Life for Christine*, 1980; *Little Miss Perkins*, 1982; *Loving Women*, 1983; *Redundant! Or, The Wife's Revenge*, 1983.

RADIO PLAYS: *Spider*, pr. 1972; *Housebreaker*, pr. 1973; *Mr. Fox and Mr. First*, pr. 1974; *The Doctor's Wife*, pr. 1975; *Polaris*, pb. 1978; *Weekend*, pr. 1979 (in "Just Before Midnight" series); *All the Bells of Paradise*, pr. 1979; *I Love My Love*, pr. 1981.

NONFICTION: *Letters to Alice on First Reading Jane Austen*, 1984; *Rebecca West*, 1985.

EDITED TEXT: *New Stories 4: An Arts Council Anthology*, 1979 (with Elaine Feinstein).

Fay Weldon is a major contemporary writer on women's issues, noted for short fiction and novels, as well as for plays for stage, radio, and television. She was born Fay Birkinshaw on September 22, 1931, in Alvechurch, Worcestershire, England, to Frank Thornton Birkinshaw, a doctor, and Margaret Jepson Birkinshaw, a writer of romantic novels. Her maternal grandfather and an uncle were also writers. Weldon was reared in New Zealand. When she was five, her parents were divorced; she spent the rest of her childhood in an all-female household, consisting of her mother, her grandmother, and her sister, and then was educated at a girls' school. After returning to England, Weldon attended Hampstead Girls' High School, London. In 1949, she went to St. Andrews University in Fife, Scotland, and received her master's degree in economics and psychology in 1954. In the 1950's, Weldon worked as a report writer for the British Foreign Office, spent some time as a market researcher for the London *Daily Mirror*, and then became an advertising copywriter. In 1960, she married Ronald (Ron) Weldon, an antique dealer, painter, and jazz musician.

Although Weldon had worked on novels in the 1950's, her career as a successful writer should be dated from the year 1966, when three of her plays were produced on British television. Her first novel, *The Fat Woman's Joke*, which was published a year later, grew out of the teleplay *The Fat Woman's Tale*. Witty, satirical, and conversational, it set the pattern for her later works, which have consistently dealt with women's problems as seen through women's eyes. In 1969, Weldon's first play was produced in London; it was followed by six others during the next decade. Meanwhile, she continued to write novels, short stories, and numerous teleplays, including an award-winning episode of the popular series *Upstairs, Downstairs*. In the 1970's, she also wrote a number of radio plays; in 1973, she won the Writers' Guild Award for one of them, *Spider*, and in 1978, she won the Giles Cooper Award for *Polaris*. In every genre, she was praised for skillful plot development, witty and realistic dialogue, and an accurate delineation of the plight of all women, single or married, who are victims of their biological drives and of the men who dominate society. Although her themes remain the same, critics are impressed by Weldon's seemingly endless powers of invention. In the early work *Remember Me*, for example, a dead divorced wife comes back to haunt her ex-husband; in *Puffball*, a pregnant woman, alone in Somerset, is beset by a witch; and in what is perhaps Weldon's most famous later novel, *The Life and Loves of a She-Devil*, an abandoned wife takes an elaborate revenge on her husband and on the wealthy romance writer who stole him from her.

In addition to her own fiction and plays, Weldon has written acclaimed scripts based on the works of other writers, including *Aunt Tatty*, based on a short story by Elizabeth Bowen, and the five-part dramatization of Jane Austen's *Pride and Prejudice* (1813), which was shown in England and in the United States in 1980. Her interest in Austen led to the publication of an unusual book, *Letters to Alice on First Reading Jane Austen*, which is cast as a series of letters from the novelist to a fictional niece. In addition to analyses of Austen's novels and details about her life, the book includes Weldon's comments on the art of fiction and on her own work. In 1986, Weldon's book *Rebecca West* was structured similarly. In this case, Weldon supposes herself to be writing fictitious letters to another writer, Rebecca West, after the birth in 1914 of West's son by H. G. Wells. In keeping with her feminist posture, she praises West's determined unconventionality but also reminds her that a satisfying life does not depend on Wells or on any other man.

It is interesting that men and women both are targets of Weldon's satire, men because they so often insist on bolstering their own insecurities by bullying the women who love them or who are involved with them, and women because they conspire in their own subjugation, assuming that thus they will keep the men they so desperately need in order to maintain their own identities. Extreme feminists criticize Weldon because her men are not monsters. Most of them are weak. Like Bobbo in *The Life and Loves of a She-Devil*, they collapse as soon as women cease to adore them. Critics also complain that Weldon's women are often as foolish as the men. Rational rather than vituperative, witty rather than shrill, Weldon's short stories and novels have drawn criticism from some feminists. Others disagree, pointing out that her incisive social commentary may lay the groundwork for a new maturity and respect in relationships between men and women, based on a new balance in the lives of women such as Weldon herself.

BIBLIOGRAPHICAL REFERENCES: For reviews of Weldon's work, see the following: Patricia Craig, "Movement of the Spheres," *The Times Literary Supplement*, July 15, 1988, 787; Grace Ingoldby, "Dear Reader," *New Statesman*, CXIII (February 6, 1987), 27-28; Paddy Kitchen, "Conjuror's Trick," *The Times Educational Supplement*, May 11, 1984, 27; John Naughton, "Family Lives," *The Listener*, CV (May 28, 1981), 717; Terrence Rafferty, "She-Devil," *The New Yorker*, LXIV (August 1, 1988), 66; Carol E. Rinzler, "Hell Hath No Fury," *The Washington Post Book World*, September 30, 1984, 1-2; Lorna Sage, "Aunt Fay's Sermons," *The Observer*, May 13, 1984, 23; Carol Sternhell, "Fay Weldon's Dangerous Dreams," *The Village Voice*, XXVIII (July 19, 1983), 34; and Harriet Waugh, "Unbelievable," *The Spectator*, CCXLIX (October 2, 1982), 24-25. Good examples of unsympathetic reviews are Martin Amis, "Prose Is the Leading Lady," *The New York Times Book Review*, October 2, 1977, 13; Mary Hope, *The Spectator*, March 4, 1978, 24; and Michiko Kakutani, review of *The Life and*

Loves of a She-Devil, *The New York Times*, August 21, 1984, C17. A helpful scholarly article is Agate Nesaule Krouse, "Feminism and Art in Fay Weldon's Novels," *Critique: Studies in Modern Fiction*, XX (1979), 5-20.

Rosemary M. Canfield Reisman

EUDORA WELTY

Born: Jackson, Mississippi
Date: April 13, 1909

PRINCIPAL WORKS

SHORT FICTION: *A Curtain of Green*, 1941; *The Wide Net and Other Stories*, 1943; *Selected Stories*, 1943; *The Golden Apples*, 1949; *The Bride of the Innisfallen, and Other Stories*, 1955; *Thirteen Stories*, 1965; *The Collected Stories of Eudora Welty*, 1980; *Moon Lake and Other Stories*, 1980; *Retreat*, 1981.

NOVELS: *The Robber Bridegroom*, 1942; *Delta Wedding*, 1946; *The Ponder Heart*, 1954; *Losing Battles*, 1970; *The Optimist's Daughter*, 1972.

POETRY: *A Flock of Guinea Hens Seen from a Car*, 1970.

CHILDREN'S LITERATURE: *The Shoe Bird*, 1964.

CRITICISM: *The Reading and Writing of Short Stories*, 1949; *Place in Fiction*, 1957; *Three Papers on Fiction*, 1962; *A Sweet Devouring*, 1969; *The Eye of the Story: Selected Essays and Reviews*, 1978; *Miracles of Perception: The Art of Willa Cather*, 1980 (with Alfred Knopf and Yehudi Menuhin).

MEMOIRS: *Ida M'Toy*, 1979; *One Writer's Beginnings*, 1984.

OTHER NONFICTION: *Music from Spain*, 1948; *One Time, One Place: Mississippi in the Depression, a Snapshot Album*, 1971.

Eudora Welty is one of the greatest writers of Southern fiction. She was born in Jackson, Mississippi, on April 13, 1909, the daughter of Mary Chestina Andrews Welty, a teacher originally from West Virginia, and Christian Webb Welty, president of a life insurance company, who had moved to Jackson from Ohio. After she left Jackson High School, Welty attended Mississippi State College for Women for two years and then transferred to the University of Wisconsin, where she received her bachelor of arts degree in 1929. She spent the following two years at Columbia University, studying advertising; unfortunately, at the beginning of the Depression, she could not find a position, and she returned to Jackson. In 1931, her beloved father died.

At this time, Welty began to write regularly, while working at various jobs, several with newspapers, one with a radio station. The position that was most important for her literary career was one as a publicity agent for the Works Progress Administration, which sent her all over Mississippi, taking photographs and interviewing people, developing a sense of place and collecting ideas for her stories. In 1936, she had a one-person show of her photographs in New York City; that same year, her first story, "Death of a Traveling Salesman," appeared in a small magazine called *Manuscript*. Soon her work was being accepted by *The Southern Review*, then edited by Robert Penn Warren and Cleanth Brooks, and by other publications of national circulation. In 1941, "A Worn Path" and "Why I Live at the P.O." were published in *The Atlantic Monthly*, and "A Worn Path" won second prize in the O. Henry Memorial Contest; that year, too, her first collection of short stories, *A Curtain of Green*, appeared, with an introduction by Katherine Anne Porter. With her literary reputation established, Welty was now able to devote full time to her writing.

From that time on, Welty's short stories were published regularly, both in magazines and in collected editions, and just as regularly won prizes. Welty herself received Guggenheim fellowships in 1942 and in 1949; the second enabled her to travel in France, Italy, and England. In 1946, Welty's novel *Delta Wedding* appeared serially in *The Atlantic Monthly* and then was published in book form. Other novels followed, winning critical acclaim, such as the William Dean Howells Medal of the American Academy in 1955 for *The Ponder Heart*, which was dramatized and ran successfully on Broadway in 1956. During the years that followed, Welty lectured at various colleges and universities, becoming more widely known;

however, it was not until the publication in 1970 of *Losing Battles* that Welty attained national fame. The book which followed in 1972, *The Optimist's Daughter*, based on the long illness and death of Welty's mother, won the Pulitzer Prize.

As her short stories and novels continued to appear, Welty became one of the most beloved writers in America and throughout the world. Works such as *The Eye of the Story* have established her importance as a critic; for the understanding of her own work and of the process of fiction, however, the most valuable critical comments are undoubtedly found in the memoir *One Writer's Beginnings*. In *One Writer's Beginnings*, Welty explains how her childhood observation prepared her for the kind of writing she was to do. For example, she says, she noticed that one friend of her mother, whose stories delighted her, always structured her stories in scenes. From the monologues of that same lady, she learned that economical speech does not reveal so much about a character as the rambling, digressive talk that is so typical of the South and which Welty reproduces perfectly. These lessons from her childhood are evident in one of Welty's most popular short stories, "Petrified Man." Essentially, the story is one long scene in a beauty shop. Through her own vivid descriptions and through the revealing, gossipy talk of the three characters, Welty not only produces an exact record of life at a point in time and space but also illustrates her theme: that women can dominate men to the point of turning men into freaks.

Writing from within a society that takes family ties and obligations seriously, Welty frequently chooses a time of crisis or ceremony for a story or a novel, when family and community are brought together and all of their intricate relationships can be revealed. In "The Wide Net," the disappearance of a young wife, who has left a suicide note, is the excuse for a group of men to come together in order to drag the river for her body. It is ironic that in this seemingly tragic situation, the men find themselves having a good time, and even the young husband briefly forgets the reason for the activity. Typically, both he and his wife (who has not actually killed herself) have learned something by the end of the story: he, that however worrisome she is, he cannot be happy without her, and she, that by cultivating her irrationality, she can enchant and control him. Similar revelations come to the young characters involved in ritual events, such as the marriage in *Delta Wedding*, the courtroom trial in *The Ponder Heart*, and the funerals in "The Wanderers" and in *The Optimist's Daughter*. These characters learn that change is part of life, that joy and sorrow are intertwined, and that only through mutual respect and forgiveness can the family and the community survive.

In the 1960's, Welty was attacked by liberal critics for her failure to crusade for civil rights. Her answer can be found in the essay "Must the Novelist Crusade?" in *The Eye of the Story*, where she insists that direct social action or propagandistic writing would simply destroy the imaginative writer, whose mission is to explore the underlying meaning of human life. By awakening her readers to the dignity that can be seen in the humblest human being, to the importance of tolerance, and to the strength for good that can be exerted by a family or a community, Welty has established her lasting place in literature and may well have accomplished more for humanity than some of her more confrontational contemporaries.

BIBLIOGRAPHICAL REFERENCES: In addition to Welty's own works, *The Eye of the Storm* and *One Writer's Beginnings*, see Katherine Anne Porter's introduction to *A Curtain of Green*, 1941, and Robert Penn Warren, "The Love and the Separateness in Miss Welty," *The Kenyon Review*, VI (Spring, 1944), 246-259, reprinted in his *Selected Essays*, 1958. An excellent early book-length work is Ruth M. Vande Kieft, *Eudora Welty*, 1962. A good later summary is Peggy Whitman Prenshaw, "Eudora Welty," in *The History of Southern Literature*, 1985, edited by Louis D. Rubin, Jr., et al. See also Alfred Appel, Jr., *The Fiction of Eudora Welty*, 1965; Joseph A. Bryant, Jr., *Eudora Welty*, 1968; *Eudora Welty: A Form of Thanks*, 1979, edited by Louis Dollarhide and Ann J. Abadie; Elizabeth Evans, *Eudora Welty*, 1981; Zelma Turner Howard, *The Rhetoric of Eudora Welty's Short Stories*, 1973; Michael Kreyling, *Eudora Welty's Achievement of Order*, 1980; Carol S. Manning, *Eudora Welty and the Love of*

Storytelling, 1985; and *Eudora Welty: Critical Essays*, 1979, edited by Peggy Whitman Prenshaw.

Rosemary M. Canfield Reisman

ARNOLD WESKER

Born: London, England
Date: May 24, 1932

PRINCIPAL WORKS

PLAYS: *Chicken Soup with Barley*, pr. 1958; *The Kitchen*, pr. 1959; *Roots*, pr., pb. 1959; *I'm Talking About Jerusalem*, pr., pb. 1960; *The Wesker Trilogy*, pb. 1960 (includes *Chicken Soup with Barley, Roots, I'm Talking About Jerusalem*); *Chips with Everything*, pr., pb. 1962; *The Four Seasons*, pr. 1965; *Their Very Own and Golden City*, pr. 1965; *The Friends*, pr., pb. 1970; *The Old Ones*, pr. 1972; *The Wedding Feast*, pr. 1974; *The Journalists*, pb. 1975; *Love Letters on Blue Paper*, pr. 1976 (televised), pr. 1977 (staged); *The Merchant*, pr. 1976; *The Plays of Arnold Wesker*, pb. 1976; *Caritas: A Play in Two Acts*, pr., pb. 1981.

SHORT FICTION: *Love Letters on Blue Paper: Three Stories*, 1974; *Fatlips: A Story for Children*, 1978; *Said the Old Man to the Young Man: Three Stories*, 1978.

NONFICTION: *The Modern Playwright*, 1960; *Fears of Fragmentation*, 1970; *Say Goodbye—You May Never See Them Again: Scenes from Two East-End Backgrounds*, 1974 (with John Allin); *Words as Definitions of Experience*, 1976; *The Journalists: A Triptych*, 1979.

MISCELLANEOUS: *Six Sundays in January*, 1971.

Arnold Wesker, one of the many English dramatists of the stage revolution that began with John Osborne's *Look Back in Anger* in 1956, made his reputation with a trio of plays about the working classes called *The Wesker Trilogy*, composed of *Chicken Soup with Barley*, *Roots*, and *I'm Talking About Jerusalem*. More to the point, his name became associated with the term "kitchen-sink drama," owing to the realistic depiction of life in his first play, *The Kitchen*, concerning the routine of daily life in a restaurant kitchen. This same realism is in his play about military life, *Chips with Everything*, which joins those works previously mentioned as the fifth of Wesker's best-known plays. All are highly detailed, humorous, and compassionate studies of life among the poor. All are drawn from his own personal and family life, and all are based on his strong convictions about the necessity for social change.

Born in East London (Stepney) to Joseph (a tailor) and Leah Perlmutter Wesker, of Russian-Hungarian-Jewish extraction, Wesker held assorted jobs as carpenter, plumber, bookshop assistant, farm worker, and pastry cook. He spent two years in the Royal Air Force and enrolled in a course at the London School of Film Technique, entering his first play, *The Kitchen*, in *The Observer* play competition in 1956, the year the stage revolution began. Although the play was rejected by theater managers at the time, like so many of his contemporaries whose plays were staged in provincial theaters and who maintained an association with a particular theater, Wesker found his home in the Belgrade Theatre, Coventry. As a moralist and social activist, he worked hard in Centre 42, an organization with the purpose of bettering life for the working classes, especially in regard to the importance of art in their lives. As a result of his political activism, he spent some time in prison for his part in a protest staged by the Campaign for Nuclear Disarmament. *The Kitchen* has its roots in Wesker's own experiences and in those of his mother, who supplemented the family income with restaurant kitchen jobs. The structure of the play takes on the order in which workers arrive at a restaurant in the course of a day, the rhythms of life in the kitchen increasing to a frenzied pitch with the lunch and dinner rushes.

Like *The Kitchen*, Wesker's trilogy is drawn from his own experience, this time from his own family and community life in London's East End. In all three plays, characters of the same family continue from one generation to the next. The first of the three plays to be staged, *Chicken Soup with Barley*, begins in the 1930's in the context of the fascistic anticommunist marches that took place in the Jewish East End. Despite the domestic quarrels of the family of Harry and Sarah Kahn, larger issues and events unify them and their idealistic son and daughter, Ronnie and Ada. World War II, the Russian invasion of Hungary, Harry's paralyzing stroke, Sarah's desperate attempt to keep the family together—all these events affect the moral and political idealism of Ronnie. In the second play of the trilogy, *Roots*, the scene is Norfolk, where Beatie Bryant and her family are awaiting the arrival of her fiancé, Ronnie, who upsets the expectations of the family by his decision not to marry Beatie. She, in turn, has experienced her own self-discovery, in contrast with the narrow-mindedness of her family and neighbors. *I'm Talking About Jerusalem* continues the Kahn family chronicles, this time in Norfolk, where Ronnie is helping Ada and her husband Dave move into a new home. More disillusionment sets in as all three, along with an old friend who is visiting them, confront a variety of personal failures. Dave is involved in petty thievery; Ronnie talks about his failed relationship with Beatie; Harry is confined to a mental institution; and a voice on the radio announces the Conservative victory of 1959. The four friends in their current situation present a vivid contrast with their optimistic idealism in *Chicken Soup with Barley*, a play in which their vision of a humane society based on brotherhood had been so strong. In all the anguish, though, idealism, although diminished, remains in the form of their recognition of the small gains that have been realized.

Originally written as a novel, *Chips with Everything* is based on Wesker's experience in the Royal Air Force. Written in Brechtian style, the play is drawn from letters Wesker wrote asking recipients to keep those letters. Pip Thompson, the main character, although middle-class, is an idealist who insists on forgoing his middle-class prerogatives for a commissioned rank. His sympathies for the military underclass and his opposition to authority, on the other hand, are challenged by officers and by his own personal revulsion to the vulgarity of the very class he champions. *Chips with Everything* was hailed by new critics such as Kenneth Tynan and rejected as proselytizing propaganda by critics who opposed Wesker's left-wing view of the outdated English class system. Between the two extremes are those critics who see Wesker's plays as compassionate, humane, and moral.

Wesker's later plays are clearly distinguished from his early plays by the focus on personal relationships, bordering at times on the sentimental or fanciful. *The Friends*, for example, is concerned with a group of friends who react to the central character, Esther, who is dying of leukemia. All the friends of Esther are in the interior decorating industry, and their aesthetic community is the integrating principle of the drama. A Chekhovian situation prevails as various characters are catalyzed into revealing their inner states of being by the idea of death. The vision here is highly personalized, and the sharp focus of the early plays seems diffused. Lyrical in tone and poetic in imagery, the style of the later plays contrasts sharply with the realism and social criticism of the early dramas. Yet the strong affirmation of family, community, and social idealism remains the thematic hallmark throughout Wesker's plays.

BIBLIOGRAPHICAL REFERENCES: A complete study of both Wesker's plays and play productions is to be found in Glenda Leeming, *Wesker the Playwright*, 1983; her *Wesker on File*, 1985, in Methuen's "on file" series, contains an extensive bibliography of writings by and about Wesker, with a brief and concise summary and comment on each of Wesker's plays. Earlier book-length studies include Harold U. Ribalow, *Arnold Wesker*, 1965; Ronald Hayman, *Arnold Wesker*, 1973 (rev. ed.); Glenda Leeming and Simon Trussler, *The Plays of Arnold Wesker*, 1971 (a discussion of plays up to 1970); Glenda Leeming, *Arnold Wesker* (for the British Council in the Writers and Their Work series), 1972. See also "Theatre in the Raw," in Laurence Kitchen, *Mid-Century Drama*, 1962; John Garforth, "Arnold Wesker's Mission," in *The Encore Reader*, 1965, edited by Charles Marowitz, Tom Milne, and Owen Hale; John Russell Brown, "Arnold Wesker: Theatrical Demonstration," in *Theatre Language: A Study of Arden, Osborne, Pinter, and Wesker*, 1972; Catherine Itzin, "Arnold Wesker," in *Stages in the Revolution*, 1980; and Glenda Leeming, "Articulacy and Awareness," in *Contemporary English Dramatists*, 1981, edited by C. W. E. Bigsby.

Susan Rusinko

JESSAMYN WEST

Born: North Vernon, Indiana
Date: July 18, 1902

Died: Napa, California
Date: February 23, 1984

PRINCIPAL WORKS

SHORT FICTION: *The Friendly Persuasion*, 1945; *Except for Me and Thee: A Companion to "The Friendly Persuasion,"* wr. 1949, pb. 1969; *Cress Delahanty*, 1953; *Love, Death, and the Ladies' Drill Team*, 1955; *Crimson Ramblers of the World, Farewell*, 1970; *The Story of a Story and Three Stories*, 1982; *Collected Stories of Jessamyn West*, 1986.

NOVELS: *The Witch Diggers*, 1951; *South of the Angels*, 1960; *A Matter of Time*, 1966; *Leafy Rivers*, 1967; *The Massacre at Fall Creek*, 1975; *The Life I Really Lived: A Novel*, 1979; *The State of Stony Lonesome*, 1984.

AUTOBIOGRAPHY: *To See the Dream*, 1957; *Hide and Seek: A Continuing Journey*, 1973; *The Woman Said Yes: Encounters with Life and Death—Memoirs*, 1976; *Double Discovery: A Journey*, 1980.

PLAY: *A Mirror for the Sky*, pb. 1948.

POETRY: *The Secret Look: Poems*, 1974.

EDITED TEXT: *The Quaker Reader*, 1962.

Jessamyn West is noted for her perceptive short stories and novels, particularly for those which deal with nineteenth century Quakers establishing homes on the Midwestern frontier and for those which re-create the Southern California frontier of her own childhood in the early twentieth century. Born in North Vernon, Indiana, on July 18, 1902, the first child of Eldo Roy and Grace Anna Milhous West, Mary Jessamyn West moved to rural Orange County, California, with her parents when she was only six years old. There, spending much of her time outdoors, she learned to love nature. She also developed a passion for reading, as well as a fierce sense of personal responsibility that was certainly influenced by her being the oldest of three children. After she was graduated from Fullerton High School in 1919, she continued her education, receiving her bachelor of arts degree in English from Whittier College in 1923. That year she married Harry Maxwell McPherson, a teacher, who also had a Quaker background. After working for five years as a teacher and as a secretary in Hemet, California, in 1929 she resigned to work on a doctorate in English literature at the University of California, Berkeley. It was there that she developed her enthusiasm for Henry David Thoreau, whose influence can be seen in her work. Unfortunately, when her work was almost concluded, she was diagnosed with advanced tuberculosis. After some time in a sanatorium, West was sent home, and during this period of enforced inactivity, she began to write.

By the time West published her first short story, she was thirty-six years old. It is not surprising that seven years later, when her first book appeared, *The Friendly Persuasion*, it was the work of a mature writer. West gathered her material during her illness, when her mother, who was nursing her, reminisced about her childhood in Indiana. The book was above all the story of a happy marriage, based on mutual respect and faith in God. The arguments between the fun-loving, strong-willed Jess Birdwell and his equally strong-willed, strict wife, Eliza Cope Birdwell, a Quaker minister, were always resolved through prayer and love. Critics praised West for her appealing characters, for her original and precise style, and above all for her convincing depiction of the gentle Quaker way of life. Coming at the end of World War II, such stories brought their readers much-needed reassurance. After an unsuccessful poetic opera based on the life of John James Audubon and a novel set on an Indiana poor farm, West returned to the form which had made her famous, the series of related sketches. *Cress Delahanty* was West's first essay into her other source of material: life in rural Orange County, California, in the period of her own youth. The adolescent heroine was praised, as the Birdwells had been, and again critics noted West's skill in pointing out the human truths that are evident in slight occurrences.

In the years which followed, West wrote primarily fiction, sometimes separate short stories, as those collected in *Love, Death, and the Ladies' Drill Team*, and sometimes novels, such as *South of the Angels*; only in *Except for Me and Thee*, did she return to the form of related sketches. She also did some screen writing, including the script for *Friendly Persuasion* (pb. 1955, released in 1956), which won the Palme d'Or at the Cannes Film Festival and received six Academy Award nominations. Her book *To See the Dream* tells of her experiences during the making of the film. In the later years of her life, West wrote several important autobiographical books. Early in the 1970's, she retreated for three months to a trailer by the Colorado River, where she wrote the meditative, reminiscent *Hide and Seek*. Unlike that work, *The Woman Said Yes*, published in 1976, raised a storm of controversy, because in it she admitted not only having considered suicide when she was in ill health but, also, actually having aided her cancer-stricken sister to kill herself, a situation that she had treated fictionally in *A Matter of Time*. In 1983, West completed her last work, the novel *The State of Stony Lonesome*. She died of a stroke in Napa, California, on February 23, 1984.

The predominant theme of West's work is the tension between the needs of the individual and the demands of love. In *The Friendly Persuasion* and in *Except for Me and Thee*, for example, the ebullient Irish Quaker Jess Birdwell must frequently decide whether to take an action that appears harmless to him yet offends the sensibilities of his loving but firm Quaker minister wife, Eliza. In keeping with her Quaker background, West stresses the importance of the individual conscience. When a character follows the demands of his conscience, he can triumph over pain. Yet each person must test his deeds and his words by their motivation. If they proceed from hatred, they will destroy him; if they proceed from love, they will enable him to triumph over heartbreak. It was perhaps this test that West used when she responded to her sister's desire for death. In this situation, she made her own decision and acted as her conscience moved her.

West was always beloved by the reading public and praised by critics. Since her death, though, the academic world seems to have rediscovered her, finding that her work is much more complex than a quick reading may suggest. Although her characters may be ordinary, it has been pointed out that their feelings and their motivations are complicated; although her plots may not at first glance appear dramatic, they involve the most serious decisions of the human spirit. Even her language, rich in metaphor and humor, lyrically descriptive and highly symbolic, deserves further study. No longer considered a local-color writer, West is now viewed as a historian of the human condition.

BIBLIOGRAPHICAL REFERENCES: Full-length critical studies of Jessamyn West include Alfred S. Shivers, *Jessamyn West*, 1972, and Ann Dahlstrom Farmer, *Jessamyn West*, 1982. John T. Flanagan's articles are sound and penetrating—see his "The Fiction of Jessamyn West," *Indiana Magazine of History*, LXVII (December, 1971), 299-316, and "Folklore in Five Middlewestern Novelists," *The Great Lakes Review*, I (Winter, 1975), 43-57. See also Eudora Welty, "A Search, Maddening and Infectious," *The New York Times Book Review*, LVI (January 14, 1951), 5; Dan Wickenden, "Humor and Pathos and Understanding," *New York Herald Tribune Book Review*, XXX (January 3, 1954), 3; Carlos Baker, "The Pathetic, the Curious, the Ironic," *The New York Times Book Review*, LX (October 16, 1955), 4; William Hogan, "West to Eden," *Saturday Review*, XLIII (April 23, 1960), 23; Christopher G. Katope, "West's 'Love, Death, and the Ladies' Drill Team,'" *The Explicator*, XXIII (December, 1964), Item 27; Laurence LaFore, "Men and Women at War with Their Environment," *The New York Times Book Review*, LXXVI (January 10, 1971), 34; Carlos Baker, "Sweet Alyssum and Bleeding Heart," *The New York Times Book Review*, LXXVI (May 11, 1971); and Nancy Hale, "Women's Insights," *The New York Times Book Review*, LXXXIV (December 16, 1979), 16-17.

Rosemary M. Canfield Reisman

PAUL WEST

Born: Eckington, Derbyshire, England
Date: February 23, 1930

Principal Works

NOVELS: *A Quality of Mercy*, 1961; *Tenement of Clay*, 1965; *Alley Jaggers*, 1966; *I'm Expecting to Live Quite Soon*, 1970; *Caliban's Filibuster*, 1971; *Bela Lugosi's White Christmas*, 1972; *Colonel Mint*, 1972; *Gala*, 1976; *The Very Rich Hours of Count von Stauffenberg*, 1980; *Rat Man of Paris*, 1986; *The Place in Flowers Where Pollen Rests*, 1988.

SHORT FICTION: *The Universe and Other Fictions*, 1988.

POETRY: *Poems*, 1952; *The Spellbound Horses*, 1960; *The Snow Leopard*, 1964.

MEMOIRS: *I, Said the Sparrow*, 1963; *Words for a Deaf Daughter*, 1969; *Out of My Depths: A Swimmer in the Universe*, 1983.

LITERARY CRITICISM: *The Growth of the Novel*, 1959; *The Modern Novel*, 1963; *Sheer Fiction*, 1987.

LITERARY STUDIES: *Byron and the Spoiler's Art*, 1960; *Robert Penn Warren*, 1964.

ESSAYS: *The Wine of Absurdity: Essays on Literature and Consolation*, 1966.

EDITED TEXT: *Byron: A Collection of Critical Essays*, 1963.

Paul Noden West is one of America's most imaginative and innovative contemporary writers and one of the twentieth century's finest literary stylists. He was born in Eckington, England, on February 23, 1930, the son of Alfred and Mildred (Noden) West. From his earliest days, West was surrounded by book lovers—parents, grandparents, and relatives—who viewed the written word as sacred and who considered nearly any book a worthy addition to an ever-growing canon of literary experiences, experiences they considered as valid as those of everyday life for authenticating the self and one's existence in the world. West quickly assimilated this reverence for the word and literary text as experience and applied it with intensity to his studies at the University of Oxford and Columbia University. Between the childhood encouragement to sample literature from around the world and the Oxford mentoring that exhorted him to experience literature, learning, and activities outside the traditional academic setting, it is not surprising that West developed an eclectic, comparative taste in literature, in what he considers as literature, in how he teaches his literature and creative writing courses at The Pennsylvania State University, and most significantly, in the versatility and variety of his literary craft.

Even a cursory examination of West's works reveals their thematic variety and stylistic richness as well as the originality of his imagination. His themes include psychic abuse, failed relationships, societal indifference, and spiritual inadequacy, but a positive side exists in his writing as well. Self-discovery and survival are strong forces in his works. The dialectical tensions between the forces of genocide and the keepers of peace reinforce the paradoxical nature of existence in an indifferent, imperfect, yet potentially rich universe of opposing experiences and forces. This thematic richness and variety is the product of West's interconnected beliefs about the human condition. Throughout his works, West juxtaposes a picture of a universe in flux, filled with a plurality of experience, to one of an arbitrary and imperfect world, self-absorbed and heedless of its members. West reveals that the tension and confrontation between these paradoxical sides of an absurd world produce both the darker sides of human behavior and being and the potentiality in life. Consequently, his works suggest the need to perceive the universe and life more inclusively and recognize the productive potential of the imagination to construct possibilities that create meaning in, provide ways of coping with, and allow for a measure of happiness in an absurd world.

West's particular significance in contemporary literature rests strongly with his stylistic genius. He ranks among the most accomplished stylists of the twentieth century—James

Joyce, Vladimir Nabokov, Marcel Proust, Virginia Woolf—at crafting simultaneously lyrical and dense, elegant and economical sentences, tours de force that create the detail and deep structures West insists on in writing while also capturing the exciting, arbitrary nature of words for reflecting that very same quality in a universe in flux. West considers mimesis, the conventional treatment of novelistic elements, and the traditional handling and parameters of subject matter as myopic notions. West's fiction demands fluidity of the novel as an organic, dynamic genre and of the reader as collaborator in the creative process of constituting the text as aesthetic object. It is for these contributions to contemporary literature that West's peers awarded him the prestigious American Academy and Institute of Arts and Letters Literature Award in 1985.

BIBLIOGRAPHICAL REFERENCES: For valuable general appraisals of West's works and their place in contemporary literature, see Brian McLaughlin, "Paul West," in *British Novelists Since 1960*, 1983, edited by Jay L. Halio; *Contemporary Literary Criticism*, Vol. 14, 1980, edited by Sharon Gunton; *Contemporary Novelists*, 1976, edited by James Vinson; and *World Authors, 1950-1970*, 1975, edited by John Wakerman. See also Frederick Busch, "The Friction of Fiction: A Ulysses Omnirandum," *Chicago Review*, XXVI (1975), 5-17. Bradford Morrow's interview of West in *Conjunctions*, XII (Fall, 1988), 141-171, provides a keen synthesis of West's views on his own work, his teaching career, the writers whose work he admires, and the state of fiction. Of great value is West's beautifully written and richly informative autobiographical portrait in *Contemporary Authors*, Autobiography Series, Vol. 7, 1988.

Joseph F. Pestino

REBECCA WEST
Cicily Isabel Fairfield

Born: London, England
Date: December 21, 1892

Died: London, England
Date: March 15, 1983

PRINCIPAL WORKS

NOVELS AND NOVELLAS: *The Return of the Soldier*, 1918; *The Judge*, 1922; *Harriet Hume: A London Fantasy*, 1929; *War Nurse: The True Story of a Woman Who Lived and Loved on the Western Front*, 1930; *The Harsh Voice*, 1935; *The Thinking Reed*, 1936; *The Fountain Overflows*, 1956; *The Birds Fall Down*, 1966; *This Real Night*, 1984; *Cousin Rosamund*, 1985; *Sunflower*, 1986.

BIOGRAPHY: *St. Augustine*, 1933.

LITERARY CRITICISM: *Henry James*, 1916; *The Strange Necessity: Essays and Reviews*, 1928; *Ending in Earnest: A Literary Log*, 1931; *The Court and the Castle*, 1957.

TRAVEL SKETCH: *Black Lamb and Grey Falcon: Record of a Journey Through Yugoslavia in 1937*, 1941.

HISTORY: *The Meaning of Treason*, 1947 (revised as *The New Meaning of Treason*, 1965); *A Train of Powder*, 1955.

MEMOIRS: *Family Memories*, 1988.

JOURNALISM: *The Young Rebecca: Writings of Rebecca West*, 1982.

ANTHOLOGY: *Rebecca West: A Celebration*, 1977.

Rebecca West is best known for her contribution to nonfiction writing, in which she has shown a remarkable facility for blending the different genres of history, travel, biography, and literary criticism. Ranking just below her masterpieces such as *Black Lamb and Grey Falcon* and *The Meaning of Treason* are her works *The Fountain Overflows* and *The Birds Fall Down*. Indeed, it does her a disservice to separate her fiction and nonfiction, since all of her mature writing is informed by a strongly novelistic sensibility.

Rebecca West was born Cicily Isabel Fairfield. Her father, Charles Fairfield, was of Anglo-Irish descent and made something of a reputation for himself as a staunch defender of individualism in debates with George Bernard Shaw and Herbert Spencer, two of the most important and influential thinkers in Victorian England. When her father died in 1902, however, West found herself in rather straitened circumstances, one of four daughters whom her mother had somehow to support. She never forgot the feeling of shabbiness in her early years and by the age of nineteen was determined to make her mark as an actress, changing her name to Rebecca West after a character in Henrik Ibsen's play *Rosmersholm* (pb. 1886; English translation, 1889). West was soon advised, however, that she had minimal talent as an actress. Almost immediately she took up her pen as a militant feminist journalist daring to attack even the most advanced thinkers of her time, such as H. G. Wells, who eventually became her lover. She bore him a son, and they later parted in bitterness, with West feeling keenly the special burdens placed on women in male-dominated, double-standard societies.

In addition to West's feminist journalism (collected in *The Young Rebecca*), there is her searching criticism of Augustine, a highly sexed man and yet a saint, cushioned in life by his devoted mother and also a worldly man capable of abandoning a mistress of long standing once he dedicated himself to the Church. In her acclaimed *Black Lamb and Grey Falcon*, a travel account and historical study of the Balkans on the eve of World War II, various female characters are given dominant roles and West herself speaks in her own voice about her youthful impressions of Eastern Europe. Her husband, Henry Maxwell Andrews, accompanied her on this trip, and through his incisive contributions to the dialogue and his quietly supportive presence, it is clear that West found a male companion entirely comfortable with her formidable intelligence and restless quest to understand her time in history.

Many critics have doubted that there is a major theme or thread in West's work. In this they are misled by the many different genres in which she has written. In fact, in her fiction and nonfiction, West's concerns have been the same: war, treason, marriage—the institutions and events that bind society together or rend it apart. In her early novel *The Return of the Soldier*, two women (a wife and cousin) are perplexed by the return of their soldier, who in his shell-shocked state does not remember them but rather longs for a woman he loved many years earlier. The gap that suddenly opens up in his life and in theirs—between the loving husband and relative and his amnesiac alter ego, the young, impulsive lover of another woman from a lower social class—is evocative of West's effort to capture both the personal and historical dimensions of experience in the war-torn world of the twentieth century.

Whether writing about the Nuremberg Trials in *The Meaning of Treason* or about petty criminals in *A Train of Powder*, West conveys an extraordinary sense of the range of human society. She understands both the historical forces that inform individual actions and the peculiarities of individual behavior that her father so cherished. Some of her novels, it is thought, are overwhelmed by her intellectuality, but on balance she must be considered as one of the greatest imaginative minds of the twentieth century.

BIBLIOGRAPHICAL REFERENCES: Victoria Glendinning, *Rebecca West: A Life*, 1987, has written the first complete biography, which is elegantly written, carefully documented, and authorized by the author's estate. An earlier biographical study written with West's cooperation is Gordon N. Ray, *H. G. Wells and Rebecca West*, 1974. Other book-length studies of West's life and work include Motley F. Deakin, *Rebecca West*, 1980; Peter Wolfe, *Rebecca West: Artist and Thinker*, 1971; and George Evelyn Hutchinson, *A Preliminary List of the Writings of Rebecca West 1912-1951*, 1957. West's volume *Rebecca West: A Celebration*, 1977, with an introduction by Samuel Hynes, provides excellent selections, a critical overview of West's work, and a bibliography. Books that have chapters concentrating on West's writing are George Evelyn Hutchinson, *The Itinerant Ivory Tower*, 1953; Patrick Braybrooke, *Novelists: We Are Seven*, 1926; Joseph Collins, *The Doctor Looks at Literature*, 1923; and Grant Overton, *When Winter Comes to Main Street*, 1922.

Carl Rollyson

EDITH WHARTON

Born: New York, New York
Date: January 24, 1862

Died: St. Brice sous Forêt, France
Date: August 11, 1937

PRINCIPAL WORKS

NOVELS AND NOVELLAS: *The Touchstone*, 1900; *The Valley of Decision*, 1902; *Sanctuary*, 1903; *The House of Mirth*, 1905; *Madame de Treymes*, 1907; *The Fruit of the Tree*, 1907; *Ethan Frome*, 1911; *The Reef*, 1912; *The Custom of the Country*, 1913; *Summer*, 1917; *The Marne*, 1918; *The Age of Innocence*, 1920; *The Glimpses of the Moon*, 1922; *A Son at the Front*, 1923; *Old New York*, 1924; *The Mother's Recompense*, 1925; *Twilight Sleep*, 1927; *The Children*, 1928; *Hudson River Bracketed*, 1929; *The Gods Arrive*, 1932; *The Buccaneers*, 1938.

SHORT FICTION: *The Greater Inclination*, 1899; *Crucial Instances*, 1901; *The Descent of Man*, 1904; *The Hermit and the Wild Woman*, 1908; *Tales of Men and Ghosts*, 1910; *Xingu and Other Stories*, 1916; *Here and Beyond*, 1926; *Certain People*, 1930; *Human Nature*, 1933; *The World Over*, 1936; *Ghosts*, 1937; *The Collected Short Stories of Edith Wharton*, 1968.

AUTOBIOGRAPHY: *A Backward Glance*, 1934.

NONFICTION: *The Decoration of Houses*, 1897 (with Ogden Codman, Jr.); *Italian Villas and Their Gardens*, 1904; *Italian Backgrounds*, 1905; *A Motor-Flight Through France*, 1908; *Fighting France from Dunkerque to Belfort*, 1915; *French Ways and Their Meaning*, 1919; *In Morocco*, 1920; *The Writing of Fiction*, 1925.

POETRY: *Verses*, 1878; *Artemis to Actaeon*, 1909; *Twelve Poems*, 1926.

CORRESPONDENCE: *The Letters of Edith Wharton*, 1988.

Edith Newbold Jones Wharton is one of the masters of American realistic fiction. She was born in New York City on January 24, 1862, into a family that held a high place in New York society. Throughout her life, Wharton valued the refined manners and charms of fashionable society, but she was also deeply conscious of its superficiality and pettiness. By the time she was a teenager, private tutoring and extensive travel in Europe had made her fluent in German, French, and Italian as well as English. Wharton's writings frequently reveal her wide range of intellectual interests, which encompassed history, art, sociology, and science as well as literature. Her artistic and intellectual interests were not shared by Edward Wharton, the man she married on April 29, 1885. The couple spent much of each year in Europe, but they also lived in New York City and Newport, Rhode Island, and eventually in Lenox, Massachusetts. The unsatisfying nature of her married life, both physically and intellectually, may explain why the issues of marriage and divorce dominate many of her best novels and short stories.

After a nervous breakdown, Wharton turned to the writing of fiction in the mid-1890's, partly as a form of therapy. In 1878, a collection of her verse had been privately printed. Although Wharton tried her hand at poetry at other times, she was rarely more than a competent craftsman of conventional verse. Her collaboration with the architect Ogden Codman, Jr., in the writing of *The Decoration of Houses* reflected her interest in architectural form and interior design, an interest that also shapes her fiction, which frequently uses the description of rooms and houses as an index to a character's moral and social standing. Wharton published nonfiction at various points throughout her career, producing a number of impressive essays and reviews as well as several vivid books of travel. Her literary reputation, however, rests almost entirely on her fiction.

Wharton's early short stories and first novella, *The Touchstone*, won the admiration of many critics, although some thought that she was imitating Henry James too closely, and others complained of a lack of human warmth in her treatment of issues and characters. Her first long novel, *The Valley of Decision*, was an unsuccessful attempt to explore the social turmoil of Italian civilization at the dawn of the Napoleonic era. In 1905, Wharton won both popular and critical acclaim for *The House of Mirth*, which charts the moral development and social decline of Lily Bart. In 1907, Wharton moved to France, where, except for tours abroad and brief visits to the United States, she spent the rest of her life. The sharp contrast between French and American values is the subject of her novella *Madame De Treymes*. Less successful was her attempt to deal with social issues, most notably labor unrest and euthanasia, in *The Fruit of the Tree*. A passionate affair with Morton Fullerton hastened the collapse of Wharton's marriage, which finally ended in divorce in 1913. Wharton's literary reputation was enhanced by her continued triumphs in the short-story form, where her achievements ranged from powerful ghost stories to ironic masterpieces of social comedy.

The publication of *Ethan Frome* in 1911 showed decisively that Wharton's subjects were not limited to fashionable New York. In this novella, which some still rank as her best work, Wharton provided a powerfully tragic vision of a wasted life set within a New England rural landscape that is both emotionally stark and symbolically fascinating. Wharton engaged in other experiments with the novel form. *The Reef* is a densely textured psychological novel that is similar in some ways to the later novels of James. Her next novel, *The Custom of the Country*, is a satire that focuses on the pretensions of a pretty but vulgar young woman who destroys others in her rise to social prominence and wealth. The outbreak of World War I in 1914 led Wharton to charity work on behalf of the refugees who were crowding into her beloved Paris and to literary work, both fiction and nonfiction, in support of the Allied cause. Her two World War I novels, *The Marne* and *A Son at the Front*, are not highly regarded, but this period also saw the publication of *Summer*, a powerful novel about the seduction and betrayal of a New England girl, which can be seen as a passionate counterpart to the coldly delineated tragedy of *Ethan Frome*.

After the war, Wharton returned to the subject of New York society, attempting to capture its social history during the last three decades of the nineteenth century in *The Age of Innocence*, which won the Pulitzer Prize. The novel tells of Newland Archer, a dilettante whose infatuation with the vibrant Ellen Olenska threatens his engagement to the bland but virtuous May Welland. The four novellas that make up *Old New York* all deal with individuals in conflict with social values; the two that focus on women, *The Old Maid* and *New Year's Day*, are quite effective.

Wharton spent her final years at her two homes in France. A few critics have been interested in her portrayal of the literary artist Vance Weston in *Hudson River Bracketed* and *The Gods Arrive*, but the other novels written in the 1920's and 1930's have been generally dismissed. This period, however, also saw the composition of some of Wharton's finest short stories, her memoir *A Backward Glance*, and an attempt to define her literary principles in *The Writing of Fiction*. At the time of her death in 1937, there was some sentiment that Wharton may have been overrated, but the literary artistry of *The House of Mirth*, *Ethan Frome*, and *The Age of Innocence* continued to attract critics and readers. The publication of R. W. B. Lewis' biography in 1975 and the advent of feminist criticism aroused new interest in Wharton's life and works. She is now widely recognized as one of the two or three most important women writers of fiction in the literary history of the United States and praised as an artist who endowed the novel of manners with a remarkable blend of social analysis and psychological depth.

BIBLIOGRAPHICAL REFERENCES: R. W. B. Lewis, *Edith Wharton: A Biography*, 1975, was hailed upon publication as the definitive study of Wharton's life, although serious questions have been raised concerning the factual accuracy of Lewis' account. Louis Auchincloss, *Edith Wharton: A Woman in Her Time*, 1971, provides useful glimpses of her social milieu. Blake Nevius, *Edith Wharton: A Study of Her Fiction*, 1953, was the most perceptive of the critical studies written before Lewis' biography. Other useful earlier essays are collected in *Edith Wharton: A Collection of Critical Essays*, 1962, edited by Irving Howe. Later critical commentary has been gathered together in *Edith Wharton*, 1986, edited by Harold Bloom. The most widely praised critical study is the psychologically oriented *A Feast of Words: The Triumph of Edith Wharton*, 1977, by Cynthia Griffin Wolff. Other useful books include Millicent Bell, *Edith Wharton and Henry James*, 1965, and Margaret McDowell, *Edith Wharton*, 1976.

Alfred Bendixen

PATRICK WHITE

Born: London, England
Date: May 28, 1912

Principal Works

NOVELS: *Happy Valley,* 1939; *The Living and the Dead*, 1941; *The Aunt's Story,* 1948; *The Tree of Man*, 1955; *Voss*, 1957; *Riders in the Chariot*, 1961; *The Solid Mandala*, 1966; *The Vivisector,* 1970; *The Eye of the Storm*, 1973; *A Fringe of Leaves*, 1976; *The Twyborn Affair,* 1979; *Memoirs of Many in One*, 1986.

SHORT FICTION: *The Burnt Ones*, 1964; *The Cockatoos: Shorter Novels and Stories*, 1974.

PLAYS: *The Ham Funeral*, pr. 1961; *Four Plays*, pb. 1965; *Big Toys*, pr. 1977; *Signal Driver: A Morality Play for the Times*, pr. 1982; *Netherwood*, pr., pb. 1983.

AUTOBIOGRAPHY: *Flaws in the Glass: A Self-Portrait*, 1981.

Patrick Victor Martindale White is not only a major Australian novelist but also one of the outstanding English-language writers of the twentieth century. A second-generation Australian, he was born in London in 1912, when his parents were on a visit there. Both his parents belonged to landholding families in the Hunter Valley of New South Wales. After his early education in Australia, he took a degree in modern languages in England at the University of Cambridge. He returned to Australia to train for life as a pastoralist but was able to persuade his father to let him return to London in order to become a writer. His first novel, *Happy Valley,* was published in England in 1939. *The Living and the Dead* was hurriedly completed in America when White was recalled to England for war service, and it is accordingly the least satisfactory of his novels. *The Aunt's Story,* begun in England but completed en route to Australia after the war, represents a major advance and is one of his two best novels. (*The Eye of the Storm*, written twenty-five years later, is the other.)

After settling in Australia, White entered his major creative period. Believing that Australia lacked a spiritual dimension, he tried to provide that in his next two novels, writing about the two great Australian movements, the pioneer settlement of the land in *The Tree of Man* and the exploration of the continent in *Voss*. Though perhaps not his best novel, *Voss* is often and validly considered the Great Australian Novel. *The Tree of Man* brought world attention to White, and his reputation continued to rise with *Voss* and *Riders in the Chariot*, his most ambitious novel, embracing Judaism as well as Christianity, Europe as well as Australia, and aboriginal as well as Caucasian aspects of Australian life.

The Solid Mandala marks the beginning of White's decline, which continued with the publication of *The Vivisector.* His achievement was such, however, that he was already a strong contender for the Nobel Prize in Literature when *The Vivisector* appeared. The Nobel Prize committee looked with disfavor upon the negative portrait of an artist in *The Vivisector* (the artist dissects his subjects for his own purposes), and it may be this disfavor that spurred White on to a recovery of his powers in *The Eye of the Storm*, the novel that secured for him the Nobel Prize in 1973, the first time that the award was given to an English-language writer outside the United Kingdom or the United States. Yet the Nobel Prize seems to have constrained White, as it has so many laureates, for the novels that followed *The Eye of the Storm* are rather slight or unattractive. *A Fringe of Leaves* tells a good story well but is one of White's less important works, while *The Twyborn Affair* and *Memoirs of Many in One* are decidedly strange and unprepossessing. White later announced that he had finished writing.

White has written two volumes of short stories but shows no special talent for short fiction. His short stories lack the spiritual dimension of his novels and reveal his less pleasant side. They show at times a derisive enjoyment of the characters' distress and an interest in disturbed states of mind. White also wrote a number of plays, the theater being his first love. His early plays might have had more significance had they been performed when they were written—*The Ham Funeral* is an early and interesting example of what was later called the Theater of the Absurd—but the delay has lessened their impact and discouraged White's theatrical career. Late in his life, with his reputation established, he again turned to the theater, but the late plays are marred either by a heavy moralizing or a certain vulgarity.

It is as a novelist and especially as one of the great stylists of the English language that White will be remembered. He has written at least four major novels (*The Aunt's Story*, *The Tree of Man*, *Voss*, and *The Eye of the Storm*) and one flawed masterpiece (*Riders in the Chariot*), an achievement few novelists in English can equal. White's novels were concerned very early with establishing an arbitrary and unclear distinction between the living and the dead (the title of his second novel) or the elect and the nonelect. Mostly his elect are social outsiders with some special gift of perception or creativity—visionaries of a kind. Among their ranks are Theodora Goodman, Stan Parker, Laura Trevelyan, the four riders in the chariot, Arthur Brown, Hurtle Duffield, and Elizabeth Hunter. A corollary of this theme is his series of Christ figures, of whom Voss is the first and Arthur Brown the last. After *The Solid Mandala*, White's elect figures are stripped of their association with Christ and accorded merely human status, with some unpleasant characteristics, such as those of Hurtle Duffield and Elizabeth Hunter.

One becomes aware in a number of White's novels of an ongoing battle between the protagonist and his or her mother or a mother figure. That is most obviously the case in *The Aunt's Story*, *Voss*, *The Eye of the Storm*, and *The Twyborn Affair*. *The Eye of the Storm* contains the greatest elevation of the mother in Elizabeth Hunter (a thinly disguised version of White's own mother) and the greatest self-abasement of her offspring; however White's growing self-disgust had already manifested itself in *The Solid Mandala*. This self-disgust is developed at greater length in the portrait of the artist in *The Vivisector* and resumed in the two novels *The Twyborn Affair* and *Memoirs of Many in One*. There is no mellowing or maturing in the late White, only disintegration. His best work was done in the years 1948 to 1960; after that date, *The Eye of the Storm* shows a resurgence of his massive talents.

BIBLIOGRAPHICAL REFERENCES: John Colmer, *Patrick White*, 1984, is a good succinct introduction to White. Carolyn Bliss, *Patrick White's Fiction*, 1985, provides an incisive overview of White that is unlikely to be surpassed. David Tacey, *Patrick White: Fiction and the Unconscious*, 1988, applies Jungian archetypical analysis to White's fiction. For a discussion of travel in White's writing, see Peter Knox-Shaw, *The Explorer in English Fiction*, 1987. John A. Weigel, *Patrick White*, 1983, is a helpful introductory volume in the Twayne World Authors series. See also Mari-Ann Berg, *Aspects of Time, Ageing, and Old Age in the Novels of Patrick White, 1939-1979*, 1983; Peter Wolfe, *Laden Choirs: The Fiction of Patrick White*, 1983; Karin Hansson, *The Warped Universe: A Study of Imagery and Structure in Seven Novels by Patrick White*, 1983; A. M. McCulloch, *A Tragic Vision: The Novels of Patrick White*, 1983; Hilary Hetay, *The Articles and the Novelist: Reference Conventions and Reader Manipulations in Patrick White's Creation of Fictional Worlds*, 1983; May-Brit Ackerholt, *Patrick White*, 1988; R. F. Brissenden, "The Plays of Patrick White," *Meanjin Quarterly*, XXIII (September, 1964), 243-256; and J. F. Burrows, "Patrick White's Four Plays," *Australian Literary Studies*, II (June, 1966), 155-170.

John B. Beston

JOHN WHITING

Born: Salisbury, England
Date: November 15, 1917

Died: Duddleswell, England
Date: June 16, 1963

Principal Works

PLAYS: *Paul Southman*, pr. 1946 (radio play), pr. 1965 (staged); *A Penny for a Song*, pr. 1951; *Saint's Day*, pr. 1951; *Marching Song*, pr., pb. 1954; *The Gates of Summer*, pr. 1956; *A Walk in the Desert*, pr. 1960 (teleplay); *The Devils*, pr., pb. 1961; *Conditions of Agreement*, pr. 1965; *The Collected Plays of John Whiting*, pb. 1969; *No More A-Roving*, pr. 1975.

RADIO PLAYS: *Eye Witness*, 1949; *The Stairway*, 1949; *Love's Old Sweet Song*, 1950.

SCREENPLAYS: *The Ship That Died of Shame*, 1955 (with Michael Relph and Basil Dearden); *The Good Companions*, 1957 (with T. J. Morrison and J. L. Hodgson); *The Captain's Table*, 1959 (with Bryan Forbes and Nicholas Phipps); *Young Cassidy*, 1965.

MISCELLANEOUS: *The Art of the Dramatist and Other Pieces*, 1969.

John Robert Whiting, while virtually unknown to general audiences, is recognized by serious critics as a major force in twentieth century drama. He was born in Salisbury, England, on November 15, 1917, the son of a retired army officer turned lawyer. An indifferent student who claimed that he "had never passed an examination," Whiting left his upper-middle-class schooling at age seventeen to train as an actor at the Royal Academy of Dramatic Art. With the outbreak of World War II, he enlisted in the Royal Artillery. After marrying actress Jackie Mawson in 1940, he returned to acting at the end of the war, joining John Gielgud's company in 1951.

In spite of this lengthy association with the theater, Whiting exhibited no interest in writing plays until a casual conversation with a friend in 1946 inspired him to make the attempt. During the following five years he wrote four plays—half of his entire canon of stage drama—as well as four radio plays for the British Broadcasting Corporation. His first stage play was *A Penny for a Song*, a comedy set during the Napoleonic Wars. Directed by Peter Brook, it was performed in March, 1951. A vivid, theatrical play, it traces the rise and fall of Sir Timothy Humpage as he attempts to preserve happiness and a sense of purpose—illusions for Whiting—at the expense of self-deception. "We find reality unbearable. . . . And so we escape, childlike, into the illusion," one of the characters says. In September of 1951, his second stage play, *Saint's Day*, was performed at the Arts Theatre Club. It closed after three weeks amid hostile popular criticism and audience rejection, a pattern which was to continue during most of Whiting's life. With a central theme of self-destruction, the play sets forth in bleak terms the tragedy of the elderly poet Paul Southman, who had isolated himself and his family from the local community. In this dense, dark play, Southman learns, "We are here—all of us—to die. Nothing more than that."

Whiting's next play, *Marching Song*, appeared in 1954. Describing it as formally austere and antitheatrical, Whiting used the figure of General Rupert Forster, who was guilty of war crimes involving the slaughter of children, to present images of death and violence, underscoring the nihilistic forces operating in the universe. Whiting wrote no more full-length stage plays until 1960, a withdrawal directly resulting from negative reactions to his work. He did, however, write many screenplays.

In 1960, Whiting was invited to write *The Devils*, an adaptation of Aldous Huxley's book *The Devils of Loudun* (1952). Successfully performed in 1961, the play explored the diabolic possession of a group of nuns through the influence of a charismatic priest named Grandier, who was horribly tortured. Another of Whiting's self-destructive characters, he was a tragic figure, flawed by his refusal to accept responsibility for his actions. Epic in style, the play achieved its effects through a relentless series of visual and verbal grotesqueries, stressing that "the purpose of man [is] loneliness and death."

John Whiting's death by cancer on June 16, 1963, abruptly ended his reestablished dramatic career. Other plays discovered among his papers and performed posthumously include *Conditions of Agreement* and *No More A-Roving*, both written in 1946.

All Whiting's best plays, the editor Simon Trussler has suggested, are "most readily understood as parables and paradigms of human behavior." Whiting was concerned with exploring the human soul in its abstracted, self-destructive preoccupation with the processes of dying. At the center of his plays stand tormented men who are caught in webs of unmotivated cruelty. In their isolation, they radiate hatred toward others and especially toward themselves. Southman, in *Saint's Day*, and Forster, in *Marching Song*, commit suicide; Grandier, in *The Devils*, provokes others to torture him to death. The structures of Whiting's plays are marked by density, austerity, and ambiguity; the tone is dark and pessimistic. Whiting characteristically uses potent and provocative stage pictures to frame the words of the text, as in the opening scene of *The Devils* in which a corpse hangs from the gallows and a sewer worker labors in his pit.

During his lifetime, Whiting's plays were neither popular nor the subject of much literary criticism. He allied himself with the tradition of the intellectual elite, writing plays that were obscure and difficult even for a discriminating audience. Embedded within his theater were structural and thematic references and allusions that were often part of a private mythology. Yet in his recurrent concern with the nature of violence and the limits of personal responsibility, Whiting anticipated the work of later writers. In his utilization of Brechtian techniques in *The Devils*, he paved the way for further experimentations in the theater. Whiting's contributions to the development of British theater were significant, although they have been underestimated. In 1965, the Arts Council of Great Britain instituted the John Whiting Award, an annual stipend given to younger British dramatists whose work is only beginning to be known.

BIBLIOGRAPHICAL REFERENCES: Simon Trussler, *The Plays of John Whiting*, 1972, is a brief, well-written overview of the plays. In *John Whiting*, 1969, Ronald Hayman deals with the biography as well as the works. Eric Salmon, *The Dark Journey: John Whiting as Dramatist*, 1979, is the most comprehensive book of criticism on Whiting. Salmon deals in depth with the biography and with unpublished manuscripts. He also corrects the dating of the plays listed in the earlier works. See also Jacqueline Hoefer, "Pinter and Whiting: Two Attitudes Towards the Alienated Artist," *Modern Drama*, IV (February, 1962), 402-408; John Dennis Hurrell, "John Whiting and the Theme of Self-Destruction," *Modern Drama*, VIII (September, 1965), 131-141; Charles R. Lyons, "The Futile Encounter in the Plays of John Whiting," *Modern Drama*, XI (December, 1968), 283-298; Tom Milne, "The Hidden Face of Violence," reprinted in *The Encore Reader: A Chronicle of the New Drama*, 1965, edited by Charles Marowitz et al.; J. C. Trewin, "Two Morality Playwrights: Robert Bolt and John Whiting," in *Experimental Drama*, 1963, edited by William A. Armstrong; Simon Trussler, "The Plays of John Whiting," *Tulane Drama Review*, XI (Winter, 1966), 141-151; Gabrielle Scott Robinson, "Beyond the Waste Land: An Interpretation of John Whiting's *Saint's Day*," *Modern Drama*, XIV (February, 1972), 463-477, and "The Shavian Affinities of John Whiting," *Shaw Review*, XVII (1974), 86-98; and Jane Goodall, "Musicality and Meaning in the Dialogue of *Saint's Day*," *Modern Drama*, XXIX (December, 1986), 567-579.

Lori Hall Burghardt

BENJAMIN LEE WHORF

Born: Winthrop, Massachusetts
Date: April 24, 1897

Died: Wethersfield, Connecticut
Date: July 26, 1941

PRINCIPAL WORKS

ESSAYS: "An Aztec Account of the Period of the Toltec Decline," 1928; "A Central Mexican Inscription Combining Mexican and Maya Day Signs," 1932; "The Phonetic Value of Certain Characters in Maya Writing," 1933; "The Punctual and Segmentative Aspects of Verbs in Hopi," 1936; "Some Verbal Categories of Hopi," 1938; "Science and Linguistics," 1940; "Linguistics as an Exact Science," 1940; "The Relation of Habitual Thought and Behavior to Language," 1941; "Languages and Logic," 1941; "Language, Mind, and Reality," 1942; *Language, Thought, and Reality: Selected Writings*, 1956.

When he died in 1941, Benjamin Lee Whorf's work was little known outside a limited circle of linguists, but his reputation as a powerful and influential thinker has since grown considerably. Born into an unusually eclectic and artistic suburban Boston household, he lived virtually all of his adult life in central Connecticut. Like his fellow Greater Hartford area resident Wallace Stevens, Whorf pursued a highly successful career in the insurance field at the same time that he pursued other, more literary, interests. He has become best known for his development of the theory of linguistic relativity, the idea that the basic structural qualities of a given culture's language largely determine the fundamental character of that society.

Educated in Winthrop public schools, Whorf was graduated from the Massachusetts Institute of Technology (MIT) with a bachelor of science in chemical engineering in the fall of 1918. Early the following year, he accepted a position as a trainee with the Hartford Fire Insurance Company and advanced rapidly in the new field of fire prevention engineering from special agent to assistant secretary, the position he held at the time of his death. An interest in fundamentalist religion seems to have driven his study of language; in the early 1920's, after he had married and established residence in the Hartford area, he began to teach himself Hebrew so that he could better understand biblical tradition. His interest in the qualities of a language which might influence cultures using that language soon led him to study other languages, including Mayan and Aztec.

As he advanced in the insurance business, so did his "hobby" of linguistic analysis prosper. His first published article, "An Aztec Account of the Period of the Toltec Decline," attracted considerable attention among linguists and students of Indian culture. Whorf more firmly established his growing reputation as a brilliant translator of hieroglyphs with published work on the Mayan civilization. Beginning to emerge from this early work were developing statements on the nature of some languages as being derived largely from a limited number of stems, or from a slightly larger group of morphemes (the smallest individual units of meaning in a language). Whorf's developing fascination with the puzzles of Aztec and Mayan culture was partially satisfied in 1930, when he won funding from the Social Sciences Research Council to travel to central Mexico and spend time in areas where the inhabitants still used a language and observed other cultural practices very close to the ancient Aztec language and traditions.

Following the period of his fellowship, in which he pursued anthropological and architectural as well as cultural and linguistic researches, Whorf worked diligently at organizing and arranging his data. In 1931, the renowned linguist Edward Sapir accepted an appointment at Yale University; Whorf immediately enrolled in order to study American Indian linguistics under Sapir. Sapir's study *Language* (1921) emphasized the tremendous potential inherent in language as social determinant and in grammar as the basis of poetry. In some of his work, Sapir was following the lead of Franz Boas, the pioneering linguist whose *Handbook of*

American Indian Languages (1911) was the first American work to demonstrate how language patterns—most important, grammatical patterns—which underlie a culture might actually determine much of that culture. Such study of interrelations among language, thought, and culture provided the basis of the theory of linguistic relativity and led to its being called the "Sapir-Whorf hypothesis" or the "Whorfian hypothesis." When Whorf's fascination with Indian ethnography was tempered by the stabilizing influence of Sapir's disciplined linguistic precision, he began to do his greatest work.

From 1935 to his death, Whorf worked feverishly at publishing his ideas. Articles on Hopi Indians demonstrated how the Hopi's unique grammar underlay a highly unusual conception of the universe. He was able to show how the Hopi are concerned largely with space, while Indo-European languages emphasize temporal concerns. From observing how such an orientation can be detected in the organization of the different societies, Whorf drew conclusions on the psychological potential of sounds and grammars. His article "The Relation of Habitual Thought and Behavior to Language," written in 1939 and published in 1941, offers his most developed statement of how the syntax, grammar, and characteristic thought construction of a language determine the way that its speakers conceive of the universe in which they exist. Though he was suffering from lung cancer the last two years of his life, he worked until his death at expanding his statements regarding linguistic relativity into a book, the projected title of which—"Language, Thought, and Reality"—was used for a collection of his works published posthumously.

BIBLIOGRAPHICAL REFERENCES: *Language, Thought, and Reality*, 1956, edited by John B. Carroll, is the most useful single work on Whorf. Carroll provides critical and biographical introductions and, in addition to Whorf's major essays, publishes for the first time many of Whorf's other writings from various stages of his career. A useful later study is Joel Sherzer, "A Discourse-Centered Approach to Language and Culture," *American Anthropologist*, LXXXIX (1987), 295-309, which considers Whorf's ideas in relation to contemporary discourse theory. Another study which brings to bear later theoretical schools is Mark A. Clarke et al., "Linguistic Relativity and Sex/Gender Studies: Epistemological and Methodological Considerations," *Language Learning*, XXXIV (1984), 34-74. A general introduction which does not contain a bibliography is Peter Farb, "How Do I Know You Mean What You Mean?" *Horizon*, X (1968), 52-57. A study which places linguistic relativity in relation to other linguistic theories is Alan S. Kaye, "Schools of Linguistics: Competition and Evolution," *Studies in Language*, X (1986), 187-199. See also "The Sapir-Whorf Hypothesis," in Geoffrey Sampson, *Schools of Linguistics*, 1980; "Subjective, Objective, and Conceptual Relativisms," in Maurice H. Mandelbaum, *Philosophy, History, and the Sciences: Selected Critical Essays*, 1984; J. H. Stam, "An Historical Perspective on 'Linguistic Relativity,'" in *Psychology of Language and Thought*, 1980, edited by R. W. Reiber; Terry Kit-Fong Au, "Chinese and English Counterfactuals: The Sapir-Whorf Hypothesis Revisited," *Cognition*, XV (1983), 155-187; and T. D. Crawford, "Plato's Reasoning and the Sapir-Whorf Hypothesis," *Metaphilosophy*, XIII (1982), 217-227.

Peter Valenti

JOHN EDGAR WIDEMAN

Born: Washington, D.C.
Date: June 14, 1941

PRINCIPAL WORKS

NOVELS: *A Glance Away*, 1967; *Hurry Home*, 1970; *The Lynchers*, 1973; *Hiding Place*, 1981; *Sent for You Yesterday*, 1983; *The Homewood Trilogy*, 1985 (includes *Damballah*, *Hiding Place*, *Sent for You Yesterday*); *Reuben*, 1987.
SHORT FICTION: *Damballah*, 1981.
MEMOIRS: *Brothers and Keepers*, 1984.

John Edgar Wideman's literary achievements since the publication of his first novel, *A Glance Away*, provide a compelling example of the diverse cultural and creative influences operating within the imaginations of contemporary black authors. Having grown up in the black community of Homewood in Pittsburgh, Pennsylvania, Wideman began his odyssey away from those roots—a central theme of his writing—when in 1959 he was awarded a Benjamin Franklin scholarship to the University of Pennsylvania, where he became a Phi Beta Kappa scholar and distinguished himself in creative writing and intercollegiate basketball. His assimilation into the world of academe continued when, as a Rhodes Scholar, he attended New College, Oxford, from 1963 to 1966 and as a student of English examined the origins of the novel, particularly eighteenth century innovations such as Laurence Sterne's *The Life and Opinions of Tristram Shandy, Gent.* (1759-1767), which furthered his interest in the possibilities of contemporary narrative form.

Wideman received a Kent Fellowship to the Iowa Writers' Workshop at the University of Iowa in 1966. Since 1967, he has served on the faculties of several universities, including the University of Pennsylvania, the University of Wyoming, and the University of Massachusetts, Amherst. As a novice teacher of Afro-American Studies at the University of Pennsylvania, he immersed himself for the first time in the complex literary tradition forged by black American writers, an experience he claims "absolutely transformed" his subsequent creative endeavors. Wideman's prose experimentation synthesizes and comments upon twentieth century aesthetic concerns. His early works, *A Glance Away*, *Hurry Home*, and *The Lynchers*, are stylistically indebted to T. S. Eliot, James Joyce, and William Faulkner, for they share modernist preoccupations with myth and ritual, fractured narrative, surreality, and polyphonic voicings. Yet Wideman also demonstrates a postmodernist affinity for fantasy and other modes of imaginative entry into the convoluted reality constructions of the psyche, seeing such means as an expressive medium for conveying the incoherencies of daily life, particularly the jarring and irreconcilable paradoxes of racism. Although not restricting himself to realist or naturalistic tableaux that elicit moral outrage, Wideman has made the black American experience the locus of his creative exploration and postmodernist experimentation his means of investigating the essential conundrum of racial categorization itself.

Many of Wideman's fictional techniques express his belief in the accessibility of a collective racial memory transcending temporal and spatial divisions through the sustaining energies provided by family, community, or culture. His aim is to expose the inner dynamics propelling his characters' lives and to articulate that mystery through the creation of a chorus of distinct but overlapping private voices whose thoughts assume the immediacy of speech. Wideman's efforts to fuse a novelistic whole from seemingly disparate narrative strands in such works as the PEN/Faulkner Award-winning *Sent for You Yesterday* or *Reuben* rest in part upon a similar theoretical supposition that from fragmentation the imagination can generate potentially healing linkages and echoes, an activity always bathed in postmodernist suspicion that the cloudiness of human vision isolates one completely from real communion with others.

Wideman has achieved the loudest critical acclaim for *The Homewood Trilogy*, comprising a short-story collection, *Damballah*, and two novels, *Hiding Place* and *Sent for You Yesterday*. Set in the Homewood of his youth, Wideman's imaginative return to his cultural past is a journey through which he explores the intricate and mysterious interweavings of history, memory, and tradition. *Damballah* and *Hiding Place*, published concurrently, offer fictive meditations on the multigenerational past of a black family as it recapitulates the social history of Homewood itself. *Sent for You Yesterday*, the culminating work in the series, draws its title from a blues song and itself becomes a "blues" rendering of Homewood's history as it has been mythically sustained in the collective memory of the community and particularized in the integrative imagination of the narrator.

With the publication of *Brothers and Keepers*, Wideman made explicit the links between his biography and the fictional plottings of his previous work, particularly *The Homewood Trilogy*. In *Brothers and Keepers*, Wideman steps out from behind the mask of fiction to write a painfully analytic and introspective first-person account of his relationship with Robby (his brother, Robert Wideman), a former drug addict and petty criminal serving a life sentence in prison. Although nonfiction, the book employs a familiar array of Wideman's literary devices: a sophisticated alternation of voices shifting between formal English and street colloquialism, a dislocated chronology and colliding narrative forms, a metafictional foregrounding, and a dissection of the creative process itself and its power to obscure and slant far more effectively than it can elucidate or represent. The themes that dominate Wideman's fiction also operate in this text, particularly the power of family and community to support the individual, and the countervailing pressures working to erode the cultural health of the black community and the faith of even its most resilient members.

The family tragedy surrounding Wideman since the 1970's deepened in 1988, when his eighteen-year-old son Jacob was convicted of murdering a teenage traveling companion and received a life sentence in the Arizona prison system. Wideman's career-long meditations upon the mysteries of human character in and above its social milieu thus have profound and haunting personal dimensions that explain the power of his creative investigations.

BIBLIOGRAPHICAL REFERENCES: The discussion with John Wideman in John O'Brien, *Interviews with Black Writers*, 1973, provides a solid introduction to Wideman's concerns as a literary artist; it is complemented by Wilfred D. Samuels, "Going Home: A Conversation with John Edgar Wideman," *Callaloo*, VI (1983), 40-59. Several overviews of his fiction extending through *Sent for You Yesterday* have appeared: James W. Coleman, "The Literary Development of John Edgar Wideman," *CLA Journal*, XXVIII (1985), 326-343; Jacqueline Berben, "Beyond Discourse: The Unspoken Versus Words in the Fiction of John Edgar Wideman," *Callaloo*, VIII (1985), 525-534; and Bernard W. Bell, "The Contemporary Afro-American Novel, 2: Modernism and Postmodernism—John Wideman," in *The Afro-American Novel and Its Tradition*, 1987. Kermit Frazier, "The Novels of John Wideman: An Analysis," *Black World*, XXIV (1975), 18-38, examines Wideman's early career. John Bennion, "The Shape of Memory in John Edgar Wideman's *Sent for You Yesterday*," *Black American Literature Forum*, XX (1985), 143-150, examines that novel's complex narrative experiments. Michael G. Cooke offers a brief analysis of *Damballah* in *Afro-American Literature in the Twentieth Century*, 1984. Wideman's own brief discussion of the logic of *The Homewood Trilogy* introduces the Avon paperback of that work (1985). See also Ishmael Reed, "Of One Blood, Two Men: *Brothers and Keepers*," *The New York Times Book Review*, November 4, 1984, 1, for a review of that work. Michael Gorra, "American Selves," *The Hudson Review*, XLI (1988), 407-408, reviews *Reuben* as a superior example of postmodernist prose; Walter Kendrick assesses it less kindly in *The New York Times Book Review*, November 8, 1987, 3.

Barbara Kitt Seidman

RUDY WIEBE

Born: October 4, 1934
Date: Fairholme, Saskatechewan, Canada

PRINCIPAL WORKS

NOVELS: *Peace Shall Destroy Many,* 1962; *First and Vital Candle*, 1966; *The Blue Mountains of China*, 1970; *The Temptations of Big Bear,* 1973; *The Scorched-Wood People*, 1977; *The Mad Trapper,* 1980; *My Lovely Enemy,* 1983.

PLAY: *Far as the Eye Can See*, pr., pb. 1977.

SHORT FICTION: *Where Is the Voice Coming From?*, 1974; *Alberta: A Celebration*, 1979; *The Angel of the Tar Sands and Other Stories*, 1982.

Rudy Wiebe was born in 1934 on his family's farm in a small Mennonite community in Fairholme, Saskatchewan; his parents were émigrés from the Soviet Union. Wiebe began writing seriously during his undergraduate years at the University of Alberta (1953-1956) and took an M.A. in creative writing from that institution in 1960. He has held various teaching posts since that time, including one at Goshen College, Indiana (1964-1967), but in 1967 he began teaching full-time as a professor of English at the University of Alberta. It is Wiebe's work as a novelist that has given him his fine reputation in his native land, though he has also carved out a formidable career as a short-story writer, playwright, and editor/critic. He has candidly described himself as "one who tries to explore the world that I know, the land and people of Western Canada, from my particular worldview: a radical Jesus-oriented Christianity." To perform this function, Wiebe has characteristically chosen experimental modes of narration, particularly the use of multiple, omniscient narrators, whose cacophonous voices establish the theme that the struggle for personal identity is resolvable only through wrestling with one's family and cultural past. As Wiebe explains, "I believe fiction must be precisely, peculiarly rooted in a particular place, in particular people." His first language was Low German, and this cultural background—coupled with his devout Mennonite faith—forms the thematic landscape in which his fiction is constructed. He has thus come to be widely praised as one of Canada's most innovative "Prairie" writers.

The characters in Wiebe's first three novels share the common plight of being "strangers in a strange land," a religious remnant fighting for their faith and family identity in a modern world gone mad. Mennonite Christianity, evolving out of the radical Anabaptist tradition, is a fiercely independent faith that demands of its practitioners a separation from the world, compelling them to leave their native land, customs, and language in search of a country where they can live out their faith. Wiebe's first novel, *Peace Shall Destroy Many,* the title of which alludes to the Book of Daniel, is an ironic juxtaposition of two men's wartime legalism and arrogance: the arrogant militarism of Adolf Hitler and the arrogant pacifism of Deacon Block, a Western Canadian Mennonite. Welcomed by critics for its evocation of time and place but equally criticized for its overt moralizing, this novel served notice that a new, yet unharnessed narrative power had emerged in Canadian letters. *First and Vital Candle* and *The Blue Mountains of China* both extend and display Wiebe's unique narrative powers, again focusing on the theme of living out the Christian vision of society and culture when the signs, symbols, and very language of Christianity are seen as defunct and irrelevant. The former novel contains powerful evocations and celebrations of American Indian and Eskimo life, filtered through the consciousness of Abe Ross, a man in search of his lost faith. In *The Blue Mountains of China*, Wiebe experiments further with his quasi-epic mode of narration. The novel has no conventional plot; each chapter is a somewhat self-contained and idiosyncratic account of the events, relationships, and inner thoughts of five principal characters, all Mennonites searching for the "land God had given them for their very own, to which they were called." Wiebe's epigraph to *The Blue Mountains of China* perhaps serves as a sardonic reminder of the common thread running through all of his novels: "They are still trying to find [this land], and it isn't anywhere on earth."

Native Western Canadians—the American Indians and Eskimos of Manitoba, Saskatchewan, and parts farther north—often populate Wiebe's fiction because they represent spiritual values markedly different from those of the world which has displaced them. The otherness and isolation characteristic of the radical Mennonite Christian community which Wiebe has attempted to chronicle are often mirrored in these non-Christian characters as well, who are themselves outcasts and wayfarers when measured against the mind-set of their times. That is certainly the case with Wiebe's next novel, one of his most important, *The Temptations of Big Bear*, for which he received the Canadian Governor General's Literary Award in 1973. Here Wiebe fictionalizes the life and times of the great Prairie Indian chief Big Bear, who suffers, along with his tribe, the fate of all those who attempt to fight against the treacheries of the modern world, and the ethnocentrism of its leaders and social planners. Wiebe's 1977 novel *The Scorched-Wood People* will most likely be regarded as his masterpiece. Wiebe novelistically investigates the historical particulars surrounding the subjugation of the Metis, a proud people of mixed French and Indian descent. In a radical indictment of the prevailing Scottish and English Canadian politics, Wiebe depicts the Metis as a people better equipped to rule their land because of their close connection with their heritage. In contrast, white Canada is seen as thoroughly cut off from its own Christian heritage, as a consequence of which it has been guilty of cultural imperialism on a vast scale.

Wiebe has been criticized by some critics as too easily falling into didacticism and employing a sometimes opaque style, but the strong Christian viewpoint which permeates all of his writing is presented engagingly and without distracting sermonizing. Wiebe shares with such fellow Canadian writers as Alice Munro and Robertson Davies a keen eye for the distinctiveness of Canadian life and landscape and remains one of North America's most eloquent and gifted fiction writers. Wiebe's international reputation can only grow as twentieth century fiction writers and critics continue to cast their attention on the life and meaning of the disfranchised indigenous peoples of North America.

BIBLIOGRAPHICAL REFERENCES: Patricia Morely's early work, *The Comedians: Hugh Hood and Rudy Wiebe*, 1977, is a helpful comparison of the work of these two Canadian novelists, but two of the best book-length critical works on Wiebe are W. J. Keith, *Epic Fiction: The Art of Rudy Wiebe*, 1981, and *A Voice in the Land: Essays By and About Rudy Wiebe*, 1981, edited by W. J. Keith. A valuable interview with Wiebe is found in Donald Cameron, *Conversations with Canadian Novelists*, Vol. 2, 1973, while Magdalene Redekop, "Rudy Wiebe," in *Profiles in Canadian Literature*, Vol. 2, 1981, edited by Jeffrey Heath, provides essential biographical material. Two articles which are particularly insightful in their analysis of Wiebe's religious worldview and the way it informs his fiction are R. P. Bilan, "Wiebe and Religious Struggle," *Canadian Literature*, LXXVII (Summer, 1978), 50-63, and Ina Ferris, "Religious Vision and Fiction Form: Rudy Wiebe's *The Blue Mountains of China*," *Mosaic: A Journal for the Study of Literature and Ideas*, XI (Spring, 1978), 79-85. Two articles that deal with the larger thematic issues considered in Wiebe's fiction are Francis Manbridge, "Wiebe's Sense of Community," *Canadian Literature*, LXXVII (Summer, 1978), 42-49, and Hildegard E. Tiessen, "A Mighty Inner River: 'Peace' in the Fiction of Rudy Wiebe," *Canadian Forum*, II (Fall, 1973), 71-76. See also *The Canadian Novel: Here and Now*, 1978, edited by John Moss; George Woodcock, "Riel and Dumont," *Canadian Literature*, LXXVII (Summer, 1978), 98-100; and Sam Solecki, "Giant Fictions and Large Meanings: The Novels of Rudy Wiebe," *Canadian Forum*, LX (March, 1981).

Bruce L. Edwards

ELIE WIESEL

Born: Sighet, Transylvania
Date: September 30, 1928

Principal Works

NOVELS AND NOVELLAS: *L'Aube*, 1960 (*Dawn*, 1961); *Le Jour*, 1961 (*The Accident*, 1962); *La Ville de la chance*, 1962 (*The Town Beyond the Wall*, 1964); *Les Portes de la forêt*, 1964 (*The Gates of the Forest*, 1966); *Le Mendiant de Jérusalem*, 1968 (*A Beggar in Jerusalem*, 1970); *Le Serment de Kolvillàg*, 1973 (*The Oath*, 1973); *Testament d'un poète juif assassiné*, 1980 (*The Testament*, 1981); *Le Cinquième Fils*, 1983 (*The Fifth Son*, 1985); *Le Crépuscule, au loin*, 1987 (*Twilight*, 1988).

PLAYS: *Zalmen: Ou, La Folie de Dieu*, pb. 1968 (*Zalmen: Or, The Madness of God*, 1974); *Le Procès de Shamgorod tel qu'il se déroula de 25 février 1649*, pb. 1979 (*The Trial of God: As It Was Held on February 25, 1649, in Shamgorod*, 1979).

MEMOIRS: *Un di Velt hot geshvign*, 1956 (*La Nuit*, 1958; *Night*, 1960).

TRAVEL SKETCH: *Les Juifs du silence*, 1966 (*The Jews of Silence*, 1966).

MISCELLANEOUS: *Entre-deux soleils*, 1970 (*One Generation After*, 1970); *Ani Maamin: Un Chant perdu et retrouvé*, 1973 (*Ani Maamin: A Song Lost and Found Again*, 1973); *Contre la mélancolie*, 1978 (*Four Hasidic Masters and Their Struggle Against Melancholy*, 1978); *Images from the Bible*, 1980; *Five Biblical Portraits*, 1981; *Somewhere a Master*, 1982; *Discours d'Oslo*, 1987; *The Six Days of Destruction: Meditations Towards Hope*, 1988 (with Albert H. Friedlander).

Eliezer (Elie) Wiesel was born in Sighet, Transylvania, on September 30, 1928. His early education was completely within Jewish tradition; he attended a religious primary school (*heder*) and then went to a local *yeshiva* for Torah and Talmudic studies. In 1944, at the age of sixteen, Wiesel was interned in several German concentration camps, where his mother and father and his younger sister all perished. Upon his release from Buchenwald in April, 1945, he went to France as a displaced person. Within three years, after working as a choir director and Bible teacher, he was able to begin university studies at the Sorbonne, where he majored in philosophy, literature, and psychology.

Wiesel's first work involved journalism. As a writer for French newspapers covering Israel's 1948 war for independence and related Middle Eastern events, he traveled extensively. These travels eventually brought him to the United States in 1956. In the same year, Wiesel published his first literary work, a massive autobiographical account of his experience of the Holocaust, *Un di Velt hot geshvign* (and the world has remained silent). From this work, written in Yiddish and published in Argentina, Wiesel quarried the book that made him famous: *Night*, a brief but unforgettable Holocaust memoir, written in French and soon widely translated.

Because of visa complications, Wiesel was unable to return to France. After applying for immigrant status in the United States, he served as United Nations correspondent for a New York Yiddish newspaper. At the same time, he was working on his first novel, which appeared first in French, then in English translation. Over the next few years, he published a novel almost every year. He became an American citizen in 1963. By 1964, Wiesel had gained sufficient recognition as an author to abandon his salaried work as a journalist. For the next few years, until his first academic appointment, he was able to earn a living through his writing and private lecturing. An important experience that would affect both his work as a novelist and as a lecturer occurred in 1965, when he visited the Soviet Union. There he observed conditions of Jewish life under the Soviet regime, a subject which became the focus of a series of articles published in 1966 under the title *The Jews of Silence.* This work was followed by another novel, *A Beggar in Jerusalem*, based on Wiesel's impressions of Israel's experience of the June, 1967, Arab-Israeli War. The book was originally published in French, and earned for the author the distinguished French literary prize, the Prix Médecis.

In 1969, Wiesel married Marion Erster Rose, also a concentration-camp survivor. Marion soon contributed directly to her husband's literary pursuits by translating his works into English. By this date, Wiesel had completed his first drama, *Zalmen*, which would wait six years before being performed for the first time in Washington, D.C. In 1970, another autobiographical work reflecting on the experience of the Holocaust, *One Generation After*, gained international recognition and prepared the way for Wiesel's first academic appointment, in 1972, to a distinguished professorship of Jewish studies at the City College of New York. From this point, and without interrupting his active career as a writer, Wiesel was to be involved in a number of academic and humanitarian public-service posts. In 1976, he was appointed to a special chair in the humanities at Boston University, a position he maintained while lecturing (in 1982-1983) at Yale University. In addition, Wiesel was named by President Jimmy Carter to chair the President's Special Commission on the Holocaust (1979).

Increasingly, recognition was extended to Wiesel as a writer driven by an intense dedication to the cause of world peace. This recognition came first in the form of the Belgian International Peace Prize, which was awarded to Wiesel in 1983. In quick succession after this, Wiesel received special awards from French President François Mitterrand and American President Ronald Reagan (1984). The crowning achievement, however, came when Wiesel was recognized by the Swedish Academy of Sciences as the 1986 recipient of the Nobel Peace Prize. During the award presentation, Wiesel was described as an "important leader and spiritual guide in an era when violence, repression, and racism continue to dominate in the world." In turn, Wiesel dedicated his Nobel Peace Prize to all the remaining survivors of the Holocaust.

BIBLIOGRAPHICAL REFERENCES: A very readable biography of Wiesel is Ellen N. Stern, *Elie Wiesel: Witness for Life*, 1982. This book takes more the form of a life narrative than a critique of the literary content of his work. Stern's account may be supplemented by Harry J. Cargas, *Harry James Cargas in Conversation with Elie Wiesel*, 1976. There is also a long and valuable interview with Wiesel in *The Paris Review*, XXVI (Spring, 1984), 130-178. For a literary analysis of Wiesel's work, see Ellen S. Fine, *Legacy of Night: The Literary Universe of Elie Wiesel*, 1982. Many of the books and articles on Wiesel center on his role as a witness to the Holocaust and the religious dimension of his writings. Among the most noteworthy of these are John K. Roth, *A Consuming Fire: Encounters with Elie Wiesel*, 1979; Michael Berenbaum, *The Vision of the Void: Theological Reflections on the Works of Elie Wiesel*, 1979; Robert McAfee Brown, *Elie Wiesel: Messenger to All Humanity*, 1984; and Graham B. Walker, *Elie Wiesel: A Challenge to Theology*, 1987. See also *Responses to Elie Wiesel*, 1978, edited by Harry James Cargas; and *Confronting the Holocaust: The Impact of Elie Wiesel*, 1979, edited by Alvin H. Rosenfeld and Irving Greenberg.

Byron D. Cannon

THORNTON WILDER

Born: Madison, Wisconsin
Date: April 17, 1897

Died: Hamden, Connecticut
Date: December 7, 1975

PRINCIPAL WORKS

NOVELS: *The Cabala*, 1926; *The Bridge of San Luis Rey*, 1927; *The Woman of Andros*, 1930; *Heaven's My Destination*, 1934; *The Ides of March*, 1948; *The Eighth Day*, 1967; *Theophilus North*, 1973.

PLAYS: *The Trumpet Shall Sound*, pb. 1920; *The Angel That Troubled the Waters and Other Plays*, pb. 1928; *The Long Christmas Dinner and Other Plays in One Act*, pb. 1931; *Our Town*, pr., pb. 1938; *The Merchant of Yonkers*, pr. 1938 (revised as *The Matchmaker*, pr. 1954); *The Skin of Our Teeth*, pr., pb. 1942; *Our Century*, pr., pb. 1947.

The winner of three Pulitzer Prizes, Thornton Niven Wilder remains one of twentieth century America's leading playwrights and novelists. Born on April 17, 1897, in Madison, Wisconsin, he was the son of Amos Parker Wilder, editor of the *Wisconsin State Journal*, and Isabella Thornton Niven Wilder. Though his father disapproved of writers, all five Wilder children—Amos, Charlotte, Isabel, Janet Frances, and Thornton—became authors. His father's peripatetic career, ranging from Madison to Hong Kong to New Haven, Connecticut, guaranteed Wilder a sophisticated upbringing. After attending high school in Chefoo, China, and Ojai and Berkeley, California, Wilder went to Oberlin College for two years, receiving his bachelor's degree in 1920 from Yale University. During World War I, Wilder was a corporal in the Coast Artillery Corps. His education continued with a year in Rome at the American Academy, where he collected material for his first published novel, *The Cabala*, originally entitled "Memoirs of a Roman Student," a description of aristocratic life in contemporary Italy. The receipt of a master's degree in French from Princeton University in 1926 completed Wilder's education.

From 1921 to 1928, Wilder was housemaster and French teacher at the Lawrenceville School in New Jersey. Torn between teaching and writing, Wilder submitted a play, *The Trumpet Shall Sound*, to the American Laboratory Theatre in 1926. Most critics were less than enthusiastic, *The New York Times* reviewer calling it "a rather murky evening." Resigned to being an educator, Wilder, nevertheless, was working on the novel that would change his life, *The Bridge of San Luis Rey.* Set in colonial Peru, it pioneered a new type of fiction, one in which diverse characters are arbitrarily brought together by an accident, in this case, the collapse of an ancient bridge. Exploring the philosophical themes of fate and freedom, this novel not only caught the popular imagination but also won for Wilder his first Pulitzer Prize.

Resigning his post at Lawrenceville in 1928, Wilder turned his attention to full-time writing. His novel *The Woman of Andros*, set in pre-Christian Greece, explores the questions, "How does one live?" and "What does one do first?" Wilder was shown to be an author who was fond of taking philosophical themes from the Bible or the classics (both ancient and modern) and then developing them with a new twist. Having become a celebrity, Wilder made "walking tours of Europe" with prizefighter Gene Tunney and lecture tours of America to garner material for future works. *The Long Christmas Dinner* was Wilder's experiment with a play that would have a minimum of props, no curtain, and maximum attention to plot and personality. Travels in the heartland prompted Wilder to move to the Midwest.

From 1930 to 1936, Wilder was a lecturer in literature at the University of Chicago, where "boy wonder" Robert M. Hutchins was stressing a program in the humanities centered in a core course of Great Books. Wilder was to be resident six months annually, teaching a large course on literature and a small seminar on writing, the remainder of the year to be free for writing. The Chicago years were mingled glory and tragedy. Lionized by North Shore society, Wilder was often shunned by more scholarly members of the university community. In

1930, he was stunned by Michael Gold's accusation, in the essay, "Wilder: Prophet of the Genteel Christ," in *The New Republic*, that he avoided topics of social relevance. The next novel, *Heaven's My Destination*, became a Book-of-the-Month Club selection.

Wilder believed the theater was "the greatest of all art forms" and "the most immediate way in which a human being can share with another the sense of what it is to be a human being." That conviction and economic circumstance led him to settle permanently in New Haven in 1937 and to turn his attention once more to drama. It was a wise decision. His play *Our Town* won for him his second Pulitzer Prize. Set in New Hampshire at the start of the twentieth century, *Our Town* explores "ordinary lives," finding in them "extraordinary meaning." Perhaps Wilder's most widely known work, *Our Town* experimented with simplicity of stage set and complexity of theme.

In World War II, Wilder served in the Air Force Intelligence Corps, seeing action in Italy and rising to the rank of major. Profoundly disturbed by this crisis in Western civilization, Wilder wrote the play for which he won his third Pulitzer Prize, *The Skin of Our Teeth*, which opened in New York's Plymouth Theatre on November 18, 1942. An "allegorical comedy of man's struggle for human survival," it was both praised as "the best pure theater" of the 1940's and panned as "a philosophy class conducted in a monkey house." Traumatic for Wilder was the accusation, made by Joseph Campbell and Henry Robinson, that his play was plagiarized from James Joyce's novel *Finnegans Wake* (1939). Once more Wilder was vindicated but deeply shaken.

Wilder toured Latin America, lectured in postwar Europe, and was visiting professor at a number of institutions, including Harvard University. *Our Century*, a play in three brief vignettes, appeared in 1947, followed the next year by his novel *The Ides of March*, a study in identity featuring Julius Caesar. In 1955, Wilder did a revision of an earlier play, *The Merchant of Yonkers*, producing it as *The Matchmaker*. The play had previously failed; now it proved popular. Reworked as the popular musical *Hello, Dolly!* (1964) starring Carol Channing, it gave Wilder even more exposure.

A time of "summing up" began. Wilder's novel *The Eighth Day* explores the dilemma of man's struggle against benevolent and malevolent forces. A mystery set in the Midwest, its theme is that man is yet young, the eighth day of creation is at hand, and "there are no Golden Ages and no Dark Ages" for there is "the oceanlike monotony of the generations of men under the alternations of fair and foul weather." This work won the National Book Award and prepared the way for Wilder's finale, the novel *Theophilus North*. The chief character often mirrors Wilder's own personality and career. Torn by many contradictory dimensions and aspirations, the hero finds unity in his "desire to be a lover." Favorably received, the novel was Wilder's own obituary, for "the kindly grandad of American letters" died at Hamden, Connecticut, on December 7, 1975.

The recipient of honorary degrees from Harvard University, the University of Zurich, and other colleges, as well as the Legion of Honor, the Order of Merit (West Germany, Peru), and many other distinctions, Wilder is assured his place in American and world literature. Perceiving him as "sophisticated and urbane," critics commented on Wilder's "consecration to perfection," his "commitment to the classics," and his "passion for absolute excellence." A lifelong Congregationalist, always a teacher, whether in the classroom or in the theater, Wilder embodied the humanist ideals of the classical tradition and reinterpreted them in the light of twentieth century realities.

BIBLIOGRAPHICAL REFERENCES: Good book-length biographies of Thornton Wilder include Gilbert A. Harrison, *The Enthusiast: A Life of Thornton Wilder*, 1983; Linda Simon, *Thornton Wilder: His World*, 1979; and Richard H. Goldstone, *Thornton Wilder: An Intimate Portrait*, 1975. Earlier studies are Rex Burbank, *Thornton Wilder*, 1961; Malcolm Goldstein, *The Art of Thornton Wilder*, 1965; Bernard Grebanier, *Thornton Wilder*, 1964; Donald Haberman, *The Plays of Thornton Wilder: A Critical Study*, 1967; Mildred Christophe Kuner, *Thornton*

Wilder: The Bright and the Dark, 1972; Herman Stresau, *Thornton Wilder*, 1971; and Helmut Papajewski, *Thornton Wilder*, 1968. Invaluable is J. M. Edelstein, *A Bibliographical Checklist of the Writings of Thornton Wilder*, 1959. A vast periodical literature exists concerning Wilder. Some helpful introductory essays are Wayne H. Morgan, "The Early Thornton Wilder," *Southwest Review*, XLIII (1958), 245-253; D. P. Edgell, "Thornton Wilder Revisited," *Cairo Studies in English*, II (1960), 47-59; and Heinz Kosok, "Thornton Wilder: A Bibliography of Criticism," *Twentieth Century Literature*, IX (1963), 93-100. Two views of Wilder's famous play are George D. Stephens, "*Our Town*—Great American Tragedy?" *Modern Drama*, I (1959), 258-264, and Winfield Townley Scott, "*Our Town* and the Golden Veil," *The Virginia Quarterly Review*, XXIX (January, 1953), 103-117. See also Henry Adler, "Thornton Wilder's Theater," *Horizon*, XII (1945), 89-99. Concerning his philosophy, consult Hermine I. Hopper, "The Universe of Thornton Wilder," *Harper's Magazine*, CCXXX (June, 1965), 72-78; E. K. Brown, "A Christian Humanist," *University of Toronto Quarterly*, IV (April, 1935), 356-370; Robert W. Corrigan, "Thornton Wilder and the Tragic Sense of Life," *Educational Theater*, XIII (October, 1961), 167-173; Edmund Fuller, "Thornton Wilder: The Notation of a Heart," *The American Scholar*, XXVIII (Spring, 1959), 210-217; Michael Gold, "Wilder: Prophet of the Genteel Christ," *The New Republic*, LXIV (October 22, 1930), 226-267; and Marvin Gardner, "Thornton Wilder and the Problem of Providence," *University of Kansas City Review*, VII (1940), 83-91. Two personal appraisals are Robert M. Hutchins, "Remarks at a Memorial Service for Thornton Wilder, January 18, 1976," *The Center Magazine*, VII (September/October, 1977), 19, and Marshall Spraguc, "Remembering Mr. Wilder," *The New York Times Book Review*, January 27, 1974, 31.

C. George Fry

JOHN A. WILLIAMS

Born: Jackson, Mississippi
Date: December 5, 1925

PRINCIPAL WORKS

NOVELS: *The Angry Ones*, 1960 (also known as *One for New York*); *Night Song*, 1961; *Sissie*, 1963; *The Man Who Cried I Am*, 1967; *Sons of Darkness, Sons of Light: A Novel of Some Probability*, 1969; *Captain Blackman*, 1972; *Mothersill and the Foxes*, 1975; *The Junior Bachelor Society*, 1976; *!Click Song*, 1982; *The Berhama Account*, 1985.

JOURNAL: *Flashbacks: A Twenty Year Diary of Article Writing*, 1970.

BIOGRAPHY: *The Most Native of Sons: A Biography of Richard Wright*, 1970; *The King God Didn't Save: Reflections on the Life and Death of Martin Luther King, Jr.*, 1970.

OTHER NONFICTION: *Africa: Her History, Lands, and People*, 1962; *This Is My Country Too*, 1965.

John Alfred Williams is one of the most important black American writers in the twentieth century. He was born in Jackson, Mississippi, on December 5, 1925, the son of a laborer, John Henry Williams, and a domestic, Ola Jones Williams. Williams spent his boyhood in Syracuse and describes it as an urban idyll in which various racial and ethnic groups were crowded into one area. In April, 1943, he left high school and joined the U.S. Navy. It was a formative experience since he came into contact for the first time with organized racism. The treatment of blacks by whites in the military became a touchstone for Williams, and he alludes to it in many of his later novels, even though his first attempt to write a book on those experiences never came to fruition. After being discharged from the navy in 1946, Williams began completing his education. He finished high school, attended Morris Brown College for a short time, and was graduated from Syracuse University in 1950. A degree in journalism, however, did not provide immediate employment on newspapers, magazines, or in public relations. Instead, he worked in a steel mill and a supermarket and as an insurance agent. The problems that Williams and other black writers have had with publishers is a major theme in his novels. He kept writing all this time in the face of rejection and deception, and finally a novel was accepted by a publisher.

Williams' first novel, *The Angry Ones*, was published in 1960, and it deals primarily with the difficulties of an educated and articulate black man in a white world. It is an early novel with a simple reversal structure; Williams avoided this structure and easy optimism in his later novels. Williams wrote two other early novels, *Sissie* and *Night Song*, but the breakthrough into his middle period came with the addition of historical contexts in the 1967 *The Man Who Cried I Am*. *The Man Who Cried I Am* is his best novel, and it is very pessimistic. The protagonist and another black writer are killed because they learned of a conspiracy to kill or relocate blacks. It is Williams' first investigation of where power is located and how it works against blacks. *Sons of Darkness, Sons of Light* continues Williams' investigation of a black man in a world in which the centers of power are controlled by whites; however, the historical vision has become more immediate and the race war that was contemplated by the repressive power structure in *The Man Who Cried I Am* has become a reality. *Captain Blackman* is also a novel deeply connected with history, but the perspective has been expanded. In the beginning of the novel, Captain Blackman is in a firefight in Vietnam; suddenly, the time frame shifts, and he is a black man caught up in the events of the Revolutionary War. Williams traces his actions in all the wars that America fights; in each case, his contribution is ignored by those he has fought for and his condition is not improved.

Mothersill and the Foxes explores a new aspect of myths dealing with blacks: sex. Williams attacks the ludicrousness of these myths, which are another side of racism. *The Junior Bachelor Society* also confronts racial conflict, but the context is not war or politics but sports. *!Click Song* is a long, autobiographical novel in which a black writer struggles with a white establishment. It contrasts the treatment given to a black writer and a Jewish one. The black writer meets nothing but opposition while the white writer is supported by the establishment, even to the point of critical approval of his novel about black people. It is more hopeful in using personal relationships as a focus, however, and it moves away from Williams' genocidal vision of the fate of blacks in America. *Sissie* is an unusual novel in Williams' canon: it is the one novel that is set entirely in a black world. This world is nurturing and loving, although it is filled with conflict. *Night Song* is also unusual since it deals not with the usual isolated black man but a jazz musician who is modeled after a historical figure, Charlie Parker.

The most important element in Williams' fiction is the struggle of blacks against the conscious and unconscious racism of a white society. Williams not only dramatizes the social and psychological problems engendered by racism but also places that struggle in a historical perspective and context. Williams often shows the positive black contribution to their country's wars, economy, arts, and other areas that are wiped out, ignored, or hidden. He shows that the American dream remains hollow for blacks oppressed by overt and hidden sources of power. Williams is in the tradition of Richard Wright and Ralph Ellison in exposing white myths of black life and people. He takes the conflicts of black and white that these writers presented and carries them more than a few steps further into an analysis of the use and abuse of power in America. Williams does not give political answers to the problems he presents but takes the necessary step to make blacks and whites aware of the world they live in, who runs it, and how they run it. With that knowledge, and the demystification of myths about blacks, some kind of beginning might be made. It may only be between a black man and a white woman, as in *!Click Song*, but Williams shows how to begin.

BIBLIOGRAPHICAL REFERENCES: Earl A. Cash, *John A. Williams: The Evolution of a Black Writer*, 1975, was the first full-length study of Williams' writing, but Gilbert H. Muller, *John A. Williams*, 1984, is both more thorough and more informative about Williams' fiction and themes. For further study, see Addison Gayle, Jr.'s study of Williams and other black writers, *The Way of the New World: The Black Novel in America*, 1975; Barbara Foley, "History, Fiction, and the Ground Between: The Uses of the Documentary Mode in Black Literature," *PMLA*, XCV (May, 1980), 389-403; Phyllis R. Klotman, "An Examination of the Black Confidence Man in Two Black Novels: *The Man Who Cried I Am* and *Dem*," *American Literature*, XLIV (January, 1973), 596-611; Noel Schraufnagel, *From Apology to Protest: The Black American Novel*, 1973; C. Lynn Munro, "Culture and Quest in the Fiction of John A. Williams," *College Language Association Journal*, XXII (1978), 71-100; and *The Black American Short Story in the Twentieth Century: A Collection of Critical Essays*, 1977, edited by Peter Bruck.

James Sullivan

TENNESSEE WILLIAMS
Thomas Lanier Williams

Born: Columbus, Mississippi
Date: March 26, 1911

Died: New York, New York
Date: February 25, 1983

Principal Works

PLAYS: *Battle of Angels*, pr. 1940; *The Glass Menagerie*, pr. 1944; *A Streetcar Named Desire*, pr., pb. 1947; *Summer and Smoke*, pr. 1947; *The Rose Tattoo*, pr., pb. 1951; *Camino Real*, pr., pb. 1953; *Cat on a Hot Tin Roof*, pr., pb. 1955; *Orpheus Descending*, pr. 1957; *Suddenly Last Summer*, pr., pb. 1958; *Sweet Bird of Youth*, pr., pb. 1959; *Period of Adjustment*, pr. 1959; *The Night of the Iguana*, pr., pb. 1961.

NOVELS: *The Roman Spring of Mrs. Stone*, 1950; *Moise and the World of Reason*, 1975.

SHORT FICTION: *One Arm and Other Stories*, 1948; *Hard Candy: A Book of Stories*, 1954; *The Knightly Quest*, 1967; *Eight Mortal Ladies Possessed*, 1974.

POETRY: *In the Winter of Cities*, 1956; *Androgyne, Mon Amour*, 1977.

NONFICTION: *Memoirs*, 1975; *Where I Love: Selected Essays*, 1978.

SCREENPLAYS: *The Glass Menagerie*, 1950 (with Peter Berneis); *A Streetcar Named Desire*, 1951 (with Oscar Saul); *The Rose Tattoo*, 1955 (with Hal Kanter); *Baby Doll*, 1956; *The Fugitive Kind*, 1960 (with Meade Roberts); *Suddenly Last Summer*, 1960 (with Gore Vidal).

Tennessee Williams is considered one of the greatest American playwrights, ranking along with Eugene O'Neill and Henry Miller. He was born the son of Cornelius Coffin Williams, a traveling salesman, and Edwina Dakin Williams, the daughter of a minister and his wife. Williams, his mother, and his older sister, Rose, lived with Williams' maternal grandparents until his father was transferred to his firm's main office in St. Louis in 1918. The move was shattering to both Williams and his sister, and it was almost certainly at least partially responsible for Williams' emotional instability and for his sister's retreat from reality—which resulted in a prefrontal lobotomy and institutionalization. *The Glass Menagerie* is an autobiographical presentation of two days in the St. Louis years after the children were grown, but it omits the children's father and their younger brother.

Unable to bear life at home, Williams began his lifelong wanderings, though he also attended college at the University of Missouri and Washington University, and finally completed a degree at the University of Iowa. He presently attracted the attention of an important literary agent, Audrey Wood, received grants, and, after having written one-act plays, poetry, and short stories, had his first full-length play, *Battle of Angels*, produced in Boston in 1940, where it failed. His first successful play was *The Glass Menagerie*, first produced in Chicago, where it attracted attention and praise from the critics; after several months it was moved to New York, where it was met with great success.

Williams' next play, *A Streetcar Named Desire*, is still considered his greatest, and won for him his first Pulitzer Prize. Its central character, Blanche Dubois, is one of the best remembered and most vividly characterized in modern drama. The daughter of an aristocratic Southern family which has gone downhill for generations and finally lost all of its wealth and its estate, she has become a prostitute, and, after losing her job as a teacher, spends months with her sister and brother-in-law in a New Orleans slum, finally being taken to an insane asylum.

Williams' other most important plays include *Summer and Smoke*, *Camino Real* (though a failure on Broadway), *Cat on a Hot Tin Roof* (for which he won his second Pulitzer), and *The Night of the Iguana*. He continued to write plays after *The Night of the Iguana*, but none had the quality of his earlier plays.

As Williams' *Memoirs* make clear, he was very frankly homosexual, and over the years he had many companions. Several of his plays (including, in the play's background, *Cat on a Hot Tin Roof*) contain homosexual characters. He continued traveling widely all of his life, his most frequent stopping places being New Orleans, New York, Rome, and Key West, where he owned a home. He finally died in a New York hotel from choking on a medicine bottle cap.

Williams' more important plays are usually set in the South, either in Mississippi or in New Orleans, the only notable exceptions being *The Glass Menagerie* (St. Louis), *Camino Real* (a mythical Central America), and *The Night of the Iguana* (Mexico). His plays frequently center on three character types: the "gentleman caller" (actually called that in *The Glass Menagerie*), usually a young man, whether "gentleman" or not, who "calls upon" a young woman; a frequently but not invariably innocent and vulnerable young woman; and a usually tougher and more experienced older woman. The pattern is obvious in both *The Glass Menagerie* and *A Streetcar Named Desire*, though in the latter play the tougher woman, Stella, is younger than her vulnerable sister, Blanche, and the gentleman caller, Mitch, is not the most important male character in the play. In *Cat on a Hot Tin Roof*, there is only the tough young woman, whose husband is ironically the opposite of a gentleman caller in that his fear of being homosexual (probably unfounded) has led him to ignore his wife sexually and has led his wife desperately (and perhaps successfully at play's end) to lure, or force, him back.

Williams' best plays are also notable for their use of impressionistic sound and lighting effects: the music from a nearby tavern in *The Glass Menagerie*; the roar of trains passing in *A Streetcar Named Desire*; the spotlight in *The Glass Menagerie*, centering on the seriously upset Laura while her mother and brother quarrel; and Blanche's covering of the naked ceiling light bulb with a shade in her sister's apartment in *A Streetcar Named Desire*. The earlier playwright who was the principal influence on Williams is Anton Chekhov, who is also noted for his impressionism and for presenting characters such as Blanche (and perhaps Amanda in *The Glass Menagerie*), characters who have fallen from the level of significant aristocracy. Yet Williams is also noted for his use of extreme violence, which relates him to the American, and more particularly Southern, gothic style, exemplified in the violence in some of the novels of William Faulkner. Examples of such violence in Williams' work include cannibalism in the background of *Suddenly Last Summer* and imminent castration in *Sweet Bird of Youth*.

All Williams's major plays fit the impressionistic, and in general realistic, pattern, except *Camino Real*, which is expressionistic, dealing with both real and fictional characters in a mythical Central America. In that play, people struggle with their inability to give life meaning and their inability to love; a few characters who succeed in overcoming their problems manage to escape. Two of the plays in Williams' major period are comedies: *The Rose Tattoo*, a successful play about a Sicilian woman on the Mississippi coast who is seriously disturbed by the loss of her husband in an accident and who finally finds a man to take his place, and the lightweight and insignificant *Period of Adjustment*.

BIBLIOGRAPHICAL REFERENCES: The most important collection of critical essays on Williams is *Tennessee Williams: A Tribute*, 1977, edited by Jac Tharpe and containing fifty-three essays by a great variety of important critics. Another important collection is *Tennessee Williams: A Collection of Critical Essays*, 1977, edited by Stephen S. Stanton. Other important works about Williams' life include Donald Spoto, *The Kindness of Strangers: The Life of Tennessee Williams*, 1985, and two books of memoirs, Dotson Rader, *Tennessee: Cry of the Heart*, 1985, and Harry Lasky, *Tennessee Williams: A Portrait in Laughter and Lamentation*, 1986. An important bibliographical source is Drewey Gunn, *Tennessee Williams: A Bibliography*, 1980. Also valuable are Nancy Tischler, *Tennessee Williams: Rebellious Puritan*, 1961; Edwina Williams, *Remember Me to Tom*, 1963, the memoirs of Williams' mother; Esther Jackson, *The Broken World of Tennessee Williams*, 1965; Signi Falk, *Tennessee Williams*, 1978; Felicia

Moore, *Tennessee Williams*, 1979; Foster Hirsch, *A Portrait of the Artist: The Plays of Tennessee Williams*, 1979; and John McCann, *The Critical Reputation of Tennessee Williams*, 1983.

Jacob H. Adler

WILLIAM CARLOS WILLIAMS

Born: Rutherford, New Jersey
Date: September 17, 1883

Died: Rutherford, New Jersey
Date: March 4, 1963

Principal Works

POETRY: *Poems*, 1909; *The Tempers*, 1913; *A Book of Poems, Al Que Quiere!*, 1917; *Kora in Hell: Improvisations*, 1920; *Sour Grapes: A Book of Poems*, 1921; *Spring and All*, 1922; *The Complete Collected Poems of William Carlos Williams, 1906-1938*, 1938; *Paterson*, 1948-1958; *Collected Later Poems*, 1950, 1963; *Collected Earlier Poems*, 1951; *The Desert Music and Other Poems*, 1954; *Journey to Love*, 1955; *Pictures from Brueghel*, 1962; *The Collected Poems of William Carlos Williams: 1909-1939*, 1986; *The Collected Poems of William Carlos Williams: 1939-1962*, 1988.

NOVELS: *A Voyage to Pagany*, 1928; *White Mule*, 1937; *In the Money*, 1940; *The Build-Up*, 1952.

ESSAYS: *In the American Grain*, 1925; *Selected Essays of William Carlos Williams*, 1954.

AUTOBIOGRAPHY: *The Autobiography of William Carlos Williams*, 1951.

CORRESPONDENCE: *The Selected Letters of William Carlos Williams*, 1957.

MISCELLANEOUS: *Imaginations*, 1970.

William Carlos Williams was a major American modernist poet to whom recognition came late in his career, and who influenced many subsequent poets in their search for a contemporary voice and form. Williams was born in Rutherford, New Jersey, on September 17, 1883, to a mother born in Puerto Rico and an English father. Both parents figure in a number of Williams' poems. In 1902, Williams began the study of medicine at the University of Pennsylvania and while a student formed important friendships with Ezra Pound and the painter Charles Demuth. In 1910, Williams began his forty-year medical practice in Rutherford, marrying Florence Herman in 1912.

Williams' first book of poems, entitled *Poems* and privately printed by a local stationer, was replete with the kind of archaic poetic diction and romantic longing typical of much American magazine poetry at the time. (In later years, Williams refused to allow the book to be reprinted.) As a result of Pound's directive that he become more aware of avant-garde work in music, painting, prose, and poetry, Williams' next book, *The Tempers*, reflected Pound's pre-Imagist manner—a variety of verse forms, short monologues, and medieval and Latinate allusions. Williams responded with enthusiasm to the Imagist manifestos of 1912 and 1913, and much of his subsequent poetry reflects the Imagist emphasis upon concrete presentation, concision, and avoidance of conventional rhythms. Williams developed these principles in his own way, arguing that the new conditions of America itself and the primitive state of its literature demanded eschewing European literary conventions and traditions, and developing an American poetics of international standard, yet expressive of the American language and landscape. *A Book of Poems, Al Que Quiere!* reflects Williams' working out of these and associated strategies, his developing an aesthetic that insists upon the ultimately creative reward of despair and destruction, and the importance of passionately engaging the object world of the native landscape with a kind of preconscious energy that breaks the conventions of perceptual habit. The 1920's volumes *Sour Grapes*, *Spring and All*, and *The Descent of Winter* (the latter two works can be found in the collection *Imaginations*) bring these concerns to fruition.

After 1913, Williams formed friendships with a number of important writers and painters working in and around New York, including Marsden Hartley, Wallace Stevens, and Charles Sheeler. He saw his hopes for native expression confirmed in the arrival in New York of such major modernist figures as Marcel Duchamp and Francis Picabia at the time of World War I. He was doubly disappointed in the early 1920's by the exodus of these figures and many

American artists to Paris and by the success of T. S. Eliot's *The Waste Land* (1922). Both events signified to Williams the triumph of the international school of modernism against which he had spiritedly set himself in the 1918 "Prologue" to his *Kora in Hell*.

Williams labored on his writing for the next twenty years, largely unrecognized except by readers of the short-lived small magazines that printed experimental American work. What some critics consider Williams' finest book, the prose and poetry sequence *Spring and All*, was printed in Paris in an edition of only three hundred and not reprinted in full until 1970, seven years after his death. The sequential format suggesting multiple but loosely linked relationships among the twenty-seven poems and interspersed prose well illustrates Williams' inventiveness—both on the level of individual poems and of overall formal structure. This book contains the famous "The Red Wheelbarrow," later printed by Williams as a separate poem, and often anthologized as the quintessential Imagist expression.

In the 1930's, Williams' work took a more overtly political turn, although he had always shared the view of Pound and Eliot that the work of the poet was central to the health and potential of a civilization and that the state of a culture was reflected in its response to its serious artists. These concerns form a central theme of *Paterson*, his long poem initially conceived and published in four books (1944 to 1951; Williams added a fifth book in 1958). The past and present of this New Jersey city is examined in a collagelike mix of poetry and prose—including newspaper accounts, histories, and letters Williams himself received while writing the work—to dramatize the lack of creative response to the rich potential of the landscape. The theme is an extension of that in Williams' book of historical essays, *In the American Grain*. Paterson's once-famous falls serves as a central motif representing the unrealized promise of native language and expression, its insistent and ever-present roar ignored amid the scenes of exploitation, sterile love affairs, and mindless escapism documented throughout the poem.

In 1951, Williams suffered the first of a series of strokes that forced him to retire from medicine and, gradually, came to affect his vision and typing ability. Williams' restricted life, and his severe depression of 1952-1953, color the tone and subject matter of the poems in *The Desert Music* and *Journey to Love*. These poems are written in the three-step line Williams had initially used in part of the second volume of *Paterson*, and many of his critical statements of the 1950's are concerned with his concepts of the "variable foot" and "the American idiom" behind this development in his poetics. Essentially, both concepts are restatements of his career-long concern with a nonliterary language to treat the local American scene and a rejection of the conventional rhythms and forms of English poetry. Nevertheless, the descending three-step line proves an ideal structural and visual form for these more meditative poems, many of which delve into memory to discover formerly unrealized significance. Williams' major achievement of these years is generally considered "Asphodel, That Greeny Flower"—a poem of reconciliation to Florence Williams, considered by W. H. Auden "one of the most beautiful love poems in the language."

Never one to rest in any one mode, for his final book of poems, *Pictures from Brueghel*, Williams returned to the more concentrated, pictorial strategies of his early career. The book was awarded the Pulitzer Prize for poetry shortly after the poet's death.

In the 1950's, Williams became an important figure for poets seeking an alternative to the neoclassical poetics of T. S. Eliot and his followers, and such figures as Robert Lowell, Allen Ginsberg, and Denise Levertov have acknowledged a large debt to his example. Since that decade, too, Williams' career-long achievement has gradually come to be more and more fully recognized. Although still not accorded the status of Eliot and Stevens by some critics of modernism, on the whole these two—along with Williams and Pound—are considered the four major figures of American modernist poetry.

BIBLIOGRAPHICAL REFERENCES: An excellent general introduction to Williams' work remains James E. Breslin, *William Carlos Williams: An American Artist*, 1970. Paul Mariani's biography *William Carlos Williams: A New World Naked*, 1981, is also essential reading. Williams' important relationships with the modernist painters have been the subject of a number of studies, including Bram Dijkstra, *The Hieroglyphics of a New Speech*, 1969; Henry Sayre, *The Visual Text of William Carlos Williams*, 1983; Christopher MacGowan, *William Carlos Williams's Early Poetry: The Visual Arts Background*, 1984; and Peter Schmidt, *William Carlos Williams: The Arts, and Literary Tradition*, 1988. A highly readable and intelligent study of Williams' innovative poetics is Stephen Cushman, *William Carlos Williams and the Meanings of Measure*, 1986. Benjamin Sankey, *A Companion to William Carlos Williams' "Paterson,"* 1971, provides helpful background to the literary, personal, and geographical allusions in the poem. See also "William Carlos Williams," in J. Hillis Miller, *Poets of Reality*, 1966; Emily Wallace, *A Bibliography of William Carlos Williams*, 1968; Joel Conarroe, *William Carlos Williams' "Paterson": Language and Landscape*, 1970; and Mike Weaver, *William Carlos Williams: The American Background*, 1971.

Christopher MacGowan

A. N. WILSON

Born: Stone, England
Date: October 27, 1950

Principal Works

NOVELS: *The Sweets of Pimlico*, 1977; *Unguarded Hours*, 1978; *Kindly Light*, 1979; *The Healing Art*, 1980; *Who Was Oswald Fish?*, 1981; *Wise Virgin*, 1982; *Scandal: Or, Priscilla's Kindness*, 1983; *Gentlemen in England: A Vision*, 1985; *Love Unknown*, 1986; *Stray*, 1987; *Incline Our Hearts*, 1988.

BIOGRAPHY: *The Laird of Abbotsford: A View of Sir Walter Scott*, 1980; *The Life of John Milton*, 1983; *Hilaire Belloc*, 1984; *Tolstoy*, 1988.

ESSAYS: *Pen Friends from Porlock*, 1987.

RELIGION: *How Can We Know?*, 1985.

The British have had a long and distinguished line of satirical novelists intent upon putting society in its place which began almost as soon as the novel in the works of Henry Fielding in the eighteenth century, continues in the works of Tobias Smollett, and is carried on in the novels of Charles Dickens, reaching its most elegant expression in the early twentieth century with Evelyn Waugh, who has been succeeded first by Kingsley Amis, and second by Andrew Norman Wilson, who carries on the tradition within a much wider career as scholar, essayist, social critic, and sometime religious commentator.

Wilson's wittily jaundiced eye for the middle to the upper classes of Britain is consistent with his own social background. He was educated at the lower-school level at one of the great English public schools, Rugby School, and went on from there to New College, Oxford. He was a prizewinning student and has had a career as an academic at the University of Oxford. He has also been rewarded for his literary work, winning the John Llewelyn Rhys Memorial Prize in 1978 for *The Sweets of Pimlico* and in 1980 for *The Laird of Abbotsford*, the Somerset Maugham Award and the Arts Council National Book Award in 1981 for *The Healing Art*, and the W. H. Smith Annual Literary Award in 1983 for *Wise Virgin*.

Wilson is also a public personality, partly because of his further career as a journalist, writing for the quality press of England. He has had a long association with *The Spectator*, the conservative weekly journal of political comment, literary review, and social attack, often of a scurrilously witty stamp. Indeed, it is necessary to understand a peculiar mark of social satire in that it is not necessarily confined to writing of a liberal or leftish bent, and can often be at its best in the hands of writers who espouse old social structures and old social values. Jonathan Swift was not a liberal, but he was devastatingly sensitive to the excesses of his society. Wilson, if less powerful than Swift, has strong inclinations to looking upon society as debased and sloppy in its political leanings to the left, but he is also aware of how badly responsible aspects of conservative power misuse their opportunities. A novel such as *The Healing Art* exposes, with mordant wittiness, the slipshod irresponsibilities of the medical profession, and *Scandal* looks balefully at the immodest and often stupid behavior of politicians.

Wilson has never been simply one kind of novelist. The early novel *The Sweets of Pimlico* is hardly satiric at all although it deals with upper-middle-class social life in the center of London. It has a kind of offbeat comic zaniness about it which might have been taken as the beginning of an exclusively comic career, and his two religious novels, *Unguarded Hours* and *Kindly Light* (which ought to be read as one), if touched with a scrupulously detailed awareness of the shambles of modern Christianity, are so cheerfully forgiving that the satire might well be missed without too much damage. Wilson also uses black comedy as in *Wise Virgin*, in which an irascible blind scholar gets what he deserves for being an emotional thug, but in *The Healing Art* that inclination to run a sick joke into the ground is distinctly unpleasant and upsetting. What is always a pleasure is the way in which he brings his enthusiasms into his art. His deep affection for Anglicanism as it used to be, his general concern for the failing Christian church can produce a sensitive, sensible discussion in *How Can We Know?* or can be made an integral part of his deliberately old-fashioned fake Victorian work, *Gentleman in England*, which is a fond re-creation of London life in the 1870's, historically accurate and stylistically as bloated as a Victorian sofa.

Scandal and *Love Unknown* have that easy, sophisticated capacity to scent out the fools and villains of the English class system which never goes away, but his 1988 novel, *Incline Our Hearts*, setting out to look like a satire on the misery which the affluent English impose on their children by sending them away to school, turns into a tale of doppelgänger intrigue in which the narrator begins to explore the nature of his real personality. It reads as if it is unfinished, and it may well be that Wilson plans to come back to this set of characters again, perhaps with more emotional development. Wilson has established himself as a satirist, a comic, and a master manipulator of form. He may yet prove to be a writer of deep emotion.

Wilson is also a critic but not a pedant. His essays on literature and his critical biographies fall into a civilized area between the popular works of oversimplification and the barbarisms of academic footnoting and hairsplitting. His conservatism reveals itself as a generous civility tempered by a sense that he would not suffer fools gladly. He would, however, address them with gentlemanly fastidiousness and style.

BIBLIOGRAPHICAL REFERENCES: Suzanne Lowry, *The Young Fogey Handbook*, 1985, was originally written as a comic attack upon young, upper-class London society; Wilson has been called the finest example of the literary young fogy, and his novels are loaded with touches of young fogyism. For reviews of *Wise Virgin*, see Nancy Forbes, *The Nation*, CCXXXVII (December 3, 1983), 577, and Pat Rogers, *The Times Literary Supplement*, November 5, 1982, 1121. An analysis of *Hilaire Belloc* can be found in Leslie E. Gerber, *Magill's Literary Annual*, I, 1985, 385-389. Reviews of *Gentlemen in England* include *Publishers Weekly*, CCXXVIII (December 13, 1985), 46, and *Time*, CXXVII (March 17, 1986), 81. *Love Unknown* is reviewed in Robert A. Morace, *Magill's Literary Annual*, I, 1988, 507-511. See also Charles H. Pullen, "A. N. Wilson," in *Critical Survey of Long Fiction Supplement*, 1987, edited by Frank N. Magill.

Charles Pullen

ANGUS WILSON

Born: Bexhill, England
Date: August 11, 1913

PRINCIPAL WORKS

NOVELS: *Hemlock and After*, 1952; *Anglo-Saxon Attitudes*, 1956; *The Middle Age of Mrs. Eliot*, 1958; *The Old Men at the Zoo*, 1961; *Late Call*, 1964; *No Laughing Matter*, 1967; *As If By Magic*, 1973; *Setting the World on Fire*, 1980.

SHORT FICTION: *The Wrong Set, and Other Stories*, 1949; *Such Darling Dodos, and Other Stories*, 1950; *A Bit off the Map, and Other Stories*, 1957; *Death Dance: Twenty-Five Stories*, 1969.

PLAY: *The Mulberry Bush*, pr., pb. 1956.

BIOGRAPHY: *Émile Zola: An Introductory Study of His Novels*, 1952; *The World of Charles Dickens*, 1970; *The Strange Ride of Rudyard Kipling*, 1977.

CRITICISM: *The Wild Garden: Or, Speaking of Writing*, 1963; *Tempo: The Impact of Television on the Arts*, 1964; *Diversity and Depth in Fiction: Selected Critical Writings of Angus Wilson*, 1983; *Reflections in a Writer's Eye*, 1986.

Angus Frank Johnstone-Wilson came to prominence shortly after World War II, first as a short-story writer and then as a novelist. Born on the south coast of England in the small resort town of Bexhill, not far from Brighton, he was the last child of William and Maude Johnstone-Wilson. His father was a Londoner but descended from a wealthy Scottish family; his mother came from South Africa. The youngest of six brothers, the next oldest being thirteen years his senior, Angus was reared in adult company and was a lonely, highly imaginative, and even more highly strung youngster. Childhood has always loomed large in his fiction, although his first novel, *Hemlock and After*, is the story of a man in middle age who faces—and fails—an important crisis in his life. It was not until *Setting the World on Fire* that Wilson wrote a novel that approached a *Bildungsroman*; it is a story about two brothers growing up in postwar England. Though his heroes are not typically teenagers or young men, protagonists favored by American novelists such as Ernest Hemingway, J. D. Salinger, and John Knowles, he is very concerned with young people both in his short fiction and in novels such as *No Laughing Matter* and *As If By Magic*.

Although the elder Johnstone-Wilsons had once been affluent, the postwar period saw them, like many others, fallen on harder times. Their shabby genteel existence colored Angus' earliest years as the family moved from hotel to hotel, often only a step or two ahead of their creditors. If his mother does not appear directly in his fiction, his father often does, especially in the early stories, as a kind of raffish old sport, for example, in the character of Mr. Gorringe in "A Story of Historical Interest" or Trevor in "The Wrong Set." Wilson's sympathies with women other than his mother, whom he dearly loved, appear otherwise in extended portraits, such as those of Meg Eliot in *The Middle Age of Mrs. Eliot* and Sylvia Calvert in *Late Call*. Both of these women confront the bleak emptiness in their lives after being widowed, each in a different way and each successfully when she is finally able to face the loneliness that Wilson views as an essential part of the human condition.

Independence and security, which Meg Eliot seeks, often tend to be mutually exclusive, as Wilson discovered in his own life. For years before and after the war, he worked in the British Museum's Department of Printed Books, rising to become Assistant Superintendent of the Reading Room. As his writing took more and more of his time and he found himself increasingly committed to it, however, he finally made the momentous decision to give up his job at the museum—and the pension that went with it—for the much less secure career of a professional writer. The decision came when he realized that he would have to devote more time to the production of his play *The Mulberry Bush* and to writing his second novel than his job at the Reading Room afforded or than his few weeks' annual holiday provided. Thus, with a scant few hundred pounds in the bank, he left to embark on his writing full-time.

What Meg Eliot and Sylvia Calvert achieve through courage in the face of loneliness and deprivation is precisely what Bernard Sands in *Hemlock and After* fails to do and what Gerald Middleton in *Anglo-Saxon Attitudes* accomplishes only after a long period of dry despair and failure. This achievement lies at the heart of Wilson's humanism, an attitude and conviction that has often linked him with humanists such as E. M. Forster, despite important and telling differences between them. Wilson is a much greater activist, both in his life and in his fiction, than Forster was, as evidenced by the character Alexandra Grant in *As If By Magic* and in Wilson's vigorous participation in Amnesty International, the Royal Literary Fund, the National Book League, and the National Arts Council.

Wilson has also been compared with Charles Dickens, a writer whom he has loved throughout his life and whose critical reputation he has done much to restore in the twentieth century. In addition to the biography of Dickens, he has written several perceptive and incisive essays, and as a professor at the University of East Anglia in the 1960's and 1970's, his curriculum has included Dickens, along with Fyodor Dostoevski, another writer he greatly admires. In addition to Wilson's humanist concerns, his fiction reflects a great interest in the form and technique of the contemporary novel. *No Laughing Matter* is a tour de force and perhaps his masterpiece. In it, he utilizes a variety of fictional techniques rivaled only by James Joyce in *Ulysses* (1922). In fact, Wilson has never stopped experimenting with the form as well as the content of his novels, so that critics have often been puzzled by what came next. For example, his futuristic *The Old Men at the Zoo* was a radical departure from *The Middle Age of Mrs. Eliot*, the Jamesian novel that immediately preceded it. He has developed the interior monologue to a hitherto unrealized flexibility and precision, and his acute ear for different voices and accents has earned for him the soubriquet of mime (he actually is an excellent mimic and has been all of his life). The cinematic opening of *No Laughing Matter* is difficult reading at first, but thereafter the playlets interspersed throughout the novel lend a liveliness and immediacy few fictions in the twentieth century have attained.

BIBLIOGRAPHICAL REFERENCES: Jay L. Halio, *Angus Wilson*, 1964, was the first book written on Angus Wilson, partly in response to A. O. J. Cockshut's essay, "Favoured Sons: The Moral World of Angus Wilson," *Essays in Criticism*, IX (1959), 50-60. Since then, several more books and many articles have appeared, such as Karin Wogatzky's monograph, *Angus Wilson, "Hemlock and After": A Study in Ambiguity*, 1971; K. W. Gransden, *Angus Wilson*, 1969; and Peter Faulkner's more comprehensive study, *Angus Wilson: Mimic and Moralist*, 1980. Collections of essays on Wilson include a special issue of *Twentieth Century Literature*, XXIX (1983), and Jay L. Halio, *Critical Essays on Angus Wilson*, 1985. Wilson's fiction figures significantly in many studies of the contemporary novel. See, for example, "Angus Wilson: Studies in Depression," in C. B. Cox, *The Free Spirit*, 1963; "Angus Wilson's Qualified Nationalism," in James Gindin, *Postwar British Fiction*, 1962; "Angus Wilson: Between Nostalgia and Nightmare," in Bernard Bergonzi, *The Situation of the Novel*, 1970; and "The Fiction of Pastiche: The Comic Mode of Angus Wilson," in Malcolm Bradbury, *Possibilities: Essays on the State of the Novel*, 1973. See also Edmund Wilson, "The Emergence of Angus Wilson," *The Bit Between My Teeth*, 1965; Arthur Edelstein, "Angus Wilson: The Territory Behind," in *Contemporary British Novelists*, 1965, edited by C. Shapiro; Malcolm Bradbury, "The Short Stories of Angus Wilson," *Studies in Short Fiction*, III (1966), 117-125; Guido Kums, "Reality and Fiction: *No Laughing Matter*," *English Studies*, LIII (1972), 523-530; John Oakland, "Angus Wilson and Evil in the English Novel," *Renascence*, XXVI (1973), 24-36; and "Angus Wilson: Diversity, Depth, and Obsessive Energy," in Kerry McSweeney, *Four Contemporary Novelists*, 1983.

Jay L. Halio

AUGUST WILSON

Born: Pittsburgh, Pennsylvania
Date: April 27, 1945

Principal Works

PLAYS: *Ma Rainey's Black Bottom*, pr. 1984; *Fences*, pr., pb. 1985; *Joe Turner's Come and Gone*, pr. 1986; *The Piano Lesson*, pr. 1988.

Roughly midway through his long-range project—a cycle of ten plays about the black American experience, one taking place in each decade of the twentieth century—August Wilson is chronicling the struggle of the black family to reconcile its necessary integration into white society with its desire (and, Wilson would say, need) to retain its heritage. Himself a child of mixed parentage, he was born in 1945 in Pittsburgh's Hill District to a German baker and Daisy Wilson, a black displaced North Carolinian. Reared by his mother and his black stepfather, David Bedford, Wilson dropped out of high school at the age of fifteen, preferring the public library, where he read all the works he found on a shelf marked "Negro"—novels and essays by Richard Wright, Langston Hughes, Ralph Ellison, and others—as well as great poets such as Dylan Thomas, John Berryman, Carl Sandburg, Robert Frost, and Amiri Baraka.

Wilson's sensitivity to the problems of black America was generated from the influences of the Black Power movement in the late 1960's, and he has continued to refer to himself as a Black Nationalist. Although cofounding the Black Horizon on the Hill Theatre company with his longtime friend Rob Penny, Wilson was a poet first, publishing in black literary journals as early as 1971. It was his connection with Penumbra, a black theater in St. Paul, that brought Wilson to Minnesota, where he lives with his wife, Judy Oliver, and his daughter by a previous marriage, Sakina Ansari.

Perhaps the most influential person in Wilson's playwriting life is Lloyd Richards, who, as director of the National Playwrights Conference at the O'Neill Center in Waterford, Connecticut, first encouraged Wilson to pursue a life of writing for the stage. After working on *Ma Rainey's Black Bottom* in the staged reading process at the conference in 1982, Richards brought the play to Yale Repertory Theater for a 1984 production, which eventually went on to Broadway. This collaboration was followed by work at the conference on *Fences*, which was later brought to Yale and subsequently followed *Ma Rainey's Black Bottom* to Broadway, where *Fences* won the Pulitzer Prize in 1987.

The course of Wilson's work follows a carefully laid out plan, to write one play for each decade of black America's modern history. (Wilson has not followed any particular order in his work, moving back and forth through the decades as ideas present themselves.) *Ma Rainey's Black Bottom*, representing the decade of the 1920's, is the story of a salty jazz singer and her fellow musicians, caught in a compromise between financial survival and purity of art; like all Wilson's plays, it dramatizes the conflict of all blacks to retain their identity against the forces of assimilation. *Fences*, which takes place in the 1950's, treats its protagonist, Troy Maxson, as an archetypal breadwinner in the black family, imperfect and human, fighting his son's attempts to gain freedom from the cycle of hopelessness in which Troy is trapped. Brent Staples, a black writer, once remarked about Maxson's generation, "Our fathers had by circumstances become nearly impossible to love." The Maxson role, which has been compared in thematic power to Willy Loman in Arthur Miller's *Death of a Salesman* (pr., pb. 1949), was played by James Earl Jones in Richards' production. *Joe Turner's Come and Gone* dramatizes the transition of a freed slave from his "ownership" by Joe Turner to his struggles to find his wife in a Pittsburgh slum community; the action of the play takes place in 1911. *The Piano Lesson* also takes place in Pittsburgh, this time in 1936, and centers on two family members arguing about selling the family heirloom, a bloodstained piano that represents their cultural past. Like all the plays in this series, it received its development at the National Playwrights Conference and its premiere performance at Yale Repertory Theater.

The value of Wilson's contribution to the stage literature of black America lies in his clear vision of the importance of retaining the distinct black heritage that gives life and dignity to the individual, rather than subsuming that "blackness" in attempts to integrate or assimilate the individual into a white world. His work is far from mere agitprop or political pamphleteering. The broad appeal of his work, which has earned for him a wide audience and every important literary award (including Guggenheim and Rockefeller fellowships to continue his work), lies in his humanity, in the grace of his characterization, and in his uncanny ability to find the cadences of ghetto speech, rendering into poetry what has long been seen as substandard English. The structure of his plays drive the plots and character development forward with great force, drawing the audience into the world of the play with seamless craftsmanship. Wilson's association with the play development process of the National Playwrights Conference and his mentorship with Lloyd Richards are reflected in this maturity of dramaturgical skill.

The accuracy of his vision is attributable only to his talent and his sensitivity to the suffering of the people around whom he grew up. Critics treat Wilson's body of work with considerable respect and seriousness, comparing him favorably to Alex Haley as a chronicler of the black experience, and citing his early successes as indicative of a long and fruitful career. In addition to his personal success, observers of regional theaters in general are noting the process by which Wilson's texts are refined in not-for-profit theater productions before venturing onto the ruthless Broadway stage; that process may well serve as a model for future development of the promising playwright, rather than merely the promising play.

BIBLIOGRAPHICAL REFERENCES: Chip Brown, "The Light in August," *Esquire*, CXI (April, 1989), 116-127, profiles Wilson with an emphasis on his early years. Dinah Livingston, "Cool August: Mr. Wilson's Red-Hot Blues," *Minnesota Monthly*, XXI (October, 1987), 25-32, is a very useful interview with the playwright. Hilary Devries, "A Song in Search of Itself," *American Theatre*, January, 1987, reviews Wilson's progress through his long-range project, describes Wilson's view of black America through the first three plays, and notes his connections with the O'Neill Center. Samuel G. Freedman, "A Voice from the Streets," *The New York Times Magazine*, March 15, 1987, previewing *Fences* in its Yale Repertory production before its Broadway success and Pulitzer Prize, draws a colorful picture of Wilson's youth. Herbert Mitgang, "Wilson, From Poetry to Broadway Success," *The New York Times*, October 22, 1984, describes the development of *Ma Rainey's Black Bottom* in an interview with Wilson. See also Frank Rich, review of *Fences*, *The New York Times*, March 27, 1987, and his article "A Season of Eastern Sissy Playwrights," *The New York Times*, June 5, 1988. Accounts of Wilson's career can be found in Les Stone, "August Wilson," in *Contemporary Authors*, Vol. 122, edited by Hal May and Susan M. Trosky; *Contemporary Literary Criticism*, Vol. 39, edited by Sharon K. Hall; and *Current Biography Yearbook*, 1987, edited by Charles Moritz. See also Alex Poinsett, "August Wilson: Hottest New Playwright," *Ebony*, XLIII (November, 1987), 68, and William A. Henry III, "Exorcising the Demons of Memory: August Wilson Exults in the Blues and Etches of Slavery's Legacy," *Time*, CXXXI (April 11, 1988), 77.

Thomas J. Taylor

EDMUND WILSON

Born: Red Bank, New Jersey
Date: May 8, 1895

Died: Talcottville, New York
Date: June 12, 1972

Principal Works

LITERARY CRITICISM: *Axel's Castle: A Study in the Imaginative Literature of 1870-1930*, 1931; *The Triple Thinkers: Ten Essays on Literature*, 1938; *The Boys in the Back Room: Notes on California Novelists*, 1941; *The Wound and the Bow: Seven Studies in Literature*, 1941; *Classics and Commercials: A Literary Chronicle of the Forties*, 1950; *The Shores of Light: A Literary Chronicle of the Twenties and Thirties*, 1952; *A Piece of My Mind: Reflections at Sixty*, 1956; *Patriotic Gore: Studies in the Literature of the American Civil War*, 1962; *The Bit Between My Teeth: A Literary Chronicle of 1950-1965*, 1965; *A Prelude: Landscapes, Characters, and Conversations from the Earlier Years of My Life*, 1967.

PLAYS: *Discordant Encounters: Plays and Dialogues*, pb. 1926; *This Room and This Gin and These Sandwiches*, pb. 1937; *The Little Blue Light*, pb. 1950; *Five Plays*, pb. 1954; *The Duke of Palermo, and Other Plays, with an Open Letter to Mike Nichols*, pb. 1969.

POETRY: *Note-Books of Night*, 1942; *Night Thoughts*, 1961.

NOVELS: *I Thought of Daisy*, 1929; *Memoirs of Hecate County*, 1946.

SOCIAL CRITICISM: *The American Jitters: A Year of the Slump*, 1932; *The American Earthquake: A Documentary of the Twenties and Thirties*, 1958; *Apologies to the Iroquois*, 1960; *The Cold War and the Income Tax: A Protest*, 1963.

HISTORY: *To the Finland Station: A Study in the Writing and Acting of History*, 1940; *The Scrolls from the Dead Sea*, 1955 (also known as *The Dead Sea Scrolls, 1947-1969*); *Upstate: Records and Recollections of Northern New York*, 1971.

TRAVEL SKETCHES: *Travels in Two Democracies*, 1936; *Europe Without Baedeker: Sketches Among the Ruins of Italy, Greece, and England*, 1947; *Red, Black, Blond, and Olive: Studies in Four Civilizations: Zuñi, Haiti, Soviet Russia, Israel*, 1956.

CORRESPONDENCE: *Letters on Literature and Politics, 1912-1972*, 1977; *The Nabokov-Wilson Letters: 1940-1971*, 1979.

JOURNALS: *The Twenties: From Notebooks and Diaries of the Period*, 1975; *The Thirties: From Notebooks and Diaries of the Period*, 1980; *The Forties: From Notebooks and Diaries of the Period*, 1983; *The Fifties: From Notebooks and Diaries of the Period*, 1986.

Edmund Wilson was an authentic man of letters, a rarity in the twentieth century. Primarily known as a literary critic, he was also a novelist, poet, playwright, historian, and social critic. Wilson was the son of a distinguished New Jersey attorney, a somewhat distant man who inculcated in his only son the virtues of decency and honor; the young man attended Hill School and Princeton University, where he became a close friend and adviser of the novelist F. Scott Fitzgerald and the poet John Peale Bishop. After service in France during World War I, Wilson began a career as a writer and editor for various journals published in New York, including *Vanity Fair*, *The New Republic*, and, eventually, *The New Yorker*. The latter association began in 1943 and continued until his death. Wilson was already a well-known critic when he published his book-length study of literary modernism, *Axel's Castle*. The first such study to treat the Symbolist and Freudian elements in literature as significant and coherent, *Axel's Castle* was an eloquent defense of such writers as James Joyce and Gertrude Stein, as well as a clear exposition of their methods and achievements. During the same period of time, Wilson caused something of a scandal with his novel, *I Thought of Daisy*. Based loosely on the character of Wilson's great early love, the poet Edna St. Vincent Millay, *I Thought of Daisy* chronicles the life and loves of what in the Roaring Twenties was called a flapper, a young woman who goes from one man to another in search of enjoyment with little regard for the future or for the consequences of her actions. The novel shared with his later work of fiction, *Memoirs of Hecate County*, a frankness about sex regarded as shocking at the time of its publication.

Wilson was not very interested in theories of criticism. He had been taught by his famed Princeton teacher Christian Gauss that literature, like all art, is the product of particular times and places, and that it is a critic's job to explain literary works in terms of their relationship to the times that produced them. Wilson therefore regarded his interest in the ideas and the history of his time and of earlier times as essential aspects of his work. In the early 1930's, he traveled widely in the United States, looking for the manifestations of the Great Depression; this search led to his book *The American Jitters*. His interest in modern psychological theory led to the critical study *The Wound and the Bow*, which argues that every writer's works are profoundly influenced by some wound or trauma suffered in the past.

Wilson made his reputation as a defender of the new literature of his own time, but later in his career, he became much more interested in history and in earlier writing. Never committed to any political party or theory, he became fascinated by Marxism during the 1930's, an interest that took the form of research into the history of the development of socialism from Karl Marx and the French and German socialists of the nineteenth century down to the beginning of the Russian revolution. The result was *To the Finland Station*. During the 1940's and 1950's, he took an interest in the discoveries of the ancient Qumrān scrolls of the Essene sect, and traveled to Israel to see them and discuss them with specialists, a project that led to his controversial study *The Dead Sea Scrolls*. Wilson's major interest, however, was always in his own country and its history. He spent years studying the literature and history of the Civil War, a project that led eventually to the book many other critics regard as his finest work, *Patriotic Gore*. This work examines some lesser-known writers who showed, in Wilson's view, aspects of America's past which history had neglected; it included writers such as Oliver Wendell Holmes, Harold Frederic, Mary Chesnut, and Thomas Wentworth Higginson. It was Wilson's conclusion that the war was fought for cynical reasons having to do with power and that Abraham Lincoln was far from the hero history has made him out to be.

Wilson was amazingly prolific. In addition to writing books on specific subjects, he was a regular reviewer for different journals, and his reviews were collected in such volumes as *Classics and Commercials*, *The Shores of Light*, and *The Bit Between My Teeth*. Some of these reviews later led to more extended studies. The collections contain an inclusive history of Wilson's view of literature from the early 1920's until 1970. Leon Edel, after Wilson's death, edited the journals Wilson had kept for most of his adult life, *The Twenties*, *The Thirties*, *The Forties*, and *The Fifties*. These chronicled the somewhat tangled details of Wilson's personal life, including his four marriages. *Upstate* concerns his experiences in Talcottville and the surrounding area, where he lived during the summers of his later years, in an old stone house inherited from his mother's family.

Everything Wilson wrote, however intimate or remote the subject matter, is couched in his characteristic prose: His style was somewhat formal, but it was lucid, precise, and often exciting. He tended to be magisterial in his judgments, as if the conclusions he reached were inarguable. Since he was human, he sometimes erred, especially in his judgments of poetry. He was, nevertheless, a careful and exact observer of his own time, and his comments on the literature and history of the middle years of the twentieth century are a substantial and fascinating record of a time of radical change as seen through the eyes of an observer who is very much a part of his own times. Wilson saw those times with a clear eye. He thought and wrote about them interestingly and well.

BIBLIOGRAPHICAL REFERENCES: One thorough study of Wilson's work, emphasizing his criticism, is David Castronovo, *Edmund Wilson*, 1985. Sherman Paul, *Edmund Wilson: A Study of Literary Vocation in Our Time*, 1965, remains valuable for its perceptions, although it was written while Wilson was still alive and therefore does not cover later publications. Charles

Frank concentrated on Wilson's fiction in *Edmund Wilson*, 1970, while George H. Douglas, *Edmund Wilson's America*, 1983, focused attention on the author's view of the relations between the American past and his own time. Richard Hauer Costa, in *Edmund Wilson: Our Neighbor from Talcottville*, 1980, gives insights into the warmth and capacity for friendship of a man often regarded as frighteningly brusque. John Wain edited a collection of essays about the personal and professional sides of the author, *Edmund Wilson: The Man and His Work*, 1978; it includes biographical essays by Alfred Kazin and Angus Wilson and critical articles by Larzer Ziff and John Wain. See also Harry Levin, "The Last American Man of Letters," *The Times Literary Supplement*, October 11, 1974, 1128-1130; Kerry McSweeney, "My Single Aim Has Been 'Literature': Edmund Wilson's Letters," *Critical Quarterly*, XXI (Autumn, 1979), 63-72; Leon Edel, "Edmund Wilson in Middle Age," *Grand Street*, I (Summer, 1982), 99-109; and Lewis Dabney, "Edmund Wilson and *The Wound and the Bow*," *The Sewanee Review*, XCI (Winter, 1983), 155-165.

John M. Muste

LANFORD WILSON

Born: Lebanon, Missouri
Died: April 13, 1937

PRINCIPAL WORKS

PLAYS: *So Long at the Fair*, pr. 1963; *Home Free!*, pr. 1964; *The Madness of Lady Bright*, pr. 1964; *No Trespassing*, pr. 1964; *Balm in Gilead*, pr., pb. 1965; *Days Ahead: A Monologue*, pr. 1965; *Ludlow Fair*, pr., pb. 1965; *The Sand Castle*, pr. 1965; *Sex Is Between Two People*, pr. 1965; *This Is the Rill Speaking*, pr. 1965; *The Rimers of Eldritch*, pr. 1966; *Wandering: A Turn*, pr. 1966; *Untitled Play*, pr. 1967; *Miss Williams: A Turn*, pr. 1967; *The Gingham Dog*, pr. 1968; *The Great Nebula in Orion*, pr. 1970; *Lemon Sky*, pr., pb. 1970; *Serenading Louie*, pr. 1970; *Sextet (Yes)*, pb. 1970; *Stoop: A Turn*, pb. 1970; *Ikke, Ikke, Nye, Nye, Nye*, pr. 1971; *Summer and Smoke*, pr. 1971; *The Family Continues*, pr. 1972; *The Hot l Baltimore*, pr., pb. 1973; *Victory on Mrs. Dandywine's Island*, pb. 1973; *The Mound Builders*, pr. 1975; *Brontosaurus*, pr. 1977; *5th of July*, pr., pb. 1978; *Talley's Folly*, pr., pb. 1979; *A Tale Told*, pr. 1981 (revised as *Talley & Son*, pr. 1985); *Angels Fall*, pr., pb. 1982; *Thymus Vulgaris*, pb. 1982; *Three Sisters*, pr. 1984; *A Betrothal*, pb. 1986; *Burn This*, pr., pb. 1987.

TELEPLAYS: *The Migrants*, 1973; *Taxi!*, 1978.

Lanford Eugene Wilson, a model of the playwrights of the generation bred and nurtured in the fertile Off-Off-Broadway lofts and churches of the 1960's, may be the most prolific American writer for the stage since Eugene O'Neill. His Pulitzer Prize-winning *Talley's Folly*, a later play in his canon, brings him about halfway through his lifelong chronicling of the fictitous Talley family and its richly variegated American environment. Born in Lebanon, Missouri, on April 13, 1937, Wilson was affected by the early divorce of his parents. After spending his childhood with his mother and stepfather in Springfield and Ozark, Missouri, he moved to San Diego, where his reacquaintance with his father (after thirteen years), however imperfect, served as the basis for his examination of his life through drama in the creative years that followed, culminating in the anguishingly autobiographical *Lemon Sky*. Gradually working his way eastward, Wilson found himself in New York at the moment of the birth of Off-Off-Broadway theater, which welcomed his unique American theater voice.

Three New York theaters were integral to Wilson's growth as an artist and person during those formative years. The Caffé Cino, operated with great daring and foresight by Joe Cino, staged Wilson's first effort, *So Long at the Fair*, and some other one-acts, including *This Is the Rill Speaking*, *Wandering*, and *The Madness of Lady Bright*, which won an Obie for its star, Neil Flanagan. Ellen Stewart's equally daring and innovative La Mama Experimental Theatre Club staged some of Wilson's longer works; *Balm in Gilead* and *The Rimers of Eldritch* demonstrate Wilson's multicharacter scene study approach to depicting whole slices of American culture in decay, a layering technique refined in subsequent work such as *Hot l Baltimore*.

The third theater to influence Wilson's work was the Circle Repertory Company, which he cofounded in 1969 with Tanya Berezin, Rob Thierkield, and Marshall Mason, who had directed Wilson's play *The Sand Castle* at Café La Mama in 1965. This relationship has continued through Wilson's career; as playwright in residence at the Circle Repertory, Wilson has created, developed, and directed more than a dozen plays, many of which have moved on to Broadway and brought awards and honors to the theater and its playwright in residence.

Wilson's mature output has centered on the continuing saga of the Talley family, in some respects intensely autobiographical, but, more important, a metaphorical construction that dramatizes the best and worst of the American family tradition. *5th of July*, a rambling front-porch drama with kaleidoscopic focus, was followed by *Talley's Folly*, a thirty-year step backward to examine in closer detail the odd love of two characters, Matt Friedman and Sally

Talley (who appears as a mature aunt in the first play). *A Tale Told* takes place at the same moment, but in the main house on the hill above the boathouse where Matt and Sally are declaring their love. Wilson's *Angels Fall* examines other themes (nuclear devastation), but *Talley & Son*, a rewriting of *A Tale Told*, brought the family back to the Circle Repertory Company in 1985. In the same year a brilliant revival of *Lemon Sky*, directed by Mary B. Robinson, was performed to rave reviews at the Second Stage Theatre. *Burn This*, opening on Broadway in 1987, returns to an urban setting to tell a story of postmodern non-love non-triangles, with John Malkovich's portrayal of Pale the most memorable part of the production.

Critics have seen in Wilson's themes and techniques a complex but dramatically exciting vision of the American family situation, the traditions of former generations implanted on the next, in conflict with a world changing more rapidly in its external indifference than in the basically unchanging human interrelationships that make up the private lives of the family members. His plays take place in two essential environments: the family setting, in which ties to former and future generations (represented by impending and dissolving marriages) are reinforced; and hard-edged urban settings peopled with failures, isolated from their families but forming alliances among themselves for security and hope. His predilection for seedy hotel lobbies and all-night restaurants as settings has invited comparison with William Saroyan and Eugene O'Neill; the roving, unfocused plots, stripping away the layers of complex family relationships with slowly revealed exposition and attention to details of characterization, show the influence of Anton Chekhov, Henrik Ibsen, and Lillian Hellman; the sense of isolation, especially in the shorter works, owes something to Eugène Ionesco, an early influence for Wilson; the "poetic realism" of his language (sometimes referred to as "lyric realism" by spokespersons of the Circle Repertory Company) is reminiscent of Tennessee Williams.

As early as 1975, Wilson was being called "a young genius on the rise." His subsequent successes, not only on Broadway and at Circle Rep but in the regional theaters throughout the United States, seem to ensure his high reputation among future critics and audiences. With David Mamet, Sam Shepard, and Arthur Kopit, he belongs to the generation of playwrights whose voices began to be heard during the Vietnam War, a kind of American absurdist school, nurtured by both Off-Off-Broadway and the regional theater movement. If he continues the prolific output of sensitive, complex family dramas offering insight and entertainment to a wide audience, his place in American theater history is assured.

BIBLIOGRAPHICAL REFERENCES: For a good overall introduction to Wilson, consult Gene A. Barnett, *Lanford Wilson*, 1987, a volume in the Twayne series. Another overview of Wilson can be found in Mark Busby, *Lanford Wilson*, 1987. Comparisons of Wilson with his contemporaries are in Bonnie Marranca and Gautam Dasgupta, *American Playwrights: A Critical Survey*, 1980. Further bibliographical references are in Kimball King, *Ten Modern American Playwrights: An Annotated Bibliography*, 1982. See also Robert Kerkvist, "Lanford Wilson—Can He Score on Broadway?" *The New York Times*, February 17, 1980, D1; two articles in *Horizon*, XXIII (May, 1980), 30-37, by Mel Gussow and Peter Buckley; Scot Haller, "The Dramatic Rise of Lanford Wilson," *Saturday Review*, VIII (August, 1981), 26-29; and Ross Wetzeon, "The Most Populist Playwright," *New York*, XV (November 8, 1982), 42-45.

Thomas J. Taylor

STANISŁAW IGNACY WITKIEWICZ

Born: Warsaw, Poland
Date: February 24, 1885

Died: Jeziory na Polesiu, Poland
Date: September 18, 1939

Principal Works

PLAYS: *Mister Price: Czyli, Bzik tropikalny*, wr. 1920, pr. 1926 (*Mr. Price: Or, Tropical Madness*, 1972); *Oni*, wr. 1920, pb. 1962 (*They*, 1968); *Straszliwy wychowawca*, wr. 1920, pr., pb. 1935; *Pragmatyści*, pb. 1920 (*The Pragmatists*, 1971); *Tumor Mózgowicz*, pr., pb. 1921 (*Tumor Brainiowicz*, 1980); *Metafizyka dwugłowego cielęcia*, wr. 1921, pr. 1928 (*Metaphysics of a Two-Headed Calf*, 1972); *Gyubal Wahazar: Czyli, Na przełęczach bezsensu*, wr. 1921, pb. 1962 (*Gyubal Wahazar: Or, Along the Cliffs of the Absurd*, 1971); *Bezimienne dzieło*, wr. 1921, pb. 1962 (*The Anonymous Work*, 1974); *Kurka wodna*, pr. 1922 (*The Water Hen*, 1968); *Nowe wyzwolenie*, pb. 1922; *Nadobnisie i koczkodany: Czyli, Zielon pigułka*, wr. 1922, pb. 1962 (*Dainty Shapes and Hairy Apes: Or, The Green Pill*, 1980); *W małym dworku*, pr. 1923; *Mątwa: Czyli, Hyrkaniczny światopogląd*, pb. 1923 (*The Cuttlefish: Or, The Hyrcanian World View*, 1970); *Szalona lokomotywa*, wr. 1923, pb. 1962 (*The Crazy Locomotive*, 1968); *Matka*, wr. 1924, pb. 1962 (*The Mother*, 1968); *Jan Maciej Karol Wścieklica*, pr. 1925; *Wariat i zakonnica: Czyli, Nie ma złego, co by na jeszcze gorsze nie wyszło*, pb. 1925 (*The Madman and the Nun: Or, There Is Nothing Bad Which Could Not Turn into Something Worse*, 1966); *Sonata Belzebuba: Czyli, Prawdziwe zdarzenie w Mordowarze*, pb. 1938 (*The Beelzebub Sonata: Or, What Really Happened at Mordowar*, 1980); *Szewcy*, pb. 1948 (*The Shoemakers*, 1968).

NOVELS: *Pożegnanie jesieni*, 1927; *Nienasycenie*, 1930 (*Insatiability: A Novel in Two Parts*, 1977); *Jedyne wyjście*, 1968; *622 upadki Bunga: Czyli, Demoniczna kobieta*, 1972.

CRITICISM: *Nowe formy w malarstwie i wynikające stąd neporozumienia*, 1919; *Szkice estetyczne*, 1922; *Teatr: Wstęp do teorii czystej formy we teatrze*, 1923.

MISCELLANEOUS: *Witkacy, malarz*, 1985 (*Witkacy, the Painter*, 1987); *Przeciw nicości: fotografie Stanisława Ignacego Witkiewicza*, 1986.

Stanisław Ignacy Witkiewicz was a talented and important writer and dramatist, who also left his mark in painting and dramatic and aesthetic theory, as well as philosophy. He was born on February 24, 1885, in Warsaw, as the only child of the noted painter and art critic Stanisław Witkiewicz. Taking his son's education under his own aegis, Stanisław Witkiewicz secured the best private instructors for his child and supervised his schooling at home. The future artist passed his maturity exam in 1901. Upon completion of his secondary studies, Witkiewicz set off for Germany and Italy for practical experience in painting. He also painted in Cracow and Zakopane. Accepted into the prestigious Cracovian Akademia Sztuk Pięknych (Academy of Fine Arts), he attended lectures there only for a short while, against his father's wishes. Witkiewicz soon began to write creatively. The years from 1910 to 1911 saw the composition of his first mature literary work, the novel *622 upadki Bunga* (the 622 downfalls of Bunga: or, the demonic woman), which, however, was not published until after the author's death.

Somehow tangled up in the unusual circumstances of his fiancée's suicide, in 1914 Witkiewicz left Poland for Australia in the company of his friend, sociologist Bronisław Malinowski. The outbreak of World War I, however, in this same year prompted the young artist to enlist in the Russian army, in search of the novelty of wartime experiences and the unusualness of military life. According to many, he served with bravery. The Bolshevik Revolution of 1917 exerted a great influence on Witkiewicz. Those close to the artist report that the dramatist and painter often referred to his fear of the Communist regime in the Soviet Union and considered Soviet iconoclasm a grave threat to European culture.

Witkiewicz published his views on graphic technique in two critical volumes of aesthetics published in 1919 and 1922 respectively: *Nowe formy w malarstwie i wynikające stąd neporozumienia* (new forms in painting) and *Szkice estetyczne* (aesthetic sketches). The complete and definitive bound collection of Witkiewicz's artwork (with many color plates) is *Witkacy, the Painter*, published in 1985. Witkacy was Witkiewicz's pseudonym. The first period of Witkiewicz's literary career occurred during the *Młoda Polska* (young Poland) period, a time of great change in Polish artistic spheres. For a long time, Witkiewicz was unable to define and stabilize his manner and style of thought, which was, for this particular period, quite shocking to the large number of Polish literati and theatergoers. The first few years of the 1920's saw the beginning of Witkiewicz's career as a playwright, which was to bring him his greatest fame. Between the years 1919 and 1923, the artist created the lion's share of his thirty dramatic works, among which are *They, W małym dworku*, and *The Water Hen*. His later *The Shoemakers*, though, became his best-known drama.

In his theoretical tract *Teatr*, Witkiewicz laid out his dramatic aesthetic, which he called "pure form." Similar to his theories of graphic art, Witkiewicz's theatrical aesthetic is based on the premise that, in drama, it is not content but form which is all important. Pondering the course of Western aesthetics, Witkiewicz noted the decline and, as he saw it, disappearance of religion and metaphysics as aids to humankind's struggle with the eternal question of life. Only art remained to humankind in its last hour of culture, before the eventual triumph of the leveling philosophy of totalitarianism would put an end to Western culture by "replacing metaphysics with ethics" and herding the questioning individual into the happy mass of the unthinking, animally satisfied collective. According to Witkiewicz, the modern artist is to abandon logic and mix the most varied elements into his work in order to create an artistic whole of satisfying formal completeness, without regard to the particular logical associations of the elements which go into the play's makeup.

As for prose, Witkiewicz did not understand the novel as an art form but rather as an arena for polemic and philosophizing. As well as *622 upadki Bunga*, written in 1910-1911, Witkacy wrote several other novels, among which the most notable are the antiutopian *Pożegnanie jesieni* (farewell to autumn) and *Insatiability*. This latter work, reputedly his best novelistic endeavor, deals with the problem which agonized him for the majority of his mature life: the undermining of Western civilization's cultural heritage by the insidious suffocation of the individual soul in a dully satisfying stagnation. Caught in the pincers of the totalitarian onslaught which propelled Poland into World War II, and fearing that the dreaded hour of the death of culture had now come round, Witkiewicz committed suicide on September 18, 1939, in a forest in eastern Poland.

BIBLIOGRAPHICAL REFERENCES: A definitive work in English on Witkiewicz is Daniel Gerould, *Witkacy: Stanisław Ignacy Witkiewicz as an Imaginative Writer*, 1981. Also of interest is Bernard F. Dukore, "'Who Was Witkacy?': Witkiewicz East and West," *Theatre Quarterly*, V, no. 18 (1975), 291-315; as well as Czesław Miłosz, "Stanisław Ignacy Witkiewicz: A Polish Writer for Today," *Tri-Quarterly*, Spring, 1967, 143-154. See also Janusz Degler, "Witkacy Worldwide," *Polish Perspectives*, XX (December, 1977), 29-37; Bernard F. Dukore, "Spherical Tragedies and Comedies with Corpses: Witkacian (sic) Tragicomedy," *Modern Drama*, XVIII (1975), 291-315; Czesław Miłosz, "The Pill of Murti-Bing," in *The Captive Mind*, 1953, as well as the same author's "Stanisław Ignacy Witkiewicz," in *The History of Polish Literature*, 1983; and the special Witkiewicz issues of *Le Théâtre en Pologne*, no. 3, 1970, and nos. 6/7, 1978.

Charles Kraszewski

LUDWIG WITTGENSTEIN

Born: Vienna, Austria
Date: April 26, 1889

Died: Cambridge, England
Date: April 29, 1951

PRINCIPAL WORKS

PHILOSOPHY: *Tractatus Logico-Philosophicus*, 1922 (English translation, 1922, 1961); *Philosophical Investigations*, 1953; *Remarks on the Foundations of Mathematics*, 1956; *The Blue and Brown Books*, 1958; *Philosophische Bemerkungen*, 1964 (*Philosophical Remarks*, 1975); *Lectures and Conversations on Aesthetics, Psychology, and Religious Belief*, 1966; *Zettel*, 1967; *Philosophische Grammatik*, 1969 (*Philosophical Grammar*, 1974); *On Certainty*, 1969; *Vermischte Bemerkungen*, 1977 (*Culture and Value*, 1980); *Remarks on the Philosophy of Psychology*, 1980; *Last Writings on the Philosophy of Psychology*, Vol. 1: *Preliminary Studies for Part II of "Philosophical Investigations,"* 1982.

Ludwig Wittgenstein has been a controversial figure in philosophy, but he is second only to Bertrand Russell among philosophers of the twentieth century. Though his academic career was spent largely in England, he was born in Vienna on April 26, 1889, to a very wealthy and very talented family, originally Jewish but for two generations Christian. He was educated at first by tutors but in 1903 was sent to a *Realschule*, or technical school, at Linz, where for a year it is possible that he could have associated with Adolf Hitler. The choice of a nonclassical school indicates that his father considered Ludwig suited to a career in some such subject as engineering; in fact, he did study engineering in Berlin and, after 1908, in Manchester, where he interested himself in aeronautics. (He was to put his technical knowledge to good use in the war and later practiced briefly as an architect.) His interests, however, shifted to mathematics and philosophy, and on the advice of the distinguished philosopher Gottlob Frege, a professor at the University of Jena, he went to the University of Cambridge to study under Bertrand Russell. Russell was at first puzzled by his "German" but before long thought that he should abandon the field of logic to Wittgenstein, who combined abject feelings of unworthiness with an arrogant aggressiveness on professional subjects. G. E. Moore and others were likewise much impressed.

In early 1914, Wittgenstein was meditating in an isolated hut in Norway, but by the time the war broke out he was back in Austria and immediately volunteered for active service. He proved to be a loyal, brave, and capable soldier and officer, who ended the war in an Italian prisoner-of-war camp. His period of active service was far from being an intellectual vacuum. In part as a result of reading such authors as Leo Tolstoy, he developed a mystical bent that annoyed Russell when they were reunited. Furthermore, he carried around with him throughout the war notebooks in which he recorded his philosophical reflections, which eventually became his first major work, *Tractatus Logico-Philosophicus*, which was published in 1922.

There followed a fallow period in Wittgenstein's career. His feelings of unworthiness (verging on the suicidal) led him to consider a religious life; eventually he chose instead to become an elementary schoolteacher in rural Austria. It was at this time, too, that he renounced his claims to his inheritance from his father. Wittgenstein pursued his teaching with great dedication, but ultimately he was drawn back to philosophy. In the late 1920's, he was associated with the logical positivists of the Vienna Circle, a clique with which he has sometimes been mistakenly identified. In 1929, he returned to the University of Cambridge, was granted a Ph.D. on the basis of the *Tractatus Logico-Philosophicus*, and was elected to a research fellowship at Trinity College.

At this point began the most fruitful period of Wittgenstein's life. His brilliant if eccentric teaching soon made him famous. Furthermore, he began multiplying the manuscripts that would be published after his death. In 1939, he was elected to the professorship of philosophy at Cambridge on the retirement of G. E. Moore. When World War II broke out, Wittgenstein, who had by then become a British subject, faithfully served out the war as a medical orderly. After the war, he returned to his professorship but found it burdensome and resigned in 1947. After a retreat in rural Ireland and a pleasant trip to the United States, where he stayed with his former student Norman Malcolm, he fell ill with cancer and died on April 29, 1951.

Given his complexity, his obscurity, and his frequent changes of opinion, it is no simple matter to give a short summary of Wittgenstein's doctrine. Still, some critics have seen a paradoxical combination of change and continuity in Wittgenstein, a contrast and yet a resemblance between the doctrine of his early work and his more mature work of the 1930's; the link is a preoccupation with language. In the *Tractatus Logico-Philosophicus*, under the influence of Frege and Russell, Wittgenstein dreamed of a rigorously logical system of propositions which would picture in their logical structure the structure of the world; his aim was to eliminate from the language any logical flaws which would interfere with the picture. In his later work, language has a different, one might say a social, function; it is a tool which human beings use in their "language games," games which obey rules as various and flexible as those of athletic games. The meaning of a word is defined not by its correspondence to something outside itself but by its "use" in the game. Of course this theory would sound more convincing if expounded with Wittgenstein's overwhelming personality in his barren upstairs rooms at Cambridge.

BIBLIOGRAPHICAL REFERENCES: There are the beginnings of a definitive life in Brian McGuinness, *Wittgenstein, a Life: Young Ludwig, 1889-1921*, 1988, the first volume of a projected two-volume authorized biography. McGuinness is especially good on Wittgenstein's family background and military service. He seems somewhat embarrassed by Wittgenstein's homosexuality, which he prefers to treat in footnotes, perhaps in reaction to W. W. Bartley III's controversial *Wittgenstein*, 1985 (rev. ed.). See also Norman Malcolm, *Ludwig Wittgenstein: A Memoir, with a Biographical Sketch by G. H. von Wright*, 1984 (rev. ed.). The secondary literature on Wittgenstein is vast. An excellent source is *The Philosophy of Wittgenstein*, 1986, edited by John V. Canfield, a fifteen-volume collection reproducing more than 250 articles, thematically grouped. See also Anthony Kenny, *Wittgenstein*, 1973, which is not easy but does succeed in imposing a pattern on Wittgenstein's disorderly production; A. J. Ayer, *Wittgenstein*, 1985, a critical and relatively lucid work by a logical positivist; and J. N. Findlay, *Wittgenstein: A Critique*, 1984, well written but somewhat more advanced. *Philosophy in the Twentieth Century*, Vol. 2: *The Rise of Analytical Philosophy in England*, 1962, edited by William Barrett and Henry D. Aiken, contains a helpful introduction by Aiken and selections from Moore, Russell, and Wittgenstein.

John C. Sherwood

P. G. WODEHOUSE

Born: Guildford, Surrey, England
Date: October 15, 1881

Died: Long Island, New York
Date: February 14, 1975

Principal Works

NOVELS: *The Pothunters*, 1902; *A Prefect's Uncle*, 1903; *The Gold Bat*, 1904; *The Head of Kay's*, 1905; *Love Among the Chickens*, 1906; *The White Feather*, 1907; *Mike: A Public School Story*, 1909 (also known as *Enter Psmith*, *Mike at Wrykyn*, *Mike and Psmith*); *Psmith in the City: A Sequel to "Mike,"* 1910; *A Gentleman of Leisure*, 1910 (also known as *The Intrusion of Jimmy*); *The Prince and Betty*, 1912; *The Little Nugget*, 1913; *Something Fresh*, 1915 (also known as *Something New*); *Psmith Journalist*, 1915; *Uneasy Money*, 1916; *Piccadilly Jim*, 1917; *Their Mutual Child*, 1919 (also known as *The Coming of Bill*); *A Damsel in Distress*, 1919; *The Little Warrior*, 1920 (also known as *Jill the Reckless*); *Indiscretions of Archie*, 1921; *The Girl on the Boat*, 1922 (also known as *Three Men and a Maid*); *The Adventures of Sally*, 1922 (also known as *Mostly Sally*); *The Inimitable Jeeves*, 1923 (also known as *Jeeves*); *Bill the Conqueror: His Invasion of England in the Springtime*, 1924; *Sam the Sudden*, 1925 (also known as *Sam in the Suburbs*); *The Small Bachelor*, 1927; *Money for Nothing*, 1928; *Summer Lightning*, 1929 (also known as *Fish Preferred*); *Very Good, Jeeves*, 1930; *Big Money*, 1931; *If I Were You*, 1931; *Doctor Sally*, 1932; *Hot Water*, 1932; *Heavy Weather*, 1933; *Thank You, Jeeves*, 1934; *Right Ho, Jeeves*, 1934 (also known as *Brinkley Manor: A Novel About Jeeves*); *Trouble Down at Tudsleigh*, 1935; *The Luck of the Bodkins*, 1935; *Laughing Gas*, 1936; *The Code of the Woosters*, 1938; *Uncle Fred in the Springtime*, 1939; *Quick Service*, 1940; *Money in the Bank*, 1942; *Joy in the Morning*, 1946; *Full Moon*, 1947; *Spring Fever*, 1948; *Uncle Dynamite*, 1948; *The Mating Season*, 1949; *The Old Reliable*, 1951; *Pigs Have Wings*, 1952; *Ring for Jeeves*, 1953 (also known as *The Return of Jeeves*); *Jeeves and the Feudal Spirit*, 1954 (also known as *Bertie Wooster Sees It Through*); *French Leave*, 1956; *Something Fishy*, 1957 (also known as *The Butler Did It*); *Cocktail Time*, 1958; *Jeeves in the Offing*, 1960 (also known as *How Right You Are, Jeeves*); *Ice in the Bedroom*, 1961; *Service with a Smile*, 1961; *Stiff Upper Lip, Jeeves*, 1963; *Biffen's Millions*, 1964; *Galahad at Blandings*, 1965 (also known as *The Brinkmanship of Galahad Threepwood: A Blandings Castle Novel*); *Company for Henry*, 1967 (also known as *The Purloined Paperweight*); *Do Butlers Burgle Banks?*, 1968; *A Pelican at Blandings*, 1969 (also known as *No Nudes Is Good Nudes*); *The Girl in Blue*, 1970; *Jeeves and the Tie that Binds*, 1971 (also known as *Much Obliged, Jeeves*); *Pearls, Girls, and Monty Bodkins*, 1972 (also known as *The Plot That Thickened*); *Bachelors Anonymous*, 1973; *The Cat-Nappers: A Jeeves and Bertie Story*, 1974 (also known as *Aunts Aren't Gentlemen*); *Sunset at Blandings*, 1977.

SHORT FICTION: *Tales of St. Austin's*, 1903; *The Man Upstairs, and Other Stories*, 1914; *The Man with Two Left Feet, and Other Stories*, 1917; *My Man Jeeves*, 1919; *The Clicking of Cuthbert*, 1922 (also known as *Golf Without Tears*); *Ukridge*, 1924 (also known as *He Rather Enjoyed It*); *The Heart of a Goof*, 1926 (also known as *Divots*); *Meet Mr. Mulliner*, 1927; *Mr. Mulliner Speaking*, 1929; *Mulliner Nights*, 1933; *Blandings Castle and Elsewhere*, 1935 (also known as *Blandings Castle*); *Young Men in Spats*, 1936; *Lord Emsworth and Others*, 1937 (also known as *The Crime Wave at Blandings*); *Eggs, Beans, and Crumpets*, 1940; *Nothing Serious*, 1950; *A Few Quick Ones*, 1959; *Plum Pie*, 1966.

PLAYS: *A Gentleman of Leisure*, pr. 1911 (with John Stapleton); *A Thief for a Night*, pr. 1913 (with Stapleton); *Brother Alfred*, pr. 1913 (with Herbert Westbrook); *The Play's the Thing*, pr. 1926; *Her Cardboard Lover*, pr. 1927 (with Valerie Wyngate); *Good Morning, Bill*, pr. 1927; *A Damsel in Distress*, pr. 1928; *Baa, Baa, Black Sheep*, pr. 1929 (with Ian Hay); *Candlelight*, pr. 1929; *Leave It to Psmith*, pr. 1930; *Who's Who*, pr. 1934 (with Guy Bolton); *The Inside Stand*, pr. 1935; *Don't Listen, Ladies*, pr. 1948 (with Bolton); *Carry On, Jeeves*, pb. 1956 (with Bolton).

NONFICTION: *Performing Flea: A Self-Portrait in Letters*, 1952 (also known as *Author! Author!*); *Bring on the Girls! The Improbable Story of Our Life in Musical Comedy with Pictures to Prove It*, 1953; *America, I Like You*, 1956 (revised as *Over Seventy: An Autobiography with Digressions*, 1957).

Pelham Grenville Wodehouse is a name that conjures up the most lighthearted and sunniest of comic worlds described by a master stylist of the English language. Born on October 15, 1881, in Guildford, England, he was the third son of a British civil servant serving in Hong Kong. To give their children an English education, his parents sent them to England; there they attended various boarding schools and visited relatives during the summer holidays. Wodehouse's upbringing explains the relative scarcity of parental figures and the corresponding preponderance of aunts in his most popular works, especially in those featuring Bertie Wooster and Jeeves. Bertie is firmly ruled by the strength of will of his female relatives, whether as likable as Aunt Dahlia or as terrifying as Aunt Agatha—both characters based on Wodehouse's own aunts, undoubtedly an affectionate tribute to these important figures from his childhood. Wodehouse, who early acquired the lifelong nickname "Plum," claimed that he started writing stories when he was five years old. His father, however, wanted his son to have a more secure future and obtained a position for Wodehouse as a clerk in the Hong Kong and Shanghai Bank. To please his father, Wodehouse remained with the bank for two years, all the while writing short pieces for magazines. Then he landed a much more congenial job writing a column for a newspaper, the *Globe*, and in 1902, became a full-time writer. In 1904, he was asked to write lyrics for a new play, and thereupon launched on another long career, as a lyricist.

Wodehouse traveled to the United States a few times and was particularly impressed with the possibilities there in 1909, when he sold two short stories on the day he arrived. On his third visit, in 1914, he met and married Ethel Rowley, an Englishwoman. Writing under a number of pen names, Wodehouse became a theater critic for *Vanity Fair.* Over the years, with Jerome Kern and Guy Bolton, Wodehouse was part of a legendary trio that produced several successful Broadway shows. In his literary biography of Wodehouse, Benny Green argues that Wodehouse's contribution to fifty-two dramatic works over a period of fifty years and his collaboration with other Broadway greats, such as Cole Porter, Florenz Ziegfeld, and George and Ira Gershwin, helped shape Wodehouse's prose fiction. A tragic incident that reveals the nature, appeal, and, for some critics, the problem with Wodehouse as a writer occurred during World War II. Wodehouse was established as a master comic stylist and had created the major characters who would continue to be the mainstay of his work: Psmith, who first appeared in the schoolboy stories and later as an adult; Ukridge, an impoverished but creative zany; Mulliner, the narrator of Hollywood stories; two elderly earls—the bouncy and youthful Lord Ickenham and the dreamy but dedicated pig breeder Lord Emsworth; the dim-witted young men of the Drones Club; and the most famous Drone Club member, Bertie Wooster, and his stupendously well-read and intelligent personal valet, Jeeves.

Wodehouse, who by all accounts was an extremely good-natured, innocent, and apolitical man, found himself a prisoner of the Germans during the occupation of France, where he and his wife were living at the time. He agreed to a request from some American companies to tape broadcasts to his concerned fans in the United States. Unfortunately for his reputation, Wodehouse described his unpleasant experiences in the humorous style so peculiarly his own, ridiculing the Germans and making light of his own miseries. He was branded a traitor by those who never heard the broadcasts but assumed that his agreeing to do them at all was suspect. While those who heard or read the broadcasts stoutly defended him, the storm of protest hurt Wodehouse. Though completely cleared of any charges, Wodehouse moved to the United States permanently in 1947, where he continued to write in much the same fashion as before the war.

The unworldly innocence apparent in this incident characterizes Wodehouse's work. As

Richard J. Voorhees notes, Wodehouse was born in the Victorian Age, came to manhood in the Edwardian, and continued to write, until the age of ninety-three, as if he still lived in that earlier time. His enduring appeal lies not only in the fantasy world he created but also in his careful and imaginative use of the full resources of the English language.

BIBLIOGRAPHICAL REFERENCES: Benny Green, *P. G. Wodehouse: A Literary Biography*, 1981, traces the connections between Wodehouse's personal experiences and his fictional creations. For further study, see Robert A. Hall, Jr., *The Comic Style of P. G. Wodehouse*, 1974, for a detailed analysis of the type of stories and the stylistic devices in Wodehouse's work. Iain Sproat, *Wodehouse at War*, 1981, vindicates Wodehouse's innocence in the infamous Nazi broadcasts. Other helpful studies include Richard J. Voorhees, *P. G. Wodehouse*, 1966; R. B. D. French, *P. G. Wodehouse*, 1966; David Jasen, *A Bibliography and Reader's Guide to the First Editions of P. G. Wodehouse*, 1970, and *P. G. Wodehouse: The Life of a Master*, 1973; *Homage to P. G. Wodehouse*, 1973, edited by Thelma Cazalet-Keir (a collection of essays by various admirers); O. D. Edwards, *P. G. Wodehouse*, 1977; Geoffrey W. Jaggard, *Wooster's World*, 1967; Richard Usborne, *Wodehouse at Work*, 1961; John Hayward, *P. G. Wodehouse*, 1941; Herbert Warren Wind, *The World of P. G. Wodehouse*, 1972. See also "In Defense of P. G. Wodehouse" in George Orwell, *The Collected Essays, Journalism, and Letters of George Orwell*, 1968; S. Metcalf, "The Innocence of P. G. Wodehouse," in Gabriel Josipovici, *The Modern English Novel: The Reader, the Writer, and the Work*, 1976; "The Lesson of the Young Master," in John W. Aldridge, *Time to Murder and Create: The Contemporary Novel in Crisis*, 1966; John Larnder, "Wodehouse Past and Present," *The New Yorker*, May 22, 1948, 104-106; Clarke Olney, "Wodehouse and the Poets," *The Georgia Review*, XVI (1962), 392-399; Lionel Stevenson, "The Antecedents of P. G. Wodehouse," *Arizona Quarterly*, V (1959), 226-234; and Richard J. Voorhees, "The Jolly Old World of P. G. Wodehouse," *The South Atlantic Quarterly*, LXI (1962), 213-222.

Shakuntala Jayaswal

LARRY WOIWODE

Born: Carrington, North Dakota
Date: October 30, 1941

Principal Works

NOVELS AND NOVELLAS: *What I'm Going to Do, I Think*, 1969; *Beyond the Bedroom Wall: A Family Album*, 1975; *Poppa John*, 1981; *Born Brothers*, 1988.
POETRY: *Even Tide*, 1977.

Larry Alfred Woiwode (pronounced "why-wood-ee") was born in Carrington, North Dakota, on October 30, 1941. He was reared in nearby Sykeston, a predominantly German settlement in rugged, often forbidding, terrain. It is this area that is probably the source of the author's appreciation for the effect of nature upon the individual. When he was ten years old, Woiwode and his family moved to Manito, Illinois, another evocatively Midwestern environment that fostered his descriptive powers. He attended the University of Illinois on and off between 1960 and 1964, but failed to complete his B.A. He left with an associate of arts degree in rhetoric and subsequently married Carol Ann Patterson in 1965. He then moved his family to New York, where he supported them with free-lance writing, publishing in *The New Yorker* and other periodicals while he worked on two novels simultaneously.

Woiwode's first novel, *What I'm Going to Do, I Think*, appeared in 1969 and won for him the prestigious William Faulkner Foundation Award as the most notable first novel of 1969; it brought to him immediate and favorable critical attention. An absorbing study of two newlyweds, the title accentuates the protagonists' self-doubt and indecision as each contemplates the responsibility of couples and parents in an age in which a transcendent faith in an all-wise, benevolent God is absent. As an intense, psychological study of two troubled individuals, *What I'm Going to Do, I Think* is a marked contrast to Woiwode's later work in both narrative strategy and characterization, but it shares with all Woiwode's output a commitment to portraying the value of "walking by faith, not by sight" in human relationships, of trusting one's parents, spouse, and children to help one navigate through a hostile world.

Woiwode's second novel, *Beyond the Bedroom Wall*, is an expansive, comic novel that reads as a discontinuous montage of events, images, and personality. Published in 1975, but actually begun earlier than his first published novel, *Beyond the Bedroom Wall* is an engaging homage to the seemingly evaporating nuclear and extended families of mid-twentieth century America. True to its subtitle, *A Family Album*, Woiwode parades before the reader sixty-three different characters before the beginning of chapter 3. Critics have remarked upon the sentimental, "old-fashioned" quality Woiwode achieves in this family chronicle; namely, his eloquent evocation of once-embraced, now-lamented values—values which often cannot bear scrutiny "beyond the bedroom wall," beyond the support of a nurturing family intimacy. Critic and novelist John Gardner placed Woiwode in the company of some of literature's great epic novelists—Charles Dickens and Fyodor Dostoevski, among them—for his rejection of fashionable pessimism and his affirmation of seeking one's dreams without sacrificing family life. Woiwode's eye for the rich details of daily life enables him to move through four generations, creating an authentic and vividly realized family history.

As Woiwode continued to write in the 1970's, he held teaching posts at various colleges, including the University of Wisconsin at Madison and Wheaton College (Illinois), while he worked on a book of poems and a third novel. The collection of poems, *Even Tide*, was published in 1977, receiving modest but positive critical reception for its informal, conversational quality and its diversity of concrete religious imagery. *Poppa John*, published in 1981, is more a novella than a novel. Judged by most critics as less successful because its title character, a soap-opera actor summarily dismissed and out of a job at Christmastime, is never fully realized, *Poppa John* still contains some of Woiwode's most lyrical scenes.

Since 1983, Woiwode has served as a faculty member at the State University of New York at Binghamton and completed work on another novel. In *Born Brothers*, published in 1988, Woiwode returns to the characters introduced in his most successful work, *Beyond the Bedroom Wall*, the Neumiller family. In some ways a sequel, in other ways not, *Born Brothers* chronicles the lives of Charles and Jerome Neumiller and their sometimes stormy sibling rivalry, this time with middle brother Charles himself as narrator rather than younger brother Tim. Here Woiwode has revitalized the relationship between memory and imagination that he evoked in the earlier narrative, frankly exhorting the reader to regard remembrance of what was as a healthier and more healing endeavor than fantasizing about what might be.

Understanding Woiwode's writing involves recognizing the essentially religious character of his narratives and their thematic structure. Woiwode rejects the notion that there can be legitimate novels of "ideas" that do not devolve into mere propaganda; he chooses to handle this problem not by creating characters who spout philosophical soliloquies but by creating authentically ordinary characters who settle comfortably into the mundane world that is life.

As a novelist, Woiwode thus stands apart from most of his contemporaries in refusing to drown his characters in the angst-ridden excesses that have become so conventional in the modern American novel. His characters are not helpless victims of their times, but participants in them. The characters in Woiwode's two best works, *Beyond the Bedroom Wall* and *Born Brothers*, recognize that the answers to life's dilemmas are found in securing trust in personal friendships and family relationships. Woiwode's willingness to reaffirm these traditional values and to point toward a transcendent moral order grounded in biblical faith makes him unique among a generation of writers whose concern is to depict their characters' dehumanization and alienation in an absurd world.

BIBLIOGRAPHICAL REFERENCES: Michael E. Connaughton, "Larry Woiwode," in *American Novelists Since World War II*, 1980 (second series), edited by James E. Kibler, Jr., provides a useful overview of Woiwode's first two novels and their interpretive context. Two interviews with Woiwode, "An Interview with Larry Woiwode," *Christianity and Literature*, XXIX (1979), 11-18; and "Larry Woiwode," in *Contemporary Authors*, New Revision Series, Vol. 16, 1985, edited by Linda Metzger and Deborah Straub, provide insights from the author himself regarding his narrative craft. See also Webster Schott, "Lost Innocents in Hemingway Country," *The New York Times Book Review*, LX (May, 1969), 46; John Gardner, review of *Beyond the Bedroom Wall*, *The New York Times Book Review*, CXXV (September 28, 1975), 1-2; Peter S. Prescott, "Home Truths," *Newsweek*, September 29, 1975, 85-86; and these reviews of *Born Brothers*: *Cleveland Plain Dealer*, December 5, 1988, C5; *The New Republic*, CXCIX (September 12, 1988), 47-50; *The New York Times Book Review*, August 14, 1988, 14; *Publishers Weekly*, CCXXXIV (June 10, 1988), 88; *Library Journal*, CXIII (August, 1988), 177.

Bruce L. Edwards

CHRISTA WOLF

Born: Landsberg an der Warthe, Germany
Date: March 18, 1929

PRINCIPAL WORKS

ESSAYS: *Lesen und Schreiben: Aufsätze und Betrachtungen*, 1971 (*The Reader and the Writer: Essays, Sketches, Memories*, 1977); *Fortgesetzter Versuch: Aufsätze, Gespräche, Essays*, 1979.

NOVELS: *Der geteilte Himmel: Erzählung*, 1963 (*Divided Heaven: A Novel of Germany Today*, 1965); *Nachdenken über Christa T.*, 1968 (*The Quest for Christa T.*, 1970); *Kindheitsmuster*, 1976 (*A Model Childhood*, 1980); *Kein Ort: Nirgends*, 1979 (*No Place on Earth*, 1982); *Kassandra: Erzählung*, 1983 (*Cassandra: A Novel and Four Essays*, 1984).

SHORT FICTION: *Moskauer Novelle*, 1961; *Unter den Linden: Drei unwahrscheinliche Geschichten*, 1974; *Gesammelte Erzählungen*, 1982.

Christa Wolf is undoubtedly one of the most prominent novelists of East Germany. Born on March 18, 1929, in the eastern part of Germany, she joined the German Socialist Party at the age of twenty and was a student of German literature at the Universities of Jena and Leipzig from 1949 to 1953. Wolf married in 1951 and gave birth to a daughter in the following year, and to a second daughter in 1956. She worked as a literary critic until 1959, then began living as an independent writer in (East) Berlin in 1962. She has received numerous prestigious literary honors in both German nations. Wolf is a highly talented narrative artist who remains deeply committed to the humanistic ideals of German socialism.

Wolf's writings are a creative and refreshing turn from the East German literature of the 1950's, which was by and large dominated by the style of Socialist Realism, a programmatic literature dictated by the political and social goals of socialist society. Literary works were expected to provide positive models of behavior for the socialist individual—self-sacrifice for the group's goals, for example—and any problematic themes, such as alienation within socialist society, were to be avoided. Wolf's works began to examine difficult and even embarrassing issues of socialist society. She has written eloquently concerning the legitimacy of the individual's subjective experience, such as a woman's concerns, within the context of a genuine commitment to socialist ideals.

Wolf's first major novel, *Divided Heaven*, suggests her ongoing commitment to the East German nation and its socialist program. Despite its somewhat immature, even trivial plot, the painful decision of the novel's heroine, Rita, not to follow her lover to West Germany but to remain in the East with the factory workers' brigade that she has come to know and trust exemplifies the kind of inner conflict that plagues some of Wolf's later characters: a deeply felt commitment to the goals of the socialist country in which she believes, versus a personal need for individual fulfillment. This theme is continued in the innovatively written *The Quest for Christa T.*, in which the narrator seeks to reconstruct from letters, notes, and personal memories the inner life of her recently deceased friend, the schoolteacher Christa T. The latter was a dedicated member of her society who believed in—but at times also honestly doubted the possibility of—the practical implementation of the socialist ideals of the equality and perfectibility of man. She was at the same time a staunch and romantic individualist who had her own wishes and desires in life. This dilemma—personal self-sacrifice for the good of the community versus the existential need for self-realization—seems to undermine Christa T.'s life and health and she succumbs to a fatal disease. Both these novels provoked a controversial reaction in East Germany, in response to the often explicit critique leveled at this socialist society, especially in its early years.

In the novel *A Model Childhood*, Wolf continues her examination of East German society, namely its coming to terms with the country's fascist past during the Nazi period. It is a strongly autobiographical text that draws on, in the form of a fictional narrator, Wolf's own childhood years in National Socialist (Nazi) Germany. She suggests that many of the attitudes and stereotypes of this time have continued. The lyrical story *No Place on Earth* depicts a fictional meeting between two brilliant but tragic eighteenth century German Romantic writers, Heinrich von Kleist and Karoline von Günderode, who represent male and female attitudes in the society and literary culture of that era. Wolf's narrative technique makes use of extensive quotations from these and other authors of the German Romantic period. These two characters illustrate, in part, the fundamental alienation of the writer-intellectual within society and the essential differences as well as complementary aspects between man and woman. The work also expresses a utopian wish for the equality and harmonious integration of conflicting social as well as gender relationships. All Wolf's narrators are women, and the plots involve major aspects of women's issues. In this text, her themes become more explicitly feminist as well as universalist.

Cassandra utilizes the figure of the prophetess and seer from the legendary Greek story of the siege of Troy in an exploration of both feminist and antiwar concerns. Within the decidedly patriarchal context of the Trojan War (fought over the possession of a woman), Cassandra—Priam's daughter who was cursed by Apollo because she refused his love and who was killed by the invading Greeks—represents, to a degree, the fate of all women in history: to be made the object of others', that is, primarily male, manipulations. The novel, which is structured as a long monologue by Cassandra, seeks to lay open to rational discussion the patriarchal assumptions that distort the writing of history and promote the oppression of all peoples by equating aggression and possessiveness with visions of nature and the divine. These views also provoked controversy and heated debate within the East German society.

Wolf has also been a prolific writer of essays and reviews on various literary and cultural topics. A trained scholar of literature, she has written on the works of Ingeborg Bachmann, the Austrian woman writer who committed suicide in 1973. She has forcefully defended the meaning and utility of literature within modern society. Wolf has also commented extensively on her approach to narrative art and emphasized—again in contrast to the style of Socialist Realism—the primacy of the individual's personal experience as the touchstone of all literary composition.

BIBLIOGRAPHICAL REFERENCES: For basic critical discussions in English, see Inta Ezergailis, *Woman Writers: The Divided Self: Analysis of Novels by Christa Wolf, Ingeborg Bachmann, Doris Lessing, and Others*, 1982, and G. Buehler, *The Death of Socialist Realism in the Novels of Christa Wolf*, 1984. For important interpretive works in German, see Marion von Salisch, *Zwischen Selbstaufgabe und Selbstverwirklichung: Zum Problem der Persönlichkeitsstruktur im Werk Christa Wolfs*, 1975; Alexander Stephan, *Christa Wolf*, 1976; *Christa Wolf: Materialienbuch*, 1979, edited by Klaus Sauer; Sonja Hilzinger, *Kassandra: Über Christa Wolf*, 1982; Dieter Sevin, *Christa Wolf: "Der geteilte Himmel," "Nachdenken über Christa T.,"* 1982; *Wolf: Darstellung, Deutung, Diskussion*, 1984, edited by Manfred Jurgensen. See also Myra Love, "Christa Wolf and Feminism: Breaking the Patriarchal Connection," *New German Critique*, XVI (1979), 31-53; Alexander Stephan, "The Emancipation of Man: Christa Wolf as a Woman Writer," *GDR Monitor* II (1979/1980), 23-31; Jeanette Clausen, "The Difficulty of Saying I in the Works of Christa Wolf," in *Gestaltet und gestaltend: Frauen in der deutschen Literatur*, 1980, edited by Marianne Burkhardt; K. McPherson, "In Search of the New Prose: Christa Wolf's Reflections on Writing and the Writer in the 1960's and 1970's," *New German Studies*, I (1981), 1-13; H. Fehervary, "Christa Wolf's Prose: A Landscape of Masks," *New German Critique*, XXVII (1982), 57-88; and Marilyn S. Fries, "Christa Wolf's Use of Image and Vision in the Narrative Structuring Experience," *Studies in GDR Culture and Society*, II (1982), 59-86.

Thomas F. Barry

TOM WOLFE

Born: Richmond, Virginia
Date: March 2, 1931

PRINCIPAL WORKS

SOCIAL CRITICISM: *The Kandy-Kolored Tangerine-Flake Streamline Baby*, 1965; *The Pump House Gang*, 1968; *The Electric Kool-Aid Acid Test*, 1968; *Radical Chic and Mau-Mauing the Flak Catchers*, 1970; *The New Journalism*, 1973; *The Painted Word*, 1975; *Mauve Gloves & Madmen, Clutter & Vine, and Other Stories, Sketches, and Essays*, 1976; *The Right Stuff*, 1979; *In Our Time*, 1980; *From Bauhaus to Our House*, 1981; *The Purple Decades: A Reader*, 1982.

NOVEL: *The Bonfire of the Vanities*, 1987.

Thomas Kennerly Wolfe, Jr., is one of the most prominent and popular writers of fiction and social commentary of the last third of the twentieth century. He was born in Richmond, Virginia, on March 2, 1931, the son of Thomas Kennerly and Helen (Hughes) Wolfe. He received a bachelor's degree from Washington and Lee University (1951) and a Ph.D. from Yale University (1957). In 1978, he married Sheila Berger, art director of *Harper's Magazine*. They would have a daughter, Alexandra. While Wolfe was establishing himself as a writer of satirical essays on contemporary American culture, he worked as a reporter for various newspapers and magazines, beginning in the late 1950's with the *Springfield Union* and continuing in the 1960's with *The Washington Post*, *New York Herald Tribune*, *New York* Sunday magazine, and *New York World Journal Tribune*. With success came independence, yet Wolfe continued to act as contributing editor for *New York* and *Esquire* magazines and as contributing artist for *Harper's Magazine*. As an artist, he has exhibited in one-man shows and illustrated many of his own works.

With the exception of an occasional short story, Wolfe wrote no fiction until *The Bonfire of the Vanities*. Until then, his fame rested exclusively on his witty and incisive social commentaries, written in a style characterized as "new journalism," a term that has come to be associated with Wolfe since the publication in *Esquire* of "The Kandy-Kolored Tangerine-Flake Streamline Baby." New journalism is a blend of journalistic objectivity and fictional subjectivity, written in a colloquial style, often with the reporter intruding into the narrative. *The Kandy-Kolored Tangerine-Flake Streamline Baby*, a collection of twenty-two essays including the celebrated *Esquire* piece, was published in 1965. It was followed in 1968 by *The Pump House Gang* and *The Electric Kool-Aid Acid Test*, the latter an account of Ken Kesey and his "Merry Pranksters," a notorious group of counterculture "hippies" dedicated to lysergic acid diethylamide (LSD) and the pursuit of the psychedelic experience. Wolfe achieved notoriety in 1970 with *Radical Chic and Mau-Mauing the Flak Catchers*, two long essays satirizing contemporary liberal sacred cows. Of the two, it was "Radical Chic" that created the greatest furor because it held up to ridicule the prospect of affluent, cultivated Jews catering to revolutionary Black Panthers at a fancy social gathering in the exclusive Park Avenue apartment of Leonard and Felicia Bernstein.

What impressed most critics about "Radical Chic" was Wolfe's thorough reporting and his total detachment. Although his style calls attention to his presence in the midst of what he observes, Wolfe lets the participants speak for—and thus incriminate—themselves. It was these same qualities that infuriated the targets of his later two books: *The Painted Word*, an exposé of the world of contemporary art, and *From Bauhaus to Our House*, an attack on the ideology behind all that is slablike and ugly in modern architecture. Insiders in both art and architecture accused Wolfe of betraying the ignorance and the philistinism of an outsider who could not possibly hope to understand modern art or architecture; most others praised Wolfe for his painstaking research and persuasive logic. Critics were generally in agreement about the virtues of *The Right Stuff*, Wolfe's tribute to heroism as exhibited in the remarkably cool style of the first American astronaut team.

Comparatively late in his career, Wolfe took the literary world by storm with *The Bonfire of the Vanities*, a first novel which, after appearing in serialized form in *Rolling Stone*, remained more than a year on *The New York Times* best-seller list. Wolfe's theme—the existence of class distinctions in a supposedly egalitarian society—is so thoroughly explored in this novel that Wolfe has been compared favorably to Charles Dickens and Honoré de Balzac. Wolfe's critics fall into two camps: those who distrust the new journalism and those who deplore his political neutrality. The former say that Wolfe blurs the traditional distinction between fiction and nonfiction, to the detriment of both; the latter claim that Wolfe started out as a liberal critic of American society only to turn reactionary. Wolfe's detractors, however, are definitely in the minority, something quite remarkable for a writer fond of widespread lampoon. His humor goes far toward explaining his appeal, yet Wolfe's real talent lies in the invigorating energy of his style. Indeed, his admirers contend that he has breathed new life into both the fiction and nonfiction of the late twentieth century.

BIBLIOGRAPHICAL REFERENCES: Serious critical commentary about Wolfe has been mainly the work of reviewers, some of it quite astute. For example, John Gregory Dunne, "Hog Heaven," a review of *The Right Stuff*, *The New York Review of Books*, XXVI (November 8, 1979), 9, analyzes Wolfe's emphasis on status as a contemporary American preoccupation, and John Sutherland, "Big Bad Wolfe," a review of *The Bonfire of the Vanities*, *London Review of Books*, X, no. 4 (1988), 15-16, identifies the gothic elements in Wolfe's vision, comparing it with Edgar Allan Poe's in "The Masque of the Red Death." Among the few scholarly articles that have been written about Wolfe, two are of particular interest. In John Hersey, "The Legend on the License," *The Yale Review*, LXXV, no. 2 (1986), 289-314, the writer attacks new journalism and its leading practitioners—Wolfe, Norman Mailer, and Truman Capote—for making it increasingly difficult for people to distinguish between truth and lies. A more favorable appraisal of Wolfe's literary credentials is to be found in Thomas L. Hartshorne, "Tom Wolfe on the 1960's," *Midwest Quarterly*, XXIII (1982), 144-163. Wolfe figures prominently in Thomas Reed Whissen, *The Devil's Advocates: Decadence in Modern Literature*, 1989, as the leading exponent of the decadent temper in contemporary literature.

Thomas Whissen

TOBIAS WOLFF

Born: Birmingham, Alabama
Date: June 19, 1945

PRINCIPAL WORKS

SHORT FICTION: *In the Garden of the North American Martyrs*, 1981; *Back in the World*, 1985; *The Barracks Thief and Selected Stories*, 1986.

NOVELLA: *The Barracks Thief*, 1984.

AUTOBIOGRAPHY: *This Boy's Life: A Memoir*, 1989.

Tobias (Jonathan Ansell) Wolff is one of the most highly respected writers of short fiction to achieve prominence in the 1980's. He was born in Birmingham, Alabama, on June 19, 1945, the son of Arthur and Rosemary (Loftus) Wolff, and grew up in the state of Washington, where he and his mother had moved some six years after his parents' divorce in 1951. Wolff left his home in rural Washington to attend preparatory school at the Hill School in Pennsylvania but failed to graduate from that institution. After enlisting in the U.S. Army, Special Forces, serving from 1964 to 1968, during which time he served in Vietnam, Wolff earned a bachelor's degree from the University of Oxford in 1972 and a master's degree from Oxford in 1975. He spent the 1975-1976 academic year at Stanford University, having won a Wallace Stegner Fellowship in creative writing. He earned a master's degree from Stanford in 1978, the same year in which he received his first National Endowment for the Arts fellowship. Like many other contemporary writers, Wolff has supported himself by teaching. He has served on the faculties of Stanford University, Goddard College, Arizona State University, and Syracuse University and has been a reporter for *The Washington Post*. Wolff published his first collection of stories, *In the Garden of the North American Martyrs*, in 1981. The book received exceptionally laudatory reviews, and the following year it earned for Wolff the St. Lawrence Award for Fiction. In the stories' range of characters, situations, and literary techniques, this collection revealed Wolff to be a writer not merely of promise but of manifest achievement as well.

Wolff's second book, the novella *The Barracks Thief*, confirmed his narrative gifts. Originally a novel-length manuscript, it was subjected to intense revision that eliminated inessential characters as well as unnecessary passages of exposition and that introduced greater complexity of narrative technique—including Wolff's startling yet successful shifts from third-person to first-person points of view. Widely admired by reviewers, *The Barracks Thief* won for Wolff the PEN/Faulkner Award in 1985 as the best work of fiction published during the preceding year. The year 1985 also saw the publication of Wolff's second collection of stories, *Back in the World*. Frequently set in either California or the Pacific Northwest, all the stories in this volume use third-person points of view that tend to distance the reader from the characters. Although this collection did not generate as enthusiastic a response from reviewers as did Wolff's first two books, it continued to develop a number of his characteristic themes and situations.

Since the publication of *Back in the World*, Wolff has also published *The Barracks Thief and Selected Stories*, a volume that reprints six of the twelve stories from his first collection, and *This Boy's Life*, an autobiographical memoir that appeared in 1989. In vivid, often humorous, sometimes painful scenes, Wolff's memoir recounts his experiences from age ten through enrollment at Hill School. With utter candor, he records the duplicity with which he created an assortment of identities for himself and describes the difficult relationship he had with his stepfather. Among the book's major strengths are its honesty, its hopefulness amid disillusionment, and its repudiation of self-pity.

In a revealing essay on the fiction of Paul Bowles, Wolff describes the characters of Bowles's extraordinary first novel, *The Sheltering Sky* (1949), as "refugees of a sort peculiar to our age: affluent drifters dispossessed spiritually rather than materially." The same might be said of many of Wolff's characters. Against what Wolff calls, in the same essay, "that voice in each of us that sings the delight of not being responsible, of refusing the labor of choice by which we create ourselves," Wolff seeks to bring his characters into the realm of responsibility, where questions of good and evil, justice and injustice, are central. His stories—written in a style marked by clarity, grace, and an unpretentious metaphorical richness—take their place in the tradition of realism, not among the metafictions of Donald Barthelme, Robert Coover, and John Barth.

Some of Wolff's fiction assumes the shape of moral parable, as in the title story of his first collection and in "The Rich Brother," the concluding story in *Back in the World*, with its fablelike opening and its affirmation of the responsibilities that brotherhood imposes. Other stories, such as "Next Door" and "The Liar," the opening and closing pieces in his first book, culminate in visionary glimpses of a world that impinges on ordinary reality but rarely coincides with it, a world of tranquillity, love, and compassion. Yet despite the clear ethical concerns of his stories, Wolff often strives to complicate the moral judgments of his readers. In *The Barracks Thief*, for example, the novella's shifting narrative perspectives enlist the readers' sympathy for Lewis, the thief. In "Coming Attractions," a teenage girl who makes a practice of shoplifting and who keeps whatever lost belongings she finds in the movie theater where she works, is shown, at story's end, struggling selflessly to raise a bicycle from a swimming pool so that she can give it to her younger brother. Such unanticipated acts of generosity occur regularly in Wolff's fiction, suggesting the mysterious depths of human motivation and the regenerative potential of people's capacity for change. Although Wolff's characters are frequently flawed, directionless human beings, Wolff presents many of them in situations in which they discover unsuspected or obscured dimensions of themselves, as does the protagonist of "The Other Miller." Wolff's stories, grounded in their author's belief that "storytelling is one of the sustaining arts," thus serve to evoke moral and spiritual alternatives to the spiritlessness of so much of contemporary life. They affirm the possibilities of renewal.

BIBLIOGRAPHICAL REFERENCES: For valuable insights into Wolff's literary aims and concerns, see the interviews by Michael Burke in *FM Five*, III (1986), 10-11, and Jean W. Ross in *Contemporary Authors*, Vol. 117, 1986, edited by Hal May. Also helpful in this connection are Wolff's introduction to *Matters of Life and Death: New American Stories*, 1983, an anthology he edited; and his essay "A Forgotten Master: Rescuing the Works of Paul Bowles," *Esquire*, May, 1985, 221-222. See also Jonathan Gill, "Fourth Grade Never Dies Out," *The New York Times Book Review*, XCIV (January 15, 1989), 28; Tom Jenks, "How Writers Live Today," *Esquire*, CIV (August, 1985), 123; Francine Prose, " 'The Brothers Wolff' (Authors Tobias & Geoffrey Wolff)," *The New York Times Magazine*, CXXXVIII (February 5, 1989), 22; David Gates, "Our Stories, Our Selves (The 'I' in Autobiographies)," *Newsweek*, CXIII (January 27, 1989), 64; Paul Gray, review of *This Boy's Life*, *Time*, CXXXIII (February 6, 1989), 70; Patricia T. O'Connor, review of *Back in the World*, *The New York Times Book Review*, CXI (October 5, 1986), 58; and Shelley Cox, review of *In the Garden of the North American Martyrs*, *Library Journal*, CVI (October 1, 1981), 1947. For additional insight on Wolff's extraordinary family, his brother Geoffrey's portrait of their father, *The Duke of Deception: Memories of My Father*, 1979, is invaluable.

John Lang

VIRGINIA WOOLF

Born: London, England
Date: January 25, 1882

Died: Rodmell, England
Date: March 28, 1941

Principal Works

NOVELS: *The Voyage Out*, 1915; *Night and Day*, 1919; *Jacob's Room*, 1922; *Mrs. Dalloway*, 1925; *To the Lighthouse*, 1927; *Orlando: A Biography*, 1928; *The Waves*, 1931; *The Years*, 1937; *Between the Acts*, 1941.

LITERARY CRITICISM: *The Common Reader*, 1925; *A Room of One's Own*, 1929; *The Common Reader: Second Series*, 1932 (also known as *The Second Common Reader*); *Contemporary Writers*, 1965; *Books and Portraits*, 1977.

ESSAYS: *The Death of the Moth and Other Essays*, 1942; *The Moment and Other Essays*, 1947; *The Captain's Death Bed and Other Essays*, 1950; *Granite and Rainbow*, 1958; *The London Scene: Five Essays*, 1975.

SHORT FICTION: *Monday or Tuesday*, 1921; *A Haunted House and Other Short Stories*, 1943; *Mrs. Dalloway's Party: A Short Story Sequence*, 1973.

CORRESPONDENCE: *The Flight of the Mind: The Letters of Virginia Woolf, Vol. 1, 1888-1912*, 1975; *The Question of Things Happening: The Letters of Virginia Woolf, Vol. 2, 1912-1922*, 1976; *A Change of Perspective: The Letters of Virginia Woolf, Vol. 3, 1923-1928*, 1977; *A Reflection of the Other Person: The Letters of Virginia Woolf, Vol. 4, 1929-1931*, 1978; *The Sickle Side of the Moon: The Letters of Virginia Woolf, Vol. 5, 1932-1935*, 1979; *Leave the Letters Till We're Dead: The Letters of Virginia Woolf, Vol. 6, 1936-1941*, 1980.

AUTOBIOGRAPHY: *A Writer's Diary*, 1953; *Moments of Being*, 1976; *The Diary of Virginia Woolf*, 1977-1984.

BIOGRAPHY: *Roger Fry: A Biography*, 1940.

The preeminent literary figure of the Bloomsbury circle, Adeline Virginia Stephen Woolf is an important modern experimental writer. The second daughter of Leslie Stephen (knighted in 1902) and his second wife, Julia Prinsep Duckworth Stephen, she was born in Kensington, London, on January 25, 1882. Even as a child she exhibited the two traits that would characterize her life: a highly creative imagination and keen intelligence, coupled with extreme nervousness that resulted in breakdowns under stress. Because of this nervousness she did not attend school, but her father, one of London's leading literati, gave her free rein to use his library at Hyde Park Gate. The family spent its summers at Tallant House, St. Ives, on the Cornish coast, the setting for *To the Lighthouse*. At the suggestion of Violet Dickinson, Woolf began sending samples of her writing to Margaret Lyttleton, editor of the women's pages for the weekly *The Guardian*; her first article, a review of William Dean Howells' *The Son of Royal Langbrith* (1904), appeared in that periodical on December 14, 1904. Even after she became an established writer she continued to review, especially for *The Times Literary Supplement*; some of these pieces developed into essays such as those collected in *The Common Reader*.

The year 1904 not only marked the launching of Woolf's literary career but also witnessed the beginning of the Bloomsbury circle. Following the death of their father in February of that year, Virginia, her sister Vanessa, and her brother Adrian set up house in Gordon Square. Their home became a gathering place for many of their brother Thoby Stephen's University of Cambridge friends, among them Roger Fry, John Maynard Keynes, Lytton Strachey, Clive Bell, whom Vanessa would marry, and Leonard Sidney Woolf, who married Virginia in 1912. Woolf's first novel appeared in 1915; *The Voyage Out* and *Night and Day*, published four years later, are conventional. With *Jacob's Room*, however, she began to experiment with fiction; she was free to try out new techniques because in 1917 she and her husband had established the Hogarth Press. Intended initially as a hobby, it became an important conduit for modern writers, including T. S. Eliot and Katherine Mansfield (whom the Woolfs met because of the press), Sigmund Freud, Harold Laski, Robert Graves, and E. M. Forster.

Over the next two decades, a steady stream of work flowed from Woolf's pen: six more novels; biographies of Roger Fry and Elizabeth Barrett Browning's dog, Flush; two volumes of *The Common Reader*; and numerous short stories, essays, and letters. Writing was a relief, but it was also a struggle, against both the blank page and mental breakdown. Overwhelmed by the Blitz and fears for her Jewish husband's life in the event of a Nazi conquest of England, Woolf committed suicide on March 28, 1941. As this event so tragically demonstrates, Woolf was not oblivious to the great world events of her time. War intrudes into *Jacob's Room*, *Mrs. Dalloway*, and *Between the Acts*, and feminism into *The Years*, but Woolf's concern is largely with the intimate and the interior. As early at 1919, in her essay "Modern Fiction," she attacked the Edwardians as "materialists" for their emphasis on external reality. As much as Ezra Pound and the Imagists in poetry, she adhered to the creed, "Make it new!" She urged writers to "look within," to focus on the psychological state of their characters.

Hence, in the tradition of Samuel Richardson and Jane Austen, she concentrates on the small but revealing action—or inaction. A look can charge the air and make everyone in the room twitch. Like the Victorians, she is a realist, but for her reality is, as she states in *A Room of One's Own*, "now . . . in a dusty road, now in a scrap of newspaper in the street, now in a daffodil in the sun." In Woolf's fiction, children, artists, women, and those who reject outworn beliefs and conventions can perceive that reality. Even for them, though, the luminous moment cannot last, for evil and stupidity can easily overwhelm goodness and intelligence. Thus, in *Between the Acts*, the child George enjoys a perfect moment of happiness as he holds a flower. Then he is bowled over by his grandfather and an Afghan hound.

Woolf treats a small world of artists, scholars, intellectuals—the people she knew from Bloomsbury—but within that world she confronts all the important issues: love and hate, freedom and bondage, solitude and society. Her novels, like her criticism, focus on the small detail, the seemingly insignificant element that can illuminate a character and, indeed, the world. Dismissed or ignored by many critics during the mid-twentieth century, Woolf has since that time gained recognition as one of the principal innovators in modern literature. Her experimental fiction helped to liberate the novel from the tyranny of plot, encouraging other writers to follow her in the exploration of consciousness. Woolf's works have been translated into more than fifty languages; three journals are devoted to analyzing her life and works; and virtually every available scrap of her writing, even the reading notes she made for her book reviews, has been published. Woolf commented that her father gave her only one piece of advice about writing—to say clearly, in the fewest words possible, precisely what she meant. Among scholars and lay readers alike, the consensus is that she mastered this lesson well.

BIBLIOGRAPHICAL REFERENCES: The number of books devoted to Woolf is enormous and steadily growing. Quentin Bell, Woolf's nephew, has written the standard biography, *Virginia Woolf: A Biography*, 1972, which offers little analysis of the works. Leon Edel, *Bloomsbury: A House of Lions*, 1979, provides an excellent introduction to this fascinating group. John Lehman, *Virginia Woolf and Her World*, 1975, offers a good pictorial biography. In *Recollections of Virginia Woolf by Her Contemporaries*, 1972, Joan Russell Noble has collected twenty-eight sketches of the writer by those who knew her. See also Lyndall Gordon, *Virginia Woolf: A Writer's Life*, 1984, and Louise DeSalvo, *Virginia Woolf: The Impact of Childhood Sexual Abuse on Her Life and Work*, 1989. Useful critical studies of the works include Jean Alexander, *The Venture of Form in the Novels of Virginia Woolf*, 1974, and Bernard Blackstone, *Virginia Woolf*, 1952. Blackstone's *Virginia Woolf: A Commentary*, 1949, introduces the literature well. The thirteen essays in Ralph Freedman, *Virginia Woolf: Re-*

valuation and Continuity, 1980, offer new insights; for a sensitive reading of the fiction, see Hermione Lee, *The Novels of Virginia Woolf*, 1977. Edward Bishop, *A Virginia Woolf Chronology*, 1989, is a very useful reference tool. Hundreds of shorter studies of Woolf are available. Among the best are Morris Beja, "Virginia Woolf: Matches Struck in the Dark," in *Epiphany in the Modern Novel*, 1971; Sisir Chattopadhyaya, "Virginia Woolf and the Capture of the Moment," in *The Technique of the Modern English Novel*, 1959; Margaret Church, "The Moment and Virginia Woolf," in *Time and Reality: Studies in Contemporary Fiction*, 1963; and Nellie Elizabeth Monroe's early but still sound "Experimental Humanism in Virginia Woolf," in *The Novel and Society: A Critical Survey of the Modern Novel*, 1941.

Joseph Rosenblum

HERMAN WOUK

Born: New York, New York
Date: May 27, 1915

PRINCIPAL WORKS

NOVELS AND NOVELLAS: *Aurora Dawn*, 1947; *The City Boy*, 1948; *The Caine Mutiny*, 1951; *Marjorie Morningstar*, 1955; *Youngblood Hawke*, 1962; *Don't Stop the Carnival*, 1965; *The Lomokome Papers*, 1968; *The Winds of War*, 1971; *War and Remembrance*, 1978; *Inside, Outside*, 1985.

PLAYS: *The Traitor*, pr., pb. 1949; *The Caine Mutiny Court-Martial*, pr. 1953; *Nature's Way*, pr. 1957.

SCREENPLAY: *Slattery's Hurricane*, 1956 (with Richard Murphy).

TELEPLAYS: *The Winds of War*, 1983; *War and Remembrance*, 1988.

RELIGION: *This Is My God*, 1959.

Herman Wouk is one of the most important modern American novelists, a writer who creates fiction which is both enjoyable entertainment and serious literature. He was born in New York City on May 27, 1915, and is the son of Abraham Isaac and Esther Levine Wouk, both Russian-Jewish immigrants. His father started in the United States as a poor laundry laborer and gradually built a successful chain of laundries. Wouk has used the experience of living in a family constantly beset by business worries, as well as much else from his youth, as integral parts of several of his novels. He attended Townsend Harris Hall in the Bronx from 1927 to 1930, and he went on to graduate with honors from Columbia University, majoring in comparative literature and philosophy, in 1934. While at Columbia, he was editor of the college humor magazine, *Columbia Jester*, and wrote two of the popular annual variety shows.

In 1935, he got his first professional position, as a radio comedy writer, but was disappointed to learn that his job consisted primarily of copying old jokes onto file cards. Eventually, however, he proved his ability, and, over the next several years, gradually assumed greater responsibilities, even assisting the famous Fred Allen with his weekly radio show. In 1941, he began writing scripts to promote the sale of United States war bonds, but his radio career was ended when he enlisted in the U.S. Navy in 1942. In 1943, while serving as deck officer aboard a destroyer/minesweeper, Wouk began writing his first novel, *Aurora Dawn*, in his spare time. He was unable to complete it, however, until May of 1946. In the meantime, in December of 1945, he was married to Betty Sarah Brown, a convert to Judaism. The Wouks had three children, Abraham Isaac (who died in 1951 at age five), Nathaniel, and Joseph.

Aurora Dawn is a satirical look at the business of radio and advertising, and follows the adventures of Andrew Reale, an ambitious young radio comedy scriptwriter. It is written in the stylized manner of an eighteenth century novel, such as Henry Fielding's *Tom Jones*, (1749). *Aurora Dawn* was not treated very kindly by the reviewers, who saw it as an unsuccessful attempt at social criticism. There are at least a few readers, however, who believe that it is one of Wouk's best novels: It is riotously funny, gently sarcastic, and very wise—Wouk frequently injects ironic philosophical asides which comment sagely upon the human condition. *Aurora Dawn* was popular enough to be chosen as a Book-of-the-Month Club selection, and even some of Wouk's worst critics at least recognized his potential. This potential was more widely acknowledged after the appearance of Wouk's second novel, *The City Boy*, which is the humorous, but also poignant, story of a fat eleven-year-old Jewish boy, Herbie Bookbinder. While *The City Boy* has been favorably compared with Mark Twain's *The Adventures of Tom Sawyer* (1876) as a universal tale of maturation, it also adumbrates Wouk's later concern with the unique experience of Jews in America.

Wouk next turned his hand to drama with *The Traitor*, which opened on Broadway in April, 1949. Since the play's theme of the decision of an atom bomb scientist to divulge secrets to the enemy seemed to parallel the real-life events of the then-recent Klaus Fuchs spy case, it was widely assumed that Wouk was attempting to cash in on public interest in this scandal. The play was not a great success. In 1951, Wouk published what is generally considered his greatest novel, *The Caine Mutiny*, which won a Pulitzer Prize. It is the suspenseful drama of a Navy lieutenant who took over command of his insane captain's ship. *The Caine Mutiny* was so well-received that Wouk later turned it into a play, *The Caine Mutiny Court-Martial*, which was also very popular. A highly acclaimed film of the book, starring Humphrey Bogart, was produced in 1954.

Both of Wouk's next two novels, *Marjorie Morningstar* and *Youngblood Hawke*, were also made into films. *Marjorie Morningstar* portrays the attempts of a young Jewish girl in New York to succeed in a non-Jewish society. As in most of Wouk's novels, social commentary is gently integrated into a fascinating plot with very endearing characters. *Youngblood Hawke*, however, is an exception. It seems to highlight many of the stereotypic qualities of Jewish family life—an overly introspective hero with an overbearing mother, for example—without any of the characters being Jewish. In between *Marjorie Morningstar* and *Youngblood Hawke*, Wouk produced his third play, *Nature's Way*, an unsuccessful comedy about a young songwriter who leaves his wife and goes to Italy with a homosexual friend. He also wrote *This Is My God*, an informative discussion of Jewish beliefs, customs, and traditions, as well as the problems Jews have in observing them while trying to fit into the secularized society of modern America.

From 1962 to 1969, Wouk was a member of the board of trustees for the College of the Virgin Islands, and this experience provided much of the background material for his most disappointing novel, *Don't Stop the Carnival*. This work fails on several levels: None of its characters is either very interesting or very likable; the usual Wouk humor has become cynical and heavy-handed; and the plot becomes bogged down in trivia. Wouk's next work, *The Lomokome Papers*, is not really a novel, but a novella, and was published only in paperback. It is a strange sort of science-fiction fable whose point is very unclear. Wouk seemed to be saving his creative juices for one of his best efforts, *The Winds of War*, an epic that spans the period from 1939 to the bombing of Pearl Harbor on December 7, 1941. The hero, Victor ("Pug") Henry, is a naval officer who becomes entangled in international diplomacy through his assignment as an unofficial envoy of President Franklin D. Roosevelt. Alternating with the adventures of Pug and his family are chapters of a history of the war written from the viewpoint of a fictitious German general, Armin von Roon. *The Winds of War* was both an artistic and a popular success; in 1983, it was made into an equally popular eighteen-hour television miniseries. In 1988, its sequel, *War and Remembrance*, also received this treatment, but with much less spectacular results. Ironically, Wouk has indicated that *The Winds of War* was only a "prologue"; *War and Remembrance* was the real story he intended to write. Generally, *War and Remembrance* is a much darker tale: Its heroes no longer seem so heroic, and its main focus, the horrors of the Holocaust, is extremely somber.

Wouk's *Inside, Outside* is a semiautobiographical story of an ambitious Jewish liberal who, ironically, serves as a political aide to the Richard Nixon Administration in its final year. As the government crumbles, he ruminates upon his heritage, and the book consists largely of flashbacks of his immigrant father's difficulties in adjusting to American life. In one sense, *Inside, Outside* seems like the culmination of all that Wouk has been trying to do: to portray in fiction the social history of Jews in modern America. Yet, as a tale, it often fails, perhaps precisely because of its heavy emphasis on this history. Nevertheless, Wouk's characters, as usual, remain fascinating, and, overall, he continues to be one of America's greatest storytellers.

BIBLIOGRAPHICAL REFERENCES: Arnold Beichman has done a wonderful study of Wouk's work, *Herman Wouk: The Novelist as Social Historian*, 1984, which incorporates much biographical detail. Short biographical sketches are included in John K. Hutchins, "Happy Success Story of Herman Wouk," *New York Herald Tribune Book Review*, XXXII (September 4, 1955), 2; Jane Howard, "Herman Wouk Surfaces Again," *Life*, LXXI (November 6, 1971), 54; Mark J. Charney, "Herman Wouk," *Dictionary of Literary Biography Yearbook: 1982*, 1983, edited by Richard Ziegfeld; and H. Colby, "Herman Wouk," *Wilson Library Bulletin*, XXVI (March, 1952). Maxwell Geismar, *American Moderns from Rebellion to Conformity*, 1958, contains a long review of *Marjorie Morningstar* and a separate essay on Wouk himself. Among Wouk's novels, *The Caine Mutiny* has received the most critical and analytical attention. Detailed discussions are included in Allen Guttman, *The Jewish Writer in America: Assimilation and the Crisis in Identity*, 1971; Edmund Fuller, *Man in Modern Fiction*, 1958; and Peter G. Jones, *War and the Novelist: Appraising the American War Novel*, 1976. Guttman also analyzes *Marjorie Morningstar.* An especially hostile view of Wouk's work, particularly *Youngblood Hawke*, is offered by Stanley E. Hyman, *Standards: A Chronicle of Books for Our Time*, 1966. W. Tasker Witham, *The Adolescent in the American Novel: 1920-1960*, 1975, focuses on *The City Boy* and *Marjorie Morningstar.* Irwin Ross, in the *New York Post* (beginning January 22, 1956), wrote an informative six-article series on Wouk and his work. *The Winds of War* and *War and Remembrance* are analyzed as political statements in Michael Mandelbaum, "The Political Lessons of Two World War II Novels: A Review Essay," *Political Science Quarterly*, XCIV (Fall, 1979), 515-522. See also Albert Van Nostrand, *The Denatured Novel*, 1956, a brilliantly witty discussion of the development of popular novels, including *The Caine Mutiny.* William H. Whyte, *The Organization Man*, 1956, is a famous sociological work which discusses *The Caine Mutiny* within the context of the tensions between individuals and organizations. Leslie Fiedler, *Love and Death in the American Novel*, 1960, includes a provocative discussion of *Marjorie Morningstar.* A general assessment of the quality of Pulitzer Prize-winning novels, including *The Caine Mutiny*, is offered in W. J. Stuckey, *The Pulitzer Prize Novels: A Critical Backward Look*, 1966.

Thomas C. Schunk

RICHARD WRIGHT

Born: Natchez, Mississippi
Date: September 4, 1908

Died: Paris, France
Date: December 5, 1960

PRINCIPAL WORKS

NOVELS: *Native Son*, 1940; *The Outsider*, 1953; *Savage Holiday*, 1954; *The Long Dream*, 1958; *Lawd Today*, 1963.

AUTOBIOGRAPHY: *Black Boy*, 1945; *American Hunger*, 1977.

SHORT FICTION: *Uncle Tom's Children*, 1938; *Eight Men*, 1961.

SOCIAL CRITICISM: *Twelve Million Black Voices*, 1941; *Black Power*, 1954; *The Color Curtain*, 1956; *Pagan Spain*, 1957; *White Man, Listen!*, 1957.

PLAY: *Native Son: The Biography of a Young American*, pr. 1941 (with Paul Green).

Richard Wright's literary reputation has been largely determined by the political and racial concerns of his fiction. From the time he published *Native Son* until his death, he was viewed primarily as the literary spokesman for black radicalism. It has only been since the 1970's that critics have begun to examine his writing in a broader perspective. Born on September 4, 1908, to Ella and Nathan Wright on a farm near Natchez, Mississippi, Richard Wright led a difficult childhood of economic deprivation, familial disruption, and frequent relocations. The family was living in Memphis when Wright's father abandoned them in 1914. His mother's poverty and increasing illness made it necessary to rely on relatives and to move frequently. For a short time, Wright and his younger brother were placed in an orphanage. For the remainder of his youth, the family traveled between Elaine, Arkansas; West Helena, Arkansas; Greenwood, Mississippi; and Jackson, Mississippi.

Wright received the bulk of his formal education at Smith-Robinson High School in Jackson, from which he was graduated as valedictorian in 1925. While in high school, he wrote "The Voodoo of Hell's Half Acre," a story that was published in the *Southern Register*, a local black newspaper. After graduation, he worked in Memphis and began an intensive period of reading H. L. Mencken, Sinclair Lewis, and Theodore Dreiser. In 1927, he traveled to Chicago. There he worked at a variety of jobs, but in 1931, he was forced to go on relief. He continued writing and sold the story "Superstition" to *Abbott's Monthly Magazine*. He subsequently found work at Michael Reese Hospital, the South Side Boys' Club, and the Illinois Federal Writers' Project. In 1932, he began attending meetings of the John Reed Club, a Communist literary society. That connection led him to publish numerous crudely didactic poems in leftist journals. In 1933, Wright officially joined the Communist Party. It was not long, though, before the cynicism of the Communist movement, particularly its decision to eliminate the literary aspects of the John Reed Clubs, angered Wright.

Despite his arguments with the Communist Party in Chicago, Wright was named Harlem editor of the *Daily Worker* and moved to New York in 1937. During his last two years in Chicago, he had begun to publish the stories that first brought him national attention. His first novel, which was posthumously published as *Lawd Today*, was rejected, but winning first prize in *Story* magazine's fiction contest made it easier for him to find a publisher for *Uncle Tom's Children*. *Uncle Tom's Children*, in turn, helped Wright get a Guggenheim Fellowship. With this financial support, he was able to finish *Native Son*, and that sensational novel became the first best-seller written by a black author. In *Native Son*, Wright consciously eliminated the sentimentality that had made *Uncle Tom's Children* too easy for liberal white readers. In Bigger Thomas, he created one of the least attractive protagonists in American literature, an uncompromising portrait of black anger and frustration.

Buoyed by the success of his novel, Wright entered an artistically active period during which he collaborated with Paul Green on a dramatic version of *Native Son*, collaborated with Edwin Rosskam on *Twelve Million Black Voices*, a pictorial history of black Americans, and began work on another novel, the final section of which was published as "The Man Who Lived Underground." He also worked on his autobiography, the first part of which was published in 1945 as *Black Boy.* Some critics consider this powerful retelling of his early years Wright's best work. Disappointed by the continued racism of American society after World War II, Wright emigrated to France in 1947. The influence of Jean-Paul Sartre and other existentialists is evident in *The Outsider*, which Wright published in 1953. During the 1950's, he published three books of political commentary based on his travels and lectured on contemporary issues. His last two novels, *Savage Holiday* and *The Long Dream*, were critical failures. He died of a heart attack in 1960, and unsubstantiated rumors that his death was directly or indirectly caused by agents of the United States government have become a persistent part of his legend.

Wright introduced white America to an assertive black literature and encouraged a generation of black authors that followed his lead. *Native Son* and several of his short stories are considered masterpieces of social realism, and *Black Boy* is one of the most influential American autobiographies. Critics have become more appreciative of Wright's existential novel, *The Outsider*, but most agree that his most important work was behind him when he left the United States.

BIBLIOGRAPHICAL REFERENCES: One of the most authoritative biographies is Michel Fabre, *The Unfinished Quest of Richard Wright*, 1973, translated by Isabel Barzum. Margaret Walker, *Richard Wright: Daemonic Genius*, 1988, part memoir, part biography, part literary criticism from the perspective of a fellow novelist, is an indispensable source. For further biographical study, see Keneth Kinnamon, *The Emergence of Richard Wright: A Study in Literature and Society*, 1972; Constance Webb, *Richard Wright: A Biography*, 1968; and John A. Williams, *The Most Native of Sons: A Biography of Richard Wright*, 1970. Important book-length critical studies include Joyce Ann Joyce, *Richard Wright's Art of Tragedy*, 1986; Michel Fabre, *The World of Richard Wright*, 1985; Robert Felgar, *Richard Wright*, 1980; Robert A. Bone, *Richard Wright*, 1969; Russell Carl Brignano, *Richard Wright: An Introduction to the Man and His Works*, 1970; Katherine Fishburn, *Richard Wright's Hero: The Faces of a Rebel-Victim*, 1977; Edward Margolies, *The Art of Richard Wright*, 1969. Three useful collections of essays are *Critical Essays on Richard Wright*, 1982, edited by Yoshinobu Hakutani; *Richard Wright's "Native Son": A Critical Handbook*, 1970, edited by Richard Abcarian; and *Twentieth Century Interpretations of "Native Son,"* 1972, edited by Houston Baker. See also James Baldwin, "Many Thousands Gone," in *Notes of a Native Son*, 1955; Ralph Ellison, "The World and the Jug," in *Shadow and Act*, 1964; and Ian Walker, "Black Nightmare: The Fiction of Richard Wright," in *Black Fiction: New Studies in the Afro-American Novel Since 1945*, 1980, edited by A. Robert Lee.

Carl Brucker

MARGUERITE YOURCENAR
Marguerite de Crayencour

Born: Brussels, Belgium
Date: June 8, 1903

Died: Northeast Harbor, Maine
Date: December 17, 1987

PRINCIPAL WORKS

NOVELS AND NOVELLAS: *Alexis: Ou, Le Traité du vain combat*, 1929 (*Alexis*, 1984); *La Nouvelle Eurydice*, 1931; *Denier du rêve*, 1934 (*A Coin in Nine Hands*, 1982); *Le Coup de grâce*, 1939 (*Coup de Grâce*, 1957); *Mémoires d'Hadrien*, 1951 (*Memoirs of Hadrian*, 1954; also known as *Hadrian's Memoirs*); *L'Œuvre au noir*, 1968 (*The Abyss*, 1976); *Anna, Soror . . .*, 1981; *Comme l'eau qui coule*, 1982 (*Two Lives and a Dream*, 1987).

SHORT FICTION: *La Mort conduit l'attelage*, 1934; *Nouvelles orientales*, 1938 (*Oriental Tales*, 1985).

PLAYS: *Électre: Ou, La Chute des masques*, pb. 1954 (*Electra: Or, The Fall of the Masks*, 1984); *Rendre à César*, pb. 1961 (*Render unto Caesar*, 1984); *Le Mystère d'Alceste*, pb. 1963; *Qui n'a pas son Minotaure?*, pb. 1963 (*To Each His Minotaur*, 1984); *Théâtre*, pb. 1971 (partially translated as *Plays*, 1984).

POETRY: *Le Jardin des chimères*, 1921; *Les Dieux ne sont pas morts*, 1922; *Feux*, 1936 (*Fires*, 1981); *Les Charités d'Alcippe et autres poèmes*, 1956 (*The Alms of Alcippe*, 1982).

NONFICTION: *Pindare*, 1932; *Les Songes et les sorts*, 1938; *Sous bénéfice d'inventaire*, 1962 (*The Dark Brain of Piranesi and Other Essays*, 1984); *Souvenirs pieux*, 1974; *Archives du Nord*, 1977; *Les Yeux ouverts: Entretiens avec Matthieu Galey*, 1980 (*With Open Eyes: Conversations with Matthieu Galey*, 1984); *Mishima: Ou, La Vision du Vide*, 1980 (*Mishima: A Vision of the Void*, 1986); *Le Temps, ce grand sculpteur*, 1983 (*That Mighty Sculptor, Time*, 1988); *La Voix des choses*, 1987.

TRANSLATIONS: *Les Vagues*, 1937 (by Virginia Woolf); *Ce que savait Maisie*, 1947 (by Henry James); *Fleuve profond, sombre rivière*, 1964; *La Couronne et la lyre*, 1979; *Le Coin des "Amen,"* 1983 (by James Baldwin); *Blues et gospels*, 1984.

MISCELLANEOUS: *Œuvres romanesques*, 1982.

The first woman ever elected to the French Academy, Marguerite Yourcenar is one of the most original writers of post-World War II France. She was born in Brussels, Belgium, on June 8, 1903, the only daughter of aristocratic and wealthy parents, Michel and Fernande de Crayencour. Several days after her birth, her mother died of puerperal fever and peritonitis; she was reared then by a series of nurses and maids, as she and her father moved from Belgium to northern France to Paris. Her father, as she lovingly and admiringly portrays him in her autobiographical *Archives du Nord* (northern archives), was an adventurous and unconventional man who loved the cosmopolitan excitement of European casino and spa towns. Well-read in literature himself, he revealed to his daughter the beauty of French, English, Latin, and Greek masterpieces, while private tutors taught her the other school subjects. She was thus able to pass the *baccalauréat* examinations in 1919. Two years later, at age eighteen, she published *Le Jardin des chimères* (the garden of chimeras) at her father's expense, under the pen name Marguerite Yourcenar (an incomplete anagram of her patronymic), followed the next year by another work of poetry, *Les Dieux ne sont pas morts* (the gods are not dead). The publication in 1929 of *Alexis* not only saw the first favorable reviews but also was followed in quick succession by other novels and short stories, mostly written in the confessional letter-monologue genre. These involve psychological studies of men in conflict with their sexuality, with life and art, and with love.

In 1939, Yourcenar, who had come to the United States on a lecture tour, could not return to Nazi-occupied Europe. At the recommendation of the English poet Stephen Spender, she was able to secure a part-time instructorship in French and art history at Sarah Lawrence

College in Bronxville, New York (a position she held until 1950), while she contributed articles and poems to émigré periodicals. At the end of the war, she decided to remain in the United States and became an American citizen in 1947, at the same time officially changing her name to Marguerite Yourcenar. In 1950, she moved to Mount Desert Island, off the coast of Maine, with Grace Frick, her longtime friend and cotranslator.

The first work to be a critical and popular success was the 1951 prizewinning *Memoirs of Hadrian*, the fictional first-person narrative of the great Roman emperor. In an altogether different style, the dark and brooding *The Abyss*, published in 1968 and translated into eighteen languages, received the coveted Prix Fémina and finally brought Yourcenar fame and recognition. It was made into a film by André Delvaux in 1988. In between had appeared essays, plays, and translations, including an anthology of Negro spirituals entitled *Fleuve profond, sombre rivière* (wide, deep, troubled water)—to be followed in 1984 by *Blues et gospels* (blues and gospels).

In recognition of her literary contributions, Yourcenar was awarded honorary degrees from such prestigious institutions as Harvard University, elected to the Belgian Royal Academy (1970), honored with numerous prizes, decorated with the rank of officer (promoted later to commander) in the prestigious French Légion d'Honneur. On March 6, 1980, by a vote of twenty to twelve, she became an "Immortal" member of the French Academy, thereby breaking an all-male tradition dating back to 1635. Despite increasingly severe pulmonary illnesses, she continued to write, mainly essays, short stories, translations, and critical studies. She died at her Maine home on December 17, 1987.

During a 1968 interview with the noted French author Françoise Mallet-Joris, Yourcenar declared, "I believe in the nobility of refusal." Indeed, all of her protagonists rebel against moral or cultural limits and engage in deviant behavior or radical thought, but often find themselves unable to resolve the conflicts between society's demands and their passions. Yourcenar is recognized for the loftiness of her thought, the breadth of her culture, and the humanity of her creations, and her works continue to enjoy great popularity.

BIBLIOGRAPHICAL REFERENCES: Pierre L. Horn, *Marguerite Yourcenar*, 1985, provides an introduction to Yourcenar. For specific aspects of her works, see C. Frederick and Edith R. Farrell's good collection of papers and articles reprinted in their *Marguerite Yourcenar in Counterpoint*, 1983. As the subtitle implies, Georgia Hooks Shurr, *Marguerite Yourcenar: A Reader's Guide*, 1987, is a very general overview of the author. See also Emese Soos, "The Only Motion Is Returning: The Metaphor of Alchemy in Mallet-Joris and Yourcenar," *French Forum*, IV (1979), 3-16; Janet Whatley, "*Mémoires d'Hadrien*: A Manual for Princes," *University of Toronto Quarterly*, L (1980/1981), 221-237; Harry C. Rutledge, "Marguerite Yourcenar: The Classicism of *Feux* and *Mémoires d'Hadrien*," *Classical and Modern Literature: A Quarterly*, IV (1984), 87-99; Helen Watson-Williams, "Hadrian's Story Recalled," *Nottingham French Studies*, XXIII (1984), 35-48; and Colette Gaudin, "Marguerite Yourcenar's Prefaces: Genesis as Self-Effacement," *Studies in 20th Century Literature*, X (1985), 31-55.

Pierre L. Horn

YEVGENY ZAMYATIN

Born: Lebedyan, Russia
Date: February 1, 1884

Died: Paris, France
Date: March 10, 1937

Principal Works

NOVELS AND NOVELLAS: *Uyezdnoye*, 1913 (*A Provincial Tale*, 1966); *Na kulichkakh*, 1914 (*A Godforsaken Hole*, 1988); *Ostrovityane*, 1918 (*The Islanders*, 1972); *My*, 1927, 1952 (*We*, 1924); *Bich Bozhiy*, 1939.

SHORT FICTION: *Povesti i rasskazy*, 1963; *The Dragon: Fifteen Stories*, 1967.

PLAYS: *Ogni svyatogo Dominika*, pb. 1922 (*The Fires of Saint Dominic*, 1971); *Obshchestvo pochetnykh zvonaret*, pr. 1925; *Blokha*, pr. 1925 (*The Flea*, 1971); *Atilla*, pb. 1950 (*Attila*, 1971); *Afrikankiy gost'*, pb. 1963 (*The African Guest*, 1971); *Five Plays*, pb. 1971.

ESSAYS: *Litsa*, 1955 (*A Soviet Heretic: Essays by Yevgeny Zamyatin*, 1970).

Yevgeny Ivanovich Zamyatin is an important Russian satirist, one of the formulators of the dystopian genre, and a masterful essayist, dramatist, and writer of short fiction. He was born on February 1, 1884, in Lebedyan, Tambov Province, in the central farmland of Russia. His family belonged to the educated middle class, his father being a priest and teacher in the local school and his mother a pianist. Zamyatin was educated from 1893 to 1902 locally and at Voronezh. In 1902, he commenced the study of naval engineering at the St. Petersburg Polytechnic Institute, spending his summers touring Russia and the Middle East. As a result of a certain innate rebelliousness, Zamyatin early became a Bolshevik, was briefly imprisoned in 1905, and was several times exiled from St. Petersburg. He completed his studies in 1908, accepting a lectureship at the Institute in Naval Architecture. During World War I, he spent some eighteen months in England but returned during the Revolution. He had long before ceased to be a Bolshevik but sympathized with the cause. After witnessing massive impoverishment and government brutality, however, he frequently satirized the state and its officials. He was most overtly critical of authoritarian regimes in the dystopian novel *We*—his masterpiece, a work never published in Russia.

Throughout his career, he continued to lecture at the institute. He produced innumerable stories, fables, sketches, and essays, and served on the editorial boards of several publishing houses and journals, editing such authors as H. G. Wells, O. Henry, and Jack London. He was a creative and influential author and lecturer, guiding the Serapion Brotherhood, a group of young writers in the early 1920's intent upon experimentation in fiction and freedom of self-expression. Indeed, Zamyatin himself was independent by nature. Most of his own writing was experimental and satiric; he frequently used the sharp, jagged imagery of the expressionists, together with touches of caricature and the grotesque; his work was usually tragic and, more often, satiric—filled with irony and literary parody. He commenced early, about 1908, with short tales and fables, later moving to the novella and the longer story in the 1920's. In this later period, he also wrote essays and a number of plays. Because of Communist pressures, however, much of his work was never published or performed, and most stories appeared individually in journals only. He remained throughout fiercely autonomous as a writer, even once asserting that major authors are outsiders: the doubter, the recluse, the lunatic, the seditious.

Accordingly, his own work was increasingly criticized by party-liners. The formation of a strong writers' union in 1929 permitted more censorship. Many writers were refused publication, silenced, arrested; a number committed suicide. Amazingly, Zamyatin, after writing a candid letter to Joseph Stalin in 1931, was permitted with his wife to emigrate, settling in Paris; he remained, until his death in 1937, a gentlemanly outsider. Of his demise, no notice was taken by the Soviet press, and his name is not included in major Soviet volumes on modern Russian literature.

Typical of his early stories is *A Provincial Tale*. Such tales, filled with slang and dialect, depict life in provincial Russia in gloomy terms. From the outset, Zamyatin published numerous shorter pieces and fables as well as stories and tales. Most reveal a cruel world, wrought with impressionistic, almost nightmarish imagery. At its best, life is tragic; in a lengthy later tale, "Yola" (1928; the yawl), a romantic fisherman in the North has saved for years to purchase his own fishing yawl. No sooner has he obtained it than a squall sinks man and boat together.

A persistent theme is revealed in the satiric story about England, *The Islanders*, which examines bourgeois philistinism. In it, Vicar Dooley seeks to institute a means of effecting "compulsory" salvation. Zamyatin is well aware of the attraction to absolutists who mechanically force some preconceived belief upon others. In "Rasskaz o samon glavnom" (1923; "A Story About the Most Important Thing"), the ardent Bolshevik, Dorda, is ominously portrayed as nothing more than a revolver in a black metallic holster. In fact, Zamyatin understood how easily man can sacrifice his humanity, becoming subhuman. He had told the tale of Attila the Hun three times: as a story (1924); as a play (1927); and in an unfinished novel, *Bich Bozhiy* (the scourge of God), which he was still writing when he died.

His masterpiece is his one completed novel, *We*. Here is his most powerful literary conception—a dystopian novel set in the Superstate's future, when all men have become mere numbers, reduced to slavery and adulation of nation and leader. A small group of subversives yearns to overturn the mechanized, lifeless dictatorship, but even they become somewhat mechanical, shedding their humanity while rigidly pursuing their goals. At the close, the rebels have breached some of the walls of the Superstate, although their revolution has been stalled. In order to keep citizens docile, the leaders lobotomize them, reducing them to robots; however, rebels always tend to rise against such tyranny. Indeed, one of Zamyatin's guiding principles maintained that humankind incessantly required fresh revolutions to offset entropy.

This last theory did much to antagonize the Communists. For that very reason, Zamyatin became a voice unwanted and often unheard, a prophet unwelcome in the Soviet Union. Yet his influence and creative zest have endured. Originally confined and prevented from addressing much of an audience, Zamyatin has, with every decade, been widening his sphere of influence; appropriately, he has acquired his largest audience long after his demise.

BIBLIOGRAPHICAL REFERENCES: Alex M. Shane, *The Life and Works of Evgenij Zamjatin*, 1968, is a good critical survey of Zamyatin's ideas, writings, and style; this volume includes an important chronology of the fiction and a first-rate extended bibliography. For other useful sources, consult Christopher Collins, *Evgenij Zamjatin: An Interpretive Study*, 1973, which stresses Zamyatin's revolutionary ideas and aesthetic tendencies, and D. J. Richards, *Zamyatin: A Soviet Heretic*, 1962, a short biography. George Woodcock, "Utopias in Negative," *The Sewanee Review*, LXIV (1956), 81-97, singles out *We* as the first major dystopian novel, well ahead of Aldous Huxley's *Brave New World* (1932) and George Orwell's *Nineteen Eighty-Four* (1949). See also Edward J. Brown, "Zamjatin and English Literature," in *American Contributions to the Fifth International Congress of Slavists*, II (1963), 21-39; Christopher Collins, "Zamjatin's *We* as Myth," *Slavic and East European Journal*, X (1966), 125-133; Milton Ehre, "Zamjatin's Aesthetics," *Slavic and East European Journal*, XIX (1975), 288-296; Richard A. Gregg, "Two Adams and Eve in the Crystal Palace: Dostoevsky, the Bible, and 'We,'" *Slavic Review*, XXIV (1965), 680-687; James Connors, "Zamyatin's *We* and the Genesis of *1984*," *Modern Fiction Studies*, XXI (1975), 107-124; and Richard L. Chapple, *Soviet Satire of the Twenties*, 1980.

John R. Clark

Cyclopedia of World Authors II

Index

AUTHOR INDEX

AUTHOR INDEX

AUTHOR INDEX

AUTHOR INDEX